Monetary Policy with Very Low Inflation in the Pacific Rim

NBER–East Asia Seminar on Economics
Volume 15

Monetary Policy with Very Low Inflation in the Pacific Rim

Edited by **Takatoshi Ito and Andrew K. Rose**

The University of Chicago Press

Chicago and London

Takatoshi Ito is professor of economics at the Research Center for Advanced Science and Technology, University of Tokyo, and a research associate of the National Bureau of Economic Research. Andrew K. Rose is the Bernard T. Rocca Jr. Professor of International Trade at the Haas School of Business, University of California, Berkeley, the director of its Clausen Center for International Business and Policy, and a research associate of the National Bureau of Economic Research.

The University of Chicago Press, Chicago 60637
The University of Chicago Press, Ltd., London

Printed in the United States of America
15 14 13 12 11 10 09 08 07 06 1 2 3 4 5
ISBN-10: 0-226-37897-7 (cloth)
ISBN-13: 978-0-226-37897-8 (cloth)

Library of Congress Cataloging-in-Publication Data

Monetary policy with very low inflation in the Pacific Rim / edited by Takatoshi Ito and Andrew K. Rose.
p. cm.
Includes bibliographical references and index.
ISBN 0-226-37897-7 (alk. paper)
1. Monetary policy—Pacific Area. 2. Inflation (Finance)—Pacific Area. I. Ito, Takatoshi, 1950– II. Rose, Andrew, 1959–

HG1480.7.M662 2006
339.5′3091823—dc22

2005054661

∞ The paper used in this publication meets the minimum requirements of the American National Standard for Information Sciences—Permanence of Paper for Printed Library Materials, ANSI Z39.48-1992.

Relation of the Directors to the Work and Publications of the National Bureau of Economic Research

1. The object of the NBER is to ascertain and present to the economics profession, and to the public more generally, important economic facts and their interpretation in a scientific manner without policy recommendations. The Board of Directors is charged with the responsibility of ensuring that the work of the NBER is carried on in strict conformity with this object.

2. The President shall establish an internal review process to ensure that book manuscripts proposed for publication DO NOT contain policy recommendations. This shall apply both to the proceedings of conferences and to manuscripts by a single author or by one or more coauthors but shall not apply to authors of comments at NBER conferences who are not NBER affiliates.

3. No book manuscript reporting research shall be published by the NBER until the President has sent to each member of the Board a notice that a manuscript is recommended for publication and that in the President's opinion it is suitable for publication in accordance with the above principles of the NBER. Such notification will include a table of contents and an abstract or summary of the manuscript's content, a list of contributors if applicable, and a response form for use by Directors who desire a copy of the manuscript for review. Each manuscript shall contain a summary drawing attention to the nature and treatment of the problem studied and the main conclusions reached.

4. No volume shall be published until forty-five days have elapsed from the above notification of intention to publish it. During this period a copy shall be sent to any Director requesting it, and if any Director objects to publication on the grounds that the manuscript contains policy recommendations, the objection will be presented to the author(s) or editor(s). In case of dispute, all members of the Board shall be notified, and the President shall appoint an ad hoc committee of the Board to decide the matter; thirty days additional shall be granted for this purpose.

5. The President shall present annually to the Board a report describing the internal manuscript review process, any objections made by Directors before publication or by anyone after publication, any disputes about such matters, and how they were handled.

6. Publications of the NBER issued for informational purposes concerning the work of the Bureau, or issued to inform the public of the activities at the Bureau, including but not limited to the NBER Digest and Reporter, shall be consistent with the object stated in paragraph 1. They shall contain a specific disclaimer noting that they have not passed through the review procedures required in this resolution. The Executive Committee of the Board is charged with the review of all such publications from time to time.

7. NBER working papers and manuscripts distributed on the Bureau's web site are not deemed to be publications for the purpose of this resolution, but they shall be consistent with the object stated in paragraph 1. Working papers shall contain a specific disclaimer noting that they have not passed through the review procedures required in this resolution. The NBER's web site shall contain a similar disclaimer. The President shall establish an internal review process to ensure that the working papers and the web site do not contain policy recommendations, and shall report annually to the Board on this process and any concerns raised in connection with it.

8. Unless otherwise determined by the Board or exempted by the terms of paragraphs 6 and 7, a copy of this resolution shall be printed in each NBER publication as described in paragraph 2 above.

Contents

Acknowledgments

The East Asia Seminar on Economics (EASE) is co-organized by the National Bureau of Economic Research (NBER) in Cambridge, MA; the Productivity Commission of Australia; the Hong Kong University of Science and Technology; the Korea Development Institute in Seoul; the Chung-Hua Institution for Economic Research in Taipei; and the Tokyo Center for Economic Research. We thank all our co-organizers.

The local sponsor was the Tokyo Center for Economic Research (TCER), and we also gratefully acknowledge support from Academy Hills for a wonderful meeting facility, and the Center for Global Partnership (CGP), which is part of the Japan Foundation, for generous financial support. All Nippon Airways (ANA) also provided partial support for the NBER economists for their travel to Japan.

The NBER helped us organize the program and prepare manuscript into publication. Brett Maranjian and Helena Fitz-Patrick have been quite efficient in their respective work at the NBER. Chieko Ishizaka and Naoko Tamiya provided executive assistant services in hosting the conference in Tokyo. We are thankful for their efforts.

Introduction to EASE-15: Monetary Policy with Very Low Inflation in the Pacific Rim

Takatoshi Ito and Andrew K. Rose

This volume contains papers from the fifteenth annual *East Asian Seminar on Economics.* EASE-15 was held in Tokyo, Japan on June 25–27.

EASE-15 was organized around the topic of "Monetary Policy with Very Low Inflation Rates." Until about a decade ago, this would have seemed to be an issue of only academic—meaning negligible—interest. However, the advent of extremely low inflation since the late 1990s has brought this macroeconomic issue to the forefront of policy discussions. As usual, academic interest has responded to this demand with a lag. Academic interest in the area is particularly high in Asia, for a number of reasons.

First and foremost, a number of important Asian countries have experienced deflation in the last fifteen years. Japan is perhaps the most prominent of these countries, but mainland China, Taiwan, and Hong Kong amongst others have also experienced persistently negative inflation rates. Some of these episodes are the result of fast growth on the supply side of the economy, which seems to have relatively benign effects. But inadequate aggregate demand policy can produce what is commonly referred to as a "liquidity trap" where the presence of a "zero-lower bound" (ZLB) on interest rates makes conventional monetary policy ineffective. A decade ago the ZLB might have been treated as a theoretical curiosum, but in the intervening period it has become a binding constraint. Second, the expecta-

Takatoshi Ito is professor of economics at the Research Center for Advanced Science and Technology, University of Tokyo, and a research associate of the National Bureau of Economic Research. Andrew K. Rose is the Bernard T. Rocca Jr. Professor of International Trade at the Haas School of Business, University of California-Berkeley, director of its Clausen Center for International Business and Policy, and a research associate of the National Bureau of Economic Research.

tion of falling prices encourages agents to defer costly purchases, thereby discouraging growth. Third, inflation has fallen globally since the early 1990s, in large part as a result of newly independent central banks implementing explicit inflation targets strategies. Most of these policies have been successful, so that inflation rates above 3 percent are now rare in rich (and an increasing number of developing) countries. But inflation targets have been set low; perhaps so low that a few bad shocks can lead to the threat of deflation. For all these reasons, monetary policy in environments of very low inflation is a topic of great interest.

While most of the conference shared a domestic focus, certain international aspects of the topic are also relevant. For instance, a number of economists such as Lars Svensson have advocated the use of exchange rate policy during periods of deflation. Such policies resemble "beggar thy neighbor" devaluations and are therefore worthy of scrutiny (which economists like Svensson have supplied). Since monetary policy is first and foremost a domestic concern, the focus of EASE-15 was domestic. Nevertheless, the first paper in the volume relies on the international dimension of problem. McCallum is concerned with developing a monetary policy rule which helps the authorities to avoid deflation altogether. (This focus differs sharply from much of the recent literature which is oriented towards designing mechanisms to allow economies which are already in a liquidity trap to escape deflation in the presence of a ZLB.) McCallum's rule is based on a mainstream model and is simplicity itself. Monetary authorities in much of the world use the short interest rate as an instrument of monetary policy. McCallum argues that simply using a weighted average of the interest rate and the depreciation rate (with a small weight on the latter) provides a considerable amount of extra stabilization. Further study of the issue is warranted since his proposal bears a similarity to the much-denigrated "monetary conditions index" which has been almost universally derided of late. Still, his proposal is attractive since the presence of the exchange rate as a guide for monetary policy would be minimal except in the extreme circumstance of a ZLB. As such, his rule is worthy of serious study.

The second paper in the volume is by Robinson and Stone. They build on previous work which has recognized the fact that bubbles in asset prices present a tradeoff for the monetary authorities. On the one hand, asset bubbles (such as the technology bubble of the 1990s that so dramatically affected the NASDAQ) tend to both cause and predict inflation, leading central bankers to lean in the direction of tightening policy at times of bubbles. On the other hand, bubbles tend to collapse, leaving recessionary pressures in their wake. Since monetary policy takes effect only with a lag, a sensible central banker expecting an asset price crash might want to start loosening monetary policy in advance of the actual crash, so as to minimize the deflationary fallout from a meltdown. These countervailing forces are analyzed by Robinson and Stone; the innovation here is to explicitly recognize the complications that a low-inflation environment throws off in the form of a ZLB. Unfortunately their careful analysis delivers only weak results, since they find the offsetting effects of asset prices to be so finely balanced that small reasonable perturbations in the characteristics of the model lead to very different results. Alternatively expressed, only unusually confident central bankers should pay much attention to asset prices.

The third paper in the study is also concerned with instruments and strategies for monetary policy. Hur focuses on an uncommon target for the monetary authorities, namely the term structure of interest rates. This topic has been unfashionable since the American authorities in the 1960s tried unsuccessfully to raise short-term interest rates (to attract capital inflows) while simultaneously lowering long-term term rates (to stimulate investment) in "Operation Twist." However, since the policy interest rate became zero in 2001 in Japan, the quantitative easing in Japan produced flattening of the yield curve. The term structure became a focus of Japan's monetary policy under ZLB. Hur's empirical model uses U.S. data and shows how the interest rates of different maturities respond to the past monetary aggregate changes (taking account not only of growth rates but higher derivatives). The interaction and relationship between different interest rates, such as the expectation hypothesis, is not explicitly modeled. This paper will stimulate further research on the term structure as a monetary policy target when the short term rate becomes (near) zero.

The next four papers concern the deflation experience in Japan. Japan is not only the second-largest economy in the world, but also the country that has been most obviously and importantly affected by deflation, the ZLB, and the liquidity trap. Accordingly, it is natural and appropriate that four EASE-15 papers are concerned with Japanese monetary policy. We present them in order from the broadest and most backward-looking historical summary, to the most abstract and forward-looking hypothetical experiment.

Ito and Mishkin provide a long comprehensive survey of Japanese monetary policy over the last two decades (though their focus, along with that of the others, is on the deflationary experience of the last decade). Ito and Mishkin provide a comprehensive history of monetary policy. While they pay attention to fiscal policy, they are especially and appropriately interested in monetary policy. While the collapse in asset prices (especially stock and housing market) since 1990 helped to precipitate the crisis, it has been the ineffective efforts of the Bank of Japan (BOJ) to reflate the economy that are mostly criticized for recent slow Japanese growth. Ito and Mishkin are thus highly critical of numerous aspects of BOJ policy.

Fukao's interest is also monetary in nature, but his focus is more on determining the causes of the Japanese deflation. Using a Phillips curve equation that links inflation and output, Fukao decomposes the slow-down into its ultimate causes. While the growth in productivity has not been trivial, Fukao's analysis attributes most of the slowdown to a financial crisis in Japanese banking which results from non-performing loans. He also quantifies the considerable fiscal strains that the slowdown has caused for the governments budget, and produces fascinating (if terrifying) Japanese budget forecasts.

The critical approach is shared by Iwamura, Kudo and Watanabe, who are also interested in Japanese policy but over a shorter period of time. Iwamura et al. use both theoretical and empirical tools to analyze Japanese macroeconomic stabilization over the past five years. They are even more critical of the Japanese authorities, since their evidence indicates that bond market participants did not expect monetary policy to remain loose, undermining the efficacy of official BoJ policy of late. But they also direct some of their fire towards the fiscal authorities. Loose fiscal policy is the standard "Keynesian" policy recommendation during a period of deflation. Indeed, that is the textbook prescription when an economy is affected by the ZLB and liquidity trap. There is a critical caveat though; "Ricardian Equivalence" must not hold. Since government bonds represent discounted claims to expected future taxes, consumers can, in principle, treat government bonds as equal and offsetting claims and liabilities. When Iwamura et al. test for Ricardian equivalence, they find the standard result, namely that it has limited empirical relevance. Accordingly, they allocate shared responsibility for slow Japanese growth and the continuing deflation to the monetary and fiscal authorities.

Like Iwamura et al., Ball is also interested in the interaction between monetary and fiscal policy for Japan. The Ball chapter addresses another important policy tool, fiscal stimulus, in a "liquidity trap" situation. An important practical objection to fiscal stimulus in the case of Japan has been the already-large Japanese public debt. The question is whether the debt/GDP ratio could be lowered eventually by temporary fiscal stimulus. He adopts a hybrid methodological approach, calibrating and simulating a simple new Keynesian macroeconomic model. Starting from initial conditions similar to those actually prevailing for Japan, he shows that an expansionary fiscal policy completely financed by money creation could have favorable short-run effects for Japan. The "helicopter drops" of money are substantial but not unprecedented and are envisaged to take place over three years. He finds that such a policy could reflate Japanese macroeconomic growth and raise interest rates to positive levels without dire long-run fiscal consequences.

The next three papers are also concerned specific topics in Japan, Korea, and Taiwan. Choi and Cook are concerned with the Japanese stock market, while Cho is interested in the Korean housing market. These are the two most important asset markets for two of the most important economies in East Asia, providing us with a highly complementary set of papers.

Choi and Cook are interested in the effects of stock market liquidity.

They use a now-conventional technique to measure the liquidity of individual stocks traded on Japanese equity markets. They use a methodology developed by others, but are primarily concerned with the results of low liquidity at both the firm level and, more interestingly, for the economy as a whole. They use the conventional macro-econometric VAR technique and show that negative shocks to liquidity result in significant downturns in the macroeconomy, lowering growth, investment, employment, and inflation.

Cho discusses the effect of a Korean housing institution mechanism known as *chonsei.* A chonsei is essentially an interest-free loan made from a renter to a landlord for a period of two years. The ratio of chonsei to housing prices is thus determined by economic factors such as inflation and interest rates. Thus, monetary policy has a strong effect on the chonsei/housing price ratio, and the resulting implicit wealth transfers. Cho analyzes the determinants of chonsei prices using a simple theoretical model. He finds that chonsei may lead the central bank to conduct looser, less aggressive monetary policy in order to minimize costly chonsei price volatility.

The Yang and Shea paper describes the deflation experience in Taiwan, and how monetary policy was conducted to mitigate the problem. Several factors are identified to be causes of the deflationary trend in Taiwan, including political tension with Mainland China, declining goods prices in the world market, appreciation of the currency, and bursting of the IT bubble in Taiwan. Monetary policy responded to deflationary pressure by lowering the interest rate aggressively, but its effectiveness was limited.

All in all, the volume provides new innovative approaches to deflationary problems in Japan and East Asian countries. Various aspects on why prices have been falling, on the role of asset markets in price movements, and on the role of monetary policy to fight deflation were examined in the papers in this volume. We hope that the papers collectively enhance understanding of deflationary problems and remedies not only in East Asia but potentially in other regions in the world in the future.

I
Monetary Policy Strategies

1

A Monetary Policy Rule for Automatic Prevention of a Liquidity Trap

Bennett T. McCallum

1.1 Introduction

Among monetary economists, a major topic of interest during recent years has been the possibility of a liquidity trap (i.e., a situation in which monetary-policy stimulus cannot be obtained by the usual method of lowering the setting of the central bank's interest rate instrument because that rate is at its lower bound of zero). It would be better, I suggest, to use the term "zero lower bound situation," rather than "liquidity trap," since the latter seems to imply a priori that there is no available mechanism for generating monetary-policy stimulus. In any event, dozens of papers on the subject have appeared, including notable items by Rotemberg and Woodford (1997); Wolman (1998); Krugman (1998); Reifschneider and Williams (2000); McCallum (2000); Goodfriend (2000); Orphanides and Wieland (2000); Svensson (2001, 2003); Benhabib, Schmitt-Grohe, and Uribe (2001); Jung, Teranishi, and Watanabe (2001); Coenen and Wieland (2003); Woodford (2003); Eggertsson and Woodford (2003, 2004); and Auerbach and Obstfeld (2003, 2004). Recent experiences in Japan have, of course, added intense concern from the practical perspective.

One of the more prominent results to come out of this literature is an irrelevance proposition pertaining to open market purchases, put forth by Eggertsson and Woodford (2003), according to which "quantitative eas-

Bennett T. McCallum is the H. J. Heinz Professor of Economics at the Tepper School of Business of Carnegie Mellon University, and a research associate of the National Bureau of Economic Research.

The author is indebted to Vitor Gaspar, Stefan Gerlach, Marvin Goodfriend, James Harrigan, Edward Nelson, Maurice Obstfeld, Vincent Reinhart, and two reviewers for helpful comments.

ing" is to no avail. Instead, "the key to effective central bank action to combat a deflationary slump is *the management of expectations*" (2003, 8). At face value, this proposition seems to contradict results by Auerbach and Obstfeld (2003), Coenen and Wieland (2003), and others who find a role for open market purchases of "unconventional" assets.[1] It will be argued below, however, that there is no actual theoretical inconsistency; that the different papers presume different types of policy experiments.[2] One crucial distinction is whether or not the policy experiment considered involves a change in the policy rule. If there is a credible rule change in an expansionary direction, then—as is shown below—monetary policy can be effective in bringing an economy out of a zero lower bound (ZLB) situation.

This last statement supposes, however, that the policy change in question is fully understood and believed so that a new rational-expectations equilibrium becomes operative immediately. That, however, appears to be a highly dubious proposition. Accordingly, it would seem to be of some importance to consider how a central bank could regularly follow a policy rule that, if sustained, would keep the economy out of a ZLB situation automatically. A major objective of the present chapter is, accordingly, to develop one such rule. That task will be undertaken in section 1.3, after section 1.2 begins by expanding upon the topics just mentioned. Then in sections 1.4 and 1.5, a small open-economy model, based on optimizing behavior but with nominal price stickiness, will be specified and calibrated. Simulation results with this model and variants of our proposed policy rule are reported in section 1.6, so as to explore the properties of the rule (which are found to be highly promising). Three relevant analytical issues are discussed in section 1.7, where it is argued that the Eggertsson and Woodford irrelevance result does not apply to our model. A brief conclusion follows.

1.2 Alternative Policy Experiments

It is expositionally useful to begin with the policy experiment of Eggertsson and Woodford (2003), henceforth referred to as E&W. It involves analysis of the stabilization properties of an interest rate policy regime that is specified to incorporate "quantitative easing." That term is taken by E&W (2003) to mean that the monetary-base supply function, which supports (i.e., implements) their interest rate rule given money-demand behavior, includes an unusual nonlinear component that calls for extra open market purchases whenever the interest rate equals zero. These purchases are evidently reversed, however, as soon as the interest rate rises above zero. (The interest rate in question, here denoted R_t, is "the riskless nominal

1. Assets, that is, that are not perfect substitutes for the short-term security that is normally used in open market operations.

2. This point is also made by Eggertsson and Woodford (2003, 2004), but with a different emphasis.

interest rate on one-period obligations . . ." [E&W 2003, 10]). One could simply view this function as a base-money-supply policy rule, include the base-money stock as a variable, and solve the model in a standard and familiar rational expectations (RE) fashion, if it were not for the nonlinear component and the restriction that the interest rate must be nonnegative.[3] What E&W do with the resulting model is to show that the behavior of prices and output in the model's RE equilibrium is independent of the parameters that describe the quantitative-easing component of the base-supply rule. Whatever the extent of the additional base-money supply specified by this component, then, there will be no effect on inflation or output in the RE equilibrium. That is the E&W irrelevance proposition. Note, crucially, that it pertains to the properties of a single ongoing RE equilibrium for a given policy rule that involves certain specified behavior when the ZLB is operative, not to the adoption of a new rule. The irrelevance proposition is arguably not surprising, given that any "extra" base money supplied when $R_t = 0$ is removed immediately as soon as $R_t > 0$.[4]

The policy experiment considered by Auerbach and Obstfeld (2003) is quite different. It begins with a policy rule in place, one that specifies a constantly growing level of the monetary base, and the economy in a ZLB situation with the interest rate R_t equal to zero. Then the authors postulate a change in the base-money rule, either a one-time upward shift in the path of the base or an increase in its slope (the rate of growth of the base)—in either case a change that is sustained permanently. The experiment presumes a forseen upward jump in the natural real rate of interest after five periods that would bring the ZLB episode to an end in any event, but each of the two considered policy-rule changes would have effects on the path of prices and, possibly, output in the interim. The increased base growth-rate policy also has the effect of bringing the ZLB episode with $R_t = 0$ to an end sooner than would otherwise be the case. The Auerbach and Obstfeld results are of particular interest because the model utilized is in most respects similar to that of E&W.

In light of the foregoing discussion, I would suggest that the basic difference in outcomes is that the E&W experiment concerns the effects of an unusual design feature of one maintained policy rule, whereas the Auerbach and Obstfeld experiment has to do with effects of a *change* from one policy rule to another. In one case the monetary rule utilizes an interest rate instrument and in the other case the monetary base, but it appears that this distinction is not crucial. As hinted above, E&W could utilize a policy rule

3. The model used by E&W is rather standard, relative to the recent monetary-policy literature, but is slightly more "monetarist" than most in that the utility function, which includes real money balances as an argument, is not assumed to be separable.

4. It is my impression that proponents of quantitative easing for Japan have almost invariably had in mind a new policy that, among other features, would entail a target inflation rate high enough to imply a positive steady-state interest rate on overnight bank loans.

specified as a base rule that includes an analogous quantitative easing component and develop a similar irrelevance result for that case. Furthermore, for a change in a monetary rule to be effective when an economy is in a ZLB situation, it is not necessary for the rule to be one that governs base quantities; it could as well be an interest rate rule that is altered.

For an extremely simple illustration of this last point, it will be sufficient to use a closed-economy model with full price flexibility. Consider the following two-equation system, which is so familiar as to require very little explanation at this point:[5]

$$(1) \qquad y_t = b_0 + b_1(R_t - E_t\Delta p_{t+1}) + E_t y_{t+1} + v_t$$

$$(2) \qquad R_t = \mu_0 + \Delta p_t + \mu_1(\Delta p_t - \pi^*) + \mu_2 y_t.$$

Here y_t and p_t denote the logs of an output variable and the price level, so Δp_t is inflation while R_t is the one-period nominal interest rate. The term v_t represents a preference shock that is generated by an exogenous stochastic process, which is assumed to be AR(1)—i.e., autoregressive of order one—with parameter ρ. Equation (2) is a Taylor-style rule in which the central bank is depicted as setting an interest rate instrument R_t each period so as to tighten policy when inflation exceeds its target value π^* and/or when output is high. In equations (1) and (2), y_t should be interpreted as the output gap, $y_t - \bar{y}_t$, with $\bar{y}_t$ for simplicity assumed constant at the value zero. With flexible prices we then have $y_t = 0$ in each period. Thus there are only two endogenous variables to be determined by the system, R_t and Δp_t. This model should be understood to also include the requirement that Δp_t must not approach $-\infty$ as $t \rightarrow \infty$, because of a transversality condition that obtains in the underlying optimizing model.

To obtain a RE solution, we first substitute out R_t and using $y_t = 0$ obtain

$$(3) \qquad 0 = b_0 + b_1[\mu_0 - \mu_1\pi^* + (1 + \mu_1)\Delta p_t - E_t\Delta p_{t+1}] + v_t.$$

The minimum-state variable (MSV) solution is of the form

$$(4) \qquad \Delta p_t = \phi_0 + \phi_1 v_t,$$

implying $E_t\Delta p_{t+1} = \phi_0 + \phi_1\rho v_t$. Then substitution into equation (3) and application of a standard undetermined-coefficient procedure yields the requirement that

$$(5) \qquad 0 = b_0 + b_1[\mu_0 - \mu_1\pi^* + (1 + \mu_1)(\phi_0 + \phi_1 v_t) - \phi_0 - \phi_1\rho v_t] + v_t$$

holds identically for all realizations of v_t. That implies unique values for ϕ_0 and ϕ_1, and yields the MSV solution

5. Explanation of a model that includes equations (1) and (2) as a special case will be provided below. The present system differs from the model of E&W primarily by positing flexible prices, which is irrelevant to the current point.

$$(6) \qquad \Delta p_t = \pi^* - \frac{(b_0 + b_1\mu_0)}{\mu_1} - [b_1(1 - \rho + \mu_1)]^{-1}v_t.$$

Of course, Taylor (1993) and many others prescribe that the central bank set $\mu_0 = r$, the long-run average real rate of interest, and we observe from equation (1) that this rate equals $-b_0/b_1$. So adherence to this recommendation implies that the second term on the right-hand side of equation (6) vanishes and we have $\Delta p_t = \pi^* - [b_1(1 - \rho + \mu_1)]^{-1}v_t$ as the MSV solution for inflation.

Suppose, then, that an economy is of the form displayed in equations (1) and (2) except that it also includes the requirement that $R_t \geq 0$. Then equation (6) would be the RE solution if the parameter values and the distribution of v_t were such that this inequality was never binding. But suppose that such is not the case and that the economy is in a ZLB situation with $R_t = 0$. Then also suppose that in some period there is a policy change that amounts to an increase in the target inflation rate π^* to a value high enough that the ZLB will never be effective in the future. In that case, the new RE equilibrium will yield immediately an inflation rate high enough to escape the ZLB situation. By contrast, an increase in the value of the policy parameter μ_1 would in that situation have no necessarily constructive effect toward bringing the economy out of the ZLB.[6] This contrast is analogous to that of the Auerbach-Obstfeld and E&W results.

The simplicity and starkness of the foregoing example will probably lead many readers to object, and say something like "But that is totally implausible; the economy's agents would be very unlikely to know about, understand, and believe in the policy change even if the central bank has every intention of carrying it out." With that objection I would entirely agree. More generally, many proponents of the hypothesis of rational expectations find it attractive mainly for consideration of alternative *maintained* policy rules (i.e., for application to situations prevailing after some time has passed—since any previous rule change—and the economy has settled into a new stochastic equilibrium). To these economists—e.g., Lucas (1980, 205); Lucas and Sargent (1981, xxxvii); Kydland and Prescott (1977)—immediate application of RE after a policy change seems dubious. Partly for this reason, E&W (2003); McCallum (2000); Jung, Teranishi, and Watanabe (2001); Reifschneider and Williams (2000), and a few others have concentrated attention on rules for preventing a ZLB situation, rather than (or in addition to) schemes for escaping a ZLB "trap" in which an

6. The solution for R_t is $R_t = r + \pi^* - [(1/b_1)(1 + \mu_1)/(1 - \rho + \mu_1)]v_t$. Here the coefficient on v_t is positive, but the direction of effect depends upon the sign of v_{t-1}. Furthermore, if $\rho = 0$, the magnitude of the coefficient is independent of μ_1. Alternatively, one might ask whether an increased value of μ_1 would, with a sustained rule, help to prevent ZLB situations. The simulation results presented below suggest that the answer is no, since larger values of μ_1 evidently imply (given other parameter values) increased variability of R_t.

economy finds itself. In that spirit we move on to the discussion of a new rule proposal.[7]

1.3 A Rule for Use at or Away from the ZLB

Let us now turn to the main topic of the present chapter, which is the development and exploration of a monetary-policy rule that is appropriate for use at all times, whether or not short-term nominal interest rates are at their ZLB.[8] The very simple basic idea is to combine two component rules, designed for normal and ZLB conditions, by means of a weighted average of their respective instrument settings. The first of these two component rules could be written as a standard Taylor-type formulation as follows:

$$(7) \qquad R_t = r + \Delta p_t + \mu_1(\Delta p_t - \pi^*) + \mu_2(y_t - \bar{y}_t) + e_t, \quad \mu_1, \mu_2 \geq 0.$$

Here R_t is a short-term nominal interest rate instrument and, for simplicity, we have entered the current value of inflation and the output gap as the variables to which the rule responds.[9] In equation (7) π^* is the target for inflation and r is the long-term average real rate of interest, while e_t is a random policy shock that reflects unsystematic behavior by the monetary authority. We suppose that in normal times, when the ZLB on R_t is not binding, the central bank wishes to utilize equation (7) as its monetary-policy rule, so as to keep Δp_t close to π^* and y_t close to $\bar{y}_t$ on average.

When R_t is at its lower bound of zero, however, the central bank will be unable to respond as implied by equation (7) if the gap measures $\Delta p_t - \pi^*$ and $y_t - \bar{y}_t$ together call for a reduction in R_t. In previous work, including McCallum (2000) and (2003), I have accordingly suggested a rule for adjusting the foreign exchange rate, s_t in logarithmic terms, in such occasions. The version of this rule given in the more recent of these two papers is as follows:

$$(8) \qquad \Delta s_t = \Delta q + \Delta p_t - \mu_1(\Delta p_t - \pi^*) - \mu_2(y_t - \bar{y}_t) - e_t, \quad \mu_1, \mu_2 \geq 0.$$

Here we have minus signs on the two gap measures because an increase in the value of $\Delta s_t - \Delta p_t$ represents a loosening, not a tightening, of monetary policy.[10]

Next we take a weighted average of the two preceding expressions, after

7. There is some interest in a policy of "helicopter drops," for example, repeated gifts of money to the public, in contrast to monetary-policy actions that involve only open market actions by the central bank. A brief analysis is presented in the appendix.

8. Obviously, if such a rule is in force during a ZLB episode, there is no need to devise an "exit strategy."

9. It would be possible to use instead expected future values or lagged expectations of current values, and so on.

10. Here and in what follows $S_t = \log^{-1} s_t$ is the home-country price of foreign exchange. Also, Δq is the trend rate of growth of the real exchange rate minus the average inflation rate abroad.

changing the signs on all terms in equation (8). Let $1 - \theta$, with $0 \leq \theta \leq 1$, be the weight on the R_t instrument. Then the resulting rule is as follows:

$$(9) \qquad [(1-\theta)R_t + \theta(-\Delta s_t)] = (1-\theta)r - \theta\Delta q + (1-2\theta)\Delta p_t + \mu_1(\Delta p_t - \pi^*) + \mu_2(y_t - \bar{y}_t) + e_t.$$

To facilitate understanding of the latter, first suppose that the interest rate R_t equals zero—i.e., is at its ZLB. Then equation (9) becomes a rule for setting the value of the rate of exchange rate depreciation, Δs_t. The formula might look a bit strange, but when $R = 0$, an implied steady-state relationship is $r = -\Delta p$. Then using the latter with equation (9) and rearranging we obtain

$$(10) \qquad \Delta s_t = \Delta q + \Delta p_t - \left(\frac{\mu_1}{\theta}\right)(\Delta p_t - \pi^*) - \left(\frac{\mu_2}{\theta}\right)(y_t - \bar{y}_t) - \left(\frac{1}{\theta}\right)e_t.$$

Clearly, the latter is of exactly the same form as the Δs_t rule (8), although it has a different numerical value for two of the response coefficients.

What about the interpretation of equation (9) when R_t is not at the ZLB? To gain an intuitive idea regarding this case, suppose that the nominal exchange rate were to behave in conformity with the current inflation rate and the long run average rate of real exchange rate depreciation. Suppose, that is, that $\Delta s_t = \Delta p_t + \Delta q$ holds on a period-by-period basis. Then substitution into equation (9) yields

$$(11) \qquad R_t = r + \Delta p_t + \left[\frac{\mu_1}{(1-\theta}\right](\Delta p_t - \pi^*) + \left[\frac{\mu_2}{(1-\theta)}\right](y_t - \bar{y}_t) + \left[\frac{1}{(1-\theta)}\right]e_t,$$

which has the form of a standard Taylor-type rule! So equation (9) works in a highly intuitive manner in both of these reference cases.

How would the composite rule (9) be implemented? To do so, the central bank would make purchases (or sales) each period in the money market or foreign exchange market—or preferably both—so as to adjust $(1 - \theta)R_t - \theta s_t$ to the value indicated by equation (9), taking s_{t-1} as given. In this regard, note that buying money-market securities tends to drive R_t downward and s_t upward, so both components of the weighted average $([1 - \theta]R_t + \theta[-\Delta s_t]) \equiv MC_t$ move in the same (downward) direction. Alternatively, buying foreign exchange would tend to drive s_t upward and R_t downward, so again both components move in the desired direction. Clearly, when instead a

11. Of course there are limits on a central bank's ability to increase MC_t, since it will hold only finite stocks of foreign and domestic assets. But for ZLB concerns, decreases are of prime interest.

monetary tightening is desired, it would be possible to sell money-market securities and/or foreign exchange, moving MC_t in the upward direction.[11]

Since the rule is designed to be used at all times, operational procedures should be the same both at and away from the ZLB, so that market participants will understand that one rule is in effect. Accordingly, it would be desirable to have a secondary rule for determining what fraction of open market purchases will, during a given period, be made in the foreign exchange market. One possibility would be to have a fixed fraction, such as 0.25. (Note that this fraction does not need to equal θ, and probably should not.) Such an arrangement would imply that the central bank would be making a large volume of purchases from the money market when at the ZLB, even though those purchases would not (in principle) have any effect on the value of MC_t. Other rules that would increase the fraction as R_t gets closer to zero would not have this latter property, but would be more difficult for market participants to understand.

It is likely that at this point many readers have guessed the reason for using the symbol MC_t to denote our composite measure. It is because this measure has some resemblance to a "monetary conditions index." The latter concept has been viewed rather unfavorably by most monetary economists in recent years, but that does not necessarily make it an undesirable policy indicator. It is my impression that the typical mode of presentation has made the concept appear to be dimensionally incoherent,[12] for most proponents have used written expressions such as $(1 - \theta)R_t - \theta s_t$, rather than $(1 - \theta)R_t + \theta(-\Delta s_t)$.[13] But in such cases the authors may actually have had in mind an exchange rate expressed in relation to some reference value, which leaves open the possibility that the dimensions of the two terms are in fact consistent. That is not to suggest that the numerical specifications of monetary-conditions indexes considered or used by actual central banks have been ones that are well designed. In section 1.6 below it will be argued that a very small weight—on the order of 0.025—should be attached to the exchange rate term, whereas personal experience tells me that the Reserve Bank of New Zealand was at one time discussing a possible monetary-conditions index with a weight close to $1 - 0.025 = 0.975$ (i.e., a weight almost forty times as large). In short, the present discussion is not intended to express approval of previous discussions of monetary-condition indexes, but merely to acknowledge the extent of similarity between them and the policy rule (9) here under investigation.

Another matter that requires brief attention is the notion of interest rate smoothing, which is widely viewed as a practice much utilized by actual

12. Thus I, for one, have been disturbed by the practice of taking a weighted average of two terms that have the units 1/years and yen/dollar, for example. But if the latter is expressed in rate of change form, as in equation (9), it too can have the units 1/years.

13. See, for example, Ball (1999), Gerlach and Smets (2000), and the recent contribution by Detken and Gaspar (2003).

central banks. Can inertial behavior of R_t be accommodated by rules such as (9)? Certainly there would be no analytical problem created by writing a partial-adjustment equation for MC_t, with the adjustment moving the actual value of MC_t toward a value such as that on the right-hand side of equation (9). Alternatively, one could apply smoothing only to the R_t component, by writing equation (7) in a partial-adjustment form before taking a weighted average of equations (7) and (8).[14] In this case the rule would be written as

$$(9') \quad [(1-\theta)R_t + \theta(-\Delta s_t)] = (1-\mu_3)(1-\theta)r - \theta\Delta q - [(1-\theta)(1-\mu_3)+\theta]\mu_1\pi^* + [(1-\theta)(1-\mu_3)(1+\mu_1)+\theta(\mu_1-1)]\Delta p_t + [(1-\theta)(1-\mu_3)+\theta]\mu_2(y_t-\bar{y}_t) + \mu_3 R_{t-1} + e_t,$$

which will be used below. Here (and in what follows) μ_3 is the interest rate smoothing parameter ($0 < \mu_3 < 1$).

1.4 Model Specification

In order to explore the properties of a rule such as (9) or (9′), one needs to combine it with an appropriately specified model of an economy and then conduct analytical exercises to determine how the economy is predicted to perform with different variants of the rule. Clearly, the model needs to pertain to an open economy, and most contemporary analysts would prefer that it be a rational-expectations model based on optimizing behavior by the economy's individual households and firms while also incorporating some form of nominal price stickiness. The model that will be used below is one that was developed by McCallum and Nelson (M&N; 1999) and utilized subsequently by them (2000) in an exploration of relationships between Consumer Price Index (CPI) inflation and exchange rate depreciation. This M&N model is not econometrically estimated, but is calibrated to match important selected characteristics of the economies of interest. It differs from many other contributions in the area, however, in the manner in which imported goods are treated. In particular, the M&N model treats imports not as finished goods, ready for immediate consumption, but instead as raw-material inputs to the home economy's producers. This alternative modeling strategy leads to a cleaner and simpler theoretical structure, relative to the standard treatment, and is empirically attrac-

14. If policy is "superinertial," as featured in Rotemberg-Woodford (1997) and Woodford (2003, 100–1), then the partial-adjustment formulation in (9′) is not appropriate, but this does not create any difficulties for the analysis developed below.

tive. Since the optimizing, general equilibrium analysis is spelled out in McCallum and Nelson (1999), here I will take an informal expository approach designed to facilitate understanding of the model's structural equations.

It is well known that optimizing analysis leads, in a wide variety of infinite-horizon models possibly involving imperfect competition, to a consumption Euler equation that can be expressed or approximated in the form

$$c_t = E_t c_{t+1} + b_0 + b_1 r_t + v_t, \quad b_1 < 0 \tag{12}$$

where c_t is the log of a Dixit-Stiglitz consumption-bundle aggregate C_t of the many distinct goods that a typical household consumes in period t. In equation (12), r_t is the real interest rate on home-country one-period bonds (private or government) and v_t is a stochastic shock term that pertains to household preferences regarding present versus future consumption. In closed-economy analysis, relation (12) is often combined with a log-linearized, per-household, overall resource constraint to yield an "expectational" or "optimizing" IS function. That step presumes that investment and capital are treated as exogenous. The simplest version of that assumption is that the capital stock is fixed; since endogenizing capital greatly complicates the analysis, the constant-capital specification will be used here.

For an open-economy extension, one might be tempted to write the economy's per capita resource constraint as $y_t = \omega_1 c_t + \omega_2 g_t + \omega_3 x_t - \omega_4 \text{im}_t$, where y_t, g_t, x_t, and im_t are logarithms of real output, government consumption, exports, and imports, with ω_1, ω_2, ω_3, and ω_4 representing steady-state shares of output for consumption, government purchases, exports, and imports. But if imports are exclusively material inputs to the production of home-country goods, and $Y_t = \ln^{-1} y_t$ is interpreted as units of output, not value added, then the relevant resource constraint is

$$y_t = \omega_1 c_t + \omega_2 g_t + \omega_3 x_t. \tag{13}$$

For import demand to be modeled in an optimizing fashion, assume that output of consumer goods is affected by producers all with production functions of the same constant elasticity of substitution (CES) form, with labor and material imports being the two variable inputs. Then the cost-minimizing demand for imports is[15]

$$\text{im}_t = y_t - \sigma q_t + \text{const}, \tag{14}$$

where σ is the elasticity of substitution between materials and labor in production, and where "const" denotes *some* constant.[16] Also, q_t is the log price of imports in terms of produced consumption goods. We will refer to

15. In the model used below there is also a small adjustment included for the effects of imperfect competition.

16. That is, the expression "const" in different equations appearing below will typically refer to different constant magnitudes.

$Q_t = \ln^{-1} q_t$ as the real exchange rate. Let P_t and S_t be the home-country money price of goods and foreign exchange, with P_t^* the foreign money price of home-country imports. Then if p_t, s_t, and p_t^* are logs of these variables, we have

$$(15) \qquad q_t = s_t - p_t + p_t^*.$$

Symmetrically, we assume that export demand is given as

$$(16) \qquad x_t = y_t^* + \sigma^* q_t + \text{const},$$

where y_t^* denotes income abroad and σ^* is the price elasticity of demand from abroad for home-country goods. Since the economy is small, we take y_t^* to be exogenous.

Now consider output determination in a sticky-price version of the model. Taking a log-linear approximation to the home-country production function, we have

$$y_t = \alpha_1 a_t + \alpha_1 n_t + \alpha_2 \text{im}_t + \text{const},$$

where n_t and a_t are logs of labor input and a labor-augmenting technology-shock term, respectively. For simplicity suppose that labor supply is inelastic, with 1.0 units supplied per period by each household. Thus with full price flexibility we would have $n_t = 0$ and the flexible-price, natural rate (or "potential") value of y_t will be $\bar{y}_t = \alpha_1 a_t + \alpha_2 \text{im}_t + \text{const}$ so that $\bar{y}_t = \alpha_1 a_t + \alpha_2(\bar{y}_t - \sigma q_t) + \text{const}$, or

$$(17) \qquad \bar{y}_t = (1 - \alpha_2)^{-1} \alpha_1 a_t - \left[\frac{\sigma \alpha_2}{(1 - \alpha_2)} \right] q_t + \text{const}.$$

But while $\bar{y}_t$ would be the economy's output in period t if prices could adjust promptly, we assume that prices adjust only sluggishly. Then, if the economy's demand quantity as determined by the rest of the system differs from $\bar{y}_t$, the former quantity y_t prevails—with workers departing from their (inelastic) supply schedules so as to provide whatever quantity is needed to produce the demanded output, with im_t given by equation (14).

In such a setting, the precise way in which prices adjust has a direct impact on demand and, consequently, on production. There are various models of gradual price adjustment utilized in the recent literature that are intended to represent optimizing behavior in the context of nominal-adjustment costs. In the analysis that follows, I will use

$$(18) \qquad \Delta p_t = (1 + \beta)^{-1}(\beta E_t \Delta p_{t+1} + \Delta p_{t-1}) + \kappa(y_t - \bar{y}_t) + u_t, \quad \kappa > 0,$$

where β is a discount factor and u_t is a behavioral disturbance. This form of equation has been fairly prominent,[17] primarily because it tends to impart a more realistic degree of inflation persistence than does the Calvo-

17. See Fuhrer and Moore (1995); Gali and Gertler (1999); and Woodford (2003).

Rotemberg model (which is theoretically more attractive). For an extensive discussion of relevant issues, see Woodford (2003, chap. 3).

A standard feature of most open-economy models is a relation implying uncovered interest parity (UIP). Despite its prominent empirical weaknesses, accordingly, the basic M&N model incorporates one:

$$R_t - R_t^* = E_t \Delta s_{t+1} + \xi_t. \tag{19}$$

We include a time-varying "risk premium" term ξ_t, however, that may have a sizeable variance and may be autocorrelated. In the main investigation below, moreover, a crucial departure from pure UIP will be assumed to prevail.

In previous applications of this model it has been assumed, as in most recent research in monetary economics, that the monetary authority conducts policy by adjusting a one-period nominal interest rate in response to prevailing (or forecasted future) values of inflation and the output gap, $\tilde{y}_t = y_t - \bar{y}_t$, as in equation (7) above. For present purposes, however, we will be using the rule (9′), now written as

$$\begin{aligned}[(1-\theta)R_t + \theta(-\Delta s_t)] = {} & (1-\mu_3)(1-\theta)r - \theta\Delta q \\ & - [(1-\theta)(1-\mu_3) + \theta]\mu_1\pi^* \\ & + [(1-\theta)(1-\mu_3)(1+\mu_1) + \theta(\mu_1 - 1)]\Delta p_t \\ & + [(1-\theta)(1-\mu_3) + \theta]\mu_2(y_t - \bar{y}_t) + \mu_3 R_{t-1} \\ & + e_t,\end{aligned} \tag{20}$$

of which equation (7)—possibly with smoothing—is a special case when $\theta = 0$.

To complete the model, we need only to include the Fisher identity, $(1 - r_t) = (1 + R_t)/(1 + E_t\Delta p_{t+1})$, which we approximate in the familiar fashion:

$$r_t = R_t - E_t \Delta p_{t+1}. \tag{21}$$

Thus we have a simple log-linear system in which the ten structural relations (12)–(21) determine values for the endogenous variables y_t, $\bar{y}_t$, Δp_t, r_t, R_t, q_t, s_t, c_t, x_t, and im_t. Government spending g_t and the foreign variables p_t^*, y_t^*, and R_t^* are taken to be exogenous—as are the shock processes for v_t, a_t, e_t, and ξ_t.[18]

One might note parenthetically a few features of the model. First, it would be possible to append a money-demand function such as

$$m_t - p_t = \gamma_0 + \gamma_1 y_t + \gamma_2 R_t + \eta_t, \tag{22}$$

18. During the past few years, several quantitative optimizing open-economy models have been developed that are more sophisticated and complex than ours. Outstanding examples include Kollmann (2002); Laxton and Pesenti (2003); and Smets and Wouters (2002).

and one of this general form—perhaps with c_t replacing y_t—could be consistent with optimizing behavior. But, as many writers have recognized, that equation would serve only to determine the values of m_t that are needed to implement the R_t policy rule. Second, with the structure given above, a useful measure of the foreign trade balance on goods and services account—i.e., net exports—is

$$\text{net}_t = x_t - (\text{im}_t + q_t), \tag{23}$$

where it is assumed that $\omega_3 = \omega_4$. This measure is used in what follows. Also, it is possible to calculate the log of the gross domestic product (GDP) deflator as

$$p_t^{\text{DEF}} = \frac{[p_t - \omega_3(s_t + p_t^*)]}{(1 - \omega_3)}. \tag{24}$$

Finally, it might be said that an advantage of the M&N strategy of modeling imports as material inputs to the production process is that the relevant price index for produced goods is the same as the consumer price index, which implies that the same gradual price-adjustment behavior is relevant for all domestic consumption. Such advantages would not constitute a satisfactory justification, of course, if in fact most imports were consumption goods. This is not the case, however, at least for the United States. Instead, an examination of the data suggests that (under conservative assumptions) intermediate productive inputs actually comprise a larger fraction of U.S. imports than do consumer goods (including services).[19]

There is one way in which the model developed in M&N (1999) differs significantly from the ten-equation formulation just presented. Specifically, the former includes a somewhat more complex form of consumption versus saving behavior, one that features habit formation. Thus in place of the time-separable utility function that leads to equation (12), M&N assumed that each period-t utility term includes $C_t/(C_{t-1})^h$, with $0 \leq h < 1$, rather than C_t alone. That specification gives rise to the following replacement for (12):

$$c_t = h_0 + h_1 c_{t-1} + h_2 E_t c_{t+1} + h_3 E_t c_{t+2} + h_4(\log \lambda_t) + v_t. \tag{25}$$

In the latter, λ_t is the Lagrange multiplier on the household's budget constraint, which obeys

19. For the year 1998, imported consumer goods amounted to \$453 billion while imports of business inputs came to \$624 billion, approximately. These figures are based on an examination of categories reported in the August 1999 issue of the *Survey of Current Business.* For several categories it is clear whether they are composed predominantly of consumer or business goods. For others, judgmental assignments were required. Those assignments are as follows, with the reported figure being the fraction of the category classified as "business inputs": Automotive vehicles, engines, and parts, 25 percent; Travel, 25 percent; Passenger fares, 25 percent; Foods, feed, and beverages, 50 percent; and Other private services, 75 percent.

$$\log \lambda_t = \text{const} + E_t \log \lambda_{t+1} + r_t, \quad (26)$$

and there are constraints relating the h_j parameters to others in the system.[20] Inclusion of this feature results in a model in which there is somewhat more persistence in consumption and output fluctuations than with the basic formulation. In the present study, accordingly, I have again included this habit-formation modification in the base-case model.

1.5 Calibration and Model Properties

Calibration of the model draws on M&N (1999) but differs in a few ways that are appropriate for present purposes. For the parameter governing spending behavior, I retain here the $h = 0.8$ value taken from an early version of Fuhrer (2000), but for my base case have adopted the assumption that γ, the counterpart of $-b_1$ in equation (1), equals 0.5 rather than 0.1667, in order to reflect the greater responsiveness of investment spending (since the latter is not included explicitly in the model).[21] For σ, the elasticity of substitution in production (and therefore the elasticity of import demand with respect to Q_t), I now use 0.6 (instead of 0.333) so that, with the same absolute value used for the elasticity of export demand with respect to Q_t, the Marshall-Lerner condition is satisfied. In equation (6), the imported inputs-share parameter α_2 is taken to equal ω_3, the share of exports in domestic production. The steady-state value of this share of imports (and exports) to domestic production is taken to be 0.15 in our base case, and can be altered to represent differing degrees of openness. For the base-case share of government consumption I take $\omega_2 = 0.2$. Finally, in the price-adjustment relation, the specification is that $\kappa = 0.03$. The latter value is based on my reading of a wide variety of studies, plus conversion into non-annualized fractional terms for a quarterly model. Also, quasi-realistic parameters for a Taylor-style interest rate policy rule will be specified as $\mu_1 = 0.5$, $\mu_2 = 0.5$, and $\mu_3 = 0.8$, the latter reflecting considerable interest rate smoothing. Below I refer to these as "standard" values, but also include cases with other values for μ_1 and μ_3.

The stochastic processes driving the model's shocks must also be calibrated, of course. For both foreign output and the technology shock, I have specified AR(1) processes with AR parameters of 0.95, rather than the 1.0 values used in M&N (1999). The innovation standard deviations (SDs) are 0.03 and 0.007, respectively.[22] The UIP risk premium term ξ_t and

20. For details and additional discussion, see M&N (1999); Amato and Laubach (2004); and the basic study by Fuhrer (2000).

21. The parameter in question, γ, is the intertemporal elasticity of substitution in consumption when $h = 0$.

22. These and other values given in this paragraph are given in terms of quarterly fractional units.

the consumption shock v_t are generated by AR(1) processes, each with AR parameter 0.5 and innovation SDs of 0.02 and 0.01. Government consumption (in logs) follows an AR(1) process, with AR parameter 0.97 and innovation SD of 0.02. Finally, the u_t and e_t shock processes are taken to be white noise with SD values of 0.002 and 0.0017, respectively.

Before using the foregoing model to discuss the policy rule (20) developed above, we should briefly investigate its properties with $\theta = 0$ (i.e., with a Taylor-style R_t rule) to establish, if possible, that they are at least moderately consistent with our understanding of the characteristics of actual economies. Consider first the values shown in table 1.1, where each cell reports standard deviations, in annualized percentage units, of quarterly observations on the four variables Δp_t, $\tilde{y}_t$, R_t, and Δs_t. These SDs are averages across 400 simulations of length 200 (with fifty start-up periods discarded), so they approximate population magnitudes. Since constant terms are all set to zero, the SD values not only indicate the variability of the four variables but can also be thought of as representing root-mean-square targeting errors, for cases in which the policy rule is intended to keep some variable close to a chosen target value. Looking across the first row of cells, we see that increased values of μ_1, the policy coefficient attached to inflation, lead to reductions in the average targeting errors for inflation—just as the Taylor-style rule is intended to do. Over part of the range, increased μ_1 values also reduce the variability of the output gap, but with large μ_1 magnitudes there is a readily apparent trade-off (between inflation and output gap stabilization). We also see that increased activism with the interest rate instrument, represented by larger μ_1 values, gives rise to greater variability of the interest rate instrument itself, R_t. Exchange rate depreciation variability is almost unaffected by the magnitude of μ_1 when small, but increases sharply when μ_1 becomes extremely large. All of these features of the simulation results are consistent with one's understanding of how the model should work.

With respect to the magnitudes themselves, we focus on the second cell

Table 1.1 **Results with standard interest rate rule**

	$\mu_1 = 0.05$	$\mu_1 = 0.5$	$\mu_1 = 5.0$	$\mu_1 = 50.0$
$\mu_3 = 0.8$	3.28	2.35	1.36	0.74
	2.19	1.96	1.69	2.35
	2.82	2.48	3.82	11.26
	18.59	18.51	19.35	27.70
$\mu_3 = 0.0$	6.27	2.92	1.35	0.58
	2.07	1.68	1.54	3.01
	7.03	4.70	7.80	28.16
	19.14	18.56	21.97	46.82

Note: Cell entries are standard deviations of Δp_t, $\tilde{y}_t$, R_t, and Δs_t.

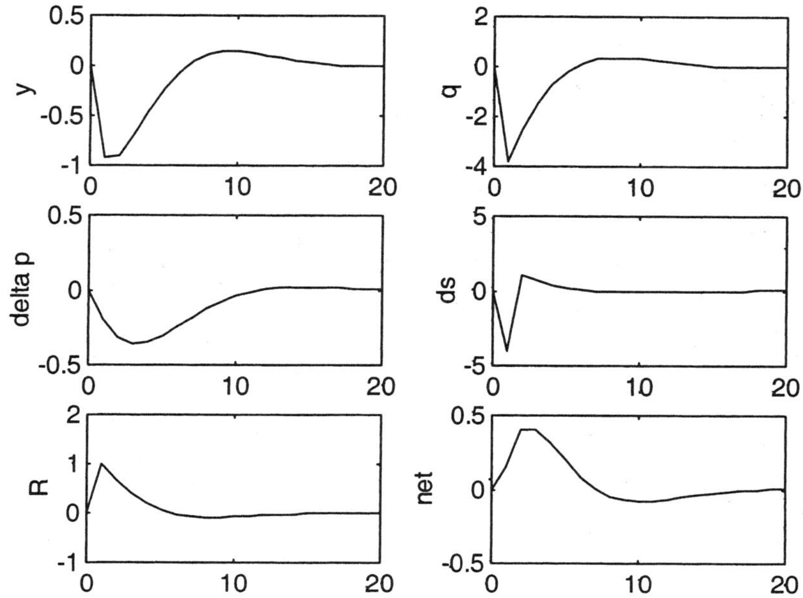

Fig. 1.1 Impulse responses, R_t rule, shock to policy rule

in the top row, where $\mu_1 = 0.5$ and the R_t smoothing parameter equals 0.8, because these are the policy-rule values that are intended to be roughly representative of those found in actual economies, such as those of the United States, the euro area, the United Kingdom, and so on. Doing so, we note that the reported SD values [2.35, 1.96, 2.48, 18.51] are encouragingly similar to statistics for actual economies including the United States over 1955–1996 [2.41, 2.23, 2.80, 12.48] or the euro area 1980–2002 [1.44, 0.83, 1.63, 19.28] or the United Kingdom 1972–2001 [6.8, 2.3, 3.1, 14.6].[23]

Also revealing are properties of impulse-response functions. In that regard, figure 1.1 reports the responses of six model variables to a unit shock in the monetary-policy rule for the reference case just described. Since that type of shock is an unexpected upward blip in the interest rate instrument, R_t, it represents an unsystematic and unexpected tightening in monetary policy. Figure 1.1 indicates that such an event would induce a fall in output that is gradually eliminated, a fall in the inflation rate that returns smoothly to its original level over a number of periods (quarters), a sharp appreciation in nominal and real exchange rates, and an increase in net exports.

23. For details, see McCallum (2004), which also shows reasonably good matches with respect to the first autocorrelations of these four variables for the economies mentioned (and also Japan).

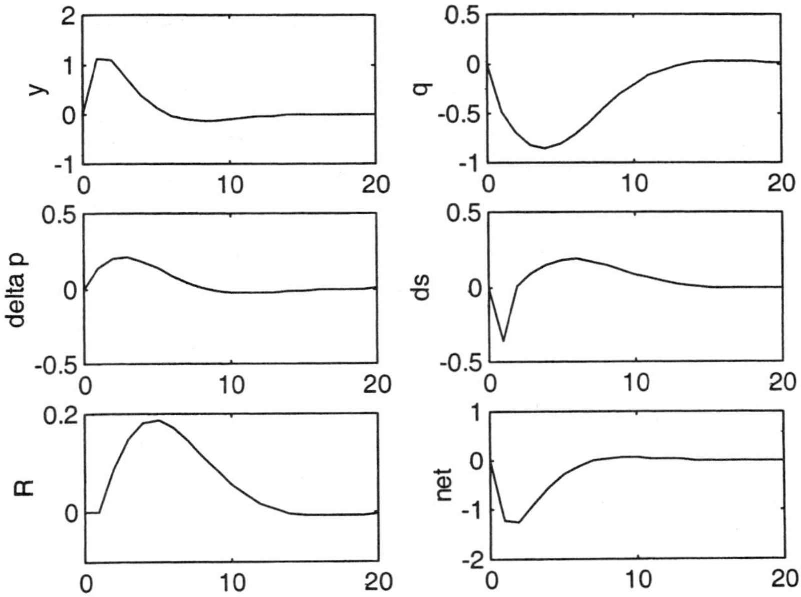

Fig. 1.2 Impulse responses, R_t rule, shock to IS function

These are all responses that accord with economists' standard understanding of the effects of an unexpected tightening of monetary policy. Next, in figure 1.2, we depict the impulses in response to a positive disturbance in the IS function—i.e., an increase in consumers' desire to consume in the present (relative to the future). In this case, both output and inflation rise and only gradually return to their original values. The nominal interest rate rises, as governed by the policy rule, to help stabilize these movements in output and inflation. The real exchange rate appreciates and only slowly returns to its original level. Also, net exports fall, as a result of the increased income levels that imply an increased magnitude of import demand.

In figure 1.3, we find responses to a positive technology shock. Real income increases and returns to its initial level only very slowly, since the shock is highly persistent—close to a random walk. Inflation falls slightly, and monetary policy lets the one-period interest rate fall in order to stabilize inflation—to which it responds more strongly than output. The trade balance deteriorates, since import demand is boosted by the increased level of income, and the real exchange value of domestic goods falls, since they are relatively cheaper to produce than they were before the shock. Finally, in figure 1.4 we depict a shock to uncovered interest parity (i.e., an unexpected and unsystematic exogenous depreciation of the nominal exchange rate). Since prices are sticky, this translates into an unexpected deprecia-

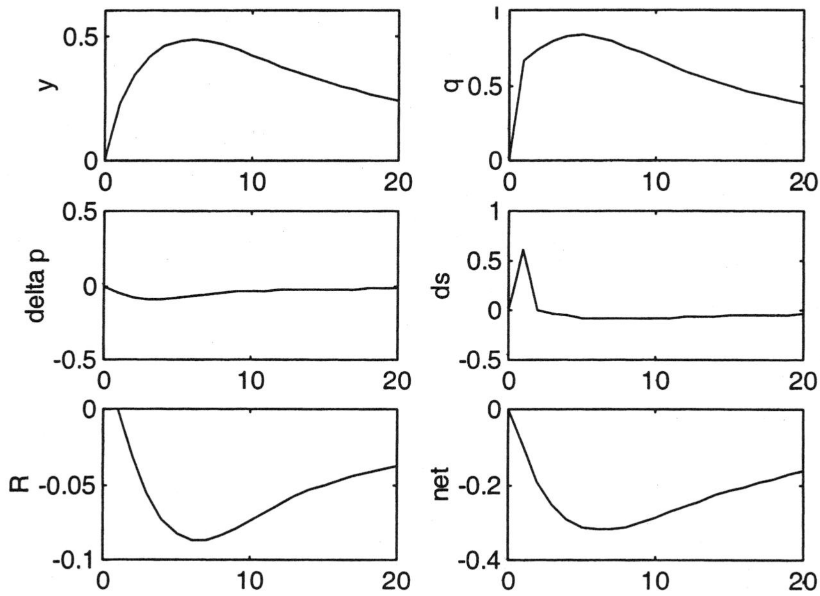

Fig. 1.3 Impulse responses, R_t rule, shock to technology

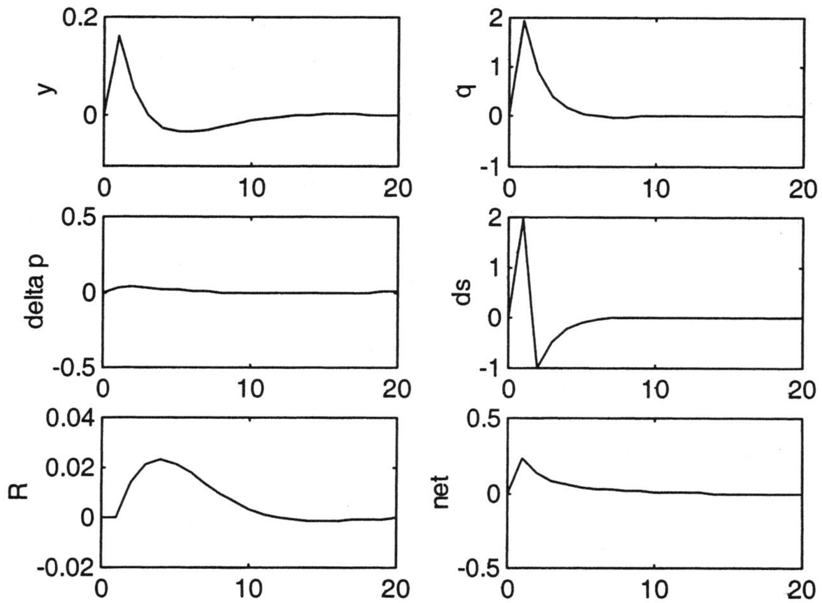

Fig. 1.4 Impulse responses, R_t rule, shock to exchange rate

tion also in the real exchange rate. That induces an increase in net exports and therefore an increase in domestic output, with a very small rise in inflation.[24]

In sum, the responses in figures 1.1–1.4 seem reasonably consistent with those that one would expect from a sensible macro/monetary model of an open economy, and thereby provide substantial encouragement to use of that model for the purpose at hand—i.e., to investigate the stabilizing properties of the MC policy rule (20).

1.6 Simulation Results

The objective now is to present results, based on analysis of the model just described, illustrating the properties of the MC equation (20) as a monetary-policy rule. Ideally, one would like to conduct this analysis with an extended version of the model that includes the nonlinear constraint $R_t \geq 0$. At present I do not have the necessary computational resources to proceed in this fashion, so only linear-model results will be reported below. They seem to be sufficient, however, to make the two essential points. These are as follows:

1. Under conditions implying that monetary policy via an interest rate rule would be immobilized by the ZLB constraint, the MC rule will provide policy actions that are strongly stabilizing.
2. Under conditions such that the ZLB constraint is not relevant, the MC rule would not significantly—if at all—hinder monetary policy.

Together, these two points establish the potential desirability of the MC rule (20).

To develop point (1), the procedure is to conduct simulations in which equation (20) is the policy rule and the interest rate R_t is held fixed at a constant value. For this to be done, one of the structural equations of the model must as a computational matter be eliminated. As in McCallum (2000), the one chosen is the UIP condition (19). As in that previous case, however, the actual *conceptual* step is not the elimination of UIP, but instead its modification to a more general condition, involving some element of the "portfolio balance" theory, together with recognition that it is operationally redundant.[25] (An extended explanation is given below.) The relevant simulation results are presented in tables 1.2 and 1.3. In the first of these the policy parameters μ_2 and μ_3 are held fixed at the values 0.5 and

24. Note parenthetically that this type of response does not reflect how net exports would behave in response to a change in the monetary-policy rule. McCallum (2003) estimates that an increase in the inflation target rate, intended to be permanent, would induce a *decrease* in net exports (the opposite of a "beggar-thy-neighbor" effect).

25. In this case the exogenous variability provided by the UIP shock term ξ_t is not eliminated, but instead is transferred to the policy rule (and included in addition to the e_t term).

Table 1.2 Results with MC rule (20) when $R_t = 0$ (with $\mu_3 = 0.8$)

	$\mu_1 = 0.05$	$\mu_1 = 0.5$	$\mu_1 = 5.0$	$\mu_1 = 50.0$
$\theta = 1.0$	34.41	9.87	2.32	0.79
	13.28	4.53	2.38	2.73
	31.75	10.38	11.02	38.21
$\theta = 0.1$	3.44	2.65	1.31	0.48
	2.44	2.27	2.20	3.54
	8.33	9.45	19.81	65.56
$\theta = 0.025$	1.60	1.38	0.78	0.26
	1.81	1.86	2.47	4.64
	14.69	17.26	36.44	103.75
$\theta = 0.01$	1.16	1.02	0.57	0.16
	1.63	1.81	2.94	5.33
	22.17	26.10	53.72	128.61

Note: Cell entries are standard deviations of Δp_t, $\tilde{y}_t$, and Δs_t.

Table 1.3 Results with MC rule (20) when $R_t = 0$ (with $\mu_3 = 0$)

	$\mu_1 = 0.05$	$\mu_1 = 0.5$	$\mu_1 = 5.0$	$\mu_1 = 50.0$
$\theta = 1.0$	34.41	9.87	2.32	0.79
	13.28	4.53	2.38	2.73
	31.75	10.38	11.02	38.21
$\theta = 0.1$	1.51	1.30	0.74	0.24
	1.79	1.83	2.55	4.77
	15.78	18.42	38.99	108.04
$\theta = 0.025$	1.03	0.90	0.48	0.11
	1.63	1.90	3.31	5.66
	28.46	33.24	67.52	141.37
$\theta = 0.01$	0.95	0.82	0.0	0.08
	1.71	2.06	3.72	5.94
	36.29	42.46	83.21	152.08

Note: Cell entries are standard deviations of Δp_t, $\tilde{y}_t$, and Δs_t.

0.8, respectively, so that the results are comparable to those in the upper cell row of table 1.1. With $\theta = 1$, as in the first cell row of table 1.2, the MC rule is simply a rule for setting the rate of depreciation (or appreciation) of the exchange rate. The figures in this cell row indicate that with μ_1 at the "realistic" value of 0.5, both inflation and the output gap are excessively variable (in relation to actuality and to the comparable values in table 1.1). But the entries in the first cell row of table 1.2 also show clearly that inflation is effectively stabilized by moving to increased (more aggressive) values of μ_1, a result implying that effective stabilization can be provided by the exchange rate rule. Crucially, use of smaller values for θ in the rule have effects that, when $R_t = 0$, are in important respects similar to those from adoption of larger μ_1 magnitudes. Thus while keeping $\mu_1 = 0.5$ we look with interest to the other cell rows in table 1.2, where smaller θ values are specified, and find much improved performance. With $\theta = 0.1$, for example, the SD values for inflation and the output gap are reduced to magnitudes close to those in the second column of table 1.1. In fact, with $\theta = 0.025$, the MC rule SD values with $\mu_1 = 0.5$ dominate[26] those in table 1.1. The same is true, moreover, for $\mu_1 = 0.05$. With large values of μ_1, however, small θ settings have the effect of making Δs_t excessively responsive to fluctuations in inflation and the output gap, leading to large SD values for this instrument variable.

The foregoing comparisons are all based on the assumption that $\mu_3 = 0.8$—i.e., that there is considerable smoothing of short-term interest rates. Table 1.3 provides values analogous to those of table 1.2 but with $\mu_3 = 0$—i.e., no smoothing. In this case there is apparently no possibility of literally dominating the table 1.1 results—for example, obtaining lower variability for all four variables Δp_t, $\tilde{y}_t$, R_t, and Δs_t. Results are quite encouraging, nevertheless, with small values of θ and μ_1. In any event, the main point of interest is not whether performance is better than with an R_t instrument in the absence of any ZLB problem. It is, instead, whether the rule (20) can provide stabilizing power even with R_t immobilized by the ZLB constraint. Table 1.3, like table 1.2, indicates that such stabilization is indeed provided, since the SD of inflation falls sharply as we move to the right (by increasing the μ_1 parameter values) or downward (by decreasing θ).

The second task, involving point (2), is to show that, in the absence of a ZLB situation, use of MC rule (20) would not seriously hinder the stabilizing effects of monetary policy, relative to the standard case with an interest rate instrument. The relevant simulations now do not impose any ZLB feature at all.[27] The results for the case with interest rate smoothing ($\mu_3 = 0.8$) are shown in table 1.4. These are to be compared with the SD values in the top cell row of table 1.1, which are for the standard interest rate rule with smoothing. Consider column two, with the realistic value of 0.5 for μ_1. With $\theta = 1.0$, we have the case in which the MC rule amounts to a pure exchange-rate rule and we find that variability of inflation and the output gap is distinctly higher than in table 1.1 for the same μ_1 value. But if we set $\theta = 0.1$, as in row two of table 1.4, the MC results improve sharply and would no longer be considered to be significantly worse, relative to the case with a pure R_t rule. So this result tends to establish the point at hand, that serious deterioration is not induced by use of the MC rule when it is unnecessary. Furthermore, the results are even better than that, for with $\theta = 0.025$,

26. I.e., are *all* smaller than.

27. The outcomes are, accordingly, more favorable than if the possibility of a ZLB were correctly recognized (i.e., if the constraint $R_t \geq 0$ was actually imposed). But in light of point (1), the outcomes reported are *relatively* more favorable for the reference case with $\theta = 0$ and so our conclusion is conservative (i.e., the error works against our conclusion).

Table 1.4 Results with MC rule (20) with no ZLB ($\mu_3 = 0.8$)

	$\mu_1 = 0.05$	$\mu_1 = 0.5$	$\mu_1 = 5.0$	$\mu_1 = 50.0$
$\theta = 1.0$	10.39	3.63	1.45	0.62
	2.63	2.41	2.17	3.15
	12.84	9.32	10.97	19.87
	9.36	1.65	6.22	29.87
$\theta = 0.1$	2.92	2.26	1.29	0.69
	2.16	1.94	1.73	2.51
	2.61	2.69	4.26	12.63
	16.94	16.42	17.30	24.41
$\theta = 0.025$	3.13	2.31	1.34	0.73
	2.19	1.96	1.69	2.39
	2.61	2.41	3.88	11.60
	18.22	18.01	18.87	27.91
$\theta = 0.01$	3.20	2.31	1.36	0.74
	2.19	1.95	1.68	2.37
	2.73	2.41	3.84	11.39
	18.38	18.39	19.19	27.69

Note: Cell entries are standard deviations of Δp_t, $\tilde{y}_t$, R_t, and Δs_t.

the SD values from rule (20) are as low or lower (than in table 1.1) for all four variables. Thus the MC rule is unambiguously more effective than the R_t rule in this particular case, even without taking any account of the former's crucial advantage, namely, to be usable in cases in which the ZLB constraint is in effect.[28]

Analogous results are presented in table 1.5 under the assumption that $\mu_3 = 0$, rather than $\mu_3 = 0.8$. The conclusions are much the same. With respect to the results in both tables 1.4 and 1.5, it must be recognized that comparisons that do not impose any ZLB constraint are not the same as the ones that would be fully appropriate theoretically (i.e., comparisons of the R_t and MC rules with solutions that have the ZLB constraint binding occasionally). But it would appear that the comparison being made is conservative (in the sense of working against our argument) since there is less weight assigned to the interest rate component by the MC rule than with the reference case, and this component's stabilizing power should actually be excluded.

The main findings presented to this point are that the MC rule does provide effective stabilization even with R_t at the ZLB and that the MC rule can perform as well as the R_t rule when the ZLB is irrelevant. There are many ways in which one would like to check the robustness of these find-

28. A minor caveat should be mentioned, namely, that the results of our simulations are subject to sampling error. Differences of less than 2–3 percent of reported values should not, accordingly, be taken too seriously.

Table 1.5 **Results with MC rule (20) with no ZLB ($\mu_3 = 0.0$)**

	$\mu_1 = 0.05$	$\mu_1 = 0.5$	$\mu_1 = 5.0$	$\mu_1 = 50.0$
$\theta = 1.0$	10.39	3.63	1.45	0.62
	2.63	2.41	2.17	3.15
	12.84	9.32	10.97	19.87
	9.36	1.65	6.22	29.87
$\theta = 0.1$	5.79	2.74	1.28	0.55
	2.03	1.67	1.57	3.05
	6.91	4.94	7.74	27.14
	18.28	17.57	20.67	45.76
$\theta = 0.025$	6.19	2.88	1.33	0.57
	2.06	1.65	1.55	3.01
	6.98	4.69	7.72	27.96
	18.97	18.47	21.52	46.89
$\theta = 0.01$	2.30	2.91	1.33	0.58
	2.07	1.67	1.54	3.02
	6.98	4.69	7.68	28.20
	19.10	18.58	21.72	47.17

Note: Cell entries are standard deviations of Δp_t, $\tilde{y}_t$, R_t, and Δs_t.

ings with respect to alterations in the model utilized. One that will be considered here is to introduce a somewhat more realistic assumption with respect to information available to the model's monetary policymakers. In particular, it will now be assumed that the central bank cannot observe current values of inflation and the output gap when choosing instrument settings for the current period. In rule (20), that is, $E_{t-1}\Delta p_t$ and $E_{t-1}\tilde{y}_t$ will be used in place of actual values of Δp_t and $\tilde{y}_t$. Results are shown in table 1.6, all based on the policy-rule parameter values $\mu_1 = 0.5$, $\mu_2 = 0.5$, and $\mu_3 = 0.8$. In the first column we find SD values under the assumption that the ZLB is irrelevant. The case of a pure interest-rate rule appears in the last cell row ($\theta = 0$), and the other rows show that with small values of θ there is no substantial deterioration in performance from use of the MC rule (20). Then in column two we have results for the case in which the ZLB condition $R_t = 0$ is imposed. Here again we see that the MC rule is effective, in the sense that SD values for inflation and the output gap are reduced as the specified value of θ is decreased, despite the assumed immobilization of the interest rate.

The one other model modification that is explored in the present chapter concerns the economy's openness, as measured by ω_3, the average share of output that is exported (and imported). In the simulations for table 1.6, this share is doubled to 0.30. The results reported in columns three and four are analogous to those in columns one and two. And again they are supportive of the suggestion that the MC rule (20) could be useful in im-

Table 1.6 **MC rule (20) with model alterations ($\mu_1 = 0.5$; $\mu_3 = 0.8$)**

	Case with $E_{t-1}\Delta p_t$ and $E_{t-1}\tilde{y}_t$ in policy rule		Case with $\omega_3 = 0.30$	
	No ZLB	ZLB, $R_t = 0$	No ZLB	ZLB, $R_t = 0$
$\theta = 1.0$ (Δs_t rule)	3.66	9.85	3.23	9.69
	2.51	4.61	2.21	4.70
	9.31	0.00	9.26	0.00
	1.46	10.30	1.55	10.33
$\theta = 0.1$	2.49	3.00	2.13	2.32
	2.08	2.54	2.26	2.30
	2.56	0.00	2.68	0.00
	16.77	10.43	15.56	7.82
$\theta = 0.025$	2.58	1.75	2.16	1.12
	2.07	2.18	2.32	1.86
	2.25	0.00	2.24	0.00
	18.54	17.78	17.23	11.18
$\theta = 0.01$	2.61	1.41	2.19	0.89
	2.30	2.07	2.35	1.92
	2.29	0.00	2.27	0.00
	18.78	25.29	17.51	15.08
$\theta = 0.0$ (R_t rule)	2.62		2.20	
	2.09		2.36	
	2.33		2.28	
	18.99		17.67	

Note: Cell entries are standard deviations of Δp_t, $\tilde{y}_t$, R_t, and Δs_t.

proving macroeconomic performance for an economy that has some danger of a ZLB constraint arising.

1.7 Analytical Issues

There are three additional issues, largely bypassed in the foregoing presentation, that need to be discussed. The first of these has to do with the "elimination" of the UIP condition (19) in the solutions in which the ZLB constraint is imposed. In that regard, most analysts (including myself) would normally include UIP as one component of an open-economy macroeconomic model—despite the existence of much empirical evidence that is, at least on the surface, strongly inconsistent with UIP on a quarter-to-quarter basis. So how can UIP legitimately be avoided in the exercises above? The answer is as follows.

It is well known that to be consistent with the data, UIP relations must include a discrepancy term, typically referred to as a risk premium. Thus included in equation (19) is a risk premium ξ_t that has a sizeable variance relative to other shock terms and furthermore is serially correlated. Often

ξ_t is treated as exogenous, but there are plausible reasons for believing that it would be related to the relative amounts of outside domestic and foreign nominal liabilities outstanding. For example, a hypothesis widely entertained during the 1970s might be expressed as

$$\xi_t = \lambda[B_t - (B_t^* + s_t)] + \zeta_t, \tag{27}$$

where B_t and B_t^* are logs of domestic and foreign government debt (including base money) and ζ_t is an exogenous stochastic shock term. Substituting and recognizing that lags could be involved, we then write

$$R_t - R_t^* = (E_t s_{t+1} - s_t) + \lambda(L)(B_t - B_t^* - s_t) + \zeta_t, \tag{28}$$

which is similar to equations prominent in several older writings of Dornbusch (e.g., 1987, 7). This "portfolio balance" hypothesis receded from its initial prominence because various empirical studies failed to find empirical support. But it is, I suggest, implausible to believe that no such relation obtains in fact, even with weak or transitory effects of the $B_t - B_t^*$ variable. Indeed, models of this type have quite recently been utilized by several leading researchers,[29] while Mussa (2000) has recognized that the absence of any effect of the type hypothesized—i.e., the absence of $B_t - B_t^*$—implies that a nation can enrich itself to an unlimited extent by printing money and buying up foreign assets. And if a relation such as equation (28) does exist, then our procedure above is fully justified. For equation (28) indicates that, even with $R_t = 0$, s_t can be affected by central bank purchases of foreign exchange since they alter the value of $B_t - B_t^*$. Yet the precise specification of relation (28) need not be known, and the relation need not be included in the model, for exactly the same reason that money-demand functions are not needed in analyses that presume use of an interest rate instrument. Thus appending some version of equation (28) to the model would have no effect on the implied behavior of Δp_t, x_t, y_t, or Δs_t; it would merely specify the magnitude of open market purchases of foreign exchange needed to implement the MC policy rule (20). In the present context, this conclusion is important because it implies that our model, with the implicit adoption of equations (27) and (28), features additional state variables relative to the case in which pure UIP holds, and is therefore not one to which the Eggertsson and Woodford (2003, 2004) invariance proposition applies.

A second issue neglected above concerns the argument, developed in the context of a closed economy model, of Benhabib, Schmitt-Grohe, and Uribe (2001). In a series of papers, these authors have suggested that a ZLB situation could arise for reasons quite different from those presumed above. In our analysis, as in that of Krugman (1998); Eggertsson and Woodford

29. Essentially the same relation as (28) is central to the analyses of Flood and Marion (2000); Flood and Jeanne (2005); and Blanchard, Giavazzi, and Sa (2005). Microeconomic support is provided by Jeanne and Rose (2002), and the notable body of work by Evans and Lyons (e.g., 2002) is indirectly supportive.

(2003, 2004); Auerbach and Obstfeld (2004); Coenen and Wieland (2003); and most other writers on the ZLB issue, it is assumed that the relevant RE solution is one in which inflation fluctuates around the target value specified by the usual interest rate policy rule. If the target inflation rate plus the steady-state real rate of interest is a moderately high value, such as 4–5 percent per year, unusually large shocks would be required to push the system to the vicinity of the ZLB. By contrast, Benhabib, Schmitt-Grohe, and Uribe suggest that there are multiple RE equilibria and the relevant one may instead be located at the ZLB value of R_t, even in the absence of shocks. My position, argued most extensively in McCallum (2002), is that this ZLB equilibrium is not plausible, because it fails to be E-stable in the sense developed by Evans and Honkapohja (2001). Such a failure implies that this (apparent) RE equilibrium would not be *learnable* in a setting that recognizes that individual agents are not miraculously endowed with knowledge of the economy's parameters, but need to learn about them over time by observation of the economy's behavior. The usual RE equilibrium, focused upon by the other papers mentioned above, is by contrast E-stable and learnable under standard assumptions. On the basis of this contrast, I would argue that the usual RE equilibrium is the only one of these two that is plausible as a description of the behavior of an actual economy.

Finally, a third issue relates to the view that anti-ZLB strategies involving the exchange rate are politically objectionable because they require sharp depreciation, which (some say) serves to improve the trade balance and thereby reduce the country's imports from its trading partners. For this reason, such strategies have been said to rely upon "beggar-thy-neighbor" effects that are globally undesirable. The premise of this argument seems highly dubious, however, for a successful anti-ZLB policy will prevent a decline or stagnation in a country's real income level, which is the more important determinant of its imports. Furthermore, the exchange rate responses induced by the MC rule (20) pertain to nominal exchange rates and will have highly temporary real effects, except through income, if the rule is effective. Quantitative simulation results exemplifying this claim are reported as a major feature of McCallum (2003, 16–23) for an expansionary increase in the target inflation rate π^*, with policy being conducted via the pure exchange-rate rule (8).[30] On the general point, see also Svensson (2003, 163–4).

1.8 Conclusions

Let us close with a brief summary of the chapter's arguments. It begins by emphasizing the difference between policy-rule changes, intended to help

30. Somewhat contradictory results are briefly reported by Coenen and Wieland (2003), but their policy experiment is quite different (with no policy response until after the ZLB constraint has been in effect for ten quarters) and their model does not recognize distinct import and export quantities.

escape an existing ZLB situation, and maintained policy rules designed so as to avoid the "liquidity trap" aspects of a ZLB situation. Analysis assuming that rule changes would be quickly recognized, understood, and believed—so that a new RE equilibrium would be relevant immediately—seems implausible. Accordingly, the chapter focuses not on policy changes for escaping a liquidity trap, but on the design of a policy rule that should retain stabilization effectiveness for monetary policy even if the economy is temporarily shocked into a situation in which the ZLB on nominal interest rates makes demand stimulation via interest rate reductions infeasible.

The particular policy rule considered in detail is one that uses as its instrument or indicator variable a weighted average of the usual short-term interest rate and the rate of depreciation of the nominal exchange rate. With a small weight attached to the depreciation term, inclusion of the latter would be nearly irrelevant in normal situations. But when the ZLB condition $R_t = 0$ prevails, then adjustments in the weighted average—which has some similarities to a monetary-conditions index—call for large movements in the depreciation rate (effected by central bank purchases of foreign exchange). These would affect aggregate demand by another channel, and would provide stabilization power—with no need for any additional exit strategy.

Stabilizing properties of this MC rule are studied by means of stochastic simulations with a model of a small open economy developed by McCallum and Nelson (1999). The latter differs from other small-scale models based on optimizing behavior (but with sticky prices) by treating imports as inputs to the economy's production processes, rather than as consumer goods, but that difference is not particularly germane to the topic at hand. The simulations indicate that: (a) under conditions implying that monetary policy via an interest rate rule would be immobilized by the ZLB constraint, the MC rule would provide strong stabilizing policy actions; yet (b) under conditions such that the ZLB constraint is not relevant, the MC rule would not significantly—if at all—hinder monetary policy. Together, these two sets of results are supportive of the idea that a monetary policy of the MC type could be useful for an economy with a low target inflation rate.

Appendix

Helicopter Drops

The object here is to discuss very briefly the effectiveness of "helicopter drop" policy for escaping a ZLB situation. Would such a policy be successful? I suggest that it would be ineffective if the economy possesses Ricardian properties, as in the case of the canonical model used by E&W (2003) and many others. The first step of the argument is as follows.

A "helicopter drop" is a transfer (gift) of money to households. In this regard, note that a transfer of \$K is equivalent to the combination of two operations, namely,

1. A lump-sum tax reduction of \$K financed by the sale of \$K of T-bills to households (i.e., a gift of \$K of T-bills to households), and
2. An open market purchase of \$K worth of T-bills.

But, it is well known that an operation of type (1) has no effect if the economy is Ricardian and also that one of type (2) has no effect at the ZLB (where base money and T-bills are perfect substitutes at the margin). Thus the combined operation—the helicopter drop—will have no effect in the ZLB situation.

The second part of the argument pertains to a sequence of such operations. Wouldn't an ongoing sequence of helicopter drops violate a transversality condition if there were no inflationary effect, since the nominal money stock will be growing without bound in the proposed experiment? Well, yes, it could if the ZLB situation were to go on forever. But analysis of ZLB issues typically pertains to situations in which an economy, assumed to have a positive *steady-state* nominal interest rate, is temporarily at the ZLB as the result of some negative shock. In such cases, the economy will escape the ZLB of its own accord at some point in the finite future, after which time p_t will tend to grow in line with m_t. So, since transversality results pertain only to the infinitely distant future they are not relevant. (This argument does not deny that one could obtain effects from repeated helicopter drops by using a non-Ricardian model, such as the overlapping-generations model considered in McCallum [2000, 876–80].)

References

Amato, J. D., and T. Laubach. 2004. Implications of habit formation for optimal monetary policy. *Journal of Monetary Economics* 51:305–25.

Auerbach, A. J., and M. Obstfeld. 2003. The case for open-market purchases in a liquidity trap. NBER Working Paper no. 9814. Cambridge, MA: National Bureau of Economic Research, July.

———. 2004. Monetary and fiscal remedies for deflation. *American Economic Review Papers and Proceedings* 94:71–75.

Ball, L. 1999. Policy rules for open economies. In *Monetary policy rules,* ed. J. B. Taylor, 127–44. Chicago: University of Chicago Press.

Benhabib, J., S. Schmitt-Grohe, and M. Uribe. 2001. The perils of Taylor Rules. *Journal of Economic Theory* 96:40–69.

Blanchard, O. J., F. Giavazzi, and F. Sa. 2005. The U.S. current account and the dollar. NBER Working Paper no. 11137. Cambridge, MA: National Bureau of Economic Research, February.

Coenen, G., and V. Wieland. 2003. The zero-interest-rate bound and the role of the exchange rate for monetary policy in Japan. *Journal of Monetary Economics* 50:1071–1101.

Detken, C., and V. Gaspar. 2003. Maintaining price stability under free-floating: A fearless way out of the corner? ECB Working Paper no. 241. Frankfurt: European Central Bank.

Dornbusch, R. 1987. Exchange rate economics: 1986. *Economic Journal* 97 (385): 1–18.

Eggertsson, G. B., and M. Woodford (E&W). 2003. Optimal monetary policy in a liquidity trap. NBER Working Paper no. 9968. Cambridge, MA: National Bureau of Economic Research, September.

———. 2004. Policy options in a liquidity trap. *American Economic Review Papers and Proceedings* 94:76–79.

Evans, D. D., and R. K. Lyons. 2002. Order flow and exchange rate dynamics. *Journal of Political Economy* 110:170–180.

Evans, G. W., and S. Honkapohja. 2001. *Learning and expectations in macroeconomics.* Princeton, NJ: Princeton University Press.

Flood, R. P., and O. Jeanne. 2005. An interest rate defense of a fixed exchange rate? *Journal of International Economics,* forthcoming.

Flood, R. P., and N. P. Marion. 2000. Self-fulfilling risk predictions: An application to speculative attacks. *Journal of International Economics* 50:245–68.

Fuhrer, J. C. 2000. Habit formation in consumption and its implications for monetary-policy models. *American Economic Review* 90:367–90.

Fuhrer, J. C., and G. R. Moore. 1995. Inflation persistence. *Quarterly Journal of Economics* 110:127–59.

Gali, J., and M. Gertler. 1999. Inflation dynamics: A structural econometric analysis. *Journal of Monetary Economics* 44:195–222.

Gerlach, S., and F. Smets. 2000. MCIs and monetary policy. *European Economic Review* 44:1677–700.

Goodfriend, M. 2000. Overcoming the zero bound on interest rate policy. *Journal of Money, Credit, and Banking* 32:1007–35.

Jeanne, O., and A. K. Rose. 2002. Noise trading and exchange rate regimes. *Quarterly Journal of Economics* 117:537–69.

Jung, T., Y. Teranishi, and T. Watanabe. 2001. Zero bound on nominal interest rates and optimal monetary policy. Hitotsubashi University. Working Paper. Tokyo, Japan.

Kollmann, R. 2002. Monetary policy rules in the open economy: Effects on welfare and business cycles. *Journal of Monetary Economics* 49:989–1015.

Krugman, P. 1998. It's baaack! Japan's slump and the return of the liquidity trap. *Brookings Papers on Economic Activity,* Issue no. 2, 137–87.

Kydland, F. E., and E. C. Prescott. 1977. Rules rather than discretion: The inconsistency of optimal plans. *Journal of Political Economy* 85:473–91.

Laxton, D., and P. Pesenti. 2003. Monetary rules for small, open, emerging economies. *Journal of Monetary Economics* 50:1109–46.

Lucas, R. E., Jr. 1980. Rules, discretion, and the role of the economic advisor. In *Rational expectations and economic policy,* ed. S. Fischer, 199–210. Chicago: University of Chicago Press.

Lucas, R. E., Jr., and T. J. Sargent, eds. 1981. *Rational expectations and econometric practice.* Minneapolis: University of Minnesota Press.

McCallum, B. T. 2000. Theoretical analysis regarding a zero lower bound on nominal interest rates. *Journal of Money, Credit, and Banking* 32:870–904.

———. 2002. Inflation targeting and the liquidity trap. In *Inflation targeting: Design, performance, challenges,* ed. by N. Loayza and R. Soto, 396–437. Central Bank of Chile.

———. 2003. Japanese monetary policy, 1991–2001. *Federal Reserve Bank of Richmond Economic Quarterly* 89 (Winter): 1–31.
———. 2004. The monetary policy transmission mechanism in industrial countries. CMU Working Paper. Carnegie Mellon University, Tepper School.
McCallum, B. T., and E. Nelson (M&N). 1999. Nominal income targeting in an open-economy optimizing model. *Journal of Monetary Economics* 43:553–78.
———. 2000. Monetary policy for an open economy: An alternative framework with optimizing agents and sticky prices. *Oxford Review of Economic Policy* 16:74–91.
Mussa, M. 2000. Reflections on monetary policy at low inflation. *Journal of Money, Credit, and Banking* 34:1100–6.
Orphanides, A., and V. Wieland. 2000. Efficient monetary policy design near price stability. *Journal of the Japanese and International Economies* 14:327–65.
Reifschneider, D., and J. S. Williams. 2000. Three lessons for monetary policy in a low inflation era. *Journal of Money, Credit, and Banking* 32:936–66.
Rotemberg, J. J., and M. Woodford. 1997. An optimization based econometric framework for the evaluation of monetary policy. In *NBER macroeconomics annual 1997,* ed. Ben S. Bernanke and Julio J. Rotemberg, 297–346.
Smets, F., and R. Wouters. 2002. Openness, imperfect exchange rate pass-through, and monetary policy. *Journal of Monetary Economics* 49:947–81.
Svensson, L. E. O. 2001. The zero bound in an open economy: A foolproof way of escaping from a liquidity trap. *Bank of Japan Monetary and Economic Studies* 19:277–312.
———. 2003. Escaping from a liquidity trap and deflation: The foolproof way and others. *Journal of Economic Perspectives* 17:145–66.
Taylor, J. B. 1993. Discretion versus policy rules in practice. *Carnegie-Rochester Conference Series on Public Policy* 39:195–214.
Wolman, A. S. 1998. Staggered price setting and the zero bound on nominal interest rates. *Federal Reserve Bank of Richmond Economic Quarterly* 84 (Fall): 1–24.
Woodford, M. 2003. *Interest and prices: Foundations of a theory of monetary policy.* Princeton, NJ: Princeton University Press.

Comment James Harrigan

Japan's experience with zero interest rates, which began in February 1999, has been a disaster for the Japanese people but a boon to monetary economists, who have been presented with a fascinating pathology that most never expected to see. One of the most important theoretical results to come out of the resulting literature is the "irrelevance proposition" of Eggertsson and Woodford (2003).

McCallum discusses the Eggertsson-Woodford result in some detail, and so it is worthwhile to digress briefly on how the result is derived. In the Eggertsson-Woodford model, monetary policy is described by two opera-

James Harrigan is a research officer in the International Research Department of the Federal Reserve Bank of New York, and a research associate of the National Bureau of Economic Research.

tional rules. The first is a general Taylor rule that determines the nominal interest rate. The second element of the monetary-policy framework is a money-supply rule with two parts: when $i_t > 0$, M_t is determined by money demand, otherwise the central bank targets the money base according to some rule. In implementing policy, the central bank may hold a very general portfolio of real and nominal assets, and makes transfers to the treasury. Fiscal policy consists of a rule for total government debt at a point in time and a very general rule for the composition of debt.

The rest of the model is a standard forward-looking macromodel of the type exhaustively detailed in Woodford (2003). With this setup, Eggertsson-Woodford prove the following irrelevance result: the rational-expectations equilibrium for output, prices, interest rates, and so on, is independent of the specification of

1. the money-base targeting rule;
2. the composition of the central banks balance sheet;
3. the composition of the government's debt.

The key implication is that "unconventional" monetary policy has no effect. In interpreting this result it is crucial to keep in mind that "conventional" monetary policy includes the expected future path of the overnight interest rate. In other words, the *only* thing that matters for monetary policy is the expected future path of the overnight interest rate.

Eggertsson-Woodford elaborate on this result, in particular the perhaps surprising implication that the maturity structure of the central bank's open market operations is unimportant:

> Even if the effects of open-market operations under the conditions described in the proposition are not exactly zero, it seems unlikely that they should be large. In our view, it is more important to note that our irrelevance proposition depends on an assumption that interest-rate policy is specified in a way that implies that these [long bond] open market operations have no consequences for [overnight] interest rate policy, either immediately, or at any subsequent date either. (23)

What is the relevance of this digression to McCallum's paper? McCallum is a little vague on the details of how his proposed rule (equation [9]) would be implemented, but it seems to envision domestic money-market operations to manipulate the domestic interest rate and foreign exchange operations to manipulate the exchange rate. Both operations involve changes in the domestic monetary base, differing only in the assets which are purchased or sold to accomplish the desired change in the base.

While Eggertsson-Woodford use a closed-economy model, I strongly suspect that extending their framework to an open economy would not overturn their irrelevance result. In particular, I would expect that the irrelevance of the composition of the balance sheet of the consolidated government would survive the addition of foreign bonds to the list of government assets. This implies two things. First, unsterilized foreign exchange (FX) operations are indistinguishable in their effects from operations in domestic bond markets. Second, sterilized FX intervention would have no effect on anything. In short, one could replace "foreign bonds" for "long bonds" in the above quotation from Eggertsson-Woodford.

McCallum has a short discussion about the optimal composition of asset purchases/sales in the implementation of his proposal. He suggests that the fraction of foreign bond purchases might be a constant, or that the fraction could be increased as the zero bound looms. My conjecture that the Eggertsson-Woodford proposition will apply here suggests that the optimal fraction is undefined.

More generally, McCallum is vague about the operational channel through which the exchange rate is to be manipulated. The empirical evidence on FX intervention is somewhat mixed, but there is a near-consensus that unsterilized intervention is indistinguishable in its effects from domestic open market operations, while sterilized intervention has at best very small effects (Sarno and Taylor 2001).

On the latter, the recent experience of Japan is instructive. Between January 2003 and April 2004, the Japanese Ministry of Finance spent over ¥35 trillion (7 percent of annual GDP) on purchasing foreign bonds (virtually all of them dollar denominated).[1] The yen appreciated against the dollar by 13 percent over the same period. It is impossible to know what might have happened to the exchange rate in the absence of intervention, but it is hard to imagine this episode being taken as evidence in favor of a powerful effect of sterilized intervention.

Surprisingly, McCallum's model contains no specification at all of a rule for FX intervention operations. The government is simply assumed to be able to set the rate of change of the exchange rate to any desired level, and at the zero bound the desired level is given by equation (10). Implementing this target might be possible with a sufficiently large *permanent* expansion of the monetary base, but my discussion here suggests that the composition of that monetary-base expansion is irrelevant.[2]

1. There has been a great deal of confusion among economists and Japan watchers about how much of this historic intervention was sterilized or unsterilized, since the domestic money base increased by ¥13 trillion over the intervention period. The correct answer is that the intervention was completely sterilized, since the FX operations by the Ministry of Finance had no effect on Bank of Japan decisions about the size of the monetary base. The Bank of Japan has no legal authority or practical influence on FX operations, and the Ministry of Finance similarly has no legal authority or practical influence on monetary policy.

2. The reason that Japan's extraordinary expansion of the monetary base (up 64 percent in the three years following the start of "quantitative easing" in March 2001) hasn't eliminated deflation, or led to a depreciation of the yen, is that the private sector understands that the expansion is not permanent. When deflation ends, the Bank of Japan will absorb all excess reserves and continue their historic commitment to price stability.

References

Eggertsson, Gauti B. and Michael Woodford. 2003. Optimal monetary policy in a liquidity trap, NBER Working Paper No. 9968. Cambridge, MA: National Bureau of Economic Research, September.

Sarno, Lucio, and Mark P. Taylor. 2001. Official intervention in the foreign exchange market: Is it effective and, if so, how does it work? *Journal of Economic Literature* 39 (3): 839–68.

Woodford, Michael. 2003. *Interest and prices.* Princeton, NJ: Princeton University Press.

2

Monetary Policy, Asset-price Bubbles, and the Zero Lower Bound

Tim Robinson and Andrew Stone

2.1 Introduction

In a low-inflation economy, the bursting of an asset-price bubble can have significant and long-lasting consequences, both for the economy and for the operation of monetary policy. In Japan, the collapse of a major bubble in property and stock prices in the early 1990s ushered in over a decade of weak growth and declining price pressures—culminating, by late 1998, in ongoing consumer-price deflation. This, in turn, has seen the Bank of Japan constrained in its actions, for over five years, by the zero lower bound (ZLB) on nominal interest rates. Likewise, the tech stock crash in the United States in 2000 marked the start of an economic downturn which saw the year-ended growth rate of the core personal consumption expenditure price index decline briefly to below 1 percent, and prompted concerns for a time that the U.S. federal funds rate might also reach the zero lower bound.

These examples suggest, at the very least, that the interaction between asset-price bubbles and monetary policy is an important one for policymakers, especially if operating in a low-inflation environment. If asset-price bubble collapses represent a primary mechanism by which otherwise well-functioning economies may become seriously destabilized, even to the

Tim Robinson is the Japan Economist in the Overseas Economies Section of Economic Group at the Reserve Bank of Australia. Andrew Stone is a senior research manager in the Economic Research Department at the Reserve Bank of Australia.

We are grateful to Louise Wilkinson for coding assistance, and to colleagues at the Reserve Bank, as well as Piti Disyatat, Kenneth Kuttner, Andrew Rose, Takatoshi Ito, and other participants at the 15th Annual East Asian Seminar on Economics, for helpful comments. The views expressed in this paper are those of the authors and should not be attributed to the Reserve Bank of Australia or the National Bureau of Economic Research.

point where monetary policy becomes constrained by the ZLB, this raises key questions for policymakers as to how they might be able to forestall, or at least reduce, the fall-out from such collapses. These questions relate not just to how policymakers might wish to react preemptively, as asset-price misalignments develop, but also to choices about the framework within which policy is set.

This chapter uses a simple, stylized two-equation model, due originally to Ball (1999a) and Svensson (1997), to explore these questions. More precisely, it builds upon recent work by Gruen, Plumb, and Stone (2003), in which the Ball-Svensson model was augmented by the inclusion of an asset-price bubble. Gruen, Plumb, and Stone (2003) then used this augmented model to investigate the implications of such bubbles for optimal policy settings, under a variety of assumptions both about the bubble's stochastic behavior, and about the degree to which this behavior can be influenced by the actions of policymakers.

Gruen, Plumb, and Stone (2003) highlighted two conflicting influences on policymakers attempting to handle a developing bubble. On the one hand, they are likely to become more confident as time passes that observed asset-price rises do indeed constitute a bubble, and so become more willing to respond actively to these rises. At the same time, however, they would become increasingly conscious of the negative effects on the economy from the bubble's eventual bursting—effects which they would be anxious not to compound, given the delay with which any ex post monetary loosening would flow through to real activity.

As a result of these competing influences, Gruen, Plumb, and Stone (2003) found that, even with an *excellent understanding* both of the economy and of the parameters governing a bubble's stochastic behavior, it may be unclear whether policymakers would wish to tighten policy in the face of such a bubble, beyond the degree to which they would do so based on an efficient markets view of asset prices. Their results highlighted the stringent informational requirements therefore inherent in a preemptive policy approach to asset-price bubbles—and the need for delicate judgments, in pursuing such a strategy, about both the process driving the bubble and its likely sensitivity to monetary policy.

In this chapter we extend the work of Gruen, Plumb, and Stone (2003) by removing one simplification built into their modeling approach. This was the assumption that, whenever the economy is struck by a large negative shock, such as the bursting of an asset-price bubble, policymakers can set the real interest rate as far below neutral as desired, regardless of the current level of inflation. This is equivalent to assuming that, at all times, the nominal interest rate may be set arbitrarily, so ignoring the ZLB.

By contrast, in this chapter we impose a zero lower bound on nominal interest rates, as a constraint on the actions of policymakers attempting to deal with a developing asset-price bubble. We then examine the implications this has for both: the behavior of policymakers who believe that they understand the stochastic properties of the bubble; and the policy framework within which they must make their decisions.

With regard to the former, policymakers who wish to react preemptively to a growing bubble must now take into account whether their current actions might result in them being unable to set the real interest rate optimally in subsequent periods, whenever the bubble bursts. Moreover, in doing so, they must allow for the possibility, not merely that their actions might become constrained in the period in which the bubble actually bursts, but also that this might occur with a lag (as the bubble's collapse flows through to lower inflation, so reducing the amount by which the real interest rate can be set below neutral).[1]

In regards to the latter issue, if inflation expectations are at least partially backward-looking then, with a zero lower bound on nominal interest rates, the level of inflation immediately prior to an asset-price bubble collapse clearly becomes important. Hence, this constraint may influence decisions about aspects of the policy framework itself, such as policymakers' preferred choice of target inflation rate.

2.2 Methodology

2.2.1 The Augmented Ball-Svensson Model

The starting point for our analysis is a simple model of a closed economy, due to Ball (1999a) and Svensson (1997). This model is described by two equations:

$$y_t = -\beta r_{t-1} + \lambda y_{t-1} \tag{1}$$

$$\pi_t = \pi_{t-1} + \alpha y_{t-1}, \tag{2}$$

where y is the output gap, r is the difference between the real interest rate and its neutral level, π is the difference between consumer-price inflation and its targeted rate, and α, β, and λ are positive constants (with $\lambda \leq 1$ so that output gaps do not behave explosively with real interest rates at neutral).

As noted in Gruen, Plumb, and Stone (2003), the Ball-Svensson model "has the advantage of simplicity and intuitive appeal. . . . It assumes, real-

1. Note that our focus in this chapter is on the effect which these possibilities (i.e., the presence of the ZLB) might have on the interest rate recommendations of policymakers, *over and above* whatever direct impact the presence of the bubble itself might have on these recommendations in the absence of the ZLB. Note also that our focus on the impact of the ZLB on policymakers' thinking while a bubble is still growing is in contrast to much of the recent research on the ZLB, which has focused on how policymakers should react once the ZLB has been reached. A brief review of where this chapter sits within the recent literature on both asset-price bubbles and the ZLB is provided in appendix A.

istically, that monetary policy affects real output, and hence the output gap, with a lag, and that the output gap affects inflation with a further lag." We adopt the same baseline values for the parameters α, β, and λ as those chosen by Ball, for the case where each period in the model corresponds to one year, namely $\alpha = 0.4$, $\beta = 1$, and $\lambda = 0.8$.[2]

Next, following Gruen, Plumb, and Stone (2003), we augment the model with an asset-price bubble.[3] We assume that in year zero the economy is in equilibrium, with both output and inflation at their target values, $y_0 = \pi_0 = 0$ and that the bubble has zero size, $a_0 = 0$. In subsequent years, we assume that the bubble evolves as follows:

$$a_t = \begin{cases} a_{t-1} + \gamma_t, \text{ with probability } 1 - p_t \\ 0, \text{ with probability } p_t. \end{cases} \tag{3}$$

Thus, in each year, the bubble either grows by an amount, $\gamma_t > 0$, or bursts and collapses back to zero. We also assume that, once the bubble has burst, it does not re-form. To allow for the effect of the bubble on the economy, we modify the Ball-Svensson model to read:

$$y_t = -\beta r_{t-1} + \lambda y_{t-1} + \Delta a_t \tag{4}$$

$$\pi_t = \pi_{t-1} + \alpha y_{t-1}. \tag{5}$$

In each year that the bubble is growing it has an expansionary effect on the economy, increasing the level of output, and the output gap, by γ_t. The bubble is, however, assumed to have no direct effect on consumer-price inflation, although there will be consequences for inflation to the extent that the bubble leads the economy to operate with excess demand as it expands, and with excess supply when it bursts. When the bubble bursts, the effect on the economy is, of course, contractionary: if the bubble bursts in year t, the direct effect on output, and the output gap, in that year will be $\Delta a_t = -\Sigma_{i=1}^{t-1} \gamma_i$. Thus, the longer the bubble survives, the greater will be the contractionary effect on the economy when it bursts.

Equations (3), (4), and (5) describe the model used by Gruen, Plumb, and Stone (2003), and adopted again here. In a moment we shall want to also in-

2. Note that Ball chose these parameter values to fit the U.S. economy, based on previous studies by Ball (1994); DeLong and Summers (1988); and Rudebusch (1995). Ball (1999b) also subsequently used these same base-parameter values in an open-economy version of the model which he noted was "meant to apply to medium-to-small open economies such as Canada, Australia, and New Zealand" (although an increase in the real interest rate, for example, affects output through two channels in this open-economy model—directly and via the exchange rate—rather than just via the former channel). Finally, Ball and Svensson also added white noise shocks to each of their equations, which we have suppressed for simplicity.

3. The discussion of equations (3), (4), and (5) below directly mimics that of Gruen, Plumb, and Stone (2003) initially, but is augmented with a discussion of the rationale for some of the notable features of these equations, such as the absence of any forward-looking component to the inflation-expectations formation process embodied in equation (5).

corporate a ZLB on the nominal interest rate into the model, but before doing so it is worth remarking on a number of aspects of the model so far.

The most notable feature of equations (3), (4), and (5) is that the treatment of both the asset-price bubbles and the structure of the economy is deliberately kept extremely simple and stylized. For example, the model allows for no forward-looking element in the formation of inflation expectations, so limiting the scope for monetary policy to influence the economy through precommitment to a particular monetary-policy path or approach. Furthermore, the asset-price bubbles in the model are treated in a simple, reduced-form fashion, in terms of their impact on real activity, without any attempt to model the bubble-formation process itself.

The reason for these choices is that much of the discussion about how monetary policy should react to asset-price bubbles focuses on the extreme informational difficulties that policymakers face in determining the properties of a given bubble (current size, likelihood of collapse), or whether or not a bubble even exists. These informational difficulties are often cited as a principal reason why an activist approach to monetary policy in the face of asset-price misalignments might be difficult or suboptimal in practice. However, by using a highly simplified model of the economy, in which policymakers are also endowed with full knowledge of the stochastic properties of a developing asset-price bubble, Gruen, Plumb, and Stone (2003) were able to abstract from these informational issues. By doing so, they were able to demonstrate that there are other factors, besides informational constraints, which complicate an approach of actively responding to asset-price bubbles—to the point of sometimes making it problematic even to know whether policy ought to be set more tightly or more loosely than it would otherwise be.

Our adoption in this chapter of the same simplified modeling framework as Gruen, Plumb, and Stone (2003) should be viewed in the same spirit. In particular, the reason that we do not attempt to provide a more explicit or detailed model of asset prices in this chapter is simply that doing so is not a focus of the chapter. Rather, extending the work of Gruen, Plumb, and Stone (2003), we wish to study whether or not it is clear-cut in what way the presence of a ZLB on nominal interest rates would influence policymakers attempting to handle a developing asset-price bubble, even when in possession of a good understanding of the stochastic properties of the bubble's *likely future impact on the real economy.* The same rationale applies to our choice of a simple and transparent modeling framework which excludes any forward-looking element to the inflation-expectations formation process. Excluding such an element does not indicate that we consider the management of future expectations to be an unimportant tool in the armory of a central bank, especially as the economy approaches the ZLB. Rather, it simply reflects that our aim in this chapter is to highlight *other* factors which would—even were such management of future expectations possible—still complicate the task of policymakers trying to determine how, optimally, to respond actively to a developing bubble.[4]

Returning to the model itself, last but not least we introduce a zero lower bound on the nominal interest rate into the model described by equations (3), (4), and (5). It is at this point that our treatment diverges from that in Gruen, Plumb, and Stone (2003).

In Gruen, Plumb, and Stone (2003) the simplifying assumption is made that policymakers control the real interest rate, rather than the nominal one, and that this real interest rate can be adjusted arbitrarily, in response to shocks to the economy. Here we drop this latter assumption and require, instead, that the real interest rate never be such that the corresponding level of the nominal rate would be negative.

This requirement may be expressed mathematically by introducing variables r_t^{lvl}, i_t^{lvl}, and π_t^{lvl} for the respective levels of the real interest rate, nominal interest rate, and rate of inflation.[5] Then, writing r^*, i^*, and π^* for the corresponding neutral or target levels of these variables, the zero lower bound restriction simply becomes the requirement that

$$i_t^{\text{lvl}} \geq 0, \tag{6}$$

while the following four identities, primarily relating real and nominal variables, must also be satisfied:

$$i^* = r^* + \pi^* \tag{7}$$

$$\pi_t^{\text{lvl}} = \pi^* + \pi_t \tag{8}$$

$$r_t^{\text{lvl}} = r^* + r_t \tag{9}$$

$$i_t^{\text{lvl}} = r_t^{\text{lvl}} + \pi_t^{\text{lvl}} = i^* + r_t + \pi_t. \tag{10}$$

2.2.2 Activist and Skeptical Policymakers

Equations (3) to (10) summarize our Ball-Svensson economy, experiencing an asset-price bubble, and subject to a zero lower bound on nominal interest rates. Returning to the framework employed by Gruen, Plumb, and Stone (2003), we next introduce two different types of policymaker: skeptics, who don't try to second-guess asset-price developments, and activists, who believe that they understand enough about asset-price bubbles to set policy actively in response to them.

To draw the distinction more precisely, both types of policymaker understand how the output gap and inflation evolve over time, as summarized

4. Note that the preceding paragraphs represent a response to some of the issues, regarding the modeling framework adopted in the chapter, raised by participants at the 15th Annual East Asian Seminar on Economics, held in Tokyo in June 2003, at which this chapter was presented.

5. Variables with a "lvl" superscript thus represent *levels* variables, while those without a "lvl" superscript continue to denote the *deviations* of these levels variables from their neutral or target values.

by equations (4) and (5). Activists also understand, and respond optimally to, the stochastic behavior of the bubble, as summarized by equation (3). Skeptics, by contrast, respond to asset-bubble shocks, Δa_t, when they arrive, but assume that the expected value of future shocks is zero.

Such skeptics should not, however, be thought of as naive or ignorant for adopting this position. As an asset-price bubble grows, there is always disagreement about whether the observed asset-price developments constitute a bubble, in which case expectations about future asset-price changes may be nonzero, or are instead consistent with an efficient market, in which case the expected value of future changes in the asset price is zero.[6] In holding that the expected value of future asset-price shocks is zero, skeptical policymakers in our framework should therefore simply be viewed as believers in the efficient markets hypothesis.

Continuing, we assume that policymakers observe in each year whether the bubble has grown further, or collapsed, before setting the interest rate for that year. Given the nature of the lags in the model, this year's interest rate will have no impact on real activity until next year, and on inflation until the year after that.

We also assume that our two types of policymaker have the same preferences, and care about the volatility of both inflation and output. Explicitly, we thus assume that in each year t, policymakers (whether activist or skeptic) recommend the real interest rate, r_t, which will minimize the weighted sum of the expected future squared deviations of inflation and output from their target levels:

$$L = \sum_{\tau=t+1}^{\infty} [E_t(y_\tau^2) + \mu E_t(\pi_\tau^2)], \tag{11}$$

where μ is the relative weight on the deviations of inflation and E_t is the policymaker's year t expectation. For the baseline results in this chapter

6. In the late 1990s, precisely this debate was occurring within the U.S. Federal Reserve in relation to the U.S. stock market, as the following quotation from Stephen Cecchetti makes clear.

> From August 1997 to June 1999 I sat on the backbench at the meetings of the FOMC [Federal Open Market Committee] and received all of the material distributed to the participants. . . . The interesting thing is that during the period when I took part in this process, the board staff preparing the forecasts invariably assumed that the U.S. stock market would decline significantly—10 to 20 percent declines in the Wilshire 5000 index were commonly the basis for the forecasts. They clearly believed that the stock market was overvalued. . . .
>
> At the time this was all happening, I confess that I was scandalized. I regularly ranted about the practice of forecasting a dramatic decline in the stock market. Like the vast majority of academics, I adhered to the efficient markets view . . . While we needed to assume something about the stock market, shouldn't we assume the equity index would stay constant at its current level indefinitely? . . .
>
> This happened five years ago (which is why I can talk about it now), and in the interim I have changed many of my views. (Cecchetti 2003)

Skeptical policymakers in our framework may be characterized as those who adhere to the approach of Cecchetti—before his change of view!

we set $\mu = 1$, so that policymakers are assumed to care equally about deviations of inflation from target and of output from potential.

Finally, in the absence of a zero lower bound on nominal interest rates, it is possible to write down explicitly the form that optimal policy will take for a skeptic in our Ball-Svensson economy.[7] Ball (1999a) showed that this is given by a Taylor rule, namely

$$r_t = \beta^{-1}(\lambda + \alpha q)y_t + \beta^{-1}q\pi_t, \tag{12}$$

where the scalar q is defined by $q = (-\mu\alpha + [\mu^2\alpha^2 + 4\mu]^{1/2})/2$. For our baseline parameter values, this becomes

$$r_t = 1.13y_t + 0.82\pi_t, \tag{13}$$

which is a more aggressive Taylor rule than the "standard" one introduced by Taylor (1993), $r_t = 0.5y_t + 0.5\pi_t$.

In the presence of a zero lower bound on nominal interest rates, however, it may not be possible for a skeptic (or an activist, after the bubble has burst) to recommend policy in accordance with equation (12). Instead, optimal policy for such a policymaker must now take the form

$$r_t = \max[\beta^{-1}(\lambda + \alpha q)y_t + \beta^{-1}q\pi_t, r_t^{ZLB}], \tag{14}$$

where r_t^{ZLB} denotes the value of r_t which corresponds to $i_t^{lvl} = 0$, namely

$$r_t^{ZLB} = -i^* - \pi_t. \tag{15}$$

2.3 How Might the Zero Lower Bound Influence an Activist Policymaker?

In section 2.4 we describe our empirical results as to how the presence of a zero lower bound on nominal interest rates influences the policy recommendations of an activist policymaker, confronting a developing asset-price bubble. We also explore the implications of these results for policy questions such as the appropriate choice of inflation target, and how this may depend on key economic parameters which may vary from country to country.

Before turning to these empirical results, however, it is instructive to ask: what effect, intuitively, would we expect the existence of the ZLB to have on an activist policymaker, weighing how best to respond to an asset-price bubble? In the remainder of this section, we address this question in two stages: first for asset-price bubbles whose development (period-to-period growth and/or probability of bursting) is completely exogenous; and secondly for asset-price bubbles whose development can be influenced by policy.

7. This reflects that, in the absence of the zero lower bound, certainty equivalence holds in the model, for a policymaker who expects no future asset-price driven shocks to output. Such policymakers in fact include not only skeptics in each period, but also activists once the bubble bursts (since it is assumed never to re-form).

Note that our focus here, and throughout what follows, is on the *marginal* effect that the ZLB might have on an activist policymaker, over and above whatever impact the bubble itself would have, even in the absence of a ZLB on nominal interest rates. Thus, when we refer to the ZLB causing an activist to, for example, loosen policy in a given period, we are not necessarily implying that they would recommend policy that is actually looser than a skeptic in that period. Rather, we mean simply that they would recommend policy, in that period, which is not as tight as they would otherwise recommend, were there no ZLB.

2.3.1 The Case of Bubbles Whose Development is Exogenous

Consider an asset-price bubble whose period-to-period growth and probability of bursting are entirely exogenous, unaffected by monetary policy. Suppose also that an activist policymaker understands that he is powerless to influence the future trajectory of this bubble.

As such a bubble grows, the activist appreciates the increasing risk that, in the future, its eventual bursting will generate a large negative shock to output and, thereafter, to inflation, which might result in the activist's preferred post-bubble policy recommendations striking the ZLB. This latter effect could occur either: immediately, if the output gap is driven sufficiently negative to result in the optimal nominal interest rate falling below zero in the period of the bubble's collapse; or in subsequent periods, as the shock to output flows into lower inflation (or even deflation), so that a lower nominal interest rate is required to reach a desired real interest rate setting.

Such a situation, in which the policymaker's capacity to stabilize the economy would be constrained, would clearly be suboptimal. Indeed, in the extreme, it might even result in the economy entering a deflationary spiral from which, owing to the ZLB, monetary policy alone would be unable to rescue it. Intuitively, therefore, an activist policymaker would prefer to prevent such an outcome arising in the future—even at some definite present cost in terms of the policymaker's loss function, equation (11).

In our Ball-Svensson model, however, the only available defense against such an outcome, for an exogenous bubble, is to recommend policy so as to raise both the output gap and inflation a little, relative to what would otherwise be optimal in the absence of the ZLB. Such a cushion of extra output and inflation would reduce the likelihood of policy subsequently striking the ZLB, either in the immediate aftermath of the bubble's collapse, or in subsequent periods. Hence, one would expect an activist policymaker, concerned about the ZLB, to be marginally less hawkish than otherwise, when deciding how best to deal with a developing exogenous asset-price bubble.[8]

8. An obvious caveat to this intuition concerns whether the notion of a buffer of extra output and inflation would, in practice, prove to be illusory. The possibility of generating such a

This intuition may be neatly illustrated using a phase diagram for the Ball-Svensson model introduced by Reifschneider and Williams (2000). This phase diagram depicts how (y_t, π_t)-space may be subdivided into three distinct regions, in each of which monetary policy has a differing capacity to return the economy to steady state (output at potential and inflation at target), in the absence of future shocks. This phase diagram is shown in figure 2.1 below, for the case in which α, β, λ, and μ take their baseline values. A detailed derivation of this phase diagram, which differs from that provided by Reifschneider and Williams (2000), is set out in appendix B.

In Region I, monetary policy is able to return the economy to steady state (absent future shocks), without ever striking the zero lower bound on nominal interest rates. By contrast, in Region II monetary policy is still able to return the economy to steady state (absent future shocks), but is initially constrained in doing so by the ZLB—so that the economy's path back to $(y_t, \pi_t) = (0, 0)$ would be suboptimal (higher loss), relative to that which could be achieved if nominal interest rates were not bounded below. Finally, in Region III, monetary policy alone is unable to prevent the economy from entering a catastrophic deflationary spiral. Such a fate would only be able to be averted by the advent, as a supplement to expansionary monetary settings, of sufficiently powerful future positive shocks to the economy: either exogenous, such as a boom in world growth; or generated through other arms of policy, such as a fiscal expansion.

Now consider again an activist policymaker in our Ball-Svensson economy, confronted with a developing exogenous asset-price bubble, and with no policy tools at his disposal other than the interest rate. Clearly, he will wish to take whatever steps are necessary to prevent the economy ever entering Region III—since this would inescapably result in devastating future losses. He will also prefer to keep the economy from entering Region II, since in this region the ZLB would prevent output and inflation from being returned to steady state as efficiently as possible, so incurring additional costs in terms of his loss function, equation (11).

If we combine these observations with the fact that, whenever the bubble does burst, the nature of the resultant shock to the economy will be to shift it horizontally to the left in (y_t, π_t)-space, by an amount equal to the size of the bubble, then the incentives for our activist policymaker become clear.

buffer is clearly, to some degree, specific to our model economy, with its purely backward-looking inflation expectations. These backward-looking expectations mean that an activist policymaker can expect higher inflation engineered *in advance* of a bubble's collapse to provide increased scope (owing to the persistence of inflation) to lower real interest rates in the *aftermath* of such a collapse, thereby stimulating the economy. To the extent that inflation expectations were only partially backward-looking, this would reduce the extent of the ongoing buffer which policymakers would be able to generate, for a given shift in interest rates—and so raise the cost of this policy option, per unit of "insurance" gained against encountering the ZLB. Since, however, this caveat would likely only alter the details of the later results, but not their overall thrust, we do not pursue this issue further in this chapter.

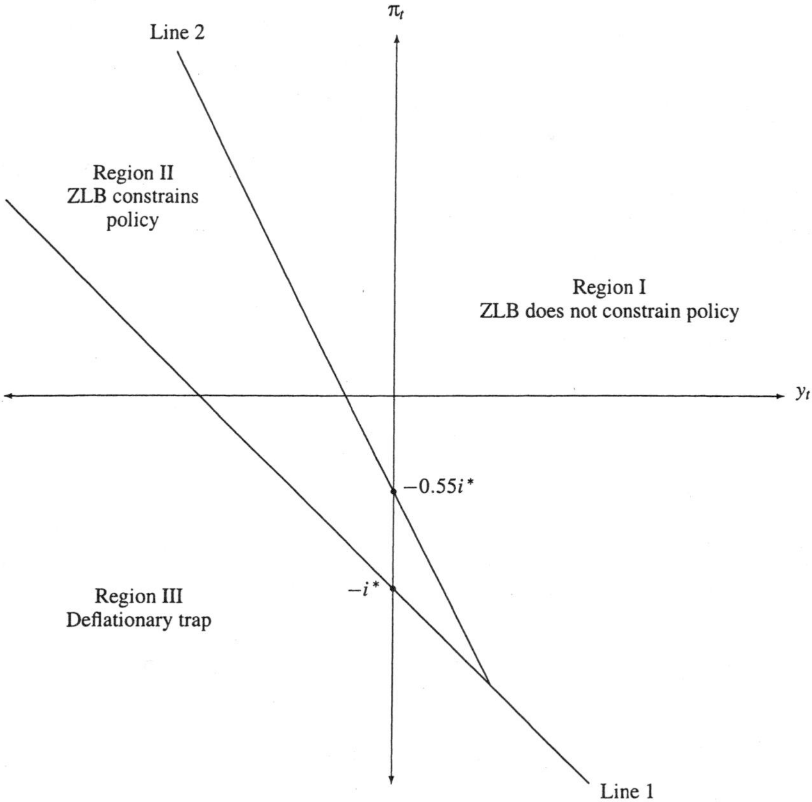

Fig. 2.1 Phase diagram for the Ball-Svensson model under optimal policy

Notes: Phase diagram for the case where the parameters α, β, λ, and μ take their baseline values. Line one passes through the point $(0, -i^*)$ and has approximate slope –0.54. Line two passes through the point $(0, -0.55i^*)$ and has approximate slope –0.62.

To ensure that the economy never enters Region III, and to also keep it out of Region II if possible, the activist will prefer to recommend policy, while the bubble survives, which pushes the economy up and to the right in (y_t, π_t)-space, relative to what he would recommend were there no ZLB. Moreover, he will prefer this even if it may take the economy further away from steady state at $(y_t, \pi_t) = (0, 0)$, and so incur an immediate cost in terms of the loss function, equation (11).

Finally, figure 2.1 also highlights two further points about the *extent* to which the ZLB will influence an activist policymaker's interest rate recommendations. The first is that, the bigger the current size of the bubble, the further such a policymaker will wish to push the economy upwards and to the right in (y_t, π_t)-space, to minimize the economy's chances of being driven into Regions II or III whenever the bubble does collapse. Hence, the bigger the current size of the bubble, the greater will be the influence that the ZLB will have on an activist's policy recommendations.

The second point rests on the observation that the locations of the boundary lines separating Regions II and III from the rest of (y_t, π_t)-space are both determined by the level of the neutral nominal interest rate, i^*. The higher is i^*, the further these boundary lines will be pushed down and to the left, away from the origin in (y_t, π_t)-space. Hence, the higher is i^*, the less of a concern will the risk of entering Regions II or III be to an activist policymaker—and so the less will such a policymaker feel the need to recommend interest rate settings, while the bubble survives, that hold both the output gap and inflation higher than they would otherwise prefer.

This latter point is, of course, simply another way of saying that the higher are both the neutral real rate of interest in the economy and the target rate of inflation, the less of a factor will the ZLB be in the minds of policymakers, when dealing with an asset-price bubble. Hence, while there are clearly costs associated with operating the economy at too high an average inflation rate, policymakers may also wish to take care not to adopt too low a figure when deciding upon an inflation target—especially if the neutral real interest rate in their economy is relatively low.

2.3.2 The Case of Bubbles Whose Development Is Affected by Policy

For an entirely exogenous asset-price bubble, we have just seen that the presence of a zero lower bound on nominal interest rates provides an incentive to an activist policymaker to recommend somewhat looser policy than otherwise, so as to shift the economy upwards and to the right in (y_t, π_t)-space. The optimal extent of such insurance against striking the ZLB will be greater the larger the current size of the bubble, and the lower the economy's neutral nominal interest rate in steady state.

For a bubble whose development (period-to-period growth and/or probability of bursting) is affected by policy, however, the situation is no longer so clear. Consider first the case of a bubble whose probability of bursting next period is increased (decreased) by setting policy more tightly (loosely) in the current period.

In this event, although the marginal effect of loosening policy would be to shift the economy away from Regions II and III in (y_t, π_t)-space, it would also be to increase the odds of the bubble surviving and growing next period, so posing a greater risk down the track. Hence, the direction in which the ZLB would influence the recommendations of an activist policymaker is no longer clear-cut. Indeed, for a bubble that is very sensitive to policy, one could imagine the ZLB providing an incentive for an activist policymaker to raise interest rates decisively early in the bubble's life—in the hope of bursting it before it can grow sufficiently to pose a serious threat to the stability of the economy upon its collapse.

A similar story holds for the case of a bubble whose period-to-period growth, while it survives, may be influenced by policy. Suppose that an activist policymaker knows that the bubble's growth next period, if it survives, will be reduced (increased) by setting policy more tightly (loosely) in the current period.

In this event, loosening policy in any given period would again have the effect of shifting the economy away from Regions II and III in (y_t, π_t)-space—by a greater amount, indeed, should the bubble survive, than the same loosening would achieve in the case of a purely exogenous bubble. However, it would also have the effect of further boosting the size of the bubble, in the event that it did not burst next period, hence increasing the size of the negative shock to the economy whenever the bubble ultimately does burst. Hence, once again, the direction in which the presence of a ZLB on nominal interest rates would, at the margin, push an activist policymaker in this situation is no longer clear.

2.3.3 An Insurance Interpretation for the Implications of the ZLB

The observation in sections 2.3.1 and 2.3.2 may be neatly summarized in terms of the phase diagram, figure 2.1, and an "insurance" paradigm for thinking about how the presence of a ZLB on nominal interest rates might influence the thinking of an activist policymaker. As illustrated in figure 2.1, the presence of a ZLB creates two zones in (y_t, π_t)-space. Regions II and III, which an activist policymaker will be either desperate (Region III) or at least anxious (Region II) to keep the economy away from. As an asset-price bubble grows, such a policymaker will therefore wish to take out some insurance against the economy being driven into either of these regions, whenever the bubble finally does collapse.

For the case of an exogenous bubble, the only such insurance that an activist can set out to purchase—that is, obtain at some definite cost in terms of their objective function, equation (11)—is to manoeuvre the economy upwards and to the right in (y_t, π_t)-space, by recommending policy be set more loosely than otherwise.

For a bubble whose development (period-to-period growth and/or probability of bursting) is affected by policy, however, alternative potential forms of insurance are available, besides this standard type. If the bubble's *probability of bursting* is influenced by policy, this alternative insurance takes the form of increasing the odds that the bubble will collapse while it is still young, before it has grown big enough to drive the economy into Regions II or III through its collapse. If instead the bubble's *growth* may be curtailed by running policy more tightly, the insurance takes the form of restraining the potential future size of the bubble, so as to again ensure that the negative shock that the bubble imparts upon bursting will not be large enough to drive the economy into Regions II or III.

In both these latter cases, these alternative forms of insurance entail setting policy more tightly than otherwise, rather than more loosely, as was the case for the standard form of insurance. For endogenous bubbles, therefore, it is no longer clear a priori which form of insurance an activist policymaker will prefer to purchase, and therefore in which direction the ZLB will alter his policy recommendations. This will depend upon the relative costliness of the different forms of insurance available—which will, in turn, vary from period to period, reflecting the state in which the activist finds the economy (i.e., current output gap and inflation rate, as well as current size of the bubble) when deciding his preferred policy settings.

2.4 Results

In this section we present the optimal policy recommendations of activist and skeptical policymakers, through time, in the presence of an asset-price bubble. As noted in section 2.2, we focus on the period in which the bubble survives and grows. Once the bubble bursts, both activists and skeptics in our Ball-Svensson model will always agree on an approach of aggressively easing policy, to counteract the contractionary effects of the burst.

As in Gruen, Plumb, and Stone (2003), we wish to examine the optimal policy recommendations of skeptics and activists over a range of plausible alternative assumptions about the stochastic nature of the bubble. To do so meaningfully, it is necessary that the two policymakers face an economy in the same state in each year. Since the current state of the economy depends on previous policy settings (as well as on the evolution of the bubble) we will assume throughout that the policy settings which are actually implemented each year are those chosen by the skeptic. We can then sensibly compare, as each year passes, the current optimal policy recommendations made by the different policymakers.

The activist's recommendations will depend on the assumptions he makes about the future possible paths of the bubble. In particular, they will reflect the economic effects implicit in these paths, and how these effects interact with both: his preferences, as reflected in the loss function, equation (11); and the potential constraint on his future actions embodied in the ZLB. By contrast, the recommendations of the skeptic—being a believer in the efficient markets hypothesis—will reflect an expectation of no future effects on the economy flowing from asset-price movements.

2.4.1 Baseline Results: The Case of Exogenous Bubbles

We begin with results for the baseline case where: the bubble's future development is unaffected by policymakers' actions; its direct expansionary effect on output in each year of its growth is a constant 1 percent ($\gamma_t = 1$); its period-to-period probability of bursting is a constant 40 percent ($p_t = p^* = 0.4$); and the model and loss function parameters α, β, λ, and μ take their baseline values (namely $\alpha = 0.4$, $\beta = 1.0$, $\lambda = 0.8$, and $\mu = 1.0$) spec-

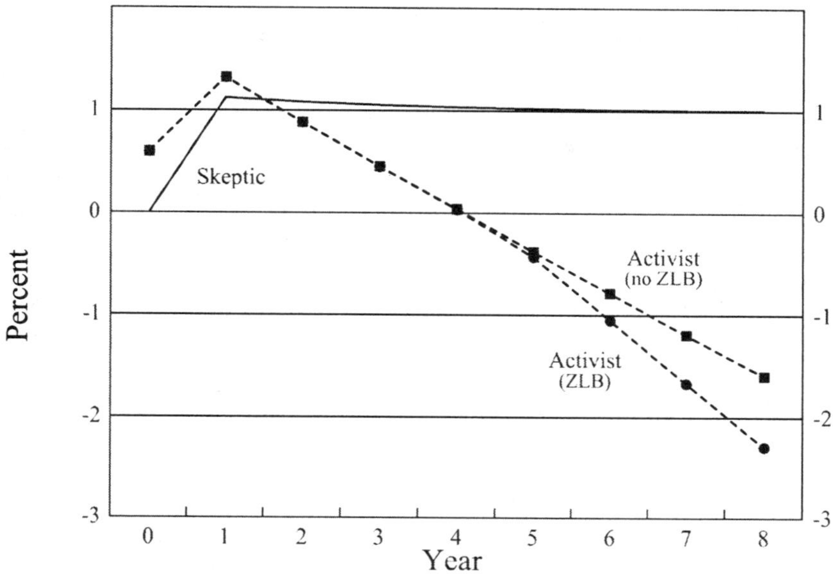

Fig. 2.2 Real interest rate recommendations while the bubble survives—policy has no effect on the bubble, i^* = 3.0

Notes: The skeptic implements policy in each year. Real interest rates are deviations from neutral.

ified earlier.[9] In subsequent subsections we will examine the effect of varying each of these sets of assumptions.

Figure 2.2 shows the optimal policy recommendations made, in each period, by the skeptic and two activists, assuming that the steady-state neutral nominal interest rate in the economy is $i^* = 3$ percent.[10] The two activists differ in the way that their actions are influenced by the ZLB. For the first, the ZLB is a genuine constraint on policy, as encapsulated by equation (6). For the (hypothetical) second, the zero lower bound is not a constraint, so that a negative nominal interest rate setting can (in some unspecified way) be achieved, if desired.

9. Note that, to ease the process of numerically determining optimal paths of contingent policy recommendations for an activist policymaker in each period, we actually make the simplifying assumption here and subsequently that, if the bubble survives until year fourteen (which is an extremely unlikely event for all the parameter values we consider), then it bursts with certainty in that year. Hence, strictly speaking, our assumption regarding p_t here is that $p_t = p^* = 0.4$ for all $t = 0, 1, \ldots, 13$, while $p_{14} = 1$. Also, for reference, if p_t were 0.4 for all t this would imply an average remaining life for the bubble of two and a half years. Since we assume $p_{14} = 1$ here, however, our exogenous bubble in this subsection has an expected remaining life in period zero of just under two and a half years.

10. Since $i^* = r^* + \pi^*$, this might represent an economy where the neutral real rate, r^*, is 2 percent, and target inflation, π^*, is 1 percent; or where $r^* = 3$ percent and $\pi^* = 0$ percent; or any other such combination.

The main features of figure 2.2—the shapes of the paths recommended by the skeptic and the "no ZLB" activist, and the fact that the recommendations of this activist, while initially above those of the skeptic, subsequently drop below them—were discussed in Gruen, Plumb, and Stone (2003). We refer the reader to that paper for a detailed analysis of the policy implications of these features, and an intuitive explanation of them (in terms of the interaction between the future possible effects of the bubble on output, and the lag with which policy affects the economy).

Our focus in this chapter, however, is on the *difference* between the two sets of activist policy recommendations shown in figure 2.2. This difference captures the impact of the presence of the ZLB on an activist policymaker's preferred recommendations. Two characteristics of this difference stand out. First, as anticipated in section 2.3, for an exogenous bubble the effect of the zero lower bound is indeed to make an activist reduce his policy recommendations in each period, at the margin, relative to what he would have recommended were there no ZLB. Secondly, even for an economy with a low steady-state neutral nominal interest rate of $i^* = 3$ percent, this effect is, however, very small at first: it is not until period six, for example, that an activist in such an economy would feel the need to lower his policy recommendation by even 25 basis points on account of concern about the ZLB.

We can explore these latter two observations further by considering how the impact of the ZLB on an activist policymaker varies with the level of the steady-state neutral nominal interest rate in the economy, i^*. Figure 2.3 below shows the difference between the policy recommendations of activist policymakers, with and without a zero lower bound constraint, for $i^* = 1$, 2, 3, 5.5, and 8 percent.[11]

We see that for neutral nominal interest rates around or above the range currently estimated for Australia, the ZLB is not a factor in an activist policymaker's thinking, even for quite large bubbles. By contrast, in an economy with an extremely low steady-state neutral nominal interest rate, such as $i^* = 1$ or 2, the ZLB would start to become a serious factor in an activist policymaker's considerations even for small- to moderate-sized bubbles.[12]

11. The choice of $i^* = 5.5$ percent is covered to include a case in the plausible range of values for Australia: corresponding to, for example, a neutral real interest rate of 3 percent and an inflation target of 2.5 percent, the mid-point of the 2 to 3 percent medium-term target band. This value also lies neatly in the middle of the 5 to 6 percent range in which most current estimates of the neutral nominal interest rate for Australia fall. The choices $i^* = 1$ and 2 percent are included to show the increasingly severe impact of the ZLB on an activist policymaker's considerations, when the neutral nominal rate is extremely low.

12. There is a technical caveat which should be borne in mind in relation to the results reported in figures 2.2 and 2.3 and subsequently. This relates to the fact that the presence of the ZLB on nominal interest rates results in an activist policymaker's expected loss ceasing to be a quadratic function of his or her contingent policy recommendations. Hence, in each period, not only must we resort to numerical methods to seek an activist's loss minimizing profile of contingent policy recommendations, but we must also be concerned about the possibility of

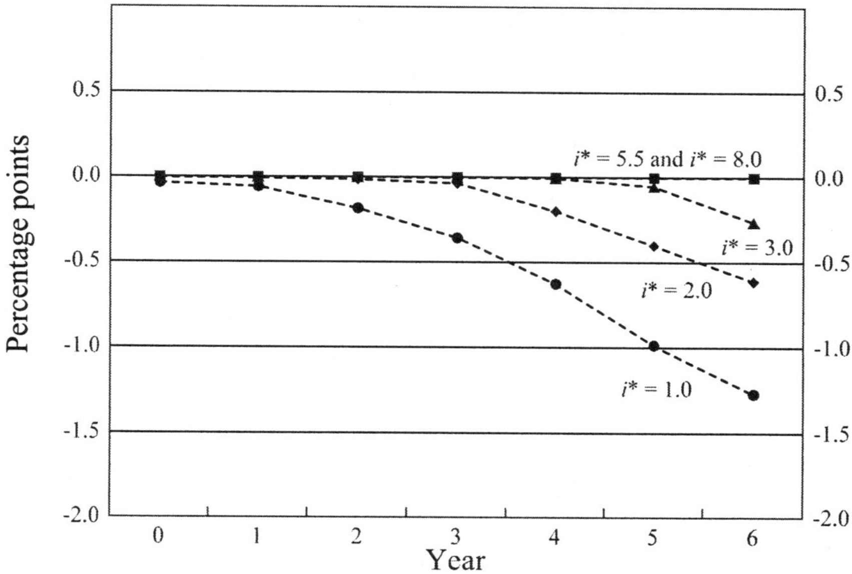

Fig. 2.3 Impact of the ZLB on an activist's recommendations—difference between recommendations with and without the ZLB

Notes: The skeptic implements policy in each year.

We now examine how these observations vary across a range of alternative assumptions about either the stochastic properties of our asset-price bubbles, or about the model parameters α, β, and λ.[13]

2.4.2 Exogenous Bubbles with Different Probabilities of Bursting

The results in figure 2.2 suggest that, for an exogenous bubble with period-to-period probability of bursting $p_t = p^* = 0.4$, the ZLB is not a

inadvertently locating a *local* rather than global minimum. To help overcome this potential problem we adopted the following safeguards throughout the simulations reported in this chapter. First, we set up the loss minimization process using two different algorithms, to provide a cross-check on our results. Secondly, having located notionally optimal sets of contingent policy recommendations for each period, in a given scenario, we then subjected these profiles to random perturbations, to see whether reoptimization starting from these perturbed settings would return the original profile, or instead give rise to an alternative with lower expected loss. Finally, these perturbation tests were separately carried out in various instances by each author, so as to try to maximize variety in the alterations tested. To the extent that these safeguards may have failed in any particular instance, this would simply highlight the practical difficulties facing an activist policymaker in trying to determine how to respond optimally to a developing asset-price bubble in such circumstances, even with perfect knowledge about both the structure of the economy and the stochastic properties of the bubble!

13. A variation which we do not examine in the main body of the chapter, but which we take up in appendix C, is the case of rational bubbles. As discussed in Gruen, Plumb, and Stone (2003), there is a sense in which the baseline bubble just described could, under plausible assumptions about the relationship between the price growth underlying an asset bubble and the

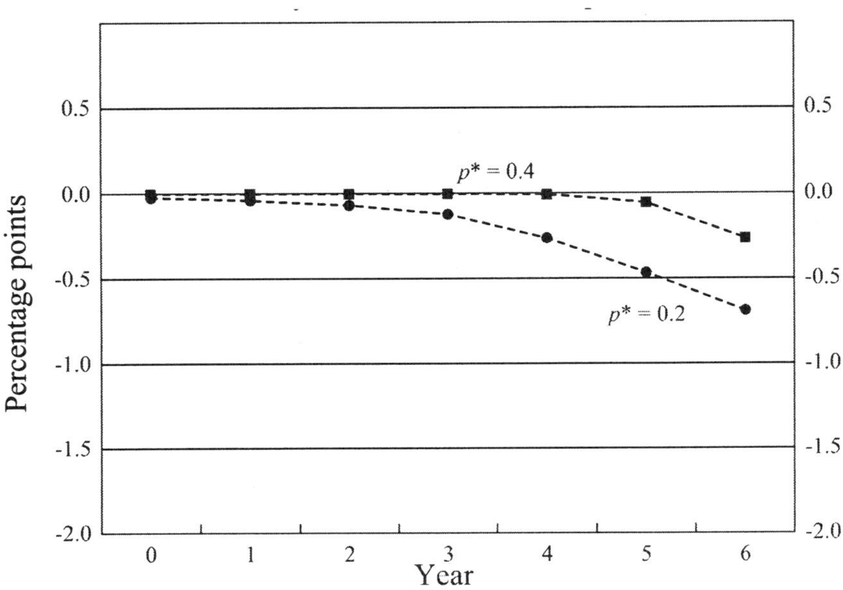

Fig. 2.4 Impact of the ZLB on an activist's recommendations—sensitivity to alternative values for p^*, $i^* = 3.0$

Notes: The skeptic implements policy in each year.

major factor in an activist policymaker's considerations, unless the steady-state neutral nominal interest rate in the economy is extremely low. It is interesting to ask whether or not this remains so as we vary the constant probability of bursting, p^*.

For small values of p^*, the probability that the bubble will continue to grow to a large size, rather than burst in the near term, increases. We would therefore expect that, the smaller the value of p^*, the greater would be the importance of the ZLB in an activist policymaker's thinking, as a possible constraint on future action.

As figure 2.4 shows, this is indeed what we find. For an exogenous bubble whose period-to-period probability of bursting is $p_t = p^* = 0.2$, the impact of the ZLB on an activist's recommendations is apparent both earlier and more forcefully than in the case where $p_t = p^* = 0.4$; in the former case the "ZLB effect" is around 25 basis points by year four, and 50 basis points by year five, whereas in the latter case it is not until year six that it even reaches

impact of that bubble on the real economy, be regarded as irrational. While we do not see this as a shortcoming per se—since there is much evidence in developed economies of irrational bubbles occurring in practice (see, for example, Shiller 2000)—it is nevertheless interesting to examine whether the imposition of a rationality assumption on our bubbles would affect the overall thrust of our findings and, if so, how. The results set out in appendix C suggest that it would not.

25 basis points.[14] Nevertheless, the scale of this "ZLB effect" is not very large in either case, nor is it dramatically different between the two cases, at least until the bubble has become quite large.

2.4.3 Bubbles Whose Growth Is Affected by Policy

In sections 2.4.1 and 2.4.2 we considered only purely exogenous asset-price bubbles. A natural extension is to assume that, by setting tighter policy this year, policymakers can reduce the extent of the bubble's growth next year, if it survives. Explicitly, we assume once again that $p_t = p^* = 0.4$ (except $p_{14} = 1$), but that now, following Gruen, Plumb, and Stone (2003),

$$\gamma_t = 1 - \phi(r_{t-1} - r^*_{t-1}), \tag{16}$$

where r^*_t, $t \geq 0$, denotes the optimal path chosen by a skeptical policymaker while the bubble survives, assuming $\gamma_t = 1$; and ϕ is a sensitivity parameter to be chosen.[15] For the results that follow we assume $\phi = 1$, so that by setting policy 1 percentage point higher than the skeptic this year, the bubble's growth next year would be reduced from 1 percent to nothing.[16]

In this setting, and for an economy with $i^* = 3$, figure 2.5 shows a comparison of the optimal interest rate recommendations of one skeptic and three activists, while the bubble survives. Two of these activists differ in their assumptions about the sensitivity parameter ϕ, with one assuming no interest rate sensitivity, $\phi = 0$, while the other assumes high sensitivity, $\phi = 1$. The third, for reference, is a hypothetical policymaker who also assumes high sensitivity ($\phi = 1$), but is unconstrained by the ZLB.

As discussed in Gruen, Plumb, and Stone (2003), we see first that being able to influence the growth of the bubble makes an activist policymaker increase their policy recommendations in each period from year one onwards, relative to what the activist would advise were he unable to influence

14. Note that an activist's policy recommendations themselves are, however, tighter in every period for a bubble with $p_t = p^* = 0.2$ than for a bubble with $p_t = p^* = 0.4$. This is true with or without the ZLB constraint on nominal interest rates—for the case without the ZLB constraint see Gruen, Plumb, and Stone (2003), figure 2.2.

15. We choose the functional form in equation (16) so that, for the benchmark policy settings chosen by the skeptic, $\gamma_t = 1$ for all t, as in the exogenous bubble case. Note also that in equation (16) the growth of the bubble *this period* depends upon *last period's* interest rate. An interesting variant, suggested to us by Kenneth Kuttner, would be to allow for monetary policy to have a contemporaneous impact on asset prices (while continuing to affect the output gap directly with a one-period lag). If suitably incorporated, such a change might allow policymakers to provide a brake on the fall of asset prices, whenever a bubble burst, so cushioning the impact of the burst on aggregate demand. Of course, knowledge that the monetary authorities might behave in this way might, however, risk creating a moral hazard problem, along the lines of the so-called "Greenspan put" discussed in relation to the recent tech stock boom and bust in the United States. For reasons of space, we do not pursue these various issues further here.

16. To continue holding the bubble's growth to zero, while it survives, would of course require policy to be set 1 percentage point higher than the skeptic in each such period—with the usual consequences of tight policy for both output and inflation.

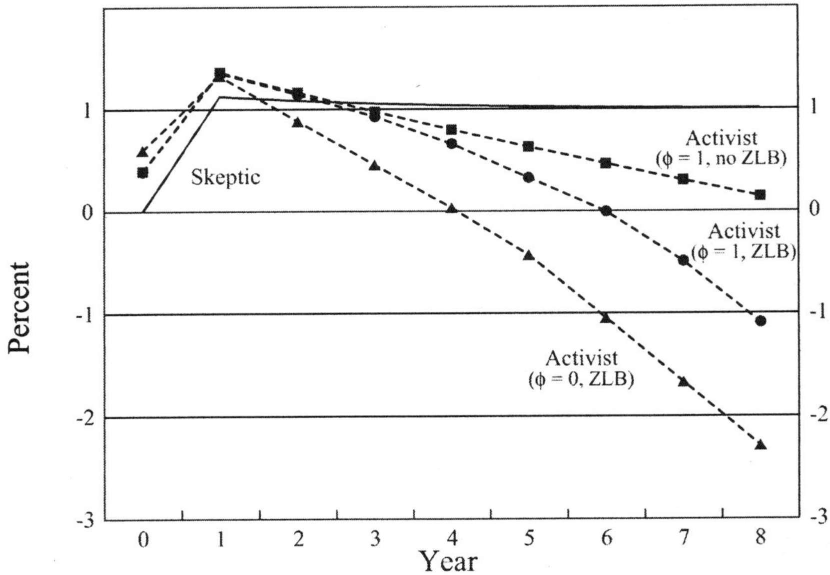

Fig. 2.5 Real interest rate recommendations while the bubble survives—policy affects the bubble's growth, $i^* = 3.0$

Notes: The skeptic implements policy in each year. Real interest rates are deviations from neutral.

the bubble's growth. However, the impact of the ZLB is still to reduce such an activist's policy recommendations, relative to what he would prefer in the absence of the ZLB. Moreover, this "ZLB effect" now manifests itself both earlier and more strongly than in the previous setting of an exogenous bubble.[17]

We can interpret these latter results in terms of the "insurance framework" for analyzing the impact of the ZLB described in section 2.3. Recall that, for bubbles whose growth is affected by policy, two alternative forms of insurance against encountering the ZLB are available to an activist policymaker: building a buffer of inflation and output against the effects of the

17. The claim of a stronger effect is based on comparing the difference between the "Activist ($\phi = 1$, ZLB)" and "Activist ($\phi = 1$, no ZLB)" lines in figure 2.5, on the one hand, with that between the "Activist (ZLB)" and "Activist (no ZLB)" lines in figure 2.2, on the other. Note also that the caveat expressed in note twelve about our earlier results, namely the possibility of our having inadvertently located local rather than global minima of our activists' loss functions, continues to apply. Indeed, if anything, it is likely to apply with even greater force in both this subsection and (especially) the next, since the ability of policymakers to influence the bubble's behavior in these two scenarios would already cause an activist's expected loss to cease to be a quadratic function of his or her contingent policy recommendations, even in the absence of the ZLB.

bubble's eventual collapse, by running policy more loosely than otherwise; or holding down the size of the bubble, and hence the size of the negative shock it will impart upon bursting, by running policy more tightly than otherwise.

The fact that the "ZLB effect" in figure 2.5 is again downwards shows first of all that, for a Ball-Svensson economy with our baseline parameters and a neutral nominal interest rate of $i^* = 3$, the former type of insurance must be more cost-effective than the latter, against a bubble whose growth can be influenced by policy according to equation (16) with $\phi = 1$. As for the observation that this "ZLB effect" is now evident both earlier and more strongly than for an exogenous bubble, this reflects the presence of two added *feedbacks* in this setting, relative to the exogenous bubble case—between an activist's recommendations, on the one hand, and the structure of equation (16), on the other.

In more detail, suppose that, in the current setting, an activist is contemplating recommending looser policy than otherwise, on account of the future risks arising from the ZLB (as figure 2.5 shows he will do). For each basis point by which he does so, the activist is aware that this will now have the effect of *increasing* the expected growth of the bubble next period, if it survives, by an equal amount. This will have two competing effects. On the one hand it will partially offset the decrease in these future risks which the activist would hope to achieve through the loosening of policy, and so require him to recommend policy be moved further, to achieve the optimal level of insurance, than he would in the exogenous bubble case. On the other, it will provide him with a greater cushion of output and (future) inflation than otherwise, and so reduce the extent of loosening he may feel is required. The results in figure 2.5, which show the magnitude of the "ZLB effect" accelerating over time relative to its size in the exogenous bubble case, suggest that it is the former feedback which dominates, in the current setting.

Once again, it is interesting to consider the sensitivity of these results to changes in the assumed steady-state neutral nominal interest rate of the economy. This is illustrated in figure 2.6, which shows the difference between the policy recommendations of activist policymakers, with and without a zero lower bound constraint, for $i^* = 1$, 3, and 8 percent. Here, these activists assume again that policy can affect the bubble's growth according to equation (16) with $\phi = 1$.

We see that, for our baseline Ball-Svensson model, the compounding effect just described becomes yet more acute if i^* is extremely low, so that for $i^* = 1$ percent the downward "ZLB effect" on an activist's recommendations is already noticeable by year two, and exceeds 1 percentage point by year four. By contrast, this "ZLB effect" is still negligible, even in year six, if i^* is set to be 8 percent, well away from zero.

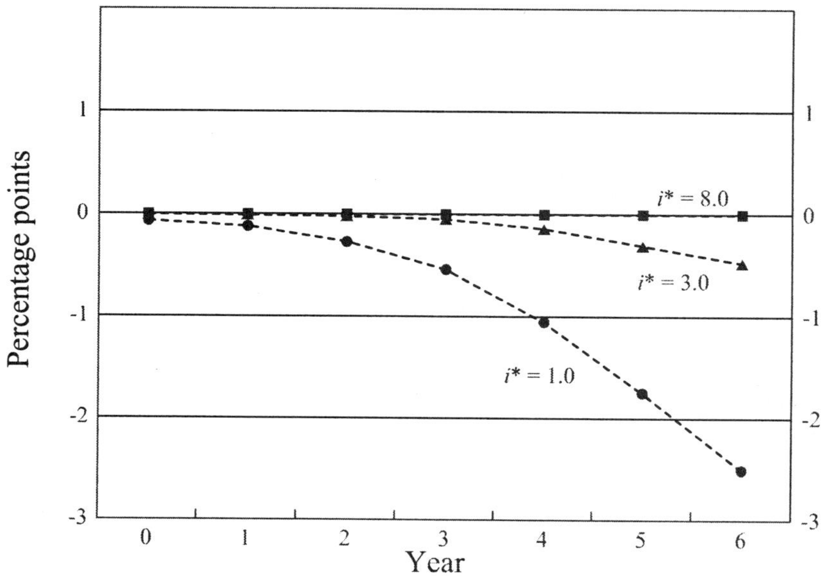

Fig. 2.6 Impact of the ZLB on an activist's recommendations—policy affects the bubble's growth

Notes: The skeptic implements policy in each year.

2.4.4 Bubbles Whose Probability of Bursting Is Affected by Policy

Next, instead of a bubble whose growth is affected by policy, consider a bubble whose period-to-period probability of bursting may be influenced by the actions of policymakers. Specifically, assume that, by setting tighter (looser) policy this year, policymakers can raise (lower) the probability that the bubble will burst next year, according to the relationship

$$(17) \qquad p_t = \frac{1}{1 + e^{a(r_{t-1} - r^*_{t-1}) + b}},$$

where r^*_t, $t \geq 0$, denotes the optimal path chosen by a skeptical policymaker while the bubble survives, assuming a constant period-to-period probability of bursting p^* (except $p_{14} = 1$); and where $b = \ln([1 - p^*]/p^*)$ and $a = -\delta/(p^*[1 - p^*])$ for some fixed sensitivity parameter δ.

We choose this functional form, which was also used in Gruen, Plumb, and Stone (2003), for three reasons. First, it ensures that, while raising last year's interest rate, r_{t-1}, raises the probability that the bubble will burst this year, p_t, it cannot drive this probability to one. Secondly, it possesses the property that $p_t = p^*$ when $r_{t-1} = r^*_{t-1}$, the benchmark policy settings chosen by the skeptic. Finally, it has the property that $\partial p_t/\partial(r_{t-1} - r^*_{t-1}) = \delta$ when this derivative is evaluated at $r_{t-1} = r^*_{t-1}$, so that the parameter δ gives the marginal sensitivity of the bubble's probability of bursting to changes in the real interest rate, at the skeptic's benchmark policy settings. For the results that follow we adopt the baseline choices $p^* = 0.4$, consistent with the bulk of our earlier simulations, and $\delta = 0.2$, corresponding to a moderate level of interest rate sensitivity.

In this setting, and for an economy with $i^* = 3$, figure 2.7 shows a comparison of the optimal interest rate recommendations of a skeptic and two activists, while the bubble survives. The two activists differ in the way that their actions are influenced by the ZLB: the first is constrained by it, while the second is not.

The most striking feature of figure 2.7 is that the impact of the ZLB is no longer in a uniform direction, over time. Up to and including year four, the effect of the ZLB on an activist policymaker is to make him recommend *tighter* policy than otherwise. However, in year five this shifts, and the effect of the ZLB becomes such as to cause an activist to recommend looser policy than otherwise, in this and subsequent years. Moreover, this shift is quite dramatic, with the "ZLB effect" on an activist policymaker moving from positive 46 basis points in year four to negative 178 basis points in year five.

Once again, we can interpret these results in terms of our "insurance framework" for analyzing the impact of the ZLB, described in section 2.3.

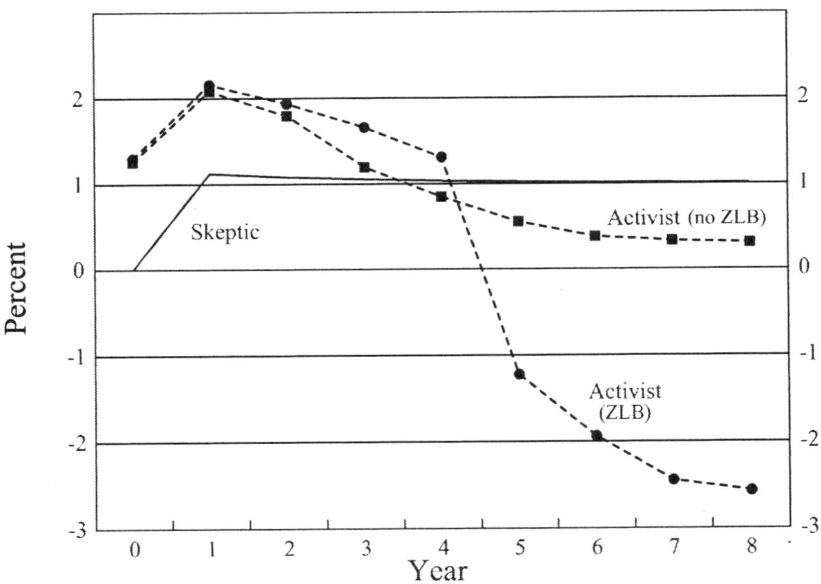

Fig. 2.7 Real interest rate recommendations while the bubble survives—policy affects the bubble's probability of bursting, $i^* = 3.0$

Notes: The skeptic implements policy in each year. Real interest rates are deviations from neutral.

Recall that, as for bubbles whose growth is affected by policy, in the current setting there are two alternative forms of insurance against encountering the ZLB available to an activist policymaker. The first is the standard approach of building a buffer of extra inflation and output against the effects of the bubble's eventual collapse, by running policy more loosely than otherwise. The second is to seek to burst the bubble before it can grow further, and so become a bigger threat to economic stability whenever it does collapse, by running policy more tightly than otherwise.

The results in figure 2.7 show that, in the current setting, the latter type of insurance must in fact be better value than the former, up to and including period four. However, in year five a threshold is crossed. In this year, assuming the bubble does not burst, an activist policymaker observes the bubble continuing to grow to a size of 5 percentage points, at the same time as the skeptic's policy settings in previous periods have failed to prepare the economy for the bubble's possible future collapse. The combination of these developments sees an activist's expected cost-benefit trade-off shift suddenly from seeking to burst the bubble, by tightening policy, to seeking to cushion the economy against any future burst, by loosening policy. The *decisiveness* of the swing from one form of insurance to the other is in part driven by the fact that, in the current setting, any loosening in current policy increases the chances of the bubble surviving next period and growing further—so increasing the likelihood, in an activist's considerations, that he may have to cope with the collapse of a very large bubble indeed some time down the track.[18]

To see how these findings change as a function of the economy's steady-state neutral nominal interest rate, figure 2.8 shows the difference between the policy recommendations of activist policymakers, with and without a zero lower bound constraint, for $i^* = 1$, 3, and 8 percent. Here, these activists assume again that policy can affect the bubble's period-to-period probability of bursting according to equation (17) with $\delta = 0.2$.

Interestingly, for the case where i^* is extremely low, at 1 percent, two differences are apparent relative to the case $i^* = 3$ just discussed. The first is that, even in the early life of the bubble, the "ZLB effect" is now marginally negative. The second is that the threshold described above, beyond which an activist shifts to recommending sharply looser policy both than they did in the previous period, and than they would do in the absence of the ZLB, is now crossed earlier. On the other hand, we see that for values of i^* far from zero, the "ZLB effect" is once again negligible, even by the time the bubble has been growing for six years.

18. The particular form of the function relating the bubble's probability of bursting next period, p_{t+1}, to this period's real interest rate deviation from neutral, r_t, will of course also influence precisely when this decisive shift in an activist's policy approach will occur, as well as the exact magnitude of the swing.

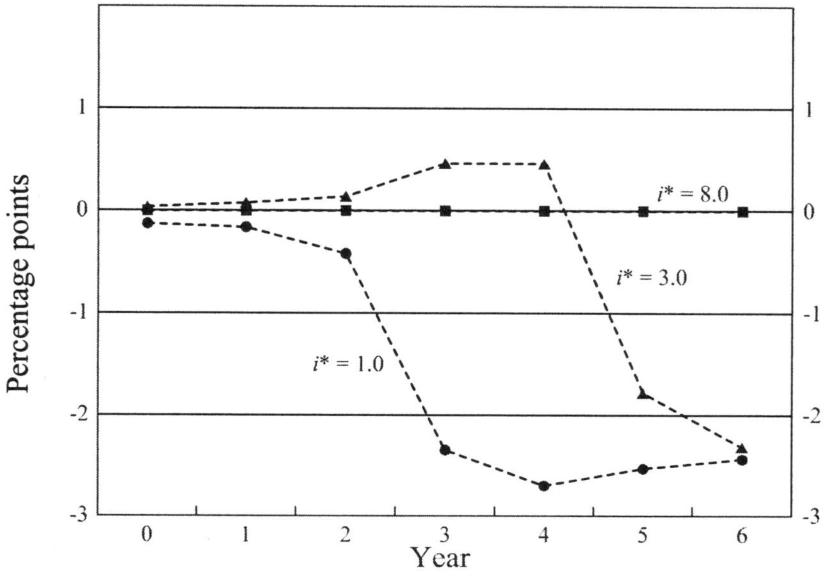

Fig. 2.8 Impact of the ZLB on an activist's recommendations—policy affects the bubble's probability of bursting

Notes: The skeptic implements policy in each year.

2.4.5 Sensitivity to Model Parameters

It is interesting to explore how sensitive the preceding results are to our choice of model parameters. We focus in particular on the two (positive) parameters β and λ. The former captures how responsive output is to real interest rates. The latter, by contrast, captures how "naturally self-correcting" our Ball-Svensson economy is, absent any policy action.[19]

Turning first to the case of β, to assess the sensitivity of an activist's policy recommendations to the value of this parameter we consider again the baseline case of an exogenous bubble with constant period-on-period probability of bursting $p_t = 0.4$ (except $p_{14} = 1$), and constant growth in the event that it does not burst, $\gamma_t = 1$. We then consider the recommendations of activists in two different economies, each of which has a steady-state neutral nominal interest rate of 3 percent, but which differ in their responsiveness to real interest rates—with values of $\beta = 0.5$ and 1, respectively. All other model and loss-function parameters are assumed to take their baseline values: $\alpha = 0.4$, $\lambda = 0.8$, and $\mu = 1.0$.

19. The smaller λ is, the more swiftly will output in the economy rebound towards potential, of its own accord, following a shock. Conversely, if $\lambda = 1$, the economy has no innate propensity to correct either a positive or negative output gap, once it opens up, so that the full burden of stabilizing the economy falls upon policymakers setting the real interest rate.

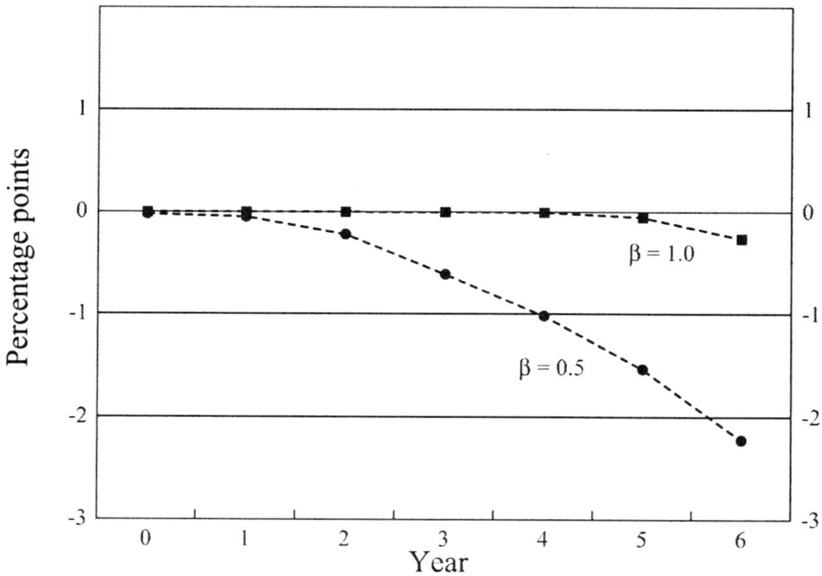

Fig. 2.9 Impact of the ZLB on an activist's recommendations—sensitivity to alternative values for beta, $i^* = 3.0$

Notes: The skeptic implements policy in each year.

We find that, for an economy with lower responsiveness, the impact of the ZLB on an activist policymaker's recommendations is correspondingly greater, when faced with an exogenous bubble. This is illustrated in figure 2.9, which shows the difference between the policy recommendations of activist policymakers, with and without a ZLB constraint, in the two economies.

The direction of this result is unsurprising, since the capacity of policy to stabilize the economy following a large negative shock to output is weaker, the smaller β is. Hence, the activist in our $\beta = 0.5$ economy is commensurately more anxious, in each period, to begin building a buffer of added inflation and output against the bubble's eventual collapse, than his or her counterpart in the $\beta = 1$ economy.

What is perhaps surprising is the magnitude of this sensitivity, with the "ZLB effect" exceeding 1 percentage point as early as period four, in the economy with $\beta = 0.5$. By contrast, in the $\beta = 1$ economy, the corresponding "ZLB effect" is still negligible in period four, and only reaches 26 basis points in period six.[20]

20. In the $\beta = 0.5$ economy the "ZLB effect" is sufficiently strong that, if the bubble were to survive this long, an activist policymaker's recommendations would actually reach the zero lower bound by year seven.

Correspondingly, to assess the sensitivity of an activist's policy recommendations to the value of λ, we consider the same baseline case of an exogenous bubble with constant period-on-period probability of bursting $p_t = 0.4$ (except $p_{14} = 1$), and constant growth in the event that it does not burst, $\gamma_t = 1$. Now, however, we consider the recommendations of activists in three different economies, each of which again has a steady-state neutral nominal interest rate of 3 percent, but which this time differ in the degree to which output is naturally self-correcting in each—with values of λ = 0.6, 0.8, and 1, respectively.[21]

In terms of our insurance framework for assessing the likely impact of the ZLB on an activist's recommendations, we would expect this impact to be greatest in the economy with $\lambda = 1.0$, and smallest in that with $\lambda = 0.6$. Policymakers in the $\lambda = 0.6$ economy can expect considerable assistance in restoring output to potential, whenever the bubble bursts, from the economy's natural tendency to rebound from such a shock. By contrast, in the $\lambda = 1.0$ economy, policymakers can expect no such assistance, and so will wish to take out commensurately more insurance against the possible effects of the bubble's future collapse.[22]

This is indeed what we find, as illustrated in figure 2.10, which shows the difference between the policy recommendations of activist policymakers, with and without a ZLB constraint, in each of our three economies. This time, however, the variation in the impact of the ZLB across our three economies is not substantial, at least until the bubble has grown very large, which suggests that our earlier results are fairly robust to plausible changes in the value of λ.[23]

2.5 Conclusions

In this chapter we have used a simple, two-equation model of a closed economy, augmented with an asset-price bubble, to investigate what impact the zero lower bound on nominal interest rates has on the recommendations of an activist policymaker, attempting to respond optimally to a given bubble. In assessing our results, it should be remembered that this

21. Here we revert to the assumption that $\beta = 1$ in all three economies, with the parameters α and μ again at their baseline values of 0.4 and 1.

22. The same conclusion can be reached more formally in terms of the phase diagram for the Ball-Svensson model discussed in section 2.3, and derived in appendix B. It may readily be checked that, for $0 \leq \lambda \leq 1$, increasing the value of λ makes the slopes of both the boundary lines separating Regions I, II, and III more negative. Hence, increasing λ brings both Regions II and III, which an activist policymaker wishes to stay away from, closer to the origin in (y_t, π_t)-space—and so increases the incentive for such an activist to recommend looser policy than otherwise, to shift the economy upwards and to the right, away from these danger zones.

23. Although we do not show them here, the same point may be seen by directly comparing the successive policy recommendations of activist and skeptical policymakers in our three economies, while the bubble survives.

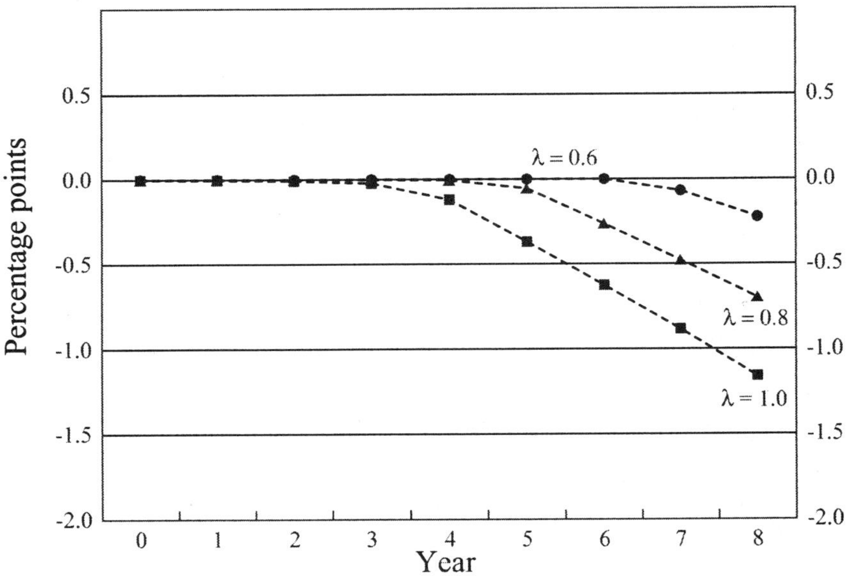

Fig. 2.10 Impact of the ZLB on an activist's recommendations—sensitivity to alternative values for lambda, i^* = 3.0

Notes: The skeptic implements policy in each year.

framework almost certainly magnifies the impact of the ZLB, most notably because it does not allow for other arms of policy (or unconventional monetary-policy operations) to help extricate the economy from a situation in which policy has become constrained by the ZLB.

For example, the possibility of encountering the ZLB in the future would clearly hold fewer fears for monetary policymakers in an economy with sound public finances, than in one burdened with high net public debt and persistent deficits. In the former, policymakers would be aware that fiscal policy could be called upon, if necessary, to aid in stimulating the economy and forestalling any risk of deflation becoming entrenched.[24] Likewise, our closed-economy setting precludes the use—as advocated for Japan by numerous authors, such as Svensson (2001) and McCallum (2000)—of exchange rate policy as a tool to help rescue an economy suffering from the effects of a severe asset-price bubble collapse.

24. This is not to say that, in an economy with sound public finances, policymakers would be unconcerned about the possibility of encountering the ZLB, since any requirement for bond-financed fiscal stimulus would result in the accumulation of net debt, which must subsequently be repaid (and which might also entail undesirable intergenerational transfers). Rather, it is to say that they would likely assess the costs of encountering the ZLB to be far lower than is implied in our framework. This would be especially so in the "deflationary trap" region of (y_t, π_t)-space, from much of which it would now be possible to escape with the aid of fiscal stimulus, so avoiding the catastrophic losses associated with a deflationary spiral.

Table 2.1 Impact of the ZLB on an activist's recommendations

Scenario	Year 1	Year 2	Year 3	Year 4	Year 5	Year 6
Policy can't affect bubble						
$p_t = 0.2$, baseline model	=	=	=	–	–	–
$p_t = 0.4$, baseline model	=	=	=	=	=	–
$p_t = 0.4$, $\beta = 0.5$	=	=	–	–	–	–
$p_t = 0.4$, $\lambda = 0.6$	=	=	=	=	=	=
$p_t = 0.4$, $\lambda = 1.0$	=	=	=	=	–	–
Policy affects bubble growth	=	=	=	=	–	–
Policy affects probability of bursting						
$p^* = 0.4$, $\delta = 0.2$	=	=	+	+	–	–

Note: Tighter (+), looser (–), or little different (=) than otherwise, $i^* = 3.0$.

Notwithstanding these caveats, our framework has the twin advantages of simplicity and transparency, while at the same time realistically capturing the key elements of the interaction between output, inflation, and real interest rates. It thus allows us to draw plausible conclusions regarding at least the direction in which the presence of the ZLB would likely influence the recommendations of an activist policymaker trying to respond optimally to a bubble. It also allows us to understand intuitively the mechanisms driving these conclusions, and how the relative importance of these mechanisms might vary as we alter either the stochastic properties of the bubble, or the parameters that characterize the economy.

Table 2.1 summarizes the results from our various numerical simulations, for the case of an economy with a steady-state neutral nominal interest rate of $i^* = 3$ percent. For each scenario the table shows, as time proceeds and the bubble grows, whether the impact of the ZLB on an activist's recommendations would be to make them tighter (+), looser (–), or little different (=) than otherwise (where "little different" here denotes an impact of less than 25 basis points).

There are two broad sets of lessons worth highlighting from this summary. The first concerns the appropriate level of the steady-state neutral nominal interest rate—the sum of the economy's neutral real interest rate and policymakers' choice of target inflation rate. From table 2.1 we see that, even for a very low neutral nominal interest rate of $i^* = 3$ percent, in most scenarios the ZLB has relatively little effect on the thinking of an activist policymaker until the bubble has become quite large.[25] Moreover, as figures 2.3, 2.6, and 2.8 confirm, even those "ZLB effects" in table 2.1 that

25. The two exceptions are: when the bubble's probability of bursting may be influenced by policy; and when the bubble is exogenous but the economy is relatively unresponsive to policymakers' actions. In these two cases the "ZLB effect" exceeds 25 basis points when the bubble is still only of a moderate size.

are not negligible dissipate rapidly as the neutral nominal interest rate is raised above 3 percent.

These observations suggest that fears of encountering the ZLB should not be overstated, unless the neutral nominal interest rate in the economy is very low. They thus have an obvious implication for policymakers anxious not to have to worry about factoring the ZLB into their thinking when trying to cope with an asset-price bubble. Such policymakers should simply avoid targeting too low an inflation rate, so as to ensure that the economy's neutral nominal interest rate is in turn not too low—for example, not below 4 percent, for our stylized, baseline economy.[26]

The results in table 2.1 also shed light on how the ZLB ought optimally to affect the recommendations of an activist policymaker, facing an asset-price bubble, for a *given* target inflation rate. We may interpret these results through the "insurance" framework for analyzing the impact of the ZLB on an activist's thinking, described in section 2.3.

As discussed there in detail, there are three forms of "insurance" that a policymaker can take out against the risk of encountering the ZLB due to the future bursting of an asset-price bubble. Two of these—to attempt to deflate the bubble before it can grow further, or to restrain its future growth—are available only if policymakers can influence the future behavior of the bubble. The third, to build a buffer of extra inflation and output against its future collapse, is always available to policymakers.

The results in table 2.1 (together with those shown in figures 2.3, 2.6, and 2.8) suggest that, for the scenarios we have considered, the third form of insurance is typically the most cost-effective, even where the first two are available.[27] The key point, however, is that this is not uniformly so—and, for different scenarios, which form of insurance is most cost-effective seems to depend delicately upon the parameters describing both the economy and the stochastic properties of the bubble. Indeed, in some instances, such as when policymakers can influence a bubble's probability of bursting, it appears that the form of insurance that represents the best value for an activist can even switch suddenly and decisively from one period to the next. Overall, therefore, whether the ZLB should cause policymakers to operate policy more tightly or more loosely than they would otherwise do, while a bubble is growing, would seem to be a subtle question—even after

26. Hence, for example, a target inflation range with a mid-point of 1 percent might well be too low for such policymakers, in our baseline economy, unless the neutral real interest rates in their economy were thought to exceed 3 percent.

27. In this regard, however, it is worth recalling the caveat noted in section 2.3.1 that the cost of this third policy option would be higher, per unit of insurance against encountering the ZLB, were inflation expectations in our model economy not assumed to be purely backward-looking. That said, this would likely only serve to further complicate the issue of which form of insurance would be judged by policymakers to be most cost-effective for different bubbles, at different times, and therefore reinforce the conclusions that follow.

abstracting from the significant informational difficulties facing policymakers in practice.

Appendix A

Recent Literature

This chapter lies at the intersection of two broad areas, both of which have been the subject of extensive research interest in recent years.

The first relates to the issue of how monetary policy should respond to asset-price bubbles. Work in this area has focused on whether policymakers ought to make allowance for perceived asset-price misalignments in setting policy; and, if so, whether such allowance ought to be explicit, through the inclusion of asset prices in either the policymaker's objective function or policy rule, or merely implicit.[28] A related issue, which has also received recent attention, is whether success in achieving low and stable inflation may, in fact, increase either the frequency with which asset-price misalignments develop, or the severity of such misalignments (Borio and Lowe 2002).

The second broad research area relates to the implications, both for the economy and for monetary policy, of deflation and the zero lower bound on nominal interest rates. An initial wave of interest in these implications was prompted by Japan's experiences with both phenomena, starting around the late 1990s. Since then, such research has gained renewed impetus recently from concerns that some other major economies, such as the United States and Germany, might have been flirting with deflation, following significant economic downturns.

Within this second broad area, the literature to date may be roughly divided into two streams. The first of these consists of theoretical analyses of the policy issues raised by deflation and the zero lower bound. These issues include the causes and implications of a liquidity trap, and the role (if any) of foreign exchange or asset-market interventions in escaping from such a trap (see, for example, Svensson 2001 and McCallum 2000). They also encompass the costs and benefits of coordinated fiscal and monetary-policy actions, such as "helicopter drops" (Bernanke 2000), or of other more abstract policy options such as Gesell taxes on money balances (Goodfriend 2000), designed to extricate an economy from deflation. Finally, they also include the role (if any) of the choice of monetary-policy regime—and in particular the decision whether or not to adopt a price-level or inflation target—in also helping an economy to escape from deflation (Krugman 1998).

28. For the two opposing views in this debate see Bernanke and Gertler (2001) and Cecchetti, Genberg, Lipsky, and Wadhwani (2000).

The second stream consists of empirical or historical examinations of these same issues. Such examinations have primarily focused on the experiences of Japan since the early 1990s (see, for example, Posen 2003 and Fukao 2003), but also include reexaminations of other relevant episodes, such as the attempt by U.S. authorities in the 1960s to increase liquidity, and lower long-term bond rates, through "Operation Twist" (see Modigliani and Sutch 1966).[29]

As noted earlier, this chapter lies at the overlap between the two broad research areas just described. From this viewpoint, the asset-price bubbles in this chapter may be regarded, at one level, as just one particular source of shocks with the potential—especially if inflation is being held at too low a level prior to such a shock—to drive the economy to a state where the zero lower bound becomes a constraint on policy. The experiences of Japan in the early 1990s, and of the United States more recently, suggest that this is certainly an important area for current research.

There is an important difference, however, between our focus in this chapter, and that of the bulk of the literature on deflation and the zero lower bound just described. The greater part of that literature concentrates on the economic implications of the zero lower bound, and on what policymakers should do to escape from this constraint, once it has been reached. By contrast, our concern in this chapter is with the ways in which the existence of the zero lower bound ought to influence policymakers *prior to* any negative shock—in our setting, caused by the collapse of a bubble—which might drive the economy into recession and deflation.

Appendix B

The Phase Diagram for the Ball-Svensson Model Under Optimal Policy

In this appendix we outline the derivation of the phase diagram (figure 2.1) discussed in section 2.3 of the main body of the chapter. This phase diagram is replicated in figure 2.11 below, now for the case of general model and loss-function parameters α, β, λ, and μ. Note that this phase diagram represents a particular case of that derived previously (in a different fashion) by Reifschneider and Williams (2000), for the Ball-Svensson model with policy determined by a general Taylor rule.[30]

29. Of course, the distinction between these two streams is to some extent artificial, since many studies have included both a theoretical and empirical component.

30. Here we consider only the case where policy is set optimally, which turns out to be a specific instance of a Taylor rule.

The basic idea of this phase diagram is that we can separate (y_t, π_t)-space into three distinct components, as follows:

(y_t, π_t)-space

- Part in which the economy will enter a deflationary spiral (DS), in the absence of future shocks to output or inflation, even with the nominal interest rate set to zero (Region III)
- Part in which the economy will not enter a deflationary spiral (Non-DS), in the absence of future shocks to output or inflation, if the nominal interest rate is set to zero
  - Part of the Non-DS Region in which the zero lower bound will initially be binding, under optimal policy to restore the economy to steady state (Region II)
  - Part of the Non-DS Region in which, absent future shocks, optimal policy will be able to restore the economy to steady state without ever striking the zero lower bound (Region I)

We begin by establishing the existence and properties of Region III. To this end observe that, in the absence of future shocks to output or inflation, the evolution of our Ball-Svensson economy may be described, in terms of nominal interest rates, by the system

$$\mathbf{Z}_t = \mathbf{M}\mathbf{Z}_{t-1} - \beta\mathbf{X}_t, \tag{18}$$

where the matrix $\mathbf{M}$, and the vectors $\mathbf{Z}_t$ and $\mathbf{X}_t$, are defined by

$$\mathbf{M} \equiv \begin{pmatrix} \lambda & \alpha \\ \beta & 1 \end{pmatrix}, \mathbf{Z}_t \equiv \begin{pmatrix} y_t \\ \pi_t \end{pmatrix}, \mathbf{X}_t \equiv \begin{pmatrix} i^{\mathrm{lvl}}_{t-1} - i^* \\ 0 \end{pmatrix}. \tag{19}$$

Now consider the question: what initial conditions for $\mathbf{Z}$ would result in the economy entering a deflationary spiral, even in the event that i^{lvl} were held at the zero lower bound? To answer this question note that, for $i^{\mathrm{lvl}} = 0$, equation (18) may be rewritten more simply as

$$\mathbf{W}_t = \mathbf{M}\mathbf{W}_{t-1}, \tag{20}$$

where $\mathbf{W}_t$ denotes the vector $\mathbf{W}_t = (y_t, \pi_t + i^*)^T$. Then, for this simplified system, the evolution of any initial $\mathbf{W}_t$ is clearly determined simply by the eigenvalues, $\xi_\pm$, and eigenvectors, $v_\pm$, of the matrix $\mathbf{M}$, which are readily computed to be:

$$\xi_\pm = \frac{1}{2}\{(1 + \lambda) \pm [(1 - \lambda)^2 + 4\alpha\beta]^{1/2}\} \tag{21}$$

and

$$v_\pm = \begin{pmatrix} 2\beta \\ (1 - \lambda) \pm [(1 - \lambda)^2 + 4\alpha\beta]^{1/2} \end{pmatrix}. \tag{22}$$

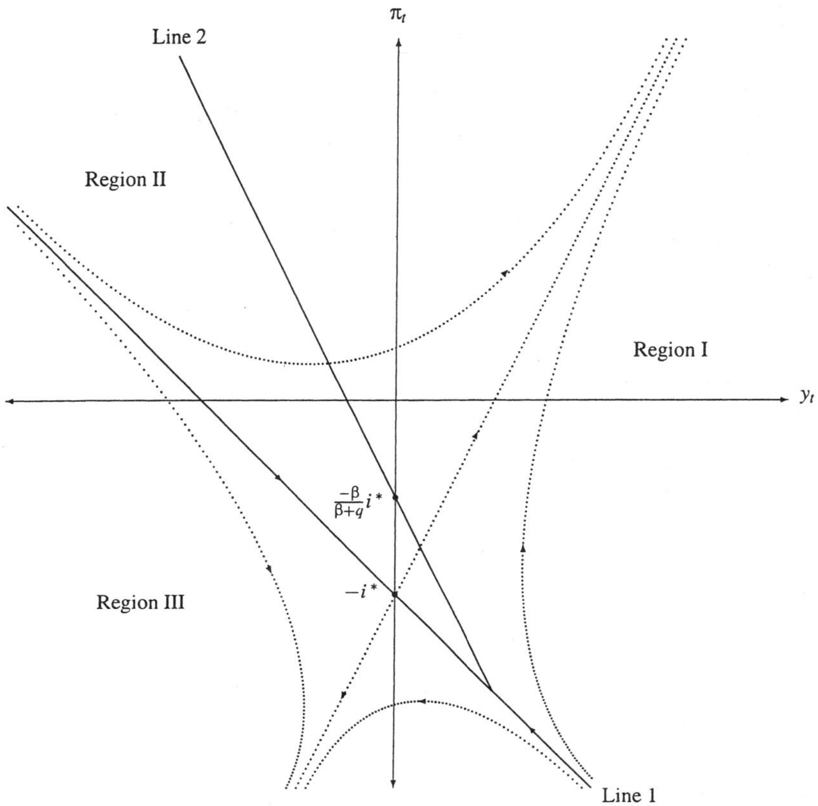

Fig. 2.11 Phase diagram for the Ball-Svensson model under optimal policy

Notes: Dotted lines with arrows denote sample trajectories for the evolution of (y_t, π_t), absent future shocks to output or inflation, in the event that the nominal interest rate is held at zero. Line one passes through the point $(0, -i^*)$ and has slope $\{(1-\lambda)-[(1-\lambda)^2+4\alpha\beta]^{1/2}\}/2\beta$. Line two passes through the point $(0, -[\beta/(\beta+q)]i^*)$ and has slope $-(\lambda+\alpha q)/(\beta+q)$, where q is the scalar defined earlier (see section 2.2).

Note that, for $\alpha, \beta, \lambda > 0$, then ξ_+ will clearly satisfy $\xi_+ > 1$; while ξ_- will satisfy $0 < \xi_- < 1$ provided $\lambda > \alpha\beta$ (which certainly holds for our baseline choice of model parameters: $\alpha = 0.4$, $\beta = 1$, and $\lambda = 0.8$).

Hence, translating back to (y_t, π_t)-coordinates, we see that (y_t, π_t)-space may be split into two halves, in one of which the economy will enter a deflationary spiral even with nominal interest rates set to zero, as shown in figure 2.11. The line separating these two halves passes through the point $(0, -i^*)$, and has slope equal to that of the eigenvector v_-, namely $([1-\lambda]-[(1-\lambda)^2+4\alpha\beta]^{1/2})/2\beta$. This slope is approximately -0.54 for our baseline choice of model parameters.

In addition, the non-deflationary-spiral component of (y_t, π_t)-space may itself be subdivided into two parts: one where the zero lower bound will initially be binding on optimal policy (Region II); and one (Region I) where it will not be binding (so that, absent future shocks, the economy may be returned to steady-state without ever setting nominal interest rates to zero).

The dividing line between these two regions will simply be given by the set of states (y_t, π_t) for which the associated unconstrained optimal *nominal* interest rate recommendation exactly equals zero. Yet we know that, for any given levels of the output gap and inflation, the unconstrained optimal *real* interest rate recommendation is simply

$$r_t^{\mathrm{lvl}} = r^* + \beta^{-1}(\lambda + \alpha q)y_t + \beta^{-1}q\pi_t, \tag{23}$$

where the scalar q is defined by $q = (-\mu\alpha + [\mu^2\alpha^2 + 4\mu]^{1/2})/2$. Hence, since $i_t^{\mathrm{lvl}} = r_t^{\mathrm{lvl}} + \pi_t + \pi^*$, the dividing line between Regions I and II will be precisely the line

$$i^* + \beta^{-1}(\lambda + \alpha q)y_t + \beta^{-1}(\beta + q)\pi_t = 0 \tag{24}$$

or, in other words,

$$\pi_t = -\frac{\beta}{\beta + q}i^* - \frac{\lambda + \alpha q}{\beta + q}y_t. \tag{25}$$

Note that this passes through the point $(0, -[\beta/(\beta + q)]i^*)$ and has slope $-(\lambda + \alpha q)/(\beta + q)$, as shown in figure 2.11.

This completes the derivation, for general model and loss-function parameters, of the phase diagram for the Ball-Svensson model under optimal policy.[31]

Appendix C

The Case of Rational Bubbles

For the baseline results presented in section 2.4.1, the asset-price bubble considered there grew at a uniform rate, $\gamma_t = 1$, and had a probability of

31. While we do not pursue this further here, it is also possible to use this phrase diagram (figure 2.11) to better understand the precise way in which being in Region II will result in additional loss for a policymaker, over and above that which he or she would expect to incur in the absence of the ZLB. The key observation is that, without the ZLB, our Ball-Svensson economy will evolve under optimal policy according to the equation $Z_t = \mathbf{U}Z_{t-1}$ where $\mathbf{U}$ is a 2×2 matrix with eigenvalues 0 and $(1 - \alpha q)$. Computation of the corresponding eigenvectors, which turn out to be $(1, -\alpha)^T$ and $(q, -1)^T$ respectively, allows the way in which optimal policy moves the economy around in (y_t, π_t)-space to be easily pictured—and hence, in turn, allows the impact of the ZLB on a policymaker, trying to stabilize an economy in Region II, to be understood geometrically in terms of the phase diagram.

collapse that was constant through time. However, under certain assumptions about the relationship between the price growth underlying an asset bubble and the impact of that bubble on the real economy, such a bubble could be regarded as irrational: that is, in violation of an arbitrage condition ruling out unexploited profit opportunities in the assets whose price rises constitute the bubble.[32]

As in Gruen, Plumb, and Stone (2003), we do not see this as a shortcoming per se, since there is much evidence in developed economies of irrational bubbles occurring in practice—see, for example, Shiller (2000). Nevertheless, it is interesting to consider whether the imposition of a rationality assumption on our bubbles would affect our overall findings and, if so, how.

To address this question we must first quantify what it means for a bubble to be rational. Such a bubble arises from the actions of a rational investor who buys the relevant assets up to the point at which expected profits are driven to zero.[33] If the probability of collapse is constant, p^*, and the capital gain to the investor in year $t + 1$ if the bubble collapses is $-a_t$, then a rational risk-neutral investor will be indifferent to holding the asset when the expected growth of the bubble, if it survives, is $\Delta a_{t+1} = a_t p^*/(1 - p^*)$. This is a geometrically growing bubble, rather than the constant-growth bubble that constituted our baseline case.[34]

Having quantified the condition for an exogenous bubble to be rational, we are now in a position to examine whether the imposition of a rationality assumption on our bubbles would fundamentally alter our earlier findings as to the impact of the ZLB on the recommendations of an activist policymaker. To this end, figure 2.12 shows the difference between the recommendations of activist policymakers, with and without a ZLB constraint, for the case of a rational bubble with size one in period zero, and with constant probability of bursting $p^* = 0.2$.[35] Results are shown for the three cases $i^* = 1$, 3, and 8 percent.

32. The required assumptions are that the effect on the output gap of a change in asset prices is proportional to the size of the change, and that rational investors and the activist policymaker agree on the exact stochastic details of the bubble. We adopt these two assumptions throughout the remainder of this appendix.

33. We assume that the assets yield an annual return equal to the real interest rate, so that the expected profit relative to holding one-year government bonds is determined by the expected capital gain on the assets.

34. This geometric growth formula for Δa_{t+1} is simply another way of stating the arbitrage condition that defines a rational bubble, namely that the bubble's expected growth over the next year, $E_t \Delta a_{t+1}$, should be zero. Note also that, if the probability of collapse is not constant, a rational bubble need not grow at a constant geometrical rate.

35. We assume that the bubble has size one in period zero, with y_0 also assumed equal to one (consistent with the scenario that the bubble has spontaneously developed in period zero, thereby perturbing the economy from the equilibrium state it occupied in the preceding period), so as to allow the rational bubble to "get started." Since the rationality condition $\Delta a_{t+1} = a_t p^*/(1 - p^*)$ may equivalently be written as $a_{t+1} = a_t/(1 - p^*)$, we see that without such an assumption a rational bubble would never be able to develop in the first place.

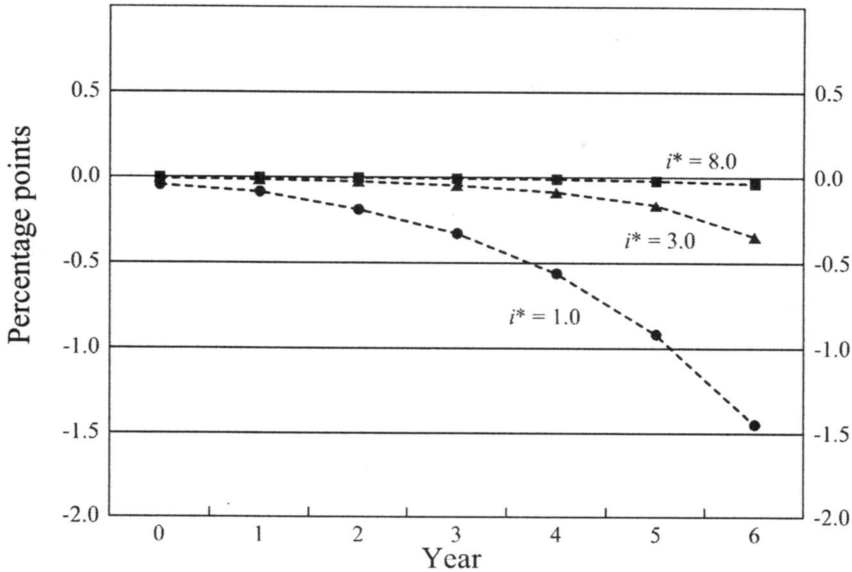

Fig. 1.12 Impact of the ZLB on an activist's recommendations—Difference between recommendations with and without the ZLB

Notes: The skeptic implements policy in each year.

Strikingly, we see that the results in figure 2.12 for this rational bubble are extremely similar to those shown earlier in figure 2.3, for our (irrational) baseline scenario.[36] This strongly suggests that the general thrust of our various findings in section 2.4, regarding the impact of the ZLB on the recommendations of an activist policymaker, is unlikely to be sensitive to the imposition of a rationality constraint on the bubbles considered there.[37]

36. The extreme closeness of this similarity is to some extent coincidental, since the constant period-to-period probability of bursting is different for the two bubbles: $p^* = 0.4$ for the baseline bubble considered in figure 2.3, versus $p^* = 0.2$ for the rational bubble considered in figure 2.12. Were we to assume also $p^* = 0.4$ for the rational bubble, the growth of this bubble would accelerate so much more quickly, while it survived, than in the $p^* = 0.2$ case, that the downward impact of the ZLB on an activist's policy recommendations would be evident both much earlier and more strongly than in figure 2.12. The important point, however, is that the *general nature* of this impact—namely to push down the optimal recommendations of an activist, and to do so increasingly strongly over time—would be unchanged.

37. This is not to say that, for an activist policymaker, the recommendations themselves (whether subject to a ZLB constraint or not) would be similar for the two different bubbles just compared: the baseline bubble in section 2.4.1 and the rational bubble specified above. Indeed, the results in section 2.3 of Gruen, Plumb, and Stone (2003) show that these recommendations would, in fact, be quite different. Rather, it merely says that, in terms of the *marginal impact* which the ZLB would have on the optimal recommendations of an activist policymaker, the general nature of this impact is similar for both types of bubble.

References

Ball, Laurence. 1994. What determines the sacrifice ratio? In *Monetary policy,* ed. N. Gregory Mankiw, 155–82. National Bureau of Economic Research Studies in Business Cycles. Chicago: University of Chicago Press.

———. 1999a. Efficient rules for monetary policy. *International Finance* 2 (1): 63–83.

———. 1999b. Policy rules for open economies. In *Monetary policy rules,* ed. John B. Taylor, 127–44. A National Bureau of Economic Research Conference Report. Chicago: University of Chicago Press.

Bernanke, Ben S. 2000. Japanese monetary policy: A case of self-induced paralysis? In *Japan's financial crisis and its parallels to U.S. experience,* ed. R. Mikitani and A. S. Posen, 149–66. Washington, DC: Institute for International Economics.

Bernanke, Ben S., and M. Gertler. 2001. Should central banks respond to movements in asset prices? *American Economic Review* 91 (2): 253–57.

Borio, Claudio, and Philip Lowe. 2002. Asset prices, financial and monetary stability: Exploring the nexus. Working Paper no. 114. *Bank for International Settlements,* July.

Cecchetti, Stephen G. 2003. What the FOMC says and does when the stock market booms. In *Asset prices and monetary policy,* ed. Tony Richards and Tim Robinson, 27–96. Proceedings of a Conference. Sydney: Reserve Bank of Australia.

Cecchetti, S. G., H. Genberg, J. Lipsky, and S. Wadhwani. 2000. Asset prices and central bank policy. *Geneva Reports on the World Economy* 2. International Centre for Monetary and Banking Studies and Centre for Economic Policy Research.

DeLong, Bradford J., and Lawrence H. Summers. 1988. How does macroeconomic policy affect output? *Brookings Papers on Activity,* 433–80.

Fukao, Mitsuhiro. 2003. Financial strains and the zero lower bound: The Japanese experience. BIS Working Paper no. 141. Basel, CHE: Bank for International Settlements, September.

Goodfriend, Marvin. 2000. Overcoming the zero bound on interest policy. *Journal of Money, Credit and Banking* 32 (4): 1007–35.

Gruen, David, Michael Plumb, and Andrew Stone. 2003. How should monetary policy respond to asset-price bubbles? Research Discussion Paper: 2003-11. *Reserve Bank of Australia,* November.

Krugman, P. R. 1998. It's baaack! Japan's slump and the return of the liquidity trap. *Brookings Papers on Economic Activity* 49 (2): 137–206.

McCallum, Bennett T. 2000. Theoretical analysis regarding a zero lower bound on nominal interest rates. *Journal of Money, Credit and Banking* 32 (4): 870–904.

Modigliani, Franco, and Richard Sutch. 1966. Innovations in interest rate policy. *American Economic Review* LVI: 178–97.

Posen, Adam S. 2003. It takes more than a bubble to become Japan. In *Asset Prices and Monetary Policy,* eds. A. Richards and T. Robinson. Proceedings of a Conference. *Reserve Bank of Australia, Sydney,* 203–49.

Reifschneider, David, and John C. Williams. 2000. Three lessons for monetary policy in a low-inflation era. *The Journal of Money, Credit and Banking* 32 (4): 936–66.

Rudebusch, Glenn D. 1995. What are the lags in monetary policy? *FRBSF Weekly Letter,* 95-05. San Francisco, CA: Federal Reserve Bank of San Francisco.

Shiller, R. J. 2000. *Irrational exuberance.* Princeton, NJ: Princeton University Press.

Svensson, Lars E. O. 1997. Inflation forecast targeting: Implementing and monitoring inflation targets. *European Economic Review* 41 (6): 1111–46.

———. 2001. The zero bound in an open economy: A foolproof way of escaping from a liquidity trap. *Monetary and Economic Studies* 19 (S-1): 277–312.
Taylor, John B. 1993. Discretion versus policy rules in practice. *Carnegie-Rochester Conference Series on Public Policy* 39:195–214.

Comment Piti Disyatat

Overview

This was a very enjoyable chapter that brings out quite clearly the trade-offs that policymakers face with respect to the possibility of hitting the zero lower bound (ZLB). The model analyzed is very simple and easy to understand and the chapter highlights neatly the key factors that influence the way in which the ZLB is factored into policymaking. That said, the simplicity of the model also causes some problems, in particular with respect to the interpretation of asset prices as detailed below.

Model Setup

The way in which the asset-price bubbles are introduced (see equation [4]) is very simplistic and makes it difficult to interpret them really as asset prices. They are more like temporary real shocks that accumulate over time and eventually reverse suddenly. As such, it may be more appropriate to refer to them as "real bubbles" since there is no asset price per se.

Unlike some other work, notably Bernanke and Gertler (1999), the impact of asset prices on the economy is not modeled. This simplification is a reflection of the chapter's focus on the impact of ZLB on policy formation rather than whether or not policy should react to asset prices. However, in practice, it is precisely the uncertainty with respect to how asset prices may affect the economy and whether asset-price movements reflect fundamentals or not that makes determining the appropriate response to them so difficult. For example, if asset-price movements reflect fundamental forces, such as improvements in productivity, they should be accommodated.

Often times, the issue is more how to respond to asset prices given observed fundamentals rather than how to react to a given set of observed fundamentals that is known to already incorporate the effects of an asset-price bubble. A direct consequence of the way in which asset price is modeled here is that policymakers react to asset price only through its impact

Piti Disyatat is a senior economist at the Bank of Thailand.
The views expressed here are those of the author and do not necessarily represent those of the Bank of Thailand or Bank of Thailand policy.

on output and inflation. In doing so, the chapter ignores the question of whether the authorities should react to them *over and above* their impact on macrovariables.

Modeling bubbles simply as real shocks may thus be too general and implicitly assumes that policymakers *know for sure* the potential impact of asset prices on the economy. While this feature is deliberate on the part of the authors, it could be motivated by recourse to Bernanke and Gertler (1999), who reached the conclusion that monetary policy should respond to asset prices not directly but only insofar as they impact on macrovariables. Thus one interpretation of the setup in this chapter is that it takes the conclusion of Bernanke and Gertler as the starting point, sweeping all of the considerations under the carpet.

Information Assumptions

Now a few words on the information assumptions. The chapter imposes the very strong assumption that policymakers know the stochastic properties of the real shock hitting the economy and can distinguish the impact on the economy of that shock. This is already somewhat a strong assumption with regards to real shocks and quite unrealistic when it comes to asset prices. More problematic, however, is the implicit assumption that the policymaker knows that the bubble will burst for sure soon (after fourteen periods with high probability). If there was some uncertainty about the bubble (whether it really exists or not) then many of the trade-offs that the activist policymaker faces will change substantially since his or her efforts to cushion against the bursting of the bubble could result in an inflation bias.

It should also be noted that the inherent difference between "activist" and "skeptical" policymakers in the chapter lies in the information set available to each type rather than any fundamental differences in views and preferences about how policy should respond to asset prices (indeed, both types of policymakers are assumed to have identical preferences and minimize the same loss function). In particular, the implicit assumption is that "skeptical" policymakers are not aware of the stochastic process governing the bubble's evolution. Otherwise, the "skeptics" would simply be extremely naive since they would be ignoring the fact that the economy will be subject to a negative real shock *for sure* in the future. In comparing the policy choices of the two policymaker types, then, the comparison is really between policymakers that have differing degrees of knowledge about the bubble process rather than any inherent differences regarding policymakers' views about market functioning as argued in the chapter.

The role of expectations is also underplayed somewhat. In particular, the framework of monetary policy and its announcement can have important implications for the formation of bubbles. As highlighted by Bernanke and Gertler, in a setting where the central bank is *known* to respond aggressively to inflation (private sector knows policy rule), the dynamic path of the bubble is attenuated simply by this expected policy response. No policy action is required ex post. Much of the stabilizing effect of prescribed policy rule comes through the public's expectations of future policy action. All this is absent here.

Optimal Policy

One of the interesting experiments in the chapter is the allowance of the dynamic path of the bubble as well as its impact on the economy to be endogenous to policy. It is important to note, however, that in the real world, the impact of policy on the path of the bubble can *itself* be dependent on the state of the economy. This is particularly relevant in section 2.4.4 where the probability of the bubble bursting is endogenized. There, the optimal-policy prescription for an activist is nonuniform in that in the early stages, the focus is on trying to pop the bubble by keeping policy relatively tight. Then, suddenly, a threshold is crossed where the aim is now to cushion the economy from the deflationary effects of the bubble bursting by adopting a relatively loose stance. This switch involves a very large swing in interest rates (from positive to negative) and occurs when the bubble is already quite advanced.

This scenario highlights the weakness of the assumption that the way in which policy affects the bubble is invariant to the state of the economy or the public's expectations. In practice, when the bubble is at an advanced stage, output and inflation are likely to be high. For the central bank to *reduce* rates in this environment would have to be explained in terms of correcting financial imbalances. If the explanation is believed then the public would have to be convinced that there is a bubble which is big and likely to burst. Their actions may then, in turn, hasten the collapse of the bubble. Thus the effect of a rate reduction may reverse sign (instead of reducing the probability of bursting the bubble, may actually *increase* it).

There is also the possibility that ex ante versus ex post volatility in desired goal variables could differ sharply. For example, the drastic policy shift recommended in section 2.4.4 may be justified ex ante, but will surely have huge repercussions on real economy and may result in substantial ex post variability. Thus the skeptic approach may be better ex post. This is a reflection of the unrealistic assumption that the "real bubble" is *known* by activist policymaker to burst after a specified time period with high probability. The trade-off that underlies the sharp reversal in the policy stance occurs precisely because of this assumption. In this respect, the chapter may be extended to compare welfare implications of activist versus skeptic policy.

Conclusion

While a significant amount of realism is lost in making strong assumptions in order to keep things simple, the chapter nevertheless succeeds in its core purpose of singling out the impact that the ZLB have on policy *prior* to it actually being reached. The chapter does so in a particularly neat and transparent way. Given the way in which asset-price bubbles are introduced, however, the impacts highlighted are more in response to uncertainty about the state of the economy in the face of real shocks than asset prices per se. The analysis in the chapter is very illuminating, but to link it to asset prices is somewhat unconvincing.

The chapter brings out clearly not only the impact of ZLB on policy setting but also the information requirements of activist monetary policy. The latter helps to elucidate the formidable information requirements for successful pursuit of activist policy. One conclusion I drew from this chapter, which could be emphasized much more by the authors, is the practical limitations of such an approach. Activist policymakers in the chapter need to know whether a bubble exists or not, how big it is, how it affects the economy, and also the likelihood of it bursting soon. This would be prohibitive in practice.

Reference

Bernanke, B., and M. Gertler. 1999. Monetary policy and asset price volatility. *Federal Reserve Bank of Kansas City Economic Review,* fourth quarter. Kansas City, KS.

Comment Kenneth Kuttner

This nicely written chapter brings together elements from two strands of recent macroeconomic research: one from the literature on the zero lower bound (ZLB) problem facing policymakers under conditions of very low inflation, and another from the literature on the optimal policy response to asset-price bubbles. Its main conclusion is that the asymmetry created by the ZLB makes it desirable for monetary policy to respond proactively to asset-price bubbles, assuming they can be identified in real time. Perhaps the most attractive feature of the chapter is its transparency. The use of a simple, familiar economic model makes the results easy to understand; but the framework's simplicity also means its shortcomings are in plain view. The analysis does, nonetheless, generate some important insights relevant to the conduct of monetary policy in near-deflationary conditions.

These comments are organized as follows. The first section presents a brief discussion of how the authors' framework, and their results, relate to

Kenneth Kuttner is the Danforth-Lewis Professor of Economics at Oberlin College, and a faculty research fellow of the National Bureau of Economic Research.

other papers in the literature on the ZLB and asset-price bubbles. The second contains a brief presentation of a simplified version of their model, capable of conveying the essence of their results in qualitative terms. The remarks conclude with a discussion of the model's shortcomings, and some suggestions for extensions and further research.

The Chapter in Relation to the ZLB and Bubble Literatures

The central question motivating the chapter is whether it is wise for central banks to respond to asset-price fluctuations in setting monetary policy. The consensus view among academic economists, as embodied in the work of Bernanke and Gertler (2001), is that central banks should respond to asset-price changes *only* to the extent that those fluctuations help forecast the things the central bank really cares about—output and inflation. Or, in the context of an earlier literature, asset prices represent a plausible "indicator" for monetary policy, but not a "target" in their own right.

This chapter's results challenge this conclusion, and argue for a more proactive policy response aimed at preventing the development of asset-price bubbles, and giving policy more "room to maneuver" in offsetting the impact of its eventual collapse. It is not alone in that regard: recent papers by Bordo and Jeanne (2002a, 2002b) and Dupor (2002, 2003) also contain similar prescriptions.

What these papers collectively demonstrate is that justifying a preemptive policy response to asset-price fluctuations requires an asymmetry, broadly speaking, in the effects of asset prices on the economy; that is, a "round trip," involving a nonfundamental asset-price bubble and subsequent burst, leaves the economy materially worse off. In Dupor's work, this asymmetry comes from the microeconomic distortions generated by "too much" investment during the bubble. In the Bordo-Jeanne analysis, the bursting of the bubble creates a credit crunch with effects similar to those of an adverse-supply shock.

The relevant asymmetry in this chapter is, of course, the zero lower bound on the short-term nominal interest rate. In this dimension, the chapter ties in nicely with a very large existing literature on the ZLB issue.[1] A central message of this research is that, because monetary policy becomes ineffective once the ZLB is reached, it should act aggressively near the bound in order to reduce the risk of running into the constraint. This chapter's policy prescriptions reflect something of a synthesis of those from the bubble and ZLB literatures. The authors conclude that central banks should fight the bubble in its early stages, but shift to an accommodative stance as the bubble progresses—essentially, bracing for the bubble's "burst" by putting more distance between the nominal interest rate and the ZLB.

1. See, for example, Clouse et al. (2003); Reifschneider and Williams (1999); and Orphanides and Wieland (1998).

A Simplified Version of the Analysis

The analysis leading to this result is conducted using a straightforward extension to the models developed in Ball (1999) and Svensson (1997). Both of these are, in turn, recognizable as dynamic versions of the textbook aggregate supply/demand model, in which the underlying "LM" relation has been replaced with a simple policy rule as suggested by Romer (2000). While this framework is perfectly serviceable for many policy questions, because it is backward-looking, it cannot deal with other proposed solutions to the ZLB problem, such as that proposed by Eggertsson and Woodford (2003).

The extension to the Ball-Svensson framework is simply the inclusion of a nonstandard aggregate demand shock, Δa_t, which is interpreted as the asset-price bubble—or more precisely, the bubble's effect on aggregate demand. What makes the shock nonstandard is its assumed law of motion

$$E_t \Delta a_{t+1} = (1 - p)\gamma - pa_t,$$

where γ is the rate at which the bubble grows, and p is the probability that the bubble bursts in any given period. In other words, while the bubble is growing, aggregate demand is higher in each period by an amount equal to γ. When it pops, however, aggregate demand is reduced by an amount equal to the bubble's accumulated growth up to that point. Older bubbles are therefore more dangerous.

Faced with a constant probability p of a progressively larger crash, what is a policymaker to do? When the ZLB is an issue, clearly the answer is to increase the inflation rate, so there is more room to drive real rates negative once the crash finally comes. This point can be illustrated quite simply in a static version of the Robinson-Stone model, using the graphical apparatus of Romer (2000). In his setup, the combination of a conventional IS equation with a simple monetary-policy rule (MPR) curve determines output in (Y, r) space; if the MPR is such that the real interest rate increases with inflation (i.e., the "Taylor principle" is satisfied), this yields a downward-sloping aggregate demand (AD) curve in (Y, π) space. The effects of the ZLB are readily discernable in the IS-MPR diagram. As shown in figure 2C.1, the ZLB creates a "floor" at $-\pi$ below which the real interest rate cannot fall (represented by the shaded area in the figure); this, in turn, creates a "kink" in the AD curve (not shown), which bends backwards at the point where the ZLB becomes binding.[2]

It is at this point that the peculiar nature of Robinson and Stone's "bubble shock" becomes relevant. In any given period, the bubble persists with probability p; in this case, the IS curve is shifted out and to the right

2. Romer's horizontal MPR rule assumes, for simplicity, that policy responds only to inflation; a rule with a response to both output *and* inflation would, of course, be upward sloping.

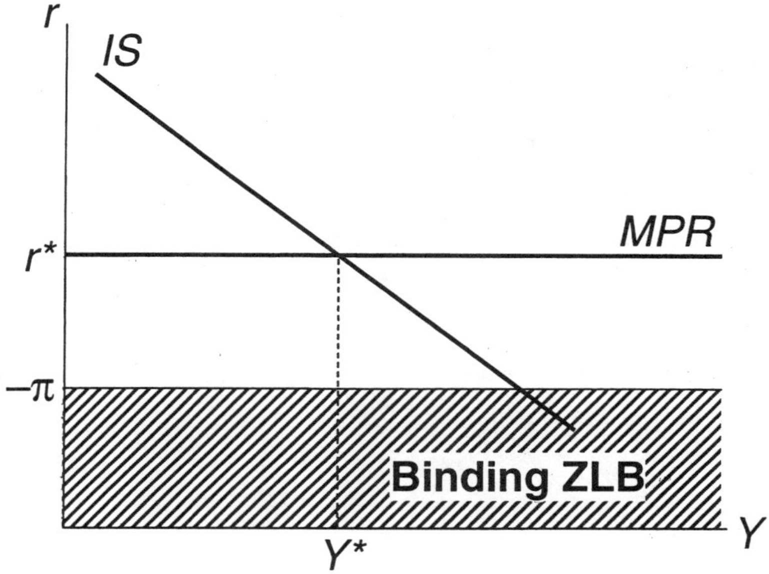

Fig. 2C.1 The IS-MPR diagram with the ZLB constraint

by an amount equal to γ, reflecting the bubble's expansionary impact on spending. Similarly, in any given period the probability of the bubble bursting is $(1 - p)$, and in this case, the IS curve shifts to the left by an amount equal to the accumulated γ during the bubble's growth phase. Eventually, if it lasts long enough, the bubble will become so large that its collapse will shift the IS curve to a point where the real interest rate r^* required to maintain full-employment output Y^* is *less* than the ZLB floor, $-\pi$, as represented by point "A" in figure 2C.2. A central bank that recognizes this threat will, of course, respond by (temporarily) increasing inflation, thereby lowering the ZLB floor, and allowing it to respond more aggressively to the bubble's collapse. While there are aspects of the Robinson-Stone analysis that this apparatus cannot deal with (notably, the optimal conduct of policy when γ is endogenous), Romer's framework does a nice job of conveying, at least qualitatively, the central point of the chapter.

Critiques and Suggestions for Future Research

As noted at the outset, one of the attractive features of the Robinson-Stone chapter is its familiar, intuitive framework which, with a minimum of technical baggage, manages to illustrate an important insight about the conduct of monetary policy. But the simplicity comes at a cost, in terms of ignoring certain effects that might mitigate or modify the chapter's central conclusions.

Perhaps the most obvious criticism has to do with the stylized, reduced-

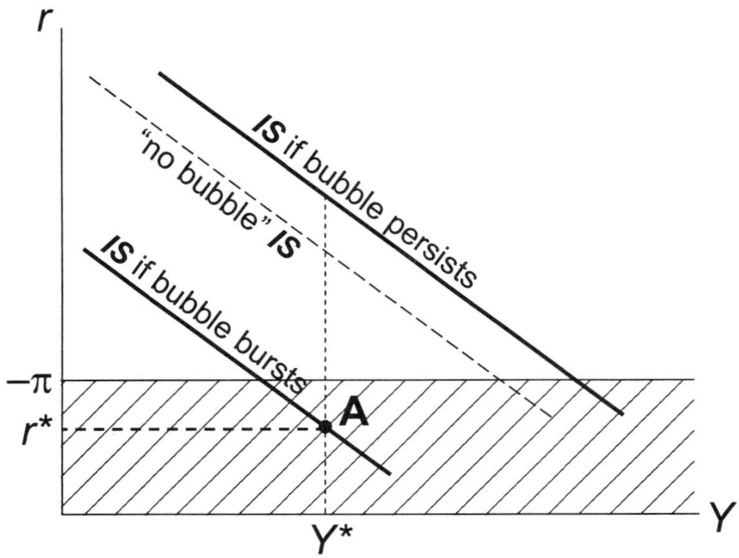

Fig. 2C.2 "Bursting" and "persisting" bubbles in the IS-MPR diagram

form way in which the bubble is modeled as a "nonstandard" demand shock. Clearly, this has a number of compelling advantages, chiefly that one need not model the asset markets at all—only the bubble's impact on spending. One has to wonder, however, whether the assumed impact on spending is, in fact, consistent with a bubble process. Specifically, if households understood the process driving the bubble, they would realize that it would eventually burst. Forward-looking consumers would presumably anticipate this eventuality by increasing their saving, or at least decreasing their propensity to consume out of wealth. This sort of behavior is consistent with the results of Ludvigson and Lettau (2004) who, for the United States, found that consumers tended to respond only to wealth fluctuations that were perceived to be permanent.

Second, the central banker in the Robinson-Stone model is assumed either to be omniscient (the "activist" case), or deluded (the "skeptical" case). The activist central banker is able to observe the bubble term directly, while the skeptic denies its existence (i.e., forecasts a zero shock). While there may be those who insist that the stock market is at all times correctly valued, surely neither case corresponds to the real-world situation in which the policymaker observes a mix of fundamental and nonfundamental shocks, and in making policy, tries to distinguish between the two. Modeling this signal extraction and/or learning aspect of the policymaker's job would seem like a worthwhile addition to any model dealing with bubbles.

Finally, the impact of monetary policy on the bubble's growth would benefit from a more sophisticated modeling approach. In this chapter, the authors simply assume that γ, the bubble's growth rate (conditional on persisting), depends on the lagged gap between the real interest rate and the "natural" rate of interest. Asset prices surely respond contemporaneously to monetary policy, however; at a minimum, therefore, the bubble's growth should depend on the current policy setting. Or even better, because asset markets are forward-looking, the bubble's growth should depend on expectations of future monetary policy.[3] In such a setting, monetary policy could check the asset-price decline resulting from the collapse of a bubble—or, through the expectations channel, perhaps prevent a bubble from occurring in the first place.

Conclusions

In the end, it would be a mistake to take the Robinson-Stone model too literally, with its highly stylized, shorthand approach to modeling asset-price bubbles. Still, the chapter clearly lays out a recognizable scenario in which, owing to the ZLB problem, bubble "preemption" and "damage control" can both play important roles. Collapses in aggregate demand resulting from bursting bubbles are surely something to worry about more when the economy is already close to the ZLB, and this chapter provides yet another rationale for steering clear of that bound, whenever possible.

References

Ball, Laurence. 1999. Efficient rules for monetary policy. *International Finance* 2 (1): 63–83.

Bernanke, Ben, and Mark Gertler. 2001. Should central banks respond to movements in asset prices? *American Economic Review Papers and Proceedings* 91 (2): 253–57.

Bordo, Michael, and Olivier Jeanne. 2002a. Monetary policy and asset prices: Does "benign neglect" make sense? *International Finance* 5 (2): 139–64.

Bordo, Michael, and Olivier Jeanne. 2002b. Boom-busts in asset prices, economic instability, and monetary policy. NBER Working Paper no. 8966. Cambridge, MA: National Bureau of Economic Research, May.

Clouse, James, Dale Henderson, Athanasios Orphanides, David H. Small, and P. A. Tinsley. 2003. Monetary policy when the nominal short-term interest rate is zero. *Berkeley Electronic Press Topics in Macroeconomics* 3 (1). Available at [www.bepress.com/gci/viewcontent.gci?article=1088&context=bejm]

Dupor, Bill. 2002. The natural rate of Q. *American Economic Review* 92 (2): 96–101.

Dupor, Bill. 2003. Nominal price versus asset price stabilization. Unpublished manuscript.

Eggertsson, Gauti, and Michael Woodford. 2003. The zero bound on interest rates and optimal monetary policy. *Brookings Papers on Economic Activity* 1:139–211.

3. While its empirical relevance is debatable, the "Greenspan put" hypothesis is an example of how policy expectations might have contributed to an overvaluation of the stock market. A similar line of reasoning suggests that a "Greenspan call," if credible, could inhibit the development of a bubble.

Lettau, Martin, and Sydney Ludvigson. 2004. Understanding trend and cycle in asset values: Reevaluating the wealth effect on consumption. *American Economic Review* 94 (1): 276–99.
Orphanides, Athanasios, and Volker Wieland. 1998. Price stability and monetary policy effectiveness when nominal interest rate are bounded at zero. Finance and Economics Discussion Series, 1998-35. Board of Governors of the Federal Reserve System, Washington D.C.
Reifschneider, David, and John C. Williams. 1999. Three lessons for monetary policy in a low inflation era. Financial and Economics Discussion Series (FEDS) 1999-44. Board of Governors of the Federal Reserve System, Washington D.C.
Romer, David. 2000. Keynesian macroeconomics without the lm curve. *Journal of Economic Perspectives* 14 (2): 149–69.
Svensson, Lars. 1997. Inflation forecast targeting: Implementing and monitoring inflation targets. *European Economic Review* 41 (6): 1111–46.

3

Money Growth and Interest Rates

Seok-Kyun Hur

3.1 Introduction

The primary purpose of our chapter is to investigate the roles of monetary policy in shaping the term-structure of interest rates. Monetary policy governing the stock of money influences the relative prices of money delivered at different times and different states. In turn, the current relative prices of money to deliver at different points of time in the future, which are, in other words, collectively called the term-structure of interest rates, influence economic decisions of private agents.

Intuitively speaking, the term-structure of interest rates is much more informative than any set of economic variables and thus will be useful as a reference for monetary policy. So far there have been continuous debates over what should be optimal targets of monetary policies. Mostly a combination of inflation and gross domestic product (GDP) gap is cited as a candidate for the target of monetary policy (Taylor 1993). Further developed models would allow autoregressive formations in inflation and GDP gap (Clarida, Gali, and Gertler 2000). Based on such criteria, a certain level of short-term interest rate (e.g., call rate in Korea, federal fund rate in the United States) is prescribed that a central bank should maintain. Though such concentration on the determination of the short-term interest rate is relatively easy to implement in practice, it only sequentially cross-checks the level of inflation and GDP gap with the current short-term interest rate. It neglects how the term-structure of interest rates as a whole reacts to the adjustment of the short-term interest rates, which might ex-

Seok-Kyun Hur is a research fellow of the Korea Development Institute.

plain why the same level of the short-term interest rate brings about different economic performances at different time and states.

Frequently we read numerous articles about predicting the future path of federal fund rate from newspapers. All of them are written on the implicit belief that monetary policy has influence on major aggregate economic activities, such as consumption, investment, and production, though its influence on these economic activities may differ in terms of directions, magnitudes, and timing. Unfortunately, a true transmission mechanism of monetary policy has not yet been thoroughly explored. A true description for the economy would be that the transmission mechanism works through multichannels, only a small number of which so far have been highlighted. To our knowledge, only a few economic models have emphasized the lagging effects of monetary policy in the context of analyzing the movements of the whole nominal bond-market equilibrium.[1]

Apart from the tradition, our chapter is based on the implicit belief that an effective monetary policy should consider the whole term-structure of interest rates rather than a yield rate of a bond with specific maturity. Furthermore, though control over the short-term interest rate has influence on the yields of bonds with longer maturities, it has not yet been clearly verified in which direction a change in the short-term interest rate shifts the whole term-structure of the interest rates. Provided that different yield curves lead to different performances of an economy, the monetary authority should perceive at least the impact of its current short-term interest rate policy on the term-structure of interest rates. However, an answer to this question would require thorough understanding of the whole economy as well as the bond market itself.

Most economic activities are determined by the anticipation of the future, which is well embedded in the term-structure of interest rates. Furthermore, the shape of the yield curve controlled by the money growth rates or the short-term interest rates plays a crucial role in determining the levels of the economic activities. Thus, we are interested in exploring how money growth rate or short-term interest rate policy shifts the term-structure of interest rates.

From the literature on durable consumption and investment[2], we under-

1. Most of the literature assumes that the shape of the term-structure curve depends on the anticipation for the future, the formation of which is hard to define or requires a somewhat arbitrary mechanism. For example, Ellingsen and Söderström (2004) explain how the yield curve responds to monetary policy. In their work, monetary policy is determined by the central bank's preference parameters over the volatilities of inflation, output, and the short-term interest rate. They claim variations in the preferences result in another yield curve by affecting people's expectation for the future. In contrast, our chapter focuses on verifying the relationship between the yield curve and the past money growth rates (or the past history of the short-term rate).

2. Refer to Hong (1996 and 1997) for durable good consumption and Breitung, Chrinko, and Kalckreuth (2003) for business investment.

stand that both of them are quite sensitive to economic fluctuations in comparison with consumption on nondurable goods and services. Intuitively speaking, since the flows of benefit from durable goods and capital continue for a certain period of time, durable goods consumption and investment entail the feature of irreversibility or indivisibility of purchase, which reduces durable goods consumption and investment decisions to optimal stopping problems. Hence, it is absurd to expect that the monetary authority can raise aggregate demands for durable goods and physical capital by merely changing the short-term interest rate. It is because in reality the falling short-term interest rate is often accompanied by an increase in the long-term interest rate, which discourages an agent from purchasing durable goods and physical capital. Thus, the monetary authority may need to find a certain pattern of a yield curve in order to reset the current yield curve to the pattern, which will boost the aggregate demand in times of depression.

On the other hand, the supply side may also depend on the term-structure of interest rates. Production requires a multiperiod binding planning horizon in addition to a time-to-build capital driven technology, in which the adjustments of production inputs are not completely flexible across time. Thus, the assignment or the employment of production inputs, not only capital but also labor, is perceived to be a function of the term-structure of interest rates.

The contents of the chapter are organized as follows: section 3.2 discusses a transmission channel of monetary policy in the economy, which relies on the lagged adjustment processes of various interest rates in the bond market. The feature of lagged adjustments resulting from delayed responses to monetary shocks is critical in that it relates the dynamics of interest rates to the past history of money growth rates or the past history of the short-term interest rates. Section 3.3 tests the models introduced in section 3.2 using the U.S. data, both monthly and quarterly. The relationship between the term-structure of interest rates and the money growth rates is estimated in consideration of endogenous money demand and velocity. Section 3.4 deduces the policy implications by discussing the time lags of monetary policy in implementing a certain yield curve as well as considering the impact of the current short-term interest rate targeting policy on the yield curve. Finally, section 3.5 concludes.

3.2 Theoretical Framework

From a survey of the current literature on the optimal monetary policy, we identify two common approaches from two distinctive traditions of thoughts—new classical and new Keynesian. The new classical approach[3]

3. Refer to Alvarez, Lucas, and Weber (2001) and Monnet and Weber (2001).

admits that market incompleteness, such as market segmentation, may cause the differential effects of monetary policy across time and across agents in the short run, whereas the new Keynesian approach[4] introduces sticky prices and wages to refute the neutrality of money. Regardless of different appearances, these two approaches have in common that they assume private agents respond to shocks in heterogeneous ways.

This section is purposed to provide a logical explanation about the delayed responses of aggregate macrovariables to monetary shocks and reveal the consequences of the delayed responses on the dynamics of the term-structure of interest rates induced by monetary policy. From the perspective of the new classical approach, we build a model, which allows a path-dependent dynamics of the interest rates governed by the past money growth rates.

To begin with, we investigate a limited bond-market participation model and show that the higher order moments of money supply can influence the term-structure of interest rates. Extended from a traditional Cash-in-Advance (CIA) model of Lucas and Stokey (1987), a general m-period-ahead CIA condition is imposed. The adoption of the CIA feature is critical because it, combined with the assumption of limited bond-market participation, brings about the more persistent redistribution effects of monetary policy on the economy. Based on these assumptions, the term-structure of interest rates is approximated by a system of linear equations of the lagged money growth rates. As is generally understood (Clarida, Gali, and Gertler 2000; Ellingsen and Söderström 2004), the expectation of the future money growth rates (or the future monetary policy) has effect on the current term-structure of interest rates. However, we emphasize the importance of the past path of monetary expansion in a sense that money shock would be realized in differential manners across heterogeneous agents in the economy.

Second, we explore the implications the nonnegativity restriction of nominal bond yield rates holds in the financial market, while showing that the linear approximation of the term-structure of interest rates by the past money growth path does not necessarily satisfy the nonnegative condition. The nonnegativity restriction of nominal bond rate is a critical barrier for the central bank to consider when it exercises open market operation policy. Especially, in a very low inflation regime, the possibility of reaching zero short-term interest rate often casts worries because zero rate is regarded as a natural lower boundary of a so called liquidity trap. It is commonly believed that the monetary policy without coordination with the expansionary fiscal policy would be ineffective in such a situation. However, the ineffectiveness of monetary expansion in case of falling into the zero nominal interest rate trap may be supported when only one type of bond is

4. For more details, refer to Clarida, Gali, and Gertler (1999) and Yun (1996).

available in the financial market other than money. Such an extreme absence of variety in the bond market is not realistic at all, and the plunge of the whole term-structure into zero has not been observed in the history, either. Hence, after complementing our term-structure model with nonnegativity restrictions, we discuss the effectiveness of monetary policy near zero short-term interest rate and explore a transitional path on which the bond-market equilibrium retrieves the positive interest rates.

3.2.1 Lagged Transmission Channel of Monetary Shocks

In this section we derive an equation linking the term-structure of interest rates with the past history of money growth rates. We introduce an economy with limited bond-market participation in order to induce a situation in which a monetary shock has differential impacts on heterogeneous agents across time (mainly redistribution effects). The impact differentials are caused by the unsynchronous timing of money shock transmitted to or perceived by the agents or by their different speed of reactions to the shock, and they lead to a nontrivial change in the term-structure of interest rates. On the other hand, in absence of such impact differentials, the yield curve would shift up or down in parallel according to the change of the present and the past money growth rates. A swing of the yield curve would be possible only by the coordinated variations of the expectation for the future monetary growth path and other real macrovariables.

Our model is an adapted version of Alvarez, Lucas, and Weber (2001). Our model assumes the following. First, there are two types of assets in the market—money and bond. Considering that the assets are a means of storing or growing values along the passage of time, the nominal return on money is always zero by construction, whereas the nominal return on bond is positive nominal interest rate. Due to the yield difference in these two types of assets, we need a mechanism guaranteeing the positive holding of money. Thus, we assign a CIA restriction, which is modified from the original one in Lucas and Stokey (1987).

Second, we assume limited bond-market participation, under which not every consumer can purchase bonds in the financial market due to transaction costs or information costs or regulation. There are two groups of consumers in the market—bond-market participants and nonparticipants, whose shares in the total population are λ and $1 - \lambda$, respectively.[5] These two groups are homogeneous in all the other aspects than the bond-market participation.

Third, the CIA condition to be introduced is defined on a multiperiod

5. It is assumed that all the bond-market participants hold all kinds of bonds with various maturities. A more realistic setup would allow that the bond-market participants should be classified into several groups by the maturities of bonds they hold (for example, short-term, medium-term, and long-term investors). Then, the equilibrium yield rate would display more dynamism.

time horizon as follows. At the current period, nominal consumption is afforded by a certain portion from the current nominal income, another certain portion from nominal income of the previous period, another certain portion from income earned two periods ago, and so on. A more intuitive interpretation of the multiperiod ahead CIA condition is that at the beginning of period t the current income (y_t) would be cashed instantly (p_t, y_t) and it would be spent for the next m periods by certain fractions of $v_{t,t+j}$, $j = 0, 1, 2, \ldots, m-1$, ($\Sigma_{j=0}^{m-1} v_{t,t+j} = 1$).

These assumptions are essential in inducing the redistributional effect of money injection across heterogeneous consumers and lowering interest rates for a certain period. In absence of heterogeneity or limited bond-market participation, there would be no redistribution of income among private agents and the interest rates would increase exactly at the speed of inflation.

Based on this story line, we derive a system of equations for our concern as follows:[6]

$$\mathbf{\Gamma}_t = \mathbf{\Phi}\mathbf{\Delta}_t + \mathbf{R}(v^t, g^t) + \varepsilon_t, \tag{1}$$

$$\mathbf{\Gamma}_t \equiv \begin{bmatrix} r_{t,t+1} \\ r_{t,t+2} \\ \cdots \\ r_{t,t+n-1} \\ r_{t,t+n} \end{bmatrix}, \mathbf{\Delta}_t \equiv \begin{bmatrix} \mu_t \\ \mu_{t-1} \\ \cdots \\ \mu_{t-m+2} \\ \mu_{t-m+1} \end{bmatrix}, \mathbf{\Phi} \equiv \begin{bmatrix} \phi_{1,1} & \phi_{1,2} & \phi_{1,3} & \cdots & \phi_{1,m-1} & \phi_{1,m} \\ \phi_{2,1} & \phi_{2,2} & \cdots & \cdots & \cdots & \phi_{2,m} \\ \phi_{3,1} & \cdots & \cdots & \phi_{i,j} & \cdots & \cdots \\ \cdots & \cdots & \cdots & \cdots & \cdots & \phi_{n-1,m} \\ \phi_{n,1} & \phi_{n,2} & \cdots & \cdots & \phi_{n,m-1} & \phi_{n,m} \end{bmatrix},$$

where $\mathbf{\Gamma}_t$ is an $n \times 1$ vector of yield rates with different maturities, $\mathbf{\Delta}_t$ an $m \times 1$ vector of money growth rates up to date for the last $m - 1$ periods, $\mathbf{R}$ an $n \times 1$ vector, and $\mathbf{\Phi}$ an $n \times m$ matrix. $\mathbf{R}(v^t, g^t)$ is the term evaluating the effects of other variables on the term structure of interest rates, such as a vector of the current and the past GDP growth rates (g^t) and is closely related to the current and the past velocities of money circulation (v^t).[7] The importance of $\mathbf{R}(v^t, g^t)$ is highlighted later in empirical analysis.

The model used for the derivation of equation (1) considers neither production nor money-market interactions. In this sense equation (1) does not represent all the equilibrium conditions. However, such a partial-equilibrium approach is worthy of trying because it can disentangle the direct effect of money growth, whereas a general equilibrium approach (including a vector autoregression [VAR] setup) evaluates both the direct and the indirect effects of money growth jointly. In addition, it is also notable

6. For more details on the derivation of the equations, see the appendix. In the appendix, we derive the system of equations with additional simplifying assumptions, such as zero GDP growth rate ($g_t = 0$ for all t) and the absence of taxation ($\tau_t = 0$ for all t). In contrast, equation (1) covers more general cases.

7. For formal definitions of g^t and v^t, see appendix.

that all yield rates other, than the federal fund rate can be converted to the functions of the federal fund rate and its lags because no-arbitrage conditions are levied in the determination of the yield rates.

Equation (1) shows path dependency in that the present term-structure of interest rates is affected not only by the money growth rate of the current period but also by those of the past $(m - 1)$ periods.[8] Theoretically, path dependency is a common phenomenon and may arise from various sources. First, it can come from the learning process. All the economic decisions in a dynamic context should involve the formation of expectation for the future, which is in turn based on the learning processes from the past experience. This is also an excuse for not including the expectation for the future in the model. Second, path dependency can arise from some sorts of market frictions, which prevent economic agents from responding to shocks in a uniform manner and with simultaneous timing. Such inevitably heterogeneous responses of the agents may lead to persistent and lagging effects of monetary policy. There are many other sources of path dependency, but here we are particularly interested in these two sources.

Another notable point from equation (1) is that the lagged adjustments of interest rates in response to monetary policy vary across different types of bonds in terms of directions as well as magnitudes of changes. This implies that the monetary authority can adjust the shape of the term structure by using the dynamic or path-dependent relation of the term structure with monetary policy.

3.2.2 Zero Lower Boundary and Liquidity Trap

The term-structure of interest rates described in equation (1) provides static information evaluated at a point of time on the dynamics of various interest rates. Considering that equation (1) is obtained from the first order log-linear approximation of equation (A2), the interest rate dynamics may violate the nonnegativity of nominal interest rates and the nonnegativity restrictions should be additionally levied on the yields of all maturities.

A nominal interest rate is the rate of return on holding nominal bonds. Due to the definition and the existence of money, zero is a natural lower boundary for the nominal interest. So far, the probability of hitting zero interest rate has been evaluated extremely low and the consideration of nonnegativity yields has not been strongly enforced. However, the recent low interest rate regime in a few economies, including the United States and Japan, has caused worries that the nominal interest rate might hit zero and the economy might fall into the natural lower bound of the liquidity trap.

In this section, we analyze the propagation mechanism of the monetary policy in case of hitting the zero short-term interest rate by levying the nonnegativity restriction on equation (1). In addition, we distinguish the liq-

8. Money growth rates for the past $m - 1$ periods can be replaced by the higher-order moments of the money growth rate (μ_t) up to $m - 1$th order.

uidity trap from the state of zero nominal interest rate and discuss an escape strategy from each of them using monetary policy.

There may be various ways of assigning the nonnegative condition to equation (1). Among them, the most intuitive one is to introduce shadow processes, which are equivalent with the yield rates when they are positive and diverge (become negative) when the yield rates are zero. In consideration of the nonnegativity condition as above, equation (1) should be modified to

$$(2) \quad \begin{bmatrix} r_{t,t+1} \\ r_{t,t+2} \\ \vdots \\ r_{t,t+n-1} \\ r_{t,t+n} \end{bmatrix} \equiv \left\{ \begin{matrix} \max\left[\sum_{j=1}^{m} \phi_{1,j}\mu_j^E + R_1(v^t, g^t) + \varepsilon_{1t}, 0 \right] \\ \max\left[\sum_{j=1}^{m} \phi_{2,j}\mu_{t-j}^E + R_2(v^t, g^t) + \varepsilon_{2t}, 0 \right] \\ \vdots \\ \max\left[\sum_{j=1}^{m} \phi_{n-1,j}\mu_{t-j}^E + R_{n-1}(v^t, g^t) + \varepsilon_{n-1t}, 0 \right] \\ \max\left[\sum_{j=1}^{m} \phi_{n,j}\mu_{t-j}^E + R_n(v^t, g^t) + \varepsilon_{nt}, 0 \right] \end{matrix} \right\}$$

$$\boldsymbol{R}(v^t, g^t) \equiv \begin{bmatrix} R_1(v^t, g^t) \\ R_2(v^t, g^t) \\ \cdots \\ R_{n-1}(v^t, g^t) \\ R_n(v^t, g^t) \end{bmatrix} \text{ and } \varepsilon_t \equiv \begin{bmatrix} \varepsilon_{1t} \\ \varepsilon_{2t} \\ \cdots \\ \varepsilon_{n-1t} \\ \varepsilon_{nt} \end{bmatrix}.$$

Looking at equation (2), we may wonder what difference it makes from equation (1), except the addition of an operator max $[x, 0]$ to each row. A more critical difference could be found in the movement of a newly defined money growth rate μ_t^E, which is the effective money growth rate and is equal to the predefined money growth rate μ_t in absence of a zero rate bond. The divergence of μ_t^E from μ_t arises when the yield rate of a bond hits, stays at, or escapes from the zero boundary. It is because a bond, once its yield rate hits zero, would be treated as an equal for money. Accordingly, the money growth rate should be modified to account for a sudden change in the categories of money stock. Likewise, when the bond yield escapes from the zero rate, the exact opposite movement in the money growth rate as well as in the money stock would be observed.

So far we haven't clarified how the zero short-term interest rate is different from the liquidity trap. The liquidity trap is a state in which monetary expansion through open market operations or helicopter money drops cannot encourage economic agents to increase bond holdings and lower the interest rate further. In other words, the liquidity trap is a mental phenomenon, in which the substitution between money and bonds is extremely sensitive to the interest rate change. Accordingly, the level of the short-term interest rate, at which the liquidity trap arises, doesn't have to be zero.

On the other hand, the zero short-term interest rate does not necessarily imply the advent of the liquidity trap. There has never been a period in which the whole term-structure collapsed into the zero line, though there were some cases in which a point on the term-structure curve hit zero. Hence, even in the (near) zero short-term interest rate environment, the monetary authority can carry out expansionary monetary policy through open market operation by using other bonds with positive yield.[9]

Comprehension of the differences between the liquidity trap and the zero interest rate gives a clue to finding escape strategies from the liquidity trap. One of them is to use the increment of money stock neither for tax reduction, nor for the purchase of bonds, but for the purchase of goods. This can be regarded as a fiscal policy in that it increases the government expenditure. On the other hand, it still holds a feature of a monetary policy in that there is no additional fiscal burden in the government account. The inflationary effect of the government expenditure expansion funded by printing money would induce private agents to consume more and faster. In other words, the inflationary policy raises the velocity of money, $1/(1 - v_{t,t})$. The faster velocity is exactly opposite to the common belief that monetary expansion through the open market operation may reduce the velocity of money in a liquidity trap.

3.3 Empirical Analysis

This section verifies the validity of the claims deduced in the previous section. Equation (1) implies that the term-structure of interest rates is governed by the past money growth rates. In this section, mainly we use several modifications of equation (1) for empirical analysis.

There is a vast empirical literature on how monetary policy influences economic variables, including interest rates, most of which adopts VAR models with varying shock-identifying conditions. As is reviewed in Christiano, Eichenbaum, and Evans (1999), these models confirm the existence of short-run liquidity effect when the monetary shocks are given to M2, NBR (nonborrowed reserves), and the federal fund rate. However, when the M1 or monetary base is used for a policy variable, the liquidity effect is statistically insignificant.

9. Orphanides appreciates the usefulness of the open market operation policy, which is to "implement additional monetary expansion by shifting the targeted interest rates to that on successively longer-term instruments, when additional monetary policy easing is warranted at near-zero interest rates" (Orphanides 2003, 23–24).

In implementing an estimation strategy for equation (1), we do not use its Vector Error Correction (VEC) version for the following reasons: first, the variables in the right-hand side of equation (1) consist of the money growth rate, the GDP growth rate, and money velocity, and their lagged variables. Due to the inclusion of the lagged variables, the equation cannot represent the cointegration relations among the variables. Second, even if the VEC model was taken, it could not explain more than the traditional Expectation Hypothesis of interest rates.

Instead of giving up a VAR or a VEC setup, we have to verify the endogeneity of regressors. To handle with the endogeneity issue, we check a few exogeneity criteria including the Durbin-Wu-Hausman test and the Granger causality test. In case those tests support the exogeneity of the regressors, we justify the exclusion of omitted equations for money-supply and aggregate-supply functions.[10] Otherwise, we compare simple ordinary least squares (OLS) estimation of equation (1) with simultaneous estimation of equation (1), money supply and aggregate supply in order to check the robustness of the single-equation estimation.

Another notable point here is that empirical results from the estimation of equation (1) should be interpreted cautiously in that they reflect partial or direct effect from money growth. In contrast, results from a VAR or a VEC setup would measure the sum of both direct and indirect effects from money growth.

3.3.1 Data

Our analysis is based on the U.S. data from July 1959 to February 2000. We use the U.S. data because the U.S. government bond market is the most developed, and the maturities as well as the volume of the bonds traded in the market are diverse and huge enough to plot a reliable yield curve.

The variables of our concern are money stock, price, and income variables in addition to five key interest rates.[11] For the key interest rates, we select federal fund rate, 3-month Treasury bill, 6-month Treasury bill, 1-year Treasury bill, and a composite of long-term U.S. government securities.[12] For the macrovariables, we use M1 for an index of money stock, GDP deflator for price index, and real and potential GDP[13] for income measures.

The data frequencies differ from one category to another. For example, all the interest rates and M1 are recorded monthly whereas GDP deflator

10. Engle and Richard (1983) show that inference concerning the parameters from a conditional probability density is equivalent with that from a joint probability density when regressors are weakly exogenous. For a test method for weak exogeneity, refer to Beyer (1998) or Hendry and Ericsson (1991).

11. Interest rates are measured in annum whereas M1, GDP deflator, and GDP measures are on a quarterly basis.

12. The composite of the long-term treasury bonds is specifically defined to be an unweighted average on all outstanding bonds neither due nor callable in less than 10 years.

13. H-P filtered real GDP is used for potential real GDP.

and GDP[14] are recorded quarterly. To reconcile the conflicts of the data frequencies while at the same time exploiting the benefit of using monthly data, we run models separately with monthly and quarterly data.

As a variable for money stock, we use seasonally adjusted M1 for a couple of reasons. First, M1 is a money aggregate closest to high-powered money. Other money-stock indicators, such as M2 and M3, are under less direct control of the monetary authority and are more likely affected by money-demand fluctuations. M1, like other money-stock variables, are still susceptible to money-demand fluctuations. Admittedly, it is hard to distinguish money-demand shock from supply shocks, but we still maintain the use of M1 because M1 fits much better than the high-powered money with the real data.

Second, the time series of M1 is seasonally adjusted, considering that the asset prices tend to have no seasonality due to the prevalence of no-arbitrage condition. Accordingly, in order to couple the interest rates with the money growth rates, it is recommendable to use the seasonally adjusted M1.

3.3.2 Test Strategies and Stationarity of Variables

Before running regressions on equation (1), we test the stationarity of each variable included in the equations by Dickey-Fuller Generalized Least Squares (DF-GLS) method. The result shows that real GDP growth rate, potential GDP growth rate, and M1 growth rate are stationary with the significance of 1–10 percent for varying lags from one to ten. On the other hand, the velocity of money circulation ($v_{t,t}$), the inflation rate (π_t, measured by GDP deflator), and the yield rates ($\mathbf{\Gamma}_t$) turn out to be nonstationary.

The stationarity test results indicate that equation (1) is not testable with the yield rates and the money growth rate only. The remainder $\mathbf{R}(v^t, g^t)$ should be a nonstationary process by construction. Hence a test strategy for equation (1) is either to take the difference for the elimination of nonstationarity or to use $\mathbf{R}(v^t, g^t)$ in the estimation procedure by representing it in a linear function of (v^t, g^t).

Given that the GDP data is not available monthly, only the first strategy is applicable to the monthly data, whereas the quarterly data can implement the second one. Thus, depending on the frequency of the data, we adopt different testable equations. For the monthly data, we use the difference method as below

$$(3)\quad \begin{aligned} \mathbf{\Gamma}_t - \mathbf{\Gamma}_{t-1} &= \mathbf{\Phi\Delta}_t - \mathbf{\Phi\Delta}_{t-1} + \mathbf{R}(v^t, g^t) - \mathbf{R}(v^{t-1}, g^{t-1}) + \varepsilon_t - \varepsilon_{t-1} \\ &= \mathbf{\Phi}(\mathbf{\Delta}_t - \mathbf{\Delta}_{t-1}) + \mathbf{R}(v^t, g^t) - \mathbf{R}(v^{t-1}, g^{t-1}) + \varepsilon_t - \varepsilon_{t-1} \\ &= \mathbf{\Phi}^*\mathbf{\Delta}_t^* + \mathbf{R}(v^t, g^t) - \mathbf{R}(v^{t-1}, g^{t-1}) + \varepsilon_t - \varepsilon_{t-1} \\ &= \mathbf{\Phi}^*\mathbf{\Delta}_t^* + \boldsymbol{\eta}_t, \end{aligned}$$

14. As for the monthly data, an index of industrial production may be used as a proxy for nominal GDP. In that case, since the monthly GDP deflator is unavailable, Consumer Price Index or Producer Price Index can be substituted for the GDP deflator.

where

$$\boldsymbol{\Phi}^* \equiv \begin{bmatrix} \phi_{1,1} & \phi_{1,2}-\phi_{1,1} & \phi_{1,3}-\phi_{1,2} & \dots & \phi_{1,m}-\phi_{1,m-1} & -\phi_{1,m} \\ \phi_{2,1} & \phi_{2,2}-\phi_{2,1} & \dots & \dots & \dots & -\phi_{2,m} \\ \phi_{3,1} & \dots & \dots & \phi_{i,j}-\phi_{i,j-1} & \dots & \dots \\ \dots & \dots & \dots & \dots & \dots & -\phi_{n-1,m} \\ \phi_{n,1} & \phi_{n,2}-\phi_{n,1} & \dots & \dots & \phi_{n,m}-\phi_{n,m-1} & -\phi_{n,m} \end{bmatrix},$$

$$\boldsymbol{\Delta}_t^* \equiv \begin{bmatrix} \mu_t \\ \mu_{t-1} \\ \dots \\ \mu_{t-m+1} \\ \mu_{t-m} \end{bmatrix}$$

$$\boldsymbol{\eta}_t \equiv \mathbf{R}(v^t, g^t) - \mathbf{R}(v^{t-1}, g^{t-1}) + \varepsilon_t - \varepsilon_{t-1}.$$

On the other hand, for the quarterly data, we use a fully linearized version of equation (1) as below:

$$\boldsymbol{\Gamma}_t = \boldsymbol{\Phi\Delta}_t + \boldsymbol{\Psi}_v v^t + \boldsymbol{\Psi}_g g^t + \varepsilon_t, \tag{4}$$

where $\boldsymbol{\Psi}_v$ and $\boldsymbol{\Psi}_g$ are vectors of the same dimension with v^t and g^t respectively.

3.3.3 Results

Equations (3) and (4) consist of several equations and they are to be estimated by seemingly unrelated regression (SUR) in principle. However, in practice SUR usually underestimates the standard errors of estimates. Hence, we run regressions equation by equation with Newey-West estimates of standard deviations instead of SUR.

Equations (3) and (4) are tested with the monthly and the quarterly U.S. data, respectively. Especially with the quarterly data, we include real GDP growth rate, the velocity of money circulation (v^t) for the estimation of equation (4). In addition, inflation rate is used as one of the instrumental variables for v_t.

Figure 3.1 displays the historical patterns of the yield rates of our concern. Overall the five key interest rates commove, but with apparent idiosyncratic fluctuations. Our chapter distinguishes itself from other literature in that it represents such term-structure dynamics by a common factor of

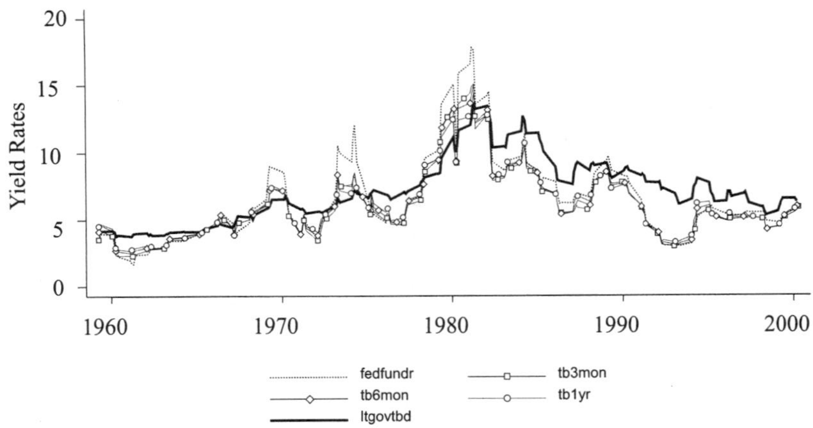

Fig. 3.1 The movements of yield rates in the United States during 1960–2000 (quarterly)

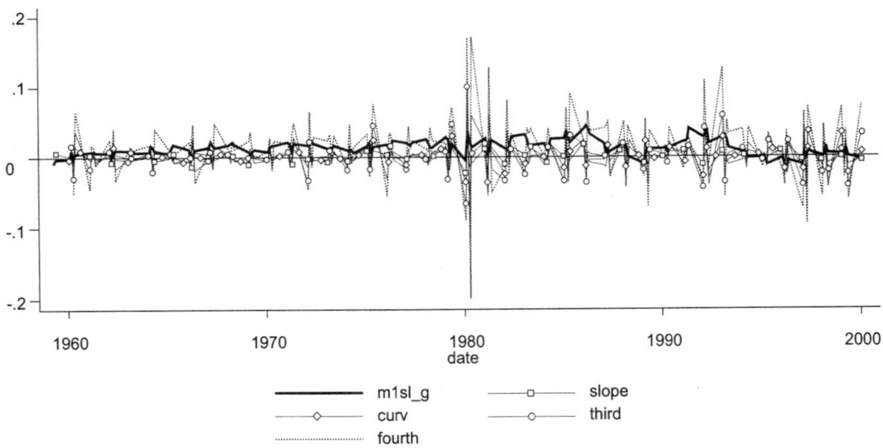

Fig. 3.2 The movements in the higher-order moments of M1 growth rate (quarterly)

the current and the past money growth rates, whose historical pattern is in turn graphically decomposed into different-ordered moments of money growth rates in figure 3.2.

Tests with Monthly Data

We test equation (3) with a little modification of $\mathbf{\Phi}^*\mathbf{\Delta}_t^*$. Since the lagged money growth rates in $\mathbf{\Delta}_t^*$ are hard to interpret intuitively, they are replaced by a vector $\boldsymbol{\theta}_t$, which contains the information on the current money growth rate and its higher-order differences.[15,16]

$$(5) \qquad \boldsymbol{\theta}_t \equiv \begin{bmatrix} \mu_t \\ \mu_t - \mu_{t-1} \\ \mu_t - 2\mu_{t-1} + \mu_{t-2} \\ \mu_t - 3\mu_{t-1} + 3\mu_{t-2} - \mu_{t-3} \\ \mu_t - 4\mu_{t-1} + 6\mu_{t-2} - 4\mu_{t-3} + \mu_{t-4} \\ \cdots \end{bmatrix}$$

The adoption of $\boldsymbol{\theta}_t$ changes equation (3) to

$$\boldsymbol{\Gamma}_t - \boldsymbol{\Gamma}_{t-1} = \boldsymbol{\Phi}^{**}\boldsymbol{\theta}_t + \boldsymbol{\eta}_t,$$

where $\boldsymbol{\Phi}^{**}$ is modified from $\boldsymbol{\Phi}^{*}$ so that it can match with $\boldsymbol{\theta}_t$.[17] We estimate equation (5) by running regressions equation by equation. The variances of the coefficient estimates are estimated by the Newey-West method.

Monetary aggregates like M1 reflect shocks not only to the behavior of the central bank, but also to money demand and the behavior of the banking sector as a whole (Christiano, Eichenbaum, and Evans 1999). Accordingly, in order to avoid the endogeneity of $\boldsymbol{\theta}_t$, we run the Wu-Hausman F-test and the Durbin-Wu-Hausman Chi-sq test by using the growth rate of monetary base as well as its higher-ordered differences for instrumental variables, but cannot reject a null hypothesis that $\boldsymbol{\theta}_t$ is exogenous in equation (5).[18]

Results from equation (5) are displayed in table 3.1. Money growth rate (μ_t) is excluded from the list of explanatory variables due to very low significance. Instead, the next three higher-order moments, slope, curvature, and the third-order moment of money growth rate, are used in the estimation of equation (5). Our findings include a couple of notable patterns. First, the signs of coefficients change alternatively from negative to positive and positive to negative. Second, the longer the maturity is, the less likely

15. The first-order moment of the money growth rate is to be called "slope" and the second one is "curvature." Higher-order moments other than the second one are to be denoted as their matching ordinal numbers.

16. The information contents in θ_t are equalized to those of Δ_t by including higher-order moments of money growth up to *m*.

17. On a quarterly basis, figure 3.2 shows how different order moments of money growth rate move in a heterogeneous way, which is also observable on a monthly basis. Another notable point is that the volatilities of the *n*-th order moments tend to increase with *n* as is shown in (table 3.5).

18. In principle, these exogeneity tests are consistent with another exogeneity test, which is based on cointegrated relations (Engle, Hendry, and Richard 1983; Hendry and Ericsson 1991; Beyer 1998).

it is to be influenced by the changes in the higher-order differences of money growth.

Reminded that table 3.1 summarizes the linear relations between the first-order differences of yield rates and the higher-order differences of money growth rate, we need to convert the results of equation (5) and evaluate directly the impact of money growth rate on the yield rates. Table 3.2 shows the liquidity effect is prevalent in the beginning and the Fisher effect shows up at later periods for all of the five key interest rates. Especially, the presence of the liquidity effect at period zero (in the first month) is meaningful in that this is the first case of confirming the liquidity effect using M1 (Christiano, Eichenbaum, and Evans 1999). On the other hand, the positive effects of money growth rate increase on the yield rates at period one

Table 3.1 Regression results of equation (5) (monthly)

	d_fedfundr	d_tb3mon	d_tb6mon	D_tb1yr	d_longbd
Slope	–127.9254***	–94.39297***	–85.78889***	–73.42162***	–30.08043***
(μ_t)	(27.96452)	(20.4626)	(18.60477)	(15.1847)	(8.06099)
Curvature	110.9467***	63.6107***	53.95926***	44.23584***	12.22965
($D.\mu_t$)	(24.56312)	(19.44036)	(17.83941)	(15.38967)	(9.06536)
Third	–29.04991***	–9.744747	–7.625036	–5.851174	–0.8182089
($D2.\mu_t$)	(7.56772)	(6.55566)	(6.007119)	(5.438865)	(3.474307)
R-square	0.1701	0.1994	0.1947	0.1795	0.1091

Note: All the numbers in parentheses are estimated standard deviation of corresponding coefficients.
***Significant at the 1 percent level.

Table 3.2 Cross-sectional variations in yield rates in response to 1 percent increase in money growth rate (monthly)

	fedfundr	tb3mon	tb6mon	tb1yr	ltgovbd
Estimates					
0	–46.03221	–40.52965	–39.45682	–35.0387	–18.67197
1	39.21423	36.9357	40.20249	37.54232	26.74801
2	–15.41497	–2.557601	–9.116989	–10.85891	–16.97112
3	44.46591	12.30309	16.74264	16.71058	17.79017
Lower (95%)					
0	–67.92918	–56.96087	–54.48401	–47.66546	–25.90708
1	10.73138	11.99402	18.2286	17.48822	13.71678
2	–52.29439	–35.40421	–35.8992	–34.92724	–32.03533
3	1.04308	–25.93205	–14.62933	–11.42724	–0.1755653
Upper (95%)					
0	–24.13525	–24.09842	–24.42963	–22.41193	–11.43686
1	67.69709	61.87738	62.17639	57.59642	39.77923
2	21.46445	30.28901	17.66523	13.20942	–1.90691
3	87.88873	50.53823	48.1146	44.84839	35.75591

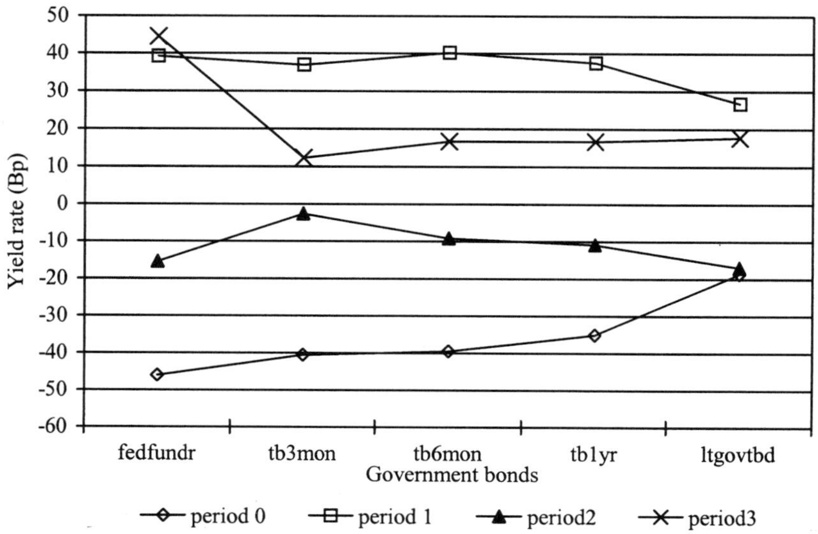

Fig. 3.3 Cross-sectional variations in the term-structure of interest rates in response to 1 percent increase in the money growth rate (monthly)

(in the second month) tend to almost absorb the previous negative liquidity effects and setting the yield rates back to the starting points, which indicates the emergence of the Fisher effect.

Additionally, figure 3.3, a graphical exposition of table 3.2, discovers a couple of interesting points. First, the longer the maturity is, the less responsive the yield rate is to the changes in money growth rate. Second, the liquidity effect prevails significantly across all the types of bonds at period zero and soon disappears, while the Fisher effect shows up at period one and stays afterwards. Third, the bonds with different maturities move generally in the same direction but with different magnitudes.

Test with Quarterly Data

As in the case of the monthly data, we modify equation (4) to

$$\Gamma_t = \overline{\Phi}\theta_t + \Psi_v v^t + \Psi_g g^t + \varepsilon_t, \tag{6}$$

where $\overline{\Phi}$ is modified from Φ so that it can match with θ_t. All the components in v^t except the current velocity of money ($v_{t-j,t-j}, j = 0, 1, 2, \ldots$) are omitted due to unobservability. From the money equation of $(m_t)(1/[1 - v_{t,t}]) = p_t y_t$, we identify $v_{t,t}$ as a function of money stock, price level, and real GDP.

In order to avoid the endogeneity of θ_t, we run the Wu-Hausman F-test and the Durbin-Wu-Hausman Chi-sq test by using the higher-ordered differences of monetary base as instrumental variables and reject a null hypothesis that θ_t is (weakly) exogenous in equation (6). In addition, the Granger causality tests on (v^t, g^t) cannot support their (strong) exogeneity in equation (6). Hence, in estimating equation (6) we jointly estimate a money-supply function (measured in growth rate), an aggregate-supply function (also measured in growth rate), and a Taylor-rule type short-term interest rate rule, which in turn are functions of various yields, GDP gaps, and inflation rates. However, by comparing the results from the joint estimation with those from the single estimation of equation (6), we could not detect any qualitative differences between the two. Furthermore, the money-supply and the aggregate-supply function are not directly derived from our model and are just imposed to eliminate the endogeneity bias. Thus, we report the results from estimating equation (6) only.

Results from running equation (6) are displayed in table 3.3. As in the case of the monthly data, we run regressions equation by equation with Newey-West estimates of standard errors. However, equation (6) differs from equation (5) in that money velocity ($v_{t,t}$) is included[19] and the yield rates, not their first-order differences, are used as dependent variables. Compared with equation (5), equation (6) has greater explanatory power.

In table 3.3, most of the first- and the second-order differences of money growth rate (μ_t) are significant at a 5 percent significance level. The negative signs of the first- and the third-order differences in money growth rate explain the presence of the short-term liquidity effect.

Converting the higher-order moments of money growth into the lagged money growth rates as in table 3.4, we find that the signs of the estimated effects of money growth along the passage of time exactly coincide with our theoretical predictions and support the short-term liquidity effect and the long-term Fisher effect. However, the signs are not supported at 95 percent confidence intervals.

Such insignificance of the liquidity effect in table 3.4 can be better understood when it is compared with the results from the monthly data set (table 3.2), which confirms the significant negative effect at period zero as well as the significant positive effect at period one. Summing up the cross-sectional variations in yield rates for the first three months in table 3.2, it is easy to understand why the signs of the first quarter variations are not statistically significant. This interpretation also indicates indirectly that the length of lag (m) is about a month or so.

Figure 3.4 graphically exposes the cross-sectional variations in the term-structure of interest rates along the passage of time in response to a 1 percent increase in money growth rates.[20] It shows that the yield rates of the bonds with different maturities move in the same direction but with vary-

19. In order to avoid endogeneity, the money velocity is instrumented by the inflation rate as well as the other explanatory variables in equation (6), including its own higher-order differences.

20. A graph of cross-sectional variation differs from an impulse-response function of a VAR setup in that it does not consider the interactions of all the endogenous variables following a shock. However, for simplicity, the cross-sectional variations are interchangeably used with the impulse responses in the chapter.

Table 3.3 Regression results of equation (6) (quarterly)

		Dependent				
Independent	Difference	fedfundr	tb3mon	tb6mon	tb1yr	ltgovbd
μ_t	D0	298.13***	237.24***	238.58***	223.96***	136.63***
		(39.09)	(32.18)	(29.90)	(26.73)	(22.94)
	D1	–762.7388	–630.98***	–653.48***	–632.83***	–446.12***
		(182.60)	(153.39)	(148.83)	(137.28)	(120.12)
	D2	707.91**	610.81**	659.82**	666.85**	558.08**
		(304.41)	(259.07)	(256.40)	(241.84)	(214.52)
	D3	–343.76	–310.45	–346.95	–360.63**	–321.70**
		(222.42)	(191.95)	(190.36)	(181.26)	(9161.96)
	D4	70.71	65.82	74.78	78.55	70.84
		(61.65)	(53.54)	(53.05)	(50.70)	(45.27)
g_t	D0	–332.07***	–248.27***	–243.46***	–221.34***	–123.54***
		(56.57)	(46.14)	(43.93)	(40.41)	(36.00)
	D1	336.26	297.87**	304.13**	294.84**	259.71**
		(189.76)	(147.81)	(140.08)	(126.57)	(103.39)
	D2	–193.66	–191.88	–199.54	–201.73	–212.86
		(214.71)	(169.66)	(157.39)	(141.42)	(116.67)
	D3	38.66	42.97	41.81	42.61	65.93
		(109.73)	(87.95)	(81.30)	(73.28)	(62.87)
	D4	4.34	4.46	6.28	6.35	–3.06
		(24.70)	(20.65)	(19.73)	(18.37)	(16.61)
$v_{t,t}$	D0	54.40***	44.50***	44.09***	42.55***	41.16***
		(7.77)	(6.43)	(6.15)	(5.64)	(4.81)
	D1	2031.07***	1612.88***	1609.21***	1489.50***	535.41***
		(283.53)	(233.48)	(216.50)	(193.11)	(154.17)
	D2	–2486.19***	–2195.61***	–2268.09***	–2179.18***	–1182.56**
		(908.18)	(747.98)	(730.03)	(675.73)	(550.75)
	D3	1600.43	1522.96	1628.05**	1605.00**	977.80
		(913.03)	(768.84)	(757.91)	(713.18)	(605.03)
	D4	–400.25	–408.53	–445.34	–442.67	–278.71
		(337.63)	(286.99)	(283.99)	(269.58)	(229.38)
Constant		–41.35***	–33.29***	–32.85***	–31.42***	–28.06***
		(6.72)	(5.58)	(5.32)	(4.87)	(4.15)
R-square		0.6136	0.5978	0.6041	0.6086	0.6516

Note: All the numbers in parentheses are estimated standard deviation of corresponding coefficients.
***Significant at the 1 percent level.
**Significant at the 5 percent level.

ing magnitudes. As seen in the monthly data, the longer the maturity is, the less responsive the yield change is.

3.4 Policy Implications

From the previous sections, it is demonstrated theoretically and empirically that the impulse-response functions of the yield rates with respect to

Table 3.4 **Cross-sectional variations in yield rates in response to 1 percent increase in money growth rate (quarterly)**

Estimates	fedfundr	tb3mon	tb6mon	tb1yr	ltgovbd
Mean					
0	–29.7439	–27.5555	–27.259	–24.1077	–2.27344
1	95.35971	77.42151	75.59565	66.85081	11.72344
2	100.8781	74.39764	67.62069	56.22627	17.99554
3	60.93011	47.15575	47.84272	46.44869	38.35082
4	70.70663	65.82379	74.77775	78.54582	70.83833
Lower (95%)					
0	–72.449	–64.1373	–61.4791	–55.3686	–31.8303
1	–21.7694	–17.9108	–17.6397	–20.025	–57.6306
2	–35.0299	–40.515	–44.4904	–48.9846	–71.6344
3	–69.2319	–64.8058	–60.3734	–54.9368	–53.129
4	–51.1602	–40.0069	–30.1012	–21.6747	–18.6497
Upper (95%)					
0	12.96119	9.026414	6.96116	7.153189	27.28343
1	212.4888	172.7538	168.831	153.7266	81.07749
2	236.7862	189.3103	179.7318	161.4371	107.6254
3	191.0921	159.1173	156.0588	147.8342	129.8306
4	192.5734	171.6545	179.6567	178.7664	160.3264

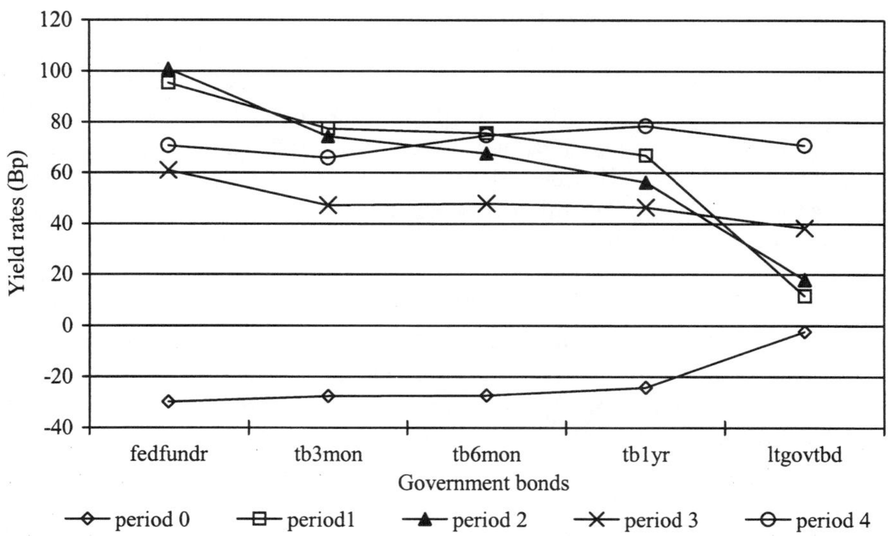

Fig. 3.4 Cross-sectional variations in the term-structure of interest rates in response to 1 percent increase in the money growth rate (quarterly)

money shocks determine the shape of the term-structure of interest rates. Using this property, the monetary authority can implement a certain shape of the term-structure of interest rates when there is no exogenous shock other than changes in money growth rate. Then, the monetary authority has to be concerned about the representability of a certain term-structure of interest rates as well as the time lags to take for the implementation.[21]

3.4.1 Implementability and Time Lags

In a type of equation (4), the dimension of the $n \times m$ matrix $\mathbf{\Phi}$ determines the representability of the term structure.[22] If dim $\mathbf{\Phi}$ is no less than the number of bond types available in the market (n), then a certain money growth rate path can lead to an arbitrary term-structure of interest rates within m periods. Otherwise, complete representability is not achievable.[23]

An easier criterion for the representability and the time lags of the implementation process is to check an impulse-response matrix, which is defined to be a stack of impulse-response-function values with respect to maturities and time horizon. Define the impulse-response matrix $\mathbf{\Xi}$ to be an $n \times T$ matrix, where T is an arbitrarily set time horizon (before all the impulse responses completely phase out) and n is the types of bond maturities available in the market. If $n > T$, then the representability of the system is limited to dim $(\mathbf{\Xi}) < n$. If $n \leq T$ and dim $(\mathbf{\Xi}) > n$, then the composite effect of the money growth rates during the last n quarters can represent any arbitrary term-structure of interest rates. Thus, we see that at least the horizons of impulse-response functions should be longer than the kinds of assets available in the market in order to guarantee the representability. The time lags of implementation is not easy to answer due to the presence of multiple solutions. However, the higher dimension of $\mathbf{\Xi}$ is more likely to raise the likelihood of attaining at a certain term-structure of interest rates within a shorter time horizon.

3.4.2 Determination of the Short-Term Interest Rate

In reality, it is more often the case that monetary authorities use the short-term interest rate rather than the money stock M1 for a control variable of monetary policy. Especially in the United States, the Federal Reserve is known to set the short-term interest rate based on the deviations of

21. Table 3.5 shows that the higher-ordered moments of money growth rate have been more volatile to the United States compared with the lower ones.

22. Representing a certain term-structure of interest rates doesn't necessarily guarantee the system would stay at the level continuously. Stability is another issue to tackle, but will be not be dealt with further in the chapter.

23. In that case, the Gaussian least square method would provide a minimum Δ_t^* from solving $\min_{\Delta_t} \varepsilon_t \varepsilon_t = (\overline{\mathbf{\Gamma}}_t - \mathbf{\Phi\Delta}_t - \mathbf{\Psi}_v v^t - \mathbf{\Psi}_g g^t)(\overline{\mathbf{\Gamma}}_t - \mathbf{\Phi\Delta}_t - \mathbf{\Psi}_v v^t - \mathbf{\Psi}_g g^t)$, where $\bar{r}_t$ is a targeted level of the yield curve.

Table 3.5 **Covariances of different-ordered moments of money growth**

	μ_t	slope	curvature	third	fourth
		Monthly, 487 observations			
μ_t	0.000025				
slope	0.000011	0.000022			
curvature	6.3e–06	0.000028	0.000057		
third	1.3e–06	0.00003	0.000087	0.000173	
fourth	–6.2e–06	0.000031	0.000089	0.00018	–0.000212
		Quarterly, 159 observations			
μ_t	0.00012				
slope	0.000039	0.000076			
curvature	0.000025	0.000101	0.000202		
third	0.000018	0.000119	0.000332	0.000645	
fourth	0.000068	0.000123	0.000461	0.001081	0.002076

inflation and GDP from certain levels.[24] Though this is the case, the relationship between money and interest rates does not change when the Federal Reserve uses the interest rate rule rather than money-aggregate targeting (Monnet and Weber 2001):

$$r_{t,t+1} = \bar{r} + \phi_{\pi}(\pi_t - \bar{\pi}) + \phi_x(y_t - y_t^p)$$

The effect of such a monetary policy of the short-term interest rate determination on the yield curve can be analyzed as a brief extension of our model.

Suppose that the short-term interest rate is prescribed by the Federal Reserve at period t as in the above Taylor-type rule. Then, by combining it with the first row of equation (6), we obtain an autoregressive equation of money growth rate μ_t as follows:

$$(7)\quad \mu_t = \frac{1}{\phi_{1,1}}\left[\sum_{i=1}^{m}\phi_{1,i+1}\mu_{1-i} + \Psi_{1v}v^t + \Psi_{1g}g^t - \phi_{\pi}(\pi_t - \bar{\pi}) - \phi_x(y_t - y_t^p) - \bar{r} + \varepsilon\right]$$

The impulse-response functions of the yield rates in regard to such federal fund rate policy can be obtained by plugging equation (7) back to equation (6) and representing it with the federal fund rate and its lags.

Table 3.6 provides the results from equation (7), showing that the Taylor-type short-term interest rate rule causes μ_t to move in an autoregressive way. Both the first and the second lags of μ_t are positive (the positivity of the second lag is valid at the 1 percent significance level) while the log GDP gap and the inflation rate hold negative signs in support of the Taylor rule.

24. Taylor (1993) estimates $r_{t,t+1} = 0.04 + 1.5(\pi_t - 0.02) + 0.5(y_t - y_t^p)$ using the U.S. data of the 1980s.

Table 3.6 **Autoregressive movements of money growth rate induced by a Taylor type short-term interest rate policy function**

Lag	LL	LR	df	p	FPE	AIC	HQIC	SBIC
				A. Lag length selection order criteria (quarterly, 159 observations)				
0	539.221				0.0000718	–6.70345	–6.60067	–6.45038
1	541.121	3.801	1	0.051	0.0000710	–6.71492	–6.60423	–6.44239
2	544.495	6.747	1	0.009	0.0000689	–6.74516	–6.62657**	–6.45316**
3	544.842	0.694	1	0.405	0.0000695	–6.73684	–6.61034	–6.42537
4	545.035	0.387	1	0.534	0.0000702	–6.72656	–6.59216	–6.39563
5	547.654	5.237**	1	0.022	.0000688**	–6.74718	–6.60487	–6.39678
6	548.655	2.002	1	0.157	0.0000688	–6.74719**	–6.59698	–6.37733

Independent	Lag	Dependent μ_t
B. Estimation results (no. of observations = 158)		
μ_t	L1	0.45 (0.24)
	L2	0.47*** (0.18)
$y_t - y_t^p$		–0.04 (0.03)
π_t		–0.16 (0.29)
$v_{t,t}$	D0	0.00 (0.02)
	D1	1.13 (1.78)
	D2	–1.96 (1.61)
	D3	0.74 (1.22)
	D4	–0.51 (0.45)
g_t	D0	–0.25 (0.33)
	D1	0.11 (0.42)
	D2	0.13 (0.50)
	D3	0.01 (0.31)
	D4	0.00 (0.07)
Constant		0.00 (0.02)
R-square		0.5243

Note: All the numbers in parentheses are estimated standard deviation of corresponding coefficients.
***Significant at the 1 percent level.

The number of lags is chosen from applying the Bayesian Information Criterion (BIC).

So far we have implicitly assumed that M1 is under the tight control of monetary authority. However, in reality, M1 is not directly controlled by the monetary authority because variations in the demand side are hardly predictable and the magnitude of the demand side effect is greater than our anticipation. Despite such a problem, we do not use monetary base instead of M1 because the money equation does not hold for the monetary base. Another solution to this is to represent equation (6) with various moments of the federal fund rate in substitution for the moments of the money growth rate as follows:

$$\Gamma'_t = \overline{\mathbf{\Phi}}'\theta'_t + \mathbf{\Psi}'_v v^t + \mathbf{\Psi}'_g g^t + \varepsilon_t, \tag{8}$$

where $\mathbf{\Gamma}'_t$ is a vector of the yield rates except the federal fund rate (r_t) and

$$\boldsymbol{\theta}'_t \equiv \begin{bmatrix} r_t \\ r_t - r_{t-1} \\ r_t - 2r_{t-1} + r_{t-2} \\ r_t - 3r_{t-1} + 3r_{t-2} - r_{t-3} \\ r_t - 4r_{t-1} + 6r_{t-2} - 4r_{t-3} + r_{t-4} \\ \cdots \end{bmatrix}.$$

The substitution of equation (8) for equation (6) can explain the propagation process of changes in the short-term interest rate policy through the bond market. The estimation results of equation (8) are summarized in tables 3.7–3.8 and figure 3.5,[25] in which the presence of liquidity effect is significantly identified at least for period zero (for the first quarter).

3.4.3 Escape from Zero Short-Term Interest Rate

Suppose that the yield rate of n-period bond, $r_{t,t+n}$, hits (or escapes from) zero at period t. Then the effective money growth rate and money stock would be $\mu_t^E \equiv \mu_t + (B_{t,t+n}/M_t)$ and $M_t^E \equiv M_t + B_{t,t+n}$ (or $\mu_t^E \equiv \mu_t - [B_{t,t+n}/M_t]$ and $M_t^E \equiv M_t$), where $B_{t,t+n}$ is the amount of n-period bond available in the market and μ_t is the ordinary money growth rate. It is noticeable that μ_t^E would jump (drop) in a more volatile way when a yield of a certain bond hits (escapes from) the zero level.

Given that the effect of increased μ_t is negative in the short-run (the liquidity effect) and positive in the long-run (the Fisher effect), then a monetary system itself has an automatic mechanism of returning to a positive interest rate as follows: once a type of bond hits zero, then the total nominal value of the bond issue is added to the effective money stock, which in turn gives downward pressure on the interest rates of bonds with near maturities. Such a tendency of the yield curve approaching the zero line would continue until the short-run negative liquidity effect coming from new entrants to the category of the effective money stock (M_1^E) dominates the long-run Fisher effect arising from the accumulation of M_1^E. So far we have assumed that the monetary authority keeps the money growth rate μ_t constant. Considering that the monetary authority is able to speed up the money growth rate μ_t, then the time required to return to the positive yield curve will be shorter.

25. The money velocity is instrumented as in equation (6).

Table 3.7 **Regression results of equation (8) (quarterly)**

		Dependent			
Independent	Difference	tb3mon	tb6mon	tb1yr	ltgovbd
fedfundr	D0	0.79***	0.86***	0.84***	0.37**
		(0.06)	(0.06)	(0.07)	(0.18)
	D1	–0.22	–0.58***	–0.85***	–0.79
		(0.16)	(0.18)	(0.22)	(0.50)
	D2	0.34	0.79***	1.14***	0.85
		(0.25)	(0.27)	(0.31)	(0.69)
	D3	–0.18	–0.44**	–0.63***	–0.41
		(0.18)	(0.20)	(0.22)	(0.48)
	D4	0.04	0.10	0.14**	0.08
		(0.05)	(0.05)	(0.06)	(0.13)
g_t	D0	25.03**	47.25***	63.88***	50.94
		(11.57)	(11.22)	(14.90)	(42.33)
	D1	–22.29	–79.22***	–123.79***	–94.11
		(28.32)	(26.06)	(32.41)	(92.45)
	D2	17.76	68.72**	106.57***	69.81
		(31.22)	(28.60)	(35.05)	(102.14)
	D3	–9.22	–27.69	–40.72**	–20.38
		(16.72)	(15.71)	(19.26)	(55.76)
	D4	3.12	5.08	5.99	0.02
		(3.92)	(3.73)	(4.58)	(12.73)
$v_{t,t}$	D0	6.97	–2.18	–4.19	48.64**
		(7.67)	(7.72)	(8.99)	(20.84)
	D1	43.14	8.21	–9.02	–153.45
		(38.53)	(35.26)	(44.19)	(131.68)
	D2	–125.45	23.17	147.98	419.76
		(91.03)	(83.08)	(99.99)	(311.95)
	D3	115.80	–24.16	–152.72	–332.50
		(88.79)	(80.45)	(97.63)	(326.31)
	D4	–43.93	–1.27	41.25	93.82
		(30.29)	(27.40)	(34.60)	(118.70)
Constant		–5.26	1.90	3.60	–35.82**
		(5.93)	(5.98)	(6.93)	(15.86)
R-square		0.3771	0.9771	0.9619	0.7011

Note: All the numbers in parentheses are estimated standard deviation of corresponding coefficients.

***Significant at the 1 percent level.

**Significant at the 5 percent level.

3.5 Concluding Remarks

Our chapter explores a transmission mechanism of monetary policy through bond market. Based on the assumption of delayed responses of economic agents to monetary shocks, we derive a system of equations relating the term-structure of interest rates with the past history of money

Table 3.8 **Cross-sectional variations in yield rates in response to 1 percent increase in federal fund rate (quarterly)**

Estimates	tb3mon	tb6mon	tb1yr	ltgovbd
Mean				
0	0.7750026	0.7304612	0.6318231	0.1020515
1	–0.0955232	–0.0884209	–0.0826153	0.0104195
2	0.0634101	0.0781971	0.0777503	0.0807758
3	0.0033343	0.0370159	0.0739016	0.1008343
4	0.0448813	0.1002093	0.1400108	0.0780675
Lower (95%)				
0	0.6850988	0.6360089	0.5231302	–0.0711424
1	–0.2279744	–0.2121276	–0.2454524	–0.3135994
2	–0.0725128	–0.0436097	–0.0861536	–0.2218558
3	–0.1220846	–0.0879021	–0.0916794	–0.2422914
4	–0.0551716	–0.0072723	0.0164971	–0.1867573
Upper (95%)				
0	0.8649064	0.8249136	0.7405161	0.2752455
1	0.0369279	0.0352859	0.0802217	0.3344384
2	0.1993331	0.2000039	0.2416543	0.3834075
3	0.1287531	0.1619338	0.2394827	0.4439601
4	0.1449343	0.207691	0.2635245	0.3428923

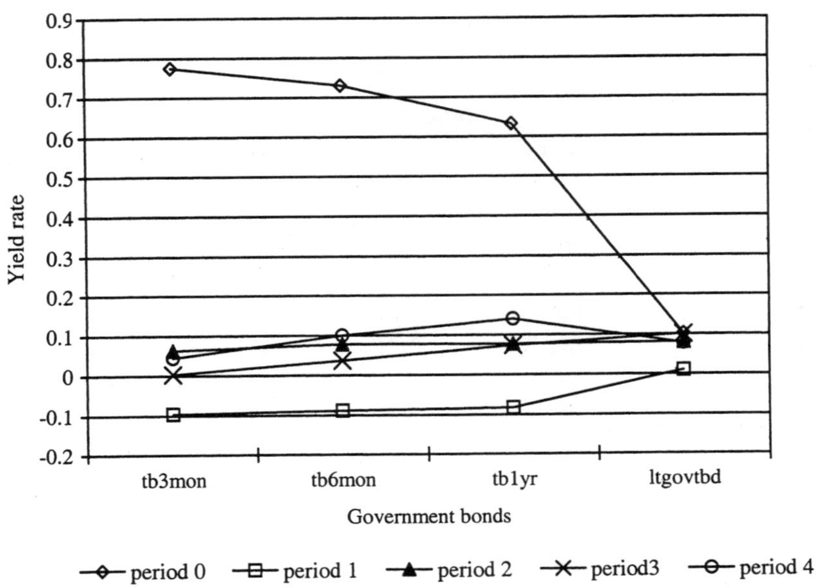

Fig. 3.5 Cross-sectional variations in the term-structure of interest rates in response to 1 percent increase in the federal fund rate (quarterly)

growth. The equations are empirically tested with the U.S. data after some modifications. Impulse-response functions of various yield rates with respect to monetary shocks as well as to the short-term interest rate (such as federal fund rate in the United States) reveal that the reactions of the yield rates may vary across the bonds with different maturities in terms of directions as well as in terms of magnitudes. Such path-dependency of monetary policy induces that monetary policy targeting a certain shape of the term-structure of interest rates could be implemented with certain time lags.

More specifically, our results for both the monthly and the quarterly data sets demonstrate that the interest rates of various maturities are significantly influenced by M1 growth rate and its higher-order differences up to the third order. The directions of influence are the same for all the bonds regardless of their maturities, but the relative magnitudes vary, which implies that the yield curve can be differently shaped depending on the past history of M1 growth rates.

When properly converted, our results confirm the sequential emergence of a liquidity effect and a Fisher effect across all the types of U.S. government bonds with different maturities using the monthly data. While the analysis into the quarterly data set fails in identifying the existence of liquidity effect and/or Fisher effect, these two observations may be reconciled by the inference that liquidity effect persists for about a month or so.

However, our results should be interpreted cautiously because they evaluate the direct effect of money shock on the interest rates and do not consider its indirect effect through other economic variables. In the same context, our chapter assumes that some endogenous variables, such as the velocity of money circulation and the bond-market participation rate, are exogenous. Furthermore, no production function is introduced. Such simplification would reduce the number of testable equations to derive and have them underidentified. Several exogeneity tests and instrumental variable regressions, which have already been adopted, are partial solutions to the symptom. Accordingly, a more complete solution including the further extension of the current model is to be sought in the future works.

Appendix

An m-*Period Extension of Alvarez, Lucas, and Weber (2001)*

Our model is an adapted version of Alvarez, Lucas, and Weber (2001). Consider an economy in which there exists two types of agents—bond-market participant and nonparticipant. Regardless of the type, both groups have the same intertemporal utility function:

$$\sum_{t=0}^{\infty}\left(\frac{1}{1+\rho}\right)^{t}U(C_t), \text{ where } U(C_t)=\frac{C_t^{1-\gamma}}{1-\gamma}.$$

Whereby the λ portion of the population participates in bond trading and the $(1-\lambda)$ portion does not. The aggregate production of this economy is y_t.

$$y_t=\lambda C_t^T+(1-\lambda)C_t^N+\frac{T_t}{P_t},$$

where C_t^T and C_t^N are consumption of the trader and the nontrader each and T_t is the nominal value for lump-sum tax payment. The budget constraint for the nontrader is

$$P_tC_t^N=\sum_{j=0}^{m}v_{t-j,t}P_{t-j}y_t, \text{ where } \sum_{j=0}^{m}v_{t,t+j}=1.$$

At each period the nontrader sells his or her product in the market and receives cash in return (P_ty). He or she allocates these proceeds across $m+1$ periods on consumption with the proportion of $v_{t,t+j}, j=0,1,\ldots,m$. Another more realistic interpretation of this m-period-ahead CIA feature is that $v_{t,t+j}, j=0,1,\ldots,m$ is the proportion of consumers who need j period time lag in responding to monetary shocks.

On the other hand, the trader spends his or her money not only on consumption but also on bond trading.

$$\begin{aligned}P_tC_t^T&=\sum_{j=1}^{m}v_{t-j,t}P_{t-j}y_t+\frac{1}{\lambda}\left[B_t-\left(\frac{1}{1+r_t}\right)B_{t+1}-T_t\right]\\&=\sum_{j=0}^{m}v_{t-j,t}P_{t-j}y_t+\frac{M_t-M_{t-1}}{\lambda}.\end{aligned}$$

Bond and money supplies satisfy

$$B_t-\left(\frac{1}{1+r_t}\right)B_{t+1}-T_t=M_t-M_{t-1},$$

where the government levies the lump-sum tax T_t on the trader only. The effect of money stock increment would be used either in purchasing bonds or in reducing tax burden. The goods market equilibrium is attained when the next equation holds:

$$P_tC_t=(1-\lambda)P_tC_t^N+\lambda P_tC_t^T=P_ty_t.$$

Combining the above equations, we obtain

$$\begin{aligned}P_ty_t&=\sum_{j=0}^{m}v_{t-j,t}(P_{t-j}y_{t-j})+M_t-M_{t-1}\\&=M_{t-1}+v_{t,t}P_ty_t+M_t-M_{t-1}\\&=V_{t,t}P_ty_t+M_t.\end{aligned}$$

Accordingly, the equation of exchange is written as

$$M_t \frac{1}{1 - v_{t,t}} = P_t y_t.$$

Thus, $v_{t,t}$ can be understood as the money velocity.

From the above equations, we represent the consumption of the trader in the function of money growth rates. Here it is noteworthy that we are interested in the consumption of the trader because in the bond market only the marginal utility of the trader matters for the determination of a yield curve.

$$C_t^T = \frac{1}{\lambda} y_t - \frac{(1-\lambda)}{\lambda} C_t^N = \frac{1}{\lambda} y_t - \frac{(1-\lambda)}{\lambda P_t} \sum_{j=0}^{m} v_{t-j,t} P_{t-j} y_{t-j},$$

where $\mu^t = (\mu_t, \ldots, \mu_{t-m})$, and $v^t = (v_{t,t} \ldots, v_{t-m,t})$. Then, the equilibrium nominal interest rate must satisfy the following marginal condition:

$$\left[\frac{\dfrac{1}{1+r_{t,t+k}}}{\dfrac{1}{1+\rho}}\right]^k = E_t\left[\frac{U'\left(C_{t+k}^T \cdot \dfrac{(1-v_{t,t})}{(1-v_{t+k,t+k})}\right.}{U'(C_t^T)\prod_{i=0}^{k}(1+\mu_{t+i})}\right].$$

Notably, the consumption plugged in the above equation is the consumption of the trader's, neither that of the nontrader's nor the aggregate consumption. This is a way of inducing the distributional effect between the trader and the nontrader groups, which in turn leads to the short-term liquidity effect.

For simplicity, we assume $y_t = y$ and $\tau_t = 0$ for all t. Then,

$$\begin{aligned} C_t^T &= \frac{1}{\lambda} y\left\{1 - (1-\lambda)\sum_{j=0}^{m} v_{t-j,t}\frac{P_{t-j}}{P_t}\right\} \\ &= \frac{1}{\lambda} y\left\{1 - (1-\lambda)\sum_{j=1}^{m-1} v_{t-j+1,t}\frac{1}{\prod_{i=1}^{j}(1+\mu_{t-i+1})}\cdot\frac{(1-v_{t,t})}{(1-v_{t-j,t-j})}\right\} \\ &\equiv c(\mu_t, \ldots, \mu_{t-m}, v_{t,t}, \ldots, v_{t-m,t})y \equiv c(\mu^t, v^t)y, \end{aligned}$$

$$\begin{aligned} \left[\frac{\dfrac{1}{1+r_{t,t+k}}}{\dfrac{1}{1+\rho}}\right]^k &= E_t\left\{\frac{U'[c(\mu^{t+k}, v^{t+k})y]}{U'[c(\mu^t, v^t)\,y]}\cdot\frac{1}{\prod_{i=0}^{k}(1+\mu_{t+i})}\cdot\frac{(1-v_{t,t})}{(1-v_{t+k,\,t+k})}\right\} \\ &= E_t\left\{\left[\frac{c(\mu^{t+k}, v^{t+k})y}{c(\mu^t, v^t)y}\right]^{-y}\cdot\frac{1}{\prod_{i=0}^{k}(1+\mu_{t+i})}\cdot\frac{(1-v_{t,t})}{(1-v_{t+k,t+k})}\right\}. \end{aligned}$$

We assume that the velocity of money ($v_{t,t}$) is constant or exogenously given and the money increase is directed towards the purchase of bonds in the financial market. On the other hand, the last line of equation (A1) enables us to briefly analyze the effect of a change in $v_{t,t}$ on the term-structure of interest rates.

Consider the liquidity trap as an extreme case, in which any interest rates would not be affected by an increase in money stock. This phenomenon can arise in the economy of equation (A1) exactly when the increase of μ_t is cancelled out by the decrease of $v_{t,t}$. Under a situation like this, the only policy option the government can take is to increase expenditure by speeding up the money growth rate. Then, the market interest rates would go higher following the money increase. It is notable that such a way of monetary expansion transmits a stimulus not through the bond market but through the goods market. The shift of the term-structure of interest rates following the monetary expansion is attributed to a new equilibrium in the goods market, which works in an opposite direction to the usual propagation mechanism of open market operation. Anyway, this suggests a way of escaping from the liquidity trap with monetary policy.[26]

Taking the first-order approximation of log $c(\mu^t, v^t)$ around the point $(0, \bar{v})$, we obtain

$$\text{(A2)} \qquad \log c(\mu^t, v^t) \cong \left(\frac{1-\lambda}{\lambda}\right)\left[\sum_{j=0}^{m}\bar{v}\left(\sum_{i=0}^{j}\mu_{t-i}\right) + f(v^t)\right]$$

$$U'[c(\mu^t, v^t)y] = \exp\left\{-y\left(\frac{1-\lambda}{\lambda}\right)\left[\sum_{j=0}^{m}\bar{v}\left(\sum_{i=0}^{j}\mu_{t-i}\right) + f(v^t)\right]\right\}y^{-y}.$$

Substituting equation (A2) into equation (A1) and taking log by both sides, then we obtain

$$\text{(A3)} \qquad \begin{bmatrix} r_{t,t+1} \\ r_{t,t+2} \\ \cdots \\ r_{t,t+n-1} \\ r_{t,t+n} \end{bmatrix} \equiv \begin{bmatrix} \phi_{1,1} & \phi_{1,2} & \phi_{1,3} & \cdots & \phi_{1,m-1} & \phi_{1,m} \\ \phi_{2,1} & \phi_{2,2} & \cdots & \cdots & \cdots & \phi_{2,m} \\ \phi_{3,1} & \cdots & \cdots & \phi_{i,j} & \cdots & \cdots \\ \cdots & \cdots & \cdots & \cdots & \cdots & \phi_{n-1,m} \\ \phi_{n,1} & \phi_{n,2} & \cdots & \cdots & \phi_{n,m-1} & \phi_{n,m} \end{bmatrix} \begin{bmatrix} \mu_t \\ \mu_{t-1} \\ \cdots \\ \mu_{t-m+2} \\ \mu_{t-m+1} \end{bmatrix} + \mathbf{R}(v^t),$$

or simply

$$\mathbf{\Gamma}_t = \mathbf{\Phi}_t\mathbf{\Delta}_t + \mathbf{R}(v^t),$$

where $\mathbf{R}_t$ is an $n \times 1$ vector, and $\mathbf{\Delta}_t$ an $m \times 1$ vector, and $\mathbf{\Phi}_t$ an $n \times m$ matrix. The coefficients of the matrix in equation (A3) are derived from equations (A1) and (A2). For $1 \leq j < m - i + 1$,

26. Though the arguments in this paragraph consider neither Ricardian equivalence nor the crowding-out effect explicitly, the equations from our model can test their validity.

$$\phi_{i,j} = -\gamma\left(\frac{1-\lambda}{\lambda}\right)\bar{v}.$$

For m: $m \geq j \geq m - i + 1 \geq 1$,

$$\phi_{i,j} = \gamma\left(\frac{1-\lambda}{\lambda}\right)\bar{v}\left(\frac{m-j+1}{i}\right) > 0.$$

Neglecting that the expectation for the future monetary policies does not change, then the coefficients of $\mathbf{\Phi}$ indicate that cross-sectionally an increase in μ_t lowers the yield rates of bonds with shorter maturities than $m + 1$ periods, while the yield rates of the bonds with maturities longer than m are raised. Combining these two, we can deduce that there is a slope change in the yield curve between m and $m + 1$. Accordingly, the liquidity effect view is supported for bonds with maturities shorter than m and the Fisher's view is valid for bonds with maturities longer than $m + 1$. In addition, the cross-time effect of μ_t changes signs from negative to positive, which also confirms that in the long run the Fisher effect prevails.

References

Alvarez, F., R. Lucas, and W. Weber. 2001. Interest rates and inflation. *American Economic Review* 91:219–25.

Bernanke, B., J. Boivin, and P. Eliasz. 2004. Measuring the effects of monetary policy: A factor-augmented vector auto-regressive (FAVAR) approach. NBER Working Paper no. 10220. Cambridge, MA: National Bureau of Economic Research, January.

Beyer, A. 1998. Modelling money demand in Germany. *Journal of Applied Econometrics* 13:57–76.

Bils, M., P. Klenow, and O. Kryvsov. 2003. Sticky prices and money policy shocks. *Federal Reserve Bank of Minneapolis Quarterly Review* 27:2–9.

Bordo, M., and J. Haubrich. 2004. The yield curve, recessions and the credibility of the monetary regime: Long run evidence 1875–1997. NBER Working Paper no. 10431. Cambridge, MA: National Bureau of Economic Research, April.

Breitung, J., R. Chrinko, and U. Kalckreuth. 2003. A vector autoregressive investment model (VIM) and monetary policy transmission: Panel evidence from German firms. Deutsche Bundesbank Discussion Paper no. 06/03. Frankfurt am Main, Germany.

Christiano, L., M. Eichenbaum, and C. Evans. 1999. Monetary policy shocks: What have we learned and to what end? *Handbook of Macroeconomics* 1A:65–148.

Clarida, R., J. Gali, and M. Gertler. 1999. The science of monetary policy: A new Keynesian Perspective. *Journal of Economic Literature* 37:1661–707.

———. 2000. Monetary policy rules and macroeconomic stability: Evidence and some theory. *Quarterly Journal of Economic Literature* 115:147–80.

Dixit, A., and J. Stiglitz. 1977. Monopolistic competition and optimum product diversity. *American Economic Review* 67:297–308.

Eichenbaum, M., and J. Fisher. 2004. Fiscal policy in the aftermath of 9/11. NBER Working Paper no. 10430. Cambridge, MA: National Bureau of Economic Research, April.
Ellingsen, T., and U. Söndeström. 2004. Why are long rates sensitive to monetary policy? IGIER Working Paper no. 256. Milano, Italy: Innocenzo Gasparini Institute for Economic Research, Bocconi University.
Engle, R., D. Hendry, and J. Richard. 1983. Exogeneity. *Econometrica* 51:277–304.
Hendry, D., and N. Ericsson. 1991. An econometric analysis of U.K. money demand in monetary trends. *American Economic Review* 81:8–38.
Hendry, S., W. Ho., and K. Moran. 2003. Simple monetary policy rules in an open economy, limited participation model. Bank of Canada Working Paper no. 2003-38. Ontario: Bank of Canada.
Hong, K. 1996. A comment on durable goods consumption. *Journal of Monetary Economics* 32 (2): 381–91.
———. 1997. Fluctuations in consumer durables expenditure and fixed investment in Korea. *International Economic Journal.*
Lucas, R. 2000. Inflation and welfare. *Econometrica* 68:247–74.
Lucas, R., and N. Stokey. 1987. Money and interest in a cash-in-advance economy. *Econometrica* 55:491–513.
Monnet, C., and W. Weber. 2001. Money and interest rates. *Federal Reserve Bank of Minneapolis Quarterly Review* 25:2–11.
Orphanides, A. 2003. Monetary policy in deflation: The liquidity trap in history and practice. FRB Working Paper. Washington, DC: Federal Reserve Board.
Taylor, J. 1993. Discretion versus policy rules in practice. *Carnegie-Rochester Conference Series on Public Policy* 39:195–214.
Thomas, J. 2002. Is lumpy investment relevant for the business cycle? FRB Minneapolis Research Department Staff Report no. 302. Minneapolis, MN: Federal Reserve Bank of Minneapolis.
Woodford, M. 2003. *Inflation and prices: Foundations of a theory of monetary policy.* Princeton, NJ: Princeton University Press.
Yun, T. 1996. Nominal rigidity, money supply endogeneity, and business cycles. *Journal of Monetary Economics* 37:345–70.

Comment R. Anton Braun

Seok-Kyun Hur's analysis challenges many current views about how monetary policy affects the yield curve, in particular, and economic activity more generally. In a world where leading central banks have long since abandoned monetary-aggregate targeting and now follow interest rate targeting rules and where academics typically model monetary policy using Taylor rules, Hur explores the link between monetary aggregates and the yield curve. Against the background of a large and growing academic literature that models money under the assumptions of monopolistic competition and costly price adjustment, Hur derives empirical restrictions from a flexible price model. Finally, rather than following the large empir-

R. Anton Braun is a professor of economics at the University of Tokyo.

ical structural vector-autoregression (SVAR) literature that seeks to isolate the effects of surprises to money supply by looking at narrow aggregates such as the composition of nonborrowed reserves in total reserves, Hur instead infers monetary policy directly from movements in M1. It is refreshing to see someone challenge so many orthodox views and as I read this chapter I had the hope that this novel approach to one of the principal questions in monetary economics would provide some new insights.

The chapter starts by positing an extension to the segmented-markets model of Alvarez, Lucas, and Weber (2001). Alvarez, Lucas, and Weber (2001) consider an economy with traders and nontraders. Nontraders can't visit the bonds market and are thus subject to a cash-in-advance constraint that requires that current consumption expenditures equal a variable fraction of current period receipts plus last period's unspent receipts. Traders, participate in both the goods market and a bonds market with centralized trade where they receive government transfers of money and adjust their holdings of money and bonds. This model delivers a liquidity effect in the short run but the Fisher effect dominates in the long run.

Hur extends Alvarez, Lucas, and Weber (2001) by imposing the restriction that nontraders are required to fund today's consumption using a distributed lag of previous period receipts. Households must store receipts received in each date in one of m separate cookie jars. This is because in any given period m cookie-jar-specific liquidity shocks arrive. At the start of each period the shopper goes to the oldest cookie jar, empties it, and goes shopping. Then the seller starts placing current period receipts in that cookie jar. Part way through the period the shopper returns home and goes to the second-oldest cookie jar and takes some fraction of the remaining receipts from it. The shopper returns once again later and proceeds to the next cookie jar and takes out some random fraction of the receipts from it. Things continue in this fashion until the shopper has removed a random fraction of the receipts from each cookie jar, including the cookie jar with current period receipts. This assumption creates what Hur refers to as path dependence: today's aggregate state depends on the vector of money growth rates over the past m periods. After some algebra a log-linear representation (equation 1) is derived that links the term-structure of interest rates to a distributed lag of previous money growth rates.

The fact that the demand for cookie jars will be very large in this economy raises a serious issue about the entire formulation. Why would nontrading households ever choose to allocate receipts to more than one cookie jar? This distinction matters. If instead nontraders are allowed to keep all of their receipts in a single cookie jar then, regardless of whether they experience a single liquidity shock or even m distinct liquidity shocks in a given period, the path dependence disappears.

Given these problems with the model formulation it is perhaps most useful to treat the empirical work in this chapter as documenting some new data facts. The principal result from the empirical work is that one can uncover liquidity effects at short horizons of one month or one quarter and a dominant Fisher effect at longer horizons by simply regressing first differences of yield rates on higher-order differences of M1. This is a potentially interesting finding. However, it flies in the face of a large body of previous results that find that M1 is highly endogenous. Unfortunately, it is impossible to tell whether the results in the chapter are a statistical artifact due to the peculiar way in which M1 is chosen to enter[1] or a substantive new contribution. Given the previous results in the literature (see, e.g., Christiano, Eichenbaum, and Evans 1999 for a nice survey) I think one must be concerned about whether the results reported in the chapter are confounding money-supply and money-demand shocks. The SVAR literature provides some simple criteria for assessing whether this is the case. According to this literature, an easing in monetary policy in addition to lowering short-term rates on impact also increases output and increases prices. If Hur's empirical work has indeed successfully identified monetary policy in higher-ordered differences of M1 growth rates, then positive shocks to monetary policy should also increase output and prices.

Finally, the chapter touches on issues related to the conduct of monetary policy when interest rates are close to zero. This is a fascinating and still largely unexplored question. The perspective taken in this chapter that growth rate of money is a relevant indicator or perhaps even *the* relevant indicator of monetary policy is compelling when nominal interest rates are zero. Hur argues that the combination of a transient liquidity effect and persistent Fisher effect creates an automatic stabilizer that keeps nominal interest rates positive and that this mechanism is enhanced when money growth rates are increased. Although this is a provocative conjecture, Japan's experience casts considerable doubt on either its veracity or quantitative importance. Japan has experienced a near-zero call rate for about seven years. Over the same period of time M1 has nearly doubled.

I enjoyed reading this chapter and was both impressed and very sympathetic to some of its unorthodox assumptions. Unfortunately, the logic of the model and the haphazard nature of the empirical analysis make it is impossible to tell what, if any, new insights this chapter sheds on our understanding about the effects of monetary policy on the term-structure of interest rates.

References

Alvarez, Fernando, Robert E. Lucas, Jr., and Warren E. Weber. 2001. Interest rates and inflation. *American Economic Review* 91 (2): 219–25. American Economic Association.

Christiano, Lawrence, Martin Eichenbaum, and Charles Evans. 1999. Monetary policy shocks: What have we learned and to what end? *In Handbook of Macroeconomics 1A,* ed. John Taylor.

1. For instance, the level of M1 growth is omitted from the monthly specification.

Comment Yuzo Honda

Summary of the Paper

Making use of the recent model by Alvarez, Lucas, and Weber (2001), as well as the consumption-based capital asset pricing model (consumption-based CAP-M), Dr. Seok-Kyun Hur derives the term-structure of interest rates as a function of past growth rates of money and of velocity variables. Then he applies this theory to U.S. data from the period July 1959 to February 2000 to test the theory's validity. Based on theoretical and empirical considerations, the author suggests using the term-structure of interest rates as a target of monetary policy.

Picking out one short-term interest rate as an operating target is the standard practice among central banks in most advanced countries. It is true that changes in the short-term interest rate are transmitted to the longer-term market interest rates through imperfect substitutions among bonds with various maturities. But the longer-term interest rates are also endogenously affected by changes in other exogenous variables in the real sector of the economy.

Despite of this fact, Hur challenges the standard practice for central banks to target one short term interest rate, and suggests that central banks might want to target the whole term-structure of interest rates, using his proposed model.

The Gap between Theory and Empirical Studies

Hur's chapter is challenging at least in the following two respects. First, he proposes an interesting microeconomic model for empirical studies. Secondly, the idea of targeting the whole term-structure of interest rates is totally new. The proposed economic model is interesting in itself. The idea of examining the responses of the whole term-structure to an exogenous shock is also interesting in the empirical part.

However, there is a gap between his theoretical model and empirical works. It seems to me that Hur needs to work more to fill in the gap. The relevant question that Hur should address is what are exogenous variables and what are endogenous variables in his theoretical model and empirical studies, respectively. In the theoretical part, money growth rates μ_t are exogenous variables. However, in reality, or in the empirical part, money growth rates are endogenous, to a first approximation.

Hur implicitly assumes the situation in figure 3C.1, in which money supply shifts exogenously with the given money demand. Money in this section is understood as M1 as in his chapter. In such a case, an exogenous increase in money supply leads to a lower interest rate, which is called the

Yuzo Honda is a professor in the Graduate School of Economics at Osaka University.

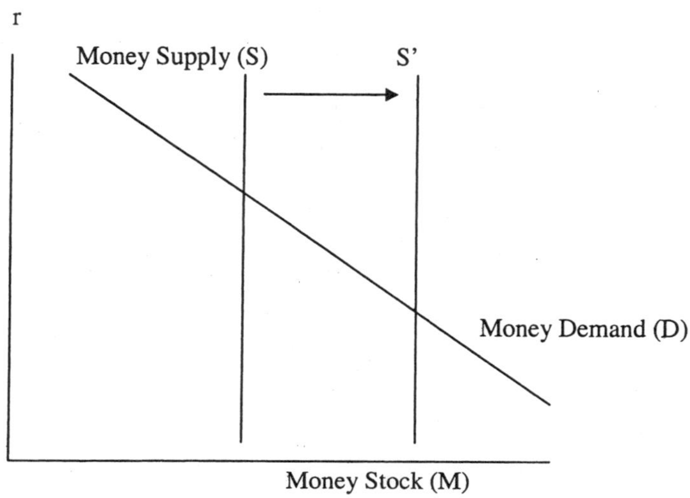

Fig. 3C.1 Money supply shifts with given money demand

"liquidity effect" in the chapter. In this model, money supply is exogenously determined by the central bank, while the short-term interest rate is endogenously determined.

Instead of figure 3C.1, consider the situation in figure 3C.2, in which the central bank changes its target interest rate with a given money-demand curve. In this model, the short-term interest rate *r* is exogenously determined by the central bank, while the amount of money stock *M* is endogenously determined.

Which is closer to the real world, figure 3C.1 or 3C.2? Although the author's theoretical model postulates the situation where money supply is exogenously given, as in figure 3C.1, money supply in reality is endogenous as in figure 3C.2 for most of the sample period. It is well known that the Federal Reserve has been using the federal fund rate as the operating target to steer monetary policy for most of the sample period (Bernanke and Blinder 1992; Bernanke and Mihov 1998).

There are, however, exceptional periods. For the period October 1979 through October 1982, the Federal Reserve used nonborrowed reserves as its primary operating target. In addition, they used monetary aggregates like M1 or M2 as intermediate targets in the 1970s, although they started to de-emphasize monetary aggregates as intermediate targets from October 1982 onwards. During these exceptional periods, there might be reasons to believe that money stock is exogenous. However, except for these relatively short periods, there seems to be little reason to believe that money supply is exogenous.

In order to fend off the above criticism, Hur adopts "Wu-Hausman

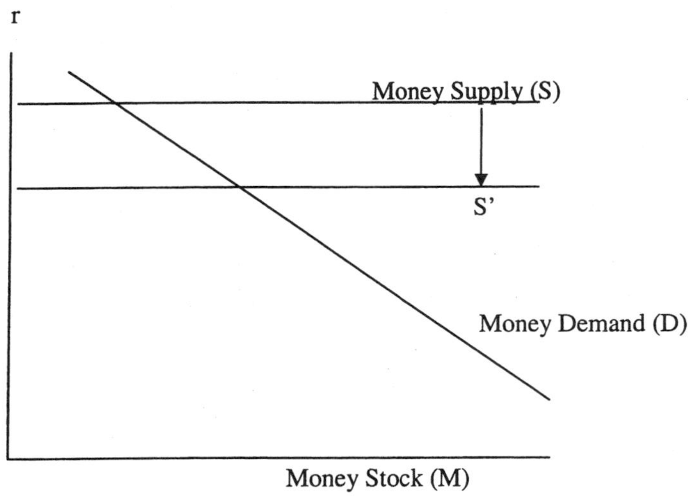

Fig. 3C.2 The central bank changes the target interest rate

F-test and Durbin-Wu-Hausman Chi-sq test" (see, for example, the subsection 3.3.3) and tests the exogeneity of money growth rates μ_t. Do these tests help? My answer is "Not Quite." These tests certainly help us to infer whether or not money growth rates μ_t are exogenous with respect to the term-structure of interest rates (or the left-hand side variables). In this sense these tests are useful. However, even if the above tests indicate that money growth rates are exogenous with respect to the term-structure of interest rates, money growth rates μ_t are still the results of the interaction between monetary-policy shocks and the activity in the real sector of the economy. Money growth rates of M1 are the mixture of policy shocks and the economic activity in the real sector. It is misleading to interpret money growth rates of M1 as monetary-policy shocks.

Alternative Approaches

There might be many approaches to overcome this gap between his theoretical model and empirical studies. One approach would be choosing only those sample periods for which the central bank actually used monetary aggregates like M1 or M2 as an intermediate target. Then exogenous money growth rates may be justified for such sample periods. It might also be worth investigating whether or not the author's theory might be justified in other countries like Germany, where monetary aggregates were used as an intermediate target for the longer period.

An alternative approach would be extending his theory and constructing a new model, into which we introduce a central bank explicitly. In this new model, we also interpret money as high-powered money (HPM) rather

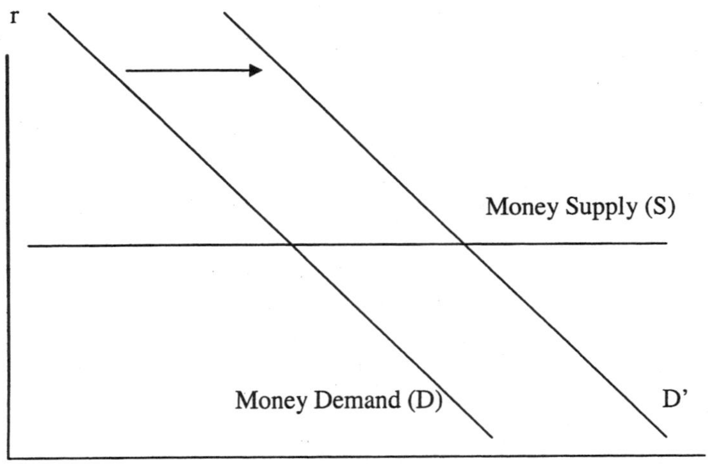

Fig. 3C.3 The central bank accommodates money supply in accordance with a money-demand shift

than M1. The central bank exogenously determines the level of the short-term interest rate as in figure 3C.3. As some exogenous shock shifts money demand out from D to D′ as in figure 3C.3, the central bank accommodates money supply in accordance with a shift in money demand. In this new model, the control variable that the central bank manipulates is the short-term interest rate. When the central bank lowers the short-term rate as in figure 3C.2, then the stock of HPM increases endogenously along the money-demand curve. I believe that a model that incorporates such features is appealing as a first approximation to real financial markets in the United States.

In short, Hur might want to explore for a new theoretical model in which one single short-term rate is exogenously determined by the central bank, while the stock of HPM as well as the whole term-structure of interest rates are jointly and endogenously determined by the interaction between the short-term interest rate and real economic activity.

Term Structure as a Target of Monetary Policy?

Hur makes a bold proposal to use the term-structure of interest rates as a target of monetary policy. I believe his suggestion is perhaps too bold, and I am not convinced by the chapter that it is a good idea to adopt the term-structure as a target of monetary policy.

There are several reasons. First, it is well known that controlling the longer end of the term-structure is more difficult (and costly). The influence of exogenous shocks from the real economy is expected to be larger at the longer end. See, for example, Cook and Hahn (1989), and Kuttner

(2001) for the case of the U.S. financial markets in which the effects of monetary-policy shocks are found to be smaller at the longer end of the term structure.

Secondly, the empirical relationship obtained is based on the history of the conduct of monetary policy by the Federal Reserve. As explained above, the Federal Reserve largely controlled the federal funds rate to steer the economy for most of this period, and the M1 was largely determined endogenously in interaction with the real economy. If the Federal Reserve adopts the growth of M1 as a policy instrument, as the author proposes, the past relationship that the author wishes to exploit might change.

Thirdly, most central banks in advanced countries have found the link between GDP and monetary aggregates less stable and less reliable in the recent years. Mainly due to this reason, most central banks gave up controlling monetary aggregates in the 1980s. Given this past history, I doubt if it is a good alternative strategy to target M1, the term-structure of interest rates, and ultimately GDP.

Finally, controlling M1 will take some time in collecting data on deposits, and we cannot use M1 as an operating target on a daily basis. If there should be any role for M1, it might be used only as an intermediate target.

References

Alvarez, F., R. E. Lucas, Jr., and W. E. Weber. 2001. Interest rates and inflation. *American Economic Review* 91 (2): 219–25.

Bernanke, B. S., and A. S. Blinder. 1992. The federal funds rate and the channels of monetary transmission. *American Economic Review* 82 (4): 901–21.

Bernanke, B. S., and I. Mihov. 1998. Measuring monetary policy. *Quarterly Journal of Economics* 113:869–902.

Cook, T., and Hahn, T. 1989. The effect of changes in the federal funds rate target on market interest rates in the 1970s. *Journal of Monetary Economics* 24:331–51.

Kuttner, K. N. 2001. Monetary policy surprises and interest rates: Evidence from the Fed funds futures market. *Journal of Monetary Economics* 47:523–44.

II

The Japanese Experience

4 Two Decades of Japanese Monetary Policy and the Deflation Problem

Takatoshi Ito and Frederic S. Mishkin

4.1 Introduction

The Japanese economy has been stagnant for more than ten years. The average growth rate from 1993 to 2003 is just above 1 percent. Since 1998, the inflation rate, either measured by gross domestic product (GDP) deflator or Consumer Price Index (CPI), has been negative. The deflation has brought the CPI price level by the end of 2003 to 3 percent below the 1997 level. During the same period, the U.S. CPI has increased by 12 percent. Due to virtually zero growth and deflation, the Japanese nominal GDP had shrunk by 4 percent from 1997 to 2002, while during the same period, nominal GDP of the United States has increased by 25 percent.

Many problems have been pointed to as contributing factors that explain the "lost decade" in Japan. The burst bubble and the nonperforming loans problem are often blamed for the poor performance of the early stage of the stagnation. By 2003, land and stock price indexes have fallen to between one-third and one-fourth of the respective peak in 1989–91. Slow policy responses to the nonperforming loan problem resulted in the banking crisis of 1997–98, and the financial sector is still weak. The consump-

Takatoshi Ito is a professor in the Research Center for Advanced Science and Technology at the University of Tokyo, and a research associate of the National Bureau of Economic Research. Frederic S. Mishkin is the Alfred Lerner Professor of Banking and Financial Institutions at the Graduate School of Business, Columbia University, and a research associate of the National Bureau of Economic Research.

This paper was written for the NBER 15th East Asian Seminar on Economics, June 25–27, 2004. The authors are grateful to Takeshi Kudo and Emilia Simeonova for their excellent research assistance. We also thank our discussants Ken Kuttner, Kazuo Ueda, Kunio Okina, and participants at seminars at the Bank of Japan, and the East Asian Seminar on Economics. Any views expressed in this chapter are the views of the authors only and not the University of Tokyo, Columbia University, or the National Bureau of Economic Research.

tion tax rate increase and repeal of income tax cut in April 1997 is often regarded as a fiscal policy mistake. Slow structural reform in regulated sectors is another problem for the Japanese economy, which has not benefited from the information and communication technology (ICT) advances that propelled the U.S. economy.

But the most likely cause for deflation in Japan is a failure of monetary policy, since inflation or deflation is ultimately a monetary phenomenon. The Bank of Japan (BOJ) was unable to stop the inflation rate from turning negative, despite its various efforts. The uncollateralized call rate (the policy interest rate that corresponds to the Federal Funds rate of the United States) was lowered to virtually zero in February–March 1999. The BOJ raised the call rate to 0.25 percent in August 2000 in false expectation of continuing economic expansion, against protests from the government and many economists. The interest rate was lowered to zero again in March 2001, with an additional measure of quantitative easing, setting the target of current account (reserves) of commercial banks at the BOJ in excess of required reserves. The target amount of current account was initially set at 5 trillion yen, while the required reserves was about 4 trillion yen. The target amount has been raised in several steps to a range of 30–35 trillion yen by January 2004. In addition to raising the target amount of current account at the BOJ, the bank expanded the amount of monthly outright purchase of long-term government bonds from 400 billion yen to 600 billion yen in August 2001, and in several steps to 1,200 billion yen in October 2002. In addition, purchases of some of private debts, including asset-backed securities (ABS), have been introduced.

By 2002, the economy and the financial institutions weakened again. Deflationary expectations were setting in, and consumption and investment were depressed. Aggregate demand fell short of potential output, and the widened output gap depressed prices, reinforcing deflationary expectations. There did not seem to be a solution to the deflationary spiral.

When the zero interest rate policy (ZIRP) was first introduced in February 1999, it was intended to continue until "deflationary concern is dispelled." It was then lifted in August 2000. When it was reintroduced in March 2001, it was declared to continue until "the inflation rate becomes stably above zero." The condition was further elaborated in October 2003, so that the necessary condition for the exit from ZIRP is that the CPI inflation rate becomes zero or above for a few months and there was no forecast by the board members of falling back to deflation. The determination to fight deflation seems to have been strengthened. Given that deflation was not over at the time of ZIRP termination and that the ZIRP had to be reinstated, the interest rate hike of August 2000 was clearly a mistake.

Lively debates have taken place as to what the BOJ could have done to prevent deflation from occurring and getting worse, and on what the BOJ could do to get out of deflation. Many academics and policymakers, including studies at the Federal Reserve Board, argue that the Bank of Japan's actions were too little too late, at least in retrospect, in preventing deflation from emerging and fighting out of deflation. Many academic critics have been arguing for nonconventional monetary policy in combating deflation: for example, purchasing long-term bonds, equities, foreign-currency-denominated bonds, and nonperforming loans. However, it has been pointed out that the transmission channel of nonconventional monetary policy is unclear.

Inflation targeting has also been proposed as a tool to promote an independent central bank and to help get out of deflation. Namely, a credible announcement of inflation targeting, of say 1 to 3 percent, would make inflation expectations become higher, so that the deflationary spiral would be broken. A combination of inflation targeting as a communication and anchoring device with nonconventional policies was advocated by academic work in the past.[1]

However, the BOJ has opposed inflation targeting, with economists in the Bank of Japan arguing that there are no clear instruments to get out of deflation, and a mere announcement without instruments would not convince market participants to change their inflation expectations. But, others in the bank have suggested that the commitment to keep the zero interest rate policy until the inflation rate becomes stably above zero has similar effects to inflation targeting.

The chapter is organized as follows. Sections 4.2 and 4.3 will review Japanese monetary policy over the last two decades. The former concentrates on the period of bubble and burst (1985–1997), and the latter examines the issue under the new law of the BOJ (1998–). Section 4.4 discusses whether estimates of Taylor rules can be used to assess Japanese monetary policy. Section 4.5 discusses the costs of deflation. Section 4.6 examines monetary-policy actions to prevent deflation, and Section 4.7 surveys the literature on monetary policy to cure deflation and discusses nonconventional monetary-policy measures. Section 4.8 concludes the chapter.

4.2 Monetary Policy and the Bubble

4.2.1 Bubble and Burst

Some researchers go back to the bubble period, 1985–90, as a source of the Japanese stagnation in the 1990s. Since the bubble occurred and burst, the Japanese economy fell into a difficult position of having nonperforming loans that led to the banking crisis. Some economists seem to believe that there was a mistake in monetary policy in the 1980s, and once the burst

1. See Ito (2000, 2001), Kazumasa Iwata (2002), and Kikuo Iwata (2001, 2002) in the books written in Japanese.

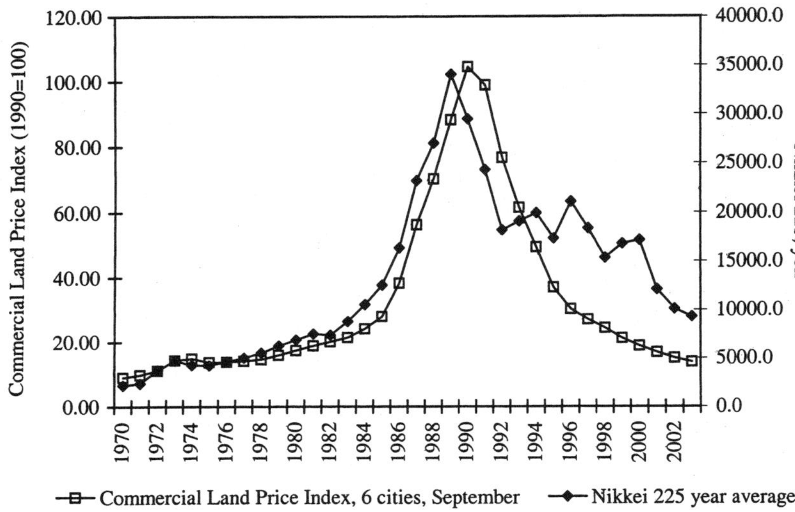

Fig. 4.1 Land prices and stock prices, 1970–2003

bubble occurred, monetary policy became powerless in the 1990s, because the transmission channel from the interest rate policy to the real economy was no longer operational. Therefore, it is entirely appropriate to start the story of deflation from the bubble years.

In retrospect, it is obvious that the Japanese economy was experiencing a bubble economy: the stock price index and the land price index quadrupled from 1983 to 1989. The stock prices index (Nikkei 225) rose from 10,000 yen at the end of 1983 to near 40,000 at the end of 1989. The economic growth rate was approaching 5 percent, surpassing the average of 4 percent from 1975 to 1989, and the tax revenues were increasing to close a fiscal gap that had plagued the economy for two decades. At the end of the 1980s, many economists as well as policymakers around the world were praising the Japanese economy for its excellent performance.[2] Although a few economists raised concerns, many financial analysts and bankers were not alarmed at the apparent high value of stocks and land compared to their cash-flow earning. Land and stock price movements from 1970 to 2003 are shown in figure 4.1.

The inflation rate had gradually come down from 12 percent in 1974 to below 4 percent in 1978. The inflation rate suddenly went up to about 8 percent in 1979 due to the second oil crisis. However, the CPI inflation rate was quickly brought down to below 3 percent in 1982. The inflation rate fluctuated at the low range of 0–3 percent for the rest of the 1980s. The infla-

2. See Ito (1992) for a comprehensive explanation of the Japanese economy up to 1991.

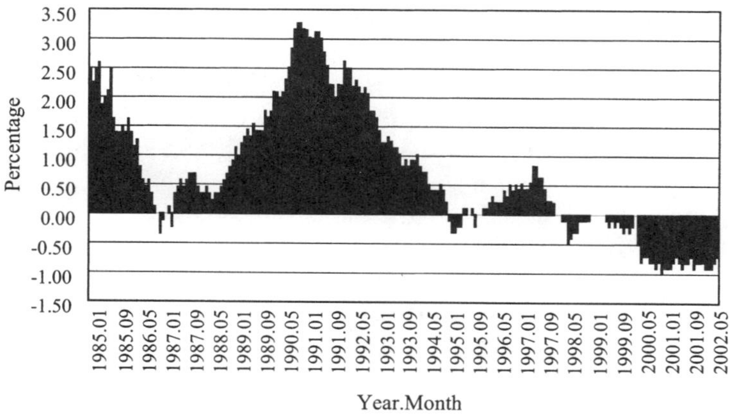

Fig. 4.2 CPI inflation excluding fresh food and consumption tax, 1985–2002

tion performance of Japan from 1976 to 1987, despite a lack of legal independence of the BOJ, was often praised in the literature.[3] Figure 4.2 shows the CPI inflation rate (excluding fresh food), that is adjusted for the consumption tax introduction in 1989, and the consumption tax rate increase in 1997.

It is remarkable that during the bubble period, the CPI inflation rate remained low. While asset prices were doubling and tripling in a few years, the CPI inflation rate remained quite reasonable, prompting a difficult choice to the BOJ. Indeed, the BOJ did not start tightening until 1989. Although the BOJ would not target asset prices, the burst bubble would make monetary policy more difficult—all with the benefit of hindsight. The yen appreciated from 260 yen/dollar in February 1985 to 150 yen/dollar in the summer of 1986, of which some part was a movement toward an equilibrium and some part was overshooting. The sharp yen appreciation caused a recession (due to a slump of exports) and imported disinflation. Interest rates were lowered from 1986 to 1987 in part to help stimulate the economy that was depressed by sharp yen appreciation.[4] Low interest rates were necessary to prevent the yen from appreciating too much.

Monetary policy was finally tightened in 1989. The official discount rate (ODR) rose from 2.5 percent, where it had been since 1987, to 3.25 percent in May 1989. The ODR rose to 3.75 percent in October and 4.25 percent in December. Despite this rapid hike of the interest rate, the CPI inflation rate

3. See, for example, Cargill, Hutchison, and Ito (1997), for the view that the BOJ might have had de facto independence and exercised it wisely.

4. See, for example, Okina, Shirakawa, and Shiratsuka (2001) for such a view. They seem to blame international policy coordination, such as the Plaza Accord of September 1995 and the Louvre Accord of February 1997, for the BOJ not acting in a timely manner.

rose from 1 percent at the beginning of 1989 to 3 percent toward the end of the same year. The official discount rate was raised to 6.00 percent in August 1990 (a 350 basis point hike in fifteen months).

Stock prices peaked at the level of 39,000 in Nikkei 225 index at the end of 1989. In tandem with the interest rate hike, regulatory tightening was applied to stop increases in land prices including: limiting the increase in bank lending to real estate related projects and companies in the spring of 1990, and raising taxes on realized capital gains from land investment. Stock prices finally turned down from the first trading day of 1990. The stock price index declined by one-third from the end of 1989, the peak, to the end of 1990. Stock prices continued to decline and the index lost 60 percent of the peak level by the summer of 1992. Land prices started to decline in 1991. The bubble had burst.

One may question whether monetary policy was too lax for too long during the bubble experience, that is the second half of the 1980s. What if monetary policy was tightened in 1988? Maybe that might have prevented the inflation rate from rising too quickly to the 3 percent level at the end of 1989. The BOJ was most likely behind the curve. However, it probably would not have had a measurable impact on the bubble process of stock prices and land prices. Even if the interest rate had been hiked earlier, it is unlikely that the expected return of purchasing an asset would not have been affected very much when the asset is in a bubble process.[5]

Those who emphasize the damage of burst bubble in the 1990s may argue that the mistake of monetary policy in the second half of the 1980s was that it allowed the bubble to get bigger and bigger. There is no clear-cut answer to the question of how monetary policy should respond to asset-price inflation with a stable CPI inflation rate, as will be seen in the general discussion in section 4.2.3.

However, the dilemma of the monetary policy at the time was that CPI inflation was indicating low inflation, mainly due to a sharp yen appreciation, from 260 yen/dollar in February 1985 to 150 yen/dollar in the summer of 1986, and to 120 yen/dollar in December 1987. When the CPI inflation rate is about 0.5 percent while the stock and land prices are increasing at 30 percent annually, what should monetary policy do? The low inflation rate, which is below typical inflation targets of around 2 percent, might suggest there is room for monetary easing, while stopping the asset-price inflation requires tighter monetary policy. There seems to be a dilemma for monetary policy.

There is a fundamental law in (linear model) economics that there should

5. See Ito and Iwaisako (1996) for an interpretation of the Japanese bubble in the 1980s as an application of stochastic bubbles. They differentiated the simulated effects of a temporary change in the interest rate and the simulated permanent change in the interest rate upon asset prices. They argue that unless the low interest rate in the late 1980s had been perceived to be permanent, the large increase in asset prices could not have been explained.

be at least two policy instruments to pursue two policy objectives. No perfect solution for the interest rate policy can be obtained to pursue both CPI price stability and asset-price stability.

Assessment of monetary policy in Japan in 1987 and 1986 is difficult. Could one justify the monetary policy that lowered the discount rate to 2.5 percent in February 1987 and maintained it at 2.5 percent, then the record low, until May 1989? One may argue that the BOJ should have applied tight monetary policy in 1987 in order to curb asset-price inflation. But it would have been difficult to justify the action given the low CPI inflation rate, the slow economic recovery from the yen-appreciation recession of 1986, and the aftermath of Black Monday in October 1987. We are not confident that preventing asset-price inflation was an overriding priority of the central bank in 1987. On the other hand, the trade-off had disappeared in 1988 when both CPI price forecasts and asset-price movements now indicated that at least modest tightening would have been justifiable. The BOJ was probably behind the curve in 1988.

4.2.2 Bubble Overkill?

In the beginning of the asset-price decline, public opinion was favorable toward monetary and regulatory policy to stop the bubble. Housing was considered to have become too expensive to ordinary citizens, so stopping the housing price from skyrocketing was considered to be a good thing. Despite the burst of the bubble, robust consumption and investment continued in 1991. The GDP growth rate remained higher than 3 percent in 1990 and 1991.

The Japanese economy slowed down considerably in 1992. Stock prices plummeted in the summer of 1992, to the level of 15,000 in Nikkei 225 index, losing more than 60 percent of the peak value in two and one-half years. The quarter-to-quarter GDP growth rate became negative in the spring–summer of 1992. Lending to the real estate sector from banks slowed down after 1991 due to regulation, but there was a loophole. Lending via nonbank financial institutions (such as leasing companies) continued and total lending to the real estate, construction, and nonbank sectors remained high until the mid-1990s. Nonperforming loans, due to nonpayment of interest by real estate companies, became a popular topic of business discussion, but was not yet showing up in any banking statistics in the first half of the 1990s.

The discount rate was lowered to 5.5 percent in July 1991, to 5 percent in November 1991, and to 4.5 percent in December 1991. The decline of the ODR continued in 1992 and 1993. A fiscal stimulus package was introduced in 1992 in response to the weakening economy. This was the beginning of a series of fiscal stimulus packages.

The economy was stagnant from 1992 to 1994, with the growth rate below 1.2 percent, three years in a row. Land prices continued to decline steadily. The CPI inflation rate declined from just above 2 percent in the beginning of 1992 to 0 percent by mid-1995. Monetary policy was relaxed in 1992 and 1993 in response to weakening of the economy. The ODR was lowered from 4.5 percent to 3.75 percent in April 1992, to 3.25 percent in July 1992, to 2.5 percent in February 1993, and to 1.75 percent in September 1993. There was no change in the ODR in 1994, but it was lowered to 1 percent in April 1995, and finally to 0.5 percent in September 1995.

The question from the viewpoint of preventing deflation is whether or not the pace of the interest rate cut from 1992 to 1995 was quick enough. The fact that the economy continued to be stagnant and the inflation rate dropped to 0 percent suggested that the BOJ might have underestimated deflationary forces.

During the period from 1992 to 1995, the nonperforming loans problem became worse and worse. Many construction and real estate companies were virtually bankrupt, since the market value of real estate in inventory had become much lower than their purchase values, and cash flows were dwindling. As a result, these companies were having trouble making interest payments on their bank loans. However, the banks, fearing that losses would become apparent and having a false belief the real estate market would rebound soon, kept lending to these companies that could not service their debt—a practice that became known as "ever-greening." The balance sheets of corporations and banks were quickly deteriorating.

Smaller financial institutions—housing loan companies, credit unions, one regional bank—failed in 1995. The banking problem was worsening, but no serious policy was introduced to address the problem. Since the seriousness was hidden behind murky accounting rules and a lenient bank supervisor (the Ministry of Finance), the public was not informed of the magnitude of the problem or a coming crisis. Since the public and politicians were not alarmed, there was little sympathy toward any suggestions for fiscal injections to recapitalize the banks.

Many economists called for introducing prompt corrective action for weak institutions and fiscal injection, if necessary, for either closing institutions or rehabilitating them. But fiscal injection was politically difficult. Instead, in 1995, the Ministry of Finance on the one hand guaranteed all deposits, suspending the deposit insurance ceiling, and on the other hand declared that no major bank would fail.

In spite of a weak economy, the exchange rate was appreciating from 1993 to 1995. The exchange rate appreciated from 100 yen/dollar to 80 yen/dollar in the spring of 1995, with no apparent macrofundamental reasons for such a sudden move. The exchange rate appreciation dampened an expectation of early recovery and contributed to disinflation and then deflation.

The economy started to grow in the second half of 1995, and the year 1996 turned out to be a good one, with the growth rate exceeding 3 percent. The yen depreciated to a level above 110 yen/dollar, providing additional support for a recovery. A fragile economic recovery of 1996 accelerated in the first quarter of 1997, as the preannounced consumption tax rate increase of April 1997 induced consumers to accelerate big-ticket consumption. In April 1997, the consumption tax rate was raised from 3 percent to 5 percent, and the temporary special income tax cut was allowed to expire, both as planned. The growth rate significantly slowed down in the second half of 1997. This was the result of the Asian currency crisis, and the banking crisis of the Japanese economy in November. The economy continued to deteriorate in 1998: the year 1998 recorded negative growth for the first time since 1976.

From 1997 to 1998, Japanese financial markets suffered from a severe crisis, as banks were losing capital due to high ratios of nonperforming loans and falling asset prices. Three large banks—Hokkaido Takushoku, Long-term Credit, and Nippon Credit—failed, and other banks were also suffering from declining capital. Banks were curtailing lending and a severe credit crunch was observed. The resulting negative effects on aggregate demand then pushed the economy into deflation.

The government finally decided to inject capital into the banks. The first capital injection in March 1998 turned out to be insufficient but the second capital injection of March 1999 finally calmed the market. Ito and Harada (2000) showed that the Japan premium—a risk premium demanded by western banks upon Japanese banks for interbank lending/borrowing—disappeared after March 1999.

4.2.3 Asset Prices and Monetary Policy

In retrospect of 1985–2003, there are several questions on what the BOJ should or could have done. The first question is whether or not the BOJ should have prevented the bubble. If all the trouble of the 1990s originates from the bubble, stronger actions should have been taken against the asset-price increases. This question relates to a new debate over the objective of central banks.[6] Some researchers, more than others, think that asset prices should be considered as a part of price stability that is the sole objective of many independent central banks. Cecchetti, et al. (2000) argued strongly to put asset prices as direct measure of the goal of monetary policy.

Bernanke and Gertler (1999) examined monetary policy in the presence of asset-price bubbles, with application to Japan. They built a model with an exogenous asset-price bubble, applied alternative monetary-policy rules, and then estimated reaction functions for the Federal Reserve (FED) and BOJ. They applied the Clarida, Gali, and Gertler (1998) model to estimate reaction functions for the FED and the BOJ. The model assumes rational expectation for estimating expected inflation rate that is used to calculate the inflation rate gap. Their results indicate that the Japanese policy was too tight from 1985 to 1988 and too lax from 1988 to 1990, fueling a

6. A few conference volumes dedicated to this question have been published, see for example, Hunter, Kaufman, and Pomerleano (2003); and Richards and Robinson (2003).

stock bubble, and too tight, again, from 1992 until at least 1996. They argue that even without explicitly targeting the asset prices, the BOJ should have tightened from 1998 to 1990, probably ending the bubble much earlier.

Okina and Shiratsuka (2002) criticized Bernanke and Gertler (1999) on the grounds that Bernanke and Gertler used a forward-looking inflation rate as expected inflation, but the inflation rate they used was not adjusted for consumption tax rate changes. Okina and Shiratsuka argued that the rapid increase of interest rate derived from the policy rule of Bernanke and Gertler mainly resulted from the introduction of the consumption tax in April 1989. The paper by Okina, Shirakawa, and Shiratsuka (2001) contains a good review of why the bubble happened, how the BOJ reacted, and what could have been done, from the angle of the central bank. In section IV (Did the BOJ's Monetary Policy Create the Bubble?) the authors take the view that the BOJ lowered the interest rate from 1986 to 1987 to support the "policy coordination" framework, and to prevent the appreciation of the yen. The paper then reviews the policy in 1988 and 1989.

There are many criticisms of the view that the central bank should pay special attention to asset prices beyond their effects on CPI. See, for example, Mishkin (2001) and Mishkin and White (2003). Ito (2003) emphasizes the role of bank supervision, rather than monetary policy, for preventing a bubble or managing a burst bubble.

The difficulty in using monetary policy (raising and lowering of the interest rate) alone to prevent a bubble can be summarized as follows. First, the central bank often would not know whether asset prices are rising due to fundamentals or due to a bubble. Second, when the bubble is in force, it would take a very high interest rate to pop the bubble, and that would throw real variables into volatile fluctuations. Those skeptics emphasize the importance of supervision policy rather than monetary policy to maintain financial stability.

Given that a bubble is created, the effects from the bursting of the bubble could be moderated by monetary policy. The question is whether the BOJ was behind the curve from 1992 to 1995. The BOJ may have been too slow to ease, possibly for fear of rekindling a bubble. Similarly, the bank may have waited too long to adopt the ZIRP, possibly because it was an unprecedented move. Would policy have been better if the bank adopted the ZIRP earlier than February 1999?

4.3 New Bank of Japan

4.3.1 Monetary Policy of the Hayami Regime, 1998–2003

When the newly independent Bank of Japan started in April 1998, hopes were high in that the BOJ would improve its performance and return to what had been viewed as successful monetary policy in the preceding two decades. However, after five years under the Hayami regime, the BOJ had lost credibility and suffered a serious confidence problem. What happened? The short answers to these questions are two-fold. First, the policy board members, led by Governor Hayami, misjudged the economic conditions, maybe because they were too eager to go back to the "normal" situation where the interest rate is positive. The interest rate hike in August 2000 was a clear mistake of this kind. Second, the governor and fellow board members took independence literally and refused to cooperate with the government when the economic conditions called for such cooperation. Since independence and early establishment of credibility were considered so important, policy actions became conservative, timid, and tentative. Cargill, Hutchison, and Ito (2000, 173) called this the "independence trap." Even when policy was finally directed toward quantitative easing in March 2001, this policy was not explained adequately, especially because the BOJ had claimed that it was likely to be ineffective. Therefore, the general public viewed the BOJ as adopting a policy that the bank did not believe in. That was hardly a good way of communicating with the market.

The old Bank of Japan, under the 1942 Law, was supposed to pursue monetary policy in order to maximize economic potential (not price stability), and the governor could be replaced by the minister of finance, if the governor did not follow the government's instructions.[7] A lack of independence is often cited as a cause for an unusually high inflation rate, about 30 percent, in 1973–74, in the wake of the first oil crisis. After the inflation of 1973–74, the BOJ had conducted prudent monetary policy, achieving a gradual decline in the inflation rate. Cargill, Hutchison, and Ito (1997; chap. 8) have praised the conduct of the BOJ, achieving a de facto independence based on reputation. Japan was known to have been an "outlier" in the relationship between the legal independence index and the historical inflation rate.

The new law, the Bank of Japan Law of 1998, guaranteed the independence of the BOJ in its policy making and board member appointments.[8] The law became effective on 1 April 1998. At around the same time, Mr. Hayami was appointed as governor, and Mr. Yamaguchi and Mr. Fujiwara two deputy governors. Two policy board members were carried over from the old law regime, but four new members were appointed in April 1998 to

7. The 1942 Law specified that the BOJ conducts its operation "in order that the general economic activities of the nation might adequately be enhanced" (Article 1). The objective of the BOJ was "for achievement of national aims" (Article 2). These wordings should be understood in the context of the war when the bill was passed. See Cargill, Hutchinson, and Ito (2000; chap. 4) for detailed comparison of the old and new Bank of Japan Laws.

8. The 1998 Law specifies two pillars, "the pursuit of price stability, contributing to the sound development of the national economy (Article 2)," and "maintenance of an orderly financial system (Article 1)." The absence of mentioning full employment, economic growth, or exchange rate objectives suggests that price stability is the primary objective. Financial-system stability is a shared responsibility with government.

replace the old members and vacancy. Mr. Hayami, age seventy-two at the time of new governor appointment, left the BOJ after serving for thirty-four years on the international side of the bank, in 1981 (seventeen years earlier) to go to a general trading company, Nissho-Iwai. After serving as president and chairman of Nissho-Iwai, he had retired from the company for several years, until he returned to the BOJ as governor. Deputy Governor Yamaguchi had climbed up the ladder in the BOJ with a reputation for his knowledge about the core business of central banking. Deputy Governor Fujiwara was a former journalist. Governor Hayami was brought back to the top position, partly because he was considered to be incorruptible in the wake of a scandal at the Bank of Japan.[9]

The Japanese economy in the spring of 1998 was in the process of falling into a serious recession and financial instability. In November 1997, financial instability became prominent: one large bank and one small bank, a large securities firm, and a medium-size securities firm all failed, and credit lines among the Japanese financial institutions, and between western financial institutions and Japanese financial institutions became severely limited. The Asian financial crisis was spreading from Thailand to Indonesia, to Korea, and to the region in general. Demand was falling and it was clear that the economy was heading into a recession.[10] The overnight call rate, the market rate corresponding to the Federal Funds rate in the United States, at the time was about 0.4–0.5 percent. This stance was maintained until 9 September 1998, when the target of the call rate was reduced to 0.25 percent.[11]

Another major step was taken on 12 February 1999. The board decided to lower the overnight call rate as low as possible, with an immediate action

9. Many bank officials were implicated for inappropriate behavior of dining and golfing with private-sector people. The scandal hit the media particularly hard in the first three months of 1997. High salaries, high severance pay, and large company housing also became a target of criticism. One bank official was arrested for taking bribes in return for leaking information to a securities firm. Governor Matsushita and Deputy Governor Fukui (who returned as governor five years later) resigned to take responsibility in March 1998, days before the new BOJ law took effect. The official who took bribes was dismissed from the Bank on April 3, 1998.

10. In the spring of 1998, it was announced that the economy had just experienced the two consecutive quarters of negative growth rates: –0.7 percent in 1997:IV and –0.3 percent in 1998:I. The currently available new SNA93 (System of National Accounts, following a United Nations recommendation of 1993) available at [http://www.esri.cao.go.jp/jp/sna/qe034-2/gdemenuja.html] does not show this: +0.7 percent in 1997:IV and –1.0 percent in 1998:I. The difference is due to the differences in the base year, the estimation methods, and the seasonal adjustment method. The point is that the BOJ and the government should have had a more negative assessment of the economy at the time of Spring 1998.

11. "The Policy Board determined to further ease the stance of money market operations for the inter-meeting period ahead as follows: The Bank of Japan will encourage the uncollateralized overnight call rate to move on average around 0.25 percent" (Bank of Japan, Announcement of Decisions, September 9, 1998).

to lower it to 0.15 percent.[12] This is the beginning of the so-called zero interest rate policy (ZIRP). It was clear that the economy was in a very weak state. At the time, the GDP growth rate was thought to have shrunk for five consecutive quarters since 1997:IV.[13]

By the spring of 1999, the decline in economic activity became clearer—the instability of the Japanese financial system became acute as the Long-term Credit Bank teetered on bankruptcy; bills to strengthen the financial system were debated in the Diet; and the international financial system was shaken by the de facto default of the Russian debts in August.[14]

After ZIRP was adopted, the board members were divided into three groups, according to the disclosed minutes. Shinotsuka, who opposed adopting ZIRP, thought that the interest rate should be raised, partly to help pensioners. Nakahara, who had proposed lowering the interest rate more aggressively than other members before February, frequently put forward a motion to adopt quantitative easing and inflation targeting, as actions beyond ZIRP. Both proposals were voted down with only one vote in favor. The majority did not recognize the need to adopt any further actions between February and September.

Since the economy was not responding to the low interest rate, the government and business sectors began to press the BOJ to adopt more aggressive quantitative easing. Just before the September 21, 1999 meeting of the policy board, speculations were abundant in press predicting that the policy board would adopt some sort of quantitative easing, possibly nonsterilized intervention in the foreign exchange market in cooperation with the Ministry of Finance. The market regarded that nonsterilized intervention to be a signal that the BOJ would fight deflation with unconventional measures. The markets also focused on whether the BOJ would increase the amount of money market liquidity on the settlement day that was two days after the intervention.

The policy board reacted strongly to this speculation in the press. The board issued the statement, in addition to a brief announcement of the monetary-policy decision, at the conclusion of the meeting, instead of waiting for quick minutes to be released two days later. In the announce-

12. "The Bank of Japan will provide more ample funds and encourage the uncollateralized overnight call rate to move as low as possible. To avoid excessive volatility in the short-term financial markets, the Bank of Japan will, by paying due consideration to maintaining market function, initially aim to guide the above call rate to move around 0.15 percent, and subsequently induce further decline in view of the market developments" (Bank of Japan, Announcement of Decisions, February 12, 1999).

13. At the time of spring 1999, the growth rates of five quarters from 1997:IV through 1998:IV were estimated as negative. The current (spring of 2004) estimates for the same period are 0.7, –1.0, –1.1, 0.8, and 0.1. The reasons for the difference are explained in note ten.

14. Some speculate that there was also implicit political pressure from the meeting between the Finance Minister of Japan and the U.S. Treasury secretary on September 4.

ment, the board emphasized that monetary policy would not respond to exchange rate movements, that nonsterilized intervention was not a useful policy, and that the press was greatly mistaken in its reports on what would happen at the upcoming meeting. The board indicated that it had done enough in easing monetary conditions, and it barely concealed the desire to go back to the positive interest rate by emphasizing the side effects of ZIRP.

The board challenged the market expectation that nonsterilized intervention was to be pursued. It took a position that the exchange rate was one of the variables to be monitored, but monetary policy should not particularly respond to the exchange rate movement, per se.[15] The board then explained that nonsterilized intervention was not a useful concept for the central bank that watches total funds in the market, whatever various sources it came from.[16] In addition, the board statement contained cautionary comments on the side effects of ZIRP, a forerunner to ending the ZIRP eleven months later.[17]

The board expressed displeasure on press reports and market reaction in strong words: "In the past few days, the market has substantially fluctuated by speculations on monetary policy. What should be clear is that the conduct of monetary policy is exclusively decided by majority vote at the Monetary Policy Meeting, a regular meeting of the Policy Board. It is never the case that our policy is determined in advance or in consultation with outside bodies. We would like to emphasize this point" (Bank of Japan, "On the Current Monetary Policy" 21 September 1999).

The quotes from the statement vividly illustrated the position of the board. Any reporting of the expected decision was considered to be a challenge to independence. The board successfully extinguished any expecta-

15. "The foreign exchange rate in itself is not a direct objective of monetary policy. One of the precious lessons we learned from the experience of policy operations during the bubble period is that, monetary policy operations linked with control of the foreign exchange rate runs a risk of leading to erroneous policy decisions. Having said this, it does not mean that monetary policy is pursued without any consideration to the development of the foreign exchange rate. The Bank considers it important to carefully monitor the development of the foreign exchange rate from the viewpoint of how it affects the economy and prices" (Bank of Japan, "On the Current Monetary Policy" September 21, 1999).

16. "In relation to the foreign exchange rate policy, we have heard arguments in favor of nonsterilized intervention. In the reserve market, however, there are various flows of funds such as currency in circulation and Treasury funds other than those resulting from the intervention. The Bank conducts its daily market operations taking into account all the money flows, in order to create ample reserves to such an extent as described above. This strong commitment of fund provision is consistent with the government's current foreign exchange rate policy" (Bank of Japan, "On the Current Monetary Policy" September 21, 1999).

17. "The Bank views the current state of the Japanese economy as having stopped deteriorating with some bright signs, though a clear and sustainable recovery of private demand has yet to be seen. In pursuing the zero interest rate policy, we need to carefully examine its adverse side effects, but deem it important to support the economic recovery by continuing easy monetary policy for the periods ahead" (Bank of Japan, "On the Current Monetary Policy" September 21, 1999).

tion in the market that the bank would be accommodative in response to desires from the government or the market. Any doubt about independence was erased on 21 September 1999. However, their own strong words might have trapped the board members: that is, they could not change their positions in the following months.

Between the fall of 1999 and the summer of 2000, there was no additional easing, except for liquidity injections to deal with Y2K concerns. The government wanted some sort of additional measures of monetary easing, while the governor increasingly mentioned the possibility of lifting ZIRP. At this point, the bank explained that the bank would continue ZIRP "until deflationary concerns subside." The economy started to show some signs of recovery in the spring of 2000, ICT-related stock prices went up and the Nikkei 225 increased by 30 percent between March 1999 and March 2000. Corporate profits rose and corporate investment showed signs of recovery. There was an argument that these corporate earnings would trickle down to households to stimulate consumption sooner or later.[18] This argument was dubbed the "dam theory": water was filling the corporate dam and would overflow sooner or later. Governor Hayami, believing that this was communication with the market, frequently suggested that there were bright signs in the economy and, as a consequence, there would be a possibility of raising the interest rate. Critics thought it was premature to talk about lifting the interest rate, and any mention of it itself diminished the effect of ZIRP by limiting its effects through expectations that easing would continue into the future.

The ZIRP was lifted in the policy board meeting of 11 August 2000.[19] At this point, the continuation of a recovery of the Japanese economy was at best doubtful. First, the ICT bubble had ended and stock prices in the United States and Japan were heading down, suggesting investment and consumption would be adversely affected in the near future. Second, the U.S. economy was beginning to show weakness, and Japanese exports to the United States were expected to decline in the future. Third, the inflation rate was still negative, and there was no sign of an end to deflation. Critics of the bank thought that ending ZIRP was a mistake. Indeed, the government exercised an option, specified in the Bank of Japan Law, to put

18. "Currently, it is our judgment that Japan's economy is at the stage where the number of firms taking the offensive has started increasing, that is, the economy is moderately recovering parallel with structural adjustment. . . . with respect to the recovery of private demand, it seems natural that the corporate sector, which has regained profitability as a result of restructuring, should take the lead by increasing investment followed by the household sector as income conditions gradually improve. This is the development we are now witnessing" (Speech given by Masaru Hayami, Governor of the BOJ, at the Japan Center for Economic Research on May 29, 2000, available at [http://www.boj.or.jp/en/press/00/ko0005b.htm#0103]).

19. Governor Hayami intended to raise the interest rate in July. However, a large department store, SOGO, failed and the economy showed some weakness. The plan of lifting the interest rate was postponed without being submitted to the meeting.

forward a motion for delaying voting of the proposal of raising the interest rate until the next meeting. The government motion was overruled by the board by an eight to one vote, and then the lifting of the zero interest rate policy was decided by a seven to two decision.

Almost as soon as the interest rate was raised in August, the Japanese economy entered into a recession. It was not known at the time, but the official date for the peak of the business cycle turned out to be October 2000. The growth rate of 2000:III turned negative, which was offset to some extent by a brief recovery in 2000:IV. But, as the economy turned into a recession, the criticism of the BOJ's actions became stronger.

The economy weakened substantially toward the end of 2000. Many urged changes in monetary policy. Some economists had recommended the return to ZIRP, and others recommended quantitative easing and unconventional monetary policy including increasing the amount of regular purchases of long-term government bonds, and newly purchasing listed mutual funds of stocks, foreign bonds, and even real estate funds. These unconventional monetary tools had been rejected by Bank of Japan economists earlier.

As 2001 started, many indicators were showing weakness and the Bank of Japan decided to ease. The question then was whether to go back to the ZIRP or to introduce a new framework, quantitative easing. In February, the bank introduced the so-called Lombard lending facility as well as cutting the official discount rate from 0.5 percent to 0.35 percent. The Lombard lending facility was to lend automatically to banks with collateral at the official discount rate, so that the interest rate would be capped at 0.35 percent. However, the market rate was at around 0.2–0.25 percent, so there was little real impact from the introduction of the Lombard facility. Pressure to ease monetary conditions did not stop because of these measures in February 2001.

The policy board meeting of 19 March 2001, turned out to be the beginning of quantitative easing as well as further easing in terms of the interest rate. The target inter-bank rate was lowered immediately to 0.15 percent, and would go down to zero, as conditions warranted. The official discount rate was cut to 0.25 percent. However, the policy change was not announced as just a return to ZIRP. It was billed as a change in the monetary *policy instrument.* The instrument was changed from the short-term interest rate to the balance of current accounts at the BOJ. The target of the current account was set at 5 trillion yen. However, by targeting an amount beyond required reserves (about 4 trillion yen), it effectively meant that the interbank rate (i.e., the call rate) would go to zero. This amounted to excess reserve targeting.[20] In September 2001, the official discount rate was cut to 0.1 percent, but this did not have any impact.

20. Earlier than it was adopted in March 2001, BOJ economist, Okina (1999a) reviewed the excess reserve targeting as a possibility of next step of further monetary easing. He pointed

The bank has also made clearer the conditions when it would lift ZIRP in the future. When the BOJ adopted ZIRP for the first time in February 1999, the condition for lifting ZIRP was when deflationary concerns were dispelled. When the ZIRP was effectively reintroduced in March 2001, the condition became more concrete: excess reserve targeting, or de facto ZIRP, would not be abandoned until the inflation rate, measured by CPI excluding fresh food, became stably above zero. The exit condition would be further clarified in October 2003, to be explained later.

From March 2001 to March 2003, quantitative easing was expanded in several steps.

- In August 2001, another measure of quantitative easing was employed. The amount of BOJ outright purchases of long-term government bonds was raised from 400 billion yen per month to 600 billion yen per month. At the same time, the current account target was raised to 6 trillion yen (or about 2 trillion yen excess reserves).
- In December 2001, the monthly purchase of long-term bonds was increased from 600 billion yen to 800 billion yen, the current account target was raised to 10–15 trillion yen.
- In February 2002, the monthly purchase of long-term bonds was increased from 800 billion yen to 1 trillion yen.
- In October 2002, the monthly purchase of long-term bonds was raised to 1.2 trillion yen from 800 billion yen, and the current account target was raised to 15–20 trillion yen.

There have been mixed reviews on these steps. Although these steps expanded quantitative easing, especially in the amount of long-term bonds from 400 billion yen per month in September 2001 to 1.2 trillion yen per month in October 2002, deflation worsened. Some argue that this shows that quantitative easing did not work. However, advocates of quantitative easing would say that these actions prevented a major decline in economic activities.

These measures are summarized in the figure 4.3. Panel A shows the expansion of purchase of long-term bonds and current account target, while panel B shows the movements of the official discount rate and the call rate.

4.3.2 Assessment of the Hayami Regime

In the initial stage (April 1998 to March 1999) of the Hayami regime, until ZIRP was adopted, many BOJ officials expressed a negative view toward further easing (zero interest rate and quantitative easing including base money expansion, government bond, and equity purchases), indicating that it was either ineffective or would have undesirable side effects, includ-

out a few problems with this option. First, "what kind of function can be expected of excess reserves" is not known with certainty and it was identified as a problem. Second, excess reserves is not reliable "as an indicator for monetary easing." Third, Okina points out an operational hurdle.

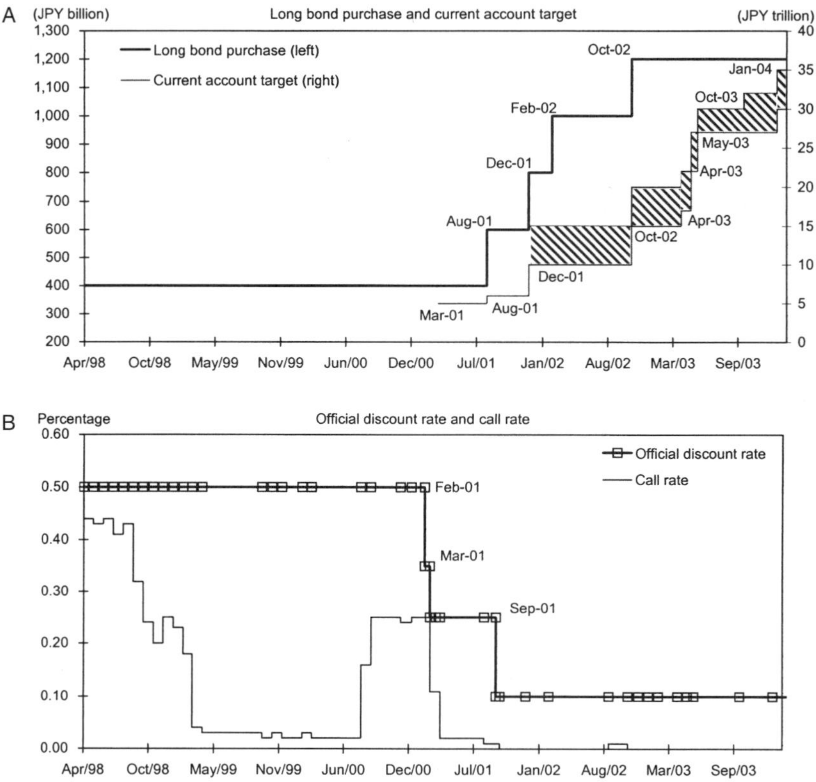

Fig. 4.3 Quantitative easing and interest rate cut

ing the risk of high inflation.[21] The call for easing by scholars was being rebuffed. (See Krugman 1998, Meltzer 1998, McKinnon and Ohno 1997 for the calls for monetary easing; and Okina 1999a, b for the rebuff.) When ZIRP was adopted in the spring of 1999, the bank maintained the view that

21. One such cautious opinion was expressed in July 1999 by Kazuo Ueda, a former University of Tokyo professor, now a newly appointed policy board member.

> "The policy to increase the money supply would first create some decline in the call rate, but automatically create further rate declines if the economy worsens and the demand for money declines. In this sense the commitment to avoid deflationary forces is stronger with money supply targeting. . . . To the extent that the money supply works through interest rates, the commitment money supply targeting delivers is already contained in the current policy stance. . . . The argument that an increase in the growth rate of the money supply increases inflationary expectations and stimulates aggregate demand by lowering real interest rates sounds attractive. It is unclear again, however, how this mechanism works when the nominal interest rate has been already driven down to zero. . . . How about a policy of letting the monetary base grow at 20 or 30 percent then? Inflation does not seem to be on the horizon. One can tighten after the inflation rate reaches 1 or 2 percent. We think such a policy would have a small chance of success for reasons already mentioned. When it does

no further steps were needed. The bank strongly resented any pressure or even suggestion from outside on further easing, as shown in the episode of their complaining about the speculation of easing before the meeting in September 1999. In the spring of 2000, Governor Hayami started to suggest ending ZIRP. Most likely, he wanted to communicate with the market on the bank's future intentions, in order to avoid a "surprise" reaction of the market and resulting volatility in the money and capital market. However, this suggestion certainly diminished any beneficial effects of ZIRP because it created expectations of higher interest rates in the future. The interest rate was raised in August 2000 despite the opinions by many scholars and the government of the need for further easing. In an international conference sponsored by the BOJ in July 2000, many scholars and foreign participants were critical of the past and current policy of the BOJ: Meltzer (2001), Goodfriend (2001), and Svensson (2001)—note the publication date of these papers was in 2001, but the conference took place in July 2000, one month before the ZIRP was reversed. Oda and Okina (2001) compare various policy options of monetary easing and their associated risks. The authors emphasized the risks more than the benefits of policy options proposed to the BOJ by "academics." They argued that "introduction of a temporary fixed exchange rate system and a huge increase in the outright purchase of medium- and long-term government bonds can induce relatively large effects, although the uncertainty in the effects as well as the accompanied costs and risks may be very large." One of the discussants, Jack Beebe (2001), felt that the "authors' views of policy feasibility and risks are unduly pessimistic. . . . Thus, the risks inherent in taking further policy actions need to be balanced against the risks of not taking them." What is striking is that the conference at which this debate took place occurred one month before the interest rate hike when ZIRP was exited, which we view was a clear policy mistake.

When the ZIRP returned with quantitative easing (current account balance of 5 trillion yen implying the excess reserve of 1 trillion yen) in March 2001, the bank did not explain why the change in policy would be effective, and this was particularly important because the bank had not been positive on its effectiveness in the past. In the summer to fall of 2001, there were calls for further easing by raising the current account target increase, increasing bond purchases, and purchasing equities and foreign bonds. Bank economists were negative on these suggested actions, saying that it was impossible to raise the current balance target (no buyers of short-term paper with zero interest rates), or no effect beyond stabilizing the financial sys-

succeed, it will probably generate a much higher rate of inflation than 1 or 2 percent. Because of lags in the effects of policy, the 20–30 percent money growth will continue to generate inflationary pressure even after the tightening starts" (Kazuo Ueda, Member of the Policy Board of the Bank of Japan, at the Meeting on Economic and Financial Matters in Kagoshima, on July 1, 1999, available at [http://www.boj.or.jp/en/press/99/ko9907a.htm]).

tem, and that risk of possible deterioration of balance sheets would be serious.[22] The policy started to change in December 2001, when the current account target was raised and long-bond purchases were raised in several steps. What was branded impossible was now possible, and the concern about the balance sheet, emphasized earlier by the bank itself, was buried without addressing it formally.

In September 2002, the bank started to purchase equities that the commercial banks held but wanted to dispose of in light of declining stock prices. Earlier, the bank had denied any possibility of purchasing stocks.[23] The action was justified by the bank on the ground that it would reduce the risk of commercial banks' balance sheets, and it was made clear that it was not intended as monetary policy, but rather as financial-market stabilization policy. (The decision was not made by the monetary policy board meeting—equivalent of Federal Open Market Committee—but the regular board meeting.) However, it was not explained why the resulting risk to the BOJ balance sheet due to financial-stabilization policy was not a big concern, while it was for monetary policy.

In October 2000, the bank paper "On Price Stability" emphasized that it would be difficult to focus on a particular price index as a guide to policy. Earlier, the bank was quite negative on the idea of inflation targeting. However, in March 2001, the board decided to adopt the ZIRP plus quantitative easing until the CPI excluding fresh food showed a positive inflation rate "stably above zero." This seemed to be a welcome switch from negative to a positive attitude toward selecting a price index and targeting a

22. "Three options for further monetary easing can be considered when money market interest rates are near zero. . . . Third, the BOJ can carry out unconventional operations by purchasing assets other than short-term Japanese government securities. . . . The third policy option is for a central bank to purchase non-traditional assets such as government bonds, foreign currencies, corporate bonds, stocks, or real estate which are more imperfectly substitutable for base money than are short-term government securities. As stated above, central bank operations that amount to the exchange of perfect substitutes produce little effect on the economy. Such non-traditional operations are effective because they directly alter the prices of the assets in question. Possible benefits and costs of this monetary policy option, however, are extremely uncertain" (Kazuo Ueda, Member of the Policy Board, at the semiannual meeting of the Japan Society of Monetary Economics held at Fukushima University in Fukushima City on September 29, 2001, available at [http://www.boj.or.jp/en/press/01/ko0112a.htm#0301]).

23. Governor Hayami denied the possibility of purchasing stocks as early as 1998, and repeatedly opposed to this saying that it violates the law. "There is intrinsically a very strict limit as to the extent to which a central bank can take on private sector risk. By shouldering such risk and seeing a subsequent deterioration in our assets, we might lose the confidence placed in us to fulfill our fundamental mission. Hence, the new Bank of Japan Law (effective April 1998) prohibits the Bank from purchasing equities bearing large credit and price risks. We thus do not think it appropriate to purchase corporate debt and equity" (A summary of the speech given by Masaru Hayami Governor, the Bank of Japan to the Kisaragi-kai meeting in Tokyo on December 22, 1998) [http://www.boj.or.jp/en/press/98/ko9812a.htm]). The switch in fall of 2002, why the governor changed the opinion and the purchase became possible without changing the law, was not explained.

numerical number, but the switch was not explained. In sum, the bank has been changing its position and action, but the switch was not explained well, and contributed to the decline in the credibility of the bank.

4.3.3 Fukui Regime

The new Governor Toshihiko Fukui took over the leadership of the Bank of Japan at the maturity of the five-year term of Governor Hayami in March 2003. Two deputy governors were also replaced. One of the two new deputy governors is Mr. Toshiro Muto who was earlier vice minister of finance; and the other Dr. Kazumasa Iwata, a former professor of economics. Iwata has been known to favor inflation targeting.

The new team moved quickly to increase the current account balance at the BOJ. The target amount was raised from 15–20 trillion yen, at the time of March 2003 to 30–35 trillion yen as of January 2004. The amount of long-term bond purchases was not changed.

The biggest change has been the rhetoric. Governor Fukui has made it explicit that the bank should maintain ZIRP until the inflation rate was clearly above zero. He seems to indicate commitment of ZIRP into the future, a sort of commitment recommended by inflation target advocates, or even better.[24]

Although the new policy is a big improvement over the last regime, there was some room for improvement. The tolerance of inflation was not indicated with precise numbers. Therefore, it was less credible than otherwise. One answer to such a criticism is the policy announcement of October 2003. It laid out the conditions for raising the interest rate:

> First, it requires not only that the most recently published core CPI should register a zero percent or above, but also that such tendency should be confirmed over a few months.
>
> Second, the bank needs to be convinced that the prospective core CPI will not be expected to register below a zero percent. This point will be described in such materials as the analysis and the forecasts of policy board members in the Outlook Report. To be more specific, many policy board members need to make the forecasts that the core CPI will register above a zero percent during the forecasting period.
>
> The above conditions are the necessary condition. There may be cases, however, that the bank will judge it appropriate to continue with quantitative easing even if these two conditions are fulfilled. (Bank of Japan, monetary policy committee announcement, 13 October 2003)

24. In his speech to economists, Fukui (2003) tried to put a spin that the exit-from-ZIRP condition that the Bank had adopted was more tolerant to inflation than a usual inflation target: "Assuming that a target has been established (for example, at 2 percent), if the expected inflation rate rises above the target and the Bank does not start tightening at that early stage, the actual inflation rate is likely to go beyond the target. Since the Bank's current policy commitments do not assume such a tightening at an early stage, they actually run a risk in the direction of greater inflation than in the case of standard inflation targeting."

Despite the good performance in the GDP growth rate in 2003:IV, the financial and capital market participants expect that ZIRP will continue for a long time. This is a big change from the Hayami regime. So far, credibility of the BOJ to maintain ZIRP seems to be on the rise.

The recent history of Japanese monetary policy has created two basic problems for the Japanese monetary authorities today. First, the BOJ's policies have left Japan in a prolonged deflationary environment in which conventional monetary policy through lowering the short-term interest rate is no longer effective because the policy rate has hit a floor of zero. Second, past Japanese monetary policy, particularly under the Hayami regime, has left the bank of Japan with a severe credibility problem in which the markets and the public are unconvinced that Japanese monetary policy can be committed to future expansion that would return the economy to health. Both of these problems present the bank with particular challenges in getting the economy out of deflation quickly, a subject we will return to later in the chapter.

4.4 Why Taylor Rules Are Not the Way to Assess Japanese Monetary Policy

In assessing the conduct of Japanese monetary policy over the last twenty years, the following questions arise:

1. Whether the BOJ should/could have taken stronger actions against the genesis of the bubble?
2. Whether the BOJ should/could have eased earlier in the 1992–1998 period in the aftermath of the burst bubble, in order to prevent the economy falling into deflation?
3. Whether the BOJ should/could have adopted the zero interest rate policy earlier than February/March 1999 in its fight against deflation (as a prevention or as a cure)?
4. Whether it was a mistake to raise the interest rate amid deflation in August 2000?
5. Whether the bank could have pursued nonconventional policy, beyond what was actually implemented in 2001–2003 to prevent a deflationary spiral (self-fulfilling expectation) from settling in?

The Taylor rule has been a popular tool to assess the monetary-policy stance. The nominal interest rate is regressed on the GDP gap and the deviation of the inflation rate from the target inflation rate, along with the constant term that represents the long-run equilibrium real interest rate and the target inflation rate. The Taylor rule might make it possible to judge whether the monetary policy was too tight or too loose for a particular period assuming that the estimated coefficients—either for an entire sample period or a part of it or, in some cases, from other countries—represent a "normal" response of the central bank. The deviation from the estimated (fitted value) target interest rate is interpreted for too tight or too loose monetary policy. The simplest version of the Taylor rule regression is as follows:

$$i_t = r^f + \pi^* + \beta_y \cdot y_t + \beta_\pi \cdot (\pi_t - \pi^*), \tag{1}$$

where i_t is the policy nominal interest rate; r^f is long-term equilibrium interest rate; π^* is the target inflation rate; π_t is the inflation rate; and y_t is the GDP gap (the log difference of the GDP and the potential GDP). In short, the nominal interest rate is regressed on the constant term, the GDP gap, and the inflation deviation, and in some cases the asset prices or the exchange rate. When equation (1) is regressed for a period in which the central bank has been operated under a stable regime, then the equation with estimated coefficients is viewed as a "reaction function" of a central bank.

Then, the fitted value of the left-hand side variable is considered to be target interest rate (normal interest rate) that the central bank on average would have pursued if the reaction function was followed without a deviation. *If the average is interpreted as optimal,* then the Taylor equation gives the normative content. When the actual interest rate is below the target policy rate (the fitted value) at period *t*, then the monetary policy is judged to be more relaxed, compared to other periods. Then monetary policy that is more relaxed is judged as too lax. Similarly, when the actual interest rate is above the target rate at period *t*, then monetary policy at *t* is judged to be too tight.

Bernanke and Gertler (1999) showed that monetary policy was too lax in 1989–1990, and too tight from 1992 to 1996. Okina and Shiratsuka (2002) criticized Bernanke and Gertler (1999) that their recommendations of early tightening in the mid 1980s to prevent asset inflation were impractical. Okina and Shiratsuka think that the forward-looking inflation rate (with rational-expectation assumption) is a source of problem.

Okina and Shiratsuka (2002, 2004) and Okina, Shirakawa, and Shiratsuka (2001) have examined monetary policy from the mid-1980s to 2002 and explored several policy options. They tend to show that monetary policy in the mid-1980s was a mistake in the sense the bubble was formed, but monetary policy in the mid- to late-1990s was basically right, and monetary policy after ZIRP does not have policy options.

Reifschneider and Williams (2000) quantified the effects of the zero bound on macroeconomic stabilization capability. They argue that under a severe contraction, open market operations alone may be insufficient to restore equilibrium. The Taylor rule should be modified to take into account the zero bound.

Harrigan and Kuttner (2004) applied the coefficients from the United States, simulated the path of the interest rate, and came to a conclusion: Had the overnight rate been set according to the Fed's policy rule, it would have been reduced to zero by mid-1993, and remained there at least through 1995.

Indeed, learning lessons from the Japanese situations was a popular exercise in the United States with an intention to avoid deflation. Clouse, et al. (2000) went through a menu of options that the central bank can think of adopting at the zero interest rate, and Ahearne et al. (2002) critically evaluated the BOJ policy. The latter came down to a conclusion that the Japanese monetary policy was too tight from 1992 to 1995. Bernanke and Gertler (1999); Jinushi, Kuroki, and Miyao (2000); McCallum (2003); and Taylor (2001) all obtained a similar conclusion that monetary loosening after 1992 was too slow (with varying changes of degree and period).

Kamada (2004) shows various estimates depending on various assumptions on output gap and data availability for decision making. Most of the simulated results show that the target rate in 2000 remained negative, suggesting that lifting ZIRP in August 2000 was a mistake, although he refrains from such an interpretation.

Clearly, researchers have come to quite different conclusions using estimates of Taylor rules. Can this evidence be considered to be reliable? We have our doubts. To illustrate this we estimate a regular Taylor equation to examine the crucial assumptions and consequences. The following is the basic data definitions: the interest rate is the call rate (collateralized call rate until June 1985, and uncollateralized call rate after that month); the price index is either the CPI excluding fresh food or the GDP deflator, measured as the change over the same month/quarter of previous year.

First, the GDP gap is estimated with an assumption that the potential GDP grows with a growth rate of moving average of the past growth rates in the sample. The potential output is further adjusted partly with the actual output with weight of 0.9 to long-run potential output and 0.1 to the output level of $t-1$:

$$Y_t^*(1 + g_{t-1}) \cdot \exp[\lambda \cdot \ln Y_{t-1}^* + (1 - \lambda) \cdot \ln Y_{t-1}], \quad (2)$$

where Y_{t-1} is the real GDP of $t-1$, λ is a set parameter of partial adjustment and here set to be 0.9, and g_{t-1} is defined as

$$g_{t-1} = \frac{1}{t-1} \cdot \sum_{j=0}^{t-1} g_j. \quad (3)$$

Although this is an ad hoc way to define potential output, it does capture a gradual decline in potential output in the 1990s without imposing perfect foresight or perfect hindsight, and allowing for the possibility that the 1990s were always below potential (lost decade) rather than imposing a restriction that some years have to be above potential. As McCallum (2003) pointed out, using a Hodrick-Prescott (HP) filter or a curve fitting method implies that some years have to be above potential and not appropriate in the situation that the last set of observations are suspected as being below potential significantly. Figure 4.4 shows our estimate of GDP gap.

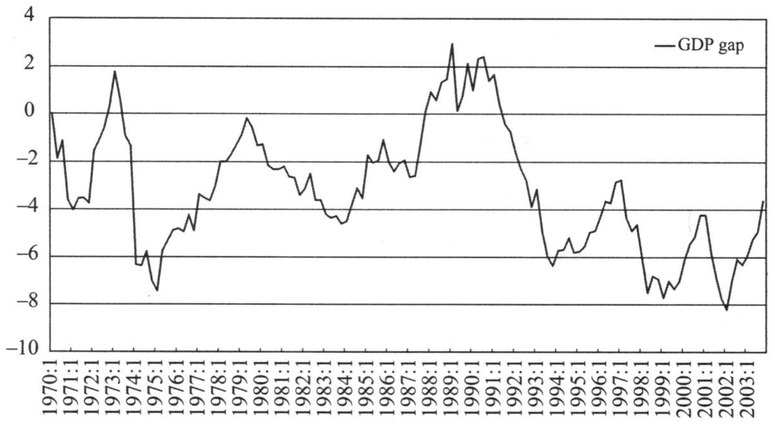

Fig. 4.4 GDP gap

We will use an inflation gap that is either backward- or forward-looking. The target inflation rate is assumed to be 2 percent. The target long-term real interest rate is implied from the estimated constant term, namely, the estimated constant term less 2 percent. In order to examine what the target rate should have been for a Taylor rule ignoring the zero bound, we estimate the equations using the data from 1982:I to 1994:IV.

Table 4.1 is the result of this estimation. The upper panel is the set of estimations with backward-looking models, while the lower panel is the set of estimations with forward-looking models. For the price index, the GDP deflator, CPI, and CPI excluding fresh food, are used. The GDP gap is not significant in the forward-looking regressions.

Figure 4.5 shows the target rate (depending on the forward and backward inflation rate) compared to the actual rate. The graph shows the following property. According to the graph, with an interpretation of the target interest rate (with backward inflation rate) to be a desirable rate, it can be said that the monetary policy was too loose from 1988–89; just about right from 1992–1995; and too loose (!) in 1996–97. However, after 1999, that target interest rate is negative, suggesting that the zero interest rate policy should be maintained. The Taylor rule estimates suggest lifting of the zero interest rate toward the end of 2000, although very briefly and very slightly above zero.[25] For the reasons we outlined in the previous section, we are doubtful about this conclusion.

Figure 4.5A, the forward-looking model, shows that the "target rate" has been consistently above the actual rate since 1995, either with the GDP definition or with the CPI definition. We again are suspicious of this result.

25. Ueda (2000) cited an internal study of the Taylor rule in his argument for arguing against lifting the zero interest rate policy. See the next footnote for detailed quotes.

Table 4.1 Taylor Rule model in Japan (1982:1–1994:4)

	Inflation rate gap	
	GDP deflator (1)	CPI ex fresh food (2)
	A. Backward-Looking model	
Constant	5.799***	6.201***
	(0.183)	(0.134)
GDP deflator or CPI ex fresh food	1.468***	1.752***
	(0.090)	(0.133)
GDP gap	0.214***	0.307***
	(0.053)	(0.040)
R-squared	0.799	0.791
DW	0.662	0.323
	B. Forward-Looking model	
Constant	5.629***	6.067***
	(0.323)	(0.266)
GDP deflator or CPI ex fresh food	1.233***	1.706***
	(0.110)	(0.276)
GDP gap	0.114	0.151
	(0.081)	(0.097)
R-squared	0.619	0.594
DW	0.253	0.162

Notes: Standard errors in parentheses are heteroskadastic-consistent.
***Significant at the 1 percent level.

The forward-looking model did not have a significant estimate of the GDP gap.

Figure 4.5B, the backward-looking model, shows that the GDP deflator model has had a negative target rate since 1998. However, it shows a positive target rate during the 1997–1998 period. The CPI model shows that the target rate has become positive since 2002. Both of these results are counterintuitive.

The above results suggest that we should be quite skeptical of estimated Taylor rules as a measure of optimal monetary-policy stance. This does not surprise us because there are theoretical reasons for doubting the usefulness of Taylor rules to assess monetary policy, many of which have been outlined by Kuttner and Posen (2004). First, the Taylor rule is essentially a reaction function, and not an optimality condition. Unless the average monetary reaction for the period of estimation is a priori known as the best practice, one cannot interpret it as the optimum, and any deviation cannot be evidence of too tight or too loose. Second, estimates are often quite sensitive to the estimation period, and that is not reassuring for us to use any particular regression results confidently without checking robustness. Third, the output gap, an important component of the Taylor rule equa-

A

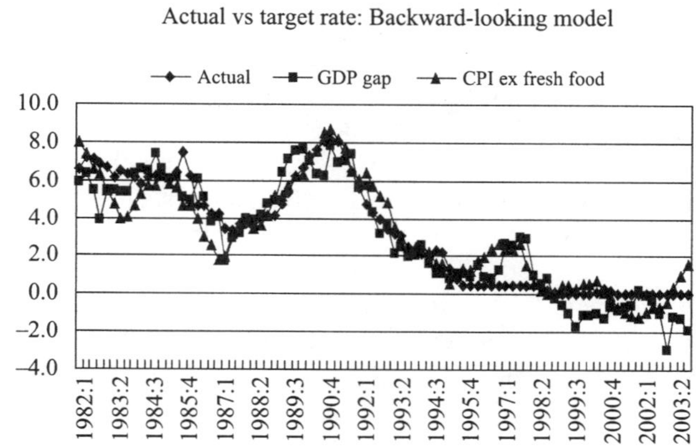

B

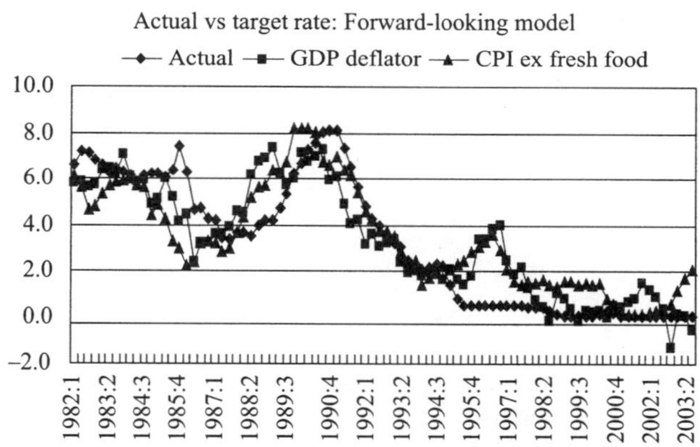

Fig. 4.5 Actual versus target rate: *A*, backward-looking model; *B*, forward-looking model

tion, is difficult to estimate. Fitting a linear trend or more sophisticated curve (e.g., HP filter) is unlikely to give us a correct output gap if years near the end of the sample are unusual (either in the upward or downward direction). For example, during the late 1990s, any conventional measure of GDP gap (or not-accelerating-inflation-rate unemployment [NAIRU]) in the United States was indicating an overheating that would require monetary tightening. However, in view of strong productivity increase, later known as a new economy, the Federal Reserve did not tighten monetary policy, and strong economic growth was extended without inflation until 2000. This episode shows the difficulty in estimating mechanically the output gap. Fourth, there are some deep conceptual problems in even deciding what an appropriate measure of the output gap is. Fifth, the regular Taylor-rule estimation does not assume that the nominal interest rate is bounded at zero. Therefore, in the case of Japan, the target rate estimated from the Taylor rule, without imposing the zero bound, often shows that the rate should be negative—this is regarded as evidence for keeping the rate at zero, as illustrated above.[26] However, this is not rigorous. If the Taylor rule is to be interpreted as an optimal monetary policy, the zero constraint of the nominal interest rate should be included in the estimation itself. Policy advice that the interest rate should be lowered more quickly than when the inflation rate is very low cannot be obtained from a regular Taylor equation that does not impose the zero bound condition.

Our examination of the Taylor-rule exercise above leaves us with a skeptical view of the use of this model to assess Japanese monetary policy. An alternative approach that we find very attractive is that in Kuttner and Posen (2004), which looks for deflation scares—sharp declines in long-term bond prices when there was no increase in the short-term policy rates. Indeed, Kuttner and Posen (2004) come to a similar view of the Hayami regime. Monetary policy during that period weakened the credibility of the BOJ to overcome the deflationary environment, and the abandonment of ZIRP in August 2000 was a clear policy mistake that led to entrenched expectations of continuing deflation.

4.5 How Costly is Deflation?

We have seen that Japan's deflation has been accompanied by weakness in the economy. However, does this mean that deflation has been harmful in Japan? Furthermore, even if deflation has had serious negative consequences for Japan, does that mean that deflation is always costly? When is a deflation likely to be harmful and thus to be avoided, and when not? There are several potential costs to deflation and we look at each of these in turn.

4.5.1 Deflation and the Labor Market

One argument for a high cost to deflation is found in the work of Akerlof, Dickens, and Perry (1996). Inflation that is at too low a level (which for them is below 2 percent) produces inefficiency and will result in an increase in the natural rate of unemployment. They argue that downward rigidity of nominal wages, which they argue is consistent with the evidence, indicates that reductions of real wages can occur only through inflation. The implication is that a very low rate of inflation might prevent real wages from ad-

26. An interpretation of negative target rate under the Taylor rule as a suggestion for keeping the zero interest rate policy in Japan has been mentioned in Ueda (September 22, 2000) who had voted against lifting ZIRP a month earlier: "the [output] gap is larger, on the deflationary side, by about 4 percent than the neutral level. With a coefficient of 50 percent on the gap in the Taylor rule formula, the gap term already contributes –2 percent to the interest rate. The inflation term also contributes negatively . . . Thus, there is no chance for the Taylor rule rate to become positive under such assumptions." A similar view was expressed by "one member" in the Monetary Policy Board meeting that reinstated ZIRP on March 19, 2001: "This member said that, according to this member's simulation applying the Taylor rule, when the economy recovered in the future, termination of the policy when the inflation rate was slightly above zero percent would not be premature."

justing downward in response to declining labor demand in certain industries or regions, thereby leading to increased unemployment and hindering the reallocation of labor from declining sectors to expanding sectors.

The evidence for the Akerlof-Dickens-Perry mechanism through which low inflation raises the natural rate of unemployment is not at all clear-cut (e.g., Lebow, Stockton, and Wascher 1995; Card and Hyslop 1997; Lebow, Saks, and Wilson 1999; Crawford and Harrison 2000; and Fares and Lemieux 2000). Also as pointed out by Groshen and Schweitzer (1996, 1999), inflation can not only put "grease" in the labor markets and allow downward shifts in real wages in response to a decline in demand along the lines of Akerlof, Dickens, and Perry (1996), but it can also put in "sand" by increasing the noise in relative real wages. This noise reduces the information content of nominal wages and hence the efficiency of the process by which workers are allocated across occupations and industries. Thus, we do have some skepticism about the Akerlof-Dickens-Perry (1996) argument which argues for keeping the inflation rate above 2 percent. However, their work does suggest that deflation might be costly.

In Japan, downward rigidity of annual compensation may not be large since regular, full-time workers have several months of compensations in bonuses. The bonuses are known to be more flexible, reflecting the performance of companies as well as individuals. Kuroda and Yamamoto (2003a, b) argued that the impact wage rigidity has on unemployment is quite small in Japan, at least among regular male workers. Wage rigidity was found to be more prominent among hourly-wage, part-time female employees. Kuroda and Yamamoto (2003c) conducted a simulation analysis to show that the downward rigidity would raise the unemployment rate by as much as 1.8 percentage points under the baseline parameters. The downward wage rigidity affects the labor-market condition most for the inflation rates between 2.4 percent and 1 percent.

Whether due to the wage rigidity or to some other reasons, the unemployment rate became as high as 5.5 percent in August 2002, compared to 4 percent in April 1998. It appears that the Phillips curve in Japan is sharply kinked at around the zero percent, CPI inflation rate.

4.5.2 Deflation, Wealth Redistribution, and Financial Instability

Unexpected deflation has the effect of shifting resources from borrowers to lenders when there are long-term debt contracts with fixed nominal interest rates. With a lower price level, and debt fixed in nominal terms, the real burden of this debt necessarily increases. One might think that losses by borrowers would be offset by gains to lenders in the macro sense, since unexpected deflation is just a wealth transfer, or a zero-sum result. But, this is not the case because deflation can lead to financial instability which can impose large costs on the economy. This provides an even more compelling reason to worry about deflation.

The transfer of resources from debtors as a result of deflation means that they suffer a loss of net worth and a deterioration in their balance sheets. Irving Fisher (1933) aptly named this phenomenon "debt deflation" and saw it as a major factor promoting the economic downturn during the Great Depression.[27] With less net worth, there is a decline in the amount of collateral a lender can grab if the borrower's investments turn sour, and the reduction in collateral therefore increases the consequences of adverse selection because, in the case of a default, losses from loans are likely to be more severe. In addition, the decline in net worth increases moral hazard incentives for borrowers to take on excessive risk because they now have less to lose if their investments go sour. The increase in moral hazard and adverse selection from deflation then means that the financial system markets will no longer be as capable of allocating capital to productive uses, with the result that investment will decline and the economy will contract. Wealth transfers are thus not neutral because they interfere with the effective functioning of the capital markets. The Great Depression is an example of when deflation had very negative consequences for the economy (Bernanke 1983; Mishkin 1978, 1991, 1997), with a recent example being that of Japan (Mishkin 1998).

Wealth redistribution from deflation also affects the fiscal position of the government. One of the largest borrowers with fixed interest rate is the Japanese government. The Japanese government has been regularly issuing long-term government bonds with fixed exchange rate. (Only in 2003, did the Japanese government start to issue inflation-indexed bonds, but the principal is protected from deflation.) Unexpected deflation during the 1990s meant that the Japanese government had an increased debt burden in real terms. In addition, since tax brackets are not adjusted for inflation, deflation meant that the government had less tax revenues (i.e., it suffered a reverse bracket creep).

4.5.3 Deflation, the Zero Bound for Nominal Interest Rates, and Increasing Difficulties in Conducting Monetary Policy

When the economy falls into deflation, as it has in Japan recently and as occurred in the Great Depression in the 1930s in the United States, there is a problem that arises from the zero bound of nominal interest rate. Lenders will not accept a negative interest rate, since hoarding cash provides a higher return. Thus nominal interest rates cannot go below a floor of zero and this can throw the economy into a disequilibrium situation.

Suppose that the economy is extremely weak and the real interest rate should be very low, possibly even zero or negative, in order to stimulate a recovery. However, when deflation is under way so that expected deflation

27. One might think that when both general price levels (for example, CPI) and asset-price levels decrease, the ratio of asset prices to CPI may not drop as much, and the debt deflation may not be so acute. However, the decrease in asset prices in Japan far exceeded CPI changes, so debt deflation was a real problem.

is substantial, a nominal interest rate that has hit the floor at zero leaves the real interest rate quite positive. Because of the zero bound, monetary policy is no longer able to get the real interest rate down to the equilibrium real rate that will put the economy back on track. The economy can be described as being in a "deflation trap" in which it operates below capacity with investment discouraged due to the deflationary environment.

Summers (1991) and a board member of the BOJ (Ueda 1999) have argued that in this situation, monetary policy becomes ineffective.[28] However, we believe this argument is a fallacy for the reasons outlined in Meltzer (1995) and in Mishkin (1996), and we discuss this further below. Monetary policy works through many other asset prices besides those of short-term debt securities, and so even when short-term interest rates hit the floor of zero, monetary policy can still be effective, and indeed was so during the Great Depression (see, Romer 1992).

Nonetheless, monetary policy becomes more difficult during deflationary episodes when interest rates hit a floor of zero because the usual guides to the conduct of monetary policy are no longer relevant. In recent years, much of the research on how central banks should optimally conduct monetary policy focus on so-called Taylor rules, in which the central bank sets the short-term interest rates at a level which depends on both output and inflation gaps. The Taylor (1999) volume is an excellent example of this type of research. However, once the interest rate hits a floor of zero, all of the research on optimal monetary-policy rules represented by work of the type in the Taylor (1999) volume is no longer useful because manipulating short-term interest rates is no longer an effective tool of monetary policy, as explained in an earlier section. We will see below that monetary policy can still be effective in stimulating the economy, but central bankers now will find themselves at sea without the usual knowledge to guide them, making it harder for them to get monetary policy exactly right.

4.5.4 Productivity-Driven Deflation

There may be one type of deflation that is not necessarily harmful to the economy: when the deflation occurs as a result of an extremely favorable productivity shock. In this case, the debt-deflation phenomenon may not operate. Think of what happens to a firm which finds the prices of the goods it produces falling because of a favorable productivity shock. It is true that the real indebtedness of the firm in terms of the firm's good prices

28. "Now let me briefly touch upon an academic, not a real-world, question of what a central bank can do beyond zero rates if it ever wanted to ease from that point on. . . . discussing money supply effects on the economy other than through interest rates. I must say they are very small once liquidity has been injected enough to maintain the zero rate. . . . I hasten to add that, once the zero rate is reached and spreads over to most of the short-term interest rates, attempts to expand the money supply themselves may become unsuccessful. We have been experiencing this lately in Japan" Ueda (1999).

rises. However, the value of the real value of the assets will also rise by the same proportion, because the firm has become more productive. In this case, the deflation is not leading to a decline in net worth and thus does not lead to the negative consequences we described earlier. This may explain the results in Atkeson and Kehoe (2004), who find that deflation was only clearly associated with economic depressions during the 1930s. Indeed, we have seen a recent episode of deflation which does not appear to have had negative consequences for the economy, China from 1997–2003.

Also, deflation that results from favorable supply shocks may not create a problem for the conduct of monetary policy. Favorable supply shocks are likely to increase the productivity of capital and thus raise the natural real rate of interest. Thus, even with deflation, the zero lower bound for interest rates will not be binding and monetary policy can be conducted using the conventional interest-rate tools.

Deflation (or disinflation) due to productivity increases would be accompanied by faster growth of output. This is likely to be what happened in the United States in the second half of the 1990s with the advent of the new economy. However, deflation driven by productivity growth does not describe the situation in Japan where stagnation has accompanied deflation.[29]

4.5.5 Bottom Line on the Costs of Deflation

The conclusion here is that deflation that occurs as a result of a decline in aggregate demand is likely to be harmful, both because it interferes with the efficient functioning of the financial markets, but also because it makes monetary policy harder to conduct. This is exactly the situation which Japan has been experiencing recently and which the world faced during the Great Depression period of the 1930s. This provides an important rationale for being concerned about the possibility of deflation. However, deflation which results from favorable supply shocks may not be nearly as harmful to the economy.

4.6 Deflation Prevention

The experience in Japan as well as the analysis in the previous section suggests that deflation can be a serious problem with high costs to the economy, particularly when it leads to a deflation trap in which conventional monetary policy is unable to help the economy to recover. Here we examine the question of how can monetary policy be designed to prevent deflation and a deflation trap from occurring. We wait until the next section to explore what can be done to get out of a deflation trap once it occurs.

Clearly, as Ahearne, et al. (2002) have pointed out, one way to prevent

29. Repeated reference to "supply-side factors" and "technological innovations" in Hayami's speeches in the early years was quite puzzling to say the least.

deflation is for monetary policy to respond particularly aggressively when negative shocks hit the economy if the economy is already in a low inflation environment. Indeed, our discussion of the Japanese experience earlier in the chapter has shown that the BOJ did not do this and was continually behind the curve in easing monetary policy when deflationary shocks first hit the economy. At one point, the BOJ even raised the interest rate amid deflation. Clearly, central bankers are human and do make mistakes, but can monetary policy be designed so that deflation and deflation traps are less likely?

Here we will see that putting in place a strong nominal anchor through an inflation targeting regime is an important strategy for reducing the probability that deflation will occur. However, a key issue for such an inflation targeting regime is what is the optimal level of inflation for the target? Once we examine this issue, we go on to look at whether or not it would be better to have the inflation targeting regime shoot for an inflation target or a price level target.

4.6.1 Inflation Targeting

As discussed and outlined in Mishkin (1999a), an inflation targeting regime involves five elements: (a) public announcement of medium-term numerical targets for the price-level path or inflation;[30] (b) an institutional commitment to price stability as the primary, long-run goal of monetary policy and to achievement of the price stability goal; (c) an information inclusive strategy, with a reduced role for intermediate targets, such as money growth; (d) increased transparency of the monetary-policy strategy through communication with the public and the markets about the plans and objectives of monetary policymakers; and (e) increased accountability of the central bank for attaining its inflation objectives.

Two features of an inflation-targeting regime can help in the prevention of deflation. The fact that a central bank that announces an inflation target and is accountable for achieving this target means that it will be under greater pressure to take steps to avoid a deflation as long as the inflation target is not too low (something that we turn to shortly).

For example, consider what might have happened if the BOJ had an inflation target of 2 percent for the CPI (the median for inflation-targeting regimes) in 1992 when the CPI inflation rate was still above 2 percent. Would that have helped the BOJ guide its policy in prevention of deflation? Or, suppose that the BOJ was given a 2 percent inflation target, in contrast to the actual 0.3 percent inflation rate, as well as instrument independence

30. To date all inflation targeters have chosen to target an inflation rate rather than the price level. However, logically an inflation targeter could just as easily choose to target the path for the price level, which trends upward at a chosen inflation rate as it targets a particular rate of inflation itself. The only difference is whether by-gones are allowed to be by-gones. We look at the question of the desirability of price level versus an inflation target later.

in 1998 under the new BOJ law. Would that have made the BOJ introduce the zero interest rate policy earlier than March 1999 and avoided lifting it in August 2000?

The inflation numbers that came in after adoption of inflation targeting would have indicated that the BOJ was not meeting its goals and pressure on the BOJ to pursue more expansionary monetary policy would have clearly increased. The likelihood that the BOJ would have lowered interest rates more rapidly and started the zero interest rate policy (ZIRP) earlier than 1999 would have been high. Furthermore, it is almost inconceivable that the BOJ would have abandoned ZIRP and raised the policy interest rate in August 2000 if an inflation-targeting regime of this type had been in place, since it was absolutely clear at the time that deflation was ongoing and a 2 percent inflation rate was nowhere in sight. An inflation-targeting regime is thus likely to have prevented BOJ's mistakes after 1998 and monetary policy would have moved in the right direction far earlier. Although this counterfactual does not imply that deflation would have been avoided, the simulations in Ahearne et al. (2002) suggest that easing monetary policy earlier and not tightening in 2000 would have promoted a stronger economy and reduced the degree of deflation. If an inflation-targeting regime and operational independence of the BOJ had been in place after the bubble economy burst, there is even a possibility that deflation could have been avoided altogether because the BOJ would have been under continual pressure not to get behind the curve as it did in the 1992 to 1998 period when inflation was clearly below 2 percent.

The second feature of inflation targeting is that it necessarily focuses on the management of expectations, which is increasingly viewed as being crucial to the successful conduct of monetary policy. One consequence of the adoption of inflation-targeting regimes is that it puts in place a strong nominal anchor that helps pin down inflation expectations (e.g., see Erceg and Levin 2001). Modern monetary theory (see Woodford 2003) shows that a strong nominal anchor that pins down inflation expectations has major consequences for the path of actual inflation and makes deflation much less likely. These theoretical results are borne out by recent experience where we have seen major successes in the ability of monetary policy to control inflation in many industrialized countries. We would argue that this is not because central banks have become so much more knowledgeable about the transmission mechanisms of monetary policy. What has changed in recent years is that central banks in industrialized countries have been able to put much stronger nominal anchors in place. The result is greatly improved performance on both the inflation and output fronts. This of course has been done by adoption of inflation targets, as in New Zealand, Canada, the United Kingdom, Sweden, and Australia, and to some extent in the European Monetary Union.

However, a strong nominal anchor can be put into place without a formal inflation target through direct communication with the public about the commitment to price stability and actions that are consistent with it. This is the strategy pursued by the Federal Reserve, which has as strong a nominal anchor as inflation-targeting central banks, although it is embodied in an individual, Alan Greenspan (Mishkin 2000).[31] This has worked well in the United States because Greenspan has understood and emphasized in his testimony and speeches that a central bank should be highly concerned about preventing deflation (Greenspan 2002, 2004). However, it can be dangerous to rely on an individual to do the right thing.

Governor Hayami clearly did not understand the dangers of deflation and continually spoke about the dangers of inflation even when the problem for Japan was the opposite. Furthermore, as we have seen, the BOJ's actions under Hayami were not oriented to preventing deflation. As a result, the BOJ has had a credibility problem, particularly under the Hayami regime, in which the markets and the public did not expect that the BOJ to pursue expansionary monetary policy in the future, which would ensure that deflation would end. These mistakes in the management of expectations are a key reason why Japan found itself in a deflation that it is finding very difficult to get out of.[32] Indeed, one of the reasons that one of us has advocated inflation targeting for the United States is that an institutional basis for the nominal anchor is likely to remain strong regardless of who is the head of the central bank (Mishkin 1999a; Mishkin and Posen 1997; Bernanke, Laubach, Mishkin, and Posen 1999; Mishkin 2004a, b). In the case of Japan, having an inflation-targeting regime would have made if far more likely that expectations would have been managed more to prevent deflation, both through actions and words, as advocated by one of us, Ito (1999).

Earlier suggestions for inflation targeting were made to help raise inflation expectation in order to get out of the deflationary trap (see Krugman 1998). Advocates of inflation targeting also suggested that it would be an appropriate monetary-policy framework for an independent central bank in order to enhance accountability and transparency of its policy. Ito (1999) further argued that inflation targeting probably enhances instrument independence. Cargill, Hutchison, and Ito (2000; chap. 5) and Ito and Hayashi (2004; chap. 5) also review major issues in the debate on inflation targeting in Japan.

31. This does not mean that there aren't reasons for the Federal Reserve to move to an inflation target. See Mishkin (2004).

32. BOJ officials have been quite skeptical of their ability to influence inflation expectation of the public. "The argument that an increase in the growth rate of the money supply increases inflationary expectations and stimulates aggregate demand by lowering real interest rates sounds attractive. It is unclear again, however, how this mechanism works when the nominal interest rate has been already driven down to zero" (Kazuo Ueda, "The Bank of Japan's Forward Looking Approach"—Remarks by Kazuo Ueda, member of the policy board of the Bank of Japan, at the Meeting on Economic and Financial Matters in Kagoshima, on July 1, 1999).

The BOJ was not warm to inflation targeting. Many policy board members as well as staff economists expressed skeptical views in recorded minutes of the policy board meetings (see Fujiki, Okina, and Shiratsuka [2001]; Okina [1999a, b]; and Ueda [2000] for a succinct view). The skeptics argued that there was no credible tool, beyond ZIRP, to raise the inflation rate. Inflation expectations in the market would not respond to a mere announcement of the target. Therefore, committing to a target when the bank did not have the tools to achieve it would cause the bank to lose credibility.[33]

At the earlier stage, that is 1999–2000, there was also an argument that the definition of deflation was not clear: which prices should be used and what numbers should be looked at in defining deflation.[34] The BOJ was also responding to new calls for more careful definitions of price stability. On 13 October 2000, two months after raising interest rates, the policy board issued a report called "On Price Stability." In the document, price stability was defined as a state that is neither deflation nor inflation. Its apparent tautology did not help settle the problem.

Only in March 2001 did the BOJ identify the price index relevant in policy discussions as the CPI index excluding fresh food (CPIexFood).[35] The relaxed monetary policy would continue until inflation rate measured by the CPIexFood would become stably above zero. In October 2003, "stably" was further defined as above zero for a few months and when there would be no risk of falling back into deflation.

It is not immediately clear to us why the BOJ was so negative toward nonconventional monetary policy and inflation targeting under the Hayami regime.[36] One possible answer was that inflation targeting was interpreted as a strategy to inflate away the nonperforming loans problem. Governor Hayami repeatedly cautioned that economic boom and inflation would make problem firms survive longer: inflation would delay structural reform.[37] This smacked of the view that "cleansing" was needed, which has a

33. "[T]he BOJ argues, as is recorded in the minutes of Monetary Policy Meetings, that 'since we cannot explicitly show the way to achieve the desired inflation rate, such action would most likely result in the BOJ losing credibility'" (Okina 1999b, 165). Critics argued that there are nonconventional monetary-policy measures that surely make the inflation rate go from negative to positive, the credibility argument is based on incorrect assumptions.

34. "Price indicators such as the GDP deflator, CPI, and Wholesale Price Index (WPI) often move differently. Even when these indicators exhibit the same movement, the extent to which the sound development of the national economy will be achieved may depend on such factors as whether property prices are stable or rising sharply" (Okina 1999a, 164).

35. The Cabinet Office also changed the definition of deflation in the appendix to the monthly report of March 2001 from "a state in which prices are falling while the economy is contracting" to "a state of continuing fall of prices" Available at [http://www5.cao.go.jp/keizai3/2001/0316getsurei/main.html]).

36. Ito (2004) examines why the BOJ did not adopt inflation targeting, based mostly on minutes of the monetary policy meetings.

37. "When the economy recovers, as is now happening, it might well be the case that efforts for structural reform might be neglected due to a sense of security. In addition, when the shadow of structural reform becomes conspicuous, for example in employment, calls to re-

strong resonance to what Federal Reserve officials said during the Great Depression in the 1930s. This view clearly misinterpreted what inflation targeting is about.

Second, another possibility is that the BOJ fell into the "independence trap," as it was called by Cargill, Hutchison, and Ito (2000). Namely, the BOJ was afraid to take bold actions when it had just gained independence. Before independence, a usual argument not to lower the interest rate quickly was that once it was lowered, it would be very difficult, politically, to raise the interest rate. Achieving independence was supposed to solve this problem. Flexible adjustments and bold actions were supposed to have become possible. On the contrary, the BOJ became much more conservative in the sense that it became reluctant to take actions, especially unprecedented ones, that might be judged a failure later, arguing that it would be important to establish credibility early. If this is the case, the BOJ was given independence precisely at the moment that it should not be given independence, because the economy called for unprecedented monetary policy.

Third, one more possible interpretation is that the bank genuinely was worried about possible deterioration of its balance sheet. Purchasing a large amount of long-term government bonds would put the balance sheet at risk if they later declined in value. A question is whether stopping nonconventional monetary policy on the grounds of a concern about the balance sheet is desirable from the point of view of avoiding deflation and maximizing potential output. The BOJ is part of the public sector, and any losses on the bank's balance sheet would be counterbalanced by gains on the central government's balance sheet. Since the BOJ should be considered as a part of the government from an accounting point of view, concern about these losses is unwarranted, unless they created political problems for the bank. The balance sheet of the BOJ should be guaranteed by the government if it makes sense for the BOJ to take risk in its operations.[38] In this sense, independence came at a wrong moment in history.

4.6.2 What is the Optimal Level of Inflation?

A key issue in any inflation-targeting regime, whether it targets a path of the price level or the inflation rate, is what is the optimal level of inflation

verse such reform and pressure for additional macroeconomic policy measures such as the expansion of aggregate demand are very likely to intensify. . . . Structural problems cannot be solved solely by macroeconomic policy measures such as monetary and fiscal policy. Now that financial and capital markets are highly globalized, any attempt to wipe out past problems by generating inflation will never be successful." (Speech given by Masaru Hayami, Governor of the Bank of Japan, at the Japan Center for Economic Research, Available at [http://www.boj.or.jp/en/press/00/ko0005b.htm] May 29, 2000)

38. Under the old BOJ law, before 1998, heavy losses on the balance sheet incurred by the BOJ were automatically filled by the Ministry of Finance. In the new law of 1998, since policies of the BOJ were subject to direction of the Minister of Finance, the clause was eliminated that emphasizes independence of the BOJ.

that the central bank should want the price level to grow to over the long run? In order to decide on the appropriate long-run inflation goal, we need to answer the deeper question of what does price stability mean? Alan Greenspan has provided a widely cited definition of price stability as a rate of inflation that is sufficiently low so that households and businesses do not have to take it into account in making everyday decisions. This definition of price stability is a reasonable one and operationally, any inflation number between 0 and 3 percent seems to meet this criterion. Some economists, Martin Feldstein (1997) and William Poole (1999) being prominent examples, argue for a long-run inflation goal of 0 percent, which has the psychological appeal of the "magic number" of zero. Indeed one concern is that an inflation goal greater than zero might lead to a decline in central bank credibility and instability in inflation expectations, which could lead to an upward creep in inflation. However, evidence in Bernanke, Laubach, Mishkin, and Posen (1999) suggests that maintaining a target for inflation above zero, but not too far above (less than 3 percent), for an extended period, does not lead to instability in the public's inflation expectations or to a decline in central bank credibility.

The BOJ (2000) attempted to define price stability in October 2000. However, it concluded that it would not be appropriate to give a numerical value to price stability, a surprisingly negative attitude toward commitment to inflation targeting:

> If some numerical values are adopted as the definition of price stability, they are expected to be valid for a very long period of time. In view of the current development of prices in Japan, it is difficult to set specific numerical values to the definition of price stability that are consistent with the sound development of the economy. Furthermore, even if some numerical values were announced, they would not serve as a reliable guidepost in the conduct of monetary policy, and the exercise would not likely contribute to enhancing transparency of the conduct of monetary policy. Therefore, it is not deemed appropriate to define price stability by numerical values. (Bank of Japan, 2000, Summary, Paragraph 5 [2])

There are several reasons why the desirable target rate should be positive. First, there is an upward bias in CPI by construction.[39] Second, it helps the economy to achieve necessary relative price adjustment if some prices and wages are sticky downward. This is a basis of the argument in Akerlof, Dickens, and Perry (1996). Third, an even more persuasive argument against an inflation goal of zero is that it makes it more likely that the economy will experience episodes of deflation. We have argued above that de-

39. The Laspayres index tends to underestimate the true inflation by keeping the basket fixed, so that the demand shift due to the relative price changes would not be reflected. The new products would not be included. Quality improvement is often ignored.

flation can be highly dangerous when it promotes financial instability and in addition can make monetary-policy decisions harder if as a result short-term interest rates hit a floor of zero. The implication is that undershooting a zero inflation target (i.e., a deflation) is potentially more costly than overshooting a zero target by the same amount. This can be dealt with by having a target rate with a buffer so that even some perturbation around the target would not force the economy into deflation.

The logic of this argument suggests that setting an inflation target a little above zero is worthwhile because it provides some insurance against episodes of deflation. Simulation evidence in Fuhrer and Madigan (1997); Orphanides and Weiland (1998); and Reifschneider and Williams (2000) bear this out, finding that inflation targets near zero (below 2 percent) increase output variability. This is why one of us has argued in Mishkin (1999a) and Bernanke, Laubach, Mishkin, and Posen (1999) for a long-run inflation goal of 1 percent above true inflation. The Boskin commission (Boskin, et al. 1996) estimated that the measurement bias in CPI inflation was about 1 percent and this is why Bernanke et al. (1999) suggested a CPI inflation goal for the United States of 2 percent.[40] In the case of Japan, the upward bias in measured CPI inflation over true inflation has been estimated to be 0.9 percent (Shiratsuka 1999), although redefinition of the price CPI in Japan may mean that the bias is now lower. Adding this to an inflation goal of about 1 percent true inflation, an inflation goal of near 2 percent for the CPI in Japan makes sense.

Another reason why central banks might be better off with a long-run inflation goal above zero, is that it is crucial that they not be perceived as being overly obsessed with controlling inflation at the expense of output stability. If a central bank is perceived as an "inflation nutter" in Mervyn King's (1996) terminology, in which the central bank puts no weight on output fluctuations in making its decisions about monetary policy, it is likely to lose the support of the public. Too low an inflation target may signal to the public that the central bank does not care sufficiently about the public's concerns. It is unstable for a central bank in a democracy to have a very different loss function than the public (Blinder 1998, and Mishkin 1999b), and pursuing too low an inflation target may weaken the support for central bank independence.[41]

40. Since the Boskin commission, the Bureau of Labor Statistics (BLS) has altered its procedures to reduce the measurement bias in CPI inflation. Also the inflation bias in the prices of consumer expenditure (PCE) deflator, which appears to be the preferred measure of inflation used by the Federal Reserve, is even lower than for the CPI. This would suggest an even lower inflation goal for this deflator.

41. By also emphasizing that the horizon for hitting an inflation target will need to be lengthened in order to not impose large output losses on the economy if inflation is far from target, the central bank can also make clear that it does put a weight on output fluctuations in making its decisions about monetary policy. See Mishkin (2004).

4.6.3 Price-Level Versus Inflation Target?

Currently, all countries who have adopted inflation targeting have chosen to target inflation *rate* rather than the price *level.* However, which of these two targets would result in better economic performance and prevent deflations is still an open question. Here we look at this question when the economy is assumed to be experiencing a positive rate of inflation. The answer to this question may be quite different when the economy is already in a prolonged deflation and we will address this situation in the following section.

There are two key advantages of a price-level target relative to an inflation target. The first is that a price-level target can reduce the uncertainty about where the price level will be over long horizons. With an inflation target, misses of the inflation target are not reversed by the central bank. The result is that inflation will be a stationary stochastic process, that is, integrated of order zero, I(0), while the price level will be nonstationary, an I(1) process. The result is that the uncertainty of where the price level will be in the future grows with the forecast horizon. This uncertainty can make long-run planning difficult and may therefore lead to a decrease in economic efficiency. Although, McCallum (1999) has argued that the amount of long-run uncertainty about the future price level that would arise from successful adherence to an inflation target may not be all that large, it still complicates the planning process and may lead to more mistakes in investment decisions.

The second possible advantage of a price-level target is that in models with a high degree of forward-looking behavior on the part of economic agents (e.g., Svensson 1999; Woodford 1999, 2003; Svensson and Woodford 2003; Clarida, Gali, and Gertler 1999; Dittmar and Gavin 2000; Vestin 2000) it produces less output variance than an inflation target. However, empirical evidence (Fuhrer 1997) does not clearly support forward-looking expectations formation, and models with forward-looking behavior have counterintuitive properties that seem to be inconsistent with inflation dynamics (Estrella and Fuhrer 1998).

The traditional view, forcefully articulated by Fischer (1994), argues that a price-level target might produce more output variability than an inflation target because unanticipated shocks to the price level are not treated as bygones and must be offset. Specifically, a price-level target requires that an overshoot of the target must be reversed and this might require quite contractionary monetary policy and, with sticky prices, this could lead to a sharp downturn to the real economy in the short run. Indeed, if the overshoot is large enough, returning to the target might require a deflation, which could promote financial instability and be quite harmful to the economy.

Although the models with a forward-looking price setting do not find that this feature of a price-level target increases output variability, they do not focus on the fact that a price-level target may lead to more frequent episodes of deflation, which leads to the problems discussed in section 4.2: deflation can exacerbate financial instability or can make monetary policy more difficult to conduct because interest rates cannot go below zero. These costs of deflation tend to make us more skeptical about theoretical results that indicate that price-level targets are able to reduce output variability when inflation is positive. Indeed, price-level targets which lead to more episodes of deflation may be more dangerous than their proponents have realized.

In addition, a price-level target may be more difficult to explain to the public because it is a moving target, in contrast to an inflation target, which is not. Because increased transparency and accountability is a highly desirable attribute for the conduct of monetary policy, this is an important advantage for an inflation target.

Another problem for a price-level target that has received little attention in the literature is the presence of measurement error in inflation. Most research on measurement error takes the view that it is *inflation* that is measured with error rather than the *price level* and this was the approach taken by the Boskin Commission.[42] This implies that the measurement error in the price level is I(1), that a price-level target results in growing uncertainty about the true price level as the forecast horizon grows. Thus many of the arguments that a price-level target results in lower long-run uncertainty about the true price level may be overstated.

The conflicting arguments above indicate that whether price-level rather than inflation targets would produce better outcomes when inflation is positive is an open question. Given this uncertainty about the benefits of price-level targeting, it is not surprising that no central bank has decided to target the price level in recent years.[43] However, the arguments made here for preferring an inflation target over a price-level target do not rule out hybrid policies, which combine features of an inflation and a price-level target and so might provide the best of both worlds.

An inflation target could be announced with a commitment to some error correction in which target misses will be offset to some extent in the future. Recent research shows that an inflation target with a small amount of error correction can substantially reduce the uncertainty about the price level in the long run, but still generate very few episodes of deflation (e.g., Black, Macklem, and Rose 1998; King 1999; Battini and Yates 1999). Furthermore, by putting a small weight on the price-level error-correction term, the trade-off between output and inflation fluctuations can be improved

42. See Boskin et al. (1996), Moulton (1996), and Shapiro and Wilcox (1996), for example.
43. However, a price-level target was used in the 1930s in Sweden (Berg and Jonung 1999).

(e.g., see also Williams 1999; Smets 2000; Gaspar and Smets 2000; McLean and Pioro 2000). Evaluating hybrid policies of this type is likely to be a major focus of future research.

One issue that would have to be addressed if such a hybrid policy was adopted is how it could be explained to the public. As is emphasized in Bernanke and Mishkin (1997), Mishkin (1999a), and Bernanke, et al. (1999), critical to the success of inflation targeting is that it provides a vehicle for more effective communication with the public. The public will clearly not understand the technical jargon of error-correction models. However, some form of an error-correction feature of an inflation-targeting regime could be communicated by not only announcing an intermediate-term inflation target, but also by indicating that there is a target for the average inflation rate over a longer period, say five years.

4.7 Deflation Cures

Once an economy begins to experience a deflation, it encounters an additional set of problems that alter the issues that confront monetary policy. First is that the economy may be in a deflation trap in which monetary policy operating through short-term interest rates is powerless to extricate the economy from the deflation because the policy interest rate cannot be driven below the zero lower bound, which leaves the real interest rate too high to stimulate recovery. Second, the central bank may have a severe credibility problem in which the markets and public are unconvinced that monetary policy can be committed to future expansion that would return the economy to health. Both of these problems are exactly what we see in Japan today. As we discussed in section 4.1, the Japanese economy is still experiencing deflation even though short-term interest rates are at zero, while past BOJ policies, particularly under Hayami, have suggested to the public that once there is a glimmer of recovery, the monetary authorities are likely to raise interest rates and tighten monetary policy.

Given these problems, what can be done to get the economy out of the deflationary spiral? We will discuss two key elements of strategies to cure deflation: (a) management of expectations through adoption of a price-level target, and (b) nonconventional policies that employ central bank purchases of other assets besides short-term bonds.

4.7.1 Price-Level Targets

According to traditional monetary theory, it might appear as though monetary policy cannot be effective in escaping the deflation trap because there is no way to drive the standard interest-rate instrument below zero. However, recent literature (Krugman 1998; Eggertsson and Woodford 2003; Auerbach and Obstfeld 2003; Svensson 2003) suggests that there is a solution to this problem: management of expectations. If the central bank can convince the markets and the public that there will be higher inflation in the future, then even with the interest rate at a floor of zero, the real interest rate will fall and this will stimulate aggregate demand through the usual channels (Mishkin 1996). But how is the central bank to do this?

Once an economy has entered a prolonged deflation as it has in Japan, lowering the real interest rate to stimulate the economy requires a substantial increase in expected inflation. This is why Krugman (1998) made the radical suggestion for the BOJ to adopt an inflation target of 4 percent for a fifteen-year period. However, a high inflation target, as suggested by Krugman, is unlikely to be credible for two reasons. First, a commitment to a high inflation target may not be credible because it is too much at variance with a goal of price stability. As documented in Bernanke, Laubach, Mishkin, and Posen (1999), no inflation-targeting central bank in an industrialized country has chosen a medium-term inflation target above 3 percent. Indeed, we suspect that the Krugman proposal may have increased the BOJ's resistance to inflation targeting because this level of inflation was well above what officials in the bank believed was consistent with price stability. Furthermore, once the economy has emerged from a deflationary spiral and starts to recover, the central bank will be tempted to renege on its commitment to a high inflation target because it would like the economy to return to an inflation rate consistent with price stability. Thus as pointed out by Eggertsson (2003), a central bank in a deflationary environment is subject to a time-inconsistency problem: it cannot credibly commit to "being irresponsible" and so continue to shoot for high inflation. The result of the time-inconsistency problem is that the markets would not be convinced the inflation would remain high, inflation expectations would not be sufficiently high to lower real rates sufficiently to stimulate the economy out of the deflation trap.

Another problem with an inflation target is that it is not "history-dependent" because it is purely forward-looking (Woodford 2000, 2003). An inflation target is not adjusted depending on the past outcome of inflation, and, as Eggertsson and Woodford (2003) have shown, will not be effective in extricating an economy from a deflation trap. When the interest rate has hit a floor of zero, a deflationary shock, which lowers the price level and puts the economy even farther below its potential, requires an even higher expected inflation in order for the real interest rate to be lowered and be even more stimulative. A price-level target does exactly this: with a price-level target, the same price-level target implies that inflation will be expected to be higher, and this produces exactly the right response of a lower real interest rate and more stimulative monetary policy.

The theoretical argument for a price-level target when an economy is in a deflationary environment is thus quite strong. But there is a further reason for adoption of a price-level target when an economy has experienced a prolonged period of deflation along with a severe balance-sheet problem that prevents the financial system from working properly as in Japan (e.g., Posen 1998; Mishkin 1998; Hoshi and Kasyhap 2005). In Japan, nonperforming loans have weakened bank balance sheets, and the lack of capital has meant that banks have been forced to cut back on lending, particularly for new investment. The result is that the financial system is unable to allocate capital to productive investment opportunities, and this is a key element in the stagnation in Japan. The deflation has also weakened corporate balance sheets, who have found their debt increase in value in real terms while their assets have not (the debt-deflation phenomenon described by Irving Fisher [1933]). The loss of net worth implies that even firms with good investment opportunities may then not be able to get funds at favorable rates because the firm is more likely to engage in risky (moral hazard) behavior because there is less at stake in the firm (Mishkin 1997). Thus restoring both financial and nonfinancial balance sheets is crucial to helping an economy like Japan's to achieve a more efficient allocation of capital that will restore it to health.

A price-level target that would get the price level to what it would have been if the economy had not experienced deflation is an important way to help restore balance sheets. A higher price level would lead to lower real indebtedness of firms and would thereby increase their net worth, making it more attractive to lend to them if they have productive investment opportunities. The improvement in firms' balance sheets would also help reduce nonperforming loans which would have a positive knock-on effect on bank balance sheets, thus making it easier for them to lend.

Furthermore, after a prolonged period of deflation, an economy may need to undergo substantial restructuring if it is to return to health. Both the BOJ and commentators on the Japanese economy have stressed the need for restructuring of the Japanese economy.[44] Indeed, the BOJ has continually argued that the economy cannot recover without restructuring and has worried that expansionary monetary policy was seen as an alternative to the needed restructuring and thus may be counterproductive. (This rhetoric seems to have stopped under Governor Fukui's leadership after March 2003.) Closing down inefficient firms and financial institutions may be exactly what the economy needs in the long run, but in the short-run it might lead to severe dislocations and unemployment. Indeed, this is probably why there has been so much resistance to the restructuring process on the part of Japanese politicians. Here is where a price-level target to raise the price level comes in. As we have seen, a higher price level would help restore financial and nonfinancial balance sheets and would help the financial system to start working again to allocate capital, which is critical to a restructuring process. Also, to the extent that a commitment

44. See, for example, Yamaguchi (1999).

to a higher price level by the monetary authorities helps raise aggregate demand, this would help cushion the short-term negative effects of the restructuring process. A price-level target that encourages more expansionary monetary policy is thus more sensibly viewed as a complement to restructuring rather than an impediment.

The analysis above suggests that a price-level target has many advantages when an economy is already experiencing deflation. Also in this case, the criticism that a price level might lead to an overshoot of the target that must be reversed, which could lead to deflation and an economic contraction, is no longer valid. When an economy is in a deflation trap and is far from the appropriate price-level target, the price level is necessarily lower than the target and so it promotes higher expected inflation which lowers real interest rates, and this then works in exactly the right direction to get the economy back on track. A price-level target thus dominates an inflation target in a deflationary environment.

Note that since October 1997, the CPI excluding fresh food has fallen by 3.7 percent to the present, while annual averages of the CPI has fallen by 2.5 percent between 1998 and 2003. This certainly understates the amount of deflation because, as is well known, measured inflation is likely to be an upward-biased measure of true inflation.[45] Most estimates of measurement error in CPI inflation in industrialized countries is around 1 percent and a similar finding has been found for Japan (Shiratsuka 1999). Hence we regard an annual increase in measured CPI at or around 1 percent as absolute price stability. So this would suggest that a target for the CPI would be 11.7 percent over current (March 2005) levels.[46] However, because the price-level target is a moving target it would continue to rise at the 1 percent rate and so the cumulative price increase when the target is reached would necessarily be higher in the future.

Let us illustrate our point for a hypothetical price target. Suppose that the price-level target was reached five years in the future, by March 2010. The cumulative increase of the CPI over the five years would need to be 17.4 percent (which includes the cumulative increase in the target over five years of 1 percent a year, 5.1 percent).[47] If this target is credible, this would mean that expected inflation would be 3.3 percent over the five years, and so seven with a nominal interest rate of zero, the real interest rate would fall to –3.3 percent, which would be highly stimulative, exactly along the lines that Eggertsson and Woodford (2003) suggest would be appropriate.

45. The CPI excluding fresh food was 101.1 in October 1997, which turned out to be a peak. In February 2004, the index became 97.5 (3.5 percent lower than six years ago). The annual average of 1998 was 100.4, while it was 98.0 in 2003. The CPIexFood level of 2003 was less than the peak by 2.4 percent.

46. $1.077 \times 1.037 = 1.117$, for example, an 11.7 percent increase.

47. $1.117 \times 1.051 = 1.174$, for example, a 17.4 percent increase.

But what should be done once the price-level target is achieved? One strand of the literature suggests that it would be optimal to continue with the price-level target. In models with a high degree of forward-looking behavior (e.g., Svensson 1999; Woodford 1999, 2003; Svensson and Woodford 2003; Clarida, Gali, and Gertler 1999; Dittmar, Gavin, and Kydland 1999, 2000; Dittmar and Gavin 2000; Vestin 2000; Eggertsson and Woodford 2003) a price-level target produces less output variance than an inflation target. Prices will have a long-run anchor. However, empirical evidence (for example, Fuhrer 1997) does not clearly support forward-looking expectations formation, and models with forward-looking behavior have counterintuitive properties that seem to be inconsistent with inflation dynamics (Estrella and Fuhrer 1998).

The other strand recommends that inflation targeting replace the price-level targeting once the price-level target is achieved. One reason, as argued by Fischer (1994), is that output variability will be less in inflation targeting in a conventional model, as opposed to a heavily forward-looking mode. A price-level target requires that an overshoot of the target must be reversed, and this might require contractionary monetary policy which, with sticky prices, could lead to a sharp downturn in the real economy. Ben Bernanke (2003) seems to have advanced this position, although he is somewhat agnostic about the switch. Another reason an inflation target may be more desirable after the price-level target is achieved is that it is a little easier to explain to the public, because it is not a moving target. Increased transparency and accountability is a highly desirable attribute for the conduct of monetary policy.

4.7.2 Nonconventional Monetary Policy

Critics of inflation targeting (Friedman 2003) have argued that the concept of "managing expectations" is problematic. Why would announcing an inflation or a price-level target pin down expectations? Aren't actions more important than words? Words by themselves are not enough, but neither are actions. This argues for the use of words plus actions in the conduct of monetary policy.

This raises the issue of what actions will actually influence the economy and help make a price-level or inflation target credible, particularly when the policy interest rate has hit a floor of zero? Once the short-term, policy interest rate is at the floor of zero, it clearly cannot be driven lower. Thus the conventional monetary-policy tool of manipulating the short-term, policy interest rate is no longer an option. Is the central bank powerless? What nonconventional policy measures can it take to affect the economy and thereby achieve its price-level or inflation target? We look at four types of measures below: (a) quantitative easing, (b) openmarket operations in long-term bonds, (c) foreign exchange rate intervention, and (d) open market purchases of private, real assets.

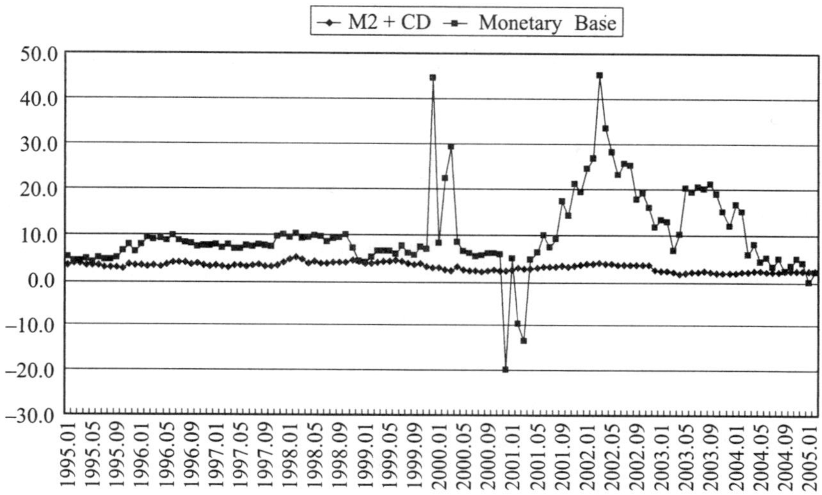

Fig. 4.6 M2 + CD and monetary base, 1995:1–2004:1

Quantitative Easing

The nonconventional monetary policy tried by the BOJ has been the so-called "quantitative easing." This involves an expansion of the monetary base, even when the policy interest rate cannot be driven any lower, either through open market operations on short-term government debt, outright purchase of long-term bonds (or equities), or through unsterilized purchases of foreign currency. The BOJ has been conducting such a policy since March 2001, and more aggressively since December 2001.

Figure 4.6 shows growth rates of monetary base (MB) and the money supply (M2 + CD, hereafter simply M2). MB had indeed expanded quickly from the end of 2001, but with little impact on M2. How to explain the deviation between MB and M2 is a challenge, and another is whether an expansion of MB without an expansion of M2 has positive impacts on the economy. The monetary base includes the amount of current account at the BOJ, the amount of excess liquidity in the system. In normal times, excess reserves would be unlikely to help stimulate the economy. However, an expansion of the monetary base might be beneficial even if it does not produce a significant increase in M2 when the interest rate is zero. First, ample liquidity in the system may help avoid a potential financial crisis that was a concern in 2002–2003. Second, liquidity may encourage financial institutions to take more risks in portfolio management, in particular taking positions in long-term bonds, equities, and foreign bonds, any of which would contribute to stimulating the economy indirectly. The economic recovery in 2003 may be partly due to ample liquidity in the system.

However, the data do not look favorable to this approach. The monetary base has increased by 20–40 percent from 2002 to 2003 and yet deflation has not stopped. One problem with coming to this conclusion based on the evidence from Japan is that, as we have seen in the earlier section of this chapter, the BOJ has created market expectations that even when it pursued expansionary monetary policy for a time, it would soon reverse it. Then it is no surprise that quantitative easing would not work.

In addition, there are good theoretical reasons why quantitative easing might be ineffective. The conventional liquidity-trap analysis suggests that when the short-term interest rate hits a floor of zero, short-term bonds become a perfect substitute for money and so expanding the monetary base will have no effect on the economy. Eggertsson and Woodford (2003) show that this result can even hold if short-term bonds and money do not become perfect substitutes, although this conclusion still is based on the specific assumptions of their model. However, as they emphasize, quantitative easing might help stimulate the economy if it provided a signal that the monetary base would be higher than it otherwise would be once the deflation is over. This is the position taken by Auerbach and Obstfeld (2003).

Given the theoretical arguments against its being effective and the fact that quantitative easing has not worked to stimulate the economy and stop deflation in Japan, there is clearly a strong case that the BOJ needs to look at other approaches to conducting monetary policy.

Open Market Operations in Long-Term Bonds

Alternative nonconventional monetary policies involve the monetary authorities in conducting open market operations in other assets besides short-term bonds. The most conventional of these is a shift toward central bank purchases of long-term rather than short-term bonds. Since long-term interest rates are more likely to figure in household and business decisions about spending, it seems that open market purchase of these bonds might succeed in lowering long-term interest rates, thereby stimulating the economy. However, in order for purchase of long-term bonds to work there would have to be significant portfolio-balance effects, so that a shift in the supply of long-term versus short-term government debt in the hands of the public as a result of the open market purchases would affect risk (term) premiums and so result in a fall in long-term rates. However, the evidence that risk (term) premiums can be affected by changing the supply of long-term bonds relative to short-term bonds in the hands of the public is, unfortunately, far from clear. One episode in which this was tried was the so-called "Operation Twist" in the United States in the early 1960s and it has generally been viewed as a failure with only a very small effect—if any—on the relative interest rates of long versus short-term bonds (see Meulendyke [1998] for a summary of the literature).

Bernanke (2002) has suggested that the apparent failure of "Operation Twist" does not mean that the central bank could not drive long-term bond rates down as long as the central bank announced that it would peg interest rates on long-term bonds at a very low interest rate (possibly zero) and stood ready to purchase any amounts of these bonds at this low rate. This peg could certainly work because the commitment is easily verifiable since the price and interest rates on long-term bonds are immediately known. However, this could require the central bank to purchase the entire stock of long-term bonds which it might not be fully comfortable about doing.

Clearly another way for the central bank to lower long-term bond rates (Orphanides and Wieland 2000) is to convince the markets that it will continue to pursue a zero interest rate policy (ZIRP) for a considerable time even after the deflation is over. Then, as is suggested by the expectations hypothesis of the term structure, because long-term bond rates are an average of the expected future short-term rates, long-term interest rates would necessarily fall. Indeed, this strategy is complimentary to Bernanke's (2002) because it is a way of committing to more expansionary policy in the future even after the economy has bounced back.

The BOJ's announcements about clarifying the conditions of exit from the ZIRP have some elements of this strategy. The BOJ has effectively announced that it will not reverse the ZIRP policy until there is clear-cut evidence that the deflation is over and that it is unlikely to recur in the future. However, this is a far weaker commitment than the strategy above suggests. It requires a commitment to stay with ZIRP not only until the deflation is clearly over, but until there is a prospect of achieving the price-level target described above in which the CPI would have to rise substantially to get to the target.[48] There is still the problem that an announcement of this type might not be believed by the markets because of the past behavior of the central bank, and this is clearly a problem for the BOJ because of the policies under Governor Hayami where the ZIRP was reversed as soon as the economy began to recover. However, this is where the purchase of long-term bonds might help. The central bank could buy substantial amounts of these long-term bonds as a signal of its confidence that their price will remain high because ZIRP will be continued well after the deflation is over. Buying long-term bonds would also provide incentives for the central bank to stick with the ZIRP policy after the deflation is over because premature abandonment of ZIRP would lead to losses on the long-term bonds that it has bought.

Foreign Exchange Intervention

Depreciation of the currency provides an additional way of exiting from a deflation trap. A fall in the value of the domestic currency makes imports more expensive and exports cheaper. The result is expenditure switching in

48. In order not to overshoot the target, ZIRP would have to be removed a little while before the target is reached, but for all practical purposes, this would be a commitment to keep ZIRP for a substantial period after the deflation is over.

which exports rise and imports fall, thereby increasing the demand for domestically produced goods, which stimulates aggregate demand. Intervention in the foreign exchange market, the selling of yen and purchase of foreign currency, has thus been suggested as a powerful way of getting the Japanese economy moving again (Bernanke 2000; McCallum 2000a, b, 2002, 2003; Meltzer 2001; Orphanides and Wieland 2000; Svensson 2001, 2003). Indeed, in recent years the Ministry of Finance and the BOJ intervened in the foreign exchange market to keep the yen from appreciating, but have not engineered a depreciation of the yen.

One problem with this transmission mechanism is that it also requires that portfolio-balance effects are operational. The exchange rate intervention in which the purchase of foreign-denominated assets are bought with domestic currency, thereby increasing the supply of domestic currency-denominated assets relative to foreign-denominated assets, only affects the exchange rate if domestic and foreign assets are imperfect substitutes. As was the case for short-term versus long-term bonds, the evidence for portfolio-balance effects are not strong (see the survey in Sarno and Taylor 2001).

However, here is where a price-level target and the management of expectations can again come to the rescue. Svensson (2001, 2003) has advocated that, along with an announcement of a price-level target along the lines we have described above, the government and/or the central bank (depending on who controls foreign exchange intervention) commit to an exchange rate peg that is consistent with that price-level target. This involves a commitment to an immediate depreciation of the domestic currency, which would then be allowed to appreciate at the rate of the foreign interest rate differential (so that the expected return on foreign and domestic assets is equalized). The peg would then be abandoned once the price-level target has been achieved and a price-level or inflation-targeting regime would be put into place. Committing to the peg is also a commitment to the higher price-level target and continued expansionary monetary policy even after the deflation is over. Thus it solves the commitment problem described above.

Since the policy calls for a substantial depreciation of the domestic currency from current levels, it would require that the government or central bank stand ready to buy large amounts of foreign-denominated assets to ensure that they are a good investment relative to domestic assets. This would just mean an accumulation of international reserves, which is always feasible. (This is in contrast to a case in which a country wants to prop up the value of its currency and thus must sell foreign assets, thereby losing international reserves, which may run out and thus force the abandonment of the peg.) The commitment to a peg also has the advantage that it provides incentives for the central bank and the government to stick with the peg until the price-level target is achieved: early abandonment would lead to an appreciation of the domestic currency, which would result in substantial losses on the holdings of international reserves.

Although we agree with Svensson that his "foolproof way" to escape the deflation trap would work, we do have our doubts about this strategy. Such a strategy suffers from two difficulties. First, the country's trading partners would be likely to be up in arms if an exchange-rate peg of this type were announced. We have seen strong U.S. complaints against the Chinese peg of the yuan at, most likely, an undervalued rate, and we expect that this outcry would be even harsher if Japan adopted Svensson's suggestion. The outcome might be trade sanctions and a rise in protectionism that could be disastrous for the world trading system.

A second problem is that adoption of an exchange rate peg might cause a shift of the nominal anchor away from the price-level or inflation target to the exchange rate. For example, as part of its inflation-targeting regime, Israel has had an intermediate target of an exchange rate band around a crawling peg, whose rate of crawl is set in a forward-looking manner by deriving it from the inflation target for the coming year. Even though the Bank of Israel downplayed the exchange rate target relative to the inflation target over time, it did slow the bank's efforts to win support for disinflation and lowering of the inflation targets (see Bernanke, Laubach, Mishkin, and Posen 1999). A recent example of this problem has occurred in Hungary (Jonas and Mishkin 2004), which has an exchange rate band as part of its inflation-targeting regime. In January 2003, the forint appreciated to the upper end of the band, and speculation about the revaluation of the parity resulted in a sharp acceleration of capital inflows that forced the National Bank of Hungary to respond by cutting interest rates by 2 percentage points and intervening heavily in the foreign exchange market. The National Bank of Hungary is reported to have bought more than 5 billion euros, increasing international reserves by 50 percent and base money by 70 percent. (See J. P. Morgan [2003].) Even though the National Bank of Hungary subsequently began to sterilize this huge injection of liquidity, market participants then assumed that maintaining the exchange rate band would have a priority over the inflation target and expected inflation in 2003 to exceed the National Bank of Hungary's inflation target by 5 percentage points.[49]

A third problem with an exchange rate target is that it can induce the wrong policy response when a country is faced with real shocks, such as a terms-of-trade shock. Two graphic examples occurred in New Zealand and Chile in the late 1990s. By early 1997, the Reserve Bank institutionalized this focus by adopting as its primary indicator of monetary policy at Mon-

49. Analysts have interpreted this as evidence that the National Bank of Hungary is determined to maintain the currency band even at the cost of temporary higher inflation. See Jonas and Mishkin (2004).

etary Conditions Index (MCI) similar to that developed by the Bank of Canada. The idea behind the MCI, which is a weighted average of the exchange rate and a short-term interest rate, is that both interest rates and exchange rates on average have offsetting impacts on inflation. When the exchange rate falls, this usually leads to higher inflation in the future, and so interest rates need to rise to offset the upward pressure on inflation. However, the offsetting effects of interest rates and exchange rates on inflation depend on the nature of the shocks to the exchange rates. If the exchange rate depreciation comes from portfolio considerations, then it does lead to higher inflation and needs to be offset by an interest rate rise. However, if the reason for the exchange rate depreciation is a real shock, such as a negative terms-of-trade shock, which decreases the demand for a country's exports, then the situation is entirely different. The negative terms-of-trade shock reduces aggregate demand and is thus likely to be deflationary. The correct interest rate response is then a decline in interest rates, not a rise as the MCI suggests.

With the negative terms-of-trade shock in 1997, the adoption of the MCI in 1997 led to exactly the wrong monetary-policy response to East Asian crisis. With depreciation setting in after the crisis began in July 1997 after the devaluation of the Thai baht, the MCI began a sharp decline, indicating that the Reserve Bank needed to raise interest rates, which it did by over 200 basis points. The result was very tight monetary policy, with the overnight cash rate exceeding 9 percent by June of 1998. Because the depreciation was due to a substantial, negative terms-of-trade shock that decreased aggregate demand, the tightening of monetary policy, not surprisingly, lead to a severe recession and an undershoot of the inflation-target range with actual deflation occurring in 1999.[50] The Reserve Bank of New Zealand did eventually realize its mistake and reversed course, sharply lowering interest rates beginning in July 1998 after the economy had entered a recession, but by then it was too late.

Chile's inflation-targeting regime also included a focus on limiting exchange rate fluctuations by having an exchange rate band with a crawling peg that was (loosely) tied to lagged domestic inflation. This focus on the exchange rate induced a serious policy mistake in 1998 because the central bank was afraid it might lose credibility in the face of the financial turmoil if it allowed the exchange rate to depreciate after what had taken place in financial markets after the East Asian crisis and the Russian meltdown. Thus instead of easing monetary policy in the face of the negative terms-of-trade shock, the central bank raised interest rates sharply and even narrowed its exchange rate band. The result was that the inflation target was undershot and the economy entered a recession for the first time in the 1990s. With

50. The terms-of-trade shock, however, was not the only negative shock the New Zealand economy faced during that period. Its farm sector experienced a severe drought, which also hurt the economy. Thus, a mistake in monetary policy was not the only source of the recession. Bad luck played a role too. See Drew and Orr (1999) and Brash (2000).

this outcome, the central bank came under strong criticism for the first time since it had adopted its inflation-targeting regime in 1990, weakening support for the independence of the central bank and its inflation-targeting regime. During 1999, the central bank did reverse course, easing monetary policy by lowering interest rates and allowing the peso to decline.

The contrast of the experience of New Zealand and Chile during this period with that of Australia, another small open economy with an inflation-targeting regime, is striking. Prior to adoption of their inflation-targeting regime in 1994, the Reserve Bank of Australia had adopted a policy of allowing the exchange rate to fluctuate without interference, particularly if the source of the exchange rate change was a real shock, like a terms-of-trade shock. Thus when faced with the devaluation in Thailand in July 1997, the Reserve Bank recognized that it would face a substantial negative terms-of-trade shock because of the large component of its foreign trade conducted with the Asian region and that it should not fight the depreciation of the Australian dollar that would inevitably result.[51] Thus in contrast to New Zealand, it immediately lowered the overnight cash rate by 50 basis points to 5 percent and kept it near this level until the end of 1998, when it was lowered again by another 25 basis points.

A more subtle approach to exchange rate intervention can avoid some of the problems of an exchange rate peg. Intervention in the foreign exchange market to depreciate the domestic currency could be an important element of nonconventional monetary policy of raising price-level expectations, without announcing a precise exchange rate target. Instead the central bank and the government could emphasize that exchange rate interventions, along with other measures, are being conducted as a method of pursuing expansionary monetary policy and to achieve a higher price level and a stronger economy. These interventions would then be unsterilized in order to make clear that their primary purpose is to produce expansionary monetary policy that raises the price level and is not focused on a target level of the exchange rate.[52] The communication strategy would also be helped by having the government and the central bank emphasize that the

51. See MacFarlane (1999) and Stevens (1999).

52. Under the Hayami regime, the BOJ resisted the suggestion that interventions be unsterilized. Since interventions are decided and conducted by the Ministry of Finance, making interventions unsterilized was seen as a dictation of monetary policy by the Ministry of Finance—a violation to independence. In 2003, under the Fukui regime, interventions became more frequent on the part of the Ministry of Finance, and quantitative easing was accelerated on the part of the BOJ. From January 2003 to December 2003, about 15 trillion yen of interventions increased the yen in the market in exchange for an increase in inventory of foreign currencies, while the ceiling of the BOJ current account target was raised by 12 trillion yen. Deputy Governor Iwata in his reply to a question in the press conference on October 1, 2003 acknowledged that these two actions, ex post, were equivalent to unsterilized interventions, although "it must be a coincident." This is a much more nuanced statement than a typical reaction during the Hayami regime (press interview, October 1, 2003, available in Japanese text through the BOJ homepage at [http://www.boj.or.jp/press/03/kk0310a.htm], translated by one of the authors of this paper).

exchange rate interventions to escape from the deflation trap would eventually help encourage purchases of foreign goods and would eventually be highly beneficial for the country's trading partners.

At the zero interest rate, the differences between sterilized and unsterilized intervention, namely the interest rate channel, disappear. However, even at the zero interest rate, we believe that the unsterilized intervention is more stimulative than sterilized intervention, primarily due to a signaling effect. Unsterilized intervention provides one more instrument to achieve quantitative easing, and conducting unsterilized intervention will make the central bank look more willing to commit to continuing ZIRP in the future.

Open Market Purchase of Private, Real Assets

An even more radical step for monetary authorities would be to purchase real assets, such as stocks, corporate bonds, or real estate. Purchase of these assets would raise their prices directly and would lead to expansion in aggregate demand though a number of channels of monetary transmission (Mishkin 1996). Purchase of real assets would also directly help restore balance sheets in the economy and help get the financial system working again, which we have seen is crucial to recovery if the country finds itself in a situation like Japan's.

However, central bank purchase of these assets is not without problems. Government purchase of private assets can be highly politicized. Which assets should the central bank buy? Different elements in the private sector would lobby for purchase of the assets that would make them profits. Some of this problem could be mitigated by the central bank buying broad-based bundles of assets or market indexes so that specific private firms do not benefit over others. However, there is still the question of how much real estate should be bought versus stocks, or how much corporate bonds versus equities. Decisions on what to buy would have important distributional consequences, which would put the central bank under intense political pressure. Not only might this result in distortionary decisions, but it could politicize the central bank and interfere with the independence that this institution has worked so hard to get.

Another problem with central bank purchase of private assets is that it involves the government in ownership of the private sector. The trend in recent years has been toward privatization because it is believed that the private sector has better incentives to produce efficiently than does the government sector. Having substantial purchases of private assets by the central bank, which after all is a government entity, goes against this trend. Maybe the problems of central bank ownership of private assets can be minimized by announcing that the central bank will have no involvement in running of the companies or real estate that it has taken a position in, but political pressures may make this hard to do.

If central bank purchases of private, real assets are sizeable, there could be adverse consequences both for the central bank and the economy. However, if nothing else worked, then this more radical step might be necessary as a way of stimulating the economy and achieving a higher price level.

Our discussion here has indicated that none of the nonconventional monetary-policy strategies are without their problems. There is thus an argument for what might be crudely described as a "kitchen sink" or "throw it against the wall and see if it sticks" approach. Because it would not be clear how well the different approaches would work, some or all of them could be tried to see which ones work best. One concern might be that the uncertainty about the impact of the different approaches might make it harder to be sure of what the outcome of using them might be. One outcome would be paralysis and then not to try any of them.

There are two responses to these concerns. The first is that having a clear-cut price-level/inflation target to pin down expectations can make it highly likely that less conventional tools of monetary policy can achieve the goal of price stability and that inflation would not spin out of control. In recent years we have seen major successes in the ability of monetary policy to control inflation in many industrialized countries. We would argue that this is not because central banks have become so much more knowledgeable about the transmission mechanisms of monetary policy. What has changed in recent years is that central banks in industrialized countries have been able to put much stronger nominal anchors in place. The result is greatly improved performance on both the inflation and output fronts. One method has been to adopt inflation targets, as in New Zealand, Canada, the United Kingdom, Sweden, and Australia, and to some extent in the European Monetary Union.[53] Alternatively, a strong nominal anchor can be put into place without a formal inflation target through direct communication with the public about the commitment to price stability and actions that are consistent with it. This is the strategy pursued by the Federal Reserve, which has as strong a nominal anchor as inflation-targeting, central banks although it is embodied in an individual, Alan Greenspan (Mishkin 2000). Adopting a price-level target and then possibly moving to an inflation target would go a long way to ensuring an escape from the deflation trap, while making it highly unlikely that inflation would spin out of control thereafter.

4.8 Concluding Remarks

This chapter reviews the experience of Japanese monetary policy over the last two decades with an emphasis on the experience of deflation from

53. The European Central Bank does not officially call their monetary policy strategy "inflation targeting," but it is pretty close: there is a strong commitment to price stability and an explicit inflation goal of "less than but close to 2%" has been announced.

the mid-1990s. The cost of deflation is quite high, and prolonged deflation makes getting out of it more difficult. A key element in escaping deflation is the management of expectations and we have seen that price-level and inflation targeting attempt to achieve exactly this. Also, because the credibility of price-level and inflation targets require actions, nonconventional policy measures become relevant when prices are declining and the zero lower bound on interest rates means that the overnight interest rate can no longer be used as the instrument of monetary policy.

We are quite critical of the conduct of the BOJ monetary policy from 1998 to 2003. The Bank of Japan's rhetoric was not helpful in fighting deflation, and the interest rate hike in August 2000 amid deflation was a serious mistake. Although rhetoric has improved since 2003 under the new Governor Fukui, more is needed to get out of deflation completely. We surveyed the literature on cost of deflation, the optimal level of inflation, and relative merits of price-level versus inflation targets. A key to curing deflation is management of expectations, and here a history-dependent policy involving a price-level target can help. However, because actions speak louder than words, management of expectations also involves nonconventional monetary policies. Admittedly, there is uncertainty about how these policies would work, but a combination of them can help the Japanese economy escape its deflationary trap.

References

Ahearne, Alan, Joseph Gagnon, Jane Haltmaier, Steve Kamin, and others. 2002. Preventing deflation: Lessons from Japan's experiences in the 1990s. Board of Governors, International Finance. Discussion Paper No. 729, June. Washington, DC: Board of Governors.

Akerlof, George, William Dickens, and George Perry. 1996. The macroeconomics of low inflation. *Brookings Papers on Economic Activity*, Issue no. 1:1–59.

Atkeson, Andrew, and Patrick J. Kehoe. 2004. Deflation and depression: Is there an empirical link? NBER Working Paper no. 10268. Cambridge, MA: National Bureau of Economic Research, January.

Auerbach, Alan J., and Maurice Obstfeld. 2003. The case for open market purchases in a liquidity trap. NBER Working Paper no. 9814. Cambridge, MA: National Bureau of Economic Research, July.

Bank of Japan. 2000. On Price Stability. [http://www.boj.or.jp/en/seisaku/05/seisak_f.htm]

Battini, N., and T. Yates. 1999. Hybrid inflation and price level targeting. Bank of England. Mimeo.

Beebe, Jack H. 2001. Comments on Oda, Nobuyuki and Okina, Kunio, "Further monetary easing policies under the non-negativity constraints of nominal interest rates: summary of the discussion based on Japan's experience." *Monetary and Economic Studies* 19 (S-1): 365–8. Bank of Japan.

Berg, Claes, and Lars Jonung. 1999. Pioneering price level targeting: The Swedish experience 1931–1937. *Journal of Monetary Economics* 43:525–51.

Bernanke, Ben S. 1983. Nonmonetary effects of the financial crisis in the propagation of the Great Depression. *American Economic Review* 73:257–76.

———. 2000. Japanese monetary policy: A case of self-induced paralysis? In *Japan's financial crisis and its parallels to U.S. experience,* ed. Ryoichi Mikitani and Adam S. Posen, 149–66. Washington, DC: Institute for International Economics.

———. 2002. Deflation: Making sure "it" doesn't happen here. Remarks before the National Economists' Club, 21 November, Washington, DC.

———. 2003. Some thoughts on monetary policy in Japan. Speech before the Japan Society of Monetary Economics, 31 May, Tokyo, Japan. Available at [http://www.federalreserve.gov/boarddocs/speeches/2003/20030531/default.htm]

Bernanke, Ben S., and Mark Gertler. 1999. Monetary policy and asset price volatility. *Federal Reserve Bank of Kansas City, Economic Review* 4th Quarter: 17–51. [Also reprinted in Federal Reserve Bank of Kansas City, New Challenges for Monetary Policy: 77–128.] Kansas City, MO.

Bernanke, Ben S., Thomas Laubach, Frederic S. Mishkin, and Adam S. Posen. 1999. *Inflation targeting: Lessons from the international experience.* Princeton, NJ: Princeton University Press.

Bernanke, Ben S., and Frederic S. Mishkin. 1997. Inflation targeting: A new framework for monetary policy? *Journal of Economic Perspectives* 11 (2): 97–116.

Black, Richard, Tiff Macklem, and David Rose. 1998. On policy rules for price stability. *Price stability, inflation targets and monetary policy.* Proceedings of a Conference held by Bank of Canada, May 1997, Ottawa, Canada: 411–61.

Blinder, Alan S. 1998. *Central banking in theory and practice.* Cambridge, MA: MIT Press.

Brash, Donald T. 2000. Inflation targeting in New Zealand, 1988–2000. Speech to the Trans-Tasman Business Cycle, Melbourne, February 9.

Boskin, Michael J., Ellen R. Dulberger, Robert J. Gordon, Zvi Griliches, and Dale W. Jorgenson. 1996. Toward a more accurate measure of the cost of living. Final Report to the Senate Finance Committee, December. Washington, DC: U.S. Government. Available at [http://www.ssa.gov/history/reports/boskinrpt.html]

Card, D. and D. Hyslop. 1997. Does inflation "grease the wheels of the labor market"? In *Reducing inflation: Motivation and strategy,* ed. C. D. Romer and H. D. Romer, 71–114. Chicago: University of Chicago Press.

Cargill, Thomas, Michael Hutchison, and Takatoshi Ito. 1997. *The political economy of Japanese monetary policy.* Cambridge, MA: MIT Press.

———. 2000. *Financial policy and central banking in Japan.* Cambridge, MA: MIT Press.

Cecchetti, Stephen G., Hans Genberg, John Lipsky, and Sushil Wadhwani. 2000. *Asset prices and central bank policy,* Geneva Reports on the World Economy no. 2. Geneva: International Center for Monetary and Banking Studies.

Clarida, Richard J., Jordi Gali, and Mark Gertler. 1998. Monetary rules in practice: Some international evidence. *European Economic Review* 42:1033–67.

———. 1999. The science of monetary policy: A new-Keynesian perspective. *Journal of Economic Literature* 37:1661–707.

Clouse, James, Dale Henderson, Athanasios Orphanides, David Small, and Peter Tinsley. 2000. Monetary policy when the nominal short-term interest rate is zero. Board of Governors of the Federal Reserve System, International Finance. Discussion Paper no. 729. Washington, DC: Board of Governors of the Federal Reserve System.

Crawford, A., and A. Harrison. 2000. Testing for downward rigidity in nominal wage rates. In *Price stability, inflation targets and monetary policy,* 179–218. Proceedings of a conference held by the Bank of Canada, May 1997 Ottawa: Bank of Canada.

Dittmar, Robert and William Gavin. 2000. What do New-Keynesian Phillips curves imply for price-level targeting? *Federal Reserve Bank of St. Louis Review* 82 (2): 21–30.

Ditmar, Robert, William T. Gavin, and Finn E. Kydland. 1999. The inflation-output variability tradeoff and price level targets. *Federal Reserve Bank of St. Louis Review*: 23–31.

Drew, Aaron, and Adrian Orr. 1999. The reserve bank's role in the recent business cycle: Actions and evolution. *Reserve Bank of New Zealand Bulletin,* 62 (1): 5–24.

Eggertsson, Gauti. 2003. Fighting deflation at zero nominal interest rates: Committing to being irresponsible. IMF Working Paper no. WP/03/64. March 1.

Eggertsson, Gauti B., and Michael Woodford. 2003. Optimal monetary policy in a liquidity trap. NBER Working Paper no. 9968. Cambridge, MA: National Bureau of Economic Research, September.

Erceg, Christopher, and Andrew Levin. 2001. Imperfect credibility and inflation persistence. Finance and Economics Discussion Series no. 2001-45. Washington, DC: Federal Reserve Board, October.

Estrella, Arturo, and Jeffrey Fuhrer. 1998. Dynamic inconsistencies: Counterfactual implications of a class of rational expectations models. Federal Reserve Bank of Boston. Working Paper no. 98/05, July. Boston, MA.

Fares, Jean, and Thomas Lemieux. 2000. Downward nominal-wage rigidity: A critical assessment and some new evidence from Canada. In *Price stability and the long-run target for monetary policy,* 3–42. Proceedings of a seminar held by the Bank of Canada, June 2000. Ottawa: Bank of Canada.

Feldstein, Martin. 1997. Capital income taxes and the benefits of price stability. NBER Working Paper no. 6200. Cambridge, MA: National Bureau of Economic Research, September.

Fischer, Irving. 1933. The debt-deflation theory of great depressions. *Econometrica* 1:337–57.

Fischer, Stanley. 1994. Modern central banking. In *The future of Central Banking,* ed. Forest Capie, Charles Goodhart, Stanley Fischer, and Norbert Schnadt, 262–308. Cambridge, UK: Cambridge University Press.

Friedman, Benjamin. 2003. Discussion of "inflation targeting": A critical view. presented at the Federal Reserve Bank of St. Louis Annual Conference, "Inflation Targeting: Prospects and Problems," October 16–17. St. Louis, MO.

Fuhrer, Jeffrey C. 1997. The (un)importance of forward-looking behavior in price specifications. *Journal of Money, Credit, and Banking* 29 (3): 338–50.

Fuhrer, Jeffrey C., and Brian Madigan. 1997. Towards a compact, empirically-verified rational expectations model for monetary policy analysis. *Carnegie-Rochester Conference Series on Public Policy* 47:197–230.

Fujiki, Hiroshi, Kunio Okina, and Shigenori Shiratsuka. 2001. Monetary policy under zero interest rate: Viewpoints of central bank economists. Bank of Japan, *Monetary and Economic Studies* February: 89–130.

Fukui, Toshihiko. 2003. Challenges for monetary policy in Japan. Speech at the Spring Meeting of the Japan Society of Monetary Economics, June 1, Tokyo, Japan.

Gaspar, Vitor, and Frank Smets. 2000. Price level stability: Some issues. European Central Bank. Mimeo.

Goodfriend, Marvin. 2001. Financial stability, deflation, and monetary policy. *Bank of Japan, Monetary and Economic Studies* 19 (S-1): 143–76.

Greenspan, Alan. 2002. Issues for monetary policy. Remarks by Chairman Alan Greenspan before the Economic Club of New York, New York City.

———. 2004. Risk and uncertainty in monetary policy. Remarks by Chairman

Alan Greenspan at the meeting of the American Economic Association, San Diego, California, January 3.

Groshen, Erica L., and Mark E. Schweitzer. 1996. The effects of inflation on wage adjustments in firm-level data: Grease or sand? *Federal Reserve Bank of New York Staff Reports,* No. 9. New York: New York.

———. 1999. Identifying inflation's grease and sand effects in the labor market. In *The costs and benefits of price stability,* ed. Martin Feldstein, 273–308. Chicago: University of Chicago Press.

Harrigan, James, and Kenneth Kuttner. 2004. Lost decade in translation: Has the U.S. learned from Japan's post-bubble mistakes? Presented at the Solution Conference, Tokyo, June.

Hoshi, Takeo, and Anil Kashyap. 2005. Solutions to the Japanese banking crisis: What might work and what definitely will fail. In *Reviving Japan's Economy,* ed. Ito, Patrick, and Weinstein, 147–95. Cambridge, MA: MIT Press.

Hunter, William C., George G. Kaufman, and Michael Pomerleano. 2003. *Asset price bubbles: The implications for monetary, regulatory, and international policies.* Cambridge, MA: MIT Press.

Ito, Takatoshi. 1992. *The Japanese economy.* Cambridge, MA: MIT Press.

———. 1999. A target for the bank of Japan. *Financial Times,* October 19.

———. 2000. *Nihon ni okeru inflation targeting seisaku* [Inflation targeting policy in Japan]. In *Zero kinri to nihon keizai* [Zero interest rate and the Japanese economy], ed. Mitsuhiro Fukao and Hiroshi Yoshikawa, 77–127. Tokyo: Nihon Keizai Shinbun Pub.

———. 2001. *Inflation targeting* (in Japanese). Tokyo: Nihon Keizai Shinbun Pub.

———. 2003. Looking forward on monetary and supervision policies to protect against bubbles. In *Asset price bubbles: The implications for monetary, regulatory, and international policies,* ed. W. C. Hunter, G. G. Kaufman, and M. Pomerleano, 547–52. Chicago: MIT Press.

———. 2004. Inflation targeting and Japan: Why has the bank of Japan not adopted inflation targeting? In *The future of inflation targeting,* ed. Christopher Kent and Simon Guttman, 220–67. Sydney: Reserve Bank of Australia.

Ito, Takatoshi, and Kimie Harada. 2000. Japan premium and stock prices: Two mirrors of Japanese banking crises. NBER Working Paper no. 7997. Cambridge, MA: National Bureau of Economic Research, November.

Ito, Takatoshi, and Tokuo Iwaisako. 1996. Explaining asset bubbles in Japan. The Bank of Japan, *Monetary and Economic Studies* 14, July: 143–93.

Ito, Takatoshi, and Tomoko Hayashi. 2004. Inflation targeting in Asia. Hong Kong Institute for Monetary Research, Occasional Paper, No. 1, March.

Iwata, Kazumasa. 2002. *Deflation spiral hassei no kanousei* [in Japanese, trans. Possibility of having a deflation spiral]. In R. Komiya, Kinyu Seisaku rongi no Soten [in Japanese, trans. Issues in the monetary policy debate]. Tokyo: Nihon Keizai Shinbun, pub.: 121–56.

Iwata, Kikuo. 2001. *Deflation no keizaigaku,* [in Japanese, trans. Economics of deflation]. Tokyo: Toyo Keizei Shinpo, Pub.

———. 2001. *Deflation no keizaigaku* [in Japanese, trans. Economics of deflation]. Tokyo: Toyo Keizai Shinpo, Pub.

———. 2002. *Yosou keisei ni hataraki kakeru kinyu seisakuo.* [in Japanese, trans. Recommending monetary policy to affect inflation expectation]. In R. Komiya, *Kinyu seisaku rongi no soten* [in Japanese, trans. Issues in the monetary policy debate]. Tokyo: Nihon Keizai Shinbun, pub.: 391–418.

Jinushi, Toshiki, Yoshihiro Kuroki, and Ryuzo Miyao. 2000. Monetary policy in Japan since the late 19870s: Delayed policy actions and some explanations. In

Japan's financial crisis and its parallels to U.S. experience, ed. Mikitani and Posen, chapter 6. Washington, DC: Institute for International Economics.

Jonas, Jiri, and Frederic S. Mishkin. 2004. Inflation targeting in transition countries: Experience and prospects. In *Inflation targeting,* ed. Michael Woodford (with Jiri Jonas). Chicago: University of Chicago Press, forthcoming.

Kamada, Koichiro. 2004. Real-time estimation of the output gap in Japan and its usefulness for inflation forecasting and policy making. Bank of Japan. Mimeo. Available at [http://www.e.u-tokyo.ac.jp/cirje/research/workshops/macro/macro paper04/kamada.pdf]. April 16.

King, Mervyn. 1996. How should central banks reduce inflation? Conceptual issues. In *Achieving price stability,* Federal Reserve Bank of Kansas City, 53–91. Kansas City, MO.

———. 1999. Challenges for monetary policy: New and old. In *New challenges for monetary policy,* Federal Reserve Bank of Kansas City, 11–57. Kansas City, MO.

Krugman, Paul. 1998. It's baack! Japan's slump and the return of the liquidity trap. *Brookings Papers on Economic Activity* Issue no. 2:137–87.

Kuroda, Sachiko, and Isamu Yamamoto. 2003a. Are Japanese nominal wages downwardly rigid? (Part I): Examinations of nominal wage change distributions. *Monetary and Economic Studies* 21 (2): 1–30. Tokyo: Bank of Japan.

———. 2003b. Are Japanese nominal wages downwardly rigid? (Part II): Examinations using a friction model. Bank of Japan, *Monetary and Economic Studies* 2 (21): 31–68.

———. 2003c. The impact of downward nominal wage rigidity on the unemployment rate: Quantitative evidence from Japan. Bank of Japan, *Monetary and Economic Studies* 21 (4): 57–85.

Kuttner, Kenneth N., and Adam S. Posen. 2004. The difficulty of discerning what's too tight: Taylor rules and Japanese monetary policy. *The North American Journal of Economics and Finance* 15 (1): 53–74.

Lebow, David E., Brian Saks, and Beth A. Wilson. 1999. Downward nominal wage rigidity: Evidence from the employment cost index. Feds Working Paper no. 1999–31. Washington, DC: Board of Governors of the Federal Reserve System, July.

Lebow, David E., David J. Stockton, and W. L. Wascher. 1995. Inflation, nominal wage rigidity and the efficiency of the labor market. Finance and Economics Discussion Series, Working Paper no. 94-45. Board of Governors of the Federal Reserve Board, October.

Macfarlane, Ian J. 1999. Statement to parliamentary committee. *Reserve Bank of Australia Bulletin,* January: 16–20.

McCallum, Bennett T. 1999. Issues in the design of monetary policy rules. In *Handbook of macroeconomics,* ed. John B. Taylor and Michael Woodford. North Holland, Amsterdam, forthcoming.

———. 2000a. Theoretical analysis regarding a zero lower bound on nominal interest rates. *Journal of Money, Credit and Banking* 32 (2): 879–904.

———. 2000b. Alternative monetary policy rules: A comparison with historical settings for the United States, the United Kingdom, and Japan. Federal Reserve Bank of Richmond, *Economic Quarterly* 86, Winter: 49–79.

———. 2002. Inflation targeting and the liquidity trap. In *Inflation targeting: Design, performance, challenges,* ed. N. Loayza and R. Soto, 395–437. Central Bank of Chile.

———. 2003. Japanese monetary policy 1991–2001. *Economic Quarterly* 89 (1): 1–31. Richmond, VA: Federal Reserve Bank of Richmond.

McLean, D., and H. Pioro. 2000. Price level targeting—The role of credibility. Paper

presented at the Bank of Canada Conference, Price Stability and the Long-Run Target for Monetary Policy, June 8–9, Ottawa, Bank of Canada, 153–200. Available at [http://www.bankofcanada.ca/en/conference/con2000/con2000.html]
McKinnon, Ronald I. and Kenichi Ohno. 1997. *Resolving economic conflict between the United States and Japan.* MIT Press.
Meltzer, Allan H. 1995. Monetary, credit and other transmission mechanism processes: A monetarist perspective. *Journal of Economic Perspectives* 9:49–72.
———. 1998. Time to print money. *Financial Times,* July 17.
———. 2001. Monetary transmission at low inflation: Some clues from Japan in the 1990s. Bank of Japan, *Monetary and Economic Studies* 19 (S-1): 13–34.
Meulendyke, Ann-Marie. 1998. *U.S. monetary policy and financial markets.* New York: Federal Reserve Bank of New York.
Mishkin, Frederic S. 1978. The household balance-sheet and the Great Depression. *Journal of Economic History* 38, December: 918–37.
———. 1991. Asymmetric information and financial crises: A historical perspective. In *Financial markets and financial crises,* ed. R. Glenn Hubbard, 69–108. Chicago: University of Chicago Press.
———. 1996. The channels of monetary transmission: Lessons for monetary policy. *Banque De France Bulletin Digest* No. 27:33–44. Paris: Bank of France.
———. 1997. The causes and propagation of financial instability: Lessons for policymakers. In *Maintaining financial stability in a global economy,* Federal Reserve Bank of Kansas City, 55–96. Kansas City, MO.
———. 1998. Promoting Japanese recovery. In *Towards the restoration of sound banking systems in Japan—the global implications,* ed. Kenichi Ishigaki and Hiroyuki Hino, 130–61. Kobe: Kobe University Press and International Monetary Fund.
———. 1999a. International experiences with different monetary policy regimes. *Journal of Monetary Economics* 43 (3): 579–606.
———. 1999b. Central banking in a democratic society: Implications for transition countries. In *Central banking, monetary policy and the implications for transition economies,* ed. Mario Blejer and Marko Skreb, 31–53, Boston: Kluwer Academic Publishers.
———. 2000. What should central banks do? *Federal Reserve Bank of St. Louis Review* 82 (6): 1–13.
———. 2001. The transmission mechanism and the role of asset prices in monetary policy. In *Aspects of the transmission mechanism of monetary policy, focus on Austria 3–4/2001,* ed. Edward Hochreiter, 58–71. Vienna: Öesterreichische National Bank.
———. 2004a. Why the Fed should adopt inflation targeting. *International Finance* 7:1, forthcoming.
———. 2004b. Can central bank transparency go too far? Reserve Bank of Australia, *The future of inflation targeting,* forthcoming.
Mishkin, Frederic S., and Adam S. Posen. 1997. Inflation targeting: Lessons from four countries. New York: Federal Reserve Bank of New York, *Economic Policy Review* 3 (3): 9–110.
Mishkin, Frederic S., and Eugene N. White. 2003. U.S. stock market crashes and their aftermath: Implications for monetary policy. In *Asset price bubbles: The implications for monetary, regulatory and international policies,* ed. William B. Hunter, George G. Kaufman, and Michael Pormerleano, 57–79. Cambridge, MA: MIT Press.
Morgan, J. P. 2003. *Emerging Europe, Middle East & Africa Weekly,* January 31.
Moulton, Brett R. 1996. Bias in the consumer price index: What is the evidence. *Journal of Economic Perspectives* 10 (4): 159–77.

Oda, Nobuyuki, and Kunio Okina. 2001. Further monetary easing policies under the non-negativity constraints of nominal interest rates: Summary of the discussion based on Japan's experience. *Monetary and Economic Studies* 19 (S-1): 323–70. Tokyo: Bank of Japan.

Okina, Kunio. 1999a. Monetary policy under zero inflation: A response to criticisms and questions regarding monetary policy. *Monetary and Economic Studies* 17:157–82. Tokyo: Bank of Japan, Institute for Monetary and Economic Studies.

———. 1999b. Rejoinder to comments made by professors McKinnon and Meltzer. *Monetary and Economic Studies* 17:192–7. Tokyo: Bank of Japan, Institute for Monetary and Economic Studies.

Okina, Kunio, Masaaki Shirakawa, and Shigenori Shiratsuka. 2001. The asset price bubble and monetary policy: Japan's experience in the late 1980s and the lessons. Background Paper for the conference: *Monetary and Economic Studies* special edition, February: 395–450.

Okina, Kunio, and Shigenori Shiratsuka. 2002. Asset price bubbles, price stability, and monetary policy: Japan's experience. Bank of Japan, *Monetary and Economic Studies* October: 35–76.

———. 2004. Policy commitment and expectation formation: Japan's experience under zero interest rates. *North American Journal of Economics and Finance* 15:75–100.

Orphanides, Athanasios, and Volker Wieland. 1998. Price stability and monetary policy effectiveness when nominal interest rates are bounded by zero. Feds Working Paper No. 1998-35. Washington, DC: Board of Governors of the Federal Reserve System, August.

———. 2000. Efficient monetary policy design near price stability. *Journal of Japanese and International Economies* 14:327–56.

Poole, William. 1999. Is inflation too low. *Federal Reserve Bank of St. Louis* Review 81 (4): 3–10. St. Louis, MO.

Posen, Adam S. 1998. *Restoring Japan's economic growth.* Washington, DC: Institute for International Economics.

Reifschneider, David, and John Williams. 2000. Three lessons for monetary policy in a low inflation era. *Journal of Money, Credit and Banking* (November): 936–66.

Richards, Anthony, and Tim Robinson. 2003. *Asset Prices and Monetary Policy.* Sydney: Reserve Bank of Australia.

Romer, Christine. 1992. What ended the Great Depression? *Journal of Economic History* 52 (4): 757–84.

Sarno, Lucio, and Mark P. Taylor. 2001. Official intervention in the foreign exchange market: Is it effective and, if so, how does it work? *Journal of Economic Literature* XXXIX (September): 839–68.

Shapiro, Matthew D., and David W. Wilcox. 1996. Mismeasurement in the consumer price index, an evaluation. In *NBER Macroeconomics Annual 1996,* ed. Ben S. Bernanke and Julio J. Rotemberg, 83–154. Cambridge, MA: MIT Press.

Shiratsuka, Shigenori. 1999. Measurement errors and quality-adjustment methodology: Lessons from the Japanese CPI. Federal Reserve Bank of Chicago, *Economic Perspectives,* 2nd Quarter: 2–13. Chicago.

Smets, Frank. 2000. What horizon for price stability. European Central Bank Working Paper No. 24. Frankfurt, Germany: European Central Bank.

Stevens, Glenn R. 1999. Six years of inflation targeting. *Reserve Bank of Australia Bulletin* May: 46–61. Sydney: Reserve Bank of Australia.

Summers, Lawrence H. 1991. How should long-term monetary policy be determined? *Journal of Money Credit and Banking* 23:625–31.

Svensson, Lars E. O. 1999. Price-level targeting versus inflation targeting: A free lunch. *Journal of Money, Credit and Banking* 31:277–95.

———. 2001. The zero bound in an open economy: A foolproof way of escaping from a liquidity trap. *Monetary and Economic Studies* 19 (S-1): 277–312.
———. 2003. Escaping from a liquidity trap and deflation: The foolproof way and others. NBER Working Paper no. 10195. Cambridge, MA: National Bureau of Economic Research, December.
Svensson, Lars E. O., and Michael Woodford. 2003. Optimal policy with partial information in a forward-looking model: Certainty-equivalence redux. NBER Working Paper no. 9430. Cambridge, MA: National Bureau of Economic Research, January.
Taylor, John B., ed. 1999. *Monetary policy rules,* 405–30. Chicago: University of Chicago Press.
Taylor, John B. 2001. Low inflation, deflation, and policies for future price stability. Bank of Japan, *Monetary and Economic Studies* (special edition) February: 35–51.
Ueda, Kazuo. 1999. Remarks. Fed Conference, Monetary Policy in a Low-Inflation Environment. 20 October, Woodstock, Vermont. Available at [www.boj.or.jp/en/press/04/press_f.htm]
———. 2000. The transmission mechanism of monetary policy near zero interest rates: The Japanese experience 1998–2000. Speech given at Japan Project Meeting, 22 September, Swedish Embassy in Tokyo. Available at [http://www.boj.or.jp/en/press/04/press_f.htm]
Vestin, David. 2000. Price level targeting versus inflation targeting in a forward looking model. Institute for International Economic Studies, Stockholm University, May. Mimeo.
Williams, J. C. 1999. Simple rules for monetary policy. Finance and economics discussion series no. 1999-12. Washington, DC: Board of Governors of the Federal Reserve System, February.
Woodford, Michael. 1999. Optimal monetary policy inertia. NBER Working Paper no. 7261. Cambridge, MA: National Bureau of Economic Research, July.
———. 2000. Pitfalls of forward-looking monetary policy. *American Economic Review* 90 (2): 100–4.
———. 2003. *Interest and prices: Foundations of a theory of monetary policy.* Princeton, NJ: Princeton University Press.
Yamaguchi, Yutaka. 1999. *Monetary policy and structural policy: A Japanese perspective.* Deputy Governor of the Bank of Japan, before Colloque Monétaire International at Banque de France, October 8–9. Paris. Available at [http://www.boj.or.jp/en/press/04/press_f.htm].

Comment Kenneth Kuttner

The broad objectives of this vast chapter are twofold. The first is to provide a definitive overview of Japanese monetary policy since the mid-1980s. The Japanese experience is then used to motivate its second objective, which is to survey recent macroeconomic research on the deflation problem, and using this, to propose policies to help solve Japan's deflation problem. With

Kenneth Kuttner is the Danforth-Lewis Professor of Economics at Oberlin College, and a faculty research fellow of the National Bureau of Economic Research.

two decades of economic history and an extensive literature to cover, the chapter's scope is a little overwhelming. The goals of these comments, therefore, are to highlight and clarify some of its major themes, and to identify a few areas where the chapter makes particularly valuable contributions. A number of unresolved issues deserving of further investigation will also be noted.

The first half of the chapter, consisting of sections 4.2 through 4.4, summarizes the policies pursued by the BOJ over the past twenty years, and some of the many critiques of those policies. Section 4.2 deals with the period prior to the BOJ's formal independence, granted in 1998, while section 4.3 takes up the performance of the independent BOJ. Section 4.4 presents and discusses the pitfalls of an effort to assess the BOJ's policies using an empirical policy-reaction function.

The detailed chronology of the BOJ's policies contained in sections 4.2 and 4.3 stands as one of the chapter's major accomplishments, and is likely to serve as an important reference for years to come. While many of the episodes covered in the Ito-Mishkin chronology have been discussed elsewhere, the presentation in this chapter is both comprehensive and compact, and benefits from Ito's firsthand policy experience while serving in the Ministry of Finance. Along with the narrative, sections 4.2 and 4.3 consider a number of the critiques that have been made of BOJ policies over the years. These include the BOJ's failure to act more aggressively to prevent the asset-price bubble of the late 1980s, its slow response to the onset of the recession in the early 1990s, the reversal of the ZIRP in 2000, and the Bank's failure to "manage expectations" effectively.

Overall, the authors are relatively sympathetic to the BOJ's predicament in the late 1980s, acknowledging that the strong Yen and generally low inflation rates presented the bank with a dilemma that, to some extent, explains its restrained response to asset-price inflation. Others, such as Jinushi, Kuroki, and Miyao (2000), are more critical of BOJ policy during this period, arguing that the bank's misplaced emphasis on the exchange rate kept it from responding to real economic conditions which, by the late 1980s, would have called for significantly tighter policy. Regardless of the assessment, clearly this episode represents an interesting case study in the potential pitfalls of exchange rate management, and probably deserves a more detailed analysis.

The bulk of the authors' criticism is reserved for the bank's Hayami-era policies—the premature abandonment of the ZIRP in 2000 is labeled a "clear policy mistake," and in the authors' view, this (and other missteps) have "left the Bank of Japan with a severe credibility problem in which the markets and the public are unconvinced that Japanese monetary policy can be committed to future expansion that would return the economy to health." The authors' assessment of this period accurately reflects the consensus view, at least among academic economists, that monetary policy could have and *should* have done more to end the country's economic stagnation. In emphasizing the potential role for monetary policy, however, the chapter gives scant attention to supply-side explanations for the slow pace of economic growth, such as that of Hayashi and Prescott (2002).

Section 4.4 supplements the narrative approach of sections 4.2 and 4.3 with a quantitative analysis based on empirical reaction-functions, or generalized "Taylor rules." There are two basic ways reaction functions are used to assess monetary policy. The first, referred to by Kuttner and Posen (2004) as the "calibration" approach, is to insert output gap and inflation measures into a reaction function with calibrated parameters (typically Taylor's) imposed a priori; if the implied interest rate path is lower than the actual policy rate, policy is deemed "too tight." The alternative, "estimation" approach is to estimate the reaction-function parameters and compare those estimates to "good" parameter values, such as Taylor's; in Japan's context, the interesting question is the extent to which policy did (or did not) react to output fluctuations.

Unfortunately, reaction-function analysis of this sort is subject to a number of methodological problems and pitfalls, as discussed in detail in Kuttner and Posen (2004). Chief among these is the choice of output gap measure, an issue that is especially germane to the case of Japan, where most simple time-series methods (including those used by Ito and Mishkin) would spuriously attribute a significant portion of a prolonged cyclical slump to a reduction in trend growth. Not surprisingly, policy assessments consequently tend to be very sensitive to the choice of method used to estimate potential output.

Ito and Mishkin run headlong into these problems in their efforts to assess BOJ policy. Their approach, which is to estimate a Taylor rule up through 1994 and calculate projections from 1995 onward, yields results that are plausible in some dimensions but odd in others. While the results suggest the BOJ should have run a tighter policy in the late 1980s, policy during the critical 1992–95 period is judged to be "about right"—and implies a significant *tightening* of policy in 1996–97. Calling these results "counterintuitive," the authors end up largely rejecting the Taylor-rule approach as uninformative, at least for the case of Japan. This conclusion is surely well founded, for all the reasons listed in the chapter, as well as those outlined in Kuttner and Posen (2004).

Nonetheless, the exercise contains one important result that deserves additional emphasis: the lack of a significant response to the output gap in the specification with a forward-looking inflation measure. A similar lack of output response has also been reported by Kuttner and Posen (2001); Jinushi, Kuroki, and Miyao (2000); and Ahearne et al. (2002). Estimates for the U.S. Federal Reserve, on the other hand, such as those reported by Clarida, Gali, and Gertler (2000), typically show an economically meaningful response to output gap fluctuations. The Fed's sharp rate cuts in

2001–03 are consistent with such a response, as the 5.5 percentage point rate reduction cannot be rationalized purely as a response to a drop in expected inflation. (With an inflation coefficient of 1.5, the observed rate reduction would imply an implausibly large 3.7 percent decline in inflation expectations.) Thus, the lack of attention to real economic conditions revealed by the estimated reaction function may well have contributed to Japan's economic malaise.

The chapter's second half (sections 4.5 through 4.7) is primarily a survey of recent research on deflation and the ZLB problem. In its survey of the literature, the chapter covers relatively well-trodden ground; it adds value, however, in interweaving its survey with a discussion on how this research might apply to the case of Japan. Drawing on this research, the authors recommend the adoption of a price-level target designed to bring prices back up to where they would have been had there been a steady, low rate of inflation. This sensible proposal can be interpreted as a simplified version of the rule advanced by Eggertsson and Woodford (2003), and it is rationalized by a similar set of considerations.

The BOJ has over the years strenuously resisted calls for an explicit price or inflation target, however; and despite BOJ Governor Fukui's apparently more sympathetic attitude to reflationary policies, the likelihood of the Ito–Mishkin proposal being adopted surely remains slim. In the past, the BOJ officials have argued that, because the bank lacked the tools to achieve an inflation target, the announcement of a target would undermine its credibility. There is a certain undeniable logic to the view that announcing a target is futile without the means to achieve it. It is worth stressing, however, that this pessimistic assessment requires either that "unconventional" policies are ineffective (a view that the disappointing experience with quantitative easing has done little to dispel), or that the ZLB will *always* bind.

Searching for a deeper explanation, Ito and Mishkin offer three hypotheses for the BOJ's resistance to an inflation target: first, BOJ officials' belief in the "cleansing" value of restrictive policy; second, a concern that a commitment to reflation would undermine its newly won independence; and third, a fear that unconventional or overly expansionary policies would jeopardize the bank's balance sheet.

These are not the only possibilities, however. The authors might add to their list of hypotheses the possibility that the BOJ may have been using monetary policy as a weapon in its tussles with the Ministry of Finance over fiscal policy. Alternatively, BOJ officials may actually have believed that Japan's deflation was "good," a symptom of enhanced productivity and efficiency. BOJ officials have also on occasion voiced concerns that once inflation began, it would quickly accelerate, as a result of the large "overhang" of liquidity in the financial system.

Some of these obstacles are probably impervious to economic reasoning; if policy is being handicapped by bureaucratic infighting, then there is not much that academic economists can do about it. But other obstacles, such as the threat of insolvency or a liquidity overhang, merit a more detailed rejoinder. Perhaps in a sequel to this chapter, the authors will take up some of these arguments and refute them in a more systematic fashion—and in doing so, advance the cause of sound monetary policy in Japan.

References

Ahearne, Alan, Joseph Gagnon, Jane Haltimaier, and Steve Kamin. 2002. Preventing deflation: Lessons from Japan's experience in the 1990s. Board of Governors of the Federal Reserve System, International Finance Discussion Paper no. 729, June. Washington, DC.

Clarida, Richard, Jordi Galí, and Mark Gertler. 2000. Monetary policy rules and macroeconomic stability: Evidence and some theory. *Quarterly Journal of Economics* 115 (February): 148–80.

Eggertsson, Gauti, and Michael Woodford. 2003. The zero bound on interest rates and optimal monetary policy. *Brookings Papers on Economic Activity* Issue no. 1: 139–211.

Hayashi, Fumio, and Edward C. Prescott. 2002. The 1990s in Japan: A lost decade. *Review of Economic Dynamics* 5 (1): 206–35.

Jinushi, Toshiki, Yoshihiro Kuroki, and Ryuzo Miyao. 2000. Monetary policy in Japan since the late 1980s: Delayed policy actions and some explanations. In *Japan's financial crisis and its parallels to U.S. experience,* ed. Mikitani and Posen, 115–48. Washington, DC: Institute for International Economics.

Kuttner, Kenneth N., and Adam S. Posen. 2001. Inflation, monetary transparency, and G3 exchange rate volatility. In *Adapting to financial globalisation,* ed. Hochreiter and Hennessy, 229–59. London: Routledge.

———. 2004. The difficulty of discerning what's too tight: Taylor rules and Japanese monetary policy. *North American Journal of Economics and Finance* 15:53–74.

Comment Kazuo Ueda

The chapter by Ito and Mishkin consists of four parts. First, it discusses the macroeconomics of the so-called lost decade. Second, it provides a narrative description of the BOJ's monetary policy during the last decade or two. Third, it presents an analysis of the Taylor rule as applied to the Japanese situation and shows the difficulties of using it as a guide for monetary policy. Fourth, it discusses the pros and cons of nonconventional operations that may be used close to the ZLB on nominal interest rates.

My quick reaction to the authors' analyses is: the discussion of the macroeconomics of the lost decade misses some important points. The narrative account of the BOJ's policy is partly accurate, partly unfair. The

Kazuo Ueda is one of the appointed members of the Monetary Policy Board of the Bank of Japan, and a professor of economics at Tokyo University.

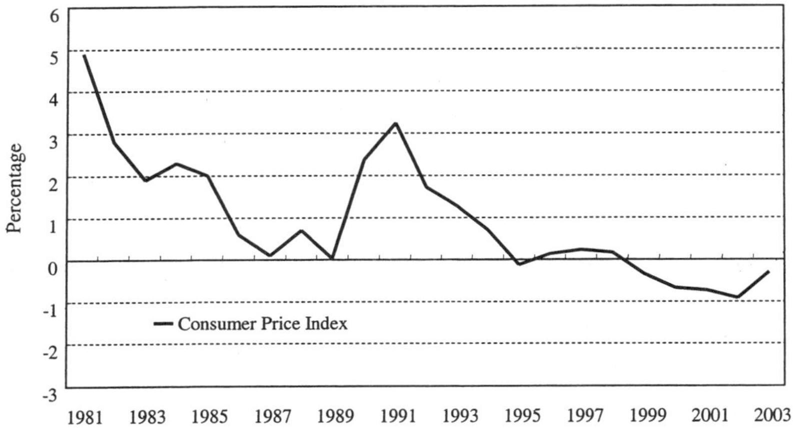

Fig. 4C.1 Rate of inflation in Japan
Source: Ministry of Public Management, Home Affairs, Posts and Telecommunications.

authors, by their focus on the Taylor rule, seem to have some misunderstanding about what the BOJ has been doing. Finally, the section on unconventional operations is well written, although I do not quite buy the authors' conclusion, which seems to be just go ahead and do them no matter what the costs are. I am afraid that, given my current position, I am unable to comment in detail on the second part of the chapter. Hence, in the following I will discuss the remaining three parts of the chapter.

Let me start with the discussion of the macroeconomics of the Japanese economy. The authors assert that macro deflation has been the number one enemy of the economy. This seems to miss the point. Figure 4C.1 shows Japan's deflation of the CPI. The deflationary tendency did not set in until the late 1990s when macroeconomic problems of the economy were already apparent. In addition, the deflation has been mild. In figures 4C.2 and 4C.3 I show estimates of ex post real interest rates in Japan for the Great Depression period and for the post-1990 period. Unlike in the former, there is no tendency for the real interest rate to rise with deflation in the late 1990s. That is, no serious debt-deflation type dynamic was taking hold in the post-1990 era.

Instead, the stagnation of the economy during the era seems to have been due to the excesses—excess capital, labor, debt, and so on—built up during the bubble period and negative financial accelerators generated by the sharp fall in asset prices as argued in Baba et al. (2004). The authors seem to realize the importance of these factors, but put too much weight on the negative effects of macro deflation.

I now turn to the discussion of policy measures recently adopted by the BOJ. The authors' focus on the technical aspects of the Taylor rule seems

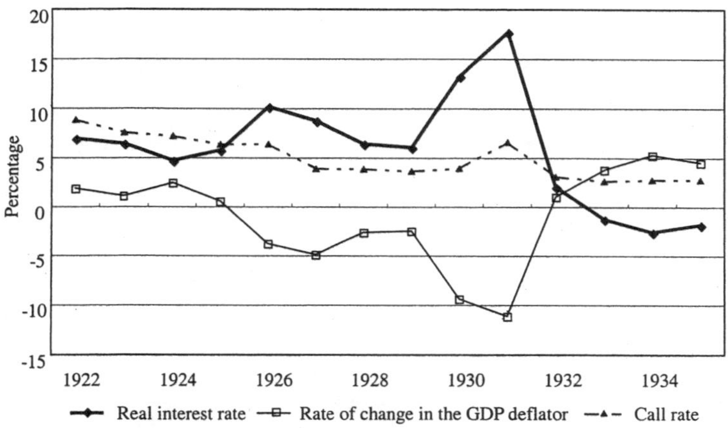

Fig. 4C.2 Estimates of real interest rates, 1922–1935
Sources: Economic and Social Research Institute, Cabinet Office; Bank of Japan.

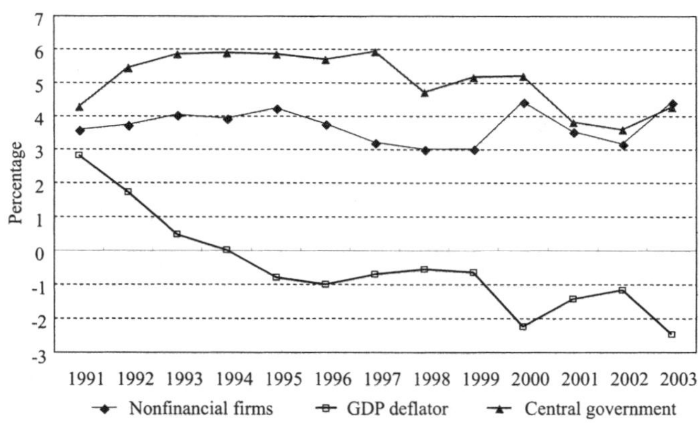

Fig. 4C.3 Estimates of real interest rates, 1991–2003
Note: Real interest rates are calculated as gross interest payments divided by total debt minus the rate of increase in the deflator for domestic demand.
Source: Economic and Social Research Institute, Cabinet Office.

to indicate that they are of the view that the BOJ has been following the rule in setting monetary policy. This is simply not correct. The Taylor rule is a useful benchmark. The BOJ has not, however, blindly followed the rule. In fact, as the authors correctly point out, it is possible to produce a fairly wide range for the optimal level of the policy interest rate using the Taylor rule, depending on assumptions about the parameters of the rule or about the method to calculate the output gap.

Focusing too much on the Taylor rule is, however, problematic not so much because of the difficulty of its implementation, but because the BOJ has attempted to use measures that produce stronger easing effects than, say, the Taylor rule. Under the Taylor rule, a central bank keeps the interest rate at zero so long as the rule says the rate should be either zero or negative. In order to produce stronger easing effects, the BOJ has made commitments regarding the duration of a zero rate. In April 1999 the BOJ announced that it would "keep the overnight rate at zero until deflationary concerns are over." The framework was in place until August 2000. Under current quantitative easing, ample liquidity provision—effectively a zero rate—is promised to continue until actual and expected CPI inflation turn positive.

The essence of such an approach is stated in Krugman (1998). Once the ZLB is hit due to, say, a large exogenous decline in the natural rate of interest, a further increase in the money supply today has no effect on the economy. Assuming, however, that there is a nonzero probability that the economy is pushed out of the ZLB as a result of an exogenous rise in the natural rate of interest tomorrow, a promise today of monetary expansion tomorrow will raise inflation expectations today and stimulate aggregate demand.

It is at once apparent that such a commitment ought to be stronger than what the market naturally assumes about future monetary policy in the absence of the commitment. Otherwise, it will not affect expectations. There are two ways to achieve this end. One is the announcement of a very high inflation target. As Krugman puts it, "the central bank needs to announce that it will be irresponsible." The other is to commit to, in the event of a rise in the natural rate of interest, slower increases in the interest rate than a baseline monetary policy, say, the Taylor rule, suggests. In this case, the target rate of inflation does not have to be very high; however, the possibility of inflation temporarily overshooting its target needs to be tolerated. Clearly, what the BOJ has been doing is closer to the second of the two approaches. In any case, these approaches are already "nonconventional" in the sense that they have not been employed elsewhere except by the BOJ and, to a lesser extent, recently by the Fed. Baba et al. (2004) shows that they have had some significant effects on the term-structure of interest rates. It is also important, however, to recognize the limitations of the approach.

Essentially, the approach requires forces other than monetary policy for stimulating the economy. As a result, it can become very strained when such forces are weak. In the Krugman version, a lower probability of the economy moving out of the ZLB tomorrow requires a correspondingly higher inflation target. Very soon, the target becomes incredible because of time inconsistency problems.[1] The second approach, for example, raising

1. To put this differently, if the announcement of high inflation targets is credible, there is no limit to the power of a permanent increase in base money to stimulate the economy. This point is made in the McCallum chapter in this volume.

interest rates more slowly than the Taylor rule as the economy improves, only starts to exert large effects on medium- to long-term interest rates when such improvements in the economy are expected to occur very soon. A central bank may have to wait a desperately long time before such improvements take place. Improvements in the economy may not materialize under the policy board that made the decision. As King (2004) points out, the difficulty here is one of "collective decisions today may fail to bind future collective decisions." In any case, these points have to be at the center of discussion in any evaluation of the BOJ's recent monetary policy.

Finally, Ito and Mishkin's discussion of the pros and cons of other nonconventional monetary-policy measures in the neighborhood of the ZLB is very reasonable. If I might add some obvious points, foreign exchange intervention may help in raising the price level. In the Japanese context, however, the BOJ is not allowed to carry out exchange rate policy, which is in the hands of the MOF. The MOF, who has the power to carry out large interventions, ironically does not have the mandate to maintain price stability. Ito and Mishkin note various problems with operations in private real assets. I agree with most of what they say here. I would have then thought that the decision on whether or not to use such operations would be a function of how desperate the situation of the economy was. In fact, the BOJ has been buying asset-backed securities since 2003 as a monetary-policy action, and equities from private banks since 2002 as a prudential policy measure. These reflected the BOJ's judgment that the economy was in a serious situation, hence the use of some risky operations were justified, but that the situation was not desperate, therefore, they should be carried out with an eye to minimizing the negative effects of such operations on private resource allocation.

References

Baba, N., N. Oda, S. Nishioka, M. Shirakawa, K. Ueda, and H. Ugai. 2004. Japan's deflation, problems in the financial system and monetary policy. Paper presented at the 3rd Bank for International Settlements (BIS) annual conference, Brunnen, Switzerland.

King, M. 2004. The institutions of monetary policy. NBER Working Paper no. 10400. Cambridge, MA: National Bureau of Economic Research, April.

Krugman, P. 1998. It's baack: Japan's slump and the return of the liquidity trap. *Brookings Papers on Economic Activity,* Issue no. 2.

5

Financial Strains and the Zero Lower Bound
The Japanese Experience

Mitsuhiro Fukao

5.1 Introduction

In this chapter, we analyze the cause of the persistent deflation in Japan by estimating the long-run Phillips curve equation using the gross domestic product (GDP) deflator and the estimated GDP gap. We also document the conduct of monetary policy in the face of a zero lower bound of interest rates. The gradually accelerating deflation has been the origin of the two serious problems of the Japanese economy, the nonperforming loan problem and the increasing national debt.

The profit margin of Japanese banks has been too small to cover the increased default risk after the crush of the bubble. Banks have not succeeded in increasing their lending margin under a strong competitive pressure from government-backed financial institutions and weakened borrowers under a deflationary economy. Moreover, under the terms and conditions of government capital injection in March 1999, banks are legally required to maintain and increase loans to small- and medium-sized firms. Because of this situation, banks often disregard the internal model-based required lending margin to make new loans to small companies. Corresponding to the flow-profit figures, the capital position of Japanese banks has been deteriorating.

National debt has been increasing rapidly. Due to the declining tax rev-

Mitsuhiro Fukao is a professor in the faculty of business and commerce at Keio University.

Earlier versions of this chapter were presented at the Bank for International Settlements conference on monetary stability, financial stability and the business cycle on March 28–29, 2003, in Basel and the fifteenth annual East Asian Seminar on Economics on June 25–27 in Tokyo. The author would like to thank Marvin Goodfriend, Oliver Blanchard, James Harrigan, Piti Disyatat, Andrew Rose, Takatoshi Ito, and other participants of the two conferences for helpful comments.

enue and the successive budgetary stimulus packages, the debt-GDP ratio had reached 157 percent by the end of 2003. With an extremely large budget deficit and declining nominal GDP, this ratio was increasing by 8 to 9 points a year. Even though the net debt-GDP ratio is still at 66 percent, it is likely to surpass 100 percent by 2008.

The Japanese economy was in a very serious situation in early 2003. In spite of the zero interest rate policy by the Bank of Japan, the GDP deflator was falling more than 2 percent per annum. The budget deficit was more than 8 percent of GDP, and fiscal consolidation was almost impossible under zero or negative nominal growth. The Nikkei 225 stock price index had fallen to only one-fifth of its peak in 1989. The capital of major banks and life insurance companies was running out very quickly due to the increasing nonperforming loans and falling stock prices.

Since short-term interest rates were already zero, conventional monetary-policy tools had lost effectiveness. Usually a potent monetary-policy weapon, an open market purchase of short-term government papers by the Bank of Japan was no longer effective because zero interest base money and zero interest short-term government papers are now perfect substitutes. Long-term bond yields had fallen to extremely low levels. A further injection of base money was not likely to push down long-term rates further.

Since the spring of 2003, the Japanese economy has shown a surprising recovery (see fig. 5.1). While it is very difficult to identify the causes of this turnaround, we can list the possible contributing factors:

1. The new governor of the Bank of Japan, Toshihiko Fukui, skillfully used "announcement effects" of monetary policy by showing that he is seriously fighting against deflation. While we could not expect much from the individual policy actions taken by the bank, Fukui succeeded in improving the expectations of the Japanese business community. We may call it the "placebo effect" of monetary policy.

2. The rescue of the failing Resona Bank in the spring of 2003 changed the perceived risk profile of shares of major Japanese banks. When the government nationalized the Long-Term Credit Bank of Japan and Nippon Credit Bank in 1998, the shareholders' equity was wiped out. On the other hand, the government saved the shareholders of Resona Bank with public money when it injected capital to the bank. This rescue operation changed the risk of bank stocks and started a "moral hazard rally" in the market.

3. The very rapid expansion of the Chinese economy induced an export boom for Japanese manufacturing companies. Japanese exports to China grew about 30 percent in 2003.

4. The massive official interventions in the foreign exchange market kept the yen relatively weak. The government bought JPY 32.6 trillion worth of U.S. dollars (about US$ 300 billion) in fiscal year 2003 that ended March 2004. This is more than 6 percent of the Japanese GDP and about twice the value of Japanese current account surplus in the same year.

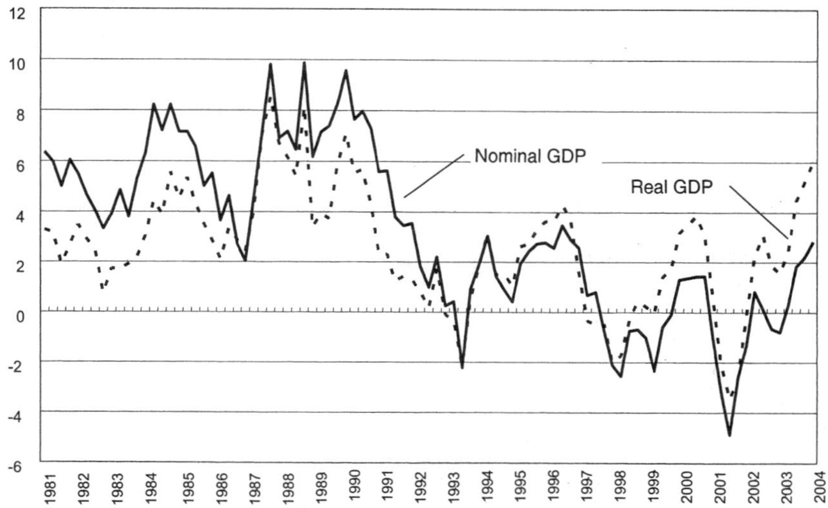

Fig. 5.1 GDP growth rate, annual rate after three-quarter moving average

As a result, the real GDP grew almost 5 percent in fiscal year 2003, and the deflationary gap has shrunk considerably. Corporate profits, private investments, and employment situations have shown a steady recovery.

However, the GDP deflator is still falling about 1.5 percent per annum at the time of this writing. Given the estimated potential growth rate of 1.5 percent, the Japanese economy still faces a risk of having a negative nominal growth again in the near future.

5.2 Gradually Accelerating Deflation

Deflation in Japan is steadily accelerating.[1] Figure 5.2 shows the GDP deflator and core consumer price index (CPI) since 1985. They are seasonally adjusted annual rates (SAAR) and show fairly erratic movements. Both of them are adjusted for value added tax (VAT) increases in 1989 and 1997. The figure also shows their trends estimated by Hodrick-Prescott (HP) Filter with the conventional parameter for quarterly time series. The trend of core CPI started to fall in 1998, and that of GDP deflator started to fall in 1995. The GDP deflator deflation rate has been larger than that of the CPI because the upward bias of CPI is more pronounced than that of the deflator. By the end of 2003, the GDP deflator deflation rate was more than 2 percent and was still accelerating. Figure 5.3 shows that the general

1. In late 2004, the GDP deflator was revised upward significantly. The government introduced chain-weight based deflator figures and the rate of deflation in 2002–2004 was revised upward by about one point. Since I could not update the analysis in this chapter all the tables and figures are based on the old statistics. As a result, you may find that my analysis of the Japanese deflation is rather pessimistic.

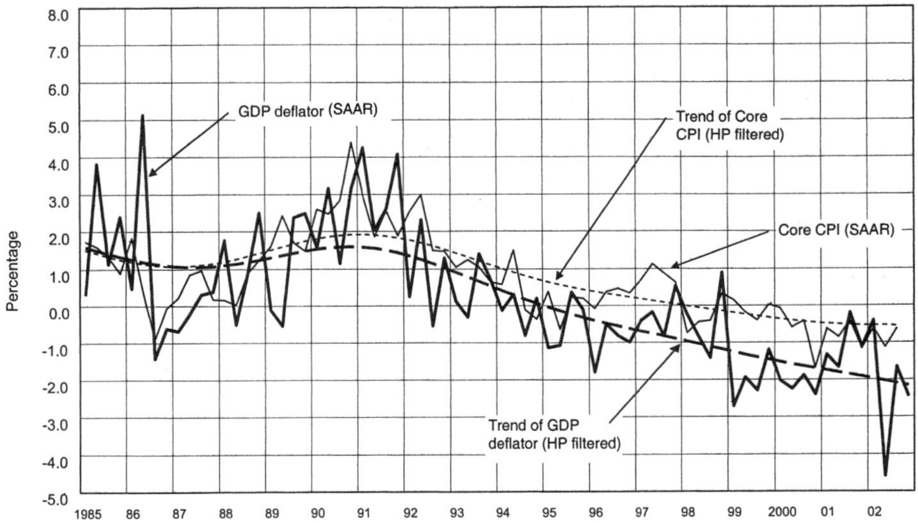

Fig. 5.2 CPI and GDP deflator deflation rates

Source: Japan Center for Economic Research (2003).

Note: GDP deflator inflation rate is adjusted for changes in consumption tax rate in 1989 and 1997.

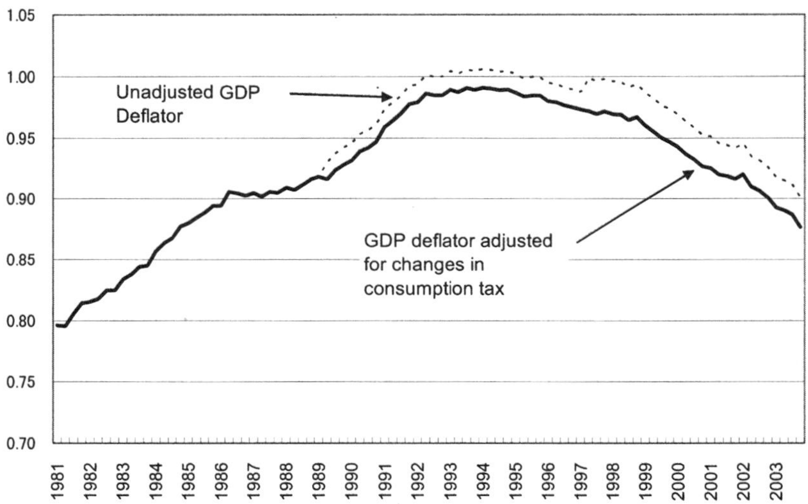

Fig. 5.3 GDP deflator price level (unadjusted 1995 = 1.0)

Note: Adjusted for changes in consumption tax in April 1989 and April 1997.

price level measured by the GDP deflator has fallen by about 12 percent from the peak in early 1994 to the first quarter of 2004.

While the public discussions on monetary policy and deflation generally focus on CPI, the development of the GDP deflator is more important for the health of the Japanese economy. The corporate profit and labor income depend on the nominal GDP that is the product of GDP deflator and real GDP. Tax revenue is also dependent on the nominal GDP. The gap between the CPI and GDP deflator widened in the 1990s, and the average gap over the past five years (1999–2003) was 1.2 percent. This means that even if the Bank of Japan can stabilize the CPI at zero inflation, the GDP deflator will be falling at 1.2 percent. Therefore, in this chapter, we look into the development of the GDP deflator deflation rate.

The Bank of Japan pointed out that the GDP deflator exaggerates the rate of deflation due to the very rapid fall in computer prices and the Paasche index bias.[2] The private investment deflator seems to overstate the deflation by about 3 percent since the first quarter of 2003 because its trend deflation rate jumped from 2 percent to 5 percent. However, the bias of the GDP deflator will be much smaller, at most by about 0.5 percent, because the weight of private investment is about 15 percent of total nominal GDP. Thus, even if we removed this downward bias of the GDP deflator, the GDP deflator is still falling by about 2 percent instead of 2.5 percent. In this context, we have to note that the Bank of Japan paper does not mention the possible upward bias in the GDP deflator (Koga 2003). Because most price indexes do not take account of the quality changes in goods and services, the GDP deflator does have some upward bias from this source. Moreover, the Bank of Japan is not disputing the validity of nominal GDP. Therefore, the correction of the downward bias of GDP deflator due to the Paasche bias means that the real growth rate will also be adjusted downward by the same amount.

The deceleration of inflation in the first half of the 1990s and the acceleration of the deflation rate in the second half of the decade strongly suggest that Japan has maintained a deflationary GDP gap since the collapse of the bubble economy in the late 1980s. I estimated the size of the GDP gap with the Financial Study Group of Japan Center for Economic Research based on the conventional production-function approach.[3] The estimation was made with the following procedure:

1. A Cobb-Douglas production function was estimated with real GDP, labor input (man-hour based), and capital adjusted for capacity utilization.

2. See Koga (2003). James Harrigan pointed out this factor at the meeting in June 2004. I had investigated this problem in the Japan Center for Economic Research (2004) paper in detail but did not include the conclusions in the earlier version of this chapter. I am summarizing the main points in my analysis in the text.

3. See the data appendix of this chapter and Japan Center for Economic Research (2004) for the details of the estimation procedure.

The factor-income share was used to calibrate the parameter of the production function. The trend of the residual of the production function corresponds to the growth of total factor productivity (TFP) of the Japanese economy:

$\ln Y_t = 0.29 \ln K_t + 0.71 \ln L_t + \ln \mathrm{TFP}_t$, where
Y_t = real GDP,
K_t = capital adjusted for capacity utilization,
L_t = labor input measured by man-hours, and
TFP_t = estimated TFP.

Since this TFP growth rate is estimated from the residual of the production function, the TFP reflects possible biases in the GDP deflator. If the GDP deflator exaggerates the deflation rate, the measured TFP growth rate also exaggerates the potential growth rate by the same amount.

2. Estimate the maximum inputs by connecting the cyclical peaks of the labor hour and capacity utilization. In this process, the peaks of labor force were identified for the working-age population and the retirement-age population separately. The peaks of working hours were identified for overtime hours and normal working hours separately because the normal working hours declined due to the changes in the labor-relations law.

3. The maximum production potential is estimated from the production function in step 1 and the maximum labor and capital inputs in step 2. The gap between this maximum GDP and the actual GDP is the unadjusted GDP gap:

$$\text{Unadjusted GDP gap} = \text{Maximum GDP} - \text{Actual GDP}.$$

Figure 5.4 shows the estimated potential GDP growth rate that is defined as the changes in the maximum GDP. The potential growth rate for the past two years has been about 1.5 percent a year. The large negative labor contribution from 1988 to 1994 and from 1997 to 2000 was due to the introduction of the five-day workweek. The TFP was estimated from the smoothed residual term of the equation, and it has been increasing at about 1 percent per annum in recent years. This potential growth rate is important because it also determines the growth rate of "natural level of GDP" in the next step.

4. The "natural level of real GDP" was calculated as a parameter, G^n, in the estimated long-run Phillips curve relationship (table 5.1). This equation assumes that the expected rate of inflation depends on the past inflation rates. The table shows that the natural level of real GDP is lower than the maximum GDP by 3.249 percent:

$$\text{Natural level of GDP} = \text{Maximum GDP} - 3.249\%.$$

At the natural level of GDP, the inflation rate will be steady. If the real GDP is below this natural level, the inflation rate gradually decelerates and be-

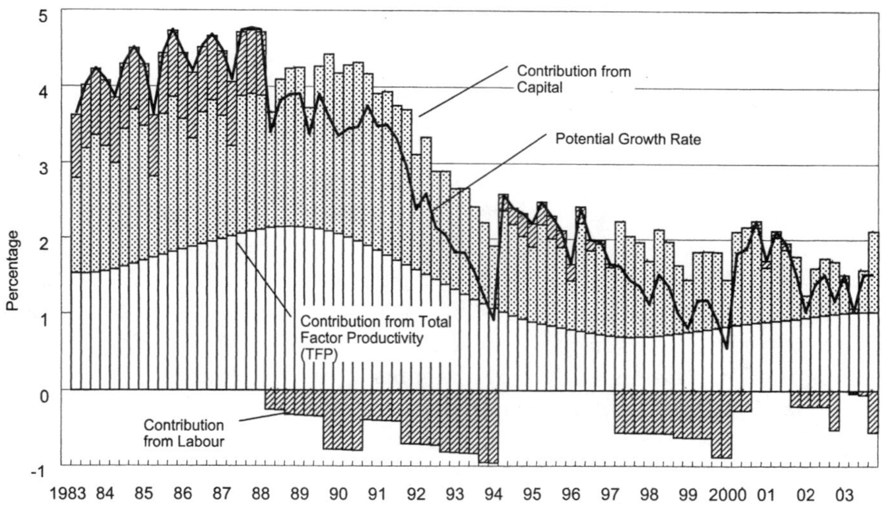

Fig. 5.4 Potential growth rate
Source: Japan Center for Economic Research (2004).

Table 5.1 Estimated price equation with GDP gap (1985/Q1–2003/Q4)

Specification

$$\pi_t = \alpha \times \sum_{i=1}^{4} \pi_{t-i}/4 + (1-\alpha) \times \sum_{i=5}^{8} \pi_{t-i}/4 + \beta \times (G_t - G^n) + \gamma \times \text{DUM} \times (G_t - G^n) + \varepsilon_t$$

$$\underset{(2.51)}{\pi_t = 0.551} \times \sum_{i=1}^{4} \pi_{t-i}/4 + \underset{(2.46)}{0.449} \times \sum_{i=5}^{8} \pi_{t-i}\,\pi_{t-i}/4 + \underset{(2.23)}{0.348} \times (G_t - (-3.249)) - \underset{(4.13)}{0.267} \times \text{DUM} \times \underset{(1.69)}{(G_t - (-3.249))} + \varepsilon_t$$

Adjusted $R^2 = 0.43$; Standard error = 1.47

Source: Japan Center for Economic Research (2004).
Notes: π = GDP-deflator inflation rate; G = unadjusted GDP gap; G^n = natural level of GDP gap; and DUM = dummy variable. From 1985 to 1993, DUM = 0; after 1994, DUM = 1.

comes negative. If the real GDP is above the natural level, the inflation rate accelerates.

In estimating the Phillips curve with the data since 1985, we found that the acceleration of deflation rate in the second half of the 1990s was much slower than the deceleration of inflation in the first half of the 1990s. This is probably due to the fact that it is easier to reduce the wage increases than to accelerate the pace of wage reductions.[4] Therefore, we assumed a structural change in the equation when the GDP deflator started to fall in 1994. The acceleration parameter under deflation, 0.081 (0.081 = 0.348 – 0.267), was only one-quarter of the parameter under inflation, 0.348.

4. See Kuroda and Yamamoto (2003) for evidence of downward wage rigidity in Japan.

5. The adjusted GDP gap is estimated by adding this natural level of GDP gap, 3.249, to the unadjusted GDP gap. In the following, we refer to this adjusted GDP gap as the GDP gap:

$$\text{Adjusted GDP gap} = \text{Unadjusted GDP gap} + 3.249\%.$$

Figure 5.5 shows the estimated GDP gap with the GDP deflator inflation rate. Since SAAR data are highly erratic, we used a three-quarter moving average of SAAR series for the chart. The GDP gap hit the peak of 2.5 percent in 1990 and started to fall. It became negative in mid-1992, and the deflationary environment has continued since then. The gap narrowed to zero in early 1997 when the planned increase of the VAT stimulated consumption on consumer durables and housing. However, the gap became very large by mid-1999 due mainly to the financial crisis from the fall of 1997 until early 1999. Although capital injection and the cyclical recovery briefly narrowed the gap in 2000, the Japanese economy fell into a deeper trough in 2002. We can see that the deflationary gap reached 6.9 percent of the natural level of GDP in the first quarter of 2002.

Our estimated GDP gap figures and the Phillips curve show that the widening GDP gap led to the acceleration of deflation from 1995 to 2003. This result indicates that the aggregate-demand shocks were more important than the aggregate-supply shocks as a cause of persistent deflation in Japan. Monetary policy should have responded more strongly to stem the deflationary pressure from the demand side.

Since then, the Japanese economy recovered slowly until mid-2003 and

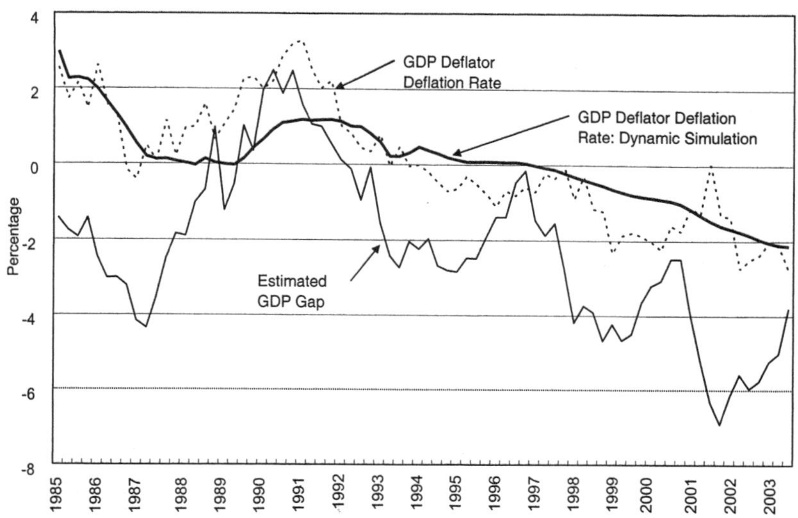

Fig. 5.5 Estimated GDP gap and deflation rate
Source: Japan Center for Economic Research (2004).

the growth rate accelerated. By the first quarter of 2004, the GDP gap had declined to less than 4 percent.

5.3 Deflation and Nonperforming Loan Problem

Banking in Japan has become an unprofitable, structurally depressed industry. Excluding capital gains realized by selling shares and real estate, Japan's banks as a group have been in the red since the year ending March 1994 (fiscal year 1993). The primary cause of this is a low profit margin and a high level of loan losses. In this section, I rely on Fukao (2003) and explain the performance of the Japanese banking sector since the mid-1990s.

Table 5.2 shows the profit-loss accounts of all commercial banks. In the ten years from fiscal year 1992 to fiscal year 2002, banks made around JPY 10 trillion each year as lending margin (row A, defined as interest and dividends earned minus interest paid). Revenue from such sources as bond and currency dealing and service charges were about JPY 3 trillion (row B). This includes all other revenue except capital gains realized on stocks and real estate. Revenues from banks' principal operations therefore amount to roughly JPY 13 trillion yen a year (row A + row B).

Total costs—including personnel and other operating expenses—were over JPY 7 trillion (row C). Operating costs declined during the 1998–2000 period because of cost-cutting measures. It is likely to be difficult to continue that pace of cost cutting. Certainly, the banks may cut labor costs further by reducing employment and cutting average compensation. But the banks have to invest heavily in information technology to remain competitive.

In the 1990s, banks stinted on improving systems because of the preoccupation with bad-loan problems, and now they have poor-quality computer systems. Thus, for example, the zengin electronic fund transfer system, which is the main payment system among bank customers, cannot handle two-byte codes, so it cannot send customer names and messages in kanji (characters). As a result, more and more payments (especially utility bills) are handled by convenience store chains, which have installed sophisticated terminals.

Since the early 1990s more and more loans held by banks have turned into nonperforming assets. Banks have suffered over JPY 6 trillion in loan losses each year since fiscal year 1994 (table 5.2, row E). As a result, banks have not reported positive net-operating profit since fiscal year 1993 (row F). However, because of occasional realization of capital gains on stocks and real estate (row G), banks have shown a positive bottom line in some years (row F + row G).

Clearly, the profit margin of Japanese banks is too small to cover the increased default risk after the crash of the bubble. Banks have not succeeded in increasing their lending margin under a strong competitive pressure from

Table 5.2 **Profitability of Japanese banking sector, by financial year (trillion yen)**

	1990	1991	1992	1993	1994	1995	1996	1997	1998	1999	2000	2001	2002	2003[a]
Lending margin (A)	7.1	8.9	9.8	9.2	9.7	10.8	10.7	10.0	9.6	9.7	9.4	9.8	9.4	9.0
Other revenue (B)	2.6	2.2	2.5	2.8	2.1	3.3	3.7	3.6	3.1	2.5	3.0	3.1	3.6	4.3
Operating costs (C)	7.1	7.5	7.7	7.7	7.8	7.8	8.0	8.0	7.5	7.3	7.1	7.0	7.0	6.7
Salaries and wages	3.7	3.9	4.0	4.0	4.0	4.0	4.0	4.0	3.6	3.5	3.4	3.2	2.8	3.1
Gross profit (D) = (A) + (B) – (C)	2.6	3.5	4.5	4.3	4.0	6.3	6.4	5.6	5.2	4.9	5.3	5.9	6.0	6.6
Loan Loss (E)	0.8	1.0	2.0	4.6	6.2	13.3	7.3	13.5	13.5	6.3	6.6	9.4	7.0	6.1
Net operating profit (F) = (D) – (E)	1.8	2.5	2.5	–0.4	–2.2	–7.0	–1.0	–7.9	–8.3	–1.4	–1.3	–3.5	–1.0	0.5
Realized capital gains (G)	2.0	0.7	0.0	2.0	3.2	4.4	1.2	3.6	1.4	3.8	1.4	–2.4	–4.1	0.6
Net profit (F) + (G)	3.8	3.3	2.5	1.7	1.0	–2.6	0.2	–4.2	–6.9	2.3	0.1	–5.9	–5.1	1.0
Asset	927.6	914.4	859.5	849.8	845.0	848.2	856.0	848.0	759.7	737.2	804.3	772.0	739.0	750.0
Outstanding loans	522.0	537.0	542.0	539.0	539.0	554.0	563.0	536.0	492.0	476.0	474.0	465.0	435.0	423.0

Source: Japan Center for Economic Research (2001). Updated by the author.

Note: Financial statement of all commercial banks. Other revenue (B) includes all the other profit such as dealing profits and fees but excludes realized capital gains of stocks and real estates. Realized capital gains includes gains of stocks and real estates.

[a]2003 numbers are for the eleven major banks.

government-backed financial institutions and weakened borrowers under a deflationary economy. Moreover, under the terms and conditions of government capital injection in March 1999, banks are legally required to maintain and increase loans to small- and medium-sized firms. Sinsei Bank, which reduced loans to small- and medium-sized firms, was ordered to increase such loans by the Financial Services Agency of Japan (FSA). Because of this situation, banks often disregard the internal model-based required lending margin to make new loans to small companies. Given these poor lending market conditions, Citibank decided to significantly reduce consumer-loan business in Japan.[5]

Corresponding to the flow-profit figures, the capital position of Japanese banks has been deteriorating. Under Japanese accounting rules for banks and lenient application by the regulators, Bank for International Settlements (BIS) capital ratios have been manipulated in many ways. First, banks have underreserved against bad loans. This tends to increase bank core capital by the same amount.

Second, banks have large deferred-tax assets on their balance sheets even though they have been losing money continually since 1993 and loss carry-forwards are limited to five years. There is little prospect of utilizing the deferred-tax asset by showing genuine profit in the near future, so it should be written off.

Table 5.3 shows the capital structure of major Japanese banks. In March 2003, more than 100 percent of tier I capital of Resona Bank and Mitsui Trust Holdings consisted of deferred tax assets (present value of the future tax shelter). More than one-half of the tier I capital of United Financial of Japan (UFJ) and Sumitomo-Mitsui Financial Group corresponds to the deferred tax asset. One-third of the tier I capital of Tokyo-Mitsubishi Group is also the deferred tax asset. This situation improved somewhat one year later. Except for UFJ Group, all the other banks' reduced deferred tax asset. Resona bank could reduce deferred tax asset by the capital injection by the government. The weakened UFJ Group is merging with the Mitsubishi Tokyo Financial Group.

Third, friendly life insurance companies hold banks' subordinated debts and bank stocks. The banks, in turn, hold subordinated loans and surplus notes of the life insurance companies. At the end of March 2003, Japanese banks provided JPY 1.9 trillion of capital to ten major life insurance companies. On the other hand, ten major life insurance companies held JPY 1.9 trillion of banks stocks and JPY 4.4 trillion of subordinated liabilities of banks.[6] This is double gearing, and the cross-held quasi capital should

5. According to the March 16, 2003, edition of Japan *Economic Journal,* Japanese edition, Citibank group would eliminate up to 500 consumer-loan offices and about 2,000 employees by the end of 2003.

6. See Fukao and Japan Center for Economic Research (2004, 133).

Table 5.3 The ratio of deferred tax asset in the core capital of major Japanese banks

	March 2004			March 2003
	Core capital (billion yen) (A)	Net DTA (billion yen) (B)	Ratio (%) (B/A)	Ratio (%) (B/A)
Mitsubishi Tokyo Financial Group	3,655	647	17.7	39.0
UFJ Group	2,149	1,397	65.0	57.1
Sumitomo Mitsui Financial Group	3,567	1,666	46.7	58.1
Mizuho Financial Group	3,941	1,333	33.8	60.8
Chuo Mitsui Group	483	269	55.7	101.5
Resona Bank	892	53	5.9	109.6
Sumitomo Trust	790	141	17.9	37.4

Source: Disclosure materials of individual banks.
Note: Net DTA means deferred tax assets minus deferred tax liabilities.

not be treated as genuine capital for either the banks or the life insurance companies.

The capital position of banks is quite sensitive to stock prices. Table 5.4 shows the capital structure of all commercial banks. Core capital based on traditional historical cost accounting is adjusted for unrealized capital gains on stocks, deferred taxes, the public capital injection, and underreserving for loan losses. Although banks showed JPY 24.8 trillion of capital on their balance sheet at the end of March 2003, this figure was inflated with JPY 10.6 trillion of deferred-tax assets, JPY 5.4 trillion of underreserving, and JPY 7.3 trillion of government capital. Removing these amounts, the privately held equity of the banking sector was only JPY 1.5 trillion. This is very small compared to the JPY 64.6 trillion of classified loans and JPY 23.2 trillion of stocks held by banks.

In the early 1990s, unrealized capital gains (the difference between table 5.4 columns [A] and [B]) were very large and banks could withstand fluctuations in stock prices. However, in the 1990s, banks sold stock to realize gains to offset huge loan losses. The increase in book value of shares (column [B]) during the 1990s shows that the banks were buying back most of the stock they had sold.

Table 5.5 shows the distribution of core capital ratios (leverage ratios) of major Japanese banks. By adjusting the underreserving and deferred tax assets, four banks had negative equity at the end of March 2003. The weighted average capital ratio declined from 3.21 percent in March 2000 to 0.30 percent in March 2003. Only two banks maintained more than 6 percent leverage ratios. One is Shinsei Bank, the former Long-Term Credit Bank of Japan (nationalized in October 1998 and privatized in March 2000). The other is Aozora Bank, the former Nippon Credit Bank (nationalized in

Table 5.4 **Stock portfolios and capital in the banking sector (trillion yen)**

	Market value of shares held by banks (A)	Book value of shares held by banks (B)	Capital account (core capital) (C)	Deferred tax asset (D)	Estimated underreserving (E)	Equity capital held by the government (F)	Net private capital (C) + ([A] – [B]) × 0.6 – (D) – (E) – (F)	Nikkei225 Index
March 1991	77.7	33.1	30.2	0.0	n.a.	0.0	57.0	26,292
March 1992	56.4	34.5	31.3	0.0	n.a.	0.0	44.4	19,346
March 1993	56.4	34.5	31.8	0.0	n.a.	0.0	44.9	18,591
March 1994	61.9	36.5	32.3	0.0	n.a.	0.0	47.5	19,112
March 1995	52.0	39.8	32.3	0.0	n.a.	0.0	39.6	13,140
March 1996	64.3	43.0	27.9	0.0	n.a.	0.0	40.7	21,407
March 1997	54.1	42.9	28.5	0.0	15.0	0.0	20.2	18,003
March 1998	50.8	45.7	24.5	0.0	5.1	0.3	22.2	16,527
March 1999	47.1	42.7	33.7	8.4	4.6	6.3	17.1	15,837
March 2000	54.5	44.4	35.2	8.1	6.6	6.9	19.7	20,337
March 2001	44.5	44.3	36.7	7.3	7.6	7.1	14.8	13,000
March 2002	34.4	34.4	29.3	10.7	6.9	7.2	4.5	11,025
March 2003	23.2	23.2	24.8	10.6	5.4	7.3	1.5	7,973

Source: Federation of Bankers Associations of Japan, various issues.

Notes: Tables represent amounts on the banking accounts of all banks in Japan. Estimated underreserving (E) = required loan loss reserve – actual loan loss reserve. Required loan loss reserve = 1 percent of normal loan + 20 percent of substandard loan + 70 percent of doubtful loan + 100 percent of estimated loss loan.

Table 5.5 **Distribution of adjusted capital/asset ratio of major Japanese banks**

		Number of banks							
	Total	Less than –2%	–2% to 0%	0% to 2%	2% to 4%	4% to 6%	More than 6%	Weighted Average (%)	Nikkei 225 index
March 2000	18	0	0	1	16	0	1	3.21	20,337
March 2001	18	0	0	10	6	0	2	1.91	13,000
March 2002	15	0	2	10	1	0	2	0.80	11,025
March 2003	14	1	3	8	0	0	2	0.30	7,873

Source: Japan Center for Economic Research (2001, 2003). The figures are updated by the author.

Notes: Major banks include city banks, long-term credit banks, and major trust banks. We excluded three new but small trust banks: Nomura Trust, Mitsui Asset Trust, and Resona Trust. Two privatized long-term credit banks after nationalization maintain "more than 6 percent" capital. Adjusted capital = core capital + unrealized capital gains and losses + loan loss reserves – estimated required loan loss reserves – deferred tax assets. Estimated required loan loss reserves = 100 percent of defaulted loans + 70 percent of risk loans + 20 percent of doubtful loans + 1 percent of normal loans. Adjusted capital-asset ratio = Adjusted capital/gross assets.

Table 5.6 **Illustrative example of banking-sector profit margin**

	Current situations	Mild inflation
Lending rate (A)	2.0	4.0
Inflation rate (B)	–2.0	2.0
Real interest rate (A) – (B)	4.0	2.0
Funding cost of banks (C)	0.2	1.0
Profit margin (A) – (C)	1.8	3.0

December 1998 and privatized in December 2000). All other banks show declining trends in the ratios.

To sum up, banks are losing money by high levels of loan losses and very thin profit margins. The banking sector is running out of capital, and the banks are surviving with government guarantees of their liabilities. In order to stabilize the banking sector, it is necessary to increase the lending margin of banks. As we will see in the next section, borrowers are already facing relatively high real interest rates due to the gradual acceleration of deflation. Therefore, an increase in the average lending rate is likely to depress the Japanese economy and will aggravate the deflation. In order to avoid this adverse effect, it is necessary to raise nominal interest rates without raising the real cost of debt for weakened borrowers. The only way to do this is to stop deflation and have a mild inflation (table 5.6). By raising trend inflation rate from minus 2 percent to plus 2 percent, for example, banks can raise average lending rate from the current 2 percent to 4 percent. At the same time, the real cost of debt for borrowers will fall from 4 percent to 2 percent.

We have to take note of the fact that a simple injection of government capital to weakened banks would not stabilize the banking sector without a bigger lending margin. Loss-making banks will deplete the injected money sooner or later. In order to revitalize the banking sector without aggravating deflation, the government has to do two things: allow banks to obtain enough lending margin that is consistent with the expected credit costs, and reduce real interest rates by stopping deflation.

Given the sharp recovery of stock prices and the improving performance of borrowing firms, banks showed better results for the fiscal year ending March 2004. The Nikkei index rose from 7,973 at the end of March 2003 to 11,715 one year later. This sharp recovery of stock prices increased the market value of stocks held by banks by about JPY 5 trillion. The recovery of the economy also reduced the loan-loss figures for most banks. On the other hand, one major bank, Resona, and one regional bank, Ashikaga, were effectively nationalized in 2003. Resona group banks alone lost as much as JPY 1,340 billion for fiscal year 2003, and Ashikaga banks also lost JPY 775 billion for the same fiscal year. This means that the banking sector is close to the break-even point but not earning enough of a profit margin to stand on its own feet. Probably, banks have to increase lending margin by about 50 to 100 basis points to make their lending reasonably profitable.

5.4 Macroeconomic Policy under Large GDP Gap and Zero Interest Rate

The Bank of Japan (BOJ) is providing a large amount of monetary base, but broadly defined money supply is not increasing much (figure 5.6). As the short-term interest rates moved close to zero, the monetary base was hoarded by banks and short-term money market dealers and was held as current deposits at the BOJ. Figure 5.7 shows a phase diagram of monetary base and nominal short-term interest rates since 1986, and it can be regarded as an empirical demand function for monetary base. When the short-term nominal interest rate was between 1 and 8 percent, the monetary base–GDP ratio moved between 7 and 9 percent. However, when the short-term interest rate reached 0.5 percent in the summer of 1995, the demand for monetary base became very elastic. The monetary base–GDP ratio increased to 11 percent when the zero-interest-rate policy was adopted in February 1999. From the start of the quantitative easing in March 2001 until the end of 2003, the ratio increased from 12.5 percent to more than 20 percent. The flat part of figure 5.7 clearly shows that the Japanese economy has been in a liquidity trap.

Figure 5.8 shows the reaction function of the BOJ in the face of the falling inflation rate. The overnight call rate was reduced in line with the GDP deflator inflation rate. A one-point fall in the deflation rate induced

Fig. 5.6 Money supply developments
Source: Japan Center for Economic Research (2003).

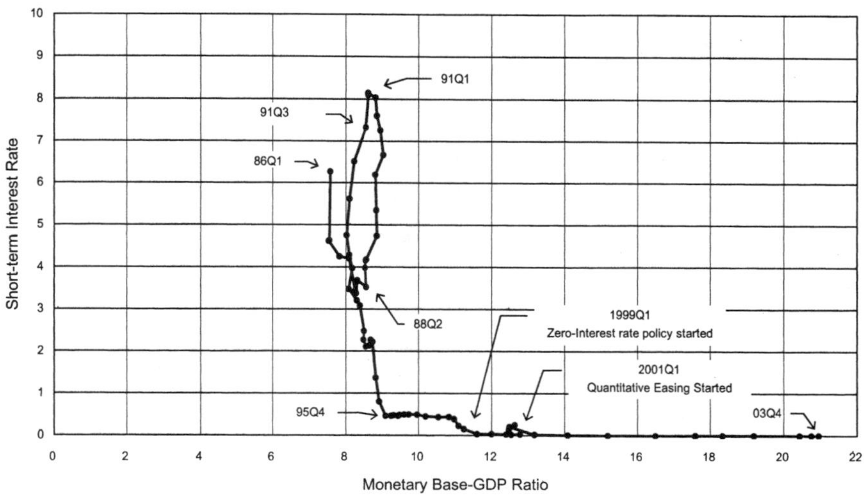

Fig. 5.7 Demand for monetary base

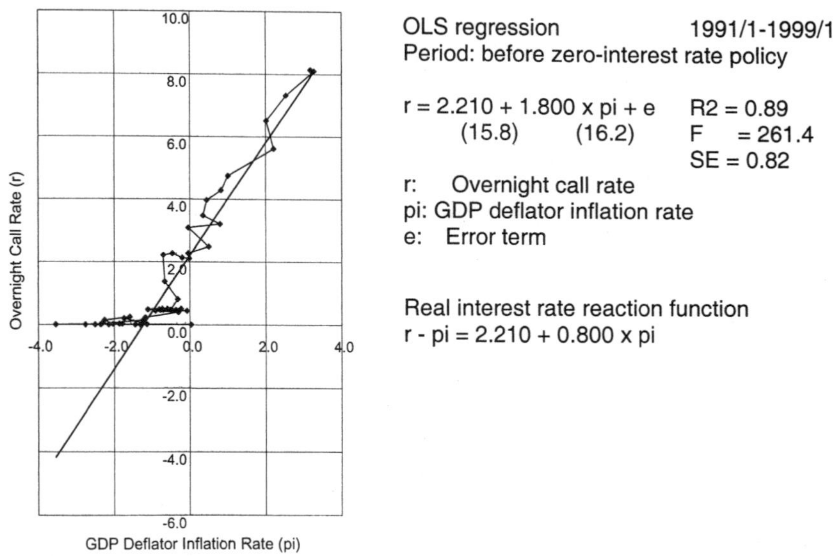

Fig. 5.8 Inflation and short-term money rate (1991–2003)

the BOJ to cut the nominal rate by 1.8 points, thereby reducing the real interest rate by 0.8 points. The BOJ ran out of room for maneuvering when the deflation rate fell down to minus 1.23 percent (1.23 = 2.21/1.80). The bank faced the zero lower bound of the nominal interest rate.

In spite of the aggressive increase of monetary base by the BOJ, real interest rates have been on a rising trend since mid-1998. Figure 5.9 shows

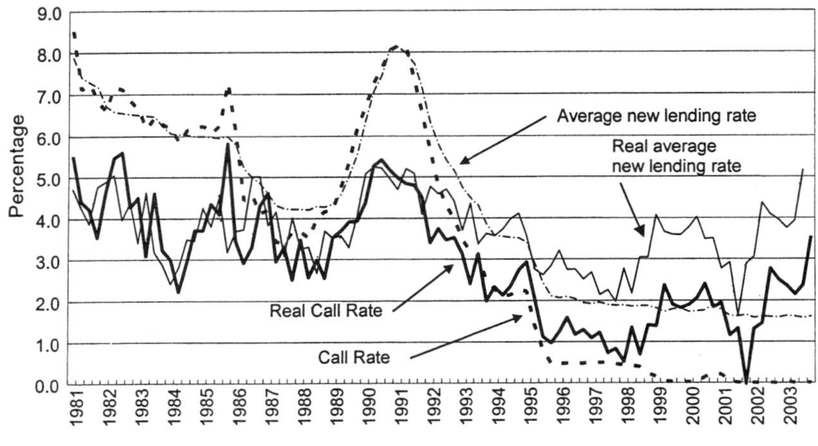

Fig. 5.9 Real and nominal interest rates

Note: Real interest rates are estimated with three-quarter moving average of GDP deflator inflation rate (SAAR).

nominal and real interest rates since 1986. This figure shows the average new lending rate of all banks and overnight call rates. The call rate indicates the short-term interest rates for high-quality borrowers. On the other hand, the average new lending rate indicates the borrowing costs for small and medium-sized enterprises (SMEs). Nominal rates are shown in dotted lines and the real rates in solid lines. While the real and nominal interest rates fell until 1998, the real rates started to rise because of the acceleration of deflation.

Moreover, we have to pay attention to the fact that the gap between the lending rates and the call rate gradually increased in the 1990s. In the 1980s, the difference between the lending rate and the call rate was very small and less than 50 basis points. By the mid-1990s, the gap increased to over 150 basis points. The increasing gap is the result of the decontrol on deposit interest rates and the decline of market interest rates toward zero. Banks lost regulatory rent from deposits in the early 1990s. As the market rates fell toward zero in the 1990s, banks had to raise loan rates to maintain their profit margin. The real new lending rate is close to 4 percent, which is close to the booming bubble period in the late 1980s. Even the real call rate is about 2 percent, which is much higher than the real short-term market rate in the United States of the same period. The high real cost of funding for SMEs is depressing economic activities.

Japan has been in a deflationary trap. High real interest rates due to deflation have been depressing the economy. The depressed economy, in turn, has accelerated deflation, and real interest rates rose further as a result. Conventional open market purchase of government notes and bonds is no longer effective. Since interest rates on short-term treasury bills (TBs) are very close to zero, they have become a perfect substitute for monetary base. An open market purchase of TBs has no expansionary effect because it is an exchange of two perfectly substitutable assets. An open market purchase of long-term government bonds is also ineffective because long-term interest rates are extremely low and the BOJ cannot push down long-term rates any lower.

Even in a liquidity trap, it is possible to consider unconventional monetary-policy measures. The BOJ can buy stocks and/or real estate as instruments of open market operations. The bank started to buy limited amounts of stocks from banks in October 2003 so as to reduce the excessive market risk of stock portfolios held by commercial banks. Because the amount was very limited (the ceiling of the total purchase was initially set at JPY 2 trillion in October 2003 and was increased to JPY 3 trillion in March 2003), its expansionary effect has been limited. The BOJ and the government can also buy foreign-currency-denominated assets to weaken the yen. Since the Ministry of Finance decides the intervention policy in the foreign exchange market, the BOJ cannot use foreign exchange as an instrument of open market operations by itself.

In 2003, the Ministry of Finance carried out massive foreign exchange intervention to keep the yen weak (fig. 5.10). Total purchase of foreign currencies, mostly U.S. dollars, amounted to JPY 20.4 trillion in 2003 and JPY 14.8 trillion in the first quarter of 2004. This is a massive intervention because JPY 35.2 trillion amounts to 7 percent of Japan's GDP. This foreign exchange intervention is accompanied by the BOJ's quantitative expansion of the monetary base. The bank increased its monetary base by JPY 21 tril-

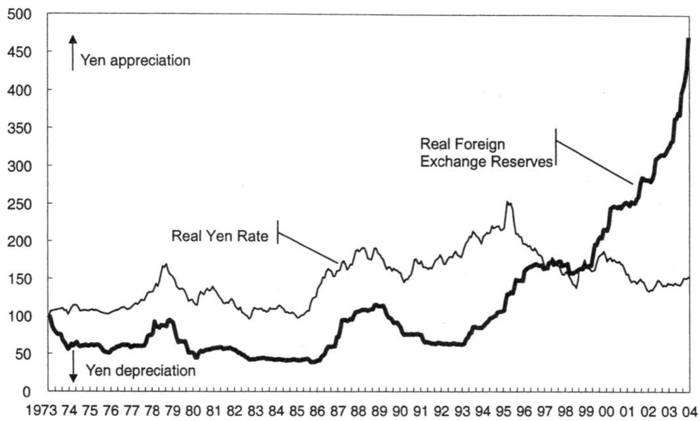

Fig. 5.10 Japanese foreign exchange reserve and real yen-dollar rate

Source: Japan Center for Economic Research (2004).

Notes: Index is equal to 100 in February 1973. Real reserve = Nominal reserve (US$) × Japanese GDP deflator/US GDP deflator/Japanese nominal GDP. Real exchange rate = Nominal yen-dollar rate × (US GDP deflator/Japanese GDP deflator).

Table 5.7 Projection on general government budget deficits

Year	Nominal GDP growth growth rate	Primary balance–GDP ratio	General government gross debt–GDP ratio	General government net debt–GDP ratio	Effective interest rate on net debt	Net interest cost GDP ratio
1999	–1.4	–5.8	120.4	36.0	3.5	1.3
2000	0.8	–6.1	130.7	43.5	3.1	1.3
2001	–1.1	–4.7	142.0	51.0	2.8	1.4
2002	–1.5	–6.0	150.2	59.2	2.1	1.2
2003	0.1	–6.3	157.6	66.6	2.1	1.4
2004	0.0	–6.3	165.3	74.3	2.1	1.6
2005	0.0	–6.3	173.2	82.2	2.3	1.9
2006	0.0	–6.3	181.4	90.4	2.7	2.4
2007	0.0	–6.3	190.1	99.1	3.0	3.0
2008	0.0	–6.3	199.4	108.4	4.0	4.3
2009	0.0	–6.3	210.0	119.0	4.0	4.8

Source: Figures until 2003 are based on International Monetary Fund, *World Economic Outlook,* and Organisation for Economic Co-operation and Development, *Economic Outlook.*

Notes: General government gross asset is assumed to be constant after 2002. Sharp downgradings of JGB are assumed after 2006.

lion from the end of 2002 to the end of March 2004. This intervention policy may have kept the yen relatively weak in 2003 and contributed to the recovery of the economy to some extent.

As a cost of this intervention policy, the Japanese government has increased its foreign exchange exposure. The foreign exchange reserves reached US$827 billion at the end of March and were equivalent to 17 percent of GDP. A 10 percent fall of the U.S. dollar induces a capital loss of 1.7 percent of GDP to the Japanese government.

Regarding fiscal policy, the extremely large budget deficit also makes it very difficult to use fiscal policy to stimulate the economy. Table 5.7 shows the budgetary situations of the general government of Japan, including the central government, local government, and the social security fund. The gross debt–GDP ratio was already 158 percent at the end of 2003. With an extremely large budget deficit and stagnant nominal GDP, this ratio is likely to increase by 8 to 9 points a year. The gross debt of the general government will reach 200 percent by 2008. Even though the net debt–GDP ratio is still at 66 percent, it is likely to surpass 100 percent by 2008. Moreover, these figures do not include off-balance-sheet liabilities such as failing national pension systems and loss-making government-owned companies.

At the time of this writing, the Japanese yen government bond (JGB) is rated AA– by Standard & Poor's and A2 by Moody's, and these are the lowest ratings among major countries. Unless the Japanese economy can get out of deflation with the current economic recovery, I expect that the JGB will be downgraded further. In that event, the government will have to shift its funding from long-term bonds to short-term notes so as to reduce interest costs. However, the shortening maturity of JGB will increase the funding vulnerability against a sharp rise in interest rates.

Such downgrading of government bonds would adversely affect the international operations of Japanese financial institutions and companies. Since sovereign credit rating usually sets the ceiling rate for private companies, they will face a rising funding cost in international financial markets.

5.5 Concluding Remarks

In this chapter, we analyzed the causes of the persistent deflation in Japan. We found that the deflation has been accelerating gradually since the mid-1990s. Because of the acceleration of deflation, real interest rates are rising and conventional monetary-policy tools have lost effectiveness.

As we explained in the introduction, the Japanese economy started to recover in 2003 due to the succession of propitious events. If the economy can overcome deflation with this recovery, the Japanese episode of zero interest rate will be over. However, we economists have to think hard to come up with monetary-policy instruments that will be effective even under a deflation. One such instrument is the idea of a Gesell tax or the famous stamp duty on money.[7] By levying taxes on the outstanding amount of government-guaranteed financial assets, it is possible to set nominal return on safe assets at a negative number. In other words, it is possible to overcome the zero lower bound on nominal interest rates by introducing a new tax on some financial assets. In the following, I summarize my proposal in my earlier paper.[8]

The government may levy a tax on the balance of all the government-guaranteed financial assets. Taxable assets include all the central and local government liabilities; all the government-guaranteed assets, such as postal saving deposits and postal life insurance policies; and all the yen liabilities of the banking sector that are effectively guaranteed by the deposit insurance system. In order to avoid tax loopholes, yen cash payments on derivative transactions by banks should also be taxed. It is necessary to levy tax on the monetary base, including banknotes and central bank deposits from private banks. In order to tax cash, the BOJ may print new bank notes and levy fees for the exchange with old bank notes. Alternatively, the government can levy stamp duty on old bank notes. Since taxable assets are the liabilities of the government bodies and the banking sector, this tax can be implemented fairly easily under the current tax collection system. The most messy part is the taxation on the bank notes. All the automated teller machines and automatic vending machines need adjustments for new notes.

7. See chapter 23 of Keynes (1936). Goodfriend (2000) also discussed the possible taxation on currency to fight against deflation.
8. See Fukao (2003) for the details of this proposal.

In order to have expansionary effects, this Gesell tax has to be somewhat higher than the rate of deflation. Given the recent deflation rate of 1 to 2 percent per annum, the tax rate can be set at around 2 percent. This tax has to be levied repeatedly as long as deflation continues. The Gesell tax can be regarded as a substitute for inflation tax on government liabilities. When an economy experiences a steady and mild inflation, the government can enjoy declining real value of its liabilities. This inflation tax has expansionary effects on the economy by encouraging rational economic agents to invest in real assets. In a deflationary economy, the increasing real value of safe assets has contractionary effects on the economy.

This Gesell tax will have very strong expansionary effects on expenditures. People will shift assets from "safe" assets to risky assets. In other words, people will shift from taxable assets to all the nontaxable assets. Since stocks, real estate, corporate bonds, foreign bonds, and consumer durables are not taxed, the demand for these assets will increase. The yen exchange rate will also depreciate against foreign currencies. This tax will also stimulate bank lending activities. Banks will shift assets from BOJ deposits and government bonds to loans and corporate bonds. Intercorporate credit will also expand because receivables are not taxed, but cash and deposits will be taxed.

This tax will also generate a large amount of revenue for the government. The total tax revenue of 2 percent tax on government-guaranteed financial assets would amount to about 28 trillion yen. The government could make use of the tax revenue to reduce its budget deficit, recapitalize deposit insurance funds, or improve its antiunemployment policy. It is possible to sweeten this tax proposal by distributing cash to all the people living in Japan. The cost of distributing 50,000 yen per person to everybody is 7 trillion yen, and this cost is only one-quarter of the revenue from this tax.

One negative aspect of this tax is the possible negative effect on the credit rating of the Japanese government. For example, Moody's Investors Service states that an imposition of tax on the government liabilities may constitute an event of partial default by the government. However, this is a relatively minor problem because only a small portion of JGB is held by foreign investors.

Appendix

Potential GDP and GDP gaps are estimated from the following data:

1. *Real GDP, GDP deflator:* Cabinet Office, Economic Social Research Institute, quarterly series.

2. *Capital stock:* Cabinet Office, Economic Social Research Institute, quarterly series. The data were adjusted to remove the gaps due to privatization of Nippon Telephone and Telegraph Co. (1985 Q2), Japan Tobacco

Co. (1985 Q2), Electric Power Development Co. (1986 Q4), East Japan Railway Co. (1987 Q2), and sales of new trunk lines from the government to railway companies (1991 Q4).

3. *Capacity utilization ratio for the manufacturing sector:* Ministry of Economy and Trade (METI), capacity utilization index for the manufacturing sector.

4. *Capacity utilization ratio for the nonmanufacturing sector:* Since there are no statistics on the capacity utilization for the nonmanufacturing sector, we estimated the ratio by using the Bank of Japan Tankan statistics on the diffusion index (DI) on capacity utilization. First, we estimated the relationship between the capacity utilization ratio for the manufacturing sector (METI data) and Tankan DI of the same sector:

$$\text{Manufacturing capacity utilization} = 109.18 - 0.53 \times \text{Manufacturing Tankan DI.}$$

By replacing Manufacturing Tankan DI with Nonmanufacturing DI, we estimated the capacity utilization ratio for the nonmanufacturing sector after 1991 Q1. Since there is no Tankan DI data for the nonmanufacturing sector before 1990 Q4, we estimated nonmanufacturing-sector DI with the following equation and manufacturing Tankan DI:

$$\text{Nonmanufacturing DI} = -5.75 + 0.44 \times \text{Manufacturing Tankan DI.}$$

Both capacity utilization ratios are normalized to be 100 at their peaks.

Figure 5A.1 shows the estimated capacity utilization for nonmanufacturing as well as manufacturing sector capacity utilization.

5. *Actual capital input:* Estimated from the following equation:

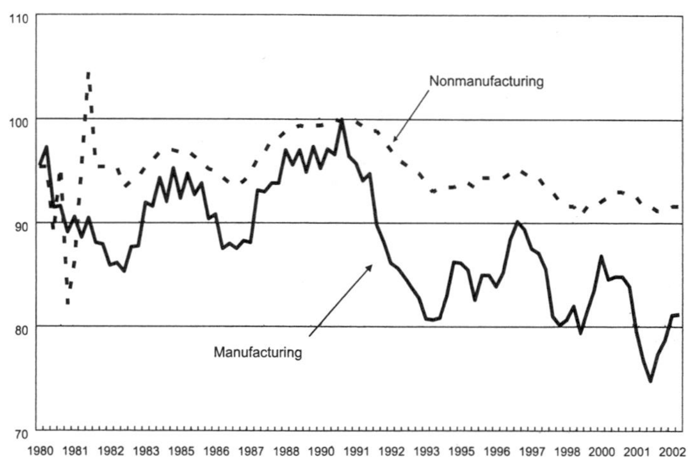

Fig. 5A.1 Capital utilization ratios of manufacturing and nonmanufacturing sectors (manufacturing: 1990:4 = 100, nonmanufacturing: 1990:1 = 100)

Source: Japan Center for Economic Research (2004).

$$\begin{aligned}\text{Actual capital input} = {} & [(\text{manufacturingsector capital stock}) \\ & \times (\text{manufacturing sector capacity utilization ratio}) \\ & + (\text{nonmanufacturing-sector capital stock}) \\ & \times (\text{nonmanufacturing-sector capacity utilization ratio})] \div 100.\end{aligned}$$

6. *Potential capital input:* Estimated from the following equation:

$$\begin{aligned}\text{Potential capital input} = {} & \text{Manufacturing-sector capital stock} \\ & + \text{Nonmanufacturing-sector capital stock}.\end{aligned}$$

7. *Actual labor input:* Actual labor input on a man-hour basis is estimated by the following equation:

$$\begin{aligned}\text{Actual labor input} = {} & \text{Number of employees and self-employed} \\ & \times (\text{Scheduled working hours} \\ & + \text{Overtime working hours}).\end{aligned}$$

Number of employees and self-employed: Ministry of Public Management, Home Affairs, Posts and Telecommunications, Statistics on Labor, all industries.

Working hours: Ministry of Health, Labor and Welfare, Monthly Labor Survey, average monthly working hours per employee in all establishments of more than five workers. Figure 5A.2 shows the development of scheduled

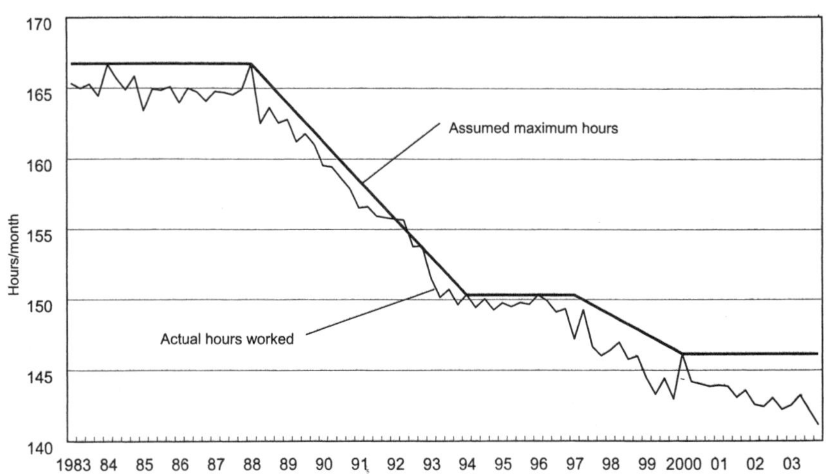

Fig. 5A.2 Regular hours per worker
Source: Japan Center for Economic Research (2004).

working hours. Because of the gradual introduction of the five-day work-week in 1988 for large companies and in 1997 for small companies, the scheduled hours declined twice.

8. *Potential labor input:* Potential labor input is estimated by connecting the past peaks of all the variables in *Actual labor input.*

References

Fukao, Mitsuhiro. 2003. Financial strains and the zero lower bound: The Japanese experience. BIS Working Paper no. 141. Basel, CHE: Bank for International Settlements.

Fukao, Mitsuhiro, and Japan Center for Economic Research. 2004. *Examining the profitability of Japanese industrial banking and life-insurance industries* (in Japanese). Tokyo: Chuo Keizai Sha.

Goodfriend, Marvin. 2000. Financial stability, deflation and monetary policy. Paper presented at the ninth international conference at the Institute of Monetary and Economic Studies, The Role of Monetary Policy under Low Inflation: Deflationary Shocks and Their Policy Responses. July 3–4, Tokyo.

Japan Center for Economic Research. 2001. *Monetary policy under deflation* (in Japanese). Financial Research Report no. 4. Tokyo: Japan Center for Economic Research.

———. 2003. *Accelerating deflation and monetary policy* (in Japanese). Financial Research Report no. 8. Tokyo: Japan Center for Economic Research.

———. 2004. *Economic analysis of deflation, yen appreciation, and long-term interest rates* (in Japanese). Financial Research Report no. 10. Tokyo: Japan Center for Economic Research.

Keynes, John M. 1936. *General theory of employment, interest, and money.* London: Macmillan.

Koga, Maiko. 2003. Why is the rate of decline in the GDP deflator so large? Economic Commentary no. 2003-2. Tokyo: The Bank of Japan.

Kuroda, Sachiko, and Isamu Yamamoto. 2003. The impact of downward nominal wage rigidity on the unemployment rate: Quantitative evidence from Japan. *Monetary and Economic Studies* 21 (4): 57–86.

Comment Piti Disyatat

Overview

The chapter provides a focused and interesting account of the causes of persistent deflation in Japan, highlighting the implications that price declines have had on the banking sector. The discussion is broadly divided

Piti Disyatat is a senior economist at the Bank of Thailand.

The views expressed here are those of the author and do not necessarily represent those of the Bank of Thailand or Bank of Thailand policy.

into two parts. The first concentrates on linking persistent and accelerating deflation to the existence of a negative output gap, while the second focuses more on the macroeconomic impact of a deflationary environment and implications for policy.

Although much of the chapter is descriptive in nature, the analysis does point out a close link between the author's estimated output gap and developments in the GDP deflator. In this regard, it would be useful if the chapter clarified a bit more the reasons behind focusing on the GDP deflator as a measure of prices rather than the CPI. On the state of the banking system, the chapter lays out clearly the main reasons why things may appear better then they are. In particular, it points out hidden weaknesses in banks' capital position and highlights the fact that Japanese banks' plight is far from over. To gain a better appreciation of how extensive the problem is, it would be nice if more information on the cross-section variation in banks' balance sheets were provided (indeed, table 5.3 indicates substantial differences across banks and suggests that things are perhaps worse for smaller banks).

The chapter could emphasize more the role that problems in the banking sector and sluggish loan growth have contributed to persistent deflation. What is needed to end deflation is an expansion in broader monetary aggregates, since these are effectively the balances that ultimately "chase" real goods and services. But it is not that central banks can directly increase broad-money supply and bank lending. They must do so through the provision of funds to financial institutions in exchange for bonds or foreign exchange. When credit markets function properly, this expansion in loanable funds leads to a rise in the supply credit that underpins the increase in broad money. However, given the ongoing banking-sector problems, monetary expansion through traditional channels may not be effective in raising broad-money aggregates. The problem stems from lingering balance-sheet weaknesses that continue to plague both the banking and corporate sectors. At the same time, excess capacity and uncertainty about future economic prospects have dampened the demand for credit. When firms are not eager to raise funds and banks are not eager to lend, higher liquidity in the banking system will not translate into higher liquidity in the economy. In this way, the slow pace of banking and corporate restructuring has contributed to the persistence of deflation in Japan.

Implications for Policy

The chapter stresses the need to improve banks' profitability through increasing lending rates while at the same time not exacerbating real debt burdens on borrowers. The only way in which this can be achieved is thus through the attainment of a positive inflation rate. The chapter does not, however, say how to achieve this. Indeed, given the large number of recommendations in the literature, it would have been nice to see where Fukao stands on this issue.

More important, however, focusing on loan margins alone is unlikely to solve the banking sector's problem since much of it is a *stock* problem associated with credit quality. Indeed, given the low demand for loans, abundant liquidity, and high degree of competition with respect to loan extension, it is unclear whether banks will actually be able to raise nominal loan rates. Other potentially more productive ways to increase spreads include (a) the moving of excess liquidity into loans; (b) the restructuring of nonperforming loans (NPLs) to yield positive returns again; and (c) the resolution of NPLs and liquidation of foreclosed assets into cash that can be invested.

The Japanese economy would certainly benefit from a reestablishment of consumer, business, and investor confidence, which cannot happen unless the macroenvironment becomes supportive. From this perspective, stopping deflation is a central element of the solution. However, it is only a first step. Many of the potential benefits lie elsewhere. The chapter could perhaps emphasize more the structural nature of the problem in Japan in which deflation is only one of the symptoms. Policy initiatives should stress the need for NPLs to be recognized at the appropriate prices and loans to bankrupt companies not rolled over. Incentives for accelerated restructuring and disposal of nonviable assets should be emphasized. At the same time, any further public injection of money must be accompanied by strict conditionality to make sure that the money is not used simply to prop up the system.

The chapter could also elaborate more on the dangers associated with the Japanese government's ballooning debt stock. Such a discussion could also usefully focus on the contingent liabilities of the government, including the possibility of large marked-to-market losses associated with the rapid accumulation of reserves that may occur should the U.S. dollar weaken further and yields on U.S. treasuries rise (as many expect). In this regard, credibility of the medium-term fiscal consolidation can be enhanced by setting clear medium-term debt targets.

Monetary Policy

To overcome the zero lower bound (ZLB) on interest rates, the chapter suggests the introduction of a tax on money holdings. However, this is unlikely to be either practical or desirable since it is the banks, not households, that are hoarding base money, and such a scheme may have adverse implications for consumer confidence. Also, if the tax encourages banks to spend money when there is simply no loan demand, banks may be encouraged to take on more risk than they should.

More substantially, it should be stressed that the ZLB does not entail ineffectiveness of monetary policy. While the ZLB indeed limits the use of traditional methods of boosting aggregate demand, it does not prevent central banks from turning to other means. In particular, short-term interest rates are simply one intermediate target of monetary policy, and should this cease to be a useful benchmark for policy, central banks can turn to other targets (such as money supply or exchange rates). The real complication of the ZLB lies in the fact that switching operational targets introduces uncertainty with respect to the size and lags of the economy's response to policy actions, making it harder to set policy targets to achieve the desired effect.

Finally, while much of the literature—this chapter included—has focused on the difficulties associated with how to conduct monetary policy against the backdrop of deflation and a ZLB constraint, it is also unclear how effective policy will be once interest rates are positive because of excess liquidity problems in banks. In particular, with loan demand still weak and plenty of funds to lend, the pass-through from changes in short-term money market rates controlled by the central bank to retail rates may be much smaller and slower than usual.

Overall, the chapter provides a succinct analysis of the key problems associated with deflation in Japan with an illuminating discussion of the state of the banking system. That said, it paints a somewhat pessimistic picture of the Japanese economy in contrast to recent data releases, which appear to indicate a brighter prospect for sustained recovery.

Comment James Harrigan

Fukao covers a lot of ground in his chapter, and I agree with much of what he says, particularly in his discussion of the financial sector. I have some questions about his analysis of the macroeconomic situation, however, and that is where I will focus my remarks.

Fukao's presentation of the Phillips curve is somewhat unusual, so it may be useful to summarize his analysis. He uses three concepts of output. The first is actual real GDP as reported in the national accounts. In the data used in the statistical model, no adjustment is made for the large and growing bias in the GDP deflator, although the importance of this is discussed elsewhere in the text.

The second concept of output used is what is called "potential GDP." This is calculated in three steps:

James Harrigan is a research officer in the International Research Department of the Federal Reserve Bank of New York, and a research associate of the National Bureau of Economic Research

1. Estimate maximum possible levels of capital and labor input, $K_t^{\max}$ and $L_t^{\max}$.

2. Calculate aggregate TFP from a Cobb-Douglas production function using actual levels of capital and labor input,

$$\ln \mathrm{TFP}_t = \ln Y_t - 0.29 \ln K_t - 0.71 \ln L_t.$$

3. Calculate the level of potential GDP as

$$\ln Y_t^{\max} = \ln \mathrm{TFP}_t + 0.29 \ln K_t^{\max} + 0.71 \ln L_t^{\max}.$$

This definition of potential GDP doesn't seem like a useful number for several reasons. First, this level is never attainable as a market equilibrium or any other system of allocating resources. Second, the interpretation of TFP is problematic. As is well known, measured aggregate TFP has an important cyclical component which partially reflects labor hoarding. As a consequence, TFP growth will fall during periods of slack resource use even if there has been no negative shock to underlying technological possibilities. Taking the trend in measured TFP, as Fukao does, will not solve this problem in the Japanese case since resource use has been slack for so long and will therefore affect the estimated trend.

The final output concept used is "natural GDP," which is defined as a constant fraction of potential GDP,

$$Y_t^n = 0.97 Y_t^{\max}.$$

The fraction 0.97 is estimated as part of the estimation of the Phillips curve relationship. The Phillips curve is unorthodox, since it imposes purely backward expectations that have a unit root (the sum of the coefficients on lagged inflation sum to one). A constant output gap leads to a constant change in inflation, and the coefficient on the output gap changes in 1994. The dynamics of inflation implied by the Phillips curve can be summarized as

$$\Delta\pi_t = 0.35 \ln \frac{Y_t^n}{Y_t} \quad 1985-1993$$

$$\Delta\pi_t = 0.08 \ln \frac{Y_t^n}{Y_t} \quad 1994-2003.$$

This statistical model is best interpreted as a reduced-form data description, rather than a structural model that explains how macro weakness has led to deflation. The reason for this is that there is no role for forward-looking expectations in this model, nor are there supply shocks.

Even as a purely reduced-form relationship, the equation is questionable. The sharp drop in the estimated relationship between inflation and output gap starting in 1994 is puzzling, especially since it appears from the *t*-statistics in the equation that it would be impossible to reject the hypothesis that the true relationship is zero. If so, the model has rather surprising implications: long-run inflation is a random walk after 1994.

More generally, Fukao's macroeconomic analysis leaves many unanswered questions. Recession, deflation, insolvent banks, and a high government debt are all jointly determined in principle and surely in practice, which leaves causation unclear. In my view, the most important unanswered questions are

- What exogenous shocks and/or policy errors caused the Lost Decade?
- What policies might extricate Japan from Lost Decade 2.0?

Fukao closes with some remarks about the fiscal position of the Japanese state that stress the large gross debt. I agree with Broda and Weinstein's (2004) view that what matters for economic analysis of fiscal policy is the government's net debt, which Fukao acknowledges is far less alarming.

Finally, I think it is inappropriate to take seriously the rating downgrades of Japanese government bonds. Taken literally, such downgrades suggest that the probability of the Japanese state defaulting on the nominal value of bonds issued in yen is strictly greater than zero. Given that the Japanese state can print an infinite amount of yen at zero cost, my estimate of default probability is zero.

Reference

Broda, Christian, and Weinstein, David E. Happy news from the dismal science: Reassessing the Japanese fiscal policy and sustainability. NBER Working Paper no. 10988. Cambridge, MA: National Bureau of Economic Research, December.

6 Monetary and Fiscal Policy in a Liquidity Trap
The Japanese Experience 1999–2004

Mitsuru Iwamura, Takeshi Kudo and Tsutomu Watanabe

6.1 Introduction

Recent developments in the Japanese economy are characterized by the concurrence of two rare phenomena: deflation and zero nominal interest rates. The year-on-year Consumer Price Index (CPI) inflation rate has been below zero for about six years since the second quarter of 1998 (see figure 6.1). On the other hand, the uncollateralized overnight call rate has been practically zero since the Bank of Japan (BOJ) policy board made a decision on February 12, 1999, to lower it to be "as low as possible" (see figure 6.2).

The concurrence of these two phenomena has revived the interest of researchers in what Keynes (1936) called a liquidity trap, and various studies have recently investigated this issue. These studies share the following two features. First, regarding diagnosis, they argue that the natural rate of interest, which is defined as the equilibrium real interest rate, is below zero in Japan, while the real overnight call rate is above zero because of deflationary expectations, and that such an interest rate gap leads to weak aggregate demand. This diagnosis was first made by Krugman (1998) and is shared by Woodford (1999); Reifschneider and Williams (2000); Jung, Teranishi, and Watanabe (2003); and Eggertsson and Woodford (2003a, b), among others.[1]

Mitsuru Iwamura is a professor at the Waseda University Institute of Asia-Pacific Studies. Takeshi Kudo is a lecturer in the faculty of economics at Nagasaki University. Tsutomu Watanabe is a professor at the Institute of Economic Research, Hitotsubashi University.

We would like to thank Laurence Ball, Marvin Goodfriend, Fumio Hayashi, Bennett T. McCallum, Shigenori Shiratsuka, Kazuo Ueda, Mike Woodford and two anonymous referees for useful suggestions and comments, and Naohiko Baba and Kazuhiko Ishid for helping us to collect the data.

1. Rogoff (1998) casts doubt on the plausibility of this diagnosis by pointing out that the investment-GDP ratio is well over 20 percent in Japan. Benhabib, Schmitt-Grohe, and Uribe

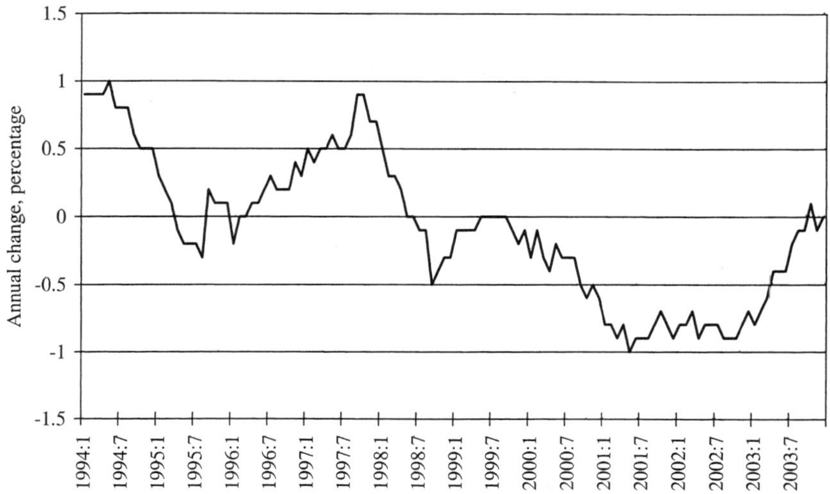

Fig. 6.1 CPI inflation

Source: "Consumer Price Index," The Ministry of Public Management, Home Affairs, Posts, and Telecommunications

Second, based on this diagnosis, these studies write out a prescription that the BOJ should make a commitment to an expansionary monetary policy in the future. Woodford (1999) and Reifschneider and Williams (2000) argue that, even when the current overnight interest rate is close to zero, the long-term nominal interest rate could be well above zero if future overnight rates are expected to be above zero.[2] In this situation, a central bank could lower the long-term nominal interest rate by committing itself to an expansionary monetary policy in the future, thereby stimulating current aggregate demand. As emphasized by Woodford (1999); Jung, Teranishi, and Watanabe (2003); and Eggertsson and Woodford (2003a, b), an important feature of this prescription is monetary-policy inertia: a zero interest rate policy should be continued for a while, even after the natural rate of interest returns to a positive level. By making such a commitment, a central bank is able to achieve lower long-term nominal interest rates, higher expected inflation, and a weaker domestic currency in the adverse periods

(2002) show the existence of a self-fulfilling deflationary equilibrium, in which deflation and zero interest rates simultaneously occur even if the natural rate of interest stays above zero. Christiano (2004) investigates the numerical conditions under which the natural rate of interest falls temporarily below zero, using a model with endogenous capital formation.

2. Note that this argument assumes that an adverse shock to the natural rate of interest is not permanent but temporary. Otherwise, future overnight rates are also constrained by the zero lower bound, so that there is no room for lowering the long-term nominal interest rate. Svensson (2001) names this a *temporary* liquidity trap to emphasize the difference from the original definition by Keynes (1936) in which the long-term nominal interest rate faces the zero bound constraint.

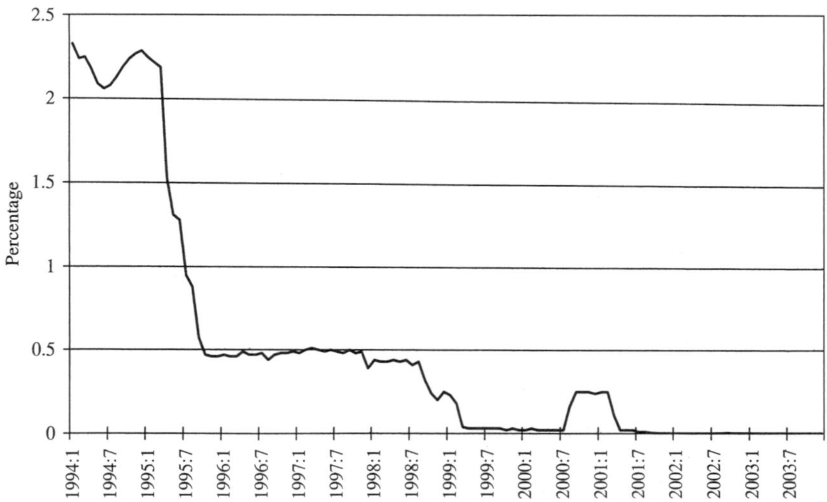

Fig. 6.2 Uncollateralized overnight call rates
Source: Bank of Japan

when the natural rate of interest significantly deviates from a normal level. This is as if a central bank "borrows" future monetary easing in the periods when current monetary easing is exhausted.

This idea of borrowing future easing has been discussed not only in the academic arena, but also in the policymaking process.[3] Just after the introduction of a "zero interest rate policy" in February 1999, there was a perception in the money markets that such an irregular policy would not be continued for long. Reflecting this perception, implied forward interest rates for longer than six months started to rise in early March. This was clearly against the BOJ's expectation that the zero overnight call rate would spread to longer-term nominal interest rates. Forced to make the bank's policy intention clearer, Governor Masaru Hayami announced on April 13, 1999, that the monetary-policy board would keep the overnight interest rate at zero until "deflationary concerns are dispelled."[4] Some researchers and practitioners argue that this announcement has had the effect of lowering longer-term interest rates by altering the market's expec-

3. For example, Governor Toshihiko Fukui stated no June 1, 2003, that the idea behind the current policy commitment is "to achieve an easing effect by the Bank's commitment to keep short-term rates at low levels well into the future. In this way, even if short-term rates come up against the lower bound, the Bank can still "borrow" from the effect of the future low rates" (Fukui 2003).

4. The BOJ terminated this commitment in August 2000, and made a new commitment of maintaining quantitative-easing policy until "the core CPI registers stably a zero percent or an increase year on year" in March 2001. See table 6.1 for the chronology of the BOJ's monetary policy decisions in 1999–2004.

Table 6.1 Chronology of monetary policy decisions in 1999–2004

Date	Event
09/09/98	The BOJ reduces the target O/N rate to 0.25 from 0.50 percent.
02/12/99	The BOJ introduces a zero interest rate policy (ZIRP).
04/13/99	Governor Hayami announces the BOJ will continue the ZIRP until "deflationary concerns are dispelled."
10/13/99	The BOJ expands the range of money market operations.
08/11/00	The BOJ terminates the ZIRP. The target O/N rate is set at 0.25 percent.
02/09/01	The BOJ introduces "Lombard-type" lending facility and reduces the official discount rate to 0.375 from 0.5 percent.
02/28/01	The BOJ reduces the target O/N rate to 0.125 percent and the official discount rate to 0.25 percent.
03/19/01	The BOJ announces to introduce "quantitative monetary easing policy" and continue it until "the core CPI records a year-on-year increase of zero percent or more on a stable basis."
08/14/01	The BOJ raises the target CAB to 6 trillion yen.
09/18/01	The BOJ raises the target CAB to above 6 trillion yen.
12/19/01	The BOJ raises the target CAB to 10–15 trillion yen.
10/30/02	The BOJ raises the target CAB to 15–20 trillion yen.
04/01/03	The BOJ raises the target CAB to 17–22 trillion yen.
04/30/03	The BOJ raises the target CAB to 22–27 trillion yen.
05/20/03	The BOJ raises the target CAB to 27–30 trillion yen.
10/10/03	The BOJ raises the target CAB to 27–32 trillion yen. The BOJ announces more detailed description of its commitment regarding the timing to terminate "quantitative easing policy."
01/20/04	The BOJ raises the target CAB to 30–35 trillion yen.

tations about the future path of the overnight call rate (Taylor 2000). Given such a similarity between the BOJ's policy intention and the prescriptions proposed by academic researchers, a natural question is whether or not the BOJ's policy commitment is close to the optimal one. The first objective of this chapter is to measure the distance between the optimal monetary-policy rule derived in the literature and the BOJ's policy in practice.

The second objective of this chapter is to think about the role of fiscal policy in a liquidity trap. The typical textbook answer to the question of how to escape from a liquidity trap is to adopt an expansionary fiscal policy, given that monetary policy is ineffective in the sense of no more room for current interest rate reductions (Hicks 1967). Interestingly, however, researchers since Krugman (1998) pay almost no attention to the role of fiscal policy. This difference comes from their assumption about the behavior of the government: the government adjusts its primary surplus so that the government intertemporal budget constraint is satisfied for *any* possible path of the price level. That is, fiscal policy is assumed to be "passive" in the sense of Leeper (1991) or "Ricardian" in the terminology of Woodford (1995). Given this assumption, the government budget constraint is automatically satisfied, so that researchers need not worry about the government's solvency condition in characterizing the optimal monetary-policy rule in a liquidity trap.[5] However, this does not necessarily imply that fiscal policy plays no role in the determination of equilibrium inflation. Rather, as pointed out by Iwamura and Watanabe (2002) and Eggertsson and Woodford (2003b), a path for the primary surplus is uniquely selected when one chooses a monetary-policy path by solving a central bank's loss-minimization problem. Put differently, even if a central bank faithfully follows the optimal monetary-policy rule derived in the literature, the economy might fail to achieve the optimal outcome if the government's behavior deviates from the one compatible with the optimal monetary-policy rule. Then one might ask whether or not the assumption of passive fiscal policy was actually satisfied during the period in which the Japanese economy was in a liquidity trap. Specifically, one might be interested in whether or not the Japanese government has adjusted the primary balance as implicitly assumed in the literature.

The rest of the chapter is organized as follows. Section 6.2 characterizes optimal policies in a liquidity trap with a special emphasis on the optimal fiscal-policy rule. Sections 6.3 and 6.4 compare the optimal commitment solution with the monetary and fiscal policy adopted in 1999–2004. Section 6.5 concludes the chapter.

6.2 Optimal Commitment Policy in a Liquidity Trap

6.2.1 A Simple Model

Household's Consumption Decision

Let us consider a representative household that seeks to maximize a discounted sum of utilities of the form

$$E_0\left[\sum_{t=0}^{\infty} \beta^t u(c_t + g_t)\right],$$

where $u(\cdot)$ is an increasing and concave function with respect to $c_t + g_t$, and β represents the discount factor. Following Woodford (2001), we assume that the private consumption expenditures c_t and the government purchases g_t are perfectly substitutable, so that government purchases have exactly the same effect on the economy as transfers to households of funds sufficient to finance private consumption for exactly the same amount. This assumption, together with the assumption of lump-sum taxes, creates a simple environment in which the government behavior affects the equilibrium only through changes in the household's budget constraint. Also, we do not treat money balances and labor supply explicitly in the utility

5. With respect to this, Krugman states, "We assume . . . that any implications of the [open market] operation for the government's budget constraint are taken care of via lump-sum taxes and transfers" (Krugman 2000, 225).

function in order to make the exposition simpler (see Woodford [2003] for detailed discussions on these issues).

The representative household is subject to a flow budget constraint of the form

$$P_t c_t + \sum_{j=1}^{\infty} E_t[Q_{t,t+j}][B^h_{t,t+j} - B^h_{t-1,t+j}] \leq P_t d_t + B^h_{t-1,t}, \tag{2.1}$$

where P_t is the price level, d_t is the household's disposable income, and $Q_{t,t+j}$ is a (nominal) stochastic discount factor for pricing arbitrary financial claims that matures in period $t + j$.[6] We assume that the government issues zero-coupon nominal bonds, each of which pays one yen when it matures, and denote the face value of bonds held by the representative household at the end of period t that will come due in period $t + j$ by $B^h_{t,t+j}$. Since the nominal market price in period t of a bond that matures in period $t + j$ is $E_t[Q_{t,t+j}]$ $(= E_t[1 \times Q_{t,t+j}])$, the second term on the right-hand side represents the amount of repayment for bonds that mature in period t. The representative household allocates the sum of disposable income and the repayment between consumption expenditures and the purchases of government bonds. The term $B^h_{t,t+j} - B^h_{t-1,t+j}$ represents the change from the previous period in the face value of bonds that mature in period $t + j$, namely, an amount of net purchase in period t. These new bonds are evaluated at the market price in period t. Note that nominal bond prices must satisfy

$$E_t[Q_{t,t+j}] = E_t[Q_{t,t+1} Q_{t+1,t+2} \times \ldots \times Q_{t+j-1,t+j}],$$

and that the one-period risk-free nominal interest rate in period $t + k$ $(k \geq 0)$, which is denoted by i_{t+k}, satisfies

$$\frac{1}{1 + i_{t+k}} = E_{t+k}[Q_{t+k,t+k+1}].$$

Under the assumption that the central bank can control the one-period risk-free interest rate, these two equations imply that the market's expectations about the future course of monetary policy, represented by the path of i_{t+k}, affects nominal bond prices.

The sequence of flow budget constraints and the No-Ponzi-game condition implies an intertemporal budget constraint, and necessary and sufficient conditions for household maximization are then that the first-order condition

$$1 + i_t = \beta^{-1}\left\{E_t\left[\frac{u'(c_{t+1} + g_{t+1})}{u'(c_t + g_t)} \cdot \frac{P_t}{P_{t+1}}\right]\right\}^{-1} \tag{2.2}$$

6. Under the assumption of complete financial markets, the existence and uniqueness of such an asset-pricing kernel follows from the absence of arbitrage opportunities.

holds at all times, and that the household exhausts its intertemporal budget constraint. We assume that some part, denoted by v_t, of the economy's output y_t is distributed to another type of household that does not make consumption decisions based on intertemporal utility maximization, so that the market-clearing condition can be written as $y_t = c_t + v_t + g_t$. Substituting this condition into equation (2.2) yields

$$(2.3) \qquad 1 + i_t = \beta^{-1}\left\{E_t\left[\frac{u'(y_{t+1} - v_{t+1})}{u'(y_t - v_t)} \cdot \frac{P_t}{P_{t+1}}\right]\right\}^{-1}.$$

Substituting the same condition into the flow budget constraint (equation [2.1] with an exact equality) and the corresponding intertemporal budget constraint leads to

$$(2.4) \qquad P_t s_t + \sum_{j=1}^{\infty} E_t[Q_{t,t+j}][B_{t,t+j} - B_{t-1,t+j}] = B_{t-1,t}$$

$$(2.5) \qquad \sum_{j=0}^{\infty} E_t[Q_{t,t+j} P_{t+j} s_{t+j}] = \sum_{j=0}^{\infty} E_t[Q_{t,t+j}] B_{t-1,t+j}$$

where s_t represents the real primary surplus, which is defined as tax revenues less government expenditures, and $B_{t,t+j}$ is the supply of government bonds.[7]

We log-linearize equations (2.3) and (2.4) around the baseline path of each variable, which is specified as follows. With respect to the maturity structure of government debt, we assume

$$(2.6) \qquad \frac{B^*_{t-1,t+j}}{B^*_{t+j-1,t+j}} = \theta^j \leq 1 \quad \text{for } j = 1, 2, \ldots,$$

where θ is a parameter satisfying $0 \leq \theta \leq 1$. We use * to indicate the baseline path of a variable. The term $B^*_{t-1,t+j}$ represents the face value of bonds at the end of period $t-1$ that mature in period $t+j$, and $B^*_{t+j-1,t+j}$ represents the face value of the same type of bonds just before redemption in period $t+j$. Equation (2.6) simply states that the government issues additional bonds, which mature in period $t+j$, at a rate θ in each period between t and $t+j-1$. Note that $\theta = 0$ corresponds to the case in which all bonds mature in one period, while $\theta = 1$ corresponds to the case in which all bonds are perpetual bonds. With respect to other variables, we assume

$$c^*_t = c^*;\ y^*_t = y^*;\ s^*_t = s^*;\ P^*_t = P^*;\ Q^*_{t,t+j} = \beta^j;\ v^*_t = 0.$$

Note that the inflation rate is assumed to be zero on the baseline path.

Log-linearizing equation (2.3) around the baseline path, we obtain

$$(2.7) \qquad \hat{x}_t = E_t\hat{x}_{t+1} - \sigma^{-1}[(\hat{\imath}_t - E_t\hat{\pi}_{t+1}) - \hat{r}^n_t],$$

7. Here we implicitly assume that the second type of household faces a flow budget constraint similar to equation (2.1), and that they exhaust their budget constraint.

where a variable with a hat represents the proportional deviation of the variable from its value on the baseline path (for example, $\hat{z}_t$ is defined as $\hat{z}_t \equiv \ln z_t - \ln z_t^*$),[8] and σ is a positive parameter defined as $\sigma \equiv -u''(y^*)y^*/u'(y^*)$. The output gap x_t is defined as $x_t \equiv y_t - y_t^n$, where y_t^n represents the natural rate of output or potential output. The inflation rate π_t is defined as $\pi_t \equiv \ln P_t - \ln P_{t-1}$. Finally, the deviation of the natural rate of interest from its baseline path, $\hat{r}_t^n$, is defined as

$$\hat{r}_t^n \equiv \sigma E_t[(\hat{y}_{t+1}^n - \hat{y}_t^n) - (\hat{v}_{t+1} - \hat{v}_t)]. \tag{2.8}$$

According to the above definition of $\hat{r}_t^n$, variations in the natural rate of interest are caused by short-term factors such as changes in v_t, as well as long-term factors such as the growth rate of potential output. Log-linearizing equation (2.4) around the baseline path, we obtain[9]

$$(1 - \beta\theta)[\hat{B}_t - \beta^{-1}\hat{B}_{t-1}] = -(1 - \beta\theta)(1 - \theta)(\beta\theta)^{-1}\hat{Q}_t - \beta^{-1}(1 - \beta)[\hat{P}_t + \hat{s}_t] \tag{2.9}$$

where $\hat{B}_t$ and $\hat{Q}_t$ are defined as

$$\hat{B}_t \equiv \sum_{j=0}^{\infty} (\beta\theta)^j \hat{B}_{t,t+1+j};\ \hat{Q}_t \equiv \sum_{j=0}^{\infty} (\beta\theta)^j E_t[\hat{Q}_{t,t+j}].$$

$\hat{B}_t$ and $\hat{Q}_t$ can be interpreted as a nominal debt aggregate, and an index of nominal bond prices.

Equation (2.7) can be seen as an "IS equation" that states that the output gap in period t is determined by the expected value of the output gap in period $t + 1$ and the gap between the short-term real interest rate and the natural rate of interest in period t. Equation (2.7) can be iterated forward to obtain

$$\hat{x}_t = -\sigma^{-1} \sum_{j=0}^{\infty} E_t[(\hat{\imath}_{t+j} - \hat{\pi}_{t+j+1}) - \hat{r}_{t+j}^n]. \tag{2.10}$$

According to the expectations theory, the expression $\Sigma_{j=0}^{\infty} E_t[(\hat{\imath}_{t+j} - \hat{\pi}_{t+j+1}) - \hat{r}_{t+j}^n]$ stands for the deviation of the long-term real interest rate from the corresponding natural rate of interest in period t, which implies that, given the path of the natural rate of interest, the output gap depends inversely on the long-term real interest rate.

New Keynesian Phillips Curve

In addition to the IS equation, we need an "AS equation" to describe the supply side of the economy. We adopt a framework of staggered price setting developed by Calvo (1983). It is assumed that in each period a fraction

8. The definition of $\hat{\imath}_t$ differs slightly from those of the other variables; namely, $\hat{\imath}_t \equiv \ln(1 + i_t) - \ln(1 + i_t^*)$.

9. The household's intertemporal budget constraint and the market-clearing condition imply that $B_{t-1,t}^l / P_t^* = (1 - \beta\theta)(1 - \beta)^{-1} s_t^*$ holds on the baseline path. We use this to obtain equation (2.9).

$1-\alpha$ of goods suppliers get to set a new price, while the remaining α must continue to sell at their previously posted prices. The suppliers that get to set new prices are chosen randomly each period, with each having an equal probability of being chosen. Under these assumptions, we obtain an AS equation of the form[10]

$$\hat{\pi}_t = \kappa \hat{x}_t + \beta E_t \hat{\pi}_{t+1}, \tag{2.11}$$

where κ is a positive parameter which is conversely related to the value of α. Equation (2.11) is the so-called New Keynesian Phillips curve, which differs from the traditional Phillips curve in that current inflation depends on the expected rate of future inflation, $E_t\hat{\pi}_{t+1}$, rather than the expected rate of current inflation, $E_{t-1}\hat{\pi}_t$.

Locally Ricardian Fiscal Policy

We assume that the government determines the (nominal) primary surplus each period following a fiscal-policy rule of the form

$$P_t s_t = \sum_{j=0}^{\infty} [E_t(Q_{t,t+j}) - E_{t-1}(Q_{t-1,t+j})] B_{t-1,t+j}, \tag{2.12}$$

where the term $E_t(Q_{t,t+j}) - E_{t-1}(Q_{t-1,t+j})$ represents the realized nominal one-period holding return, including interest payments and capital gains/losses, for a bond that matures in period $t+j$. Equation (2.12) simply states that the government creates a primary surplus by an amount just enough to cover these payments on existing liabilities. In a deterministic environment, in which there is no uncertainty about the sequence of bond prices, the absence of arbitrage opportunities implies $i_{t-1} = (Q_{t,t+j} - Q_{t-1,t+j})/Q_{t-1,t+j}$, so that equation (2.12) reduces to

$$P_t s_t = i_{t-1}\left(\sum_{j=0}^{\infty} Q_{t-1,t+j} B_{t-1,t+j}\right), \tag{2.13}$$

where the term $\Sigma_{j=0}^{\infty} Q_{t-1,t+j} B_{t-1,t+j}$ represents the market value of the existing government liabilities at the end of period $t-1$, and the right-hand side of equation (2.13) represents the interest payments on existing liabilities. Equation (2.13) is equivalent to a budget-deficit (not primary deficit but conventional deficit) targeting rule, and in that sense, is very close to the spirit of the fiscal requirement of the Maastricht treaty or the Stability and Growth Pact in the European Monetary Union. Also, the fiscal-policy rule of this form is used in empirical studies such as Bohn (1998), in order to describe the actual government's behavior.

Substituting equation (2.12) into the government's flow budget constraint (equation [2.4]), we observe that

10. See Woodford (2003) for more on the derivation.

$$\sum_{j=0}^{\infty} E_t[Q_{t,t+1+j}]B_{t,t+1+j} = \sum_{j=0}^{\infty} E_{t-1}[Q_{t-1,t+j}]B_{t-1,t+j}$$

holds each period. That is, the market value of the existing government liabilities does not change in each period as long as the government determines the primary surplus following equation (2.12). Using this property, we observe that

$$E_t[Q_{t,\tau+1}\sum_{j=0}^{\infty} Q_{\tau-1,\tau+j}B_{\tau-1,\tau+j}] = E_t[Q_{t,\tau+1}]\sum_{j=0}^{\infty} E_{t-1}[Q_{t-1,t+j}]B_{t-1,t+j}$$

holds for all $\tau > t$, which implies[11]

$$\lim_{\tau\to\infty} E_t[Q_{t,\tau+1}\sum_{j=0}^{\infty} Q_{\tau-1,\tau+j}B_{\tau-1,\tau+j}] = 0. \quad (2.14)$$

This equation states that the fiscal-policy rule (2.12) guarantees the transversality condition for *any* path of the price level. Thus the government's transversality condition does not affect the price level in equilibrium as long as the government follows the rule (2.12). Fiscal-policy rules with this feature are called "passive" by Leeper (1991), and "locally Ricardian" by Woodford (1995).

Equations (2.7), (2.9), (2.11), and the log-linear version of (2.12)

$$\hat{s}_t + \hat{P}_t = (1-\beta\theta)\hat{B}_{t-1} + (1-\beta)^{-1}(1-\beta\theta)[\hat{Q}_t - \theta^{-1}\hat{Q}_{t-1}] \quad (2.15)$$

consist of four key equations of our model.[12] Given the natural rate of interest $\hat{r}^n_t$ as an exogenous variable and the short-term nominal interest rate $\hat{\imath}_t$ as a policy variable, which is determined as we see in the next subsection, these four equations determine the equilibrium paths of $\hat{x}$, $\hat{P}$ (or equivalently $\hat{\pi}$), $\hat{B}$, and $\hat{s}$.[13] It should be emphasized that fiscal variables ($\hat{s}_t$ and $\hat{B}_t$) do not appear in the IS and AS equations ([2.7] and [2.11]), so that, given the paths of $\hat{\imath}_t$ and $\hat{r}^n_t$, these two equations determine the paths of $\hat{x}_t$ and $\hat{\pi}_t$ (or equivalently $\hat{P}_t$), independently of the fiscal variables. In this sense, equations (2.7) and (2.11) constitute an independent block in the four-equations system; namely, they first determine the paths of $\hat{x}_t$ and $\hat{\pi}_t$, and, given them, the other two equations determine the paths of the two fiscal variables ($\hat{s}_t$ and $\hat{B}_t$). This structure of the model is fully utilized when we characterize the optimal monetary-policy rule in the next subsection.

11. Here we assume that the short-term nominal interest rate might be zero in the present and subsequent periods, but that it is strictly above zero in the sufficiently remote future, so that $\lim_{\tau\to\infty} E_t(Q_{t,\tau+1}) = 0$.

12. Note that equation (2.5), which is an equilibrium condition related to government solvency, is not a part of the key equations, since it is automatically satisfied as long as the government follows the rule (2.12).

13. Since $\hat{Q}_t = -\hat{\imath}_t - \Sigma_{j=1}^{\infty}(\beta\theta)^j E_t(\hat{\imath}_{t+1} + \hat{\imath}_{t+2} + \ldots + \hat{\imath}_{t+j-1})$, the value of $\hat{Q}_t$ is determined by the path of the short-term nominal interest rate chosen by the central bank. Note that the expectations theory holds locally (i.e., as long as deviations of each variable from its baseline value are small enough).

6.2.2 Optimal Monetary Policy

Adverse Shock to the Economy

Following Jung, Teranishi, and Watanabe (2003), we consider a situation in which the economy is hit by a large-scale negative-demand shock; the central bank responds to it by lowering the short-term nominal interest rate to zero; but aggregate demand is still insufficient to close the output gap. More specifically, we assume that a large negative shock to the natural rate of interest, denoted by ε_0^n, occurs in period zero, so that the natural rate of interest takes a large negative value in period zero and subsequent periods. The deviation of the natural rate of interest from the baseline path is described by

$$\hat{r}_t^n \equiv \ln(1 + r_t^n) - \ln(1 + r_t^{n*}) = \rho^t e_0^n \text{ for } t = 0, \ldots, \tag{2.16}$$

where r_t^{n*} is the baseline value of the natural rate of interest, which is assumed to be equal to $\beta^{-1}(1 - \beta)$, and ρ is a parameter satisfying $0 \leq \rho < 1$.[14]

It is important to note that the natural rate of interest $\hat{r}_t^n$ appears only in the IS equation (2.7), and that fluctuations in the natural rate of interest could be completely offset if the central bank equalizes the short-term nominal interest rate to the natural rate of interest ($\hat{\imath}_t = \hat{r}_t^n$). In the usual situation, therefore, aggregate-demand shocks can be completely offset by an appropriate monetary policy. However, this is not true if the natural rate of interest falls below zero and the nonnegativity constraint of the short-term nominal interest rate, $i_t \geq 0$, or its log-linear version

$$\hat{\imath}_t + \beta^{-1}(1 - \beta) \geq 0 \tag{2.17}$$

is binding.

Optimization Under Discretion

The central bank chooses the path of the short-term nominal interest rates, starting from period zero, $\{\hat{\imath}_0, \hat{\imath}_1, \ldots\}$ to minimize

$$E_0 \sum_{t=0}^{\infty} \beta^t (\hat{\pi}_t^2 + \lambda \hat{x}_t^2),$$

subject to equations (2.7), (2.9), (2.11), (2.15), and (2.17). Since equations (2.7) and (2.11) consist of an independent block, and the fiscal variables ($\hat{s}_t$ and $\hat{B}_t$) do not appear in the loss function, the optimization problem can be solved in a step-by-step manner: we first minimize the loss-function subject to equations (2.7), (2.11), and (2.17) and characterize the optimal paths for

14. Here we assume that, following Jung, Teranishi, and Watanabe (2003), the stock to the natural rate of interest is known in period zero and that no new information arrives in the subsequent periods. Eggertsson and Woodford (2003a, b) extend the analysis by introducing stochastic disturbances of some special form. It is important to note that certainty equivalence does not hold in our optimization problem because of the nonnegativity constraint on nominal interest rates, so that the difference between a deterministic and a stochastic environment is not trivial.

$\hat{\imath}_t$, $\hat{x}_t$, and $\hat{\pi}_t$; then we substitute them into equations (2.9) and (2.15) to obtain the optimal paths for $\hat{s}_t$ and $\hat{B}_t$.

Under the assumption of discretionary monetary policy, the central bank reoptimizes in each period. The optimization problem is represented by a Lagrangian of the form

$$\mathcal{L} = E_0 \sum_{t=0}^{\infty} \beta^t \{L_t + 2\phi_{1t}[\hat{x}_t - \hat{x}_{t+1} + \sigma^{-1}(\hat{\imath}_t - \hat{\pi}_{t+1} - \hat{r}_t^n)] + 2\phi_{2t}[\hat{\pi}_t - \kappa\hat{x}_t - \beta\hat{\pi}_{t+1}]\},$$

where ϕ_{1t} and ϕ_{2t} represent the Lagrange multipliers associated with the IS and AS equations. We differentiate the Lagrangian with respect to $\hat{\pi}_t$, $\hat{x}_t$, and $\hat{\imath}_t$ to obtain the first-order conditions

$$(2.18) \qquad \hat{\pi}_t + \phi_{2t} = 0$$

$$(2.19) \qquad \lambda\hat{x}_t + \phi_{1t} - \kappa\phi_{2t} = 0$$

$$(2.20) \qquad [\hat{\imath}_t + \beta^{-1}(1 - \beta)]\,\phi_{1t} = 0$$

$$(2.21) \qquad \hat{\imath}_t + \beta^{-1}(1 - \beta) \geq 0$$

$$(2.22) \qquad \phi_{1t} \geq 0.$$

Equations (2.20), (2.21), and (2.22) are Kuhn-Tucker conditions regarding the nonnegativity constraint on the nominal interest rate. Observe that $\partial\mathcal{L}/\partial\hat{\imath}_t = 2\sigma^{-1}\beta^t\phi_{1t} \propto \phi_{1t}$. If the nonnegativity constraint is not binding, $\partial\mathcal{L}/\partial\hat{\imath}_t$ is equal to zero, so that ϕ_{1t} is also zero. On the other hand, if the constraint is binding, $\partial\mathcal{L}/\partial\hat{\imath}_t$ is nonnegative, and so is ϕ_{1t}.

Given the assumption that the natural rate of interest converges monotonically to its baseline value (see equation [2.16]), it is straightforward to guess that the non-negativity constraint is binding until some period, denoted by period T^d, but is not binding afterwards. By eliminating ϕ_{2t} from equations (2.18) and (2.19), we obtain

$$\phi_{1t} = -\kappa[\hat{\pi}_t + \kappa^{-1}\lambda\hat{x}_t].$$

Substituting $\phi_{1t} = 0$ into this equation leads to $\lambda\hat{x}_t + \kappa\hat{\pi}_t = 0$, which, together with the AS equation, imply $\hat{\pi}_t = 0$, $\hat{x}_t = 0$, and

$$(2.23) \qquad \hat{\imath}_t = \hat{r}_t^n$$

for $t = T^d + 1, \ldots$. Thus the central bank sets the short-term nominal interest rate at zero during the periods in which the natural rate of interest is below zero, but, once the natural rate returns to a positive level, the central bank equalizes it with the level of the natural rate of interest. In this sense, the timing to terminate a zero interest rate policy is determined entirely by an exogenous factor, $\hat{r}_t^n$.

Optimization Under Commitment

We now proceed to the commitment solution: the central bank makes a commitment about the current and future path of the short-term nominal interest rate, considering the consequences of the commitment on the private sector's expectations. The first-order conditions become

$$\hat{\pi}_t - (\beta\sigma)^{-1}\phi_{1t-1} + \phi_{2t} - \phi_{2t-1} = 0 \tag{2.24}$$

$$\lambda\hat{x}_t + \phi_{1t} - \beta^{-1}\phi_{1t-1} - \kappa\phi_{2t} = 0 \tag{2.25}$$

$$[\hat{\imath}_t + \beta^{-1}(1-\beta)]\,\phi_{1t} = 0 \tag{2.26}$$

$$\hat{\imath}_t + \beta^{-1}(1-\beta) \geq 0 \tag{2.27}$$

$$\phi_{1t} \geq 0, \tag{2.28}$$

which differ from those obtained earlier in that lagged Lagrange multipliers, ϕ_{1t-1} and ϕ_{2t-1}, appear in the first two equations. We eliminate ϕ_{2t} from equations (2.24) and (2.25) to obtain a second-order difference equation with respect to ϕ_{1t}.

$$\phi_{1t} - [1 + \beta^{-1} + \kappa(\beta\sigma)^{-1}]\phi_{1t-1} + \beta^{-1}\phi_{1t-2} = -\kappa[\hat{\pi}_t + \kappa^{-1}\lambda(\hat{x}_t - \hat{x}_{t-1})]$$
$$\text{for } t = 0, \ldots, T^c + 1,$$

where T^c is the final period of a zero interest rate policy, and initial conditions are given by $\phi_{1-1} = \phi_{1-2} = 0$. A unique solution to this difference equation is given by

$$\phi_{1t} = -\kappa A(L)[\hat{\pi}_t + \kappa^{-1}\lambda(\hat{x}_t - \hat{x}_{t-1})], \tag{2.30}$$

where L is a lag-operator and $A(L)$ is defined by

$$A(L) \equiv \frac{1}{\xi_1 - \xi_2}\left(\frac{\xi_1}{1 - \xi_1 L} - \frac{\xi_2}{1 - \xi_2 L}\right),$$

and ξ_1 and ξ_2 are the two real solutions to the characteristic equation associated with the difference equation (2.29), satisfying $\xi_1 > 1$ and $0 < \xi_2 < 1$.

Equation (2.29) has the following implications regarding the differences between the discretionary and commitment solutions. First, as pointed out by Woodford (1999) and Jung, Teranishi, and Watanabe (2003), a zero interest rate policy is continued longer in the case of commitment. To see this, we observe from equations (2.10), (2.11), and (2.30) that

$$\phi_{1t} = B(L)[(\hat{\imath}_t - \hat{\pi}_{t+1}) - \hat{r}^n_t],$$

where

$$B(L) \equiv \kappa\sigma^{-1}A(L)[\kappa(1 - \beta L^{-1})^{-1}(1 - L^{-1})^{-1} + \kappa^{-1}\lambda(1 - L^{-1})^{-1}(1 - L)].$$

Note that the real interest rate will never be below the natural rate of interest ($[\hat{\imath}_t - \hat{\pi}_{t+1}] - \hat{r}^n_t \geq 0$) in the case of discretion. Thus, if a zero interest rate policy is terminated in period T^d, ϕ_{1t} takes a positive value at $t = T^d + 1$, indicating that

$$0 \leq T^d \leq T^c < \infty.$$

The optimal commitment solution is characterized by monetary-policy inertia, in the sense that a zero interest rate policy is continued for a while even after the natural rate of interest becomes positive. This is in sharp contrast with the case of discretion, in which a zero interest rate policy is terminated as soon as the natural rate of interest becomes positive.

Second, we compare fiscal adjustments between the discretionary and commitment solutions. By log-linearizing the government's intertemporal budget constraint (2.5), we obtain

$$\sum_{t=0}^{\infty} \beta^t E_0[\hat{P}_t + \hat{s}_t] = (1 - \beta\theta)(1 - \beta)^{-1}\hat{B}_{-1} + (1 - \beta)^{-1}\left[(1 - \beta\theta)\sum_{t=0}^{\infty} (\beta\theta)^t E_0(\hat{Q}_{0,t}) - (1 - \beta)\sum_{t=0}^{\infty} \beta^t E_0(\hat{Q}_{0,t})\right].$$

In either discretionary or commitment solutions, the short-term nominal interest rate is set at zero for some periods and then returns to a normal level, which means that $E_0(\hat{Q}_{0,t})$ takes positive values in period zero and subsequent periods and then returns to zero. Given that $\theta \in [0, 1]$, this implies that the second term on the right-hand side is nonpositive, therefore the (nominal) primary surplus must be on or below its baseline path.[15] Furthermore, the degree of fiscal expansion depends on the maturity structure of government bonds: the shorter the maturity, the larger the fiscal expansion. When the maturity of bonds is very long, reductions in the short-term nominal interest rate in the current and future periods raise bond prices significantly, therefore fewer fiscal adjustments are needed.[16]

To compare the discretionary and commitment solutions in terms of *real* fiscal adjustments, we compute

$$\sum_{t=0}^{\infty} \beta^t E_0[\hat{s}^c_t - \hat{s}^d_t] = -\left\{\sum_{t=0}^{\infty} \beta^t E_0[\hat{P}^c_t - \hat{P}^d_t]\right\} + (1 - \beta)^{-1}\left\{\left[(1 - \beta\theta)\sum_{t=0}^{\infty} (\beta\theta)^t E_0(\hat{Q}^c_{0,t}) - (1 - \beta)\sum_{t=0}^{\infty} \beta^t E_0(\hat{Q}^c_{C,t})\right] - \left[(1 - \beta\theta)\sum_{t=0}^{\infty} (\beta\theta)^t E_0(\hat{Q}^d_{0,t}) - (1 - \beta)\sum_{t=0}^{\infty} \beta^t E_0(\hat{Q}^d_{0,t})\right]\right\},$$

15. Note that, given the assumption that the economy is on the baseline before the natural rate of interest falls in period zero, $\hat{B}_{-1}$ in equation (2.31) must be zero.

16. For example, in the case of $\theta = 0$, in which all bonds are one-period bonds, reductions in the short-term nominal interest rate in the current and future periods have no influence on the current bond price, so that the first term in the squared bracket $[(1 - \beta\theta)\Sigma_{t=0}^{\infty}(\beta\theta)^t E_0(\hat{Q}_{0,t})]$ is zero, and the expression in the squared bracket takes a large negative value. On the other hand, if all bonds are perpetual bonds ($\theta = 1$), the expression in the squared bracket equals to zero.

where the first term on the right-hand side is negative since $\hat{P}_t^c$ is greater than $\hat{P}_t^d$ in every period, and the second term is also negative because $T^d \leq T^c$ implies $E_0(\hat{Q}_{0,t}^c) \geq E_0(\hat{Q}_{0,t}^d)$ in every period. Thus we observe

$$\sum_{t=0}^{\infty} \beta^t E_0[\hat{s}_t^c] \leq \sum_{t=0}^{\infty} \beta^t E_0[\hat{s}_t^d]. \quad (2.31)$$

This indicates that the commitment solution cannot be achieved by monetary policy alone, and that a close coordination with fiscal policy is indispensable.[17] A more expansionary stance should be taken on the side of fiscal policy, as well as on the side of monetary policy.

6.2.3 Numerical Examples

In this subsection we numerically compute the optimal path of various variables.[18] Figure 6.3 shows the responses of eight variables to an adverse shock to the natural rate of interest in the case of discretion. The paths for the short-term nominal and real interest rates and the natural rate of interest represent the level of those variables (i_t, $i_t - \pi_{t+1}$, and r_t^n), while those of other variables are shown by the deviations from their baseline values. The natural rate of interest, which is shown in panel G, stays below zero for the first four periods until period three, and becomes positive in period four, then gradually goes back to a baseline level. In response to this shock, the short-term nominal interest rate is set at zero for the first four periods, but becomes positive as soon as the natural rate of interest turns positive in period four. Given the shock to the natural rate of interest and the monetary-policy response to it, the short-term *real* interest rate rises and the spread between $i_t - \pi_{t+1}$ and r_t^n is widened, as shown in panel G. Consequently, inflation and the output gap stay below the baseline for the first four periods during which a zero interest rate policy is adopted, and return to zero as soon as that policy is terminated.

Panels B, D, F, and H of figure 6.3 show the fiscal aspects of the model. The price level falls during the first four periods and continues to stay at a level below the baseline, while the bond price rises in period zero and subsequent periods reflecting the market expectation of monetary easing in the current and future periods. This leads to a rise in the *real* value of the existing public debt, which puts the government under pressure to increase the real primary surplus, while lower interest payments due to the zero in-

17. See Iwamura and Watanabe (2002) for a similar argument in a setting of perfectly flexible prices.

18. The values for structural parameters are borrowed from Woodford (1999): $\lambda = 0.048/4^2$; $\beta = 0.99$; $\sigma = 0.157$; $\kappa = 0.024$. We assume that $\theta = 0.8$. The initial shock to the natural rate of interest, ε_0^n in equation (2.16), is equal to –0.10, which means a 40 percent decline in the annualized natural rate of interest. The persistence of the stock, which is represented by ρ in equation (2.16) is 0.5 per quarter. The parameter values are all adjusted so that the length of a period in our model is interpreted as a quarter.

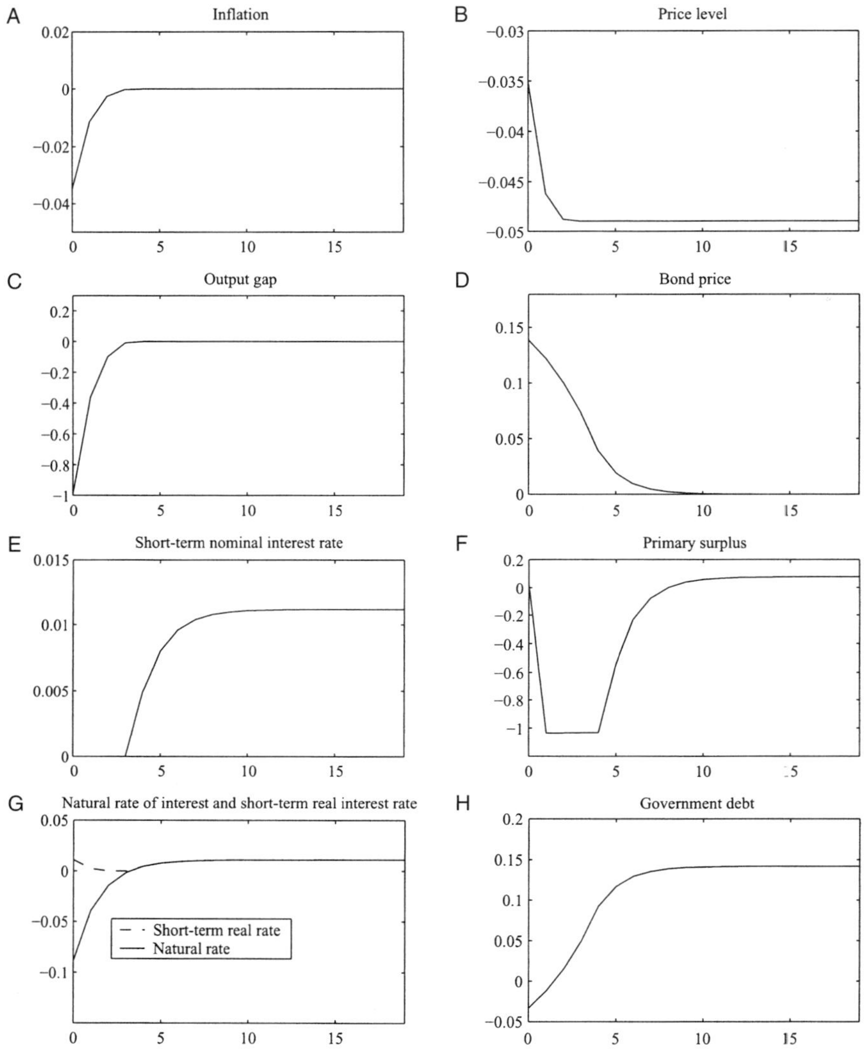

Fig. 6.3 Optimal responses under discretion

terest rate policy create room for the government to reduce the real primary surplus. Combining these two conflicting effects, the real primary surplus is below the baseline for the first eight periods until period seven, but slightly above the baseline path thereafter.

Figure 6.4 shows the responses of the same set of variables for the case of commitment. An important difference from the discretionary solution is that a zero interest rate policy is continued longer. Reflecting this, the cu-

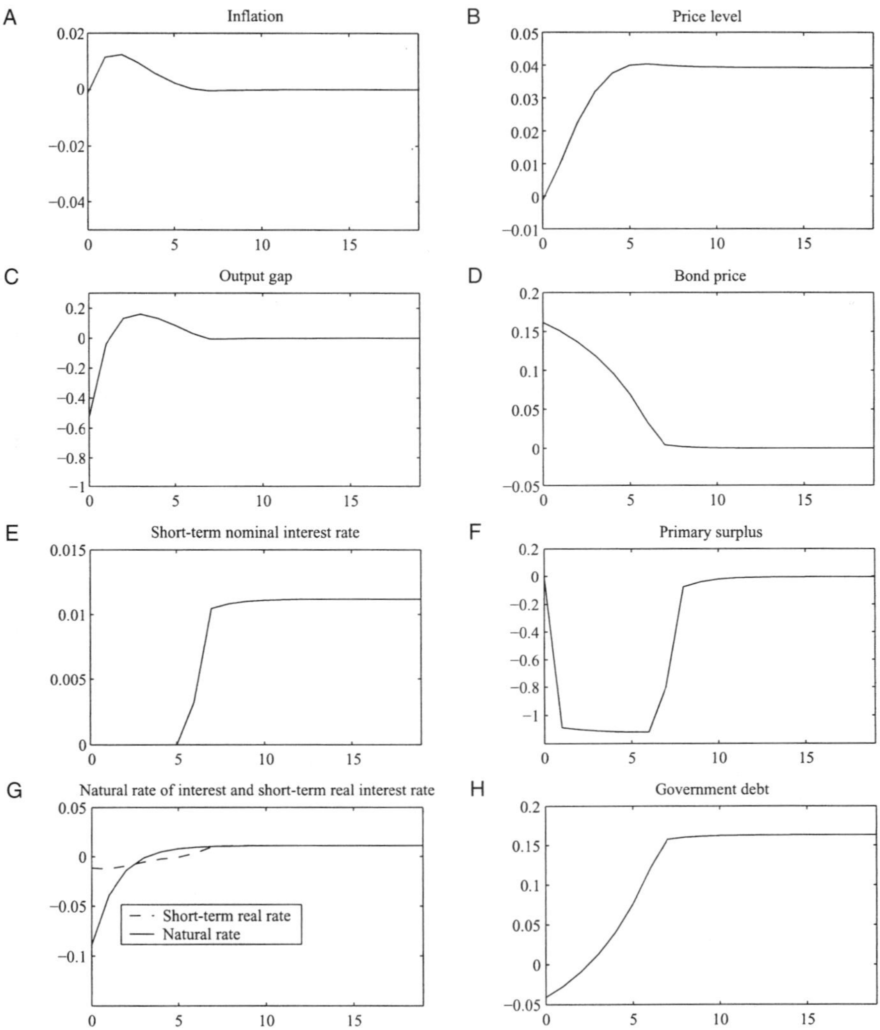

Fig. 6.4 Optimal responses under commitment

mulative sum of the deviation of the short-term *real* interest rate from the natural rate of interest becomes significantly smaller in comparison with the case of discretion, leading to a decline in the *real long*-term interest rate. This alleviates deflationary pressures on the inflation rate and the output gap. Turning to the fiscal aspects of the model, monetary-policy inertia (i.e., prolonging a zero interest rate policy) keeps the price level higher than the baseline path, which is in sharp contrast with the case of discretion. As a result, the real primary surplus stays below the baseline path even after

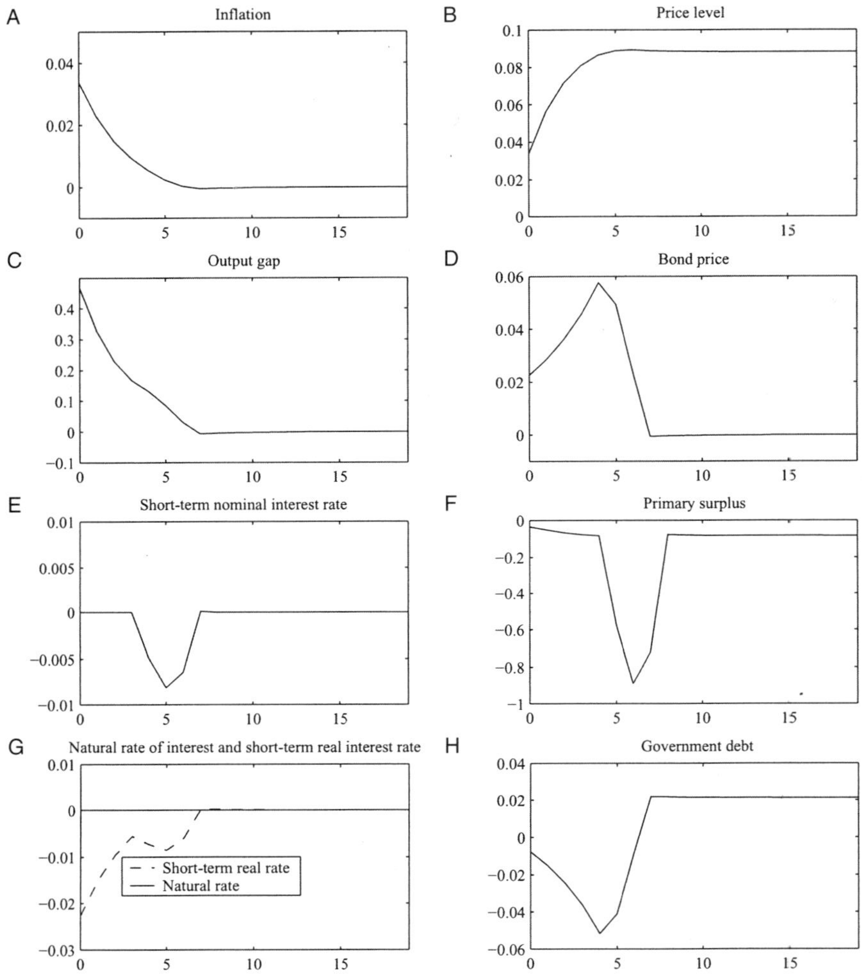

Fig. 6.5 Differences between the commitment and discretionary solutions

the zero interest rate policy is terminated. The differences between the commitment and discretionary solutions (the commitment solution minus the discretionary solution) are shown in figure 6.5.

Table 6.2 shows the amounts of fiscal adjustments needed to achieve the optimal outcomes under discretion and commitment. Nominal adjustments $(\Sigma_{t=1}^{\infty} \beta^{j}[\hat{P}_t + \hat{s}_t])$ are negative in both solutions, indicating that fiscal expansion is needed to achieve the optimal outcomes. Note that the amount of fiscal adjustments is larger in the commitment solution in which a zero interest rate policy is continued longer. Also, note that the amount of fiscal adjustment depends on the maturity structure of government debt:

Table 6.2 **Fiscal adjustments in the discretionary and commitment solutions**

	$\theta = 0.1$	$\theta = 0.4$	$\theta = 0.8$	$\theta = 1.0$
	Nominal adjustments $\sum_{t=0}^{\infty} \beta^t(\hat{P}_t + \hat{s}_t)$			
Commitment solution (A)	–7.174	–6.569	–3.937	0.001
Discretionary solution (B)	–5.345	–4.749	–2.581	0.035
(A) – (B)	–1.829	–1.820	–1.356	–0.034
	Real adjustments $\sum_{t=0}^{\infty} \beta^t \hat{s}_t$			
Commitment solution (C)	–11.009	–10.404	–7.771	–3.832
Discretionary solution (D)	–0.465	0.132	2.300	4.916
(C) – (D)	–10.544	–10.535	–10.071	–8.748

the amount of fiscal adjustment is larger when the maturity is shorter. Turning to the real adjustments ($\Sigma_{t=1}^{\infty} \beta^j \hat{s}_t$), they are positive in the discretionary solution while negative in the commitment solution. This reflects a difference between the two solutions in terms of the path of the price level. In the case of the discretionary solution, the price level is lower than on the baseline (figure 6.3), so that a larger primary surplus is needed to finance larger *real* redemption. On the other hand, the price level is higher than on the baseline in the commitment solution (figure 6.4), thus a smaller surplus is sufficient to finance smaller *real* redemption. The difference between the two solutions again depends on the maturity structure of government debt: the real amount of fiscal adjustment becomes larger when θ is smaller.[19]

6.3 Monetary Policy in 1999–2004

6.3.1 Term-Structure of Interest Rate Gaps

As emphasized by Woodford (1999); Jung, Teranishi, and Watanabe (2003); and Eggertsson and Woodford (2003a, b), history dependence is one of the most important features of the commitment solution. To see how history-dependent monetary policy affects the output gap and inflation, we rewrite the IS and AS equations (2.7) and (2.11) as

$$\hat{x}_t = -\sigma^{-1}(1 - L^{-1})^{-1}[(\hat{\imath}_t - E_t\hat{\pi}_{t+1}) - \hat{r}_t^n];$$
$$\hat{\pi}_t = -\sigma^{-1}\kappa(1 - \beta L^{-1})^{-1}(1 - L^{-1})^{-1}[(\hat{\imath}_t - E_t\hat{\pi}_{t+1}) - \hat{r}_t^n].$$

An important thing to note is that these two variables are determined solely by the current and future values of the interest rate gap (i.e., the spread be-

19. Put differently, this implies that keeping the maturity of government debt longer during peacetime (i.e., on the baseline) is an effective way of insuring against the risk of falling into a liquidity trap. See Iwamura and Watanabe (2002) for more on this point.

tween the actual real interest rate and its natural rate counterpart, $[\hat{\imath}_t - E_t\hat{\pi}_{t+1}] - \hat{r}_t^n$), and, in that sense, the interest rate gap is the key variable through which monetary policy affects the real side of the economy.[20] Given this structure, the central bank's commitment to continuing a zero interest rate policy even after the natural rate of interest becomes positive makes the private sector expect that the interest rate gap, $(\hat{\imath}_t - E_t\hat{\pi}_{t+1}) - \hat{r}_t^n$, will shrink and become negative in the future periods, thereby weakening the deflationary pressure on the current output gap and inflation.

More specifically, as shown in figure 6.3, the short-term real interest rate is never below the natural rate in the discretionary solution, thus the term-structure of interest rate gaps defined by

$$E_t \sum_{k=0}^{K} [(i_{t+k} - \pi_{t+k+1}) - r_{t+k}^n], \tag{3.1}$$

monotonically increases with K. In contrast, as shown in figure 6.4, the short-term real interest rate stays below the natural rate in periods three to six in the case of the commitment solution, and therefore the gap defined by equation (3.1) *declines* during these periods. This is a direct reflection of monetary-policy inertia, and a key feature to discriminate between the two solutions. These observations suggest a simple way to test whether the BOJ's actual policy is close to the optimal one: we estimate the term-structure of interest rate gaps to see whether or not the gap declines with K towards the end of recession.

We start by estimating the natural rate of interest using the methodology developed by Laubach and Williams (2003).[21] Equation (2.8) may be re-written as

$$r_t^n = \sigma g_t^p + z_t, \tag{3.2}$$

where the potential growth rate g_t^p is defined as $g_t^p \equiv E_t(y_{t+1}^n - y_t^n)$, and the other stationary component z_t is defined as $z_t \equiv -\sigma E_t(v_{t+1} - v_t)$. Following Laubach and Williams (2003), we assume that g_t^p is a random walk process, while z_t follows an AR process. Using these two assumptions (together with other assumptions adopted in Laubach and Williams [2003]), we estimate

20. Admittedly, this simple relationship between the interest rate gap and $\hat{x}_t$ or $\hat{\pi}\}_t$ depends on the structure of our model. However, Neiss and Nelson (2003) find a similar relationship, through simulation analysis, in a more complicated (and realistic) model with endogenous capital formation, habit persistence in consumption, and price setting of the Fuhrer-Moore type. Also, their empirical analysis using the U.K. data finds a reasonably strong negative relationship between the interest rate gap and the inflation rate.

21. Laubach and Williams (2003) use the Kalman filter method to estimate a system of equations consisting of the observation equations (i.e., the IS and AS equations) and the transition equations that describe the law of motion for the components of the natural rate of interest. The same methodology is applied to the Japanese data by Oda and Muranga (2003). We would like to thank Thomas Laubach and John C. Williams for providing us with the program code used in their paper.

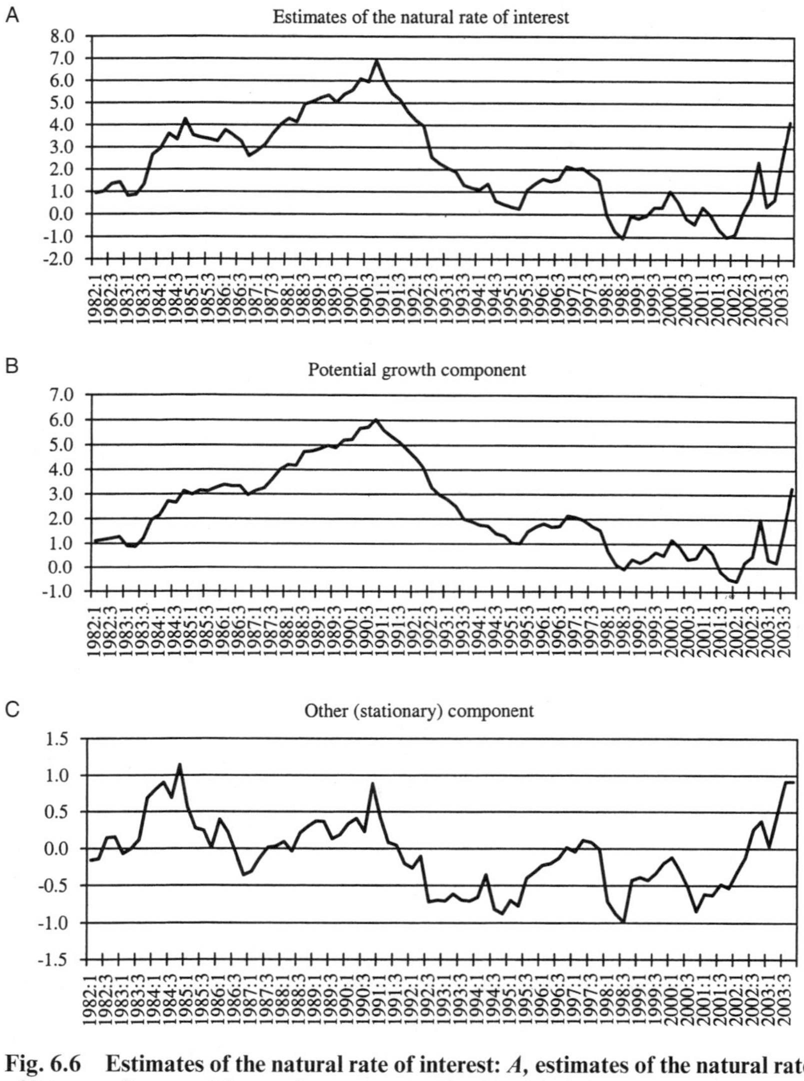

Fig. 6.6 Estimates of the natural rate of interest: *A*, estimates of the natural rate of interest; *B*, potential growth component; *C*, other (stationary) component

the natural rate of interest for the period from 1982:1Q to 2003:4Q, which is presented in panel A of figure 6.6. Note that the natural rate of interest shown here represents the annualized overnight rate. Figure 6.6 shows that the natural rate of interest was 7 percent in 1990, and then gradually declined until it reached almost zero in 1995. Furthermore, it declined below zero in 1998:1Q–1999:2Q, 2000:3Q–4Q, and 2001:2Q–2002:1Q, indicating that Krugman's (1998) prescription for the Japanese economy is not rejected by the data. Panels B and C of figure 6.6 decompose fluctuations in

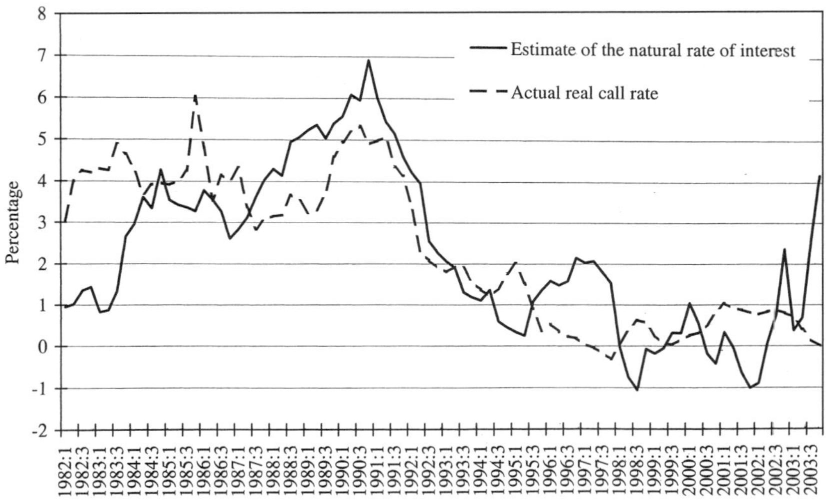

Fig. 6.7 Overnight interest rate gap

the natural rate of interest into the two components: the random walk component (σg_t^p) and the stationary component (z_t). Panel B shows that the potential growth rate was barely above zero in the 1990s, but fell below zero for the three quarters starting from 2001:3Q. Negative values for the natural rate of interest are due to very low potential growth rates, as well as adverse temporary shocks that had occurred several times after the mid-1990s.

Figure 6.7 compares the natural rate of interest with the overnight real interest rate, $i_t - E_t\pi_{t+1}$. We use the uncollateralized overnight call rate for i_t, and the actual inflation rate in period t as a proxy for the expected overnight inflation rate. Figure 6.7 shows that the real call rate is significantly lower than the natural rate of interest in the latter half of the 1980s, which is consistent with the results from the existing studies that the BOJ's policy was too expansionary, thereby contributing to the asset-price inflation during this period. It also shows that the opposite (i.e., the real call rate is higher than the corresponding natural rate) happened in the period from 1998 to 2002. The nominal call rate had already been lowered to the zero lower bound during this period, but deflationary expectations kept the real call rate above zero, thereby creating positive *overnight* interest rate gaps in these years.

Given that the time-series estimates for the natural rate of interest are to hand, we next construct a time series for the expected values of the natural rate of interest $E_t\Sigma_{k=0}^{K} r_{t+k}^{n}$, as well as a time series for the expected rate of inflation. We construct the first by utilizing the fact that the natural rate of interest consists of a random walk component and a stationary compo-

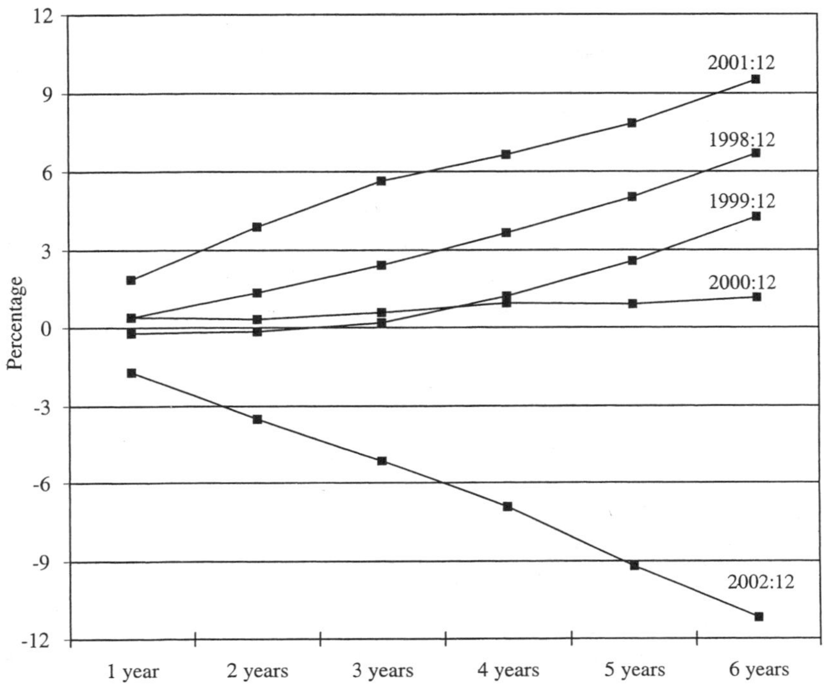

Fig. 6.8 Term structure of interest rate gaps

nent.[22] As for the expected rate of inflation, we use the five-year forecasts published in *The JCER Mid-term Economic Forecasts* by a private research institute, the Japan Center for Economic Research (JCER), in December of each year. By using these two time series, we can compare the natural rate of interest and the real interest rate for various time horizons (namely, K in equation [3.1]).

The results of these calculations are presented in figure 6.8, which shows the term-structure of interest rate gaps at the end of each year starting from 1998.[23] First, the term structure at the end of 1998, just before the introduction of the zero interest rate policy, was upward sloping although the one-year gap was very close to zero. The upward-sloping curve mainly comes from the term-structure of nominal interest rates.[24] These two findings suggest that market participants expected that the BOJ would not adopt expansionary monetary policy sufficient to offset an expected decline in the

22. Specifically, z_t follows an AR (1) process, which is estimated as $z_t = 0.8304 \cdot z_{t+1} + e_t$.

23. The definition of the term-structure of interest rate gaps is given in equation (3.1). Note that gaps are *not* annualized.

24. See Okina and Shiratsuka (2004) for the evolution of the term-structure of nominal interest rates during the zero interest rate period.

natural rate of interest. Second, the term-structure curve at the end of 1999 shifted downward from its position in 1998, and the gaps became negative for the time-horizon up to two years. This suggests that the BOJ's new regime introduced in early 1999 had successfully affected the market's expectations. More importantly, however, we see no indication of a downward-sloping curve, suggesting that the BOJ's commitment was not powerful enough to generate an expectation that the short-term real interest rate would decline below the level of the natural rate counterpart. Third, the term-structure curve at the end of 2001 was also upward sloping: to make matters worse, it shifted up substantially from its positions in the preceding years, indicating that quantitative monetary easing combined with a renewed commitment in March 2001 was not strong enough to offset a pessimistic expectation about the future path of the natural rate of interest.[25]

6.3.2 Inflation Targeting to Implement the Commitment Solution

Eggertsson and Woodford (2003a) propose a version of price-level targeting to implement the optimal commitment solution characterized by Jung, Teranishi, and Watanabe (2003). However, as mentioned by Eggertsson and Woodford (2003a), price-level targeting is not the only way to implement it, but a version of inflation targeting can also implement the commitment solution. The BOJ's commitment relates the timing to terminate a zero interest rate policy (or quantitative-easing policy) to the rate of inflation, so that it should be closer to inflation targeting rather than price-level targeting. In this subsection, we characterize a version of inflation targeting that achieves the commitment solution and compare it with the BOJ's policy commitment.

History-Dependent Inflation Targeting

We start by defining an output-gap adjusted inflation measure $\tilde{\pi}_t$ as

$$\tilde{\pi}_t \equiv \hat{\pi}_t + \kappa^{-1}\lambda(\hat{x}_t - \hat{x}_{t-1}),$$

and then denote a target for this adjusted inflation by π_t^{Tar}. We also denote the target shortfall by $\Delta_t^{\pi}(\Delta_t^{\pi} \equiv \pi_t^{\text{Tar}} - \tilde{\pi}_t)$. Given these definitions, we substitute $\phi_{1t} = \kappa\Delta_t^{\pi}$ into equation (2.29) to obtain

$$\pi_t^{\text{Tar}} = [1 + \beta^{-1} + \kappa(\beta\sigma)^{-1}]\Delta_{t-1}^{\pi} - \beta^{-1}\Delta_{t-2}^{\pi}. \tag{3.3}$$

Now let us consider the following targeting rule. The inflation target for period zero is set at zero ($\pi_0^{\text{Tar}} = 0$), and the targets for the subsequent periods are determined by equation (3.3). The central bank chooses the level of the

25. The only example of a downward-sloping curve we observe in figure 6.8 is the year 2002 (December 2002), in which the expected one-year real interest rate in each year was close to zero, but the corresponding natural rate was well above 2 percent, so that the interest rate gap declines by about 2 percent per year. This might be due to imprecise estimates of the natural rate of interest towards the end of the sample period.

overnight interest rate in each period, so that it can achieve the predetermined target level for the adjusted inflation rate. If the central bank successfully shoots the target in each period starting from period zero, then Δ_t^{π} is always zero, therefore the target in each period never deviates from zero. However, if the natural rate of interest falls below zero, the central bank cannot achieve the target even if it lowers the overnight interest rate to zero. Then, Δ_t^{π} takes a positive value, and consequently the predetermined target for the next period becomes higher than zero. Given that the natural rate of interest evolves over time following equation (2.16), the central bank fails to achieve the targets in period zero and subsequent periods even though it lowers the overnight interest rate to zero. Therefore the central bank must continue a zero interest rate policy until it achieves the target in some period, which is denoted by $T + 1$. Since Δ_{T+1}^{π} equals to zero by definition, ϕ_{1T+1} must equal to zero as well, therefore $T = T^c$ must hold. Put differently, the central bank is able to implement the commitment solution by adopting a version of inflation targeting in which the target inflation rate is updated in each period following equation (3.3).[26] It is important to note that this inflation targeting has a feature of history dependence since the current target inflation rate depends on the values of the natural rate of interest and the performance of monetary policy in the past.

Panel A of figure 6.9 shows the evolution of the target inflation rate that is needed to implement the commitment solution presented in figure 6.4. The values for the adjusted inflation rate are below its target levels in the first six periods, but the target shortfall in each period gradually decreases until it finally reaches zero in period six, when the central bank terminates the zero interest rate policy.

A Comparison with the BOJ Rule

The regime of history-dependent inflation targeting defined above has some similarities with the BOJ's commitment of continuing a zero interest rate policy (or quantitative-easing policy) until some conditions regarding the inflation rate are met,[27] but these two rules differ in some important respects. To show this, we first express the BOJ's target criterion as

26. Price-level targeting to implement the commitment solution can be derived in a similar way. We define an output-gap adjusted price-level index as $\tilde{P}_t \equiv \hat{P}_t + \kappa^{-1}\lambda\hat{x}_t$, and denote the target shortfall as $\Delta_t^P \equiv P_t^{\mathrm{Tar}} - \tilde{P}_t$. Then, substituting $\phi_{1t} = \kappa\Delta_t^P$ into equation (2.29) leads to an equation describing the evolution of the target price level (equation [3.11] in Eggertsson and Woodford 2003b). See the middle panel of figure 6.9 for the path of P_t^{Tar} to implement the commitment solution. By a similar calculation, we can characterize an instrument rule to implement the commitment solution: $\hat{\imath}_t = \max\{0 - i_t^*, i_t^{\mathrm{Tar}}\}$, where $i_t^{\mathrm{Tar}} = \hat{r}_t^n + [1 + \beta\kappa\sigma(\kappa^2 + \lambda)^{-1}]E_t\hat{\pi}_{t+1} + \sigma E_t\hat{x}_{t+1} - \lambda\sigma(\kappa^2 + \lambda)^{-1}\hat{x}_{t-1} + [1 + \beta^{-1} + \kappa(\beta\sigma)^{-1}]\Delta_{t-1}^i - \beta^{-1}\Delta_{t-2}^i$, and $\Delta_t^i \equiv i_t^{\mathrm{Tar}} - \hat{\imath}_t$. See the lower panel of figure 6.9 for the path of i_t^{Tar} that implements the commitment solution.

27. For example, Governor Fukui emphasizes the importance of intentional policy delay by stating that the BOJ will continue to implement monetary easing "even after the economy has started to improve and inflationary expectations are emerging" (Fukui 2003).

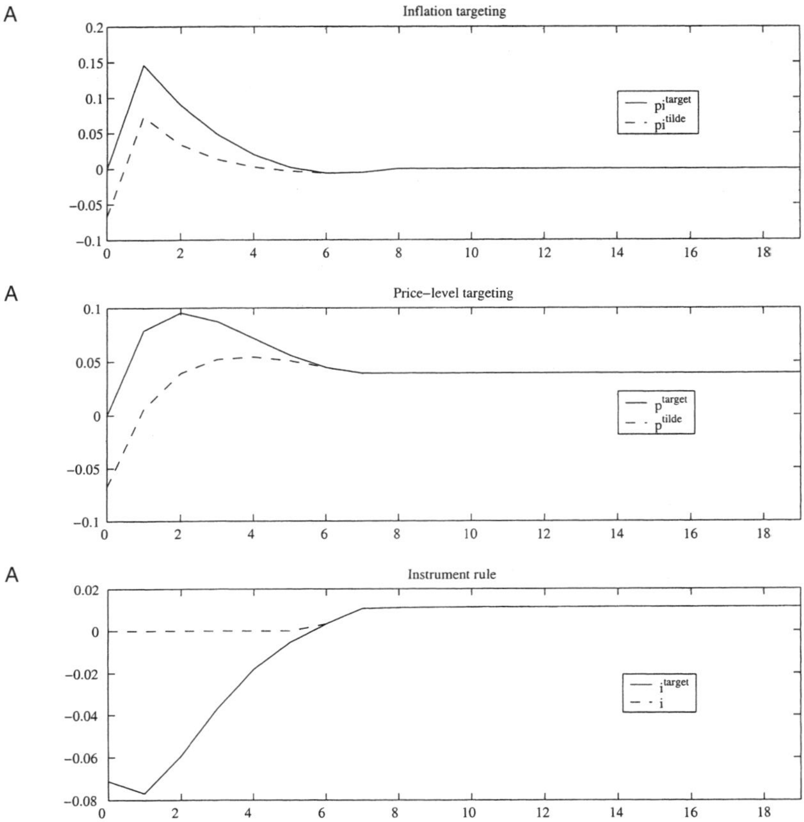

Fig. 6.9 Monetary policy rules to implement the commitment solution: *A*, inflation targeting; *B*, price-level targeting; *C*, instrument rule

$$\hat{\pi}_t = \tilde{\pi}^{\mathrm{Tar}}.$$

The BOJ chooses overnight call rate in each period so as to achieve this target criterion if it is possible; however, if it is not possible due to the zero interest rate bound, the bank simply sets the call rate at zero.

This BOJ rule differs from the regime of history-dependent inflation targeting in the following respects. First, the output gap, x, is completely ignored in the BOJ's targeting criterion, while it plays an important role in the targeting criterion of the history-dependent inflation targeting unless λ equals to zero. Put differently, under the BOJ rule, fluctuations in the output gap do not affect the timing to terminate a zero interest rate policy (or quantitative-easing policy). Second, the target inflation rate is *never* revised under the BOJ rule, while equation (3.3) requires the central bank to revise the target for the next period depending on whether or not it successfully shoots the target in the current period.[28] In fact, despite the occurrence of a series of unanticipated adverse events including the failures of major banks, the target inflation rate has never been revised since the introduction of a zero interest rate policy in February 1999: some of the BOJ board members repeatedly showed an adherence to the commitment made in the past and no intention at all to revise its target level of inflation.[29] As seen in equation (3.3), the target inflation rate should have been upwardly revised in response to these additional shocks to the natural rate of interest. The lack of history-dependent responses to unanticipated additional shocks implies the suboptimality of the BOJ rule.

To make a quantitative evaluation on the difference between the two rules, we construct a time series of π_t^{Tar} using the actual data. Specifically, we assume that the target level for the adjusted inflation rate was zero just before the introduction of a zero interest rate policy, and then compute π_t^{Tar} by substituting the actual values for the inflation rate and the output gap into equation (3.3). The basic idea of this exercise is as follows. If the BOJ rule is very close to the optimal one, then we should observe that the computed target rate is always close to $\overline{\pi}^{\text{Tar}}$, say, 2 percent per year. On the other hand, if the deviation of the BOJ rule from the optimal one is not negligible, then the exercise of computing target inflation using equation (3.3) would be a wrong one, which could yield unrealistically large numbers for the target rate of inflation.[30] The result presented in figure 6.10A clearly shows that the computed target in each period is significantly higher than zero, suggesting that the deviation of the BOJ rule from the optimal one was not small.

Figure 6.10B conducts the same exercise but now we take into account supply shocks to make the discussion closer to the reality. If deflation since the late 1990s is at least partly due to supply shocks (or equivalently, changes in relative prices), the target level of inflation that the BOJ seeks to achieve should be lowered to some extent.[31] To incorporate this type of argument into our model, we divide the items contained in the CPI into two

28. Most of the discussions about the BOJ's policy commitments have focused on whether $\overline{\pi}^{\text{Tar}}$ is high enough to escape from the liquidity trap. However, somewhat surprisingly, little has been said about the absence of state-contingent responses to additional shocks.

29. However, this does not necessarily mean that the BOJ did not make any response to additional shocks. On the contrary, it responded to them by revising the target for the current account balances very frequently: it has been revised nine times during the last three years. However, as correctly pointed out by Eggertsson and Woodford (2003a), an additional provision of liquidity to the market without any implications about the future course of monetary policy has no effects on the economy as long as the demand for liquidity reaches a satiation level ("Irrelevance proposition").

30. For example, if one substitutes the values of π and x obtained in the discretionary solution (rather than those obtained in the commitment solution) into equation (3.3), then one would obtain extremely large numbers for the target rate of inflation.

31. With respect to an appropriate policy response to supply shocks, a BOJ policy board member stated, "It would be difficult for monetary policy to control the impact of supply shocks. If monetary policy were to try to control such impacts, it is likely that sustainable price

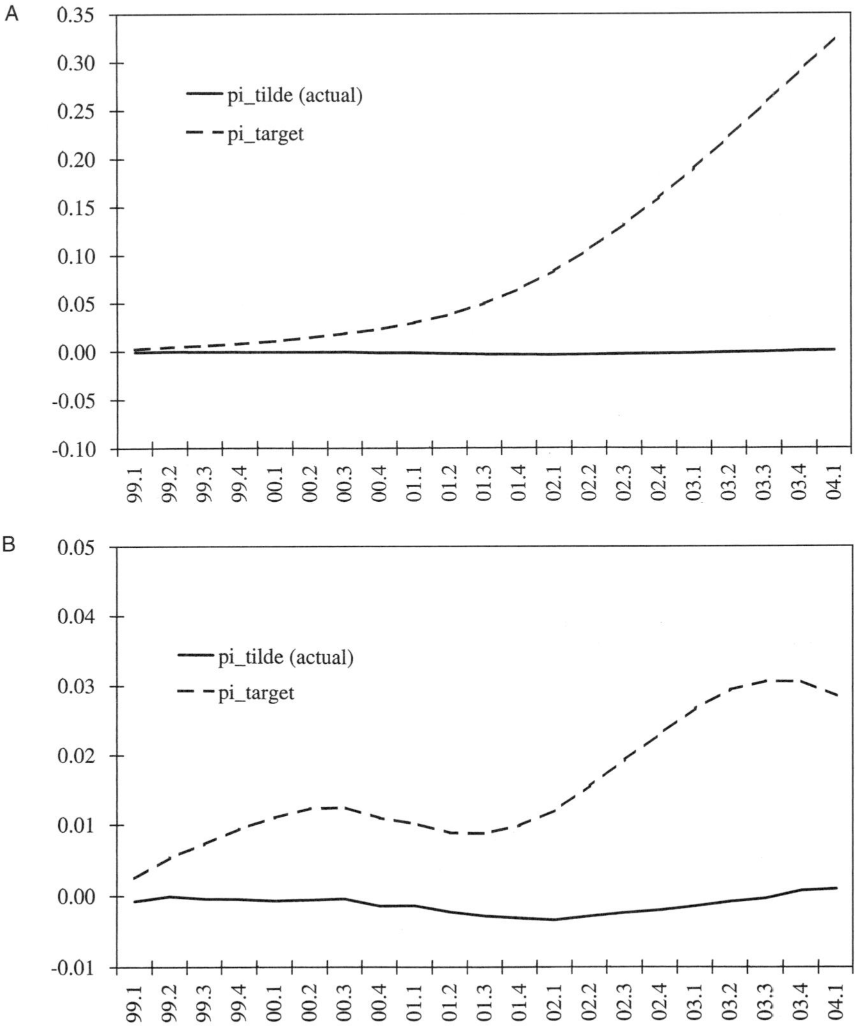

Fig. 6.10 Is the BOJ rule close to the optimal targeting rule?

subgroups, "goods" and "services," and denote the inflation rate in each sector by $\hat{\pi}_{1t}$ and $\hat{\pi}_{2t}$. The inflation rate in each sector is not necessarily identical, thus the relative price between the two sectors could change over time. This is the situation in which Aoki (2001) and Benigno (2004) discuss the optimal monetary policy under the assumption of sticky prices. Be-

stability would be impaired as production swings became larger and uncertainty regarding investment increased. Therefore, we should accept change in prices due to supply shocks to a certain extent" (Shinotsuka 2000).

nigno (2004) searches for a desirable index of the inflation rate that a central bank should target, and finds that it is not the traditional CPI inflation rate (namely, the simple average of the two inflation rates) but

$$\gamma\hat{\pi}_{1t} + (1 - \gamma)\hat{\pi}_{2t},$$

where the weight γ is defined by

$$\gamma \equiv \frac{n\alpha_1(1 - \alpha_1)^{-1}(1 - \alpha_1\beta)^{-1}}{n\alpha_1(1 - \alpha_1)^{-1}(1 - \alpha_1\beta)^{-1} + (1 - n)\alpha_2(1 - \alpha_2)^{-1}(1 - \alpha_2\beta)^{-1}}.$$

Here α_i represents the probability of no price adjustments being allowed (α_i takes a larger value for more sticky prices). Note that if the core inflation rate defined above equals to zero, the traditional CPI inflation rate ($n\hat{\pi}_{1t}$ + $(1 - n)\hat{\pi}_{2t}$, where n represents the CPI weight for the goods sector) equates to $(n - \gamma)[\hat{\pi}_{1t} - \hat{\pi}_{2t}]$.[32] Given that the central bank responds to relative price changes as recommended by Benigno (2004), this implies that equation (3.3) changes to the following rule[33]

$$(3.4)\quad \pi_t^{\mathrm{Tar}} = (n - \gamma)[\hat{\pi}_{1t} - \hat{\pi}_{2t}] + [1 + \beta^{-1} + \kappa(\beta\sigma)^{-1}]\Delta_{t-1}^{\pi} - \beta^{-1}\Delta_{t-2}^{\pi}.$$

Figure 6.10B presents the implied target inflation rate π_t^{Tar} computed using equation (3.4).[34] The implied target inflation rate is now much closer to zero as compared with the upper panel, but it still requires high inflation of more than 2 percent per quarter. This implies that a quantitative difference between history-dependent inflation targeting and the BOJ rule is not trivial even if we take supply shocks into consideration.

6.4 Fiscal Policy in 1999–2004

6.4.1 Did the Japanese government follow a Ricardian rule in 1999–2004?

It is assumed in section 6.2 that fiscal policy is passive (or locally Ricardian) in the sense that the government adjusts the primary surplus so that the government's solvency condition is satisfied for *any* path of the price level. In this subsection, we look at the behavior of the Japanese government to see whether or not this assumption has been satisfied since early 1999, when the BOJ introduced a new policy regime.

32. As pointed out by Benigno (2004), the traditional CPI inflation rate coincides with the core inflation rate if $\alpha_1 = \alpha_2$ or either of the two is equal to zero.

33. It should be noted that this rule is *not* derived by solving an optimization problem. However, Kudo, Takamura, and Watanabe (2005) explicitly solve a central bank's loss-minimization problem in a two-sector economy with asymmetric sectoral shocks, and obtain an optimal monetary-policy rule that is very close to equation (3.4) in the case in which prices are perfectly flexible in one of the two sectors.

34. The values for α_1 and α_2 are taken from the estimates in Fuchi and Watanabe (2002): $\alpha_1 = 0.389$ and $\alpha_2 = 0.853$. Other parameter values are the same as before.

Evidences from the Time-Series Data

A positive linkage between the primary surplus and the real value of public debt is one of the most important implications of Ricardian fiscal policy.[35] Everything else equal, a fall in the price level leads to an increase in the real value of public debt, and then the Ricardian government responds to it by increasing the primary surplus.

Figure 6.11A shows the gross public debt (relative to the nominal gross domestic product [GDP]) on the horizontal axis against the primary surplus (relative to the nominal GDP) on the vertical axis, for 1970–2003. This figure shows that both variables tend to deteriorate simultaneously in the 1990s, indicating a negative correlation between them. However, such a correlation may be spurious for the following reasons. First, cyclical fluctuations in economic activities lead to changes in the primary surplus, mainly through changes in tax revenues. Since we are mainly interested in the government's discretionary responses to various shocks, we need to remove the changes in primary surplus due to such an automatic stabilizer. Second, as emphasized by Barro (1986) and Bohn (1998), the government's tax-smoothing behavior could create a negative correlation between the two variables. For example, think about the consequence of a temporary increase in public expenditure. It is possible to increase taxes simultaneously in accordance with it, but changing marginal tax rates over time increases the excess burden of taxation. Therefore, an optimizing government minimizes the costs of taxation by smoothing marginal tax rates over time. This implies that a temporary increase in public expenditures would lead to a decrease in the primary surplus and an increase in the public debt.

Following Barro (1986) and Bohn (1998), we remove these two factors by estimating a regression of the form

$$(4.1)\quad \text{SURPLUS}_t = a_0 + a_1\text{GVAR}_t + a_2\text{YVAR}_t + a_3\text{DEBT}_{t-1} + v_t,$$

where SURPLUS_t is the primary surplus, DEBT_{t-1} is the amount of the public debt at the end of the previous period, GVAR_t is the level of temporary government spending measured by the deviation of the government spending from its trend, and YVAR_t is the output gap measured by the deviation of the GDP from its trend (all relative to GDP).[36] The columns (1) and (2) of table 6.3 present the ordinary least squares estimates of this equation for the sample period 1970–2003: the column (1) uses the *gross*

35. Woodford (1998) emphasizes that a positive linkage between these two variables is a necessary but not a sufficient condition for the Ricardian rule to hold, because a similar positive linkage could emerge even under the non-Ricardian fiscal-policy rules, through a response of the price level to a change in the expected future primary surplus.

36. GVAR_t and YVAR_t are defined by $\text{GVAR}_t \equiv (G_t - G_t^*)/Y_t$ and $\text{YVAR}_t \equiv (1 - Y_t/Y_t^*)(G_t^*/Y_t)$, where G_t is the real government spending, Y_t is the real GDP, and G_t^* and Y_t^* represent the trend of each variable estimated by the HP filter. See Barro (1986) for more on the definition of these two variables.

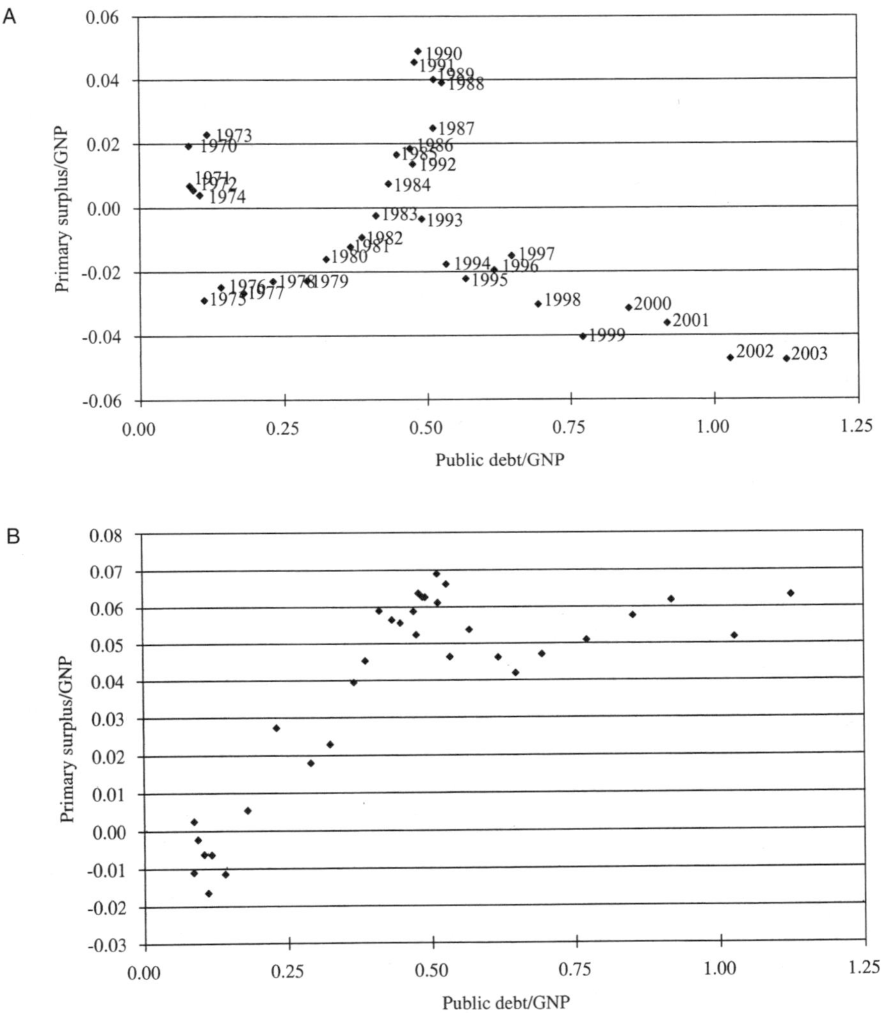

Fig. 6.11 Primary surplus versus public debt, 1970–2003: *A*, simple correlation; *B*, adjusted correlation

public debt while the column (2) uses the *net* public debt.[37] The coefficients on GVAR and YVAR are in the correct sign and statistically significant in both specifications, while the coefficient of our interest, a_3, is almost equal to zero in both specifications, rejecting the Ricardian fiscal-policy rule. To see why it is rejected, the lower panel of figure 6.11 plots the two variables

37. The difference between the gross and net figures is not trivial in Japan: for example, the debt-GDP ratio in 2003 is 1.6 for the gross debt, while 0.7 for the net debt. Broda and Weinstein (2004) argue that the net figure should be used to evaluate the Japanese fiscal situation.

Table 6.3 Estimates of fiscal policy rules

	(1)	(2)	(3)	(4)
Constant	–0.021	–0.012	–0.079	–0.052
	(0.021)	(0.016)	(0.008)	(0.005)
GVAR	–1.904	–1.810	–1.640	–1.546
	(0.842)	(0.818)	(0.311)	(0.410)
YVAR	–1.549	–1.256	–2.334	–2.453
	(0.719)	(0.649)	(0.205)	(0.220)
Gross public debt	0.017			
	(0.029)			
Net public debt		0.012		
		(0.062)		
Gross debt interest payments			2.279	
			(0.260)	
Net debt interest payments				3.559
				(0.454)
R^2	0.330	0.322	0.815	0.746
σ	0.022	0.023	0.012	0.014
DW	0.237	0.243	0.515	0.363

Note: Dependent variable is the primary surplus (relative to GDP). Figures in parentheses represent standard errors.

again, but now the primary surplus is adjusted by subtracting the business-cycle component as well as the temporary government-spending component ($\text{SURPLUS}_t - [g_0 + a_1\text{GVAR}_t + a_2\text{YVAR}_t]$). As seen in the figure, there is indeed a positive correlation between the two variables during the period 1970–1993: the adjusted primary surplus tends to increase by about 0.10 percentage points for 1 percentage point increase in the public debt, which is close to the corresponding U.S. figures reported in Barro (1986) and Bohn (1998). On the other hand, during the period 1994–2003, we observe a slightly negative correlation between the two variables even after controlling for the business-cycle factor and temporary government spending. The lack of a positive relationship in the latter period may be due to low nominal interest rates during the post-bubble period, particularly during the period of the zero interest rate policy and quantitative easing (see equation [2.13]).

To control for fluctuations in nominal interest rates in addition to the business cycle and temporary government spending, we now estimate a regression of the form

$$\text{SURPLUS}_t = b_0 + b_1\text{GVAR}_t + b_2\text{YVAR}_t + b_3\text{INTEREST}_t + v_t, \tag{4.2}$$

where INTEREST_t represents the government's debt interest payments, which corresponds to the expression on the right-hand side of equation (2.13). Note that equation (4.2) can be a good approximation to equation (4.1) as long as the interest rate is constant over time, but not so during the

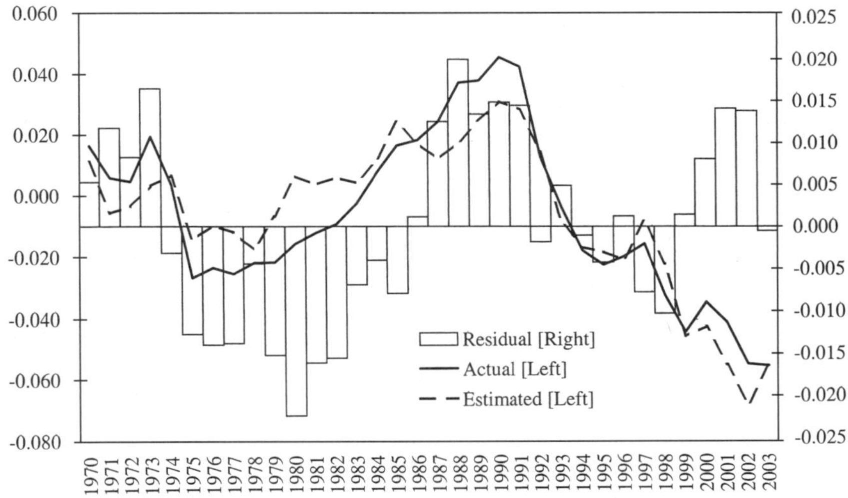

Fig. 6.12 Deviations from the Ricardian fiscal policy rule

period in which the interest rate exhibits a significant fluctuation as it did in the latter half of the 1990s. The estimate of this equation for the same sample period (1970–2003) is reported in the columns (3) (in which *gross* debt interest payments is used) and (4) (in which *net* debt interest payments is used). The coefficients on GVAR and YVAR are almost the same as before, but the coefficient on the debt interest payments is now positive and significantly greater than unity, implying that the Ricardian rule cannot be rejected. These sets of regression results indicate that the Japanese government adjusted the primary surplus in response to changes in the public debt, but only through changes in the debt interest payments.[38]

Given that the Japanese government behavior was, *on average,* consistent with the Ricardian rule during 1970–2003, figure 6.12 looks more closely at the difference between the actual and fitted values for the primary surplus, which can be interpreted as a measure for the deviation from the

38. It should be noted that these results do not necessarily imply that the Japanese fiscal situation is not so bad. First, according to our definition of Ricardian rule (equation [2.12]), a government is required to generate primary surplus only to cover debt interest payments in each period: it is not required to immediately repay the principal of debts. Given that interest rates are very close to zero, this requirement is not so difficult to fulfill even for a government with a huge amount of public debts. Second, our Ricardian government is allowed to ignore "off-balance" debts, such as public pension expenditures that are expected to rise sharply in the near future. That is, a government is allowed to postpone fiscal reconstruction until off-balance items actually change to on-balance items. Our empirical results shown in table 6.3 indicate that the Japanese government has a nice track record in the sense that it has not violated the Ricardian criterion at least so far; however, we do not have much to say about what will happen when the central bank turns to monetary tightening, or when public pension expenditures actually start to rise sometime in the future.

Ricardian rule.[39] There are three phases in which the residual takes significant positive values: 1970–74, 1987–92, and 1999–2002. It is not surprising to observe positive residuals in 1987–92, a period of famous episode of fiscal reconstruction during which the Japanese government intensively cut expenditures to achieve a target of "no net issuance of government bonds."[40] But it might be somewhat surprising to observe positive residuals in 1999–2002, during which the Japanese economy had been in the midst of deflation. This result supports the view that the Japanese government started fiscal tightening just after the Obuchi Administration ended in April 2000.[41] It also suggests that policy coordination between the government and the BOJ did not work well during this period, in the sense that the government deviated from the Ricardian rule toward fiscal tightening while the BOJ adopted a zero interest rate policy and quantitative easing.

Evidences from the Private Sector's Forecasts

By taking innovations of the log-linear version of equation (2.13), we obtain

$$\begin{aligned}(E_t - E_{t-q})\hat{s}_t &= (1-\beta)^{-1}(E_t - E_{t-q})\hat{\imath}_{t-1} \\ &\quad + (E_t - E_{t-q})\{(1-\beta\theta)[\hat{B}_{t-1} + (\beta\theta)^{-1}\hat{Q}_{t-1}] - \hat{P}_t\},\end{aligned}$$

which simply states that the forecast errors in the primary surplus should be positively correlated with those in the real public debt as well as those in the nominal interest rate. This suggests that looking at the correlation between the forecast errors for those variables is another way to test the assumptions of Ricardian fiscal policy. Suppose that the private sector did not expect a change in the monetary-policy regime from discretion to commitment,[42] and that, at the end of 1998, just before the introduction of a new monetary-policy regime, they expected the discretionary solution would continue to be realized in the coming years. Given the analysis in

39. Here we use the estimates in the column (3) of table 6.3; but we obtain the same result even when we use the specification (4) of table 6.3.

40. See Ihori, Doi, and Kondo (2001) for more on the fiscal reform during this period.

41. See, for example, Iio (2004). According to Iio (2004), the shift in fiscal-policy stance toward tightening occurred during the Mori Administration (April 2000 to April 2001) and the Koizumi Administration (April 2001 to the present). Iio (2004) argues that a change in the electoral system from the middle-size district system to the single-member district and PR party lists parallel system has strengthened the influence of the prime minister relative to other political players, thereby creating a political environment for these administrations to start fiscal reconstruction. See, for example, Persson and Tabellini (2000) for more on the relationship between electoral systems and fiscal policymaking.

42. The BOJ had been conducting monetary policy in a discretionary manner before it started a zero interest rate policy (see, for example, Ueda 1993). Also, Ueda (2000) emphasized the importance of the regime switch from discretion to commitment by stating that "the ZIRP [zero interest rate policy] was a unique experiment in the history of the BOJ not just because the level of the overnight rate was zero but because it involved some commitment about the future course of monetary policy."

section 6.2, this implies that the private sector should be surprised not only by a change in monetary policy, but also by a shift in fiscal policy toward more expansionary (or less tightening) in 1999 and subsequent years, because the price level should be unexpectedly higher and thus the real debt burden should be unexpectedly lower.

Table 6.4 compares the forecasts about fiscal-policy variables published in the December 1998 *JCER Mid-term Economic Forecast* by the JCER with the corresponding actual values. The fiscal surplus, which is measured by the net saving of the general government (relative to the nominal GDP), was expected to deteriorate over time, starting from –0.085 in FY1999 to –0.117 in FY2003. But this expectation turns out to be too pessimistic: the corresponding actual values were –0.077 in FY1999 and –0.081 in FY2003. These forecast errors seem to be consistent with the theoretical prediction obtained in section 6.2. However, what is going on behind them is quite different from the theoretical prediction. First, the rate of deflation was higher than expected: very mild deflation in terms of the GDP deflator was expected (0.3 percent per year in 1998–2003), while the actual rate of deflation turned out to be much higher (1.8 percent per year during the same period). Second, in spite of the unexpectedly high rate of deflation, the public debt, measured by the gross debt (relative to the nominal GDP)

Table 6.4 **Private sector's forecast about fiscal policy**

	Forecast	Actual
	Net saving of the general government (relative to the nominal GDP)	
FY1999	–0.085	–0.077
FY2000	–0.095	–0.066
FY2001	–0.105	–0.066
FY2002	–0.113	–0.081
FY2003	–0.117	–0.081
	Gross debt of the general government at the beginning of each year (relative to the nominal GDP)	
FY1999	1.200	1.218
FY2000	1.300	1.329
FY2001	1.510	1.430
FY2002	1.620	1.527
FY2003	1.790	1.619
	GDP deflator (FY1998 = 100)	
FY1999	99.93	98.28
FY2000	99.44	96.39
FY2001	98.98	95.18
FY2002	98.59	93.01
FY2003	98.25	91.35

Note: Forecast was published in December 1998 by the Japan Center for Economic Research (JCER).

of the general government at the beginning of each fiscal year, was lower than expected. For example, the figure for FY2003 was expected to be 1.790 but turned out to be 1.619, mainly due to a slower accumulation of nominal government debt. Third, and most importantly, the combination of an overprediction of the public debt (i.e., an unexpectedly low government debt) and an underprediction of the fiscal surplus (i.e., an unexpectedly small fiscal deficit) is inconsistent with the assumption of Ricardian fiscal policy. Together with the fact that the nominal interest rate was lower than expected,[43] this suggests the possibility that the Japanese government deviated from the Ricardian fiscal-policy rule toward tightening.

To investigate further the unanticipated improvement in fiscal deficits, table 6.5 shows how forecasts for the amount of public investment were updated over time. The amount of public investment tends to be decided on a discretionary basis; therefore the government's fiscal-policy intention should be more clearly seen in its changes. Table 6.5 shows that downward revisions were consistently made for the years of FY1999, 2000, and 2001, while no substantial revisions were made for FY2002 and 2003. This suggests that an unanticipated shift in fiscal-policy stance toward contraction took place around the year 2000.

6.4.2 Optimal Monetary Policy under the Assumption of Non-Ricardian Fiscal Policy

The above evidence suggests that the Japanese government has been deviating from Ricardian fiscal policy since the latter half of the 1990s. Given that evidence, the next question we would like to address is whether the deviation from Ricardian policy has some implications for optimal monetary-policy commitment. As shown by Iwamura and Watanabe (2002) in a model with perfectly flexible prices, the optimal commitment solution differs depending on whether the government follows a Ricardian or a non-Ricardian policy. This is because the government solvency condition implies an equilibrium relation between current and expected future inflation under the assumption of non-Ricardian fiscal policy, so that the central bank must choose between deflation now or deflation later, a tradeoff analogous to the "unpleasant monetarist arithmetic" of Sargent and Wallace (1981). It is important to note that, in this situation, Krugman's (1998) prescription of making a commitment to a higher price level in the future would not work well, as emphasized by Iwamura and Watanabe (2002).

To see how the optimal monetary-policy commitment would change, let us conduct the same exercise as we did in section 6.2.2, but now under the

43. According to the JCER forecast in December 1998, the government-bonds yield (ten years, benchmark) was expected to be 1.40, 1972, and 1.94 percent in 2001, 2002, and 2003, much higher than the actual values.

Table 6.5 **Private sector's forecast about public investment**

	The amount of public investment in:				
	FY1999	FY2000	FY2001	FY2002	FY2003
Forecasted in:					
1999.03	115.2	116.5			
1999.06	112.6	113.8			
1999.09	108.0	111.1			
1999.12	106.3	110.4	110.4		
2000.03	104.6	104.6	104.4		
2000.06	100.8	99.4	98.6		
2000.09		100.2	99.5		
2000.12		94.2	90.8	83.7	
2001.03		96.8	95.0	87.3	
2001.06		92.9	90.1	81.7	
2001.09			88.9	83.0	
2001.12			87.3	86.6	81.8
2002.03			87.9	87.5	83.3
2002.06			88.1	87.0	77.4
2002.09				89.0	79.8
2002.11				82.9	76.7
2003.02				83.4	79.3
2003.05				83.7	77.5
2003.09					77.2
2003.11					75.4
2004.02					74.1

Source: The Nomura Research Institute, various issues.

Note: Figures represent forecasts made by the Nomura Research Institute. Index, FY1997 = 100.

assumption of non-Ricardian fiscal policy. Since the government solvency condition (equation [2.31]) is no longer automatically satisfied, we have to consider equation (2.31) as an additional constraint for the central bank's loss-minimization problem. To simplify the discussion, we assume that all bonds are perpetual bonds ($\theta = 1$), then equation (2.31) reduces to[44]

$$\sum_{t=0}^{\infty} \beta^t \hat{\pi}_t = -(1-\beta) \sum_{t=0}^{\infty} \beta^t \hat{s}_t .$$

The Lagrangian becomes

$$\mathcal{L} = \sum_{t=0}^{\infty} \beta^t \{L_t + 2\phi_{1t}[\hat{x}_t - \hat{x}_{t+1} + \sigma^{-1}(\hat{\imath}_t - \hat{\pi}_{t+1} - \hat{r}_t^n)] + 2\phi_{2t}[\hat{\pi}_t - \kappa\hat{x}_t - \beta\hat{\pi}_{t+1}] + 2\mu[\hat{\pi}_t + (1-\beta)\hat{s}_t]\},$$

44. We continue to assume as before that the economy is on the baseline before period zero, so that $B_{-1} = 0$.

where μ is a new Lagrange multiplier associated with the government's solvency condition (4.3). Denoting the optimal value of L_t by L_t^*, the Lagrange multiplier μ must satisfy[45]

$$\mu = \frac{1}{2} \frac{\partial \sum_{t=0}^{\infty} \beta^t L_t^*}{\partial \sum_{t=0}^{\infty} \beta^t \hat{s}_t} \geq 0.$$

The difference equation that characterizes the timing to terminate a zero interest rate policy (equation [2.29]) now becomes

$$\phi_{1t} - [1 + \beta^{-1} + \kappa(\beta\sigma)^{-1}]\phi_{1t-1} + \beta^{-1}\phi_{1t-2} = - \kappa[\hat{\pi}_t + \kappa^{-1}\lambda(\hat{x}_t - \hat{x}_{t-1})] - \kappa\mu,$$

and its unique solution is given by

$$\phi_{1t} = -\kappa A(L)[\hat{\pi}_t + \kappa^{-1}\lambda(\hat{x}_t - \hat{x}_{t-1})] - \kappa\mu A(1), \tag{4.4}$$

where the definition of $A(L)$ is the same as before, and $A(1)$ satisfies $A(1) = (1 - \xi_1)^{-1}(1 - \xi_2)^{-1} < 0$. Then, it is straightforward to see that if a zero interest rate policy is terminated in the same period as in section 6.2 (namely, period T^c), ϕ_{1t} takes a positive value at $t = T^c + 1$, indicating that a zero interest rate policy should be continued longer in the case of non-Ricardian fiscal policy. Put differently, the property of history dependence plays a more important role in the case when the government deviates from Ricardian fiscal policy.

6.5 Conclusion

Have the Japanese central bank and the government adopted appropriate policies to escape from the liquidity trap? To address this question, we first characterize optimal policy responses to a substantial decline in the natural rate of interest, and then discuss monetary- and fiscal-policy rules to implement them. Based on this analysis, we compare the optimal policy rules with the actual policy decisions made by the Japanese central bank and the government in 1999–2004.

Our main findings are as follows. First, we find that the optimal commitment solution can be implemented through history-dependent inflation targeting in which the target inflation rate is revised depending on the past performance of monetary policy. We compare this optimal rule with the Bank of Japan's policy commitment of continuing monetary easing until some conditions regarding the inflation rate are satisfied, and find that

45. As we saw in section 6.2, the Ricardian government reduces $\Sigma_{t=0}^{\infty} \beta^t \hat{s}_t$ in response to a substantial decline in the natural rate of interest. The multiplier μ can be interpreted as a measurement of how much the government deviates from Ricardian policy.

the BOJ rule lacks history dependence in the sense that the BOJ had no intention of revising the target level of inflation in spite of the occurrence of various additional shocks to the Japanese economy. Second, the term-structure of the interest rate gap (i.e., the spread between the actual real interest rate and its natural rate counterpart) was not downward sloping, suggesting that the BOJ's commitment failed to have a sufficient influence on the market's expectations about the future course of monetary policy. Third, we find time-series evidence that the primary surplus in 1999–2002 was higher than predicted by the historical regularity. Also, by comparing the private sector's forecasts with the corresponding actual values, we find a combination of an unexpectedly low government debt and an unexpectedly small fiscal deficit. Such evidence on the government's behavior suggests that the Japanese government deviated from Ricardian fiscal policy toward fiscal tightening. The optimal commitment solution obtained under the assumption of non-Ricardian fiscal policy implies that, given such government's behavior, the central bank should continue a zero interest rate policy longer.

References

Aoki, Kosuke. 2001. Optimal monetary policy responses to relative-price changes. *Journal of Monetary Economics* 48:55–80.

Barro, Robert J. 1986. U.S. deficits since world war I. *Scandinavian Journal of Economics* 88:195–222.

Benhabib, Jess, Stephanie Schmitt-Grohe, and Martin Uribe. 2002. Avoiding liquidity traps. *Journal of Political Economy* 100:535–63.

Benigno, Pierpaolo. 2004. Optimal monetary policy in a currency area. *Journal of International Economics* 63:293–320.

Bohn, Henning. 1998. The behavior of U.S. public debt and deficits. *Quarterly Journal of Economics* 113:949–63.

Broda, Christian, and David E. Weinstein. 2004. Happy news from the dismal science: Reassessing Japanese fiscal policy and sustainability. NBER Working Paper no. 10988. Cambridge, MA: National Bureau of Economic Research, December.

Calvo, Guillermo. 1983. Staggered prices in a utility-maximizing framework. *Journal of Monetary Economics* 12:383–98.

Christiano, Lawrence J. 2004. *The zero bound, low inflation, and output collapse.* Chicago, IL: Northwestern University, Department of Economics.

Eggertsson, Gauti, and Michael Woodford. 2003a. The zero bound on interest rates and optimal monetary policy. *Brookings Papers on Economic Activity,* Issue no. 1:139–211.

Eggertsson, Gauti, and Michael Woodford. 2003b. Optimal monetary policy in a liquidity trap. NBER Working Paper no. 9968. Cambridge, MA: National Bureau of Economic Research, September.

Fuchi, Hitoshi, and Tsutomu Watanabe. 2002. Measuring the stickiness of prices in the Japanese industries (in Japanese). *Kin-yu Kenkyu* 21(1): 35–70.

Fukui, Toshihiko. 2003. Challenges for monetary policy in Japan. Speech at the Japan Society of Monetary Economics, June 1, 2003, Tokyo, Japan.

Hicks, John. 1967. *Critical essays in monetary theory.* London: Oxford University Press.

Ihori, Toshihiro, Takeo Doi, and Hironori Kondo. 2001. Japanese fiscal reform: Fiscal reconstruction and fiscal policy. *Japan and the World Economy* 13:351–70.

Iio, Jun. 2004. Two aspects of the Japanese bureaucracy in the budget process (in Japanese). RIETI Discussion Paper Series No. 04-J-007. Tokyo, Japan: Research Institute of Economy, Trade, and Industry.

Iwamura, Mitsuru, and Tsutomu Watanabe. 2002. Price level dynamics in a liquidity trap. RIETI Discussion Paper Series No. 03-E-002. Tokyo, Japan: Research Institute of Economy, Trade, and Industry.

Jung, Taehun, Yuki Teranishi, and Tsutomu Watanabe. 2003. Optimal monetary policy at the zero-interest-rate bound. *Journal of Money, Credit, and Banking,* forthcoming.

Keynes, John Maynard. 1936/1971. The General Theory of Employment, Interest and Money *Volume VII,* of The Collected Writings of John Maynard Keynes. London: MacMillan Press.

Krugman, Paul. 1998. It's baaack: Japan's slump and the return of the liquidity trap. *Brookings Papers on Economic Activity,* Issue no. 2:137–87.

Krugman, Paul. 2000. Thinking about the liquidity trap. *Journal of the Japanese and International Economies* 14:221–37.

Kudo, Takeshi, Tamon Takamura, and Tsutomu Watanabe. 2005. The zero-interest-rate bound and optimal monetary policy: The case of asymmetric sectoral shocks. Tokyo, Japan: Hitotsubashi University, Institute of Economic Research.

Laubach, Thomas, and John C. Williams. 2003. Measuring the natural rate of interest. *The Review of Economics and Statistics* 85:1063–70.

Leeper, Eric M. 1991. Equilibria under "active" and "passive" monetary and fiscal policies. *Journal of Monetary Economics* 27:129–47.

Neiss, Katharine S., and Edward Nelson. 2003. The real interest rate gap as an inflation indicator. *Macroeconomic Dynamics* 7:239–62.

Oda, Nobuyuki, and Jun Muranaga. 2003. On the natural rate of interest: Theory and measurement (in Japanese). The Bank of Japan Working Paper Series, No. 03-J-05. Tokyo, Japan: Bank of Japan.

Okina, Kunio, and Shigenori Shiratsuka. 2004. Policy commitment and expectation formations: Japan's experience under zero interest rates. *North American Journal of Economics and Finance* 15 (1): 75–100.

Persson, Torsten, and Guido Tabellini. 2000. *Political economics: Explaining economic policy.* Cambridge, MA: The MIT Press.

Reifschneider, David, and John C. Williams. 2000. Three lessons for monetary policy in a low inflation era. *Journal of Money, Credit, and Banking* 32 (Part 2): 936–66.

Rogoff, Kenneth. 1998. Comment on Krugman, "It's baaack: Japan's slump and the return of the liquidity trap." *Brookings Papers on Economic Activity,* Issue no. 2:194–9.

Sargent, Thomas J., and Neil Wallace. 1981. Some unpleasant monetarist arithmetic. *Federal Reserve Bank of Minneapolis Quarterly Review* 5 (3): 1–17.

Shinotsuka, Eiko. 2000. Japan's economy and the role of the bank of Japan. Speech at the Japan Society of Monetary Economics, May 27, 2000, Tokyo, Japan.

Svensson, Lars E. O. 2001. The zero bound in an open-economy: A foolproof way of escaping from a liquidity trap. *Monetary and Economic Studies* 19:277–312.

Taylor, John B. 2000. Recent developments in the use of monetary policy rules. In *Monetary policy and inflation targeting in emerging economies,* ed. C. Joseph and

A. H. Gunawan, 207–19. Jakarta: Bank of Indonesia and International Monetary Fund.
Ueda, Kazuo. 1993. Japanese monetary policy during 1970–1990: Rules versus discretion? In *Price stabilization in the 1990s: Domestic and international policy requirements,* ed. Kumiharu Shigehara, 191–212. Basingstoke: Macmillan Press.
Ueda, Kazuo. 2000. The transmission mechanism of monetary policy near zero interest rates: The Japanese experience 1998–2000. Speech at a Conference Sponsored by the National Bureau of Economic Research, European Institute of Japanese Studies, Tokyo University Center for International Research on the Japanese Economy, and the Center for Economic Policy Research, September 22, 2000, Tokyo.
Woodford, Michael. 1995. Price-level determinacy without control of a monetary aggregate. *Carnegie-Rochester Conference Series on Public Policy* 43:1–46.
Woodford, Michael. 1998. Comment on John Cochrane, "A frictionless view of U.S. inflation." *NBER Macroeconomics Annual* 13:390–418.
Woodford, Michael. 1999. Commentary: How should monetary policy be conducted in an era of price stability? in *New challenges for monetary policy,* Kansas City, KS: Federal Reserve Bank of Kansas City.
Woodford, Michael. 2001. Fiscal requirements for price stability. *Journal of Money, Credit, and Banking* 33:669–728.
Woodford, Michael. 2003. *Interest and prices: Foundations of a theory of monetary policy.* Princeton, NJ: Princeton University Press.

Comment Fumio Hayashi

This chapter is an extension of Jung, Teranishi, and Watanabe (2003), which was the first to show *policy duration,* the feature about optimal monetary policy requiring the central bank to continue the zero interest rate policy well after the natural interest rate becomes positive. The value-added of this chapter consists of: (a) showing that the optimal monetary policy can be expressed as a version of inflation targeting, (b) testing whether policy duration can be found in the Japanese data, (c) a discussion of whether the recent Japanese fiscal policy is "Ricardian," and (d) a derivation of optimal monetary policy when fiscal policy is not "Ricardian."

Perhaps because of its desire to cover these various issues, in sharp contrast to its predecessor, the chapter is loaded with exceedingly complex notation and numerous equations (many of which are redundant). The reader not familiar with the literature may find it hard to read this chapter. My discussion will be mainly concerned with an exposition of a stripped-down version of the chapter's model and an examination of its analytical aspects. My comments on the chapter will appear at the end.

Fumio Hayashi is a professor of economics at the University of Tokyo, and a research associate of the National Bureau of Economic Research.

A Simplified Model

Most readers should now be familiar with the "New Keynsian sticky-price model" made popular by Woodford's book (2003). Its deterministic version consists of two equations:

$$\text{IS equation: } x_t = x_{t+1} - \sigma^{-1}(i_t - \pi_{t+1} - r_t^n),$$

$$\text{AS equation: } \pi_t = \kappa x_t + \beta \pi_{t+1},$$

where x_t is the output gap (the log difference between actual output and the natural output level), i_t is the nominal interest rate between date t and date $t + 1$, π_{t+1} is the inflation rate between dates t and $t + 1$, and r_t^n is the natural real interest rate. In the stochastic version, the variables dated $t + 1$ on the right-hand sides of the IS and AS equations would be expected values (so, for example, x_{t+1} would be replaced by $E_t[x_{t+1}]$). Having actual values in place of expectations amounts to assuming perfect foresight. The central bank's objective is to find the best inflation-output trade-off by minimizing its bank's loss function

$$\sum_{t=0}^{\infty} \beta^t \left(\frac{1}{2} \pi_t^2 + \frac{1}{2} \lambda x_t^2 \right).$$

The IS and AS equations here differ from the chapter's counterparts, equations (2.7) and (2.11), in two respects. First, there is no uncertainty here, but this is actually useful, given that virtually all the results of the chapter (including the numerical solution) are for the deterministic case. Second, as in the standard exposition of the New Keysian model and unlike in the chapter, there are no hats over the variables here. The chapter employs the complex notation with hats, probably because of its desire to linearize the government budget constraint around a baseline path for the nominal interest rate. As I argue below, however, such a linearization is harmful as well as unnecessary.

In minimizing the loss function, the central bank picks the sequence of the nominal rate $\{i_t\}_{t=0}^{\infty}$, taking the sequence of the natural interest rate $\{r_t^n\}_{t=0}^{\infty}$ as given. The two-equation system consisting of the IS and AS equations can be viewed as a bivariate first-order difference equation in (π_t, x_t) with $i_t - r_t^n$ as the forcing variable. The system can be written as

$$\begin{bmatrix} \pi_{t+1} \\ x_{t+1} \end{bmatrix} = \begin{bmatrix} \dfrac{1}{\beta} & -\dfrac{\kappa}{\beta} \\ -\dfrac{1}{\beta\sigma} & 1 + \dfrac{\kappa}{\beta\sigma} \end{bmatrix} \begin{bmatrix} \pi_t \\ x_t \end{bmatrix} + \begin{bmatrix} 0 \\ \dfrac{1}{\sigma}(i_t - r_t^n) \end{bmatrix}.$$

It is easy to show that the 2×2 coefficient matrix has two real eigenvalues, one between zero and one and the other greater than one. Therefore, even if the sequence $\{i_t - r_t^n\}$ picked by the central bank is bounded, there is a continuum of bounded solutions to the system of difference equations. I gather that the convention of the literature is to assume that the central bank can select a particular solution from among the continuum of solutions. Under this convention, the central bank's problem is to choose a sequence $\{i_t, \pi_t, x_t\}_{t=0}^{\infty}$ to minimize the loss function subject to the IS and AS equations for $t = 0, 1, 2, \ldots$.

The Commitment Solution without the Zero Bound

The chapter is mainly concerned about the "commitment" solution in which the central bank adheres to the path of the nominal rate chosen in date zero. Since i_t enters the IS equation only, this minimization problem can be done in two stages, as shown in chapter seven of Woodford (2003). In the first stage, minimize the loss function with respect to sequences $\{\pi_t, x_t\}$ subject only to the AS equation. In the second stage, given the sequence $\{\pi_t, x_t\}$ so determined, use the IS equation to back out the interest rate.

Although this two-stage procedure is useful for clarifying the structure of the minimization problem, it will turn out to be useful, when we later introduce the zero interest rate bound, to incorporate both the IS and AS equations simultaneously. So, form the Lagrangian as

$$\mathcal{L} \equiv \sum_{t=0}^{\infty} \beta^t \left\{ \frac{1}{2}\pi_t^2 + \frac{1}{2}\lambda x_t^2 + \phi_{1t}[x_t - x_{t+1} + \sigma^{-1}(i_t - \pi_{t+1} - r_t^n)] + \phi_{2t}(\pi_t - \kappa x_t - \beta\pi_{t+1}) \right\}.$$

The first-order conditions (still with the nonnegativity constraint on the nominal rate ignored) with respect to i_t is $\partial\mathcal{L}/\partial i_t = 0$ ($t = 0, 1, 2, \ldots$), which implies $\phi_{1t} = 0$ for all $t \geq 0$. The rest of the first-order conditions are: $\partial\mathcal{L}/\partial\pi_0 = 0$, $\partial\mathcal{L}/\partial\pi_t = 0$ ($t \geq 1$), $\partial\mathcal{L}/\partial x_0 = 0$, and $\partial\mathcal{L}/\partial x_t = 0$ ($t \geq 1$). These latter conditions can be written as

$$\pi_0 + \phi_{2,0} = 0, \tag{6C.1}$$

$$\pi_t - \frac{1}{\beta\sigma}\phi_{1t} + \phi_{2t} - \phi_{2,t-1} = 0,\ t \geq 1, \tag{6C.2}$$

$$\lambda x_0 + \phi_{10} - \kappa\phi_{2,0} = 0, \tag{6C.3}$$

$$\lambda x_t + \phi_{1t} - \frac{1}{\beta}\phi_{1,t-1} - \kappa\phi_{2t} = 0,\ t \geq 1. \tag{6C.4}$$

(Equations [6C.2] and [6C.4] are equations [2.24] and [2.25] of the chapter without hats.)

Setting $\phi_{1t} = 0$ in these four equations, substituting (6C.4) into (6C.2) to eliminate $\{\phi_{2t}\}$, and combining the resulting equation with the AS equation, we obtain the following system of bivariate homogeneous difference equations:

(6C.5)
$$\begin{bmatrix} \pi_{t+1} \\ x_{t+1} \end{bmatrix} = \begin{bmatrix} \frac{1}{\beta} & -\frac{\kappa}{\beta} \\ -\frac{\kappa}{\lambda\beta} & 1+\frac{\kappa^2}{\lambda\beta} \end{bmatrix} \begin{bmatrix} \pi_t \\ x_t \end{bmatrix}, t \geq 0.$$

The 2×2 coefficient matrix has two real eigenvalues, one of them between zero and one and the other greater than one. So there appears to be a continuum of bounded solutions, but equations (6C.1) and (6C.3), which with $\phi_{10} = 0$ can be combined to yield $\lambda x_0 + \kappa\pi_0 = 0$, provides an initial condition that pins down the unique bounded solution. It is easy to show that that unique solution is $\pi_t = 0$, $x_t = 0$ for all $t \geq 0$. The associated shadow prices are also zero: $\phi_{1t} = 0$, $\phi_{2t} = 0$ for all $t \geq 0$. Thus, the central bank can achieve the first-best under commitment. (As shown in, e.g., chapter seven of Woodford [2003], the first-best can be achieved under discretion as well.) Unlike the proof by Woodford and others, my proof of the first-best here does not depend on the boundedness of the shadow price $\{\phi_{2t}\}$. As equation (6C.2) with $\phi_{1t} = 0$ shows, it is possible that $\{\phi_{2t}\}$ is unbounded while $\{\pi_t\}$ is bounded.

The Commitment Solution with the Zero Bound

Now I consider the commitment solution with the nonnegativity constraint $i_t \geq 0$. Noting that i_t can be calculated from the IS equation as $i_t = \pi_{t+1} + r_t^n + \sigma(x_{t+1} - x_t)$, the first-order condition with respect to i_t is now:

(6C.6)
$$\phi_{1t} \geq 0,$$

(6C.7)
$$\pi_{t+1} + r_t^n + \sigma(x_{t+1} - x_t) \geq 0,$$

(6C.8)
$$[\pi_{t+1} + r_t^n + \sigma(x_{t+1} - x_t)]\phi_{1t} = 0.$$

If the natural real interest rate r_t^n is nonnegative, then the first-best solution ($\pi_t = x_t = \phi_{1t} = \phi_{2t} = 0$ for all $t \geq 0$) also satisfies equations (6C.6)–(6C.8). so even with the zero bound the first-best is the solution. The zero bound becomes relevant only when $r_t^n < 0$ for some t.

Suppose, then, that r_t^n is initially negative but becomes positive after some date. The particular path for r_t^n is assumed by the chapter is

(6C.9)
$$r_t^n = r_\infty^n + \rho^t \varepsilon_0^n, t = 0, 1, 2, \ldots, \varepsilon_0^n < 0, r_\infty^n > 0.$$

For this path, it seems reasonable to assume that the zero bound is binding continuously for the first several periods and never binds thereafter. That is,

(6C.10)
$$\phi_{1t} > 0 \text{ for } t = 0, 1, \ldots, T^c \text{ and } \phi_{1t} = 0 \text{ for } t = T^c + 1, T^c + 2, \ldots.$$

Under this assumption, Jung-Teranishi-Watanabe (2003) and this chapter provide a set of equations that determine the whole time paths of (i_t, π_t, x_t, ϕ_{1t}, ϕ_{2t}) and show the *policy duration*—that the zero bound remains binding *after* r_t^n becomes positive (that is, the sign change for r_t^n occurs before T^c). They also show that, in contrast to this commitment solution, the zero bound ceases to bind as soon as r_t^n becomes positive under discretion. I have no alternative proof here. I only point out that the reader would have liked to see the assumption (6C.10), although intuitively plausible, verified.

Other Comments

So far we have been concerned about the choice made by the central bank. Under either commitment or discretion, the central bank picks a path $\{i_t, \pi_t, x_t\}_{t=0}^{\infty}$. Recalling that π_t is the inflation rate between date $t-1$ and t and noting that the price level in date -1, P_{-1}, is given, picking a sequence $\{i_t, \pi_t\}_{t=0}^{\infty}$ amounts to picking a sequence of the price level and the real interest rate, $\{P_t, r_t\}_{t=0}^{\infty}$. If the sequence under commitment is indicated by superscript "c" and the one under discretion by superscript "d", the chapter shows that, for the natural real rate sequence considered above,

$$P_t^c > P_t^d,\ r_t^c < r_t^d,\ t = 0, 1, 2, \ldots.$$

In the "Ricardian" regime, the fiscal authority takes the sequence $\{P_t, r_t\}_{t=0}^{\infty}$ picked by the central bank, either under commitment or discretion, as given and adjusts the real primary surplus sequence $\{s_t\}_{t=0}^{\infty}$ so that the government budget constraint in the present-value form

$$\sum_{t=0}^{\infty} \frac{s_t}{(1 + r_0)(1 + r_1)\ldots(1 + r_{t-1})} = \frac{B_{-1}}{P_0}$$

is satisfied. Here, we are assuming that the government issues only one-period bonds and B_{-1} is the nominal government bonds outstanding at date -1. Toward the end of section 6.2.2 of the chapter, it is claimed that fiscal policy should be more expansionary under commitment. That is, if $\{s_t^c\}$ and $\{s_t^d\}$ are the sequences of real primary surplus chosen by the fiscal authority under commitment and discretion on the part of the central bank, the chapter claims

$$\sum_{t=0}^{\infty} \beta^t s_t^c \leq \sum_{t=0}^{\infty} \beta^t s_t^d.$$

(This is the deterministic version of the chapter's equation [2.32].) This does not seem to hold, even when the initial debt B_{-1} is set equal to zero. Here is a counterexample. Consider special sequences with $s_0 = 1$ and $s_2 = s_3 = \ldots = 0$. With $B_{-1} = 0$, we have

$$1 + \frac{s_1^c}{1 + r_0^c} = 0 = 1 + \frac{s_1^d}{1 + r_0^d}.$$

So $s_1^c = -(1 + r_0^c)$ and $s_1^d = -(1 + r_0^d)$. Since $r_0^c < r_0^d$ as noted above, we have $s_1^c > s_1^d$. The above inequality claimed by the chapter does not hold for this example.

I conclude my discussion by listing other miscellaneous comments and questions.

- In section 6.3, the authors note that, for the numerical solution featuring the assumed path of r_t^n as described in equation (9) $i_t - \pi_{t+1} - r_t^n$ is negative for some t. They then go on to test whether or not this negative component is reflected in the term-structure of interest rates at various calendar dates for date zero, based on their estimate of r_t^n. However, their estimate of r_t^n, shown in figure 6.6, does not resemble the path assumed in the numerical solution. If the assumed path were as shown in figure 6.6, then $i_t - \pi_{t+1} - r_t^n$ might not be negative for some t. As another criticism, a more robust implication of policy duration (that i_t remains zero even after r_t^n becomes positive) is about $i_t - r_t^n$.
- Eggertsson and Woodford (2003) show in a similar model (but with r_t^n following a Markov process) that the commitment solution can be implemented by either inflation targeting or price-level targeting, with the target moving continuously to reflect the target shortfall. The chapter shows the same for the chapter's deterministic model (the chapter discusses only inflation targeting, but during the conference it was agreed that price-level targeting also works). Eggertsson and Woodford (2003) also argue that a price-level targeting that does not depend on the target shortfall nearly implements the commitment solution. Is the same true for the chapter's model?
- As the chapter's derivation of the new Keynesian model in section 6.2 aptly shows, fiscal policy is *very* neutral. First, because of Ricardian equivalence, the timing of taxes given a sequence of government expenditure g_t does not matter. Second, g_t in the model is like a school lunch program, being perfectly substitutable with private consumption. So the path $\{g_t\}$ has no effect, which explains why g_t does not show up in the IS equation. However, at least for the "Ricardian" case, the analysis of monetary policy under commitment and discretion would not be affected if g_t showed up in the IS equation. All one needs to do is to redefine r_t^n to reflect the effect of g_t.

References

Eggertsson, G., and M. Woodford. 2003. Optimal monetary policy in a liquidity trap. NBER Working Paper no. 9968. Cambridge, MA: National Bureau of Economic Research, September.

Jung, T., Y. Teranishi, and T. Watanabe. 2003. Optimal monetary policy at the zero-interest-rate bound. *Journal of Money, Credit, and Banking,* forthcoming.

Woodford, M. 2003. *Interest and prices.* Princeton, NJ: Princeton University Press.

7

Fiscal Remedies for Japan's Slump

Laurence Ball

7.1 Introduction

When an economy slumps, policymakers typically stimulate demand by reducing short-term interest rates. Japan's experience in the last decade has renewed interest in an old question: what to do when rates can't be lowered. Weak demand has produced an output slump and deflation. But short-term rates cannot fall because they are already at their lower bound of zero. Japan has experienced this "liquidity trap" since 1998. Can policy still stimulate demand?

The textbook remedy for a liquidity trap is a fiscal expansion. Japanese policy is complicated, however, by a large and rising government debt. This problem led the major rating agencies to downgrade Japan's debt in 2002. Policymakers resist a fiscal expansion because they believe it would exacerbate the debt problem.

Others, however, argue for a fiscal expansion. Kuttner and Posen (2001) suggest that this policy would not only boost output but also have benign effects on Japan's debt problem. They argue that Japan's large budget deficits have mainly been caused by its output slump. By ending the slump, a fiscal expansion would eventually raise tax revenues, and higher inflation would reduce the real value of debt. These effects would offset the direct costs of a fiscal expansion.

Several advocates of a fiscal expansion suggest a twist: money finance (e.g., Mankiw 1999; Stevens 2001). They advocate a "helicopter drop" of money—or, equivalently, a bond-financed fiscal expansion coupled with purchases of the new debt by the central bank. Monetization of the debt

Laurence Ball is a professor of economics at Johns Hopkins University, and a research associate of the National Bureau of Economic Research.

would eliminate the direct fiscal costs of the policy, leaving only the benefits from economic stimulus. Bernanke (2003) summarizes the argument for a money-financed tax cut:

> Isn't it irresponsible to recommend a tax cut, given the poor state of Japanese public finances? To the contrary, from a fiscal perspective, the policy would almost certainly be stabilizing, in the sense of reducing the debt-to-GDP ratio. The BOJ's purchases would leave the nominal quantity of debt in the hands of the public unchanged, while nominal GDP would rise owing to increased nominal spending. Indeed, nothing would help reduce Japan's fiscal woes more than healthy growth in nominal GDP and hence in tax revenues.

This paper examines these ideas. It uses a textbook-style macromodel calibrated to fit the Japanese economy. The model's initial conditions are based on the situation in 2003. I determine the fiscal transfer needed to boost output to potential, and derive the effects over time on output, inflation, and the debt-income ratio. I compare results for a bond-financed transfer, a money-financed transfer, and a baseline case with passive fiscal policy. In most exercises, I assume monetary policy follows a Taylor rule once interest rates become positive.

The results are generally favorable to fiscal expansions. For base parameter values, a transfer of 6.6 percent of gross domestic product (GDP) returns output to potential in the following year, and thereafter only small transfers are needed to keep it there. The output recovery ends deflation, and the interest rate becomes positive; then the Taylor rule guides the economy to a steady state with low positive inflation. If the fiscal transfer is financed with bonds, the debt-income ratio jumps up when the transfer occurs, but then it falls as output and inflation rise. Two years after the transfer, the debt-income ratio falls below its level under passive policy, and it remains lower in steady state. Thus the transfer improves the long-run fiscal situation as well as ending the output slump.

Does it matter if the fiscal expansion is financed with money rather than debt? Money finance prevents the debt-income ratio from jumping up when the transfer occurs. For base parameter values, this ratio remains lower with money finance than with debt finance for nine years. In year ten, however, the debt paths under the two policies converge. The initial financing of the transfer is irrelevant in the long run.

These results arise because the Taylor rule becomes operative in year ten. In that year the central bank sets a positive interest rate, which requires a contraction of the monetary base. It reduces the base by selling government bonds. The necessary contraction is larger if the initial transfer was money financed, and the extra sales of debt offset the initial savings from monetization.

The rest of this paper contains seven sections. Section 7.2 presents additional background and Section 7.3 presents the model. Sections 7.4–7.8 derive the implications of passive fiscal policy, debt-financed transfers, and money-financed transfers. Section 7.7 considers robustness and Section 7.8 concludes.

7.2 Background

7.2.1 Japan's Slump

Figure 7.1 presents annual data on Japan's economy from 1990 to 2003. I use the experience of this period to guide my modeling of the economy. The situation in 2003 is summarized in table 7.1. In simulating alternative policies, I use data from 2003 as initial conditions.

Panel A of figure 7.1 shows the log of real output. Output growth averaged 1.3 percent per year over 1990–2003, compared to 4.0 percent from 1980 to 1990. Early in the slump, some blamed it on slow growth of potential output due to "structural" factors. Today, however, most economists agree that output has fallen below potential because of deficient demand. Apparent demand shocks include a collapse in asset prices, a credit crunch, and policy mistakes (e.g., Hoshi and Kashyap 2004; Posen 2003).

There is, of course, uncertainty about the gap between output and potential output. Following McCallum (2000) and Hoshi-Kashyap, figure 7.1 presents a path for potential based on the assumption that it has grown 2 percent per year since 1990. This approach produces an output gap of –9 percent in 2003. Using production functions, some researchers have esti-

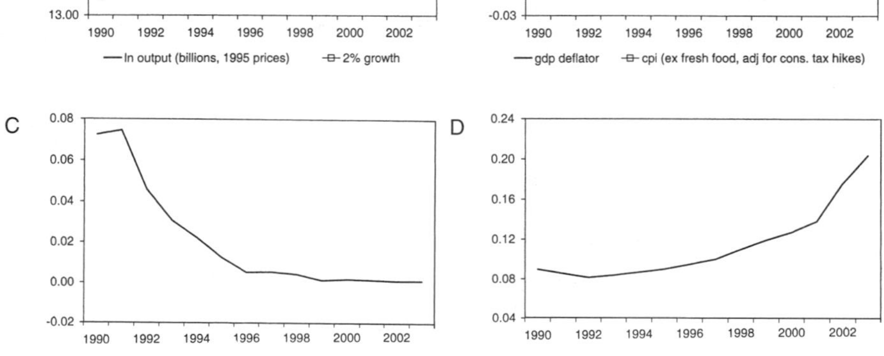

Fig. 7.1 Japan's slump: *A*, output; *B*, inflation; *C*, short-term interest rate; *D*, monetary base/GDP

Table 7.1 **Conditions in 2003 (initial conditions for simulations)**

	Conditions
Output gap	–7.5%
Inflation	–1.0%
Nominal interest rate	0
Base/GDP	0.20
Debt/GDP	0.79

mated recent gaps of around –5 percent (e.g. Ahearne et al. 2002; Leigh 2004). In my simulations, I assume an initial output gap of –7.5 percent).

Figure 7.1 also shows inflation, as measured by the GDP deflator and by core Consumer Price Index (CPI). The slump of the 90s dragged inflation down, as predicted by the accelerationist Phillips curve. In 2000, inflation reached about –1 percent (a bit higher for the CPI and a bit lower for the deflator). Since then, inflation has remained fairly constant. I use –1 percent as the initial value of inflation.

The stability of inflation since 2000 is *not* consistent with a conventional Phillips curve. Such an equation predicts accelerating deflation when the output gap is negative. The cause of this anomaly is unclear, but Blanchard (2000) suggests one possibility. The accelerationist Phillips curve is based on the assumption that expected inflation equals past inflation. This relation breaks down if people view deflation as transitory—if they expect a return to nonnegative inflation. In this case, an output slump causes deflation but not accelerating deflation. I will incorporate this idea in the chapter's model.[1]

Panels C and D of figure 7.1 show the behavior of monetary policy. The Bank of Japan (BOJ) responded to the slump and falling inflation by cutting the short-term interest rate. Leigh (2004) shows that a conventional Taylor rule captures this behavior up to 1998. At that point, the Taylor-rule interest rate became negative, and the actual rate hit the zero bound. The interest rate has stayed close to zero since then.

The monetary base grew steadily as the interest rate fell. Base growth accelerated under the policy of "quantitative easing," which entailed large open market operations. The base grew 26 percent in 2002 and 16 percent in 2003, reaching 20 percent of GDP. With the interest rate stuck at zero, this monetary expansion did not have obvious effects on output or inflation. This experience is consistent with a textbook liquidity trap.

7.2.2 A Fiscal Solution?

The classic solution to a liquidity trap is a fiscal expansion. However, Japanese policymakers are reluctant to try this policy, for two reasons.

1. Econometric research suggests that the Japanese Phillips curve broke down sometime in the 1990s. See Fukao (2004).

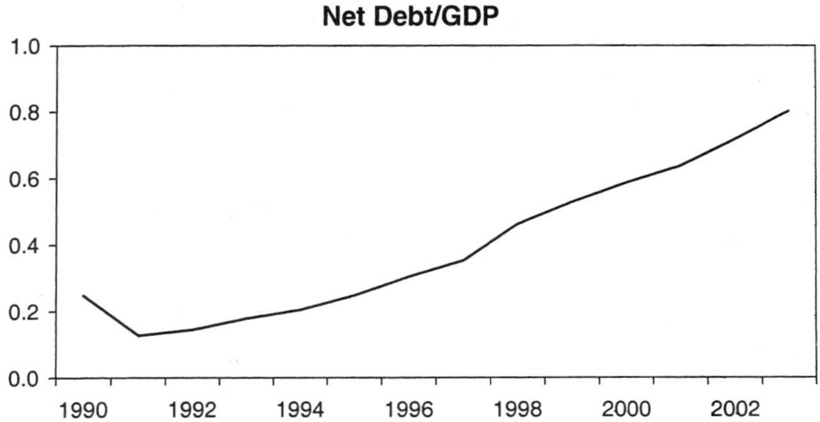

Fig. 7.2 Rising debt

First, many argue that fiscal policy is ineffective in raising output. Second, they fear that a fiscal expansion would exacerbate the problem of a growing national debt.

This chapter rejects the first reason. It is based on the view that Japan tried fiscal expansions in the 1990s without success (e.g., Friedman 2001). This view has been debunked by Posen (1998) and Kuttner and Posen (2001). They show that several "expansion" programs failed because they were not really expansions—they consisted mainly of normal expenditures. There were large fiscal deficits, but these mainly reflected revenue losses caused by the slump. In periods of true fiscal loosening, such as 1995, output responded.

Kuttner and Posen also estimate multipliers for fiscal policy in Japan. They use the structural VAR approach of Blanchard and Perotti (2002), which controls for the cyclical behavior of deficits. Kuttner and Posen find that a 100 yen tax cut raises output one year later by about 125 yen.

This chapter will worry more about the second objection to fiscal expansion: its effects on Japan's public debt. Figure 7.2 shows the path of net government debt as a percent of GDP. This ratio rose from 0.13 in 1991 to 0.79 in 2003, and forecasters predict that it will continue to rise. Long-term budget projections are bleak because of Japan's aging population. Many analysts fear an eventual fiscal crisis, possibly even default. As a result, Japan's debt has been downgraded to A2/AA–, the level for many developing countries.[2]

This chapter will look for policies that end Japan's slump without worsening its debt problem. I will ask whether a fiscal transfer can do so—

2. According to the Organisation for Economic Co-operation and Development (OECD), Japan's gross government debt for 2003 was 157 percent of GDP and government assets were 78 percent, yielding net debt of 79 percent. Broda and Weinstein (2004) suggest two adjustments to this figure. Like this chapter, they view the government and the central bank as the

whether the fiscal benefits from higher output and inflation outweigh the direct costs of the transfer. I will also consider the effects of financing the transfer with money rather than bonds.

7.3 The Model

Japan's problems are largely explained by textbook macromodels. A fall in aggregate demand has reduced output, and monetary policy is ineffective because the interest rate has hit zero. Kuttner and Posen say "the basic lesson of Japan's Great Recession for policymakers is to trust what you learned in intermediate macroeconomics class." In that spirit, I study a model with textbook equations such as an IS curve and a money-demand function. I add simple dynamics following Svensson (1997) and Ball (1999). The only unorthodox equation is the Phillips curve, which is modified to capture Japan's steady deflation.

7.3.1 Assumptions

Output: Potential output Y^* grows by g percent per year. Actual output Y deviates from potential according to an IS equation:

$$\text{(1)} \qquad \frac{(Y_t - Y_t^*)}{Y_t^*} = \frac{\lambda(Y_{t-1} - Y_{t-1}^*)}{Y_{t-1}^*} - \beta(r_{t-1} - r_{t-1}^*) + \delta\left(\frac{G_{t-1}}{Y_{t-1}^*}\right)$$

where t indexes years, G is real transfers from the government, r is the real interest rate, r^* is the "neutral" interest rate, and all parameters are positive. The real rate r is $i - \pi$, where i is the nominal rate and π is inflation. In words, the output gap depends on the lagged gap, the lagged real interest rate, and lagged transfers. The one-year lags are consistent with Japanese evidence (see Kuttner and Posen 2001).

Inflation: Inflation is determined by an expectations-augmented Phillips curve:

$$\text{(2)} \qquad \pi_t = \pi_t^e + \frac{\alpha(Y_{t-1} - Y_{t-1}^*)}{Y_{t-1}^*},$$

where π^e is expected inflation. A conventional assumption is that expected inflation equals lagged inflation, $\pi_t^e = \pi_{t-1}$. I assume instead that

$$\text{(3)} \qquad \pi_t^e = \max\{\pi_{t-1}, 0\}.$$

The conventional assumption holds when lagged inflation is nonnegative, but expectations do not follow actual inflation below zero. When $\pi_{t-1} \geq 0$,

same entity, and thus subtract government bonds owned by the central bank. This reduces net debt by 16 percent of GDP. Second, they add bad loans from the government to the private sector, which by coincidence are also 16 percent of GDP. The two adjustments cancel, so net debt is still 79 percent.

equations (2) and (3) imply that output determines the change in inflation. When $\pi_{t-1} < 0$, output determines the *level* of inflation, as suggested by Blanchard.

Section 7.7 replaces equation (3) with the assumption that π_t^e always equals π_{t-1}. This change does not greatly affect the economy's response to fiscal expansions. It does change the baseline case with passive fiscal policy. If $\pi_t^e = \pi_{t-1}$ and policy is passive, the economy falls into a spiral of accelerating deflation.

Money: The central bank controls the stock of base money, M, through open market operations. Money evolves according to

$$(4) \qquad M_t = M_{t-1} + Z_t,$$

where Z is central-bank purchases of government bonds ($Z < 0$ means sales of bonds). The demand for base money is given by

$$(5) \qquad \ln\left(\frac{M_t}{P_t Y_t}\right) = k - \gamma i_t,\ i_t > 0;$$

$$\geq k, \quad i_t = 0,$$

where P is the price level. This equation imposes a unit income elasticity of money demand (which is consistent with Japanese data). At positive interest rates, there is a constant interest rate semi-elasticity; at a zero interest rate, money demand becomes flat. Figure 7.3 shows the money-demand function in a graph.[3]

Debt: I measure Japan's fiscal problem with privately-held debt, which excludes debt held by the central bank. Thus I ignore the separate balance sheets of the government and central bank and treat them as one entity. Nominal debt D_t evolves according to

$$(6) \qquad D_t = D_{t-1} + i_{t-1}D_{t-1} + P_t G_t - Z_t - \theta(P_t Y_t - P_t Y_t^*).$$

Debt is past debt plus changes from four sources: interest payments on the past debt; current nominal transfers; open market purchases, which reduce debt; and a term for the government's primary surplus in the absence of transfers. This surplus is assumed to be zero when output equals potential ($Y_t = Y_t^*$). It varies procyclically when output fluctuates.[4]

In reality, Japan's primary surplus would probably be negative even if output were at potential. Ignoring this fact helps us isolate the effects of ex-

3. It is common to specify a demand function like equation (5) for M1 rather than the monetary base. This would not affect the analysis if one assumes a constant ratio of M1 to the base (i.e., a constant money multiplier). This multiplier is fairly stable in Japan.

4. Equation (6) implicitly assumes that government debt has a maturity of one year. In reality, much of Japan's debt is long term. Adding long-term debt to the model would strengthen the case for fiscal expansion. As shown below, an expansion raises the path of interest rates. Higher rates imply capital losses for holders of long-term debt, which are capital gains for the government.

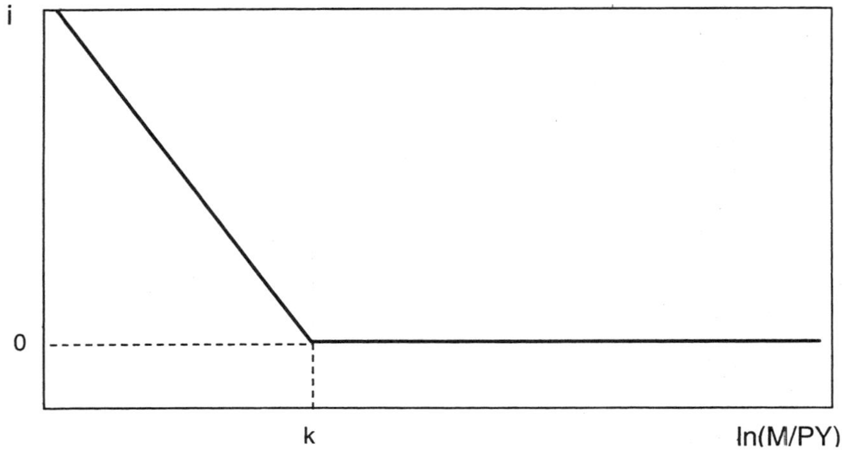

Fig. 7.3 Money demand

ogenous fiscal expansions. Section 7.7 extends the model to include a primary deficit when $Y = Y^*$.

7.3.2 Calibration

Table 7.2 presents base values for the model's parameters. Section 7.7 considers robustness to changes in these parameters.

In the IS equation, I set β, the coefficient on the real interest rate, to 1.0. This follows Ball's (1999) calibration for the United States (I have not found Japanese evidence). For the other IS parameters, I use Kuttner and Posen's econometric results. They estimate that δ, the effect of lagged transfers on output, is 1.25 and λ, the effect of lagged output, is 0.6. The effect of transfers is smaller than Blanchard and Perotti's estimates for the United States.[5]

I also use Kuttner and Posen's estimate of θ, the effect of output on the primary surplus. They find $\theta = 0.25$. This appears conservative, as taxes are 20 percent of Japanese output and marginal taxes are higher than average taxes.

The Phillips curve slope, α, is 0.2. This estimate comes from studies at the BOJ (e.g., Hirose and Kamada 2002). The Phillips curve appears flatter in Japan than in the United States, where α is often estimated around 0.4.

In the money-demand equation, the interest rate semi-elasticity, γ, is 0.1, based on estimates by Fujiki, Hsiao, and Shen (2002), and Miyao (2002). The parameter k is the point at which the money-demand curve hits an interest rate of zero. I calibrate it using the historical evidence in figure 7.1.

5. More precisely, Kuttner and Posen estimate an equation for log output, and get a coefficient of –0.25 on log taxes. Dividing by the ratio of taxes to GDP (approximately 0.2) yields the yen-for-yen effect of taxes and transfers on output.

Table 7.2 **Base parameter values**

	Values
IS	
β	1.0
λ	0.6
δ	1.25
Revenue	
θ	0.25
Phillips curve	
α	0.2
Money demand	
γ	0.1
k	ln(0.1)
Potential output	
g	0.02
Neutral rate	
r^{*}[a]	–0.02
r^{*}[b]	+0.02

[a]In year 0.
[b]Grows linearly to year 10.

When the interest rate reached zero in 1998, the ratio of the monetary base to GDP was about 0.1. This implies $k = \ln(0.1)$.

The growth rate of potential output, g, is 2 percent per year.

7.3.3 The Neutral Interest Rate

It remains to calibrate the neutral real interest rate, r^*. This is a thorny issue. There is debate about whether this parameter is positive or negative in Japan (e.g. Krugman 2000). My view is that r^* is currently negative, but unlikely to stay negative forever. My calibration will capture this idea.

The neutral interest rate is the one that produces $Y = Y^*$ in the absence of a fiscal expansion. It seems clear that r^* has been negative in the early 2000s. The actual real rate has been about 1 percent and Y has been far below Y^*. Thus r^* must be well below 1 percent. I assume an initial r^* of –2 percent, which implies $r - r^* = 3$ percent. For this value of $r - r^*$, the output gap converges to –7.5 percent if there is no fiscal transfer. Thus the calibration captures the idea that output is stuck at a low level.

It is unlikely, however, that r^* will stay negative forever. Iwamura, Mitsuru, and Watanabe (2004), and Leigh (2004) estimate that r^* was well above zero before the 1990s, but fell during the 90s slump. The fall in r^* means the IS curve shifted in. This shift reflected adverse demand shocks, such as the credit crunch and fall in confidence. It is likely that these problems will someday abate. Eventually, a cleanup of banking may spur greater lending. Or a recovery due to external demand will raise confidence and improve balance sheets. Whatever the reason, the IS curve will shift back out and r^* will return to a positive level.

I assume that r^* eventually rises to +2 percent. Of course it is hard to guess how quickly this will happen. In the base specification, I assume that r^* rises linearly from –2 percent to +2 percent over ten years. The IS curve shifts outward, but slowly. Since this assumption is arbitrary, variations on the r^* path are a top priority among robustness checks.

7.4 A Baseline Case

This section derives the path of the economy if there is no fiscal expansion: $G_t = 0$ for all t. The economy starts in year zero with the initial conditions in table 7.2. This exercise provides a baseline for measuring the effects of fiscal policy.

7.4.1 Monetary Policy

To close the model, I must specify the behavior of monetary policy. I assume an interest rate rule based on the past behavior of the Bank of Japan. Recall that the BOJ appeared to follow a Taylor rule until the interest rate hit zero. This behavior is captured by

$$(7) \qquad i_t = \max\{i_t^T, 0\},$$

$$i_t^T = r_t^* + \pi_t + \frac{a(Y_t - Y_t^*)}{Y_t^*} + b(\pi_t - \pi^*),$$

where π^* is an inflation target. The variable i^T is the interest rate dictated by a Taylor rule: it depends on the output gap and inflation. The BOJ sets an interest rate of i^T if i^T is positive, and zero if i^T is negative. BOJ officials have suggested the same rule in describing their policy (Baba et al. 2004).

When the rule delivers a positive interest rate, the money-demand equation determines M. M and lagged M determine open market purchases, Z. When $i = 0$, M is not determined by the rule, because money demand is flat. In this case, I make the additional assumption that $Z = 0$, so M equals lagged M. That is, I assume the BOJ does not pursue open market operations if they do not affect the interest rate. (Section 7.6 examines an alternative assumption.)

In the Taylor rule, the coefficients a and b are chosen as follows. Taylor rules with certain parameters are equivalent to "flexible" inflation targeting: a policy that returns inflation to π^* at a fixed rate (see Svensson [1997] and Ball [1999] for proofs in similar models). I assume that inflation moves halfway to its target each period. One can show that this implies $a = 1.1$ and $b = 2.5$.

I assume the inflation target π^* is 2 percent, which is close to the targets of many countries.

Given initial conditions and the policy rule, it is straightforward to derive the evolution of the economy. Each period, Y and π are determined by past conditions through equations (1)–(3). Inflation π determines the price level P. The policy rule determines i, M, and Z, as described above. Finally, equation (6) determines D.

7.4.2 Results

Figure 7.4 shows the paths of some key variables: the output gap, π, i, and the ratios of Z, M, and D to GDP. Starting from period zero, output

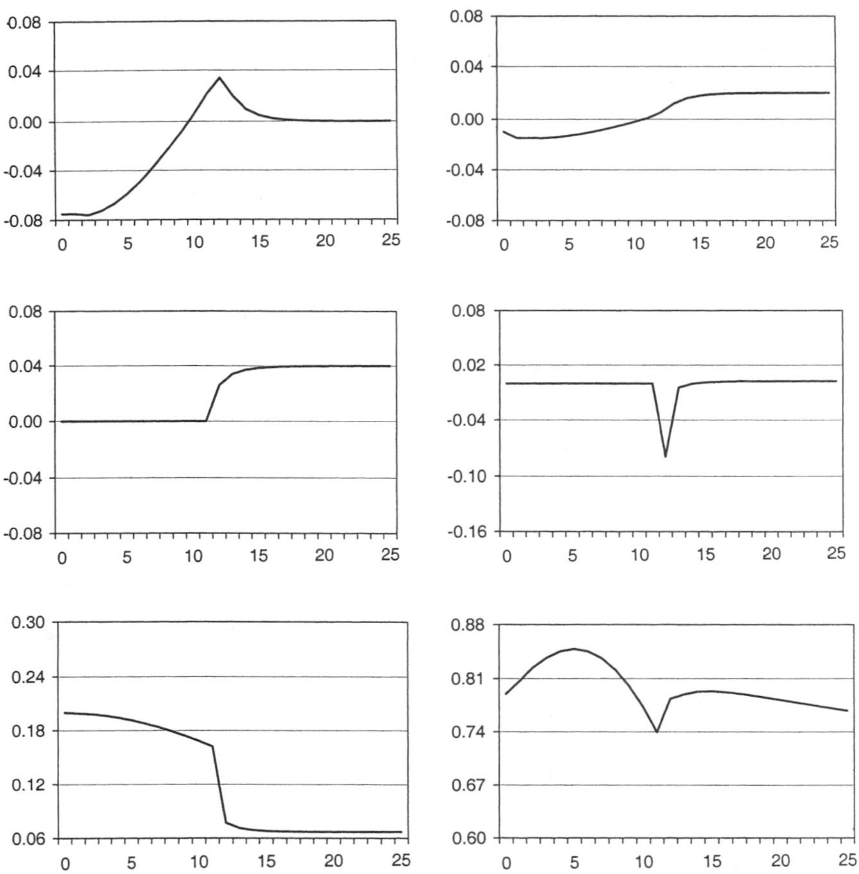

Fig. 7.4 Baseline case: output gap; inflation; nominal interest rate; OMO/GDP; monetary base/GDP; debt/GDP

stays in a deep slump for several years and then slowly recovers as r^* increases. The output gap rises above –5 percent in year six, and it becomes positive in year ten. From years one to nine, there is a cumulative output gap of –54 percent.

Inflation falls to –1.5 percent and then inches up as the economy recovers. It becomes positive in year eleven. Through that year the Taylor rule prescribes a negative interest rate, so i is stuck at zero.

In year twelve, the recovery pushes the Taylor-rule interest rate above zero. The rule begins to operate, and it guides inflation smoothly to the target of 2 percent. Output temporarily overshoots potential as inflation rises.

While the interest rate is zero, the money stock is constant and nominal GDP grows (the growth in Y exceeds the fall in P). The money-GDP ratio declines slowly. In year twelve, when the interest rate becomes positive, the money-GDP ratio falls by more than half. This occurs through a large monetary contraction: open market purchases, Z, are –8 percent of GDP. This action is needed because of the high level of money at the start of the simulation. Although the money-GDP ratio falls in years one to eleven, it remains far above the level that produces a positive interest rate. Thus a large money absorption is needed when the Taylor rule takes effect.

The debt-income ratio rises initially, because the output slump produces primary deficits. The ratio peaks at 0.85 in year five, then falls as the economy recovers. It jumps up in year twelve, when the large monetary contraction occurs. The BOJ's sales of government bonds raise the level of privately-held debt.

In steady state, the debt-income ratio falls slowly. The primary deficit is zero, and interest payments are balanced by income growth, since $r = g =$ 2 percent. The fall in the debt ratio results from seignorage revenue, as $Z >$ 0 in steady state. The ratio reaches 0.77 in year twenty-five.

7.5 A Bond-Financed Fiscal Expansion

This section examines how a bond-financed fiscal expansion changes the evolution of the economy.

7.5.1 The Policy

In this experiment, interest rate policy is the same as before: $i = \max\{i^T, 0\}$. And once again, $Z = 0$ when $i = 0$.

However, this policy is now accompanied by fiscal transfers. These transfers add to government debt through equation (6). The transfers begin in year one; given the lag in the IS curve, they start affecting output in year two. The transfers are chosen to end the slump quickly and permanently: the output gap is nonnegative in years two, three, ... Each period, the government makes the smallest transfer sufficient to achieve this result.

To state this policy formally, let G_t^* be the real transfer that produces $Y_{t+1} = Y_{t+1}^*$. G_t^* can be computed from the IS curve given the state at t. The rule for transfers is

$$G_t = \max\{G_t^*, 0\},\ t \geq 1. \tag{8}$$

If a positive transfer is needed to keep output at potential, it is made. If a negative transfer would keep output at potential, no transfer is made. In this case, output exceeds potential.

7.5.2 The Path of Transfers

Figure 7.5 shows the series of fiscal transfers implied by equation (8). In year one, the transfer is 6.6 percent of output (Y), or 6.1 percent of potential output (Y^*). Given the multiplier of 1.25, this transfer is needed to produce a zero output gap in period two, rather than the –7.6 percent gap of the baseline case. The transfer is 2.2 percent of output in year two, less than 1 percent in years three and four, and zero thereafter. The necessary transfer peters out because $r - r^*$ falls, stimulating spending. (The real rate falls because π rises, and r^* rises by assumption.) The cumulative transfer over years one through four is 9.4 percent of output.

This fiscal expansion is large by historical standards, but not gigantic. Over the 1990s, Japan experienced a series of changes in taxes and government spending (Kuttner and Posen 2001). Several of these shifts amounted to 2 percent of GDP or more; a 1998 stimulus package was 4 percent. The total effect of fiscal policy was small, because expansions in some years were offset by contractions in others (such as the 1997 tax increase). The key difference between the transfers proposed here and recent practice is that policy pushes consistently in one direction.

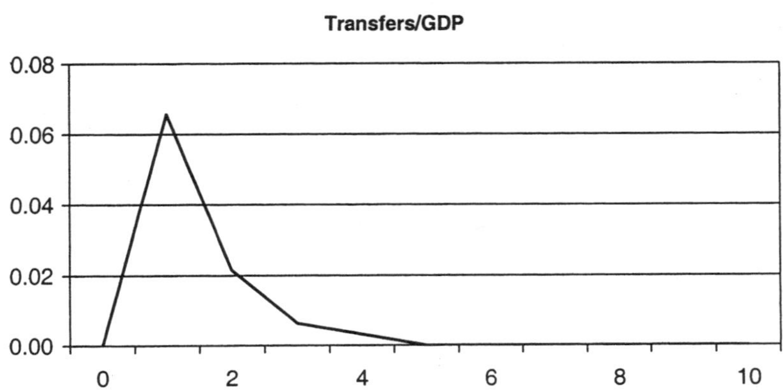

Fig. 7.5 The fiscal expansion

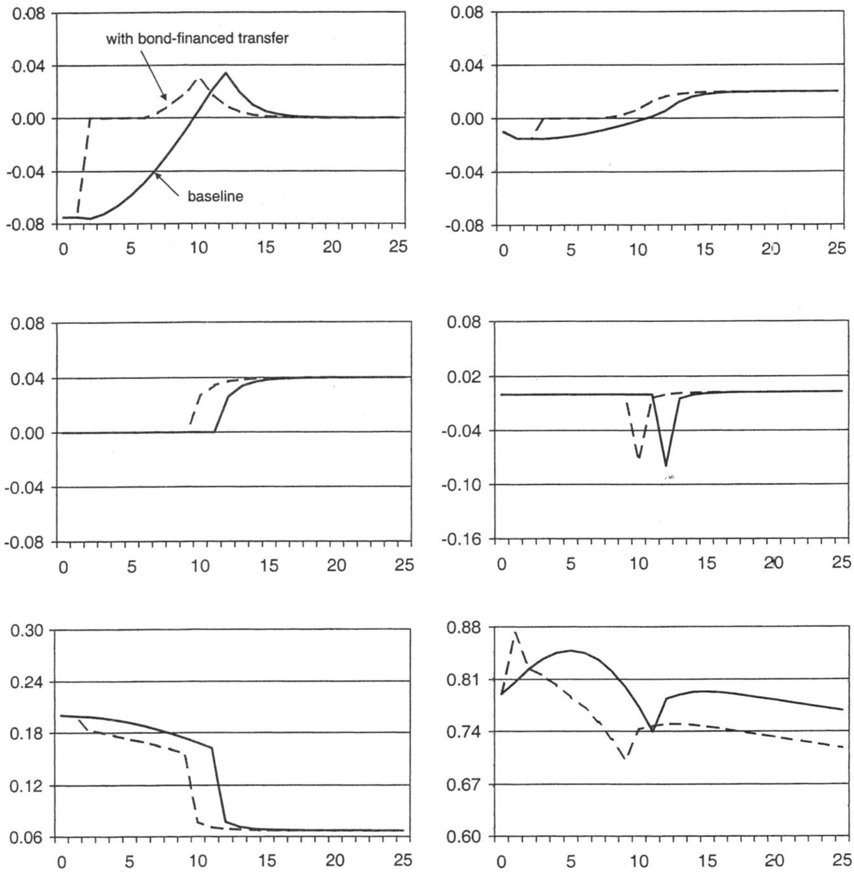

Fig. 7.6 Effects of fiscal expansion: output gap; inflation; nominal interest rate; OMO/GDP; monetary base/GDP; debt/GDP

7.5.3 Effects of the Transfers

Figure 7.6 shows the effects of fiscal transfers. It compares the economy's path under the transfer rule (8) (the dashed line) to the baseline case without transfers (the solid line). By construction, the transfers return output to potential in period two; most of the long slump in the baseline case is eliminated. The faster recovery implies that inflation and the interest rate start rising sooner than before. Nonetheless, the Taylor rule guides the economy to the same steady state, with 2 percent inflation.

The large transfer in period one causes the debt-income ratio to jump up: it reaches 0.87, compared to 0.81 in the baseline case. After that the ratio falls rapidly as the transfers fuel growth and inflation. In year two, the debt-income ratio with transfers (0.825) is very close to the ratio in the baseline case (0.824); in year three, the ratio with transfers falls below the baseline case. It remains lower in all future years, except for year eleven when it is slightly higher. (The result for year eleven reflects the fact that the nominal interest rate rises earlier with transfers. The jump in debt from the necessary monetary contraction occurs sooner.)

In steady state the debt-income ratio falls slowly in both the baseline case and the case with transfers. However, the path of the ratio is lower with transfers. In year twenty-five, the ratio is 0.72 with transfers and 0.77 without them. Thus the transfers produce a win-win: they end the output slump quickly *and* they improve the long-run fiscal situation.

To better understand these results, note that the cumulative output gap in the baseline case is –44 percent of potential output. The cumulative gap with transfers is –5 percent, so the transfers raise output by a total of 39 percent of potential. The effect of output on government revenue, θ, is 0.25; thus revenue rises by (0.25)39 percent = 9.8 percent of potential output. This gain more than offsets the initial transfers, which total 9.4 percent of potential. The transfers also reduce the debt-income ratio by raising inflation. Inflation reaches zero in period three, while it stays negative through period ten in the baseline case. The faster rise in inflation reduces real interest rates on the debt.

7.6 A Money-Financed Fiscal Expansion

This section considers fiscal transfers financed by printing money rather than issuing debt. I ask whether money finance produces lower debt-income ratios, as suggested by Bernanke and others.

7.6.1 The Policy

In this experiment, the fiscal transfers are the same as before (see the path in figure 7.5). There are positive transfers in years one through four. The government finances the transfers by issuing bonds and the central bank buys the bonds. The central bank's purchases equal the nominal level of transfers:

$$Z_t = P_t G_t,\ t = 1, \ldots, 4. \tag{9}$$

These actions raise the money stock by the amount of the transfers, and leave privately-held debt unchanged. Thus they are equivalent to a helicopter drop of money.

After year four, monetary policy behaves as in the previous experiments. Open market purchases are zero until the Taylor rule prescribes a positive interest rate, and then this rule determines policy.

7.6.2 Results

The fiscal multiplier does not depend on how transfers are financed. Thus switching from debt to money finance does not change the path of output.

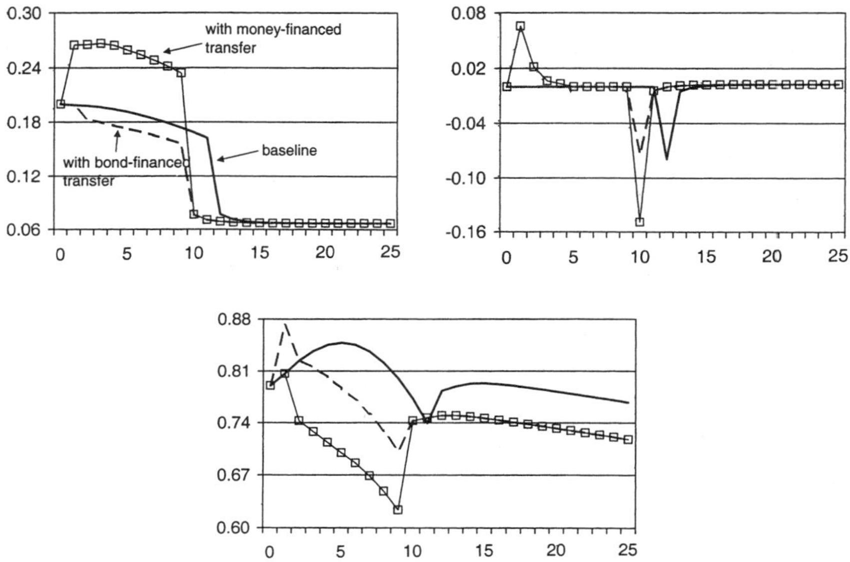

Fig. 7.7 Money-finance versus debt-finance: monetary base/GDP; OMO/GDP; debt/GDP

There is also no effect on inflation or the interest rate, since the Phillips curve and Taylor rule are unchanged. The only changes are in open market operations, the money stock, and debt. Figure 7.7 shows the paths of these variables. It compares the case of money-financed transfers (the dotted lines) to the cases of bond-financed transfers and no transfers.

When the transfers are money financed, the money-income ratio jumps up in year one. In contrast to the case of bond finance, the debt-income ratio does *not* rise sharply. In years one through nine, the money-income ratio is higher with money finance, and the debt-income ratio is lower by the same amount. Policymakers have substituted money for debt.

Things change in year ten, when the Taylor rule becomes operative. As before, contractionary open market operations are needed to reduce money to the level consistent with the Taylor rule. The necessary open market sales are larger in the case of money-financed transfers, because the money-income ratio is higher in year nine. The extra sales of debt raise the debt-income ratio to its path in the bond-finance case. In other words, the monetization of debt in years one through four is reversed in year ten: money is turned back into debt. Starting in year ten, the initial financing of transfers is irrelevant to all variables in the model.

In light of these results, does it matter how transfers are initially financed? Monetization has no effect on output or inflation, and no long-run effect on debt. However, it prevents the jump in the debt-income ratio that occurs in year one if transfers are debt financed. With money finance, the debt-income ratio never significantly exceeds its level in the baseline case. Thus monetization matters if we care about the short-run path of debt, not just its steady-state behavior.

Do we care about the short-run path of debt? To address this question, we must go beyond the model and ask why debt matters. A high debt-income ratio is dangerous because investors may start to fear default, sparking a financial crisis (Ball and Mankiw 1995). Higher debt at a point in time might increase this danger, even holding constant the long-run behavior of debt. Investors are more likely to panic when they hold more debt, because they have more to lose from an immediate default. However, the importance of this effect is unclear. The case for money-financed transfers is not as compelling as some economists suggest.[6]

7.6.3 A Permanent Monetary Expansion

In the previous experiment, the increase in money that finances transfers is reversed in the long run. This fact follows from the conventional assumption that the central bank eventually follows a Taylor rule. However, the reversal of the monetary expansion differs from some economists' suggestions. Bernanke, for example, advocates money-financed transfers for which "much or all of the increase in the money stock is viewed as permanent." Here I consider such a policy. As one might guess, the policy prevents the debt-income ratio from jumping up at any point. Unfortunately, it also produces hyperinflation.

Specifically, I assume again that transfers are governed by equation (8), and that they are financed by money creation. Monetary policy after the transfers is the same as in earlier experiments, except for a constraint: open market purchases must be nonnegative. That is, after the money stock rises, it can never fall. This constraint first binds in year eleven, when the Taylor-rule interest rate becomes positive. When the Taylor rule implies $Z_t < 0$, the central bank sets $Z_t = 0$ instead.

Figure 7.8 shows the effects of this policy. Through year nine we see the same effects of money-financed transfers as before. In year ten, the Taylor rule starts calling for large open market sales, but they do not occur. Con-

6. Goodfriend (2000) and Suda (2003) argue that a monetary expansion to finance transfers would eventually have to be reversed, with adverse fiscal consequences. Their arguments anticipate the results of this section.

Auerbach and Obstfeld (2004) present a model in which expansionary open market operations reduce debt permanently. This result contradicts my finding that monetization of debt is irrelevant in the long run. The differences between Auerbach-Obstfeld's results and mine arise from different assumptions about inflation. In the Auerbach-Obstfeld model, a monetary expansion causes inflation to rise, reducing real government debt, even when the interest rate is zero. After that, inflation falls without a fall in output. In my model, monetary policy cannot affect inflation at a zero interest rate, and a fall in inflation requires lower output and tax revenue.

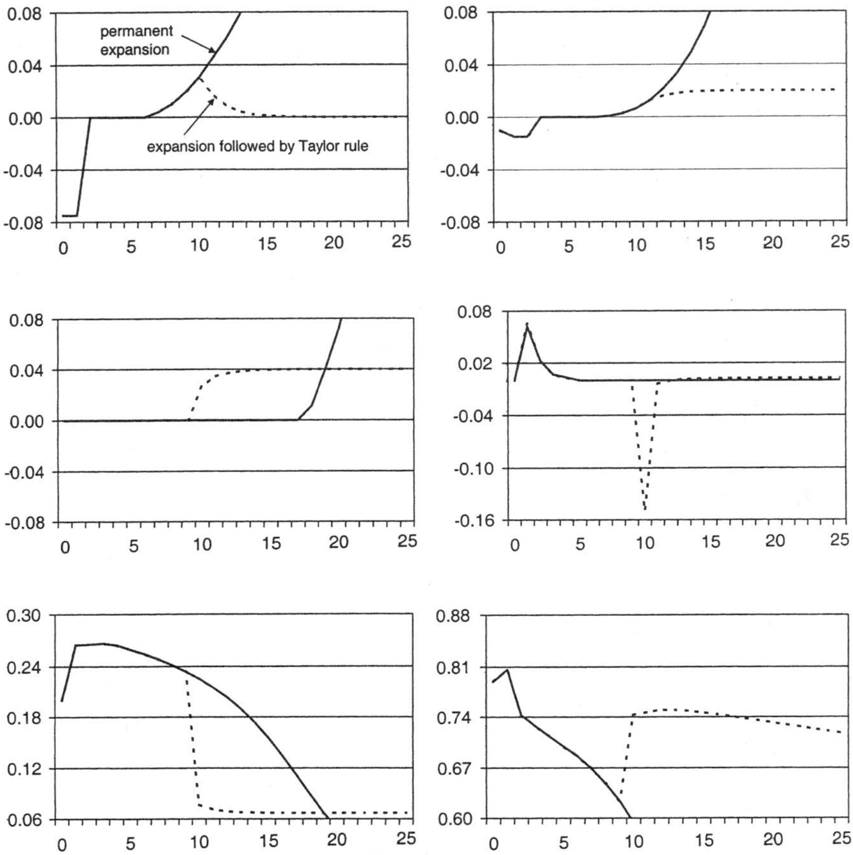

Fig. 7.8 A permanent monetary expansion: output gap; inflation; nominal interest rate; OMO/GDP; monetary base/GDP; debt/GDP

sequently, the money-income ratio stays high and the nominal interest rate stays at zero. The failure to tighten policy causes output and inflation to rise. At this point, the economy enters an unstable spiral: higher inflation reduces the real rate, which raises output, which further raises inflation. Without reducing money, the central bank cannot raise the interest rate to abort this process. Inflation reaches 7 percent in year fifteen and 90 percent in year twenty-five, and keeps rising forever.[7]

BOJ officials have criticized the idea of money-financed transfers on the grounds that they would eventually produce high inflation. Figure 7.8 shows a scenario in which this fear is realized. We have seen that policy-

7. Eventually inflation reduces the money-income ratio sufficiently that the nominal interest rate starts rising. However, it rises more slowly than inflation, so the real rate falls forever.

makers can prevent this outcome by reducing the money stock when inflation starts rising. But this action reverses the fiscal gain that money finance is intended to achieve.

7.7 Robustness

This section considers the robustness of my results. I first vary the model's parameters, and then consider broader changes in assumptions.

The chapter's main conclusions are fairly robust. A fiscal expansion always produces a faster output recovery. The long-run effects on the debt-income ratio vary across specifications. In most cases, however, a fiscal expansion reduces debt below its level under passive policy. In some cases, this gain is large. At worst, a fiscal expansion raises long-run debt by a small amount.

7.7.1 The Neutral Real Rate

As discussed in section 7.3, Japan's neutral real interest rate appears to be negative, but is unlikely to stay negative forever. So far, I have assumed the neutral rate r^* starts at –2 percent and rises linearly to +2 percent over ten years. Here I continue to assume r^* rises linearly from –2 percent to +2 percent, but vary the speed of this rise. A fast increase in r^* means the IS curve shifts out quickly.

A faster increase in r^* weakens the case for fiscal expansion. This is illustrated by figure 7.9. Like figure 7.6, this figure compares the economy's evolution with passive policy and with the fiscal rule (8). But it assumes that r^* rises to +2 percent in five years rather than ten. Fiscal expansion still raises output, but its effects on debt are a bit less favorable than before. The debt-income ratio in year twenty-five is about one percentage point higher with the expansion than without.

This result reflects the effects of the r^* path on output. If r^* rises more quickly, then output recovers more quickly in the case of passive policy. This reduces the benefits of ending the initial slump with a fiscal expansion. There are smaller output gains, and hence smaller revenue gains to offset the initial cost of the expansion.

Figure 7.10 considers a range of paths for r^*. I assume this parameter rises linearly from –2 percent to +2 percent in n years, and vary n from one to twenty. For each n, the figure shows the debt-income ratio in year twenty-five with passive policy and with a fiscal expansion. The expansion raises the debt-income ratio for $n < 6$, but only by modest amounts. The costs of expansion when n is small are lower than the gains when n is large.

7.7.2 Equation Coefficients

Table 7.3 examines robustness to varying the coefficients in the model's equations—the IS and Phillips curves and the debt equation. Starting from

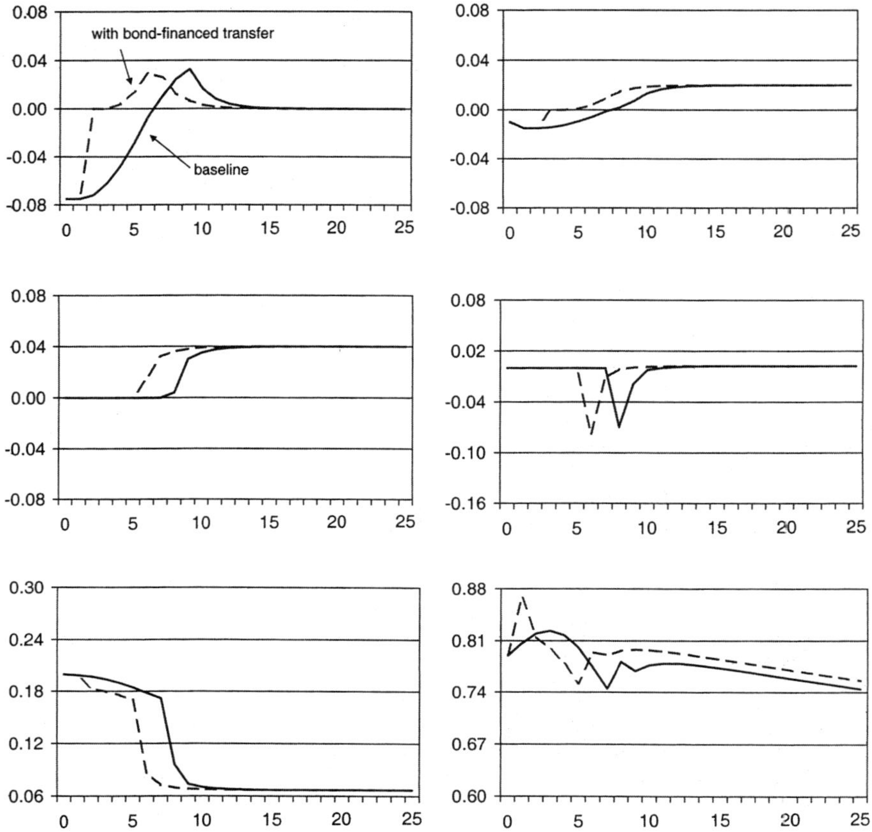

Fig. 7.9 A faster rise in r^*: output gap; inflation; nominal interest rate; OMO/GDP; monetary base/GDP; debt/GDP

the base values in table 7.2, I change one coefficient at a time, trying values that are twice as large and half as large. For each variation, table 7.3 reports the debt-income ratio in year twenty-five with passive policy and with a fiscal expansion.[8]

Not surprisingly, a key coefficient is δ, the fiscal multiplier. A larger multiplier means a smaller transfer is needed to return output to potential. This reduces the debt-income ratio in the case of expansionary policy. Recall that the base value of δ is 1.25; for this value, the debt-income ratio in year twenty-five is 5 points lower with expansionary policy than with pas-

8. As I vary the model coefficients, I also vary the coefficients in the central bank's interest rate rule, equation (7). As discussed in section 7.4, the coefficients in equation (7) are chosen so that inflation moves halfway to its target each period. The coefficients defined by this rule are functions of the IS and Phillips-curve coefficients.

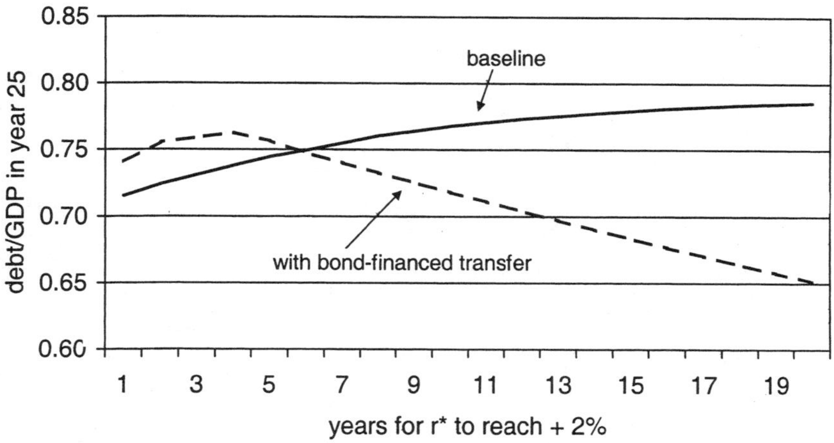

Fig. 7.10 Varying the path of r^*

Table 7.3 Varying the parameter values

	Debt/GDP in year 25	
	With baseline policy	With fiscal transfer
$\delta = 0.625$	0.77	0.79
$\delta = 2.5$	0.77	0.68
$\beta = 0.5$	0.67	0.66
$\beta = 2$	1.13	0.81
$\lambda = 0.3$	0.66	0.67
$\lambda = 1.2$	[very large]	0.86
$\alpha = 0.01$	0.65	0.64
$\alpha = 0.125$	0.73	0.72
$\theta = 0.5$	0.85	0.71

sive policy. This gain rises to 9 points for $\delta = 2.5$, but it falls to –3 points for $\delta = 0.625$. The gain is positive for all $\delta > 0.76$.

When the other coefficients change, the fiscal gains from transfers are robust. Transfers raise the long-run debt ratio in only one case ($\lambda = 0.3$), and then by a trivial amount. Often transfers reduce debt by large amounts (e.g., 41 percent of GDP for $\alpha = 0.4$).

7.7.3 Perpetual Deficits

So far I have assumed the government's primary budget is balanced if output is at potential and the transfers G are zero. This assumption does not fit Japan today. There is a large primary deficit, which is only partly cyclical. It appears this deficit would be about 5 percent of GDP if output were at potential.

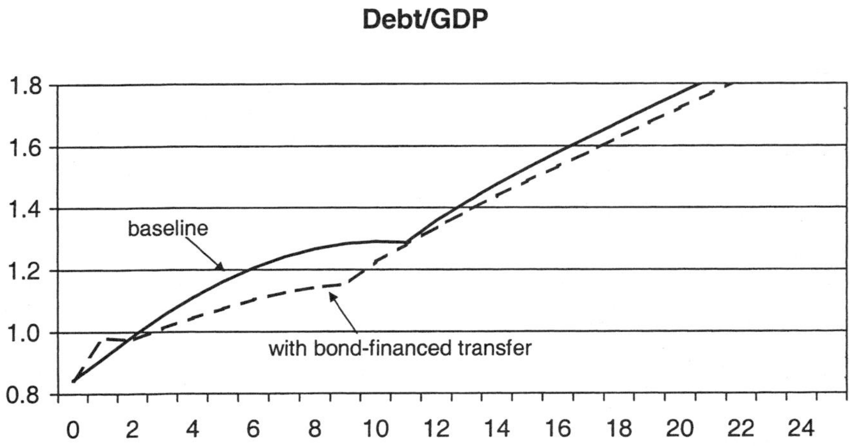

Fig. 7.11 Perpetual deficits

This fact can be captured by adding a term to the debt equation, (6). The equation becomes

$$(9)\quad D_t = D_{t-1} + i_{t-1}D_{t-1} + P_tG_t - Z_t - \theta(P_tY_t - P_tY_t^*) + (0.05)P_tY_t^*.$$

The last term is the primary deficit when output is at potential.

This modification does not change the behavior of output or inflation, but it does affect the debt path. For base parameter values, figure 7.11 shows this path for the cases of passive and expansionary fiscal policy. In both cases the debt-income ratio rises forever. A permanent budget deficit leads to disaster.

However, fiscal expansion still compares favorably to passive policy. Starting in year two, the debt-income ratio is always smaller with the expansion. This policy does not eliminate the underlying deficit problem, but it slows the growth of debt.

7.7.4 A Textbook Phillips Curve

The main model assumes that expected inflation cannot fall below zero. Here I assume that expected inflation equals past inflation, even if past inflation is negative:

$$(10)\qquad \pi_t^e = \pi_{t-1}.$$

This assumption and equation (2) produce an accelerationist Phillips curve:

$$(11)\qquad \pi_t = \pi_{t-1} + \frac{\alpha(Y_{t-1} - Y_{t-1}^*)}{Y_{t-1}^*}.$$

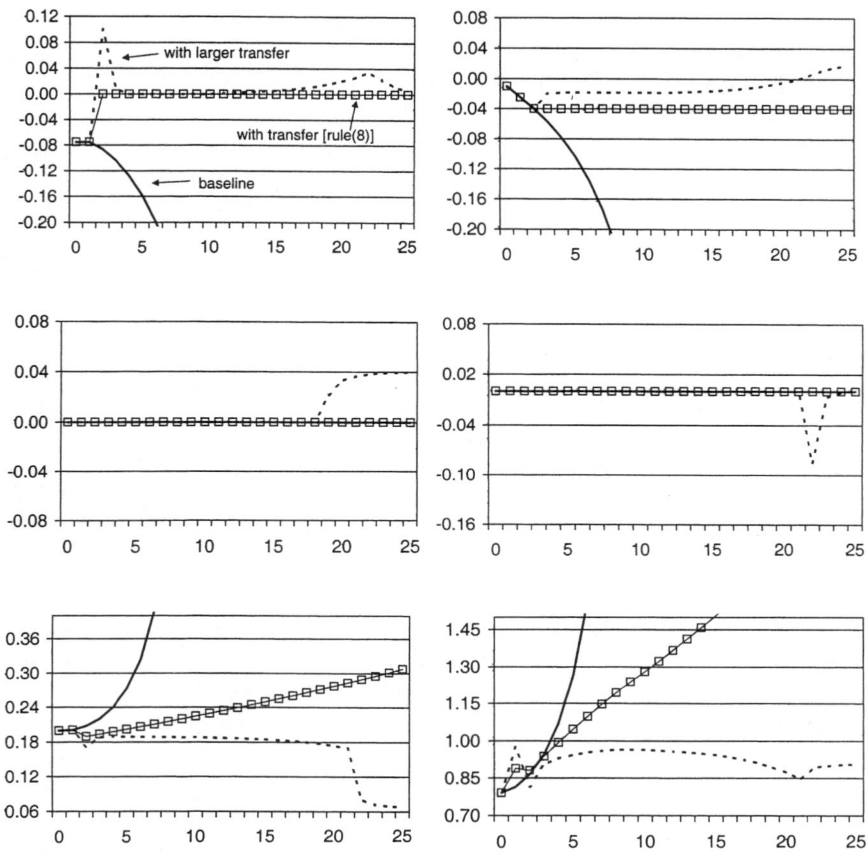

Fig. 7.12 A textbook Phillips curve: output gap; inflation; nominal interest rate; OMO/GDP; monetary base/GDP; debt/GDP

Figure 7.12 shows how this modification affects the economy under alternative policies.

The largest changes occur for the case of no fiscal expansion—the solid line in the figure. In this case, the output slump leads to a deflationary spiral. Low output reduces inflation, which raises the real interest rate, which further reduces output. Inflation and output head to minus infinity. With an accelerationist Phillips curve, passive policy is disastrous.

The dashed line in figure 7.12 shows the effects of the fiscal rule (8). The outcomes from this policy are better than from passive policy, but still not good. Inflation falls to –4 percent and then remains at that level. The nominal interest rate stays at zero, and the real rate rises to +4 percent. The economy stays in a liquidity trap. To keep output at potential, as required by rule (8), the government must provide transfers forever. This causes the debt-income ratio to rise without bound.

In this version of the model, a more aggressive fiscal expansion is better. The dotted line in figure 7.12 shows what happens if the transfer in year one is 15 percent of potential output, rather than 7 percent as dictated by equation (8). This transfer creates a boom in year two, pushing inflation from –4 percent to –2 percent in year three. With 2 percent inflation, the real interest rate is low enough for the economy to escape the liquidity trap. Eventually a nonnegative output gap can be sustained without transfers. The debt income ratio peaks at 0.91 in year twenty-six and then falls.

7.7.5 A Forward-Looking Real Interest Rate

The main model is backward-looking—there is no role for expectations of future variables. Here I introduce some forward-looking behavior. I define the real interest rate as the nominal rate minus expected future inflation, not current inflation. Since the model is nonstochastic, expected inflation equals actual future inflation. The real interest rate is

$$r_t = i_t - \pi_{t+1}. \tag{12}$$

This variation has only minor effects on the results. Once again, a fiscal expansion ends the output slump and reduces long-run debt. The debt-income ratio in year twenty-five is 0.73 with fiscal expansion and 0.79 with passive policy.

7.8 Conclusion

This chapter examines the effects of fiscal transfers in a model of the Japanese economy. Initial conditions are set to capture Japan's slump as of 2003. I determine the level of transfers needed to return output to potential, and the effects on inflation and the debt-income ratio. I assume that monetary policy follows a Taylor rule once the interest rate becomes positive.

A quick output recovery requires transfers totaling 9.4 percent of potential GDP over four years. After the recovery, the Taylor rule guides the economy to a steady state with output at potential and 2 percent inflation. If the transfers are financed with bonds, they cause the debt-income ratio to jump up. After that, the ratio falls rapidly due to higher growth, inflation, and tax revenue. In steady state, the debt-income ratio is lower than in a baseline case with no transfers. Thus the transfers produce a win-win: they end the output slump and reduce Japan's long-run fiscal problem.

I also consider transfers financed with money rather than debt. The finance method does not influence the paths of output or inflation. It also does not affect the debt-income ratio in steady state, because the initial monetization of debt is eventually reversed. However, money finance prevents the initial run-up of debt that occurs with bond-financed transfers.

Thus money finance is preferable if policymakers care about short-run as well as long-run debt levels.

The results in this paper capture the ideas of some Japan-watchers. For example, in discussing the downgrade of Japan's debt, Thomas Byrne of Moody's argues that Japan needs a fiscal expansion:

> Japan can't consolidate its way out of this (debt problem), it has to grow its way out. Any policy that ends deflation and stimulates growth (is good). A fiscal policy that didn't include a lot of wasteful spending may present near-term anxiety but, if it really did stimulate growth, it would be good over the long term. (Pilling 2002)

Byrne suggests that the long-run fiscal benefits from expansionary policy would outweigh the costs, as this paper finds. The "near-term anxiety" he mentions is presumably caused by the temporary rise in debt from a bond-financed expansion. Thus Byrne also provides a rationale for money finance, which reduces debt in the short run.

References

Ahearne, Alan, et al. 2002. Preventing deflation: Lessons from Japan's experience in the 1990s. International Finance Discussion Paper, Board of Governors of the Federal Reserve System.

Auebach, Alan, and Maurice Obstfeld. 2004. The case for open-market purchases in a liquidity trap. Berkeley, CA: University of California Press.

Baba, Naohiko, et al. 2004. Japan's deflation, problems in the financial system, and monetary policy. Bank of Japan.

Ball, Laurence. 1999. Efficient rules for monetary policy. *International Finance* 2 (April): 63–83.

Bernanke, Ben S. 2003. Some thoughts on monetary policy in Japan. Speech to Japan Society of Monetary Economics, May 31.

Blanchard, Olivier. 2000. Bubbles, liquidity traps, and monetary policy. In *Japan's financial crisis and its parallels to U.S. experience,* ed. Ryoichi Mikilan and Adam S. Posen. Institute for International Economics.

Blanchard, Olivier, and Roberto Perotti. 2002. An empirical characterization of the dynamic effects of changes in government spending and taxes on output. *Quarterly Journal of Economics* 117 (November): 1329–68.

Broda, Christian, and David E. Weinstein. 2004. Happy news from the dismal science: Reassessing Japanese fiscal policy and sustainability. Columbia University.

Friedman, Milton. 2001. No more economic stimulus needed. *Wall Street Journal,* October 10, A17.

Fujiki, Hiroshi, Cheng Hsiao, and Yan Shen. 2002. Is there a stable money demand function under the low interest rate policy? A panel data analysis. Bank of Japan *Monetary and Economic Studies* 20 (April): 1–23.

Fukao, Mitsuhiro. 2004. Financial strains and the zero lower bound: The Japanese experience. Keio University.

Goodfriend, Marvin. 2000. Overcoming the zero bound on interest rate policy. *Journal of Money, Credit, and Banking* 32 (November, part 2): 1007–35.

Hirose, Yasuo and Koichiro Kamada. 2002. Time-varying NAIRU and potential growth in Japan. Working Paper no. 02-8. Bank of Japan Research and Statistics.
Hoshi, Takeo, and Anil K. Kashyap. 2004. Japan's financial crisis and economic stagnation. *Journal of Economic Perspectives* 18 (Winter): 3–26.
Iwamura, Mitsuru, Takeshi Kudo, and Tsutomu Watanabe. 2004. Monetary and fiscal policy in a liquidity trap: The Japanese experience 1999–2004. Institute of Economic Research, Hitotsubashi University.
Krugman, Paul. 2000. Thinking about the liquidity trap. 2000. *Journal of the Japanese and International Economies* 14 (December): 221–37.
Kuttner, Kenneth N., and Adam S. Posen. 2001. The great recession: Lessons for macroeconomic policy from Japan. *Brookings Papers on Economic Activity,* Issue no. 2:93–160.
Leigh, Daniel. 2004. Monetary policy and the dangers of deflation: Lessons from Japan. Johns Hopkins University.
Mankiw, N. Gregory. 1999. Memo to Tokyo: Cut taxes, print money. *Fortune,* January 11.
McCallum, Bennett T. 2000. Alternative monetary policy rules: A comparison with historical settings for the United States, the United Kingdom, and Japan. NBER Working Paper no. 7725. Cambridge, MA: National Bureau of Economic Research, June.
Miyao, Ryuzo. 2002. Liquidity traps and the stability of money demand: Is Japan really trapped at the zero bound? Kobe University.
Pilling, David. 2002. Japan braced for a rating downgrade as economy dips. *Financial Times,* March 9.
Posen, Adam S. 1998. *Restoring Japan's economic growth.* Institute for International Economics.
———. 2003. It takes more than a bubble to become Japan. IIE Working Paper no. 03-9. City: Institute for International Economics.
Stevens, Glenn. 2001. Comment. Bank of Japan *Monetary and Economic Studies* 19 (September): 313–21.
Suda, Miyako. 2003. The effect of "quantitative monetary easing" when the nominal short-term interest rate is zero. Bank of Japan.
Svensson, Lars E. O. 1997. Inflation forecast targeting: Monitoring and implementing inflation targets. *European Economic Review* 41 (June): 1111–46.

Comment Mitsuru Iwamura

Government's Intertemporal Budget Constraint

The model discussed in the chapter is very simple, and contains no forward-looking expectations. This is not a serious shortcoming of the chapter. In most cases, backward-looking expectations are enough and even more realistic. However, this may not be good if we discuss the Japanese fiscal problem in the last ten years.

The Japanese government conducted a series of fiscal stimulus during

Mitsuru Iwamura is a professor at the Graduate School of Asia-Pacific Studies at Waseda University.

the 1990s. Through the series of fiscal package, we have learned several important things as follows.

(1) Simple Ricardian equivalence does not hold, so fiscal stimulus has some impacts on the economic activity.

(2) The effectiveness of fiscal stimulus depends on the level of the existing public debt. If the level of public debt is very high, fiscal stimulus becomes less powerful. In an extreme case, fiscal expansion leads to a decrease in private consumption. Some empirical papers report that this mechanism did exist in the latter half of the 1990s.

(3) Temporary and permanent fiscal expansions have different impacts. If it is permanent, it has a larger impact on the economic activity. However, if it is temporary, its impact is very limited. A famous example is "Shopping Coupon" or CHIIKI-SHINKOKEN in March 1999, in which the government delivered a coupon of about 20,000 yen to each family. This was a one-time money transfer. It had some effects on the consumers' behavior, but its impact was very small. People recognized well that this was a temporary transfer, so that they did not revise much their permanent income.

These three things have important implications about the value of δ in the IS equation, equation (1). Ball assumes that δ is equal to 1.25. I am not quite sure if this is an appropriate number in the case of the Japanese economy in the last five years. Before deciding the value of δ, we have to be very careful about how it depends on the level of public debt, and whether the fiscal shock is a temporary one or a permanent one.

Monetary Expansions and Base Money Market

Ball compared a bond-financed fiscal expansion and a money-financed fiscal expansion, and then he concluded monetization has no effect on output or inflation. However, suppose that the government and the central bank implement a money-financed fiscal expansion, so the supply of base money increases. I wonder what will happen on the demand for base money. Simply speaking, the demand for base money depends on the nominal interest rate. In the situation discussed in this chapter, the short-term nominal interest rate is zero, but the medium- or long-term interest rate is probably above zero. Therefore, if the medium- or long-term nominal interest rate falls in response to the money-financed fiscal expansion, people demand more base money, and consequently the market-clearing condition for base money is satisfied. In contrast, if the medium- or long-term nominal interest rates do not decline, the demand for base money does not increase, so that we have an excess supply in base money market.

This argument indicates that what is essentially important to escape from the liquidity trap is not monetary expansion itself, but a decline in the medium- or long-term nominal interest rate. If we think in this way, we can make a good connection between Ball's argument and the arguments made by previous papers like Eggertsson and Woodford. As Ball mentioned in this chapter, the main source of a liquidity trap is a substantial decline in the neutral rate, or equivalently the natural rate of interest. Then the issue is how to lower the real interest rate in accordance with its natural rate counterpart. Given the zero lower bound on nominal interest rates, we can fix this problem only by changing the expected rate of inflation or changing medium- or long-term nominal interest rates.

Furthermore, Ball argued that a permanent monetary expansion might produce hyperinflation, because such a permanent monetary expansion shall be accompanied by a monetary policy avoiding raising the interest rate forever. I fully agree with this argument and also emphasize the importance of considerations to base money market-clearing condition.

Distinction between Money and Public Debt

Ball discussed that monetization might ease investors' fear to default in virtue of preventing the jump in the debt-income ratio. Regarding this, I would call our attention to denomination of public debt.

If the public debt is denominated by foreign currency, the distinction between a bond-financed fiscal expansion and a money-financed fiscal expansion is so vital. Huge amounts of government bonds denominated by foreign currency are directly linked to the fear of default. Such experiences are so common in the cases of Latin American debt problems.

On the other hand, if such a fiscal expansion is financed by the home currency, fear to default depends on the relationship between the government and the central bank. As long as there are no serious conflicts between them, the central bank will purchase government bonds to cope with crises in the money market caused by the accumulation of government debt. Moreover, especially speaking about Japan, as government bonds occupy 67 percent of asset of the central bank (as of the end of March 2005), it is unlikely that people distinguish between money and government bonds: they must recognize these two are almost identical. They will not trust money any more when they do not trust government bonds. And once people cease to trust money, inflation will start to take place. Inflation is not good, but it will reduce real debt burden, thereby removing the threat of default.

Someone might say that money is good because the central bank is not obliged to repay it. But this is simply wrong. If that is true, the government is able to reduce debt burden just by repaying debts in terms of government money. Needless to say, this is a wrong argument, because government bonds and government money are both on the liability side of the government's balance sheet.

III Case Studies

8

Stock Market Liquidity and the Macroeconomy
Evidence from Japan

Woon Gyu Choi and David Cook

8.1 Introduction

In the early 1990s, Japanese equity prices fell drastically from heights that are now considered the effects of a stock market bubble. During the remainder of the decade, the value of the stock market stabilized at much lower values. Here, we examine the link between the liquidity of the Japanese stock market and the macroeconomy in a period of prolonged deflation, slow growth, and near-zero interest rates.

Recent research has shown that the liquidity of major world financial markets substantially varied over time and that the unpredictability of market liquidity is an important source of risk for investors. In this chapter, we document a large and persistent decline in Japanese stock market liquidity during the 1990s. In illiquid stock markets, investors are unable to sell large amounts of shares without a sharp decline in the price of the shares. We show that the impact of stock trading on share prices rose substantially after the collapse of the bubble. In addition, the volatility of liquidity shocks to the stock market increased dramatically.

A number of factors have led to a decline in asset-market liquidity during the late 1990s. First, Japanese financial intermediaries experienced a substantial deterioration in their balance sheets. If market makers and

Woon Gyu Choi is a senior economist at the International Monetary Fund. David Cook is an associate professor of economics at the Hong Kong University of Science and Technology.

The views expressed in this paper are those of the authors and do not necessarily represent those of the IMF or IMF policy. We thank Tim Chue, Burkhard Drees, Shinichi Fukuda, Takatoshi Ito, Charles F. Kramer, Andrew Rose, Makoto Saito, Sunil Sharma, Ling Hui Tan, and participants at the NBER East Asian Seminar on Economics meetings for comments. David Cook thanks the Research Grants Council of Hong Kong for financial assistance (Project No. HKUST6291/03H) and Hao Li for valuable research work.

other investors faced credit constraints, this may have reduced their ability to take advantage of high returns by providing liquidity to an illiquid market. Second, during much of this period, Japan was operating in a deflationary environment in which savers were able to earn real returns simply by holding money. This may have reduced their incentives to take speculative risks by providing liquidity to the market. Third, adverse shocks to liquidity in the world and East Asian financial markets potentially increased the exposure of Japanese firms. At the microstructure level, the Tokyo Stock Exchange implements a continuous auction-based order system in the late 1990s, dispensing with market makers (Tokyo Stock Exchange 2003).[1]

We consider some channels through which financial market liquidity shocks may affect the macroeconomy. Naturally, a rise in equity risk tends to raise the cost of capital of firms through the cost of financing channel. Using cross-sectional data, we find that exposure to liquidity risk is an important determinant of investment. Another channel pertains to the effects of shocks on the portfolio of assets. Kiyotaki and Moore (2001) construct a theory in which liquid assets are held primarily as a hedge against the illiquidity of real assets. A rise in money held for financial liquidity may reduce money available for transactions. In an economy with nominal rigidities, an increase in money demand can have real effects on the economy. Nagayasu (2003) finds evidence of a structural break in money demand in Japan during the crisis. Indeed there is a sharp decline in the velocity of money in the late 1990s. We find, using time-series data, that shocks to financial market liquidity have effects on the economy, which are similar to textbook effects of money demand shocks.

In measuring stock market liquidity, we closely follow Pastor and Stambaugh's (2003) measure of United States equity market liquidity. They measure liquidity by the degree to which the quantity of stocks traded affects the market price of stocks. In a liquid market, large sales of stocks can be made without substantially changing the price of the stocks. In an illiquid market, however, they can have an adverse impact on stock prices. Amihud and Mendelson (1986) is an early study of the relationship between market liquidity and stock returns. Campbell, Grossman, and Wang (1993) construct a model in which risk-averse market makers require a premium to buy large quantities of stock. Chordia, Sarkar, and Subrahmanyam (2002) find that aggregate liquidity fluctuations in the United States affect both bond and stock markets and are correlated with monetary policy. Stahel (2004) finds that global liquidity shocks affect stock markets in both the United States and Japan. Hamao, Mei, and Xu (2003)

1. Buy and sell orders are matched first according to price (highest buy to lowest sell offer) and second by time of placement. Also, important features of the Tokyo Stock Exchange include the intraday price limit rule and limit-order trading—for the institutional features of trading, see, for example, Ahn et al. (2002).

find a dramatic decrease in trading volumes in the Japanese stock market after the bubble burst.

Section 8.2 describes the technique for measuring stock market liquidity and some of the time-series properties of market liquidity shocks. We find that, during the 1990s, stock market liquidity fell, and the volatility of liquidity shocks increased. Moreover, the exposure of individual firms' equity shares to liquidity shocks rose during the same period. Section 8.3 presents some firm-level cross-sectional determinants of liquidity risk and the real impact of exposures to liquidity risk. We find that the liquidity of individual corporate balance sheets predicts how exposed their shares will be to liquidity shocks. Moreover, exposures to liquidity shocks help determine the capital growth and sales growth of firms during the crisis. In Section 8.4, we examine the dynamic interaction between stock market liquidity and the macroeconomy using vector autoregressions (VARs). An examination of money markets suggests that a decline in stock market liquidity leads to a rise in the demand for real money balances. Section 8.5 concludes. The data used are described in an appendix.

8.2 Measure of Liquidity Risk

8.2.1 Measuring Stock Market Liquidity

In measuring Japanese aggregate stock market liquidity, we closely follow Pastor and Stambaugh's (2003) measure for the United States equity markets. For a group of Japanese common shares indexed by k, we estimate the effect of order flows on excess daily returns for each month from January 1975 to December 2001. Using time-series ordinary least squares (OLS), we estimate the following equation:

$$(1) \qquad r^{xs}_{k,d,t} = \theta^0_{k,t} + \theta^1_{k,t} \cdot r_{k,d-1,t} + \theta^2_{k,t} \cdot \text{sign}(r^{xs}_{k,d-1,t}) \cdot vol_{k,d-1,t} + \varepsilon_{k,d,t},$$

where $r_{k,d,t}$ is the return on the stock of company k on day d of month t. Define $r^{MKT}_{d,t}$ as the equal-weighted return on Japanese stocks in the Pacific Capital Markets (PACAP) database (see the appendix). The excess return $r^{xs}_{k,d,t} = r_{k,d,t} - r^{MKT}_{d,t}$ is measured as the difference between the return on stock k and the market return. The sign$(r^{xs}_{k,d-1,t})$ variable is equal to 1 when lagged excess returns are positive and equal to –1 when lagged excess returns are negative. We define $vol_{k,d,t}$ as the value of shares traded, measured in billions of yen. The signing of the trading volume is meant to distinguish whether trades are driven by selling pressure from investors or by buying pressure. When investors are selling shares in a company to market makers or other short-term liquidity providers, such as speculators, excess returns on that company should be negative. When investors are buying from market makers, excess returns should be positive. The lagged return is included to capture inertia effects that are not volume related.

The parameter $\theta^2_{k,t}$ measures the degree to which sales affect returns and thus might be thought of as a measure of liquidity in that particular market. One would expect $\theta^2_{k,t}$ to be negative in general and more negative when liquidity is lower. This idea is rooted in Campbell, Grossman, and Wang's model (1993) in which a large value of shares traded generates reversals in returns in illiquid markets.[2] In their model, risk-averse market makers demand higher than expected returns to buy or sell a large volume of shares. When there are large sales at day $d-1$, the market makers offer a relatively low price, generating negative excess returns in period $d-1$ and predicting relatively high returns in the subsequent period. Under this theory, trading volume should be associated with return reversals, if the stock is not perfectly liquid. Technically, the Tokyo Stock Exchange (Tokyo Stock Exchange 2003) does not operate on a system in which specified market makers are responsible for the trading of individual stocks. The Campbell, Grossman, and Wang theory can apply more generally to a case in which there are a limited number of investors willing and able to engage in short-term speculation in individual stocks. It is therefore interesting to see whether the Pastor and Stambaugh (2003) model captures some features of market liquidity in a market without market makers.

We estimate $\theta^2_{k,t}$ for each stock-month for which there are at least nine usable observations during the month and for which both the previous month and the subsequent month have at least nine usable observations. To obtain a consistent sample of firms during the 1990s, we choose from the PACAP database a set of 828 nonfinancial firms for which we are able to estimate $\theta^2_{k,t}$ for at least 140 of the 144 months between January 1990 and December 2001, and for which we can obtain balance-sheet data (from the same source) in years 1990, 1995, and 2000. To avoid contaminating the sample with the results of buyouts or bankruptcies, we exclude firms whose equity permanently ceases trading at some point.

Panel A of figure 8.1 shows the number of shares, N_t, for which we are able to estimate the effect of trading value on returns for each month for the period between January 1975 and December 2001. We begin with approximately 500 different shares, a number that grows with time. By construction, the number of firms after 1989 is approximately constant. (Other panels of the figure will be discussed later.)

8.2.2 Descriptive Statistics of the Aggregate Stock Market

Table 8.1 also shows some properties of the shares of our sample in comparison with a broader index of stocks from PACAP. The equal-weighted average monthly return (excluding dividends) for shares in the overall sample of firms is about 0.8 percent per month; in our smaller sample, the

2. Chao and Hueng (forthcoming) show that return reversals are a prevalent phenomenon of the Japanese stock market.

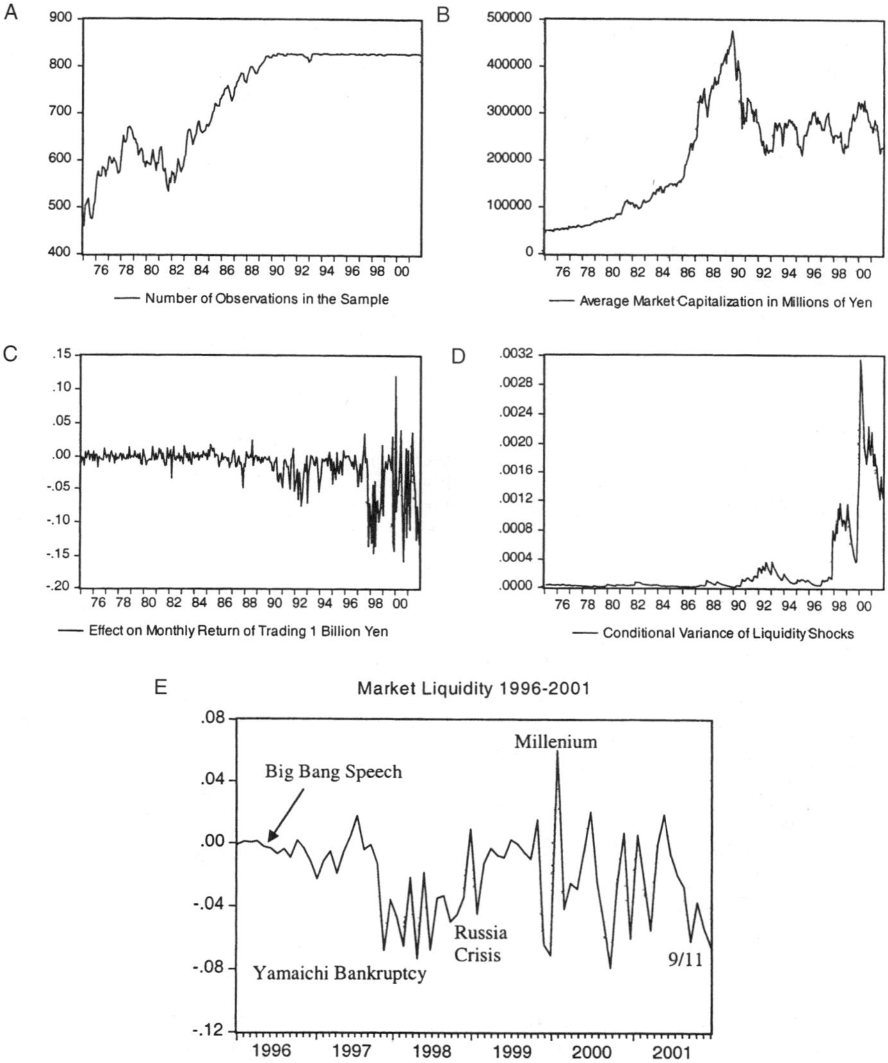

Fig. 8.1 Time-series liquidity measures

Notes: The figure shows the details of aggregate market liquidity. Panels A and B show the details of the sample of firms including the number of firms in the sample observed in any period and the market capitalization of those firms. Panel C shows the aggregate market liquidity measure, *LIQ,* which essentially is the average cost, in terms of returns, of trading 1 billion of 2001 yen. Panel D shows the conditional heteroscedasticity of shocks to an AR(2) process in *LIQ.* Panel E is a closeup of panel C with the indication of episodic dates.

Table 8.1 Descriptive statistics of stock market aggregates (%)

	Entire period (January, 1975–December 2001)	Early 1990s (January, 1990–December, 1995)	Late 1990s (January, 1996–December, 2001)
Mean return			
PACAP index r^{MKT}	0.80	–0.37	–0.55
Our sample	0.61	–0.28	–0.49
Standard deviation of market return			
PACAP index	5.90	8.04	6.97
Our sample	5.74	8.67	7.38
Monthly turnover			
TOPIX	4.38	2.19	3.22
Our sample	5.08	3.38	3.62

Notes: This table characterizes some of the statistical properties of time series from the Japanese stock markets. We compute the mean and standard deviation of returns from an equal-weighted index calculated by PACAP and those from an equal-weighted average of our sample of firms. We also compare the turnover (ratio of monthly value traded to market capitalization) for the Tokyo Stock Exchange and our sample of firms.

average return is slightly smaller at 0.6 percent per month. We will focus on two subperiods: the early 1990s (January 1990–December 1995) and the late 1990s (January 1996–December 2001). In both the early and late 1990s, mean returns are negative and slightly lower for the large sample than for our narrower sample. This may not be surprising since our sample drops those shares that stop trading at some point during the 1990s. In all subperiods, the standard deviation of the equal-weighted monthly returns in our sample is similar to that in the PACAP sample. The volatility of returns increases during the 1990s in both samples and is largest during the early 1990s.

8.2.3 Dissecting Changes in Market Turnover

To access stock market liquidity, we compare the average monthly turnover of the shares of our sample, relative to the turnover of the stocks measured in the Topix index of the Tokyo Stock Exchange. Turnover is defined as the value of shares traded in a month as percentage of end-of-period market capitalization (bottom rows of table 8.1). In the whole period, about 4 percent of the value of shares in the Topix index is traded in the average month. Our sample is slightly more liquid with about 5 percent of the value traded. While turnover is slightly higher in our sample than the Topix sample in both subperiods, it is lower in the early and late 1990s than in the entire period in both samples.

Given the overall decline in market liquidity, we look more closely at which investors left the market. Figure 8.2 shows the path, from 1988 to 2001, of average monthly purchases of stocks (relative to overall market

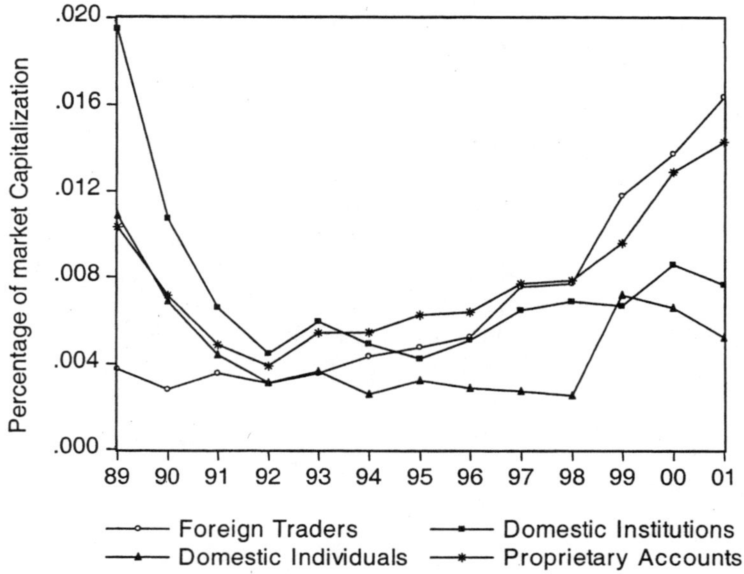

Fig. 8.2 Purchases of shares by type of investor

Notes: The figure shows Tokyo Stock Exchange data on the quantity of shares purchased by four types of investors relative to aggregate market capitalization. Data reported are yearly averages of monthly data.

capitalization) by investors trading for their proprietary accounts and by three other types of investors trading through brokerages. The three types include domestic individuals, domestic financial institutions, and foreign traders. All trading is reported relative to the aggregate market capitalization. Purchases by foreign traders grew throughout the period, while trading by all three types of domestic investors initially declined following the burst of the stock market bubble. Over the course of the 1990s, trading on proprietary accounts recovered. However, trading through brokerages by individuals and institutions persistently declined during the first half of the period. In particular, by the end of the period the share traded by domestic institutions had fallen to less than half of its initial level.[3]

8.2.4 Properties of the Liquidity Measure

The aggregate measure of the market value, m_t, of the shares for which we are able to calculate $\theta^2_{k,t}$ is given by

$$m_t = \sum_{k=1}^{N_t} mktcap_{k,t}, \tag{2}$$

3. Wang (2003) shows that institutional participation is a significant determinant of market liquidity in the United States.

where $mktcap_{k,t}$ is the end-of-month market capitalization of stock k in month t, and N_t is the number of shares in month t. Panel A of figure 8.1 shows the average market capitalization m_t/N_t during each period. In the mid-1970s, the average firm in the sample had a market capitalization of approximately 45 billion yen. During the 1970s and 1980s, average market capitalization grew rapidly to a peak of nearly 500 billion yen in late 1989 before falling rapidly to a level near 200 billion yen. During the 1990s, average market capitalization fluctuated between 200 and 300 billion yen.

Chordia, Roll, and Subrahmanyan (2002) find that average market liquidity in the United States (as measured by bid-ask spreads) shows substantial variation over time. Following Pastor and Stambaugh (2003), we measure average market liquidity, LIQ_t, as follows:

$$LIQ_t = \frac{m_t}{m_{\text{Dec, 2001}}} \cdot \frac{\sum_{k=1}^{N_t} \theta_{k,t}^2}{N_t}.$$

We average the liquidity parameter across the firms with usable observations in a particular month t. The parameter measures the effect of a billion yen trading on stock returns. To reflect the growth in size of the stock market over time, the average of $\theta_{k,t}^2$ across firms is multiplied by the ratio of the sum of the market capitalization of the firms to the market capitalization at a fixed date, December 2001.

Panel C of figure 8.1 shows the time path of LIQ_t. The aggregate market liquidity is negative in most of the time, suggesting—in accordance with theory—that heavy trading results in return reversals due to illiquidity. Further, aggregate market liquidity varies substantially. Table 8.2 (part A) shows that the mean level of liquidity is –0.014 so that sales of 1 billion yen (roughly in 2001 yen) result in expected returns of 1.4 percent in a month. The market became less liquid over time, and the average level of LIQ_t fell to –0.02 in the early 1990s and fell further to below –0.04 by the late 1990s, approximately twice the entire period mean. A simple Chow breakpoint test at January 1996 rejects the stability of the mean at any reasonable critical value. However, an Adjusted Dickey-Fuller test with twelve lags rejects the hypothesis of a unit root at the 1 percent critical value (regardless of whether a deterministic trend term is included). Although Pastor and Stambaugh (2003) document substantial and persistent variations in the U.S. equity market, such variations do not involve so prolonged a liquidity drought as observed in the Japanese market in the late 1990s.

Panel E of figure 8.1 shows more closely the time series of aggregate market liquidity over the period 1996–2001 (essentially a close-up of panel C of figure 8.1). Over this period, market liquidity seems to reflect a response to both national and international events. Perhaps coincidentally, in the periods following the November 1996 announcement of the "Big Bang" market

Table 8.2 **Liquidity measure and liquidity beta**

	Entire period (January, 1975–December, 2001)	Early 1990s (January, 1990–December, 1995)	Late 1990s (January, 1996–December, 2001)
	A. Liquidity measure		
Mean	–0.0143	–0.0200	–0.0401
Shock volatility	0.0147	0.0102	0.0274
Correlation w/ PACAP index	0.268	0.424	0.252
Covariance w/ PACAP index	0.000226	0.000342	0.000425
	B. Liquidity beta		
Mean	—	1.573	0.536
Standard deviation	—	1.150	0.567
Percent firms with significant *t*-statistics		32.6	27.3

Notes: Part A characterizes the mean and standard deviation of our measure of market liquidity, *LIQ*, as well as its correlation and covariance with the PACAP equal-weighted index. Part B characterizes the cross-sectional distribution of the partial betas from regressions of individual stock returns on the aggregate index and liquidity shocks. The characterization includes mean and cross-section standard deviation of the coefficient on liquidity shocks as well as the percentage of firms with significant *t*-statistics based on Newey and West's heteroscedasticity-autocorrelation consistent standard errors.

liberalization, there was a persistent decline in market liquidity, followed by a recovery over the summer of 1997. However, in November 1997, market liquidity suddenly plunged to a level dramatically lower than that observed in any prior period. This episode coincides with major turmoil in the Japanese financial system (as well as the East Asian financial crisis) since a number of intermediaries including the fourth largest securities firm (Yamaichi Securities) and one of the city banks (Hokkaido Takushoku) were forced into bankruptcy. This low level of liquidity persisted through 1998, including a negative spike in September coincident with the Russian crisis and the collapse of Long-Term Capital Management (LTCM).[4]

Liquidity recovered to more normal levels through 1999. However, a new persistent decline in liquidity occurred in November 1999 and was punctuated by a number of periods in which liquidity increased rapidly but temporarily. In one of these periods, January 2000, liquidity reached a level much higher than previously observed. During the turn of the millennium period, the level of bank reserves held at the Bank of Japan also spiked.

We observe another sharp decline in liquidity after September 2001, de-

4. Crises can be internationally transmitted through diverse channels. In particular, a crisis in one market causes institutional investors to sell liquid assets in other markets to meet regulator requirements (a forced-portfolio recomposition effect). Forbes (2000), using firm-level cross-country data, shows that individual company's stock market returns are affected by global trading liquidity during the East Asian and Russian crises through a forced-portfolio recomposition.

spite that Japan has undergone reforms to liberalize its financial markets in ways that may allow the additional participation of external investors and institutions. Persaud (2000), however, argues that the common use of modern risk-management practices leads to herding behavior that may reduce market liquidity despite a large number of market participants. Also, such a decline in liquidity might be associated with heightened perceptions of risk after the 9/11 terrorist attack.

8.2.5 Robust Measures

We also examine some alternative measures of liquidity. Figure 8.3 (panel A) shows the pattern of $\Sigma_k^{N_t} \theta_{k,t}^2 / N_t$, which is unadjusted for changes in market capitalization over time. According to this measure, the impact of trading a billion yen worth of shares from the mid- to the late seventies was indeed very large and comparable with more recent periods. However, during the 1980s, return reversals associated with large stock sales became

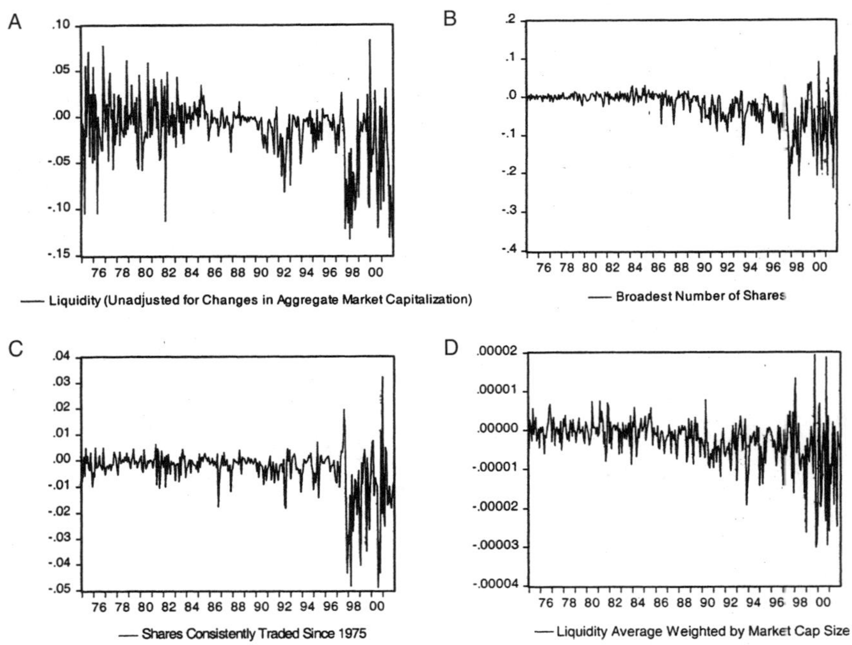

Fig. 8.3 Alternative liquidity measures

Notes: Panel A shows the average liquidity in terms of return of trading a billion yen in current currency units (i.e., unadjusted for changes in aggregate market capitalization). Panel B shows the average liquidity using a sample of all available firms including those that joined or left the sample during the 1990s. Panel C shows the average liquidity of a group of firms that were observed for the entire twenty-seven year period between 1975 and 2001. Panel D shows the weighted (by market capitalization) average liquidity of the sample.

much smaller, beginning to rise dramatically again in the 1990s just as in the benchmark series, *LIQ*.

Panels B and C show alternative measures of LIQ_t for different sets of firms. Panel B pertains to the set of firms that includes all of the nonfinancial firms available in which an estimate of $\theta^2_{k,t}$ is available in that time period. The number of firms ranges from about 500 in 1975 to about 1,400 by 2001. The measure of liquidity with this broad set of firms shows a similar pattern, compared to our benchmark measure of liquidity. During the 1970s and 1980s, stock market liquidity was relatively high. During the 1990s, the aggregate liquidity began to fall. After 1997, stock market liquidity on average dropped dramatically and the volatility of liquidity rose.

Panel C depicts a liquidity measure defined by the average $\theta^2_{k,t}$ (weighted across time by aggregate market capitalization) of a group of approximately 370 firms for which we are able to measure liquidity for at least 320 out of the 324 months in the years between 1975 and 2001. This measure of liquidity shows again a similar path with a fall in liquidity in the 1990s and a more dramatic decline after 1997 along with an increase in volatility of liquidity. The average level of liquidity of this group of more established companies was higher than that of the broader sample.

Finally, panel D displays a weighted average of $\theta^2_{k,t}$ with the weight for each firm being the end-of-month market capitalization. This measure shows the same pattern as the other measures with a marked drop in liquidity in the 1990s. In the weighted average, the size of return reversals is smaller, indicating that big-cap stocks are more liquid.

8.2.6 Measuring of Shocks to Market Liquidity

A measure of innovations to liquidity is the adjusted average of innovations to the liquidity of each firm:

$$\Delta LIQ_t = \frac{m_t}{m_{\text{Jan},1990}} \cdot \frac{\sum^{N_t}(\theta^2_{k,t} - \theta^2_{k,t-1})}{N_t}.$$

Aggregate liquidity shocks are estimated as innovations to the following dynamic process:

$$\Delta LIQ_t = \beta_0 + \beta_1 \cdot \Delta LIQ_{t-1} + \beta_2 \cdot LIQ_{t-1} + \omega_t,$$

where the predicted change in liquidity depends on the lagged change and the deviation of the lagged level from its long-run mean (impounded in β_0). The fitted residuals are a measure of liquidity shocks:

$$lshock_t = \hat{\omega}_t.$$

Table 8.2 (part A) shows that the average standard deviation of liquidity shocks varies from period to period. The standard deviation for the entire sample is about 0.015. However, much of this volatility is concentrated in the late 1990s, where the standard deviation is above 0.027 as compared with that of 0.010 in the early 1990s.

We conduct a Breusch-Pagan LM test for conditional heteroscedasticity on the residuals and reject conditional homoscedasticity with a p-value of less than 10^{-4} using any number of lags between one and twelve. We estimate a GARCH (1, 1) process for $lshock_t$:

$$\sigma_t^2 = \underset{(0.000)}{0.000} + \underset{(0.025)}{0.851}\,\sigma_{t-1}^2 + \underset{(0.030)}{0.190}\,lshock_{t-1}^2. \tag{3}$$

(standard errors in parentheses)

Panel D of figure 8.1 shows the fitted value of the conditional variance of the shock. The volatility of the liquidity shock increased sharply during the early 1990s. Such a sharp rise was followed by a much larger rise in conditional variance in 1998 and, finally, an even larger jump in 2000–2001.

We calculate the correlation between the PACAP equal-weighted stock return, r_t^{MKT}, and $lshock_t$ (part A of table 8.2). The correlation in the entire period is about 0.27. During the early 1990s, the correlation between liquidity shocks and aggregate stock returns was as high as 0.42 and fell to 0.25 in the late 1990s. However, despite the fall in correlation, the overall exposure of firms' shares to aggregate liquidity shocks rose over the decade because of the increased variance of shocks. The covariance between the aggregate return index and the liquidity shock was about 20 percent larger in the late 1990s sample than in the early 1990s sample.

8.2.7 Liquidity Risk and Asset Pricing

To check if there is some relationship between liquidity risk exposure and the average returns, we estimate a partial liquidity beta, $\beta_{k,period}^{liquid}$, by regressing the monthly excess return on the liquidity shock over the period January 1990–December 1995.

$$r_{k,t} - i_{t-1} = \alpha + \beta_{k,period}^{MKT} \cdot (r_t^{MKT} - i_{t-1}) + \beta_{k,period}^{liquid} \cdot lshock_t + e_{k,t}, \tag{4}$$

where period is equal to the early 1990s or the late 1990s, $r_{k,t}$ is the monthly return on stock k, and i_t is the collateralized overnight call money rate.

The average $\beta_{k,90-95}^{liquid}$ across firms is about 1.6 while the average $\beta_{k,96-01}^{liquid}$ is slightly greater than 0.5 (part B of table 8.2). Note that the median is very close to the mean for both figures. Although a given shock on returns has a smaller effect in the later period, the overall rise in the volatility of the liquidity shock indicates that the partial covariance of the shock (measured as the product of $\beta_{k,period}^{liquid}$ and the variance of $lshock_t$) is higher in the later period. Using Newey-West corrected, heteroscedasticity-autocorrelation consistent standard errors, we find that the percentages of firms that have significant exposures to the liquidity shocks at the 5 percent level in two subperiods are not much different: about 33 percent of the firms have liquidity

Table 8.3 **Banking risk measure, liquidity shocks, and market returns**

	lshock	r^{MKT}	r^{MKT}	r^{MKT}
lshock		0.636***		0.458**
		(3.35)		(2.13)
Δjpnprem	–0.056***		–0.270***	–0.247***
	(–2.67)		(–4.29)	(–3.53)
Adjusted R^2	0.021	0.052	0.141	0.161

Notes: Regression results with the PACAP equal-weighted stock index on liquidity shocks and the change in the Japan premium. The Japan premium, as a measure of banking risk, is defined as the spread between the interest rate paid on dollar borrowing in the Japanese interbank market and the rate paid on dollars in London. The coefficient estimates are reported with Newey-West's heteroscedasticity-autocorrelation consistent *t*-values (in parentheses).

***Significant at the 1 percent level.

**Significant at the 5 percent level.

beta's which are significantly different from zero in the first subperiod, while approximately 27 percent of the firms do in the second subperiod.

8.2.8 Banking Risk and Liquidity Shocks

We examine the connection between liquidity shocks and banking risk. Liquidity shocks may be the result of credit rationing, which prevents speculators from borrowing money that could be used to buy stocks. We can measure banking risk by the premium that Japanese banks pay to borrow from abroad. In the late 1990s, Japanese banks paid a premium to borrow in euro markets. Ito and Harada (2000) show that this premium is connected to incidents related to both the failures of Japanese financial firms and the excess returns on banking stocks. The Bank of Japan (BOJ) collects data on the Japan premium from 1997. The Japan premium is persistently high during 1997 and 1998, a period when stock market liquidity is also persistently low.[5]

Table 8.3 summarizes the regression results for the relationship between liquidity shocks, banking risk, and market returns. The estimated coefficient (along with Newey-West corrected standard errors) from a regression of liquidity shocks, *lshock,* on the first difference in the Japan premium, *Δjpnprem,* suggests that increases in the Japan premium are associated with negative shocks to stock market liquidity (table 8.3, column 1). This association is significant at the 1 percent level. However, the adjusted R^2 from the regression is less than 0.03, suggesting much of the variation in liquidity shocks is not directly caused by the Japan premium.

To examine how liquidity shocks and the Japan premium are associated

5. Banks whose credit ratings deteriorate upon adverse aggregate shocks may drop out of the international interbank market. Such dropouts are positively correlated with country risk and thus reflected in the measured Japan premium.

with innovations to stock returns, we regress the PACAP equal-weighted market return, r^{MKT}, on lshock and $\Delta jpnprem$ over the period January 1997–December 2001. Positive innovations in liquidity are associated with relatively high stock returns (column 2). The association is statistically significant in each case at the 1 percent level. Increases in the Japan premium are significantly (at the 1 percent level) negatively associated with stock returns (column 3). Also, when we include both variables (column 4), changes in the Japan premium are still significant at the 1 percent level. The effect of the liquidity shock remains significant for the equal-weighted return at the 5 percent level, even with the inclusion of the Japan premium.

8.3 Cross-Sectional Evidence on Market Liquidity and Growth

8.3.1 Firm-Level Variables and Descriptive Statistics

From PACAP, we extract additional firm-level variables that we consider as factors to explain cross-sectional exposure to liquidity risk. Descriptive statistics are reported in table 8.4. Additional information on the data used in the chapter is provided in the appendix.

First, a large percentage of shares of the firms in our sample are owned either by financial institutions or by corporations. Shares with these kinds of cross-holdings may be less liquid. We construct a variable: *percentage of stocks held by banks or corporate sector* is the number of shares owned by financial institutions plus shares owned by other businesses divided by the total number of shares in 1995. In 1995, approximately two-thirds of the shares of the mean and median firm are held by banks and other corporations.

Firms with high liquidity needs may be especially vulnerable to aggregate liquidity shocks. We construct a variable to measure short-term debt at the firm level: *short-term loans to asset ratio* is the measure of short-term loans includes accounts and notes payable, short-term loans and paper (due within one year), as well as the current portion of long-term bonds and loans which are due within the year. Short-term loans are normalized by dividing by total assets in 1995. These liabilities constitute approximately 30 percent of assets for the mean and median firm, though the number ranges between 0 and nearly 95 percent.

To control for overall leverage, we include other kinds of liabilities: *other liabilities to asset ratio* indicates the sum of all other liabilities relative to total assets in 1995. Other types of liabilities are approximately 30 percent of assets for the mean and median firm and are on average equal in size to short-term liabilities.

If a firm has more liquid assets, it will be less exposed to liquidity shocks. However, financially weak firms that do not have access to financial markets will fear financial strains caused by insufficient reserves of liquidity and thus try to hold more liquidity. Empirical studies with U.S. firm-level

Table 8.4 Descriptive statistics of firm-level variables

Variable	Mean (SD)	Median	[Min, Max]
Percent of stocks held by banks or corporate sector	0.650 (0.115)	0.661	[0.086, 0.921]
Short-term debt to asset ratio	0.304 (0.17)	0.280	[0.000, 0.942]
Other liabilities to asset ratio	0.292 (0.146)	0.276	[0.016, 0.964]
Liquid assets to assets ratio	0.308 (0.181)	0.272	[0.019, 0.986]
Log of assets	11.990 (1.279)	11.862	[8.666, 16.44]
Financial value to book assets	1.471 (0.397)	1.393	[0.780, 6.042]
Return on equity	0.018 (0.152)	0.034	[–2.859, 0.460]
Growth in net fixed assets (in log difference) End of 1995 to end of 2001	0.037 (0.419)	0.030	[–3.573, 1.696]
Growth in sales (in log difference) End of 1995 to end of 2001	–0.056 (0.306)	–0.041	[–2.961, 1.237]

Notes: The table summarizes the descriptive statistics for balance sheet data from PACAP for the period 1995–2001. We also report the growth in fixed assets and sales between 1995 and 2001.

data (Opler et al. 1999; Choi and Kim 2001; Hubbard, Kuttner, and Palia 2002) suggest that high-information-cost firms hold comparatively larger cash reserves than do other firms.[6] Thus, controlling for the size and quality of firms, we examine if firms with more liquid assets are less exposed to liquidity shocks. We construct a variable which measures firms' liquidity positions: *liquid assets to assets ratio* is the currency, bank deposits, and marketable securities held by the firm relative to total assets in 1995. About 30 percent of the average firms' assets are liquid. Naturally, this constitutes a large range.

Since liquidity shocks may be less important for large firms, which have better access to financial markets, than for small firms, we also include an asset variable as a proxy of firm size. *Assets* denotes the logarithm of the total assets (measured in millions of yen).

In addition, we include some additional balance-sheet measures to control for the overall quality of the firm. *Financial to book value* is the sum of total liabilities plus market capitalization divided by total assets in 1995. This measures the cost of purchasing the firm outright relative to the ac-

6. Almeida, Campello, and Weisbach (2004) suggest that financially weaker firms' liquidity position is more sensitive to cash-flow shocks, compared to financially stronger firms. This reflects that financially weak firms strive to accumulate reserves of liquidity to hedge against liquidity risk while financially strong firms can raise funds from financial market in the event of financial strains.

counting cost valuation of assets, which is considered as a proxy of Tobin's q-ratio. *Return on equity* indicates net income divided by book equity value in 1995. The typical financial-to-book value in the sample is approximately 1.4. The average return on equity in 1997 was approximately 4 percent but the range is extremely large. Further, PACAP categorizes firms by sector at the approximately one- or two-digit level. The appendix lists the sectors and the number of firms in our sample that fall into these shares.

8.3.2 Determinants of the Liquidity Premium

To access the determinants of the liquidity exposure of individual firms during the liquidity-trap period, we regress the partial liquidity beta, $\beta^{liquid}_{k,96-01}$, which is obtained from estimating equation (4) for January 1996–December 2001, on our firm-level variables. We scale all coefficients by multiplying each by the ratio of the cross-sectional standard deviation of that variable and dividing by the standard deviation of the dependent variable, $\beta^{liquid}_{k,96-01}$. The results are reported in table 8.5 (column 1), along with heteroscedasticity-consistent t-statistics.

In general, we find evidence on the link between firms' exposures to liquidity shocks and liquidity in their equity markets or balance sheets. Indicators of equity-market liquidity are associated with less exposure to liquidity shocks. We find that large firms (in terms of assets) have less exposure to liquidity shocks than small firms, and this is significant at the 10 percent critical value. Firms whose shares are owned in large part by financial institutions, nonfinancial corporations, or the government also have relatively high-risk exposure, though this is marginally insignificant at the 10 percent critical value (p-value $= 0.102$).

Perhaps more interestingly, firms with more liquid balance sheets are less exposed to liquidity shocks, whereas firms with more short-term debt are more exposed to the shocks. A one-standard-deviation increase in short-term debt is significantly associated (at the 1 percent level) with an increase in liquidity exposure equal to 14.3 percent of a standard deviation. By comparison, a one-standard-deviation increase in longer-term liabilities relative to assets is associated with an increase in liquidity exposure of 5 percent of a standard deviation. This association, however, is not significant at even the 10 percent level. Further, firms with large holdings of liquid assets are less sensitive to liquidity shocks. A one-standard-deviation increase in the liquid assets to assets ratio will reduce partial liquidity exposure by 8 percent of a standard error: this relationship is significant at the 5 percent level. The positive link between corporate balance-sheet liquidity and stock market liquidity perhaps indicates that stock market liquidity shocks occur simultaneously with broader shocks to liquidity in the economy including credit markets.

Higher quality firms have less exposure to liquidity shocks. Firms with high financial value relative to book value and firms that earn high profits

Table 8.5 Firm-level regressions (end of 1995 to end of 2001)

Firm Characteristics	Partial Liquidity Beta $\beta^{liquid}_{k,96-01}$	Percent growth in net fixed assets	Percent growth in sales
Partial liquidity beta: $\beta^{liquid}_{k,96-01}$		–0.130***	–0.144***
		(–2.61)	(–4.89)
Percent of stocks held by banks or corporate sector	0.061	0.020	0.015
	(1.64)	(0.48)	(0.55)
Short-term debt to asset ratio	0.143***	–0.052	–0.288***
	(2.77)	(–0.90)	(–6.34)
Other liabilities to asset ratio	0.050	–0.076	–0.093**
	(0.93)	(–1.49)	(–2.28)
Liquid assets to assets ratio	–0.083**	0.002	–0.086**
	(–2.04)	(0.05)	(–2.07)
Log of assets	–0.079*	–0.029	–0.024
	(–1.89)	(–0.63)	(–0.68)
Financial value to book assets	–0.083*	0.081	0.082**
	(–1.85)	(1.25)	(2.20)
Return on equity	–0.115**	0.077	0.123*
	(–2.49)	(1.12)	(1.80)
Industry dummies	Yes	Yes	Yes
No. of observations	774	773	772
R^2	0.167	0.084	0.272

Notes: The table reports the coefficient estimates of the regressions of measures of exposure to liquidity risk and performance on firm characteristics. All variables have been scaled by their cross-sectional standard deviation so that the coefficient represents the impact (as a share of one standard deviation of the left-hand side variable) of a one-standard-deviation increase in each right-hand side variable. Also reported are heteroscedasticity consistent *t*-statistics.

***Significant at the 1 percent level.

**Significant at the 5 percent level.

*Significant at the 10 percent level.

relative to book equity have significantly less exposure to liquidity shocks. These relationships are statistically significant at the 10 percent and 5 percent critical value, respectively. Overall, the regression has an R^2 of about 17 percent.

8.3.3 Liquidity Exposure and Growth

To examine the relationship between liquidity exposure and firm growth, we first measure the growth of a firm in terms of capital investment. *Growth in net fixed assets* is the logarithm of the ratio of net fixed assets in 2000 to net fixed assets in 1995. Over five years from 1995 to 2001, our sample firms grew at 3.7 percent (an annual growth of about 0.7 percent) in net fixed assets. The cross-sectional variation of fixed-asset growth is large with a standard deviation of almost 40 percent.

We also measure real growth in sales. The variable *growth in sales* is the logarithm of sales in 2000 relative to sales in 1995. Sales declined during the period by almost –1 percent on annual average. Again, there is large cross-sectional variation in this measure with a standard deviation of over 30 percent.

In table 8.5 (columns 2 and 3), we regress measures of firm growth on liquidity exposure and other firm-level characteristics (as well as some industry dummies). The measure of liquidity exposure is the partial liquidity beta from the late 1990s period, $\beta^{liquid}_{k,96-01}$. The additional firm characteristics are those listed in the previous section. We find that firms that have high liquidity exposure also have statistically significantly (at the 1 percent critical value) slower capital growth. One standard deviation higher in liquidity exposure is associated with 13 percent of a standard deviation decline in capital growth (which is approximately 1 percent lower fixed-investment growth per year). None of the other firm-level characteristics are significant at even the 10 percent critical value.

Firms with high liquidity exposures also tend to have lower sales growth. A one-standard-deviation increase in liquidity exposure is statistically significantly associated (at the 1 percent critical value) with a 15 percent of standard deviation decrease in sales growth (approximately 1 percent lower annual growth in sales). Variables related to market liquidity, such as size and shares cross held, are not significant. However, overall high leverage levels and, especially, high short-term debt are associated with slow sales growth. A one-standard-deviation increase in the short-term debt to asset ratio is significantly associated (at the 1 percent critical value) with a near 30 percent of a standard deviation lower level of sales growth (approximately 3 percent annual lower sales growth). Other liabilities relative to assets are also significantly associated with slow sales growth, though the effect is smaller quantitatively. Interestingly, firms with a high liquid assets to total assets ratio in 1995 have statistically significantly (at the 5 percent critical value) slower subsequent sales growth. This result perhaps reflects that holding liquid assets to hedge against liquidity risk is costly and that such a precautionary liquidity holding may postpone or hinder investment and production for sales. A high market-to-book valuation of assets ratio significantly (at the 5 percent level) predicts subsequent sales growth, and a high return on equity in 1995 also significantly (at the 10 percent level) predicts subsequent sales growth.

8.4 Time-Series Evidence on Market Liquidity and the Macroeconomy: Vector Autoregression (VAR)

Monetary assets are part of larger portfolios of assets. Agents may hold more liquid assets as a hedge when the liquidity risk of interest- or dividend-paying assets rises. In Kiyotaki and Moore (2001), money is held entirely as a hedge against the illiquidity of real assets. An increase in money demand might lead to less liquidity available for the purchase of goods and, as in standard IS-LM analysis, lead to a decline in economic activity. Thus, one may propose that a negative shock to market liquidity increases money demand and affects adversely economic activity.

To assess this proposition, we estimate a dynamic system with a VAR with terms for real shocks, money-demand shocks, and money-supply shocks during the post-bubble period (1990–2001). We use an economic activity/production index, y_t, for all sectors of the economy (excepting agriculture) as a measure of real activity. Ueda (1993) argues that Japanese monetary policy targets the call money rate, and Miyao (1996, 2002) describes the call money rate as the operating target of the Bank of Japan during the period under consideration. We include the uncollateralized overnight call money rate, $call_t$. We use broad real-money balances as a proxy for real-money demand. Specifically, the variable, mp_t, is the logarithm of the ratio of M2 plus CDs—which Ito (1994) reports as the most commonly used broad money aggregate for Japan—divided by the core Consumer Price Index (CPI) (i.e., CPI not including food and energy). Sekine (1998) argues that financial wealth is a determinant of money demand. We include the log of the Topix stock market index, *topix*, as a proxy for wealth and to control for the effects of stock market return shocks on market liquidity. This may be important as Bayoumi (2001) has shown that shocks to asset prices have substantial real effects on the Japanese economy during this period.

Since the stock market does not display much in the way of secular growth during the post-bubble period, we measure the level of liquidity as the simple average of the response of returns to signed trading volume:

$$liquidity_t = \sum_{k=1}^{N_t} \frac{\theta_{k,t}}{N_t} \tag{5}$$

We do not multiply this liquidity measure by the aggregate market capitalization that may have macroeconomic effects separate from financial liquidity. The time series for liquidity is shown in the first panel of figure 8.3.

We first conduct Adjusted Dickey-Fuller (ADF) tests on each of the variables to assess for unit roots. Using a specification with four lags and including a trend term, we are unable to reject the null hypothesis of a unit root at the 10 percent level for any of the variables with the exception of liquidity, for which the null hypothesis is rejected at any reasonable critical value. Using the Johansen trace statistic in a specification with four lags and a trend term, we are unable to reject the hypothesis that *y*, *mp*, or *call* is cointegrated with *topix*. We therefore estimate the VAR in a level specification.

We estimate a VAR in [*y*, *call*, *mp*, *liquidity*, *topix*] with twelve lags, a trend term, and a dummy variable for January 2000, the millennium period with the anomalously large, positive liquidity realization. The Akaike Information Criterion indicates a second order VAR. However, this strikes us as too few lags to capture the dynamics of the monthly system.[7] Instead, we estimate the VAR with twelve lags, which may be fairly typical for the VAR estimation with monthly data.

We identify shocks to the system using the Choleski decomposition, interpreting them as, in order: real output shocks, money-supply shocks, money-demand shocks, liquidity shocks, and stock-price shocks. Ordering the variables in this way, [*y*, *call*, *mp*, *liquidity*, *topix*], implies a number of identifying assumptions about the short-run dynamics of the model. We assume each of the shocks could have immediate effects on the price of the stock market. In particular, this ordering implies that innovations in the aggregate price of stocks have no immediate impact on stock market liquidity. However, we do allow market liquidity to respond immediately to all macroeconomic shocks. Following Miyao (2002), we treat exogenous innovations in the call money rate as monetary-policy shocks and allow the call money rate to respond immediately to real output shocks. Also, we allow money demand to respond immediately to output and the interest rate. However, real output responds only with a lag to monetary-policy shocks.

Figure 8.4 displays all of the impulse responses along with two standard-error bands. However, we concentrate on discussing the effects of liquidity shocks on the macroeconomic variables and the effects of various shocks on stock market liquidity. We find that liquidity shocks significantly affect macroeconomic variables. Liquidity shocks affect output in the real economy, but the impact of stock market liquidity on the economic activity index is small and short-lived. A one-standard-deviation increase in liquidity results in an initial increase in output of about 0.2 percent. After one period, the increase in output is not statistically significant at even the 10 percent level. Liquidity shocks never explain more than 7 percent of variation in *y* at any frequency.

Liquidity shocks have persistent and statistically significant impacts on real balances. A positive shock to stock market liquidity leads to a reduction in the demand for more liquid real balances. Indeed, variance decomposition shows that liquidity shocks explain more than 16 percent of the variation in real balances at a frequency of eighteen months. Liquidity shocks have macroeconomic effects which are consistent with persistent money-demand shocks. A positive liquidity shock also leads to a statistically significant decline in (nominal) interest rates, consistent with the reduced money demand after the shock. However, the effects of liquidity shocks on asset markets themselves seem more transitory. Liquidity shocks have very short-lived effects on the stock market index, *topix*, reverting to mean after a couple of periods.

7. In particular, a very low-order VAR suggests that liquidity shocks have fairly large and persistent effects on output and real balances. In such a low-order VAR, macroeconomic shocks have insignificant effects on liquidity.

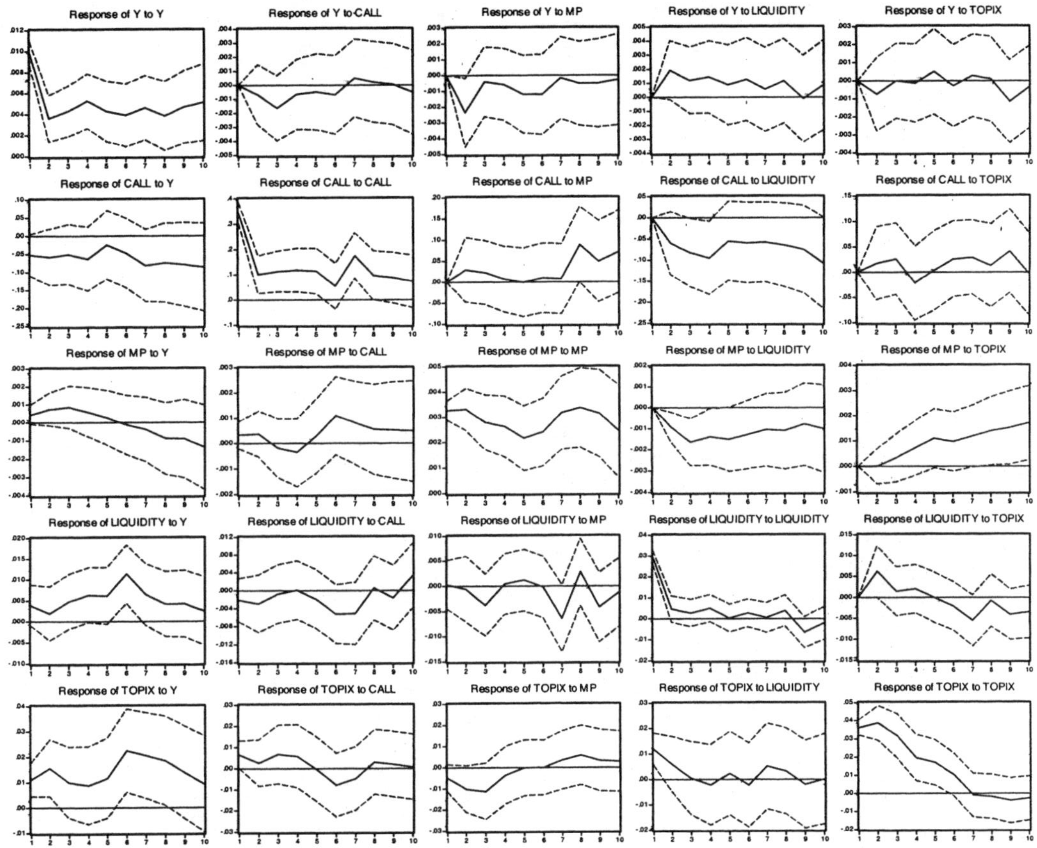

Fig. 8.4 Impulse responses of a five-variable VAR

Notes: The figure shows the impulse response functions (along with two standard-error bands) of a five-variable VAR including, in order: economic activity index, *y*; the uncollateralized call money rate, *call*; real balances, *mp*, which is M2 plus CDs divided by the core CPI; our measure of average stock market liquidity, *liquidity*; and a stock market index, *topix*. The VAR is estimated with twelve lags, a trend term, and a dummy for the anomalous millennium period.

Next, we find that market liquidity is significantly affected by shocks to output and *topix* but not by shocks to money-market variables, call rates, and real balances. Shocks to *topix* have a short-lived impact on stock market liquidity, suggesting that a rise in the stock price index attracts liquidity to the stock market at least temporarily. Shocks to economic activity also have significant impacts on stock market liquidity. A positive innovation in *y* leads to a persistent increase in topix and an increase in stock market liquidity that persists for about six months. At the eighteen month frequency, about 20 percent of the variation in stock market liquidity comes from shocks to *y*. However, neither shocks to call rates nor shocks to real balances have significant effects on stock market liquidity, while liquidity shocks significantly affect both call rates and real balances: in essence, the liquidity shocks could be thought of as general liquidity preference shocks which feed into money and asset markets.

We are also interested in the response of the nominal money supply to stock market liquidity shocks. To look at the response of narrow money, we define *mbase* as the natural log of the monetary base; to look at broad money, we define *m*2 as the log of M2 plus CDs. We estimate VARs in [*y*, *call*, *mbase*, *liquidity*, *topix*] and [*y*, *call*, *m*2, *liquidity*, *topix*] with twelve lags, a trend term, and a millennium dummy. Figure 8.5 depicts the impulse responses of the monetary aggregates to a one standard-deviation shock along with two standard-error bands. There seems to be a qualitative difference. The amount of banks' reserves held after a positive liquidity shock declines sharply and immediately. However, after just one period, the supply of reserves returns to the preshock level. By contrast, the positive liquidity shock leads to a reduction in the demand for M2 that occurs much more slowly but more persistently. Interpreted as a persistent decline

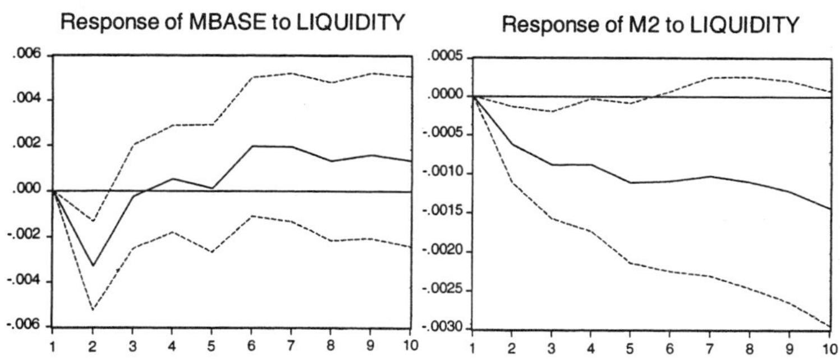

Fig. 8.5 Money and interest rate responses

Notes: The figure shows the responses (along with two standard-error bands) of two monetary aggregates to identified stock market liquidity shocks. The monetary aggregates are the monetary base, mbase, and M2 plus CDs, *m*2. Shocks are identified using VARs with twelve lags, a trend, and a millennium dummy.

in money demand that occurs due to a decrease in asset-market liquidity risk, which is not fully accommodated by a reduction in the monetary base, this could explain why the interest rates in interbank lending markets fall persistently following a liquidity shock.

8.5 Conclusions

We find evidence that during the recent deflationary period, Japanese equity markets were highly illiquid and subject to increasingly volatile liquidity shocks. Our intention in this chapter is to show some of the causes of this decline in liquidity as well as some of the interactions between stock market liquidity and the macroeconomy.

Financial market evidence suggests that these liquidity shocks affected the equity returns of firms during the slump that followed the bursting of Japan's late–1980s bubble. We find cross-sectional evidence that firms with illiquid balance sheets and illiquid markets for their equity were more exposed to these shocks and that this exposure was a predictor of the performance of the firms during this period. We interpret the high exposure to equity liquidity shocks of firms with high short-term debt as indicating that the liquidity shocks to the stock market were also correlated with liquidity shocks in broader financial markets, including credit markets. This interpretation is supported by time-series evidence that liquidity shocks have even more persistent effects on money demand than on equity market prices.

Using aggregate market liquidity, we find evidence that liquidity shocks in the Japanese stock market are associated with some macroeconomic events. Large declines in liquidity occurred simultaneously with international financial shocks, such as those that occurred in September 1998 and September 2001. Exogenous liquidity shocks seem to have a persistent negative effect on money demand and interest rates, as well as some short-term effects on output. Time-series evidence also shows that the large initial declines in liquidity occurred simultaneously with a wave of bankruptcies of Japanese financial intermediaries, including financial firms. Statistically, the Japan premium (i.e., the extra cost of short-term borrowing imposed on Japanese banks) is strongly associated with stock market liquidity. In general, exogenous negative-business-cycle shocks reduced stock market liquidity. Stabilizing aggregate demand in the face of such a liquidity shock may require the monetary authority to reduce interest rates. Since 1999, Japanese monetary policy has been characterized by zero interest rates, the lower bound that prevents the full accommodation of liquidity shocks. The policy of quantitative easing undertaken by the Bank of Japan since March 2001, which led to an unprecedented high level of current account balances, may have provided ample reserves to the financial sector. However, such a measure was not promptly transmitted into the expansion of lending and broad money (M2 + CDs) enough to stimulate the economy and to reverse lowered stock market liquidity.[8]

Since interest rates cannot fall below zero, whether or not the monetary authorities can provide an additional stimulus to the economy remains in question. Securities investors sufficiently averse to liquidity risk may avoid holding potentially illiquid stocks even at zero interest rates. However, if securities firms or other market makers are facing credit constraints due to problems in the banking sector, the direct provision of short-term loans to securities companies or securities finance companies may enhance stock market liquidity. Direct purchasing of the bills of financial institutions is one of the monetary-policy instruments available to the Bank of Japan (see Bank of Japan 2002). It has long been recognized that providing liquidity to financial markets during panics is an important part of central bank management. In the environment faced by Japan over the last decade, with a persistently illiquid market buffeted by volatile liquidity shocks, a more systematic provision of liquidity to equity markets may offer substantial benefits. Though systematically providing liquidity to the stock market may not overcome all of the risks faced by firms with illiquid balance sheets, enhancing stock market liquidity and reducing liquidity risk faced by investors could reduce the cost of equity capital in future fund raising (see, e.g., Lerner and Schoar 2004) and promote firm-level growth. However, it should be cautioned that a commitment to providing liquidity to financial markets on a permanent basis may have an inflationary bias in the long run.

Appendix

Stock Market Data

Data on individual firms' returns are from the PACAP (Pacific Capital Markets) database. For each share in our sample, we use daily returns without dividends reinvested (PACAP mnemonic: DRETND) and trading values (TRDVAL). Daily returns are daily equally weighted market returns without cash dividends reinvested (DERMND). We also use (TRDVAL) monthly data on trading values and market capitalization (MKTCAP). We also use a PACAP monthly return, which is monthly equally weighted market returns without cash dividends reinvested (MERMND). Turnover

8. The intermediary functions of the money market declined at the extremely low interest rate. With the quantitative easing policy, financial institutions—including banks, securities companies, and securities finance companies—have accumulated rapidly current account balances with the Bank of Japan. Despite the resulting large increases in monetary base, however, financial intermediation was not revived because financial institutions built up the unprecedented level of excess reserves (see Hetzel 2004).

Table 8A.1

Agriculture and forestry	1	Nonferrous metals	20
Air transportation	3	Other manufacturing	24
Chemicals	107	Petroleum	6
Communications	1	Precision equipment	18
Construction	75	Pulp and paper	12
Electric machinery	99	Real estate	15
Electric power and gas	14	Retail	39
Financial (non bank & securities)	10	Rubber	8
Fishery	5	Services	22
Foods	51	Shipping	8
Glass and ceramics	21	Textiles	34
Iron and steel	30	Transportation equipment	56
Land transportation	22	Warehousing and wharfing	7
Machinery	56	Wholesale	43
Metal products	13	Total	828
Mining	8		

and market capitalization in the stocks in the Tokyo Stock Exchange Topix Index are from CEIC DRI Asia Database.

Cross-Sectional Data

To construct cross-sectional data on firms, we use data from a PACAP database on balance sheets that contains our main measure of firm size and normalization variable on Total Assets (PACAP mnemonic: BAL22). *Short-term loans to asset ratio* is the sum of accounts and notes payable (BAL10) and short-term loans (BAL11) divided by total assets. *Other liabilities to asset ratio* is total liabilities (BAL17) divided by total assets minus *short-term loans to asset ratio.* We measure *liquid assets to assets* ratio is the sum of cash (BAL1) and marketable securities (BAL2) divided by total assets. *Financial to book value* is the sum of total liabilities and the product of number of shares of common stock (MKT5) and share price (MKT3) divided by total assets. *Return on equity* is net income (INC9) divided by total shareholder's equity (BAL21). We construct *percentage of stocks held by banks or corporate sector* as the number of shares owned by government and local government (JAF75) plus the number of shares owned by financial institutions (JAF76) plus the number of shares owned by other business corporations (JAF78) divided by total shares owned (JAF81). We also measure growth in *net fixed assets* (BAL7) and *sales* (INC1).

Industry-level dummy variables are also created to match the industries in table 8A.1.

Time-Series Data

Time-series data are obtained from the OECD Main Economics Indicators.

topix: The Tokyo Stock Exchange Topix Index
cpi: CPI Services Less Housing (1995 = 100)
m2: M2 plus CD (trillions of yen, seasonally adjusted)

Additional data are obtained from the CEIC DRI Asia database.

MB: Monetary Base (monthly average, billions of yen, seasonally adjusted with X-12)
y: All Industry Activity Index (1995 = 100, seasonally adjusted with X-12)
call: Uncollateralized Overnight Rate (%)

References

Ahn, Hee-Joon, Jun Cai, Yasushi Hamao, and Richard Y. K. Ho. 2002. The components of the bid-ask spread in a limit-order market: Evidence from the Tokyo Stock Exchange. *Journal of Empirical Finance* 9 (November): 399–430.

Almeida, Heitor, Murillo Campello, and Michael S. Weisbach. 2004. The cash flow sensitivity of cash. *Journal of Finance* 59 (August): 1777–804.

Amihud, Yakov, and Haim Mendelson. 1986. Asset pricing and the bid-ask spread. *Journal of Financial Economics* 17 (December): 223–49.

Bank of Japan. 2002. *Principal terms and conditions pertaining to the purchase of bills.* Bank of Japan. Mimeo.

Bayoumi, Tamim. 2001. The morning after: Explaining the slowdown in Japanese growth in the 1990s. *Journal of International Economics* 53 (April): 241–59.

Campbell, John Y., Sanford J. Grossman, and Jiang Wang. 1993. Trading volume and serial correlation in stock returns. *Quarterly Journal of Economics* 108 (November): 905–39.

Chao, Chaoshin, and C. James Hueng. Forthcoming. Over-reaction effects independent of risk and characteristics: Evidence from the Japanese Stock Market. *Journal of Japan and the World Economy,* forthcoming.

Choi, Woon Gyu, and Yungsan Kim. 2001. Monetary policy and corporate liquid asset demand. IMF Working Paper no. WP/01/177 Washington, DC: International Monetary Fund, November.

Chordia, Tarun, Richard Roll, and Avanidhar Subrahmanyam. 2002. Order imbalance, liquidity, and market returns. *Journal of Financial Economics* 65 (July): 111–30.

Chordia, Tarun, Asani Sarkar, and Avanidhar Subrahmanyam. 2002. An empirical analysis of stock and bond market liquidity. Emory University Working Paper.

Forbes, Kristin. 2000. The Asian flu and Russian virus: Firm-level evidence on how crises are transmitted internationally. NBER Working Paper no. 7807. Cambridge, MA: National Bureau of Economic Research, July.

Hamao, Yasushi, Jianping Mei, and Yexiao Xu. 2003. Idiosyncratic risk and the creative destruction in Japan. NBER Working Paper no. 9642. Cambridge, MA: National Bureau of Economic Research, April.

Hetzel, Robert L. 2004. Price stability and Japanese monetary policy. IMES Discussion Paper No. 2004-E-6. Tokyo, Japan: Institute for Monetary and Economic Studies, Bank of Japan.

Hubbard, R. Glenn, Kenneth N. Kuttner, and Darius N. Palia. 2002. Are there bank effects in borrowers' costs of funds? Evidence from a matched sample of borrowers and banks. *Journal of Business* 75 (October): 559–81.

Ito, Takatoshi. 1994. *The Japanese economy.* Cambridge, MA: The MIT Press.
Ito, Takatoshi, and Kimie Harada. 2000. Japan premium and stock prices: Two mirrors of Japanese banking crises. NBER Working Paper no. 7997. Cambridge, MA: National Bureau of Economic Research.
Kiyotaki, Nobuhiro, and John Moore. 2001. Liquidity, business cycles and monetary policy. London School of Economics. Mimeo.
Lerner, Josh, and Antoinette Schoar. 2004. The illiquidity puzzle: Theory and evidence from private equity. *Journal of Financial Economics* (April): 3–40.
Miyao, Ryuzo. 1996. Does a co-integrating M2 demand relation really exist in Japan? *Journal of Japan and the International Economies* 10 (June): 169–80.
———. 2002. The effects of monetary policy in Japan. *Journal of Money, Credit and Banking* 34 (May): 376–92.
Nagayasu, Jun. 2003. A re-examination of the Japanese money demand function and structural shifts. *Journal of Policy Modeling* 25 (June): 359–75.
Opler, Tim C., Lee Pinkowitz, Rene Stultz, and Rohan Williamson. 1999. The determinants and implications of corporate cash holdings. *Journal of Financial Economics* 52 (April): 3–46.
Pastor, Lubos, and Robert F. Stambaugh. 2003. Liquidity risk and expected stock returns. *Journal of Political Economy* 111 (June): 642–85.
Persaud, Avinash. 2000. Sending the herd off the cliff edge: The disturbing interaction between herding and market-sensitive risk management practices. State Street. Mimeo.
Sekine, T. 1998. Financial liberalization, the wealth effect, and the demand for broad money in Japan. *Bank of Japan Monetary and Economic Studies* 16 (May): 35–55.
Stahel, Christof W. 2004. Is there a global liquidity factor? Ohio State University. Mimeo.
Tokyo Stock Exchange. 2003. *Tokyo Stock Exchange Handbook* 2003. Tokyo.
Ueda, Kazuo. 1993. A comparative perspective on Japanese monetary policy: Short-run monetary control and the transmission mechanism. In *Japanese monetary policy,* ed. Kenneth J. Singleton, 7–30. Chicago: University of Chicago Press.
Wang, Ashley W. 2003. Institutional equity flows, liquidity risk and asset pricing. University of California, Los Angeles. Mimeo.

Comment Shin-ichi Fukuda

This chapter investigates what impacts liquidity shocks had on micro and macroeconomy in Japan during the past decade. It has three major findings: (a) empirical evidence on liquidity shocks of Japanese stock markets based on daily data, (b) microevidence on the liquidity based on the firm-level data, and (c) macroevidence based on time-series data. All of them are valuable empirical studies.

Empirical Evidence on Liquidity Shocks Based on Daily Data

The first important contribution of this chapter is on empirical evidence on liquidity shocks of Japanese stock markets. There are several previous

Shin-ichi Fukuda is a professor of economics at the University of Tokyo.

studies that tried to measure the liquidity of stock markets. But there are relatively few for Japanese stock markets. The analytical method follows Pastor and Stambaugh (JPE 2003). It estimates the parameter that measures the degree to which sales affect expected returns, and supposes that the parameter measures "liquidity." The intuition is that "order flow" should be accompanied by a return that one expects to be partially reversed in the future if the stock is not perfectly liquid. The greater the expected reversal for a given dollar volume, the lower the stock's liquidity.

By using the data of Japanese stock markets in the post-bubble period, the authors find steep drops in the liquidity and steep rises in liquidity risk. There was a clear-cut relationship between liquidity shocks and stock returns. In particular, most of liquidity shocks occurred during market downturns. The results are very reasonable. However, as for the relationship between liquidity shocks and stock returns, their causality is not clear.

The chapter reports three subperiods that had steep drops in the liquidity and steep rises in liquidity risk: 1991–1992 (the period after the crush of the bubbles), 1997–1998 (the period of banking crisis in Japan), and 2000–2002 (the deflation period). Liquidity shocks might have caused the market downturns during these periods. It is, however, possible that the market downturns in turn caused liquidity shocks during these periods. To identify the causality, we need to check which events caused the "liquidity shocks" observed in the chapter. Checking which events caused some spikes of the "liquidity shocks" may verify the causality.

Microevidence on the Liquidity Based on the Firm-Level Data

The second important contribution of this chapter is on microevidence on the liquidity shocks based on the firm-level data in Japan. In previous literature, Hasbrouck and Seppi (JFE 2001) find that idiosyncratic liquidity strongly dominates the common liquidity factor in explaining returns by using the Dow Jones Index. But few previous studies explored how cross-sectional variations of "liquidity" are related to firms' characteristics, such as their balance sheets. The chapter thus clearly provides a new empirical evidence by using the microdata in Japan from 1995 to 2001.

The chapter reports various cross-sectional variations of "liquidity" in Japanese stock markets. In particular, it showed that firms with high exposures to liquidity shocks are those whose balance sheets are illiquid, that is, high short-term debt–asset ratio and low liquid assets to asset ratio, and that large firms (in terms of assets) have less exposure to liquidity shocks than small firms. The findings are interesting. Their intuitive interpretations are, however, not necessarily straightforward.

The interpretations in the chapter are as follows. If a firm has more liquid assets, it will be less exposed to liquidity shocks. Financially weak firms will fear financial strains caused by insufficient reserves of liquidity. The interpretations look similar to those of agency cost approaches. However, "liquidity" in the chapter is "liquidity" for investors in the stock markets. The "liquidity" in the stock markets is different from "liquidity" of firms' balance sheets. We thus need a new story to explain why "liquidity" in the stock markets is so related to "liquidity" of firms' balance sheets.

"Liquidity" in the stock markets is liquidity for outside investors. We thus need to explain why those investors could not diversify idiosyncratic liquidity shocks. My interpretations of the results are as follows. "Liquidity" in the stock markets may be related with some default risk of firms. The stocks become more illiquid for the firms that have higher default risk. Default risk varies across firms. Firms whose balance sheets are illiquid (that is, firms with high short-term debt–asset ratios and small liquid assets) tend to face larger default risk. Large firms face smaller default risk than small firms. The interpretations seem consistent with empirical results in the chapter. But if this is the case, default risk rather than "liquidity" in the stock markets is the ultimate source that explains cross-sectional variations of "liquidity." The implications will be different.

On microevidence on the liquidity based on the firm-level data, the chapter provides other interesting findings: (a) Firms that have high liquidity exposure have slower capital investment; (b) Liquidity exposure is also an important determinant of sales growth. But in explaining capital investment, some important variables such as Tobin's q and profits are missing in the regressions. Thus, their interpretations may not be easy. There are two types of liquidity: (a) "liquidity" in the stock markets that reflect liquidity for outside investors and (b) "liquidity" of firms' balance sheets. The results seem to suggest that the first type is much more important than the second type for capital investment. They suggest that in Japan, there was no credit constraint in the sense of traditional agency cost approaches. However, it contradicts a large number of studies that support the importance of the second type of liquidity for capital investment. Liquidity exposure to the first type is highly correlated with that to the second. The regression has some missing variables and some measurement errors because it uses book values in the balance sheet rather than market values. It is very difficult to distinguish the effects of two types, although the regressions include proxies for both types of liquidity exposure.

Macroevidence on the Effects of Liquidity Shocks Based on Time-Series Data

The third important contribution of this chapter is on macro time-series evidence on the effects of liquidity shocks based on VARs. Several previous studies investigated how the liquidity measures of stock markets affect several variables in the stock markets. But there are few studies that investigated how the liquidity measures of stock markets affect macrovariables.

The paper provides the times-series analysis (that is, VARs and impulse-response functions) based on monthly (and quarterly) macrodata. The sample period is from 1990 to 2001. It shows that liquidity shocks have significant impacts not only on stock returns, but also on various macrovariables and monetary variables. On the impacts of a negative liquidity shock on macrovariables, it finds negative impacts on CPI, positive impacts on unemployment rate, negative but insignificant impacts on IIP, and negative impacts on changes of business investment. Except for IIP, the impacts are large and persistent. But the impacts seem to be too big and too persistent. For example, liquidity shocks explain 25 percent of the variation in CPI and unemployment rate. It is hard to believe that the shocks can explain such a large proportion of variations.

Why did we have such big impacts of liquidity shocks on macro and monetary variables? A possible reason is that only limited variables are included in VARs. If some key variables are missing, the third factors may cause spurious impacts of liquidity shocks on macro and monetary variables. In particular, many of the macro and monetary variables have some sluggishness. Even after exogenous shocks occurred, these variables take time to adjust. Stock prices and liquidity shocks, in contrast, respond to the exogenous shocks almost instantaneously. If this is the case, liquidity shocks can cause macro and monetary variables in the sense of Granger. But it does not necessarily mean that liquidity shocks affect macro and monetary variables.

What Policy Implications?

Overall, the chapter provides various interesting empirical findings. These findings imply that liquidity exposure is an important source of economic downturns in Japan. The results deserve publication by themselves. But the chapter's policy implications are not necessarily clear. Could Japan improve macro- and micro-level economic downturns by eliminating liquidity exposure? If yes, how?

In the paper, illiquid balance sheets of the firms explain a part of micro-level liquidity shocks. But its explanatory power was very small (that is, R^2 was 0.16). In conclusion, the chapter seems to suggest that lowering interest rates can eliminate macrolevel liquidity exposure. But the impulse-response functions show almost negligible impacts from monetary shocks to liquidity shocks. At least the present version of the chapter did not explain major sources of highly illiquid equity markets during the recent deflationary period. The ultimate source of economic downturns in Japan seems to be left unexplained in the chapter.

References

Hasbrouck, J., and D. Seppi. 2001. Common factors in prices, order flows, and liquidity. *Journal of Financial Economics* 59 (3): 383–411.

Pastor, L., and R. F. Stambaugh. 2003. Liquidity risk and expected stock returns. *Journal of Political Economy* 111 (3): 642–85.

Comment Makoto Saito

This chapter first applies a method proposed by Pastor and Stambaugh (2003) to daily Japanese stock data, and constructs the time-series of degrees of market liquidity as state variables for asset pricing. Then, using this measure of market liquidity, it estimates liquidity betas, or risks associated with changes in market liquidity for individual stocks. In addition, the authors conduct a cross-sectional analysis of effects of these estimated liquidity betas on performances of firms, as well as a time-series analysis of effects of aggregate market liquidity on macroeconomic variables.

Major findings of this chapter are summarized as follows. First, stock markets were extremely illiquid during the late 1990s. Second, firms with liquid balance sheets carried relatively low liquidity risks. Third, high liquidity risks were associated with low performances of firms. Fourth, aggregate liquidity measures served as a leading indicator for major aggregate variables such as output, investment, and employment.

Before commenting on this chapter, I would like to make a quick review of a method proposed by Pastor and Stambaugh (2003). They identify order-induced one-day return reversals as market impacts from individual stock data, and construct an aggregate liquidity measure by averaging such market impacts over individual return reversals. Then, they estimate an individual liquidity beta by checking whether innovations on the above-constructed liquidity measures are priced for equity premiums of individual stocks.

To my best knowledge, this chapter is the first serious application of Pastor and Stambaugh (2003) to Japanese stock data. Sincere readers of this chapter might be intellectually curious to know how innovations in aggregate liquidity are priced in Japanese stock markets in comparison with U.S. stock markets. In this regard, reporting detailed information as to the estimated liquidity betas would be appreciated greatly by such readers.

I would like to discuss this chapter in two respects. My first comment concerns a theoretical relationship between aggregate liquidity in stock markets and macroeconomic variables. This paper well documents that negative shocks on aggregate liquidity measures are followed by declines in macroeconomic activities. Then, one may want to ask which theoretical hypothesis may explain such a relationship between them. As mentioned above, Pastor and Stambaugh's liquidity measures are based on high-frequency phenomena such as one-day return reversals. In other words, the construction of this liquidity measure implicitly assumes that pricing distortion is fixed at least partially within one business day. With due consideration for this aspect, it would be rather hard to imagine that such high-frequency frictions themselves have direct and substantial impacts on macroeconomic activities.

Makoto Saito is a professor of economics at Hitotsubashi University.

One possible story for the above relationship is that there is a common shock which drives both illiquidity of stock markets and economic slowdown. For example, due to downward revisions in expectations about economic fundamentals among market participants, stock markets would become seller-dominated, and market liquidity would be deteriorated to a large extent. Circumstantial evidence for this story is that during the financial crises in both 1997 and 1998, not only stock markets, but also other markets serving for corporate financing, were extremely illiquid.

My second comment regards responses of monetary policy to illiquid financial markets, which may have something to do with issues broadly raised by this conference. I still believe that a monetary policy is quite important in terms of maintaining orderly financial markets, though not controlling business cycles, when financial markets are extremely illiquid during financial crises. One important question is how a central bank should behave in order to recover market liquidity. Which financial market should the bank target? Which policy instrument should it adopt?

During a financial crisis, liquidity often shifts from stock markets or corporate bond markets, to money markets or government-bond markets. In particular, there may emerge extremely strong demand for short-run government-issued bonds. In such a case, the open-purchase operations in which a central bank provides liquidity to commercial banks that are major market makers at money markets, would not be as effective as they are in normal market conditions. Through monetary operations, the Bank of Japan might just yield an additional demand for money market instruments in competition with other private players.

One possible effective operation may be to provide liquidity to security companies and investment banks that are major market makers at stocks and corporate bonds, or even more directly to large investors that hold long positions in stock markets by carrying short positions in money markets. A central bank's direct purchase of corporate stocks may be an alternative choice. Given the authors' empirical finding that stock markets were extremely illiquid during the financial crises in the late 1990s, discussing possible policy measures to recover market liquidity in more detail would enhance the value of this chapter substantially.

Reference

Pastor, Lubos, and Robert F. Stambaugh. 2003. Liquidity risk and expected stock returns. *Journal of Political Economy* 111 (3): 642–85.

9

Interest Rate, Inflation, and Housing Price
With an Emphasis on *Chonsei* Price in Korea

Dongchul Cho

9.1 Introduction

Since the IT bubble burst in 2000, interest rates have fallen and housing prices have risen in the global economy. According to Case and Shiller (2003), for example, the ratio of house prices to per capita income soared from around 6.5 in 2000 to around 8.5 in 2003 in California. Along with the soaring house prices, investment on house construction also increased at a substantial pace. For example, the residential investment in the United States increased by 4.9 percent in 2002 and 7.5 percent in 2003, while gross domestic product (GDP) grew at the rate of 2.2 percent in 2002 and 3.1 percent in 2003.

Korea was no exception in this global trend. During the period from 2001 to 2003, the general house price index rose by more than 30 percent. However, the prices of apartments—the most preferred housing type in recent years—rose by more than 50 percent nationwide, and by almost 100 percent in the Kangnam area (south of Han River) of Seoul. Along with the rise in house prices, construction industries enjoyed a boom. The average annual growth rate of building construction investment during the period of 2001–2003 reached 13.3 percent, while the average GDP growth rate remained only at 4.6 percent. This boom increased the portion of

Dongchul Cho is a fellow of the Korea Development Institute.

This chapter was prepared for presentation at the fifteenth NBER East Asian Seminar on Economics at Tokyo in May 2004. Earlier versions of this chapter (in Korean) were presented at the Korea Development Institute and the Bank of Korea. I am grateful to Chinhee Hahn, Takatoshi Ito, Toshiki Jinushi, Mario Lamberte, Jong-Hwe Lee, Kyung-Mook Lim, Chang-Yong Rhee, Andrew Rose, and the Conference participants for their comments. I also would like to extend my appreciation to Myung-Ki Sung, Yoon-Ki Kim, Jong-Man Ryoo, and Hyun-Sook Koh for their research assistance.

building construction relative to GDP from 8.4 percent in 2000 to 11.3 percent in 2003.

In addition to all of these standard indicators, however, the Korean housing market has a unique *chonsei* system that provides a very meaningful indicator for the market value of housing service—*chonsei* price, or an up-front lump-sum deposit from the tenant to the owner for the use of the property with no additional requirement for periodic rent payments (see section 9.2 for details). While *chonsei* prices, as well as sales prices, should reflect demand and supply in the housing market, the two prices have shown sharply different trends since the second half of 2002 (see figure 9.1). Until the first half of 2002, both prices had rapidly recovered from the collapse after the 1997 crisis. Since then, however, only the sales prices have kept rising while the *chonsei* prices have stagnated, which has sharply raised the ratio of sales to *chonsei* price or lowered the real value of *chonsei* deposit (deflated by the sales price). This phenomenon can, in a sense, be interpreted as a transfer of wealth from *chonsei* tenants to house owners.

Motivated by this observation, this chapter examines the determinants of the relative housing prices—sales and *chonsei* prices—and shows that the relative housing prices depend on the ratio of nominal to real interest rate. It is probably easy to expect that the discrepancy between the two housing prices is widened as the (expected) inflation rate increases. At the same time, however, the discrepancy can also be widened when the real interest rate declines, even though the monetary authority adamantly sticks to a pre-announced inflation target. In fact, this argument applies not only to the housing prices, but also to the prices of general nominal assets that are not hedged against inflation.

If the monetary authority has concerns over the potential wealth transfers due to the decline in real interest rate, it could, at least in theory, maintain the relative housing prices (or relative prices of real to nominal assets) by proportionately adjusting the target level of inflation rate to the decline of the real interest rate.[1] This result may find its relevancy to an economy like Korea's, in which real interest rates are secularly declining and the credit market is not yet completely accessible to households (see sections 9.2 and 9.5).

This chapter is organized as follows. Section 9.2 explains the *chonsei* sys-

1. The recent volatility in asset prices under the stable and low inflation environment has triggered a challenge on the standard inflation-targeting framework. While a majority of economists (e.g., Bernanke and Gertler 2001; Gilchrist and Leahy 2002) still support the standard monetary-policy framework represented by Taylor rules, a group of economists (e.g., Cecchetti et al. 2000; Borio and Lowe 2002; Hahm and Hong 2002) argue that the monetary authority needs to react to asset-price bubbles in order to stabilize the economy. See Bean (2003) for this debate. Although from a quite different perspective, this chapter's result could be interpreted to provide a rationale for the monetary policy that considers asset-price fluctuations.

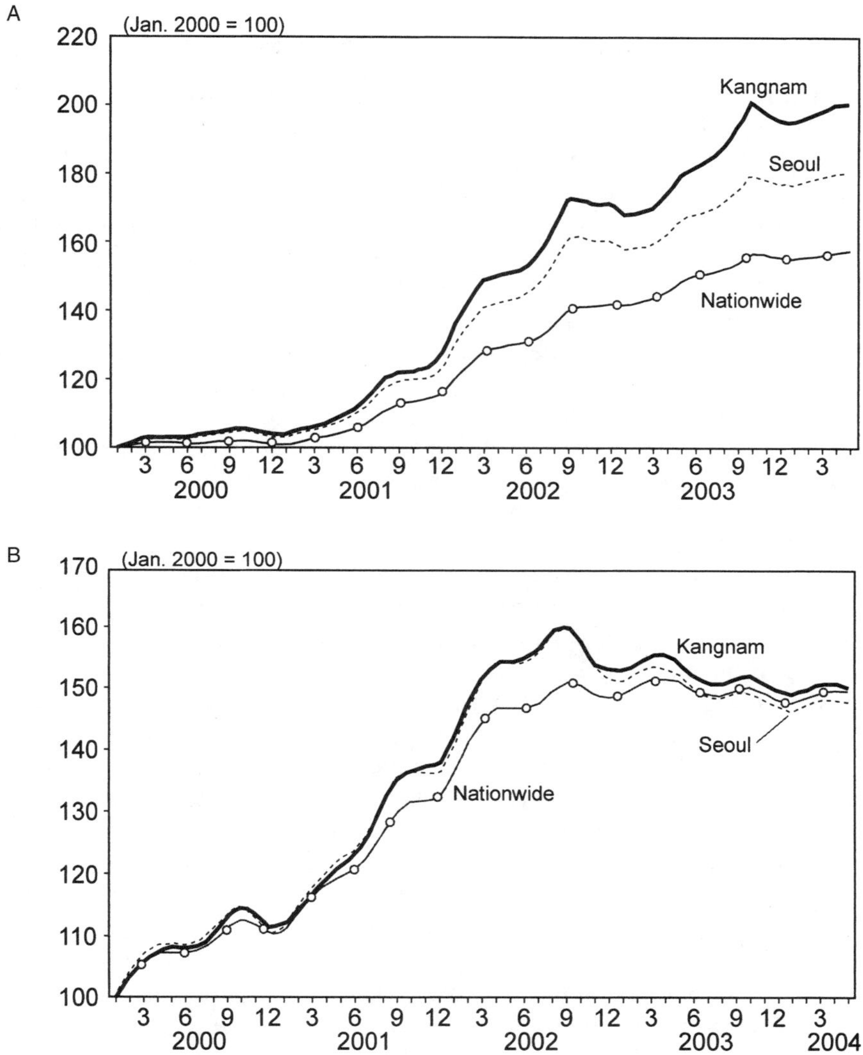

Fig. 9.1 ***A*, trends of house prices; *B*, trends of *chonsei* prices**

tem of Korea and section 9.3 contains a theoretical model that explains the determination of housing prices. The first part of section 9.3 discusses the arbitrage condition between the sales and *chonsei* prices, and the second part presents a simple general-equilibrium growth model that includes housing sector. Section 9.4 presents the results of a crude empirical analysis on the ratio of sales to *chonsei* prices in Korea, and section 9.5 concludes with brief remarks about monetary policy.

9.2 *Chonsei* System in Korea

The Korean housing market has a very unique system called *chonsei.* In this system, the tenant pays an up-front lump-sum amount of deposit (currently 30 to 70 percent of house sales prices) to the owner for the use of the property with no additional requirement for periodic rent payments. The interest earned on this lump-sum deposit, therefore, provides income to the owner during the contract period (typically two years), and the deposit is returned to the tenant when the contract expires. If the owner does not return the *chonsei* deposit at maturity, the Korean legal system grants the tenant priority to recoup the deposit from an auction for the house arranged by the court. That is, the tenant's deposit is legally protected as an asset that can be claimed against the collateral value of the property.

Although the historical origin of the *chonsei* system is not entirely clear, the literature reports that a convention similar to the *chonsei* system already existed in Korea during the Chosun Dynasty (or Yi Dynasty, 1392–1910).[2] In particular, this system was widely spread out in Seoul, where people rushed in as the feudal system collapsed after the Byung-Ja Treaty (1876) between Korea and Japan. While the court recognized the *chonsei* system as a convention during the Japanese colonial period (1910–1945), the first Korean government, in 1948, began to formally recognize the *chonsei* system under the legal framework. The legal rights and obligations of the homeowners and tenants have slightly changed over time, but the deposit has been protected if legally registered. Nevertheless, the *chonsei* contract differs from a collateral contract in that the tenant does not assume the ownership of the property even if the homeowner defaults on the deposit.

Underdeveloped financial services (mortgage services in particular) and rapid urbanization are thought to be the two most important factors that explain the popularity of the *chonsei* system in Korea.[3] During the period of "government-led development," in particular, the Korean government kept interest rates low for business firms. These interventions inevitably imposed higher-than-equilibrium interest rates on consumer credit and housing finance in the formal financial market. Under this environment, "for landlords, *chonsei* is an informal financial instrument that satisfies various household credit demands. . . . For tenants, the *chonsei* system allows households to afford homes that would not be possible for outright cash purchase" (Ambrose and Kim 2003, 62).

This *chonsei* system has been widely spread out with the rapid urbanization for the last few decades in Korea.[4] According to the *Population and Housing Census Report* (National Statistics Office 2000), the total number

2. For example, Kim (2000) and Park (2000) cite the survey reports on Korean conventions prepared by the Japanese Colonial Government (1910–1945).

3. See for example Renaud (1989) and Choi (2003).

4. See Ambrose and Kim (2003) for details.

of households in Korea is 14.31 million, out of which 7.75 million (54 percent) are homeowners and 4.04 million (28 percent) are under *chonsei* contracts (the remaining households are under monthly rents). In particular, the ratio of *chonsei* tenants increases in metropolitan areas, where housing prices are high. For example, the number of *chonsei* tenants is as large as the number of homeowners in Seoul (out of 3.09 million households, 1.26 million [40 percent] are homeowners and 1.27 million [40 percent] are under *chonsei* contracts).

Given the popularity of the *chonsei* system, it is obvious that a substantial amount of assets are held in the form of *chonsei* deposit in Korea. For example, a back-of-the-envelop calculation yields 200 to 250 trillion won, approximately 40 percent of GDP or 80 percent of the total stock value, as the outstanding amount of total *chonsei* deposit.[5] Given this size of the *chonsei* deposit, it seems natural that policymakers are concerned about the fluctuation of *chonsei* prices.[6] More important than the *chonsei* prices themselves, however, may be the ratio of sales to *chonsei* prices. This ratio is often interpreted as an indicator for the affordability of potential homebuyers because relatively young and/or poor households commonly live under *chonsei* contracts until they accumulate sufficient savings in addition to the *chonsei* deposit for the purchase of their own houses.[7] As an extreme example, if 100 percent of *chonsei* deposit is held for future purchase of houses, then a 1 percent increase of sales price over *chonsei* price simply implies a 1 percent decline in the purchasing power of *chonsei* deposit.

Apart from the policymakers' concerns, the information about *chonsei* prices is potentially very useful in identifying the factors that affect asset prices of real estate. Unlike the sales price, the *chonsei* price inherently excludes the possibility of capital gains and reflects the value of housing service assessed by the spot housing market itself. In this sense, the Korean housing market provides an important additional indicator for the real

5. According to the *1997 National Wealth Survey,* the total value of household housing (excluding land) is 485 trillion won, which is approximately 50 percent of the total building value of all sectors. Applying this ratio of 50 percent to the total land value estimate, 1,548 trillion won, yields 1,259 (= 774 + 485) trillion won as the total value of housing (including land). Using 28 percent as the ratio of *chonsei* dwellings and 60 percent as the ratio of *chonsei* to sales prices, one can obtain 212 trillion won in 1997, which is estimated to inflate to 284 trillion won as of the end of 2003, applying the *chonsei* price index. This amount is almost 40 percent of GDP (721 trillion won) or 80 percent of total equity value (355 trillion won) in 2003.

6. While many *chonsei* contracts are revolved upon maturity, the related parties write new contracts whose prices reflect market situations at that time. Therefore, new contracts involve cash transactions between owners and *chonsei* tenants, whenever *chonsei* prices change in the market. With general price inflation, it is common for tenants to deposit additional money that covers the increments in *chonsei* prices, but there were some exceptional cases. For example, housing prices including *chonsei* prices were collapsed by more than 20 percent nationwide in the swirl of economic crisis in 1998, which pushed many owners to the verge of liquidity crisis and invited the government to mobilize special rescue funds for them.

7. For the stylized facts of housing tenures and demography, see Renaud (1989) and Choi (2003).

estate prices, which are not available in other countries. The next section considers various factors that explain the discrepancy between the sales price and *chonsei* price, but the emphasis will be given to the expected capital gains that are greatly influenced by macrovariables, such as interest and inflation rates, rather than other micro or institutional factors.

9.3 Theoretical Discussion

9.3.1 Interest Rate, Inflation Rate, and Real Estate Prices

Chonsei *versus Purchase*

A household in Korea having two choices for housing service, either purchase or *chonsei,* would consider the following factors. First, there are inherent differences between homeowners and *chonsei* tenants. For example, the homeowners are free to move whenever they want, while the *chonsei* tenants do not enjoy such a freedom. This is a factor that boosts the sales price relative to *chonsei* price. In contrast, however, the homeowners should bear the cost to maintain the quality of houses that *chonsei* tenants do not have to care about. This is a factor that discounts the sales price relative to *chonsei* price. A priori, therefore, it is not clear whether the sales price should be inherently higher than the *chonsei* price.

Second, the homeowners should bear the risk of price fluctuations, while the *chonsei* tenants are relatively well-protected from such risks. As far as investors are risk averse, this is a factor that discounts the sales price relative to *chonsei* price. Third, the homeowners should pay taxes that *chonsei* tenants are free from.[8] This is another factor that discounts the sales price relative to *chonsei* price. In short, these factors cannot explain why sales prices are substantially higher than *chonsei* prices for the basically same housing services.

Therefore, the primary reason for the huge discrepancy of the sales price relative to *chonsei* price seems to lie in the expectation on capital gain. That is, the *chonsei* tenants are expected to recoup only the deposit in monetary unit upon maturity, but the owners will be able to enjoy capital gains if the house prices rise as they did in Korea. As with any other prices in monetary economy, the rise of house price is composed of two parts, the rise in the relative price of house over general prices and the rise of general prices (or inflation) itself. However, the rise of relative price can hardly be sustained in the long run, and thus this chapter focuses on the general price inflation as the underlying factor that persistently increases house price.[9] For

8. Section 9.4 provides explanation on Korea's real estate tax system.

9. Theoretically, it is possible that the relative prices of houses keep rising at a more rapid rate than general prices if the productivity growth rate of the housing sector is permanently lower than other sectors. However, this does not seem to be the case at least in Korea during

the same reason, the general price inflation can be seen as a primary factor for the sales price that remains substantially higher than *chonsei* price all the time.

An Arbitrage Condition

Focusing on the aforementioned factor of expected capital gain, the arbitrage condition between the sales and *chonsei* prices can be written as

$$(1) \qquad P_t^H = \frac{[i_t P_t^C + E_t(P_{t+1}^H)]}{(1 + i_t)},$$

where P_t^H is sales price at time t, P_t^C is *chonsei* price, i_t is nominal interest rate, $E_t(P_{t+1}^H)$ is the sales price at time $t + 1$ expected at time t. That is, the sales price at time t is the discounted sum of the return for housing services (or the opportunity cost of dwelling in the house rather than leasing the house on a *chonsei* contract), $i_t P_t^C$, and the expected sales price at time $t + 1$, $E_t(P_{t+1}^H)$.

This arbitrage condition can be recursively solved forward, and the solution will be a complicated function of the expectations about future *chonsei* prices and interest rates. Assuming a steady state with no speculative bubbles (in which the interest rate is fixed at i and the *chonsei* price increases at a constant inflation rate of π), however, equation (1) produces a simple and intuitive result:

$$(2) \qquad \frac{P_t^H}{P_t^C} = \frac{i}{i - \pi}.$$

That is, the ratio of the sales to *chonsei* price is equal to the ratio of nominal to real interest rate. Of course, this result is based on many restrictive assumptions. Nevertheless, if the sustained real interest rate is around 4 percent and *chonsei* price inflation rate is around 3 percent (a medium-term target inflation rate of the monetary authority in Korea), this ratio becomes 1.75, which is similar to the ratio of sales to *chonsei* price at the end of 2003.[10]

Financial versus Real Asset Prices

It has long been recognized that the existence of inflation raises the value of real assets relative to financial assets that are not hedged against inflation risks. In Korea, the discrepancy between the sales and *chonsei* prices for the same housing can be referred to as a typical example for this. In fact,

the 1987–2003 period: the overall housing price increased at 4.1 percent per annum, slightly lower than the CPI inflation rate of 5.0 percent, although the average apartment price increased at 6.9 percent, slightly higher than the CPI inflation rate.

10. The ratio of sales to *chonsei* prices of apartments at the end of 2003 was 1.7 for the nation and 2.0 for Seoul (Kookmin Bank 2004).

the above result can be applied to rather general asset prices. In a steady state economy where the nominal interest rate is fixed at i, the price of a financial asset that yields a constant return R in monetary unit at every point in time is determined by $\int_0^\infty e^{-is}Rds = R/i$, while the price of a real asset that provides service flow whose price increases at a constant inflation rate π can be expressed as $\int_0^\infty e^{-is}Re^{\pi s}ds = R/(i-\pi)$. Therefore, the existence of inflation pushes up the price of a real asset relative to that of financial asset providing the same service, and their ratio becomes the same as the sales to *chonsei* prices $P_t^H/P_t^C = i/(i-\pi)$.[11]

From this result, it is easily confirmed that a rise in the inflation rate would raise the price of real asset relative to that of financial asset. What has not been much discussed in the literature, however, is that the same effect can be generated by the decline of real interest rate. Defining the real interest rate as $r \equiv i - \pi$, equation (2) can be re-expressed as $P_t^H/P_t^C = 1 + \pi/r$, implying that the relative price is determined by the ratio of inflation rate to real interest rate, rather than by the inflation rate alone. Therefore, even when the monetary authority strictly maintains a pre-announced target level of inflation rate, the ratio of sales to *chonsei* price rises if the real interest rate is lowered.

In order to relate this discussion to monetary policy, however, it seems necessary to explicitly understand the general price level. In other words, the meaning of "real estate price" or "*chonsei* price" rather than the relative price of those two needs to be clarified in the context of general price inflation. At the same time, if the discussion is extended from the housing market to the macroeconomy, the real interest rate and rent need to be taken as endogenous variables. In this sense, this subsection's discussion is viewed as a partial equilibrium approach in which inflation rate, real interest rate, and rent are exogenously determined. In order to sense a general equilibrium flavor, the next subsection will examine a very simple growth model.

9.3.2 A Simple Growth Model

Consider a representative household who earns (nominal) income i_tA_t from asset A_t and spends P_tC_t and R_tH_t for consumption C_t and housing service H_t, respectively. If the instantaneous utility function is given by $\ln(C_t^\alpha H_t^{1-\alpha})$ and the time discount rate is ρ, then the household solves the following optimization problem:

$$\text{(3)} \qquad \text{Max} \int_0^\infty \ln(C_t^\alpha H_t^{1-\alpha})\, e^{-pt} d_t, \text{ s.t. } \dot{A}_t = i_tA_t - P_tC_t - R_tH_t,$$

11. The sales to *chonsei* price ratio can also be considered in this context. The prices of *chonsei* and sales are $P_0^C = \int_0^t e^{-is}R_s ds + P_0^C e^{-it}$ and $P_0^H = \int_0^t e^{-is}R_s ds + P_t^H e^{-it}$, respectively. The main difference between the two prices is that, at time t, *chonsei* renters are left with the *chonsei* deposit at time zero, while the owners are left with the house price at time t ($P_t^H = P_0^H e^{\pi}$). Comparing the two prices, one can derive $P_0^H/P_0^C = (1-e^{-it})/(1-e^{-[i-\pi]t}) \approx i/(i-\pi)$.

where $\dot{A}_t$ denotes the increase in the asset level. If the (nominal) value of the asset is the sum of (nominal) values of capital and houses,

$$(4) \qquad A_t \equiv P_t^K K_t + P_t^H H_t,$$

it is easy to show that the growth rate of consumption as well as capital becomes proportional to the real interest rate, or $i_t - \dot{P}_t^K / P_t^K$:

$$(5) \qquad \frac{\dot{C}_t}{C_t} = \frac{\dot{H}_t}{H_t} = i_t - \frac{\dot{P}_t^K}{P_t^K} - \rho.$$

Production and Capital Market Efficiencies

In this economy with no frictions, where real and nominal variables can be completely separated, the relative prices of real assets to consumption goods are entirely determined by the supply side, or the technology that stipulates how many units of real assets are accumulated at the expense of one unit sacrifice of consumption. In order to make this point clear, assume the following technology:

$$(6) \qquad \dot{K}_t + \dot{H}_t = D(BK_t - C_t).$$

For simplicity, this equation takes a linear-production function BK_t and treats capital and house as perfect substitutes at the supply side. A peculiar feature in this equation is the coefficient $0 < D \leq 1$ that measures the units of increase in future capital when present consumption is reduced by one unit. While $D = 1$ is the standard case in growth models, the case of $D < 1$ can be interpreted in line with a Tobin's q model in the sense that $D < 1$ implies a real adjustment cost in investment.[12] Another, perhaps more pertinent, interpretation of D may be the degree of capital-market efficiency. In other words, if the capital-market efficiency is low, or $D < 1$, then the capital-accumulation process is marred although the production efficiency B is maintained.

Once the model is set up as above, it is easy to derive the equilibrium relative prices by equating the resource constraint (equation [6]) and the budget constraint (equations [3] and [4]). That is, using equations (3) and (4),

$$(7) \qquad \dot{P}_t^K K_t + P_t^K \dot{K}_t + \dot{P}_t^H H_t + P_t^H \dot{H}_t = i_t(P_t^K K_t + P_t^H H_t) - P_t C_t - R_t H_t$$

is derived, and by equating this equation to equation (6), one can obtain the following four equilibrium conditions:

$$(8\text{-}1) \qquad \frac{P_t}{P_t^K} = D \Rightarrow P_t^K = \frac{P_t}{D};$$

12. Of course, while the adjustment cost vanishes when the economy approaches a steady state in Tobin's q models, equation (6) assumes that the cost exists permanently for simplicity. See Abel and Blanchard (1983) and Lim and Weil (2003) for growth models that explicitly incorporate formal Tobin's q specifications.

(8-2) $$\frac{P_t^H}{P_t^K} = 1 \Rightarrow P_t^H = P_t^K;$$

(8-3) $$\frac{i_t - \dot{P}_t^K}{\dot{P}_t^K} = DB;$$

(8-4) $$\frac{(i_t P_t^H - R_t - \dot{P}_t^H)}{P_r^K} = 0 \Rightarrow \frac{\Box i_t - \dot{P}_t^H}{P_t^H} = \frac{R_t}{P_t^H} \Rightarrow \Box R_t = BP_t.$$

These results are easily predictable from the assumptions. That is, results (8-1) and (8-2) state that the relative price of capital (or house) to consumption good is determined by *D*, while result (8-3) indicates that the real interest rate is determined by *B* multiplied by *D*, or the efficiency of the capital transformation process from present to the future. Result (8-4) is an arbitrage condition that the benefit from the purchase of house, the sum of rent R_t and capital gain $\dot{P}_t^H$, should be equal to the opportunity cost, $i_t P_t^H$.

Inflation and Chonsei *Price*

The introduction of money in this model economy does not affect any relative prices, hence any resource allocation processes. Therefore, if the monetary authority inflates a certain target price, say, consumption price P_t, at a rate of π, the asset prices will increase at the same rate. In contrast, however, the rate of inflation can affect the relative price of *chonsei.* As far as an arbitrage condition holds between the *chonsei* and rent markets, the opportunity cost of *chonsei,* $i_t P_t^C$, should be equal to the rent:

(9) $$P_t^C = \frac{R_t}{i_t} = \frac{BP_t}{(DB + \pi)}.$$

Price Responses to a Decline in Real Interest Rate

What would happen to this economy if the real interest rate permanently declines? First, the growth rate is unambiguously lowered (equation [5]). The relative prices of assets to consumption goods, however, depend on the sources of the decline in interest rate. If the real interest rate is lowered due to the decline in *B*, then the relative price of house (or capital) does not change (equation [8-1]), and only the relative price of *chonsei* declines (equation [9]). If, in contrast, the real interest rate is lowered due to the decline in *D*, then both the house (or capital) and *chonsei* prices rise, but the price of house rises more than that of *chonsei.* Figure 9.2 describes this situation.

The intuition that the decline in *B* does not change the relative price of house can be explained as follows. The price of house is ultimately determined by $P^H = \int_0^\infty e^{-(i-\pi)s} R ds = R/(i - \pi)$, and thus the fall in the real interest rate itself is a factor to raise the house price by lowering the discount

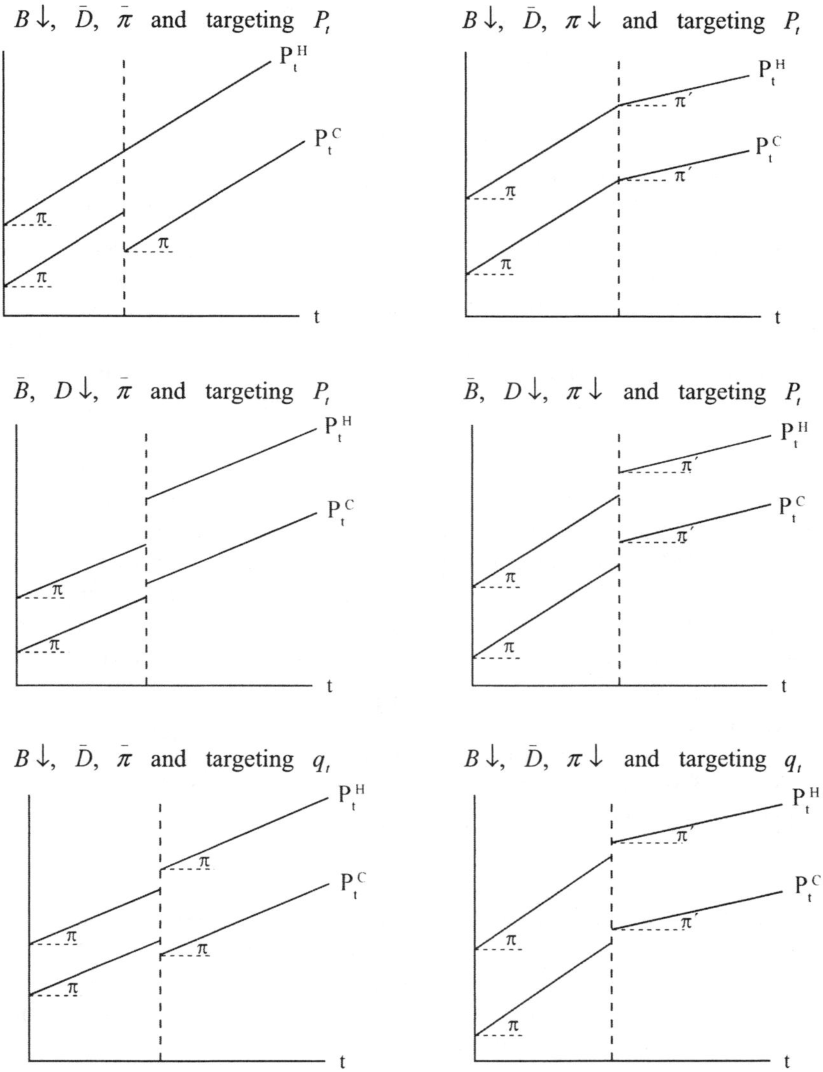

Fig. 9.2 Time paths of house price (P_t^H) and *chonsei* price (P_t^C)

rate for the future (or the return rate of alternative investment). In a general equilibrium set-up, however, the rent R is also lowered by the decline in B because consumption goods supplied by the same amount of capital are decreased while the supply of houses remains at the same level. In the particular model of this subsection, the instantaneous fall in R exactly cancels off the effect from the decline in the real interest rate, leaving the house price unchanged.[13] In contrast, if the real interest rate is lowered due to the decline in D, the supply of consumption goods and R do not change, raising the house price.

Price Index and the Target Rate of Inflation

In the previous paragraphs, it was shown that the house price does not change if the real interest rate declines due to a fall in B. Yet it is worthwhile to note that the house price here was the relative price of house to consumption goods. In other words, this "price" becomes the price in monetary unit, only when the monetary authority uses the price of consumption goods as a target. In practice, however, it seems common to include rent as an important component of the target Consumer Price Index (CPI).[14] If, for example, the monetary authority gradually increases the price index,

$$q_t \equiv P_t^{\alpha} R_t^{1-\alpha} \tag{10}$$

(instead of P_t), then the price of housing (as well as P_t) in monetary unit will rise even when a fall in B lowers the real interest rate (see figure 9.2 for the time paths of the housing prices in this case).

Although the *chonsei* price in monetary unit is also affected by the choice of target price as well as the source of the decline in real interest rate, the ratio of sales to *chonsei* prices depends only on the inflation rate as confirmed in the previous subsection. Therefore, if the monetary authority lowers the target inflation rate proportionately in response to the decline in the real interest rate, the discrepancy of the *chonsei* price from the sales price would not be expanded. Figure 9.2 also shows the time paths of housing prices when the monetary authority follows such a rule.

Quantity Responses to a Decline in Real Interest Rate

Though not a central issue in this paper, the responses of the quantity variables with respect to a decline in the real interest rate can also be traced (see the appendix for algebra). One of the results worth noting is that a fall in the real interest rate lowers the ratio of consumption to housing at the steady state, but raises the ratio of consumption to capital.

It is natural to decrease the steady-state level of capital to housing ratio as the real interest rate (or the marginal rate of return for capital) declines due to a fall in B, because the shock that lowers the marginal rate of return

13. In this case, the relative price of capital to consumption good does not change, but the shadow price of capital (as well as consumption good) jumps up. That is, an unanticipated adverse shock to productivity decreases the level of consumption, and the ex post marginal utility of consumption good is higher than the marginal utility that was expected before the shock was realized.

14. In Korea, the weight of rent is approximately 15 percent in the headline CPI that does not include owner's equivalent rent (www.nso.go.kr). If the owner's equivalent rent was included in the CPI, the weight of rent would be increased to approximately 31 percent, which is similar to that in the United States at 31.5 percent (www.bls.gov).

for capital does not directly lower the marginal utility from the housing service.[15] Therefore, the household reduces the saving for capital accumulation (hence income), but not the saving for housing. This optimization behavior leads to a decrease in the steady-state level of consumption, but not as much as the decrease in the steady-state level of capital. Recalling that the measured income is a linear function of capital, this implies that the steady-state saving rate in the aggregate falls when the real interest rate declines. At the same time, however, the saving rate for housing investment rises with a fall in the real interest rate or growth rate, which seems to be consistent with the recent experiences of the global economy as mentioned in the introduction.

Remarks

In order to learn intuitions in a straightforward way, this subsection introduces a very simple growth model in which all of the prices are instantaneously adjusted from one steady state to another. This model may be extended in various dimensions to generate rich dynamics of asset prices. For example, a Cobb-Douglas production function can be used instead of the linear-production function of this subsection (results are available upon request). In this case, a fall in the efficiency growth rate gradually lowers the real interest rate, and thus the discrepancy between the sales and *chonsei* prices is also widened at a gradual pace. Another variant would be to explicitly introduce the Tobin's q model, which would produce short-run fluctuations of asset prices. Perhaps the most interesting variation of the model, however, might be the one in which housing rents adjust to fluctuations of interest rates in a gradual manner (probably due to a slow adjustment of housing market relative to consumption goods market). This feature that relaxes the tight link between the housing and other markets would be able to generate short-run deviations of rents from interest rates, hence the fluctuations of house prices.

9.4 A Brief Look at the Data

Interest Rate, Inflation Rate, and the Ratio of Sales to Chonsei Prices

Based on the theoretical discussion of the previous section, this section takes a brief look at the actual data of the sales and *chonsei* prices of apartments from Korea.[16] While it would also be of great interest to examine the house prices in relation to general prices and macroeconomic fluctuations,

15. When the real interest rate declines due to a fall in D, the results become complicated. See the appendix.

16. See appendix B for variable explanations and data sources. The data for house prices were collected from the Kookmin Bank. This data set is an official (or at least semi-official) one that the Korean government uses. Originally, this data set was compiled by the National Bank for Housing, which was merged into the Kookmin Bank (then another government

the model's predictions regarding these issues are not sufficiently clear. At the same time, it is very likely that various sector-specific shocks have generated uneven effects across the housing market and other markets in actual data. This section, therefore, limits the scope of analysis to the relative housing prices that are presumably immune to the noises generated by micro sector-specific shocks. In addition, considering that most theoretical discussion was based on steady-state analyses, the empirical examination is also focused on the relationships of long-run trends across variables.

Figure 9.3 shows the trends of relevant variables since 1986, the first year of the available data, along with their HP-filtered trends. First, the ratio of sales to *chonsei* prices (figure 9.3A) had declined from almost three in the late 1980s to around 1.5 in 2000, and rebounded back to two since then. Second, apart from the exceptional hike during the currency crisis period in 1998, the nominal interest rate (figure 9.3B) had also declined from over 15 percent in the early 1990s to around 6 percent in 2003. Third, however, the expected inflation rate (figure 9.3C) had also been lowered from over 5 percent in the late 1980s to below 3 percent in 1998 and 1999, operating as a factor to lower the ratio of sales to *chonsei* prices. Fourth, in contrast, the portion of expected inflation in the nominal interest (figure 9.3D) has been rising from below 20 percent in 1998 and 1999 to over 40 percent in 2003, mainly due to the decline in the real interest rate in spite of stable inflation expectations, which seems to operate as an important factor for the rebound of the housing price ratio.

Taxes on Real Estate

Although the inflation and interest rates seem to be capable of explaining the *direction* of long-term trend of the housing price ratio, they are not sufficient enough to explain the *magnitude* of the changes in this ratio, particularly the ratio around three in the late 1980s and early 1990s. During this period, the portion of the expected inflation rate in the nominal interest rate was nearly 50 percent, implying that the inflation and interest rate cannot generate the housing price ratio over two. This observation invites discussions on the other factors explained in section 9.3 that can potentially affect this ratio. In order to incorporate the other factors, slightly modify the arbitrage condition, equation (1):

$$P_t^H = \frac{[(i_t + \alpha)P_t^C - \tau P_t^H + E_t(P_{t+1}^H)]}{(1 + i_t)}, \tag{1'}$$

bank) and privatized after the Korean crisis. This data set traces the prices of 16,000 sampled houses throughout the whole country every month. For apartments, the sample size is 13,020 covering Seoul, six metropolitan areas, fifty-six cities, four Goons (district unit in rural area), and ninety Gus (district unit in urban area). Currently, the quality of the houses is not considered in this data set.

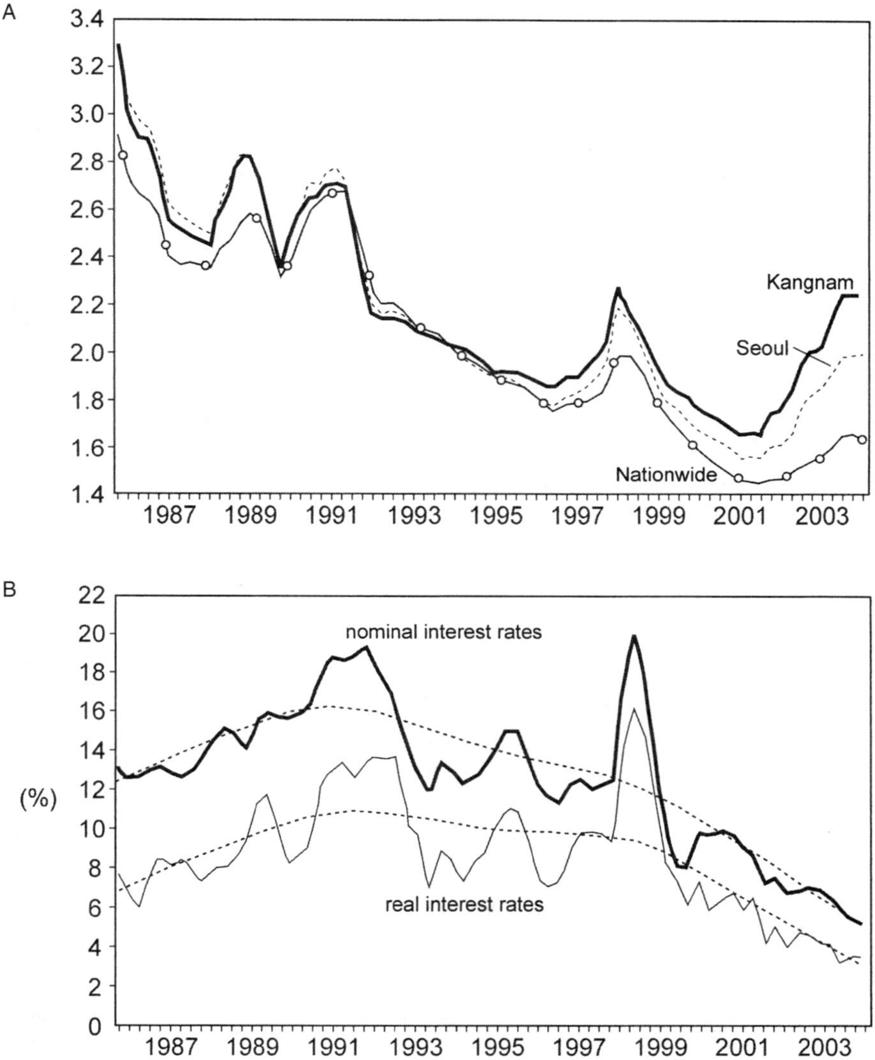

Fig. 9.3 ***A*, ratio of sales to *chonsei* prices; *B*, nominal versus real interest rates; *C*, expected inflation rate; *D*, expected inflation rate as a portion of nominal interest rate; *E*, effective tax rate on real estate; *F*, effective tax rate relative to nominal interest rate**

where τ is a tax rate for holding a house and α represents all the other factors, such as convenience for owning a house, maintenance cost, risk averseness and so forth. The reason for separating out the tax rate from other factors is that the changes in tax rate can be traced to an extent, while the changes of other factors over time are neither traceable nor believed to

C

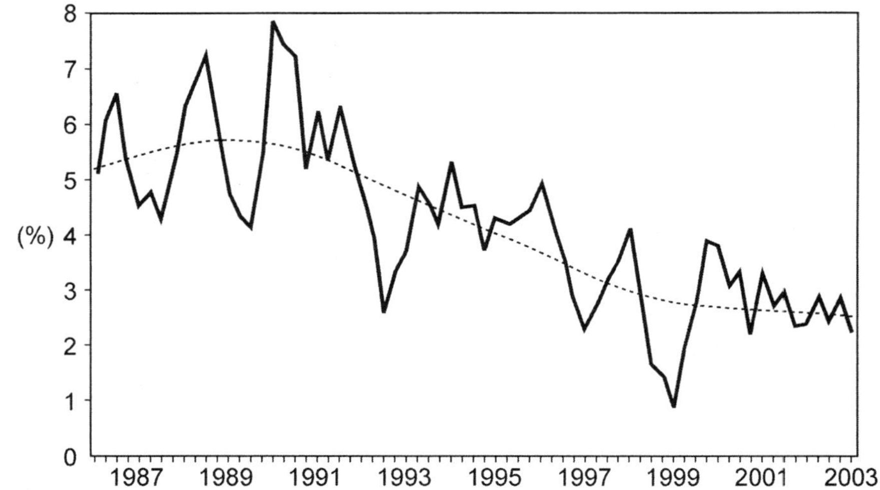

D

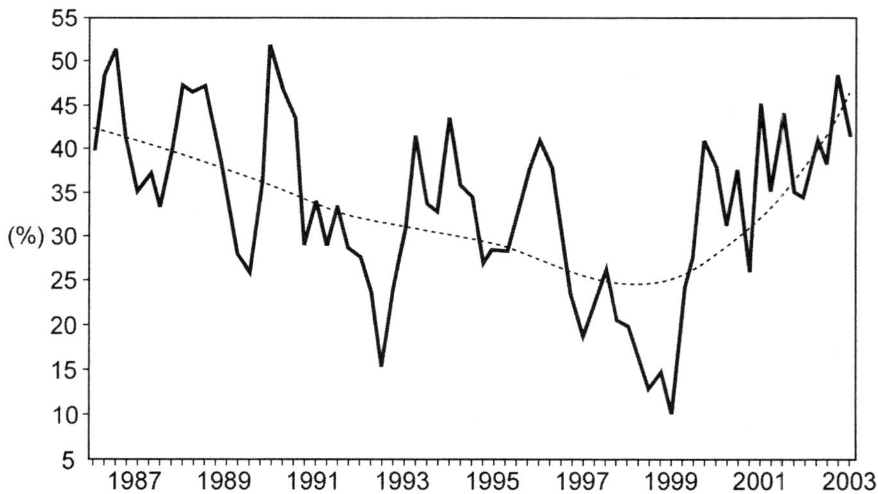

Fig. 9.3 (cont.)

be significant. Under the steady-state assumption again, equation (2) is modified to be:

$$\frac{P_t^H}{P_t^C} = \frac{i + \alpha}{i + \tau - \pi}. \tag{2'}$$

The real estate tax system is extremely complicated in Korea: one should pay acquisition and registration taxes when he or she purchases a house, property tax while he or she holds a house, and capital gains tax when he

E

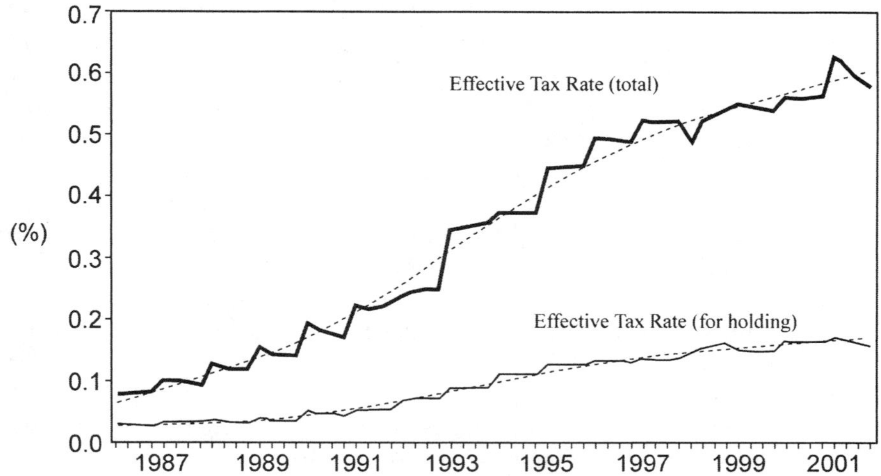

F

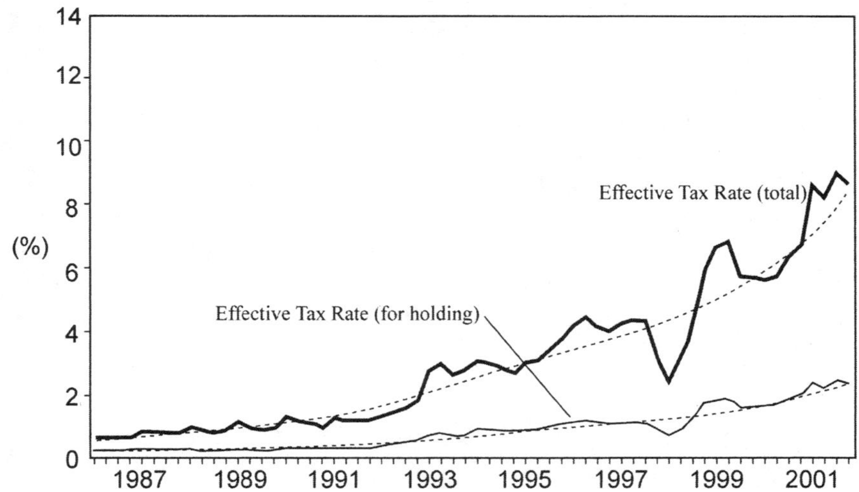

Fig. 9.3 (cont.)

or she sells a house. However, what makes the system complicated is how to calculate the actual taxes. For example, the legal tax rates for acquisition and registration are 2 percent and 3 percent, respectively, but the effective tax rates are far lower than the legal rates because the actual taxes are based on "publicly assessed values" that are far lower than market prices. Similarly, the property tax rate ranges from 0.2 percent to 7 percent progressively with property values, but the effective tax rate is estimated to be around 0.1 percent. The capital gains tax rate is 40–60 percent, but there exist many exceptional cases for reductions and exemptions.

Figures 9.3E and 9.3F show the estimated effective tax rates on real estate, or the total tax revenues divided by the estimates of total real estate value. In light of equations (1′) and (2′), these statistics have two potential shortcomings. First, since the relevant tax data for apartments are not available, these figures report the effective tax rates for the entire real estate (including land and nonapartment houses). Second, since the portion of property tax (or holding tax) in total real estate tax revenue is very low in Korea relative to those in other countries, the figures report not only the property tax rate but also the total tax rate, including taxes related to transactions. However, it should be noted that the transaction-related taxes must have theoretically different effects on real estate prices from those of holding taxes.

In spite of the shortcomings, the figures provide some basic insights. First, the effective tax rate on real estate has been rising from a very low level (figure 9.3E).[17] In conjunction with the rapid decline of nominal interest rate, the relative size of the effective tax rate to the nominal interest rate has been sharply increasing (figure 9.3F), implying that the tax factor appears to have contributed to the decline in the ratio of sales to *chonsei* prices. Second, however, the magnitude of the impact by tax seems to be small relative to the impacts by interest rates and inflation rates: during the sample period in figure 9.3, the effective holding tax rate fluctuates from 0.02 percent to 0.12 percent only (from 0.1 percent to 0.6 percent for the entire tax rate), while the fluctuations of interest rates and inflation rates are in the order of several percentage points. This observation seems to emphasize the importance of macrovariables in determining the real estate prices, although the macrovariables as well as taxes do not appear to sufficiently explain the high sales price relative to *chonsei* price in the late 1980s.[18]

9.6 Conclusion with Some Remarks on Monetary Policy

This chapter discusses the relationship between interest rates and inflation rates on one part and the house prices (typical real asset prices) relative to *chonsei* prices (typical nominal asset prices) on the other. The key point of the chapter is that the relative price of sales to *chonsei* depends on the ratio of inflation to real interest rates. Therefore, even when the monetary authority maintains a pre-announced target level of inflation rate, the relative price of sales to *chonsei* rises if the real interest rate declines.

It is not clear whether the monetary authority *should* be concerned about

17. The effective holding tax rate was merely 0.02 percent and even the entire tax revenue was less than 0.1 percent of total real estate value in the late 1980s.

18. A strong conjecture among Koreans is that there were significant bubbles in real estate prices in the late 1980s, which has not been considered in this chapter.

the changes in this ratio. At least, the growth model presented in this chapter is completely silent on this issue: there exists neither short-run fluctuation nor social cost from inflation. Probably the answer should be sought in the context of the debate about whether the monetary authority should be concerned with the fluctuations of asset prices in the first place.[19] In addition to its implication on short-run economic fluctuations, however, the changes in the relative housing price between sales and *chonsei* generate significant implications about wealth distribution in Korea. As mentioned in section 9.2, most of the *chonsei* deposit is the savings that relatively young and/or poor people have reserved for the purchase of houses in the future. Unless the capital market is perfect, therefore, a rise in the sales price relative to *chonsei* price is very likely to worsen the wealth distribution.

If the fluctuations in interest rates and the induced fluctuations in the relative house prices are cyclical, the implication about wealth distribution is temporary. If the real interest rate (and growth rate) secularly declines, however, it may permanently deteriorate the wealth distribution. In fact, the secular decline in capital productivity and real interest rates is a likely scenario in developing economies like Korea, although it may not be common in developed economies.[20] Figure 9.4, copied from Cho and Koh (1999), clearly shows the long-term declining trends of capital productivity and real interest rates in Korea for the past thirty years. In this case, the monetary authority can at least in theory prevent such an "undesirable" deterioration of wealth distribution by lowering the target inflation rate in proportion to the decline in real interest rate.

In practice, of course, it is extremely difficult to identify the components of short-term fluctuation, as opposed to secular components, from the variations of real interest rates. Given the widespread apprehension about the zero (nominal) interest rate bound, in addition, a more serious question may be how much to lower the target inflation rate in an economy with very low interest rates. That is, as the real interest rate declines toward zero, the monetary authority may have to accept either a higher discrepancy between real and financial-asset values or a higher risk of hitting the zero interest rate bound. Regarding many issues, including this thought-provoking one,

19. The recent volatility in asset prices under the stable and low inflation environment has triggered a challenge on the standard inflation-targeting framework. While a majority of economists (e.g., Bernanke and Gertler 2001; Gilchrist and Leahy 2002) still support the standard monetary-policy framework represented by Taylor rules, a group of economists (e.g., Cecchetti et al. 2000; Borio and Lowe 2002; Hahm and Hong 2003) argue that the monetary authority needs to react to asset-price bubbles in order to stabilize the economy. See Bean (2003) for this debate. Although from a quite different perspective, this chapter's result could be interpreted to provide a rationale for the monetary policy that considers asset-price fluctuations.

20. The convergence theory based on either the Neoclassical growth model (Barro 1991; Mankiw, Romer, and Weil 1992) or technology diffusion (Lucas 2000; Parente and Prescott 1994) predicts a secular decline of (capital) productivity growth rate and real interest rate.

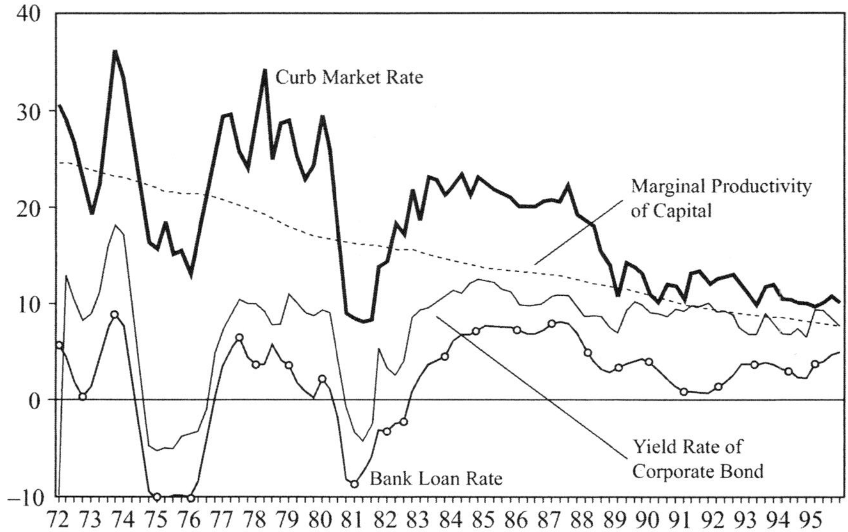

Fig. 9.4 Trends of real interest rates of Korea
Source: Cho and Koh (1999).

the chapter does not provide rigorous discussions yet, and many arguments remain at conjecture levels. No doubt that far more research is needed before drawing conclusions in this area.

Appendix A

Dynamics of the Model in the Text

The dynamics of the model in the text can be traced by solving the following three equations for C_t, H_t, and K_t:

$$\text{(5)} \qquad \frac{\dot{C}_t}{C_t} = \frac{\dot{H}_t}{H_t} = i_t - \frac{\dot{P}_t^K}{P_t^K} - \rho = r_t - \rho = DB - \rho;$$

$$\text{(6)} \qquad \dot{K}_t + \dot{H}_t = D(BK_t - C_t);$$

$$C_t = \frac{\alpha}{1-\alpha} \cdot \frac{R_t}{P_t} H_t = \frac{\alpha}{1-\alpha} r_t H_t = \frac{\alpha}{1-\alpha} DBH_t,$$

from the optimization of instantaneous allocation between consumption and housing expenditure. While C_t and H_t always move along the steady-state paths (although the steady-state level of C_t can jump at the moment when a shock arrives), K_t has a transitional dynamics governed by:

$$\frac{\dot{K}_t}{K_t} = DB - [(DB - \rho) + \frac{\alpha}{1-\alpha} D^2 B] \frac{H_t}{K_t}.$$

In a steady state, therefore, these three equations yield:

$$\frac{C}{H} = \frac{\alpha}{1-\alpha} DB;$$

$$\frac{K}{H} = \frac{1}{\rho}\left[(DB - \rho) + \frac{\alpha}{1-\alpha} D^2 B\right]; \text{ hence,}$$

$$\frac{K}{C} = \frac{1-\alpha}{\alpha} \cdot \frac{1}{\rho DB}\left[(DB - \rho) + \frac{\alpha}{1-\alpha} D^2 B\right].$$

Using these results, it can be shown that a fall in either B or D decreases the steady-state values of C/H, K/H, and K/C. Finally, the aggregate saving rate at the steady state,

$$1 - \frac{C}{BK} = 1 - \frac{\alpha}{1-\alpha} \cdot \frac{\rho D}{\left\{(DB - \rho) + \left[\frac{\alpha}{(1-\alpha)}\right] D^2 B\right\}},$$

declines with a fall in B and increases with a fall in D, but the housing investment ratio to output,

$$\frac{\dot{H}/D}{DB} = \frac{\rho}{DB} \cdot \frac{1}{\left\{1 - \left[\frac{\alpha}{(1-\alpha)}\right] D \Big/ \left[\frac{1-\rho}{DB}\right]\right\}},$$

increases with a fall in B (its direction with a fall in D becomes ambiguous).

Appendix B

Variables and Data Sources

<table>
<tr><th colspan="2">Variables</th><th>Notes</th><th>Data Sources</th></tr>
<tr><td colspan="2">House prices</td><td>Since the ratio of the sales to chonsei prices is not available prior to December 1998, this variable was extended backward using their inflation rates of the sales and chonsei prices.</td><td>Monthly House Prices, Kookmin Bank</td></tr>
<tr><td colspan="2">Nominal interest rate</td><td>Yield rate on 3-year corporate bonds.</td><td>Monthly Bulletin, Bank of Korea</td></tr>
<tr><td colspan="2">Expected inflation rate</td><td>Obtained by annualizing forecast values for the next three years (twelve quarters) of inflation at every quarter using the structural vector autoregression estimation composed of two variables, GDP and core CPI.</td><td>Kim (1996), Cho (2003)</td></tr>
<tr><td rowspan="3">Real estate taxes</td><td>On holding</td><td>1. Land: aggregate land tax, local education tax, and city planning tax.
2. Building: property tax, local education tax, city planning tax, and common facilities tax.</td><td rowspan="2">Annual Local Tax Statistics Report, Ministry of Government Administration and Home Affairs</td></tr>
<tr><td>On purchase</td><td>Acquisition tax and registration tax.</td></tr>
<tr><td>On capital gains</td><td>Capital gains tax, excessive holding land tax (existed during the 1991–1993 period only), and asset revaluation tax.</td><td>Statistical Yearbook of National Tax, National Tax Service</td></tr>
<tr><td colspan="2">Total value of real estate</td><td>This variable was extended backward using their inflation rates of house and land prices, based on the total value of real estate estimated at the end of 1997 (2,500 trillion won: 1,548 trillion won for land and 952 trillion won for buildings).</td><td>National Wealth Survey, National Statistics Office</td></tr>
<tr><td colspan="2">Effective tax rules on real estate</td><td>Ratio of the real estate tax revenues to the total value of real estate</td><td></td></tr>
</table>

References

Abel, Andrew, and Olivier J. Blanchard. 1983. An intertemporal model of saving and investment. *Econometrica* 51:675–92.

Ambrose, Brent W., and Sunwoong Kim. 2003. Modeling the Korean chonsei lease contract. *Real Estate Economics* 31:53–74.

Bank of Korea. Several Issues. Monthly Bulletin (in Korean). Seoul: Bank of Korea.

Barro, Robert J. 1991. Economic growth in a cross-section of countries. *Quarterly Journal of Economics* 106:407–43.

Bean, Charles. 2003. Asset prices, financial imbalances and monetary policy: Are inflation targets enough? In *Reserve Bank of Australia 2003 Conference on Asset Prices and Monetary Policy,* ed. Tony Richards and Tim Robinson, 48–76. Sydney: Reserve Bank of Australia.

Bernanke, B. S., and M. Gertler. 2001. Should central banks respond to movements in asset prices? *American Economic Review* 91 (2): 253–57.

Borio, Claudio, and Philip Lowe. 2002. Asset prices, financial and monetary stability: Exploring the nexus. BIS Working Paper no. 114. Basel, Switzerland: Bank for International Settlements, July.

Case, Karl E., and Robert Shiller. 2003. Is there a bubble in the housing market? *Brookings Paper on Economic Activity,* September: 299–362.

Cecchetti, S. G., H. Genberg, J. Lipsky, and S. Wadhwani. 2000. Asset prices and central bank policy. *Geneva Reports on the World Economy, 2,* International Centre for Monetary and Banking Studies, and Centre for Economic Policy Research. London, UK: Centre for Economic Policy Research.

Cho, Dongchul. 2003. Post-crisis structural changes and monetary policy scheme in Korea. KDI Working Paper no. 2003-02. Seoul: Korea Development Institute.

Cho, Dongchul, and Young-Sun Koh. 1999. Liberalization of capital flows in Korea: Big-bang or gradualism? In *Changes in exchange rates in rapidly developing countries: Theory, practice, and policy issues,* ed. Takatoshi Ito and Anne Krueger, 285–308. Chicago: University of Chicago Press.

Choi, Soon Young. 2003. Housing tenure choice and financial market constraints: The chonsei housing system of Korea. Chicago: University of Chicago Press, December, Manuscript.

Clarida, Richard, Jordi Gali, and Mark Gertler. 1997. Monetary policy rules in practice: Some international evidence. CEPR Discussion Paper no. 1750. London: Centre for Economic Policy Research, November.

Gilchrist, Simon, and John V. Leahy. 2002. Monetary policy and asset prices. *Journal of Monetary Economics* 49:75–97.

Greenspan, A. 2002. Economic volatility. Speech at a symposium sponsored by the Federal Reserve Bank of Kansas City. Jackson Hall, Wyoming.

Hahm, Jung-Ho, and Seung-Jae Hong. 2002. Asset price fluctuations and monetary policy (in Korean). The Bank of Korea Working Paper no. 139. Institute for Monetary and Economic Research.

Hayashi, Fumio, and Edward C. Prescott. 2002. The 1990s in Japan: A lost decade. *Review of Economic Dynamics* 5:206–35.

Kim, Dongjoon. 2000. A comparative and historical study on chonsei right system. Korea University. Manuscript available at [http://dres.pe.kr/dataspring/dres027.PDF].

Kim, Jun-Il. 1996. Business cycle and GDP gap. *KDI policy studies,* 217–57. Spring. Seoul: Korea Development Institute.

King, Mervin. 1999. Challenges for monetary policy: New and old. *Federal Reserve Bank of Kansas City Symposium Proceedings.* Kansas City, MO: Federal Reserve Bank of Kansas City.

Kookmin Bank. 2004. *Monthly House Prices* (in Korean). Seoul: Kookmin Bank Research Center.

Leigh, Daniel. 2003. Monetary policy and the dangers of deflation: Lessons from Japan. Johns Hopkins University, October. Manuscript.

Lim, Kyung-Mook, and David N. Weil. 2003. The baby boom and stock market boom. *Scandinavian Journal of Economics* 105 (3): 359–77.

Lucas, Robert. 2000. Some macroeconomics for the 21st century. *Journal of Economic Perspectives* Winter: 159–68.

Mankiw, N. Gregory, David Romer, and David N. Weil. 1992. A contribution to the empirics of economic growth. *Quarterly Journal of Economics* 107:407–37.
Ministry of Government Administration and Home Affairs. Several Issues. *Annual Local Tax Statistics Report* (in Korean). Seoul, Korea: Ministry of Government Administration and Home Affairs.
National Statistics Office. 1999. *National Wealth Survey* (in Korean). Daejeon: Korea National Statistics Office.
National Statistics Office. 2000. *Population and Housing Census Report* (in Korean). Daejeon: Korea National Statistics Office.
National Tax Service. Several Issues. *Statistical Yearbook of National Tax* (in Korean). Seoul, Korea: National Tax Service.
Parente, Stephen L., and Edward C. Prescott. 1994. Barriers to technology adoption and development. *Journal of Political Economy* 102:298–321.
Park, Shinyoung. 2000. The origin of the chonsei system and a prospect of chonsei market. *Journal of Housing (Jootaikji)* (in Korean). Spring: 1–11.
Renaud, Bertrand. 1989. Understanding the collateral qualities of housing for financial development: The Korean "chonse" as effective response to financial sector shortcomings. Infrastructure and Development Department Discussion Paper no. 49. Washington, DC: The World Bank, June.

Comment Toshiki Jinushi

Summary of the Paper

The chapter by Dr. Cho is inspired by the Korean *chonsei* system and analyzes the factors contributed for the divergence between its price and the house price. The *chonsei* is a special type of lease contract, in which the rentee pays the large key deposit (the *chonsei* price) on its beginning, pays no regular rent afterwards, and gets the key deposit back in the end. The rentor receives the returns on the key deposit instead of the regular rents during the lease. In Korea, the majority of the rentee is on the *chonsei* rather than the regular monthly rent contract.[1] The author explains that this system is basically the product of the imperfect mortgage markets and the rapid urbanization in Korea.

After deriving the important arbitrage condition for the *chonsei* price and the house price, the author puts the *chonsei* contract in the simple growth model with some capital-market imperfections. He analyzes how the factors, like the marginal product of the capital, the capital-market imperfections, and the inflation rate, affect the ratio between the two prices. Then, he tries to derive some lessons for monetary-policy operations from the analysis, assuming that the monetary-policy authority cares for the wealth distribution.

Toshiki Jinushi is a professor in the faculty of economics at Kobe University.

1. Cho (2004) explains that the Korean GDP estimation needs extra steps in the imputed rents calculation because of the prevalent *chonsei* system.

The Arbitrage Condition

There are two arbitrage conditions, one on the house price (P^H) and the rent (R), and the other on the *chonsei* payment (P^C) and the rent:

$$P_t^H = \frac{[R_t + E_t(P_{t+1}^H)]}{(1 + i_t)}$$

$$P_t^C = \frac{(R_t + P_t^C)}{(1 + i_t)},$$

where, the nominal interest rate is referred to as i. The second condition is derived from the choice between the *chonsei* and the regular rent contract, which means $i_t P_t^C = R_t$. These two conditions imply that the relationship between the two prices is determined as follows:

$$\frac{P_t^H}{P_t^C} = \frac{i_t}{[(i_t - E_t(\pi_t^H)]}.$$

This indicates that, thanks to the *chonsei* system, we can estimate the expected capital gain of the house price (π^H) easily from the observable variables, P^H, P^C, and i. This can be very useful information for both the policy-making and the economic analysis. However, Dr. Cho focuses on another implication of this equation. This equation shows that the ratio of the house price over the *chonsei* payment would rise as the expected capital gain of the house price rises, and that it declines as the nominal interest rate declines as long as the expected capital gain (π^H) is positive.

The Two Prices in the Growth Model with Capital-Market Imperfections

Dr. Cho constructs a simple growth model, with the house stock and housing services, and with some capital-market imperfections. The utility depends on the consumption of goods and the housing services, through the Cobb-Douglas functional form. The capital stock and the housing stock are perfect substitutes. The production function is linear with constant marginal product of the capital, B. A part of the saving does not lead to the investment because of some capital-market imperfections, whose degree is denoted by D.[2]

Based on this model, the author derives the house price equation first,

$$P_t^H = \frac{P_t}{D},$$

where P_t denotes the nominal price of the ordinary good. The house price is higher than the ordinary good, because of the capital-market imperfections. Next, he puts the inflation into the model without any influences on

2. D is one when the capital market is perfect. Thus, the imperfection indicates $D < 1$.

to the real variables. Then, the *chonsei* contract is introduced into the model, represented by an arbitration condition, $i_t P_t^C = R_t$. Because the house stock and capital stock are perfect substitutes, the nominal value of the rent should be equal to the nominal value of the marginal product of the capital, so that $R_t = B \cdot P_t$. In the end, the nominal interest rate should be equal to the real interest rate plus the inflation rate.[3] The real interest rate is equal to the marginal product of the capital discounted by the capital-market imperfections, that is, $D \cdot B$. The inflation rate, π, is externally chosen by the monetary authority. These considerations lead to the *chonsei* price equation

$$P_t^C = \frac{BP_t}{(DB + \pi)}.$$

These two equations show that the ratio of the house price over the *chonsei* price rises as the marginal product of the capital, B, declines, since it lowers the *chonsei* price. The ratio also rises as the capital-market imperfections deteriorate, D declines, since the house price rises more than the *chonsei* price. The inflation raises this ratio as well since it lowers the *chonsei,* leaving the house price intact.

Policy Implications

Based on the above analysis, the author reaches to some intriguing policy recommendations. First, under the declining marginal product of the capital, the monetary authority should lower the inflation target in order to avoid the wealth transfer from the *chonsei* rentee to the house owners. Second, the monetary-policy operation should be less active than those implied by ordinary recommended policy rules like Taylor rule in order again to avoid the wealth transfer between the house owner and the *chonsei* rentee, or more broadly between the real-asset holders and the financial-asset holders.

Comments

The *chonsei* contract is fascinating. The historical and/or institutional analysis is due to clarify its origin and evolution. I also like to see the empirical analysis of its implied "capital-gain forecast" of the house prices.

This chapter is inspired by the fact that the gap between the house and the *chonsei* prices is widening recently. But, the author intends to go beyond the mere analysis of that fact and he tries to analyze the relative price fluctuations between the real assets and the financial assets in general. It is a very ambitious research goal. In addition, it reaches to the quite unique policy implications.

3. In this analysis, the author assumes that the house price moves together with the good price, so that $\pi = \pi^H$. This assumption might not reflect the real situation in Korea.

However, I have to point out that the chapter is not dealing with the key points in the debates about how the monetary policy should respond to the asset-price fluctuations. Since the author focuses on the case where asset-price inflation is equal to the general inflation rate, he ignores all the issues related to the asset-price bubbles under the mild inflation rate. Thus, this chapter says almost nothing about the recent experiences in Japan.

The compact growth model with capital-market imperfections is nice by decomposing the real interest rate into the two parts, the marginal product of the capital and the degree of capital-market imperfections. It is understandable that the capital-market imperfections are introduced since they might have generated the *chonsei* system itself. However, their interconnection is not articulated at all. I would like to see some discussion on that point rather than just referring to the *q*-theory.

On the policy recommendations of the chapter, it is notable that those are against the currently popular view that the monetary-policy operation should be more aggressive facing the risk of deflation (see Kato and Nishiyama 2003; and Ahearne et al. 2002). If monetary authority lowers the target inflation rate under the declining marginal product of the capital, as the chapter recommends, the risk of hitting the zero bound of the nominal interest rate gets higher. In addition, the less active policy operation is called for by the chapter in order to avoid the wealth transfer between the real-asset and the nominal-asset holders. If the central bank follows those recommendations, the risk of the deflation might loom up. Though that kind of transfer is serious in Korea since the total balance of the *chonsei* deposit is huge, the deflation spiral would be the more dreadful nightmare.

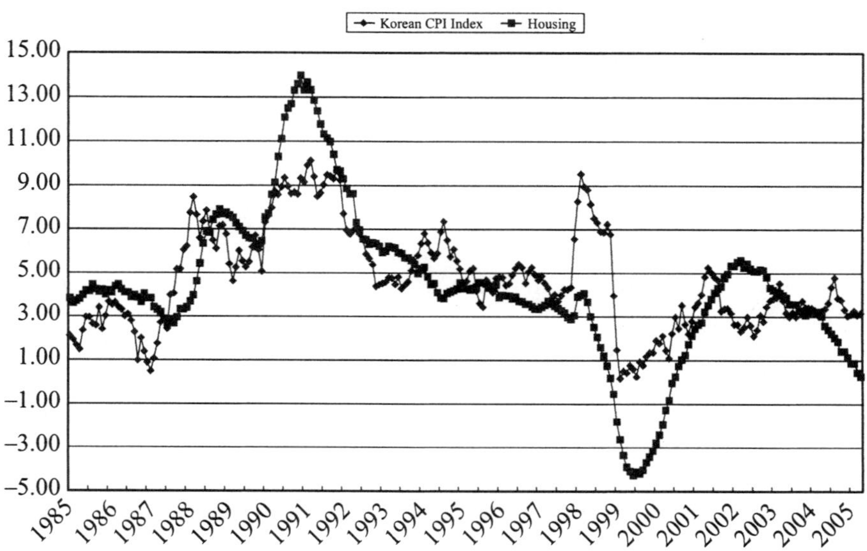

Fig. 9C.1 Korean CPI inflation: the general index and the housing index

In the end, I agree with another commenter that the *chonsei* prices are kept low recently in Korea because of the market expectations and conditions. In particular, a casual look at the Korean CPI shows that the housing part of the CPI inflation is declining recently although the general CPI inflation is picking up (fig. 9C.1). This seems to show the weak market condition for the rental housing under the strong capital gain expectation about the housing price.

References

Ahearne, A., J. Gagnon, J. Haltmaier, and S. Kamin. 2002. Preventing deflation: Lessons from Japan's experience in the 1990s. International Finance Discussion Paper no. 2002-729. Washington, DC: Federal Reserve Board, June.

Cho, Tong-Gil. 2004. Estimation of housing prices in Korea. a paper presented at the 8th OECD-NBS Workshop on National Accounts, December. Paris: Organization for Economic Cooperation and Development, and National Bureau of Statistics.

Kato, Ryo, and Nishiyama Shin-Ichi. Optimal monetary policy when interest rates are bounded at zero. IMES Discussion Paper Series 2003-E-11, Bank of Japan, October. Tokyo: Institute for Monetary and Economic Studies.

Comment Mario B. Lamberte

Summary

In this chapter the author observes in recent years a divergence in relative housing prices (i.e., the ratio of sales price of a house to house rental or *chonsei* prices). Then, the author goes on to identify factors that could explain such a divergence by first developing a partial equilibrium model in which inflation rate, real interest rate, and rent are exogenously determined. This model produces equation (2), which clearly shows that the relative housing price is determined not by inflation rate alone but by the ratio of inflation rate and real interest rate. What is interesting in this result is that even if inflation rate, which can be the monetary authorities' target, remains the same, the real interest rate could decline, thereby raising the price of house relative to price of *chonsei.*

Then, the author goes on to develop a general equilibrium model that allows inflation rate, real interest rate, and house rent to be endogenously determined. The results shown in equations (8-1) to (8-4) and equation (9) yield important insights. First, the relative price of consumption good to capital (or house) is determined by the parameter D, ($D < 1$), which is a measure of capital-market efficiency. Second, real interest rate is deter-

Mario B. Lamberte is president of the Philippine Institute for Development Studies.

mined by two parameters, *D* and *B*, where *B* is the parameter of a linear-production function. A decrease in either *D* or *B* or both can lead to reduction in real interest rate. Third, the opportunity cost of owning a house is equal to the rent and capital gains derived from the house. And fourth, the price of *chonsei* contract is determined by the parameters *B* and *D*, inflation rate, and the price of consumption goods. In this model, one has to trace the source of the decline in real interest rate because it will have a different impact on the relative prices of house (or capital) and *chonsei.* For instance, a reduction in real interest rate caused by a decline in *B* will have no impact on the price of house (or capital) but will affect the price of *chonsei* in the same direction. However, if the reduction in real interest rate comes from *D*, then both prices rise, other things being equal; however, the former rises more than the latter.

Finally, the author develops a monetary rule that takes into account the objective of minimizing fluctuations of the relative prices of house and *chonsei,* or more generally, the relative values between real and financial assets. The results shown in equation (12) suggest that monetary authorities concerned with the relative asset prices should react to output fluctuations less actively than they should by just using the traditional Taylor rule.

Comments

1. In most countries, the housing rental contract involves the amount of monthly rental and security deposit (typically equivalent to one month).[1] The housing rental contract in Korea, however, is entirely different. Under the *chonsei* system, a renter pays a lump-sum deposit for the entire lease period and gets back this deposit at the end of the contract period. However, interest earned from such deposit accrues to the homeowner, which in effect is his rental income. Given the uniqueness of this contract, I suggest that the author provides more information about this system, including its origin, legal framework, and tax incentives. Housing-market analysts and observers would certainly want to understand why it exists only in Korea and why some people choose it over straight purchase of a house.

2. I suggest that the author indicates which interest rate is used in figure 9.4 in the same manner for figure 9.3B.

3. The author was motivated by the growing divergence of house price and *chonsei* price in recent years, as shown in figures 9.1A and 9.1B, which was brought about mainly by the continuing rise of house price and a flat growth rate in *chonsei* price. The result of the author's model, specifically equation (2), predicts that as long as the real interest rate declines faster than the inflation rate, then the price of house relative to *chonsei* will increase, which indeed is borne out by the data in recent years. However, one has to look much further back to see if the result predicted by the model is robust. This can be done by looking at figures 9.3A to 9.3C. As shown, de-

1. Sometimes, landlord asks for one or two months advance in rental.

spite the decline in real interest rate and expected inflation rate in the 1990s, the ratio of house price to *chonsei* price continued to decline, which contradicts the prediction of the model.

4. This brings us to an important point; that is, the behavior of relative prices in recent years could have been affected by other factors. Consider this: when real interest rates decline to a certain level, it would make it attractive for households to buy their own house by borrowing from a bank rather than by continuing to rent an apartment or house. Given the vastly improved condition of the Korean banking system in recent years after KAMCO successfully cleaned up their bad debts, banks could have started providing mortgage loans, which could have explained the construction boom Korea experienced in recent years. At the end of 2002, the average NPL ratio of commercial banks stood at 1.9 percent, which was even lower than the pre-crisis level of 3.9 percent. If the banking system had indeed resumed lending in recent years after cleaning up their NPLs, then they might have been looking for low-risk borrowers with good collateral that will not require huge provisioning. Obviously, banks would favor those who borrow to purchase a house than those borrow to rent a house according to the *chonsei* contract. Landlords could have reacted by freezing the *chonsei* price so as not to lose their customers.

5. I have some misgivings about asking monetary authorities to be concerned about relative prices. They already have problems choosing which price index to monitor to calibrate their monetary policy. One of the author's rationale for including the relative asset prices in the Taylor rule is that uncertainty about the relative asset prices will likely shrink financial transactions and economic activity. It is not clear if this is the case. What is clear, though, from the Korean data is that the increase in relative prices between house and *chonsei* price in recent years has been associated with a construction boom. The other rationale put forward by the author is that the wealth redistribution between real asset holders and financial asset holders itself incurs a cost to society. I think this issue can be better addressed by fiscal policy rather than by monetary policy.

6. The parameters B and D play a crucial role in the model. The author in fact noted that the marginal productivity of capital in Korea has been declining, and this decline is associated with declining real interest rate. In this situation, if the monetary authorities are concerned with fluctuations in relative prices, then they should also lower the target for the inflation rate. Granting that B has changed over time, then I must also ask if D has changed over time, which the author has not touched upon. Given B, the only case in which real interest would decline is when D decreases. However, I suspect that with liberalization and deepening of the Korean financial system, D could have also improved, which could lead to a reduction in relative prices. So, policies aimed at improving capital-market efficiency will have beneficial impacts on relative prices.

10 Deflation and Monetary Policy in Taiwan

Ya-Hwei Yang and Jia-Dong Shea

10.1 Foreword

Ever since the Great Depression of the 1930s drew to a close, inflation has been one of the major headaches for financial and economic decision-makers. Inflation and the unemployment rate have been the two major elements that make up the misery index, while deflation has never seriously been considered a threat. However, by the end of the 1990s, Japan, China, and Hong Kong had been exhibiting a phenomenon of price decreases for many years running, and the rate of price increases in both European and American countries had also started to slow down. The issue of deflation therefore gradually drew the attention of economists and policymakers. The November 2002 issue of *The Economist* even went so far as to suggest that deflation had become a serious threat to the global economy.

In Taiwan the gross domestic product (GDP) deflator decreased in four out of five years from 1999 to 2003, with the exception being 2001. The Consumer Price Index (CPI) also declined in each of the years from 2001 to 2003. Rogoff, chief economist of the International Monetary Fund, published a research report in April 2003 in which Taiwan, together with Japan, Hong Kong, and Germany, was ranked as a high-risk country for

Ya-Hwei Yang is research fellow, Chung-Hua Institution for Economic Research; also adjunct professor of finance, National Taiwan University. Jia-Dong Shea is adjunct professor of economics, National Taiwan University.

The authors thank Takatoshi Ito, Andrew Rose, Toshiki Jinushi, Shigeroni Shiratsuka, the seminar participants at the "Monetary Policy with Very Low Inflation in the Pacific Rim, East Asia Seminar on Economics Volume 15," and the anonymous referee of the University of Chicago Press for their helpful comments on an earlier version of this paper. Any errors and omissions in the paper are the authors' responsibility.

The early version of this paper has been published as NBER Working Paper No. 11244, March 2005.

deflation. The core CPI, published by the Directorate-General of Budget, Accounting, and Statistics of the Executive Yuan in Taiwan, exhibited a negative growth rate in each quarter in 2003. These findings have made deflation a cause for concern among both scholars and the media. Although the Central Bank of China in Taiwan has never admitted that Taiwan is suffering from a deflation problem, it has tried very hard to promote domestic economic activity and avoid price decreases.

Several international research institutions have engaged in research on deflation; see, for instance Ahearne et al. (2002) and Rogoff (2003). The Bank of Japan (2001) also convened a symposium on the issue—*The Role of Monetary Policy under Low Inflation: Deflation Shocks and Policy Responses*—in 2000, where participating scholars emphasized the importance of monetary policy in guarding against and dealing with deflation.[1]

In Taiwan, however, there have been no government reports on the domestic deflation issue, probably for the reason that the government has denied that the problem exists. Similarly, very few studies have been performed by domestic scholars. Research reports compiled by the Department of Economic Research of the Central Bank of China (2002) and the Council for Economic Planning and Development of the Executive Yuan (2003) have merely tried to explain the causes of and responsive strategies to deflation in the light of other countries' experiences. Wu (2003), for instance, not only analyzed the reasons why the global price growth had slowed since 1997, but he also discussed the causes of low prices in Taiwan. Huang (2003) probed long-, medium-, and short-term causes that led to the price decreases in Taiwan and provided policy recommendations. However, although Wu and Huang talked about the causes of Taiwan's deflation, they simply presented narrative explanations or arguments, without engaging in any in-depth or detailed analysis.

In the early part of 2004, Taiwan's CPI reversed its downward trend and started to rise. Although the problem of deflation in Taiwan disappears gradually, there are several questions that are worth looking into. How serious has the deflation problem in Taiwan really been in the last few years? What are the fundamental reasons for the deflation? How has the Central

1. The theme of the seminar held by the Bank of Japan (2001) was *Monetary Policy under a Low Inflation Rate,* in which participants mostly emphasized the importance of monetary policy during a period of deflation. For example, Cargill thought that central banks generally focused more on policies to control the monetary environment during periods of inflation, while neglecting the seriousness of the problem of deflation, and therefore seldom utilizing monetary-policy tools to prevent the deflation phenomenon. This is considered to be one of the main reasons for the Great Depression of the 1930s. Cargill thought that Sweden differed from the United States in that it laid emphasis on the price level, paying close attention to deflation. As for Japan, he offered the same suggestion, calling for an emphasis on the importance of monetary policy during a period of deflation. Goodfriend also thought that monetary policy was the fundamental reason for deflation and economic stagnation.

Bank in Taiwan responded to deflation? How effective have the Central Bank's policies been? This chapter aims to answer these questions.

Since deflation is usually accompanied by a recession, section 10.2 of this chapter briefly introduces the changes in the political and economic environment in Taiwan that have taken place in recent years, thereby providing the background for Taiwan's unsatisfactory economic performance since 1999. Section 10.3 explains two phenomena associated with macro-price changes. One is deflation and the other is price divergence. Price divergence refers to the phenomenon that the three macro-price indexes—i.e., the CPI, wholesale price index (WPI), and GDP deflator (PGDP)—have been moving in different directions. In section 10.4, major global factors that have affected Taiwan's prices are emphasized. Section 10.5 probes the key factors causing Taiwan's PGDP to drop since 1999. The sources of the WPI-CPI divergence are also identified. Section 10.6 explains how Taiwan's Central Bank operates its monetary and exchange rate policies, and then discusses its policy responses to deflation, while also carefully reviewing their effectiveness. The final section presents the conclusions.

10.2 The Political and Economic Environment in Recent Years

Taiwan's economic growth used to be regarded by foreign scholars and decisionmakers as a "miracle" or taken as a "model" for developing countries to study or follow. Due to its sound economic fundamentals, quick policy responses, and other reasons as mentioned in Shea and Shih (1999), Taiwan was also relatively immune from the attack of the East Asian financial crisis in 1997–1998, performing better in terms of its economic growth rate, unemployment rate, currency depreciation, and falling stock prices than its East Asian neighbors.

As table 10.1 shows, however, Taiwan's economic performance since 1999 has never returned to the illustrious growth of the past three to four decades. The economic growth rate has yet to again exceed 6 percent, and its first negative growth rate of –2.18 percent in Taiwan's post-war history was recorded in 2001. The unemployment rate has also climbed steadily and remained at a level of around 5 percent in 2003. Although the stock price index and the total stock trading volume recovered a little in 2000, they have both decreased in other years. The New Taiwan dollar (hereafter the NT dollar) has also remained weak relative to the U.S. dollar during this period.

There have been several factors that have served to bring about Taiwan's unsatisfactory economic performance since 1999. The poor performance in 2001 can be partly explained by a gloomy world economy caused by the bursting of the Internet and IT bubbles in late 2000 and the 9/11 terrorist attacks in 2001. The SARS epidemic also hampered Taiwan's economic

Table 10.1 **Key economic indicators**

	Economic growth rate (%)	Changes in price indexes (%)			Unemployment rate (%)	Stock price index (1966 = 100)	Total trading volume in stock market (trillion NT$)
		GDP deflator	WPI	CPI			
1991–1995 average	7.12	2.94	1.71	3.76	1.56	5,043	10.724
1996	6.10	3.11	–1.01	3.08	2.60	6,004	12.908
1997	6.68	1.68	–0.45	0.89	2.72	8,411	37.241
1998	4.57	2.64	0.60	1.69	2.69	7,738	29.619
1999	5.42	–1.42	–4.55	0.17	2.92	7,427	29.292
2000	5.86	–1.73	1.82	1.26	2.99	7,847	30.527
2001	–2.18	0.57	–1.34	–0.01	4.57	4,907	18.355
2002	3.59	–1.01	0.05	–0.20	5.17	5,226	21.874
2003	3.31	–2.13	2.48	–0.28	4.99	5,254	20.333

	Exchange rate at year-end (NT$/US$)	ROA of domestic banks (%)	ROE of domestic banks (%)	Nonperforming loan ratio of financial institutions at year-end (%)	Growth rate of private enterprises fixed investment (%)	Direct investment abroad (million US$)	Tax burden (tax and monopoly revenue/GNP) (%)	Outstanding central government debt as a % of GNP
1991–1995 average	27.265[a]	0.71[a]	11.87[a]	3.00[a]	14.28	2,451	18.0[a]	12.36[a]
1996	27.491	0.73	11.36	4.15	3.44	3,843	16.1	16.5
1997	32.638	0.85	12.23	4.18	18.61	5,243	15.7	17.2
1998	32.216	0.71	9.29	4.93	11.88	3,836	16.0	15.8
1999	31.395	0.54	6.91	5.67	–0.68	4,420	14.7	14.5
2000	32.992	0.47	6.05	6.20	15.76	6,701	13.2	25.3
2001	34.999	0.26	3.61	8.16	–29.29	5,480	13.0	28.9
2002	34.753	–0.47	–7.35	6.84	2.50	4,886	12.3	29.0
2003	33.978	0.21	3.50	5.00	–1.47	5,679	12.2	31.3

Sources: Various data from the Directorate-General of Budget, Accounting and Statistics (DGBAS), Council for Economic Planning and Development (CEPD), Ministry of Finance (MOF), and the Central Bank of China (CBC).

[a]Figure for 1995.

growth in 2003. In addition to these three well-known factors, the deterioration in Taiwan's political and economic environment also is a fundamental reason.

Since the early 1990s, the ruling power in Taiwan has gradually shifted from those who migrated from mainland China to Taiwan in the late 1940s together with the KMT (Kuomintang) government, over to the so-called "native Taiwanese." During the process of this power transition, an ongoing confrontation between the two camps has never been resolved. Although a significant proportion of the people in Taiwan would like to maintain Taiwan's status quo, there is a major division among the people on the issue of whether Taiwan should pursue independence from China or be unified with China at some point in the future. Constant friction between the two camps and disputes between them in major elections, which Taiwan has held almost annually in recent years, have caused Taiwan to degenerate into a society that lacks any consensus or harmony. The switch in the ruling party from the KMT to the DPP (Democratic Progressive Party) for the first time in 2000 only further complicated the situation. KMT and DPP legislators have since then fought tooth and nail almost irrationally on any issue in the Legislative Yuan (the law-making body in Taiwan). The result is a semiparalyzed government without much determination or executive power. This phenomenon of political unrest is certainly a negative factor in relation to private investment.

The rise of China's economy has also affected Taiwan's own economy in many ways. China's cheap labor and land have provided Taiwan's fading labor-intensive industries with an opportunity to revitalize. A big China market has also been attractive to capital- and technology-intensive product manufacturers. Therefore, huge numbers of business people flooded into China to invest in the 1990s. This massive investment in China gave rise to concerns over whether Taiwan's economy would be "hollowed out." This hollowing-out concern plus the bad feeling regarding China on its political stance of constantly repressing Taiwan in international affairs finally led former President Teng-Hui Lee to adopt a "no hurry, be patient" policy to guide economic relations with China. However, due to the huge potential profits from investing in China and the advantage of sharing the same language and culture enjoyed by Taiwan businessmen in competing with investors from other countries, this "no hurry, be patient" policy did not effectively counter the huge flow of westward-bound investment from Taiwan to China.

After the opposition DPP candidate won the presidential election in 2000, the DPP's stance of leaning toward Taiwan's independence from China enhanced China's hostility toward Taiwan. No official dialogue between the two sides of the Taiwan Strait has ever been resumed. China has even strengthened its threat of military reprisals against Taiwan. A large number of the DPP's loyal supporters also oppose any closer economic ties with China. Tension with China of this sort has not only nearly put an end to the potential role that Taiwan can play as a medium or bridge for foreign investors entering the China market, but it has also discouraged private and direct foreign investment in Taiwan.

The financial sector in Taiwan has also encountered a number of problems. Allowing new private banks to be set up in 1991 suddenly increased the number of domestic commercial banks from seventeen in 1991 to thirty-three in 1993. Some credit cooperatives and investment and trust companies were also allowed to be converted into commercial banks in subsequent years. Therefore, the total number of domestic banks, including commercial banks and medium-business banks, increased from twenty-five in 1991 to forty-one in 1993 and to fifty-two in 1999—more than double the original number. The resulting fierce competition among banks led to credit expansion and prosperous stock and real estate markets in the mid-1990s.

In the years that followed, although Taiwan remained relatively insulated from the East Asian financial crisis, the contagion effects of the crisis still caused Taiwan's stock and real estate prices to fall and the nonperforming loans ratio of its financial institutions to rise in 1998. Furthermore, between the end of 1998 and early-1999, several listed companies and business groups, which had been found guilty of misconduct in fund management (e.g., engaging in cross-investments in the stocks of their group members, being highly leveraged, borrowing short to invest long, being involved in stock-price supporting activities, or overinvesting in the slackening housing industry), sank into heavy financial troubles. These so-called "land-mine" companies or business groups not only adversely affected the financial condition of the domestic banks, but also accelerated the downturn in stock prices.

Fierce competition among banks together with the accidents caused by these "land-mine" companies steadily lowered the return on assets (ROA) and the return on equity (ROE) of domestic banks, and raised the nonperforming loans ratios of financial institutions during the 1998–2002 period, as table 10.1 indicates. The willingness and ability of financial institutions to grant loans to the business sector therefore shrank during this same period.

All of the above-mentioned factors, including political unrest, tensions with China, out-bound investments attracted by China, and a weakened financial sector, had a detrimental impact on private and foreign investment in Taiwan. As shown in table 10.1, the growth of fixed investment on the part of private enterprises slowed down or even turned negative, while direct investment abroad grew significantly after 1999.

When faced with deflationary pressure, the government is usually expected to adopt an expansionary fiscal policy to stimulate the economy. Unfortunately, Taiwan's government has been constrained by its deteriorating financial condition, such that it has not been able to afford to expand

Table 10.2 **Contribution to the economic growth rate of expenditure items[a] (%)**

Year	Economic growth rate	Domestic demand: Subtotal	Private consumption	Public expenditure[b]	Private sector fixed investment	Increase in inventory	Net exports
1996	6.10	5.58 (91.48)	3.85	0.87	0.46	0.40	0.52 (8.52)
1997	6.68	8.43 (126.20)	4.30	0.75	2.48	0.90	–1.75 (–26.20)
1998	4.57	6.38 (139.61)	3.88	0.70	1.75	0.05	–1.81 (–39.61)
1999	5.42	1.87 (34.50)	3.25	–0.38	–0.11	–0.89	3.55 (65.50)
2000	5.86	3.89 (66.40)	2.98	–0.28	2.36	–1.17	1.97 (33.60)
2001	–2.18	–4.93 (272.02)	0.62	–0.26	–4.78	–0.51	2.75 (–126.15)
2002	3.59	0.96 (26.74)	1.23	–0.73	0.30	0.16	2.63 (73.26)
2003	3.31	0.36 (10.88)	0.42	–0.07	–0.17	0.18	2.95 (89.12)

Source: DGBAS.
Note: Figures in parentheses are contribution shares to the economic growth rate of that specific year.
[a]Calculated by real growth rate of expenditure item *x* share in GDP of previous year.
[b]Public expenditure includes government consumption, government investment, and public-enterprise investment.

public expenditure. Under China's threat of military action, Taiwan has had no room to cut its national defense expenditure. Moreover, political parties have been competing for votes by writing checks for welfare programs, cutting tax rates, and by providing tax holidays or tax exemptions to please the voters. As a result, the tax burden in Taiwan, as table 10.1 shows, has fallen year after year to reach a level of 12.2 percent in 2003, one of the lowest in the world. Outstanding central government debts as a percentage of gross national product (GNP) have also been increasing very rapidly from 14.5 percent in 1999 to 31.3 percent in 2003.

Due to such financial constraints, Taiwan's public expenditure (including government consumption, government investment, and public-enterprise investment) in fact fell during 1999–2003, bringing a negative contribution to economic growth in this period, as table 10.2 shows. We can also see from this table that the private sector's fixed investment in addition contributed little or even negatively to economic growth, except in the year 2000. Another conclusion we can draw from table 10.2 is that the major driving force behind economic growth on the expenditure side during the period 1999–2003 was net exports instead of domestic demand.

10.3 Macro-price Changes in Taiwan

10.3.1 Deflation as a New but Short-term Concern

In April 2003 Taiwan was listed by the International Monetary Fund (IMF) as a country that faced a high risk of deflation, along with Japan, Hong Kong, and Germany. The IMF calculated the deflation risk index for thirty-five countries, and classified the results into four categories as high-, medium-, low-, and very low-risk countries. Among the countries categorized as being high-risk, Japan scored the highest, followed by Hong Kong, Taiwan, and Germany.[2]

Figure 10.1 depicts the inflation rate of Taiwan's GDP deflator (hereafter PGDP) from 1961 to 2003. Except for 1965 when its value was slightly negative (–0.61 percent), the PGDP annual changes before 1998 were positive. During this period, the annual inflation rate measured by PGDP seldom exceeded 5 percent, except for the two oil crisis years. However, there has been an obvious change since 1999. That is, PGDP inflation turned negative in most of the subsequent years. The annual PGDP change was –1.42 percent in 1999, –1.73 percent in 2000, 0.57 percent in 2001, –1.01 percent in 2002, and –2.13 percent in 2003. The CPI also exhibited a negative inflation rate for three consecutive years in 2001–2003, as shown in table 10.1. The IMF and scholars in Taiwan thus became worried that Taiwan might have started to experience deflation.[3]

Since 2003, however, the global as well as domestic economic situation has improved. Starting with the second half of 2003, the global prices of raw materials like steel, cement, petroleum, coal, wheat, soybeans, butter, and paper pulp have been surging. During the first quarter of 2004, the CPI in Taiwan increased by 0.51 percent as compared with the same quarter in 2003. During that same time, the core CPI rose by 0.12 percent and the WPI increased by 2.37 percent. The government and various research institutions in Taiwan have each forecasted that both the CPI and WPI will exhibit positive growth rates in 2004. Taiwan's period of deflation is therefore generally believed to be over.

10.3.2 Divergence of PGDP, CPI, and WPI

In recent years, the macro-price indexes in Taiwan have exhibited a divergence, with the PGDP, CPI, and WPI moving in different directions. As figure 10.2 indicates, from 1999 to 2000 the PGDP declined, but the WPI and CPI rose slightly. In addition, from 2002 to 2003 both the PGDP and CPI declined, leading to a concern about deflation. The WPI, however, rose—an obvious price divergence. When there is price divergence, which

2. See Kumar (2003) and Rogoff (2003).

3. Deflation is defined as a phenomenon where general price levels continue to drop. To facilitate the analysis, the IMF defines deflation as occurring when annual price growth is negative for two consecutive years. Please see IMF (1999, 106).

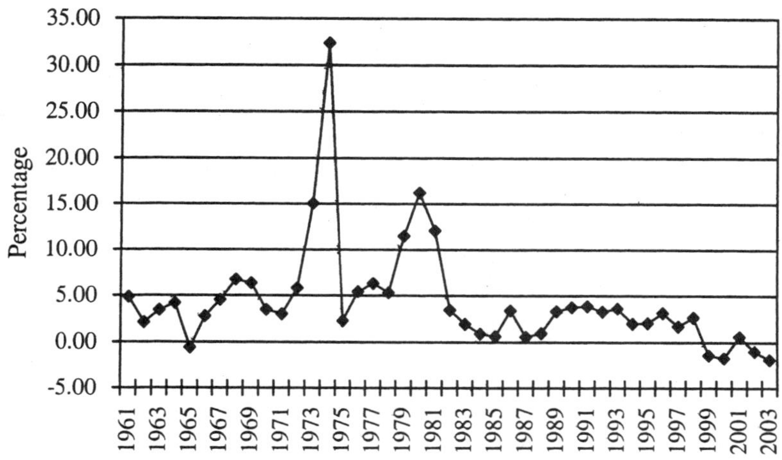

Fig. 10.1 Growth rate of PGDP
Source: DGBAS.

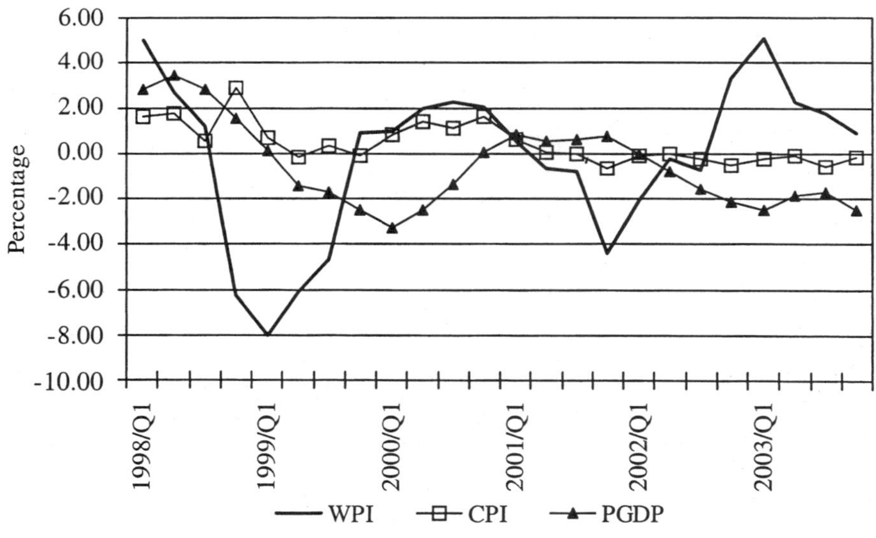

Fig. 10.2 Inflation rates of WPI, CPI, PGDP
Source: Price Statistics Monthly, DGBAS.

price index is a proper indicator for inflation or deflation becomes an issue. This paper chooses PGDP as the indicator in the discussion on deflation.

In fact, divergence of price indexes happens all the time in Taiwan. As can be seen from table 10.3 and figure 10.3, ever since 1982 price divergence has occurred many times. For example, from 1986 to 1992, the CPI and PGDP went up, while the WPI went down.

Table 10.3 **Moving directions of WPI, CPI, and PGDP (1982 to 2003)**

Year	1982	1983	1984	1985	1986	1987	1998	1989	1990	1991	1992	1993	1994	1995	1996	1997	1998	1999	2000	2001	2002	2003
WPI	–	–	+	–	–	–	–	–	–	+	–	+	+	+	–	–	+	–	+	–	+	+
CPI	+	+	–	–	+	+	+	+	+	+	+	+	+	+	+	+	+	+	+	–	–	–
PGDP	+	+	+	+	+	+	+	+	+	+	+	+	+	+	+	+	+	–	–	+	–	–
Divergence	Yes	Yes	Yes	Yes	Yes	Yes	Yes	Yes	Yes	No	Yes	No	No	No	Yes	Yes	No	Yes	Yes	Yes	Yes	Yes

Notes: From 1982 to 2003, only five years have experienced a simultaneous movement in the same direction for three price indexes. + indicates positive growth; – indicates negative growth. Yes indicates a simultaneous movement in the same direction for the three price indexes; No indicates no such comovement.

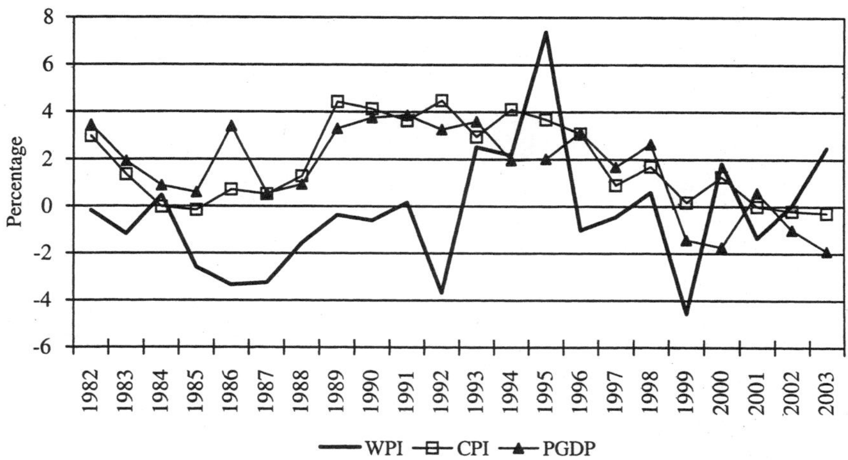

Fig. 10.3 Inflation rate of WPI, CPI and PGDP (annual)
Source: Price Statistics Monthly, DGBAS.

10.4 Global Factors Affecting Taiwan Prices

The deterioration in Taiwan's political and economic environment, as mentioned in section 10.2, has not only brought about an unsatisfactory performance in terms of economic growth in Taiwan, but also has formed deflationary pressure on Taiwan's macro prices. In addition, there have been several global factors affecting Taiwan's macroeconomy and prices.

Taiwan is a highly open economy. Ever since the 1970s, the ratios of exports and imports to GDP have almost always remained above 40 percent, sometimes even exceeding 50 percent. The macroeconomy of Taiwan has thus been deeply affected by the global economic situation and prices. For example, during the periods of the two oil crises, Taiwan encountered the problem of so-called "imported inflation." Macro-price changes in Taiwan in recent years have not only been caused by domestic factors, but have also been closely related to major factors that have affected global prices, especially the bursting of the internet bubble in 2000 and the rise of China's economy.

Excessively optimistic expectations on the future of the internet, communications, and the IT industries resulted in overinvestment and caused stock prices to soar globally in the late-1990s. After the economic bubble burst at the end of 2000, the huge excess capacities of these industries led to their prices dropping. The bursting of the bubble also caused stock prices to sink and wealth to shrink. Furthermore, the global economic situation worsened and unemployment rose. All of these factors caused world consumption to fall. In addition, excess capacity contributed to a pessimistic outlook, such that willingness to invest decreased. Therefore, the bursting of the Internet and IT bubbles brought about a weakening in world consumption and investment, which further caused global prices to fall.

As an economy highly dependent on exports, especially the exports of products from IT and IT-related industries, Taiwan suffered heavily from the bursting of the IT bubble. Taiwan's total exports dropped by 17.16 percent in 2001, which was also one of the major factors causing a negative economic growth rate of –2.18 percent in that year for Taiwan.

Ever since China accelerated its transition from a controlled economy to a market economy in 1992 and reinforced its trade and investment relations with the rest of the world, it has had a significant impact on the global economy. The rise of China's economy has affected global and Taiwanese prices in several ways.

China has a huge pool of cheap labor. Labor-intensive products produced in China and exported to the world market have forced the global prices of those products, mostly final consumer goods, to fall. On the other hand, the rise of China has caused the prices of China's major imports, mostly raw materials, agricultural products, and capital- or technology-intensive goods (regarding which, China has a comparative disadvantage) to rise. China's rapid economic development has also raised the purchasing power and hence private consumption of the Chinese people, which has further increased the demand for and the global prices of raw materials and agricultural products. To prepare for the 2008 Olympic Games in Beijing and the 2010 Shanghai World Exposition, China has begun large-scale public-construction projects, which have given rise to even higher increases in the global prices of raw materials such as minerals, cement, and petroleum.[4]

In sum, due to the rise of China's economy, the global prices of its exports (most are manufactured as final consumer goods) have been decreasing, while the prices of its imports (mainly upstream raw materials, agricultural products, and machinery and equipment) have been rising. The prices of related products in Taiwan are naturally affected.

As table 10.4 indicates, export prices and import prices in Taiwan had been moving in different directions each year in 2000–2003. The general index of export prices, together with its major component—the export prices of industrial goods—had been decreasing almost steadily except for in

4. China consumed approximately 50 percent of the world's cement, 36 percent of its steel products, and 30 percent of its coal in 2003. In 2003, China's demand for steel products amounted to about 38 million tons. In the first quarter of 2004, China imported 10.08 million tons of steel products worth U.S.$5.72 billion. The quantity of steel products imported increased by 17.5 percent compared with the first quarter of 2003, with the total value going up by 28.4 percent. In 2003, China imported 91.12 million tons of crude oil (representing annual growth of 30 percent). In the first quarter of 2004, China imported 30.14 million tons of crude oil worth U.S.$7.15 billion. The volume of crude oil imports increased by 35.7 percent compared with the first quarter of 2003 and its total value increased by 41.2 percent. This shows that unit prices for steel products and crude oil have surged.

Table 10.4 **Changes of export and import price indexes in Taiwan (%)**

	Export price indexes				Import price indexes			
		Components				Components		
Year	General index	Agricultural goods	Processed agricultural goods	Industrial goods	General index	Raw materials	Capital goods	Consumer goods
1998	5.57	40.41	9.24	5.53	0.74	–1.81	6.55	11.21
1999	–8.53	4.93	10.50	–8.93	–4.10	–4.75	–3.72	–0.92
2000	–0.88	–51.18	–18.11	–0.34	4.63	7.15	–4.53	–0.15
2001	0.32	–6.31	–10.14	0.53	–1.25	–2.21	0.15	2.85
2002	–1.49	16.22	1.11	–1.55	0.40	0.88	–1.58	–0.45
2003	–1.49	10.10	4.45	–1.62	5.14	7.00	–0.25	1.35

Source: Price Statistics Monthly, DGBAS.

2001. On the other hand, the general index of import prices, especially the import prices of raw materials, which account for 70.0 percent of the general import price index in weighting, had been rising, with an exception in 2001. These changes in export and import prices were consistent with the impacts of the bursting of the Internet and IT bubbles and the rise of China's economy on the world prices.

10.5 Causes of Deflation and Price Divergence

10.5.1 Analysis of PGDP Deflation

The GDP deflator (PGDP) measures the price of final domestic products. In order to explain the change of PGDP, we need a theoretical model as the base. According to the aggregate-demand and aggregate-supply (AD-AS) model, any factor that may cause the AD curve to move to the right (left) will lead PGDP to go up (down); while it may cause the AS curve to shift to the right (left), leading PGDP to go down (up).

We can set up the AD equation as the following:

$$(1) \qquad Y = \text{AD}(\overset{-}{\text{PGDP}}; \overset{+}{\text{GEXP}}, \overset{+}{\text{MS}}, \overset{+}{Pf}, \overset{+}{Yf}, \overset{+}{\text{EXR}}, \overset{-}{Z} \ldots).$$

In this AD equation, Y is real GDP; GEXP is government real expenditures, including government consumption expenditures, government investment, and public enterprise investment; MS is money-supply volume; Pf and Yf represent foreign export prices and the global economic situation, respectively; and EXR is the exchange rate measuring the value of the U.S. dollar in terms of the NT dollar. Z represents unquantifiable qualitative factors, including political unrest, tensions with China, and a weakened financial sector. On the right-hand side of the equation, a positive or negative symbol above each explanatory variable represents the direction of impact of that variable on Y.

A general equation of aggregate-supply (AS) can be presented as follows:

$$Y = \mathrm{AS}(\overset{+}{\mathrm{PGDP}}; \overset{-}{W}, \overset{+}{K}, \overset{+}{T}). \tag{2}$$

In this equation, W is the nominal wage rate; K is the capital stock; and T is the technology level. Because it is difficult to measure the capital stock K and technology level T, and because W, K, and T may jointly affect aggregate supply through unit output labor cost LC, the AS function can be rewritten as

$$Y = \mathrm{AS}^{*}(\overset{+}{\mathrm{PGDP}}; \overset{-}{\mathrm{LC}}). \tag{3}$$ [5]

From equations (1) and (3), the PGDP equation can be derived as

$$\mathrm{PGDP} = f(\overset{+}{\mathrm{GEXP}}, \overset{+}{\mathrm{MS}}, \overset{+}{\mathrm{EXR}}, \overset{+}{Pf}, \overset{+}{Yf}, \overset{+}{\mathrm{LC}}, \overset{-}{Z} \ldots). \tag{4}$$

Because increases in the first five explanatory variables on the right-hand side all cause the AD curve to shift to the right, and a rise in LC causes the AS curve to shift to the left, thus all six explanatory variables have a positive impact on PGDP.[6] However, Z has negative influence on PGDP.

Since the first six variables are measurable, we can look at their trends to help identify the sources of PGDP deflation in Taiwan. Since 1999, PGDP has been declining, except in 2001. This phenomenon of a declining PGDP has been caused by several factors. Figure 10.4 shows the changes in four explanatory variables (GEXP, LC, EXR, and Pf) which have contributed to PGDP deflation. As explained in section 10.2, mainly due to a finance constraint, government expenditures (GEXP) decreased during this period. Furthermore, improvements in production technology caused unit output labor costs (LC) to go down, except in 2001. The bursting of the Internet and IT bubbles and the rise of China's economy also depressed world export prices (Pf) before 2003. Furthermore, the NT dollar appreciated relative to the U.S. dollar in 1999 and 2000. All of these factors contributed to PGDP's decline.

5. In theory, it is not difficult to infer that the impact of the wage rate W on unit output labor cost LC is positive, and the impact of the capital stock K and the technology level T on LC is negative. Furthermore, because LC affects aggregate supply negatively, equation 3 implies that the impact of W on Y is negative, and the impact of K and T on Y is positive, which is consistent with equation 2.

6. We have tried to apply the Two-Stage Least Squares (2SLS) technique to estimate this equation. The empirical results support our theoretical model.

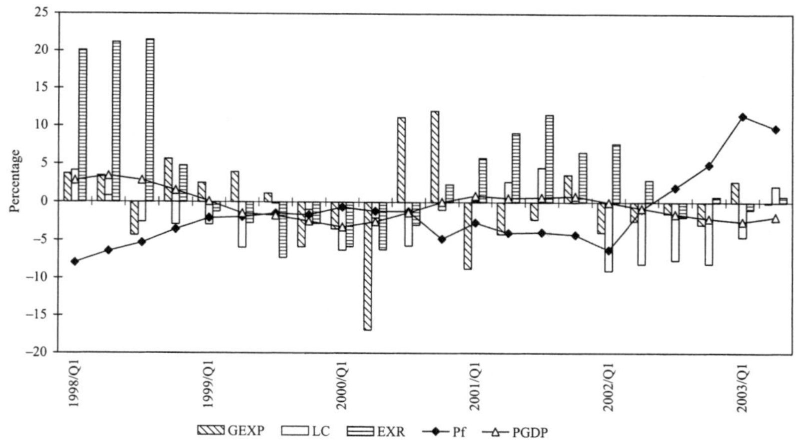

Fig. 10.4 Changes in PGDP and its determinants (annual growth rate)
Source: DGBAS.

10.5.2 Causes of WPI-CPI Divergence

This subsection intends to explain the possible factors that caused a divergence between the WPI and CPI during the period extending from the fourth quarter of 2002 to the third quarter of 2003. During this period, the CPI slowly declined, while the WPI rose.

What the WPI measures is factory prices or wholesale prices of three categories of products: domestically-produced and domestically-sold (DPDS) products, imported goods, and exported goods. It is a weighted average of the above three categories of price indexes. Let WPId, PM, and PX represent the price index of DPDS products, the import price index, and the export price index, respectively. These three components enjoy roughly equal weights in the current calculation of the WPI in Taiwan.

As figure 10.5 shows, the WPId in Taiwan fell during 1998 and 1999, began to rise slightly in 2000, and followed up with a further slight decline in 2001. Since then, the WPId has been rising. The reason why the WPId fell in 2001 was the recession in Taiwan. A lack of effective domestic demand caused the WPId to slide. Since 2003, the economy has slightly recovered. Domestic demand and the WPId are therefore rising.

In the case of import prices (PM), because agricultural products and industrial raw materials constitute the largest portion of Taiwan's imports, followed by capital goods and consumer goods, PM is mainly affected by the global prices of agricultural products and industrial raw materials as well as capital goods. It is also influenced by the global prices of consumer goods, the NT-dollar exchange rate, and customs duties. Since the 1980s, the effective customs-duty rate has decreased, resulting in decreasing import prices. Since 2001, however, the NT dollar has depreciated, pushing

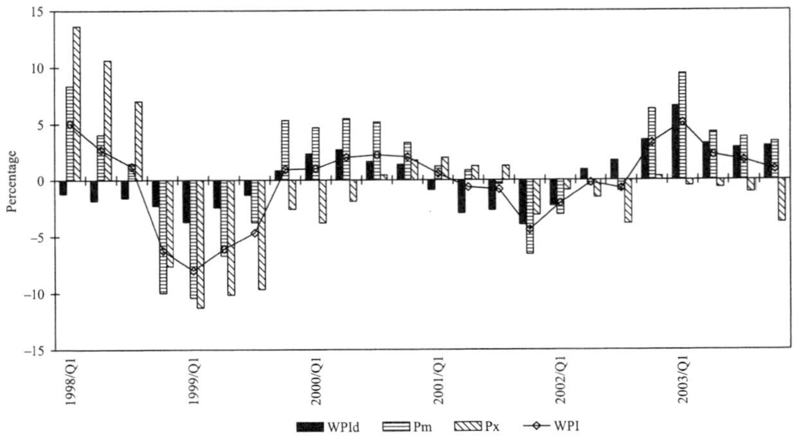

Fig. 10.5 Change in WPI and its component (annual growth rate)
Source: Price Statistics Monthly, DGBAS.

up import prices. Strong Chinese demand for raw materials and capital goods has caused the global prices of that category of goods to soar, thus raising Taiwan's import prices and hence the WPI since the fourth quarter of 2002.

As for export prices (PX), Taiwan's exports are mainly composed of industrial products, the bulk of which are information industry and electrical machinery or electronics products. The former has been affected by the bursting of the Internet bubble, and the latter by competition from China's exports in recent years. The PX has thus dropped since the second half of 2002.

Figure 10.5 summarizes the trend in the WPI and its components since 1998. During the period from the fourth quarter of 2002 to the third quarter of 2003, the WPI rose. Among its components, the wholesale price index for DPDS products (WPId) rose as well as the import price index (PM), while the export price index (PX) declined. Therefore, it is evident that the rise in the WPI was mainly caused by a rise in the prices of DPDS products and imported goods.

CPI trends have differed from those of the WPI. From the fourth quarter of 2002 to the third quarter of 2003, the WPI surged, while the CPI fell. The CPI measures the retail prices of consumer goods and services. Consumer goods can be further divided into local consumer goods and imported consumer goods.[7] In other words, CPI measures the price of local consumer goods, imported consumer goods, and service sectors. A fall in the price of services (*Ps*) accounts for a large portion of a decline in CPI.

7. Since there is no other better proxy, we adopt PGDP as the proxy measure of the prices of local consumer goods. We have tried some regression of CPI on PGDP, PMc, and *Ps,* and obtained satisfactory results.

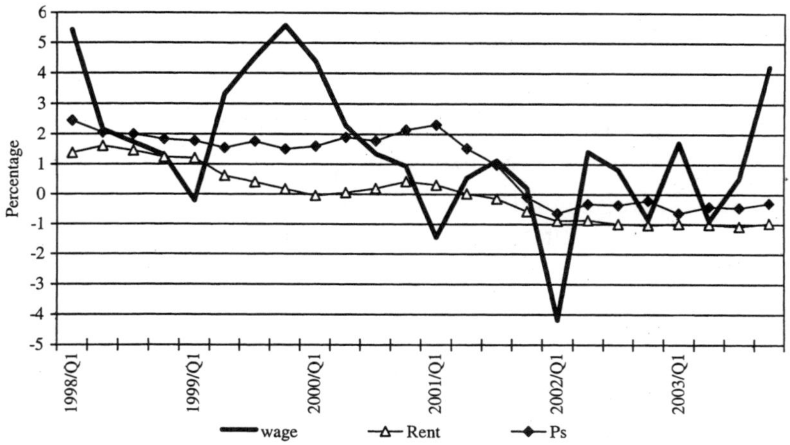

Fig. 10.6 Changes in Ps and its components (annual growth rate)
Source: Statistical Database, DGBAS.
Note: Rent is housing rentals. Wage is per capita average salary of employees each month.

Because the fall in the price of services (*Ps*) is a major factor causing the CPI to drop, we study the reasons for the decrease in *Ps*. The production costs and prices of services are mainly determined by the wage (*W*), rent (*R*), and the interest rate (*r*). Figure 10.6 indicates that *Ps* moves closely with rent *R* and the interest rate *r*. The wage has also been relatively stable since 2001.

Falling rents were mainly caused by factors such as weak domestic demand, the outward migration of companies and white-collar laborers, and an oversupply of houses and office buildings. The decline in the interest rate was due to the central banks of many countries adopting a low-interest-rate policy to stimulate their economies during this period, a path that Taiwan also followed. Stable wages were the result of competition from Chinese labor and an increase in domestic unemployment.

10.6 The Central Bank's Policy Responses to Deflation

Although the Central Bank in Taiwan (formally the Central Bank of China, hereafter the CBC) has never admitted that Taiwan has encountered the problem of deflation, the CBC implemented some measures to stimulate aggregate demand for Taiwan's products, in order to promote economic growth as well as to counter the problem of deflation.[8] The deterioration in the government's financial situation as explained in section

8. When deflation became a public concern in Taiwan in 2002 and 2003, the CBC several times tried to downplay the issue by pointing out either that the core CPI was still rising or that the falling CPI was just a temporary phenomenon.

10.2 restricted the government's ability to adopt an expansionary fiscal policy to promote the economy. The CBC's monetary and exchange rate policies therefore became the major policy instruments for the government to rely on.

10.6.1 The Formation of Monetary Policy

According to the Central Bank Act, the CBC has the obligation to maintain price as well as exchange rate stability and to assist in economic development. To achieve these final goals, the CBC chooses monetary-aggregate targeting as the basic framework of its monetary policy, instead of inflation, exchange-rate, or interest-rate targeting. Since 1992, the monetary aggregate M2 has been chosen as the intermediate target of monetary policy to achieve the final goals.

Before the end of each year, the CBC (often after having consulted with scholars and experts) sets and publicly announces the target zone of the M2 growth rate for the subsequent year based on the government's target figures of the economic growth rate and inflation rate, as well as other factors influencing the demand for money, such as the opportunity cost of holding money and the diversification of financial assets. Using a zone, rather than a specific number, as the M2 growth target, the CBC is endowed with the flexibility to maintain the stability of interest rates, the exchange rate, and other major financial indicators throughout the year.

The actual M2 growth rate is very carefully observed each month by the CBC. In order to effectively control M2, the CBC adopts reserve money as the operational target. At the beginning of each month, the CBC has a monetary estimation and forecasting meeting to determine the target value of reserve money for that month. A reference target for the inter-bank overnight call-loan rate is also derived in the meeting. The CBC then applies a variety of operational instruments, including required reserves, discounts and accommodations, open market operations, re-deposits from financial institutions, selective credit management, and moral suasion, to fine-tune the daily figures of reserve money and the inter-bank overnight call-loan rate.

Since monetary-aggregate targeting is generally regarded as outdated, the CBC occasionally has faced challenges from scholars who strongly suggest to replace monetary-aggregate targeting with interest-rate targeting or inflation targeting. By adopting a target zone for M2 growth and setting a reference target for the inter-bank overnight call-loan rate in its operations, the CBC in fact has implicitly incorporated interest-rate targeting in its framework of monetary policy.

Among CBC's operational instruments, open market operations are the most frequently-used instruments. Re-deposits from financial instruments, selective credit management, and adjusting the discount and accommodation rates are sometimes adopted. The required-reserve ratios are adjusted only occasionally for special cases as a strong monetary-policy measure. For open market operations, before 1992 the CBC relied on the issuance of savings bonds, treasury bills, and certificates of deposit (CDs) as tools to manage the liquidity situation in the financial market. However, the issuance of savings bonds and treasury bills was terminated in 1992 and 1998, respectively. In recent years, the CBC has either issued or redeemed CDs almost every day to affect the liquidity and inter-bank overnight call-loan rate. Since 1999, the CBC has depended heavily on the issuance of CDs and on receiving re-deposits from financial institutions in order to sterilize the impact of the accumulation of foreign exchange reserves on reserve money, such that the CBC's outstanding CDs and re-deposits from financial institutions have increased very rapidly. As of the end of 2003, the outstanding CDs even reached NT$2.99 trillion, equivalent to 185 percent of total reserve money, and re-deposits from financial institutions amounted to NT$2.06 trillion, or 127 percent of reserve money.[9]

10.6.2 Exchange Rate Policy

The authorities in Taiwan shifted from a fixed exchange rate system to a floating exchange rate system in July 1978. The purpose behind introducing a floating exchange rate was to make Taiwan's economy less vulnerable to external disturbances. However, in a highly open economy like Taiwan, the exchange rate is a key factor affecting its trade balance, economic growth, and domestic price level. The exchange rate is therefore frequently regarded as an important policy instrument to promote economic growth or stabilize prices. According to the Central Bank Act, the CBC also has the obligation to stabilize the external value of the NT dollar, as in the exchange rate. Hence, since the adoption of a floating exchange rate in 1978, the CBC has frequently intervened in the foreign exchange market in order to affect the level of the exchange rate or its fluctuations. The final purpose of the CBC is either to promote exports and economic growth, to stabilize domestic prices, or to stabilize the exchange rate. In other words, what is adopted by the CBC is in fact a managed floating exchange rate.

The general impression and feeling derived by scholars and experts in Taiwan over the CBC's foreign exchange operations may be summed up as follows. First, the CBC has usually adopted a strategy of repressing the NT dollar, aiming to promote exports. Therefore, the NT dollar has been characterized as being "easy to depreciate, difficult to appreciate." Second, when domestic prices face any serious inflation problem, the CBC is then more

9. Re-deposits from financial institutions constitute a very powerful and effective operational instrument for the CBC to adjust reserve money. The CBC is entitled to receive or return re-deposits from the postal savings system, three specialized agricultural banks, and other approved banks when the CBC concludes that the domestic financial situation requires it to do so. To increase (decrease) reserve money, the CBC can simply return (receive) re-deposits to (from) the financial institutions.

willing to allow the NT dollar to appreciate. Third, when major events such as political unrest, a military threat from China, and the East Asian financial crisis in 1997–1998 occurred, such that the NT dollar faced serious pressure to depreciate, the CBC was obliged to defend the exchange rate.

Since the CBC has kept information on foreign exchange intervention a secret, the impact of CBC's intervention on the exchange rate is difficult to estimate. In a recent study on the NT-dollar exchange rate, Yang and Shea (2005) set up an optimal-intervention model to introduce three variables, representing three purposes of CBC intervention, into the determination equation of the NT-dollar exchange rate, together with the standard factors affecting the exchange rate, such as the relative price level, interest-rate gap, and export-competing countries' exchange rates. The empirical estimation results of this paper show that each of the three intervention-purpose variables played a significant role in the determination of the NT-dollar exchange rate. The model incorporating the intervention-purpose variables performed far better, in terms of both explanatory power and forecasting power, than the model that excluded the intervention-purpose variables. These results clearly indicate that CBC's intervention is really a key factor affecting the NT-dollar exchange rate, and that promoting economic growth, stabilizing domestic prices, and stabilizing the exchange rate are truly the main concerns of the CBC in exchange rate management.

10.6.3 Counter-Deflation Policies

By coping with the weakening demand for money caused by the slowdown of economic growth and the increase of substituting financial assets, the CBC could not but passively and gradually adjust downward the target zone of its M2 growth rate during the period from 2000 to 2003, as shown in figure 10.7. This figure also shows that the actual growth rate of M2 fell most of the time into the target zone, which indicates that the CBC's management of money supply was, generally speaking, satisfactory during this period.

The expansionary monetary policy adopted by the CBC to stimulate domestic demand was revealed by the policy measures, which were intended to loosen the monetary environment and to guide the market interest rate in a downward direction. Between December 2000 and the end of 2003, the CBC lowered both the discount rate and the rate on accommodations on fifteen occasions, as indicated by table 10.5. In 2001–2003, the required-reserve ratios of the NT-dollar deposits and foreign currency deposits were reduced on one occasion and three occasions, respectively. As a result, the market interest rates as represented by the inter-bank overnight call-loan rate, one-year time deposit rate, and the 31–90 day Commercial Paper (CP) rate in the secondary market all moved downward in 2001–2003 as figure 10.8 shows.

As for its exchange rate policy, the CBC has been used to keeping the NT dollar undervalued in ordinary times in order to stimulate Taiwan's exports

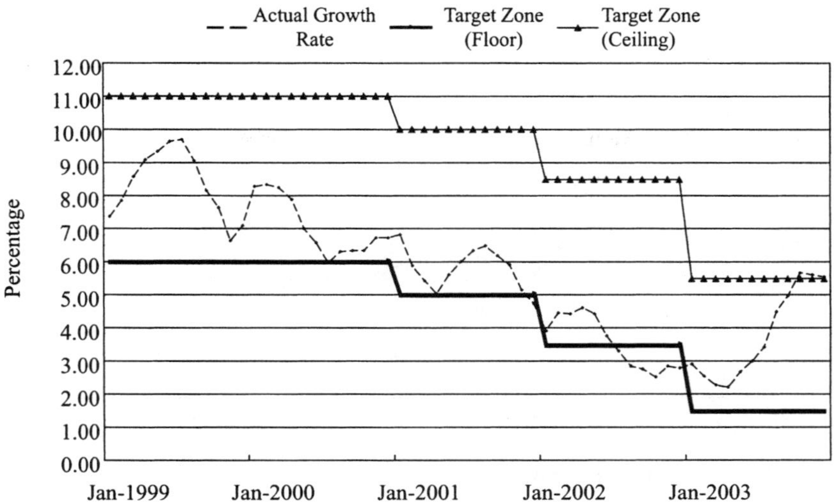

Fig. 10.7 Target zone and actual growth rate of M2
Source: The Central Bank of China.

Table 10.5 CBC interest rates (percent per annum)

Effective date of change	Discount	Accommodations with collateral	Accommodations without collateral
27 June 2000	4.750	5.125	9.625
29 Dec. 2000	4.625	5.000	9.625
2 Feb. 2001	4.375	4.750	9.625
6 Mar. 2001	4.250	4.625	9.625
30 Mar. 2001	4.125	4.500	9.625
23 Apr. 2001	4.000	4.375	9.625
18 May 2001	3.750	4.125	6.000
29 June 2001	3.500	3.875	5.750
20 Aug. 2001	3.250	3.625	5.500
19 Sep. 2001	2.750	3.125	5.000
4 Oct. 2001	2.500	2.875	4.750
8 Nov. 2001	2.250	2.625	4.500
28 Dec. 2001	2.125	2.500	4.375
28 June 2002	1.875	2.250	4.125
12 Nov. 2002	1.625	2.000	3.875
27 June 2003	1.375	1.750	3.625

Source: Financial Statistics Monthly, CBC.

and economic growth, as explained above. When faced with a slowdown in economic growth in the period 2000–2003, the CBC was naturally more eager to intervene in the foreign exchange market than in any ordinary period by purchasing foreign exchange in the market to maintain an undervalued NT dollar or to prevent it from appreciating. Deflation in this period further strengthened the justification for the CBC's foreign exchange

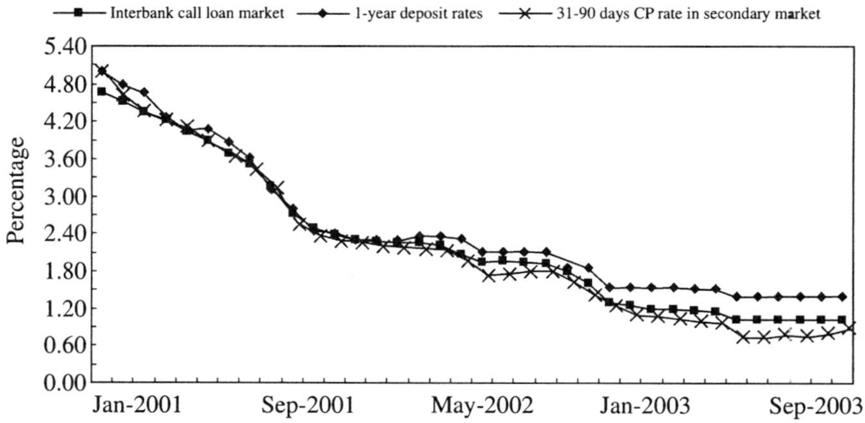

Fig. 10.8 Market interest rates
Source: Financial Statistic Monthly, CBC.

intervention. Without its intervention, the currency's appreciation would have caused domestic prices to go down, thereby worsening the deflation problem. Therefore, the CBC's foreign exchange intervention during this period was regarded as a good strategy for "killing two birds with one stone." That is, an undervalued NT dollar was believed to be beneficial both in promoting economic growth and in combating deflation.[10]

The CBC intervened heavily in the foreign exchange market to slow down the appreciation of the NT dollar during the period 2000–2003 when Taiwan enjoyed a huge balance-of-payments surplus. Although the NT dollar was still appreciating then, CBC tried to smooth its movement, otherwise the degree of appreciation would have been larger. The result of the CBC's intervention was a rapid piling up of foreign exchange reserves and a relatively stable NT-dollar exchange rate. The foreign exchange reserves held by the CBC almost doubled from US$106.7 billion at the end of the year 2000 to US$206.6 billion at the end of 2003. The NT$-U.S.$ exchange rate even fell from 32.992 to 33.978, a depreciation of 2.90 percent relative to the U.S. dollar, during the same period, when most of the currencies of Taiwan's major export-competing countries were appreciating.[11]

The by-product of foreign exchange purchasing by the CBC was a

10. Svenson (2001) proposed depreciation as a foolproof way of getting out of deflation for Japan. This policy recommendation was actually adopted by CBC.

11. During the same period from the end of the year 2000 to the end of 2003, the appreciation rates of the currencies of Taiwan's major export-competing countries relative to the U.S. dollar were as follows:

Japan	South Korea	Hong Kong	Singapore	Malaysia
7.01 percent	6.04 percent	0.51 percent	1.76 percent	0

Table 10.6 Liquidity ratio and loan/deposits ratio (%)

Year	Liquidity ratio of deposit money banks	Ratios of loans and investments over deposits for major financial institutions
1998	19.47	92.28
1999	21.71	88.31
2000	18.94	85.59
2001	22.77	81.19
2002	27.33	77.27
2003	31.32	75.19

Source: Financial Statistics Monthly, CBC.

pumping out of reserve money into the financial market. To control the growth of M2 within the target zone, the CBC was obligated to issue CDs and to receive re-deposits from financial institutions so as to sterilize the impact of foreign exchange intervention on reserve money. The CBC's outstanding CDs hence rapidly increased from NT$562 billion at the end of the year 2000 to NT$2,992 billion at the end of 2003, and re-deposits from financial institutions nearly doubled from NT$1,148 billion to NT$2,056 billion over the same three-year period.

Although lowering the target zone of M2 growth rate was a passive response to a weakened demand for money, and massive sterilization was a necessary policy measure to control the money supply after heavy foreign exchange interventions, these two measures may still seem as a contradiction to the expansionary monetary policy that the CBC is supposed to adopt. However, the falling of the market interest rates as shown in figure 10.8, together with the rising liquidity ratio of banks and the dropping of the ratio of loans and investments over deposits of major financial institutions as reported in table 10.6, all show that CBC had effectively created a relatively loose monetary environment.[12]

Despite these efforts, the CBC's effectiveness in curbing deflation and stimulating economic growth might have been limited for several reasons. First, political unrest and tensions with China had not eased, and these were major factors weakening private consumption and domestic investment in Taiwan. Second, in view of its high degree of openness, Taiwan's economic performance was closely linked with that of the global economy.

12. In addition, there are two measures about real estate market which contribute on the counter-deflation policy. First, the preferential loans for real estate are adopted, which is subsided by the Ministry of the Interior, and CBC provided the funds needed. Second, the Central Bank advises local banks to adopt interest-index housing loans. The interest-indexed housing loans are set according to the interest rates of one-year time deposits or time and savings deposits plus fixed markup. This policy makes the interest rate of real estate move together with the market interest rate. As a result, the interest rates of real estate are transparent, and it follows the decline of market interest rates. It can enhance the effects of transmitting monetary policy. These measures help lessen the interest burden of housing buyers, stimulate the real estate market, and lessen the threat of deflation.

Taiwan could hardly curb deflation caused by external factors. Third, due to the restrictions imposed by the government's deteriorating financial situation, an expansionary fiscal policy could not be implemented. By depending on the CBC's policies alone, Taiwan's economy could not have improved very much. However, we may state that CBC's efforts might have at least shielded the economy from a more serious recession and deflation in 2000–2003.

Of course, the CBC's counter-deflation policies have not been immune from complaints and criticisms. Although lowering the market interest rates had been generally regarded as a necessary and correct policy direction, it created complaints from depositors, as well as from insurance companies since it depressed their profitability. Some scholars and journalists even criticized that the CBC had intervened too heavily in the foreign exchange market on the basis that the foreign exchange reserves had accumulated too rapidly and too much. Nevertheless, the CBC's policy responses to deflation were in general well accepted by the general public and most scholars in Taiwan.[13]

10.7 Conclusion

Taiwan is a small open economy that is characterized by an export-oriented path of development. Domestic investment also serves to stimulate the growth of the economy. There have been some major changes in the political and economic environment in Taiwan in recent years. These changes—including political unrest, tensions with China, outbound investment to China, a weakened financial system, and a deteriorating government financial situation—have provided the backdrop for an economic slowdown and deflation in Taiwan. Some global factors, especially the bursting of the Internet and IT bubbles in late 2000 and the rise of China's economy, have also heavily influenced both global and Taiwanese prices.

This chapter probes the reasons influencing deflation during the period from 1999 to 2003. Reviewing the actual changes of some major economic variables affecting the aggregate demand or the aggregate supply, this chapter has identified some sources of PGDP deflation in Taiwan. During this period, government expenditures have decreased. This factor together with development of production technology that has caused unit output labor costs to fall, the collapse of the bubble economy, the influx of cheap products from China into the world market, and the NT dollar's appreciation have all contributed to a lower PGDP.

In order to fight deflation, the Central Bank adopted several measures to reduce the extent of price decreases. It lowered the discount rate and the

13. Some reports of investment banks, such as Goldman Sachs (2004), Lehman Brothers (2004), and UBS (2004), also have positive evaluation on the monetary policy of CBC in this period.

rate on accommodations on many occasions, and occasionally reduced the required-reserve ratio to guide the market interest rates in a downward direction. The Central Bank also intervened in the foreign exchange market to maintain an undervalued NT dollar, so as to promote exports and combat deflation at the same time.

Although the Central Bank tried to help solve the deflation problem, its monetary policy could not serve as the only remedy. Various factors still needed to be added to strengthen the recession situation. Therefore, the expansionary effects of a loose monetary environment do not seem to be significant. Fortunately, from 2004, the Taiwan economy is no longer under the threat of deflation.

During this period of deflation, the price configuration has experienced a change, whereby the PGDP has gone down and the CPI has slightly decreased, but the WPI has gone up. In fact, this kind of price-divergence phenomenon has not only appeared during the period of deflation, but has also appeared repeatedly on several occasions according to historical data over the years.

In analyzing the reasons why the WPI and CPI trends have diverged since 2002, we find that the WPI increase is mainly due to the huge Chinese demand for raw materials. This has caused the prices of global raw materials and Taiwan's imports to rise, which has caused the WPI to rise. Another reason is that the domestic economy has been recovering since 2003. As for the CPI decrease, this has resulted from a decrease in the prices of services and PGDP. A decrease in the prices of services is related to the decline in rents and the interest rate. A rise in domestic unemployment and competition from China's cheap labor has also kept domestic wages steady.

The deflation problem puzzled Taiwanese scholars during the period from 1999 to 2003. Fortunately, it has started to disappear gradually since 2004. The economic growth rate increased up to 5.71 percent, and inflation rates for PGDP, WPI, and CPI are –1.8 percent, 7.1 percent, and 1.7 percent in 2004, respectively. It shows the phenomenon of price divergence in 2004. Furthermore, although PGDP growth rate is negative in 2004, the first quarter of 2005 is around 0.3 percent, and it is expected to be positive for all the year of 2005. Although deflation in Taiwan seems to be over, the global and domestic factors will all continue to influence Taiwan's economy from different aspects.

References

Ahearne, Alan, Joseph Gagnon, Jane Haltmaier, and Steve Kamin. 2002. Preventing deflation: Lessons from Japan's experience in the 1990s. International Finance Discussion Paper no. 729. Washington, DC: Federal Reserve Board, June.

Bank of Japan. 2001. The role of monetary policy under low inflation: Deflationary shocks and policy responses. *Monetary and Economic Studies,* special edition, 19 (S-1 February). Sponsored by the Institute for Monetary and Economic Studies, Bank of Japan. 3–4 July. Tokyo, Japan.

Cargill, Thomas F. 2001. Monetary policy, deflation and economic history: Lessons for the bank of Japan. In *The role of monetary policy under low inflation: Deflationary shocks and policy responses,* Bank of Japan, 113–42.

Department of Economic Research, the Central Bank of China. 2002. The deflation phenomenon in Japan, Hong Kong and mainland China in recent years, (in Chinese). Staff Report. Taipei.

Goldman, Sachs. 2004. Taiwan–A showcase for Asia's road to reflation. *Asia-Pacific Economics Analyst,* February 27.

Goodfriend, Marvin. 2001. Financial stability, deflation and monetary policy. In *The role of monetary policy under low inflation: Deflationary shocks and policy responses,* Bank of Japan, 143–76.

Hsu, Hsi-Chang. 1992. Analysis on the economic significance of divergence between the consumer price index and the wholesale price index (in Chinese). *Industrial Economics.* August: 1–7. Taiwan Cooperative Bank.

Huang, Chih-Jia. 2003. A study on Taiwan's decreasing price trend in recent years. *Economic Research* (in Chinese) December. Taipei: Economic Research Department, Council for Economic Planning and Development.

International Monetary Fund. 1999. World economic outlook. Washington, DC: IMF, October.

Kumar, Manmohan S. 2003. Deflation: The new threat? IMF *Finance & Development.* June: 16–19.

Lehman, Brothers. 2004. Taiwan: Taking off. *Global Weekly Economic Monitors* March 5:1–3.

Rogoff, Kenneth. 2003. Deflation: Determinants, risks and policy options: Findings of an international task force. Washington, DC: International Monetary Fund, April.

Shea, Jia-Dong, and Tsuen-Hua Shih. 1999. Taiwan's financial policies in response to the Asian financial crisis. *Central Bank of China Quarterly* June: 1–32. Taipei: Central Bank of China.

Svensson, Lars E. O. 2001. The zero bound in an open economy: A foolproof way of escaping from a liquidity trap. *The role of monetary policy under low inflation: Deflationary shocks and policy responses,* (special edition) 19 (S-1). Bank of Japan. Monetary and Economic Studies.

The Council for Economic Planning and Development of the Executive Yuan. 2003. Analysis of the threat of global deflation and its responsive strategies, (In Chinese). Background Material, January.

Union Bank of Switzerland. 2004. The Taiwan debate is over. *UBS Investment Research* February 24. London: UBS.

The Economist. 2002. *The risk of deflation—Comparing symptoms.* November 9.

Wu, Chung-Shu. 2003. Casting off the shadow of deflation. *The Republic of China economic yearbook, Economic Daily News* (in Chinese), 15–20.

Yang, Ya-Hwei, and Jia-Dong Shea. 1996. Money and prices in Taiwan in the 1980s. In *Financial deregulation and integration in East Asia,* ed. Takatoshi Ito and Anne O. Krueger, 229–43. NBER—East Asia Seminar on Economics: Volume 5. Chicago and London: The University of Chicago Press.

Yang, Ya-Hwei, and Jia-Dong Shea. 2005. The new Taiwan dollar exchange rate and central bank intervention. *Taiwan Economic Forecast and Policy* (in Chinese) March: 23–41. Institute of Economics, Academia Sinica.

Comment Toshiki Jinushi

Summary of the Paper

The chapter by Yang and Shea gives a nice starting point for the analysis of the deflation experience in Taiwan in the early 2000s. They offer a broad political and economic background for the deflation first, and then a basic analysis of the price movements, and the description of the monetary-policy operation in the end. This comments focus mainly on the monetary-policy operation.

The Monetary-Policy Operation

The framework for the Taiwanese monetary policy has been monetary targeting for years but its operation has changed recently. The Central Bank of Taiwan seems to have smoothed the interest rate changes recently, as Young and Shea pointed out. The volatility of the interest rates got decreased evidently since around 1998 (fig. 10C1.1). Though the operation has become more pragmatic the monetary aggregate has been within the target band, except for in the latter half of 2002. Thus, we may evaluate that the Central Bank has maintained the monetary targeting well.[1]

However, the operation in 2002 is highly problematic. It is the time when the Taiwanese economy faced the deflation. Though the WPI increased slightly, both the CPI and the GDP deflator decreased. In addition, the GDP gap[2] is significantly negative after the IT bubble collapsed. As figure 10C1.2 shows, these two main concerns for the monetary policy unanimously call for the monetary ease. But, the money supply did not even meet the lower end of the target band.

This policy operation seems quite passive, even though the money demand would have been quite stagnant then. In fact, the Central Bank lowered its discount rate only twice in 2002, from 2.125 to 1.875 in June, and to 1.625 in November. The inter-bank rate followed it from around 2.30 in January to 1.60 in December.

The Central Bank did have ample chances to meet the monetary target in 2002, since it implemented massive FX market intervention against the NT dollar appreciation. However, it sterilized this by the open market operation and the re-deposit.

The Central Bank might have been in the "wait-and-see" mode, after the

Toshiki Jinushi is a professor in the Faculty of Economics at Kobe University.

Author would like to thank Mr. Singo Umino for assistance in the data collection and some calculations.

1. The Central Bank seems to have faced some difficulties so that it has changed the definition of the target aggregates. That is common in the monetary-targeting countries.

2. The GDP gap in the chart is calculated as the deviation of the actual GDP from its quadratic trend.

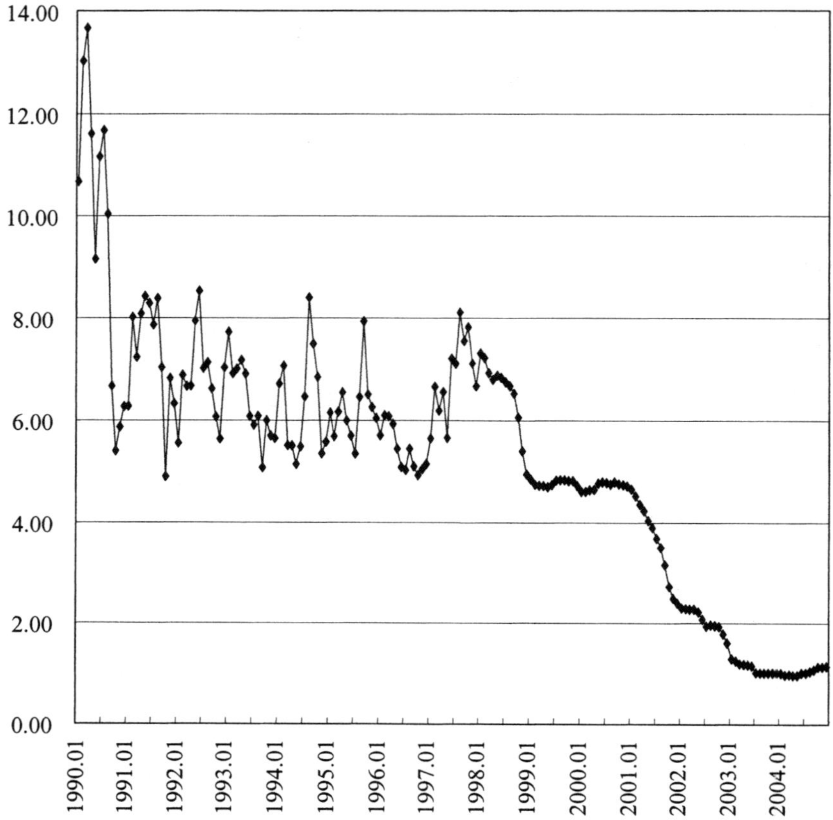

Fig. 10C1.1 Taipei inter-bank overnight rate

aggressive easing in 2001; it lowered the discount rate eleven times from 4.625 to 2.125. But, later, it found it necessary to lower interest rates through 2003. In addition, the literature had already shown that the extraordinary aggressive easing is desirable on the edge of the deflation and the zero bound of the nominal interest.

Based on these reasons, we could evaluate that the Central Bank's easing decisions were delayed in 2002. In fact, even the simple Taylor rule shows that the inner-bank rate should have been lowered more (fig. 10C1.3).[3]

The Analysis of the Deflation

Yang and Shea decomposed the factors affecting the price movements in Taiwan. Their main analysis is about the GDP deflator. They concluded

3. The calculation is based on the original coefficients of 0.5 and 0.5 and the target inflation rate of 1.835 percent (the Taiwanese average inflation rate for 1982 to 2004).

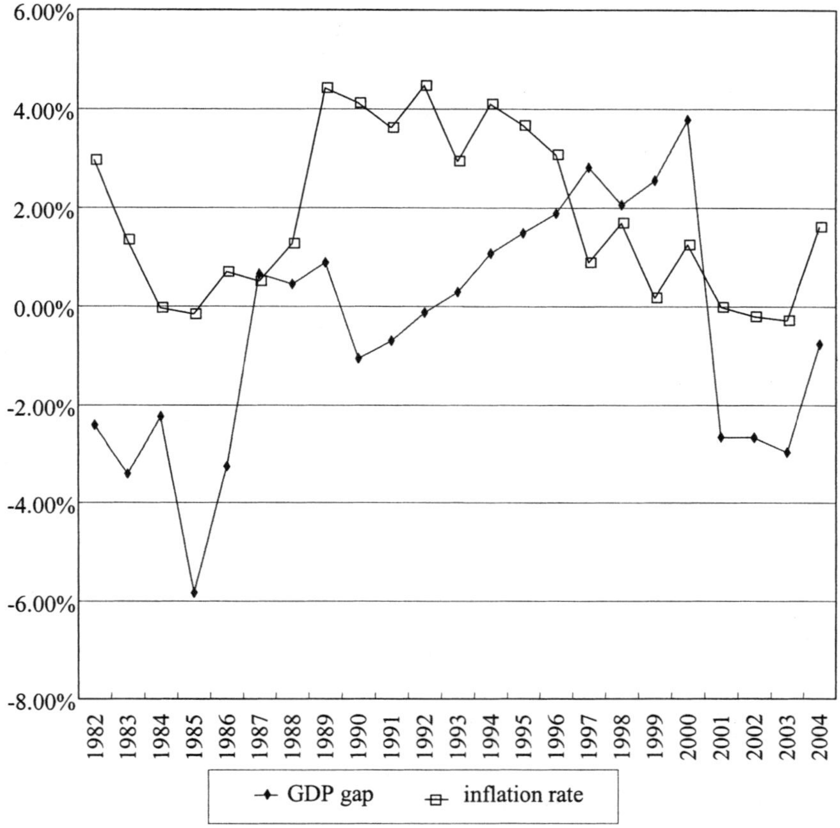

Fig. 10C1.2 GDP gap and inflation rate

that the reduction in unit labor cost, lower export prices, the NT dollar appreciation, and the low government expenditure are the main contributors for the recent deflation. Then, they focused on the divergent behavior of the price indexes, GDP deflator, CPI, and the WPI.

However, based on the discussion on the monetary operation, the focus should be put on the persistence of the factors contributing for the deflation. By doing so, they might be able to examine the reasons why the Central Bank downplayed the deflation in 2001–2003.

References

Ahearne, A., J. Gagnon, J. Haltmaier, and S. Kamin. 2002. Preventing deflation: Lessons from Japan's experience in the 1990s. International Finance Discussion Papers no. 2002-729. Federal Reserve Board, June. Washington, DC.

Kato, Ryo, and Nishiyama Shin-Ichi. 2003. Optimal monetary policy when inter-

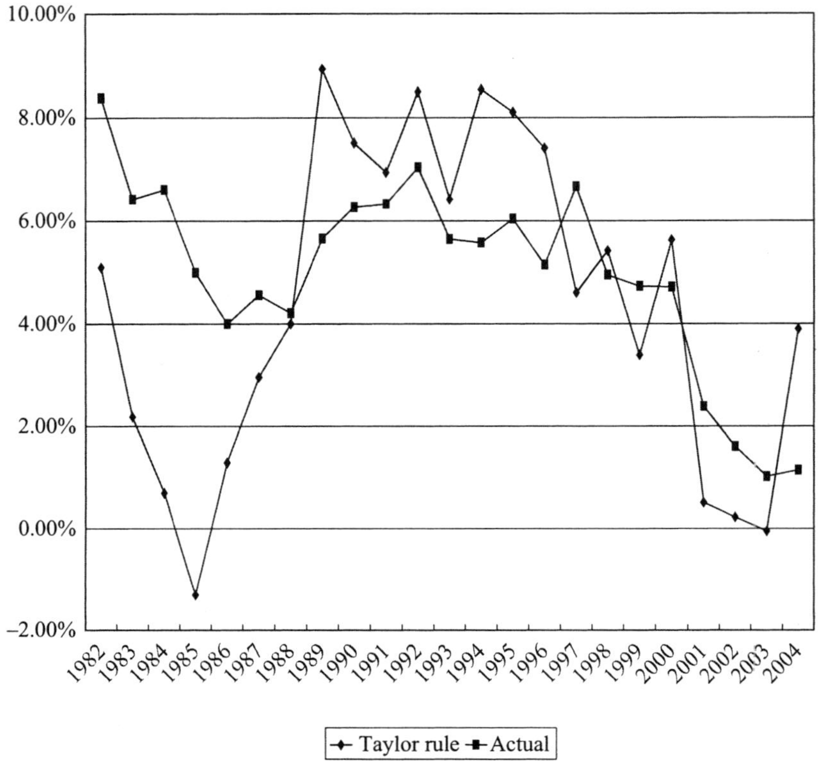

Fig. 10C1.3 The Taylor rule and the actual rate: inter-bank overnight rate

est rates are bounded at zero. IMES Discussion Paper Series 2003-E-11, Bank of Japan, October. Tokyo: Institute for Monetary and Economic Studies.

Comment Shigenori Shiratsuka

Introduction

Ya-Hwei Yang and Jia-Dong Shea provide useful information on Taiwan's experience with deflation in the early 2000s, ranging from political and economic background to price developments and monetary-policy responses. This is another story of deflation in the East Asian region, but one

Shigenori Shiratsuka is director and senior economist in the economics and finance section of the Institute for Monetary and Economic Studies at the Bank of Japan.

The views expressed in the paper are those of the authors and do not necessarily reflect those of the BOJ or the IMES.

less well-known compared with Japan's experience in the years following the mid-1990s.

As Toshiki Jinushi points out in his comments, Yang and Shea's chapter seems to suggest that deflation in Taiwan is influenced not only by temporary factors but also more persistent factors. This associates me with Japan's experience of low economic growth in the 1990s, often referred to as the "lost decade." Based on my previous papers, joint with co-authors, on Japan's experience, I will elaborate some possible explanations for deflation in Taiwan involving structural and persistent factors.

Distortion in Cross-Sectional Resource Allocation

The first point is that various structural impediments prevent the resources in the economy from reallocating in an efficient manner.

As Yang and Shea argue, sudden and significant changes in Taiwan's economic environments, such as the bursting of the IT bubbles, the rise of China's economy, and the weakened financial system, helped bring about the stagnant economic condition after 1999. In Japan's case, structural impediments have also affected the economy after the bursting of asset-price bubbles.[1,2] In addition, significant structural changes to the economic environments occurred during the 1990s: for example, the changing pattern in the division of labor between Japan and its East Asian neighbors, a rapidly aging population, and advances in information and communications technology.

Okina and Shiratsuka (2004) argue that protracted economic stagnation in Japan after the 1990s can be seen as the result of incomplete economic adjustments to significant changes in relative prices in two dimensions: the intertemporal and cross-sectional dimensions. In the cross-sectional dimension, when relative price changes occur, frictions and distortions in factor markets lead the economy to exhibit inefficient resource allocation, thereby lowering attainable output given the total amount of resources in the economy. In the intertemporal dimension, as long as economic growth remains stagnant, asset prices, which correspond to the discounted present value of future cash flow, can hardly be expected to recover, thus producing further downward pressure on trend growth through declines in capi-

1. The list of structural impediments includes rigid corporate governance, inefficiency of the nonmanufacturing sector, the issue of nonperforming assets associated with the generation and bursting of the asset-price bubble, and the savings-investment imbalance.

2. Hayashi and Prescott (2002) argue that economic stagnation in Japan in the 1990s is attributable to declines in both the TFP growth rate and working hours, while Kawamoto (2005) points out that technology growth, measured as a purified Solow residual, remains almost unchanged from the 1980s to the 1990s. In any case, these empirical studies suggest that structural impediments against more efficient resource allocation are crucial factors behind Japan's lost decade. Sekine, Kobayashi, and Saita (2003); and Caballero, Hoshi, and Kashyap (2003) provide further evidence that one of the major causes of Japan's long-term stagnation is forbearance lending to inefficient firms.

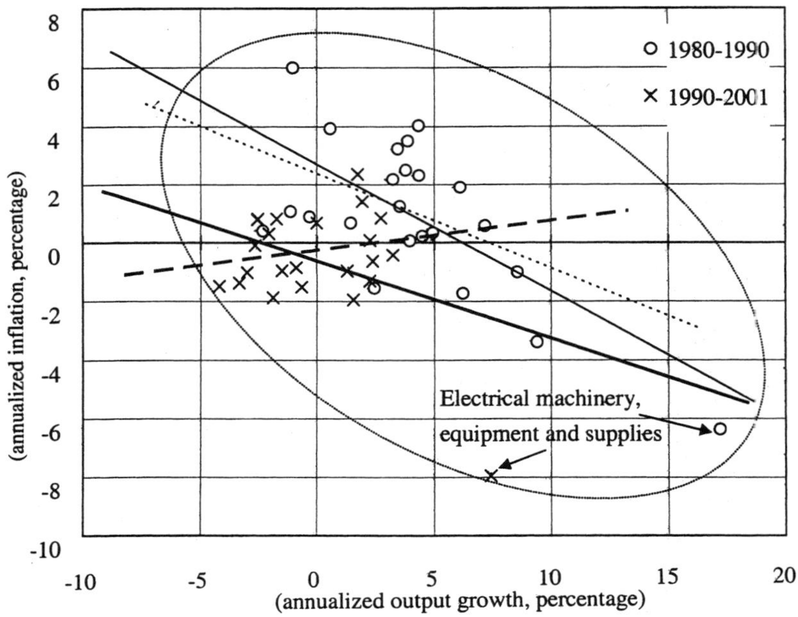

Fig. 10C2.1 Output growth and inflation by industry
Source: Okina and Shiratsuka (2004).

tal accumulation in high-productivity sectors. In addition, it should be noted that the cross-sectional and intertemporal resource misallocation interacts to amplify the negative impacts of structural factors on the economy as a whole.

Figure 10C2.1, taken from Okina and Shiratsuka (2004), depicts the relationship between output growth and price changes by industry in Japan. The horizontal and vertical axes plot annualized changes in outputs and deflators by industry, respectively. Observations shown as circles and Xs, respectively, indicate data for the period from 1980 to 1990 and from 1990 to 2001.

An overall negative relationship suggests the importance of supply-side factors in determining cross-sectional differences over time. Resources are allocated to growing industries where relative prices are declining, reflecting their relatively high productivity growth. A closer look at the figure, however, reveals that the above negative relationship varies between two periods: thin and bold solid lines for the observations for the periods 1980–90 and 1990–2001, respectively; and thin and bold dotted lines for the observations for the corresponding periods but excluding electrical machinery. The slopes of the observations for the period of 1980–90 are negative, regardless of inclusion or exclusion of the outlier observation for electrical machinery, while the slope of the observations for the period 1990–2001 turns slightly positive if the outlier observation for electrical machinery is excluded.

Increased Waiting-Option Value in Response to Political Uncertainty

The second point is that waiting-option values rise in response to increased uncertainties in the economy, thereby restraining irreversible expenditure to consumption and investment.

Yang and Shea document that uncertainties in both political and economic environments have increased significantly in the 2000s. Political conflicts with China have intensified, as Taiwan has leaned toward establishing itself as an independent nation The rise of the Chinese economy induces foreign direct investment to China, leading to the growing concerns over the hollowing out of Taiwan's manufacturing sector.

As discussed in Saito and Shiratsuka (2003), an important element in saving motive under uncertainty is an option to wait for the uncertainty to be resolved. With this motive, savings are regarded as a flexible choice for the future, while consumption is treated as a firm commitment to current expenditures or a perfectly irreversible decision. Such a waiting-option motive becomes more important when uncertainties surrounding the economy are growing. It should be noted, however, that a waiting-option motive is often confused with a precautionary motive.

The aforementioned two types of saving motives under uncertainty provide broad implications. That is, the first motive is driven by the magnitude of risks, while the second is promoted by the subsequent resolution of uncertainty. If saving motives as waiting options are present, savings increase when uncertainty is expected to be resolved subsequently. Empirical results shown in Saito and Shiratsuka (2003) indicate that saving behavior since the 1980s is more consistent with dominant precautionary savings; however, estimation results from the behavior during the 1990s offer some evidence in favor of savings as waiting options.

Conclusions

In closing, I emphasize the importance of investigating the cause of the problem more deeply for each episode of deflation. I think there are more interesting issues on deflation ripe for further investigation. The nature of deflation varies from country to country and from episode to episode. Required policy responses also vary according to such differences in the nature of the deflation.

References

Caballero, Ricardo J., Hoshi, Takeo, and Anil K. Kashyap. 2003. Zombie lending and depressed restructuring in Japan. Mimeograph.

Hayashi, Fumio, and Edward C. Prescott. 2002. The 1990s in Japan: A lost decade. *Review of Economic Dynamics* 5:206–35.
Kawamoto, Takuji. 2005. What do the purified solow residuals tell us about Japan's lost decade? *Monetary and Economic Studies* 23 (1): 113–46. Institute for Monetary and Economic Studies, Bank of Japan.
Okina, Kunio, and Shigenori Shiratsuka. 2004. Asset price fluctuations, structural adjustments, and sustained economic growth: Lessons from Japan's experience since the late 1980s. *Monetary and Economic Studies* 22 (S-1): 143–77. Institute for Monetary and Economic Studies, Bank of Japan.
Saito, Makoto, and Shigenori Shiratsuka. 2003. Precautionary motives versus waiting options: Evidence from aggregate household saving in Japan. *Monetary and Economic Studies* 21 (2): 1–20. Institute for Monetary and Economic Studies, Bank of Japan.
Sekine, Toshitaka, Keiichiro Kobayashi, and Yumi Saita. 2003. Forbearance lending: The case of Japanese firms. *Monetary and Economic Studies* 21 (2): 69–92. Institute for Monetary and Economic Studies, Bank of Japan.

Contributors

Laurence Ball
Department of Economics
Johns Hopkins University
Baltimore, MD 21218

R. Anton Braun
Faculty of Economics
The University of Tokyo
7-3-1 Hongo, Bunkyo-ku
Tokyo, 113-0033 Japan

Dongchul Cho
Korea Development Institute
Macroeconomic Policy Division
P.O. Box 113 Cheongryangri Dong
Seoul 130-012 Korea

Woon Gyu Choi
International Monetary Fund
700 19th Street, NW
Washington, DC 20431

David Cook
Department of Economics—Business School
Hong Kong University of Science and Technology
Clear Water Bay
Kowloon, Hong Kong

Piti Disyatat
Bank of Thailand
273 Samsen Road
Bangkhunphrom
Bangkok 10200 Thailand

Mitsuhiro Fukao
Faculty of Business and Commerce
Keio University
2-15-45 Mita, Minato-ku
Tokyo 108-8345, Japan

Shin-ichi Fukuda
Faculty of Economics
University of Tokyo
7-3-1 Hongo, Bunkyo-ku
Tokyo 113-0033, Japan

James Harrigan
International Research Function
Federal Reserve Bank of New York
33 Liberty Street
New York, NY 10045

Fumio Hayashi
Department of Economics
University of Tokyo
7-3-1 Hongo, Bunkyo-ku
Tokyo 113-0033, Japan

Yuzo Honda
Graduate School of Economics
Osaka University
1-7, Machikaneyama
Toyonaka, Osaka 560-0043 Japan

Seok-Kyun Hur
Korea Development Institute
207-41, Chongnyangri-Dong
Dongdaemun-Gu P.O. Box 113
Chongnyang Seoul Korea

Takatoshi Ito
Graduate School of Economics
The University of Tokyo
7-3-1 Hongo, Bunkyo-ku
Tokyo, 113-0033 Japan

Mitsuru Iwamura
Graduate School of Asia-Pacific Studies
Waseda University
1-104 Totsukamachi, Shinjuku-ku
Tokyo, 169-8050 Japan

Toshiki Jinushi
Graduate School of Economics
Kobe University
2-1, Rokkodai, Nada-ku
Kobe, 658-8501 Japan

Takeshi Kudo
Faculty of Economics
Nagasaki University
4-2-1 Katafuchi
Nagasaki-shi, 850-8506 Japan

Kenneth Kuttner
Oberlin College
Economics Department
10 North Professor Street, Rice Hall
Oberlin, OH 44074

Mario B. Lamberte
Philippine Institute for Development Studies
NEDA sa Makati Building
106 Amorsolo St., Legaspi Village
Makati, Philippines

Bennett T. McCallum
Graduate School of Industrial Administration
Carnegie Mellon University
Pittsburgh, PA 15213

Frederic S. Mishkin
Graduate School of Business
Uris Hall 817
Columbia University
New York, NY 10027

Tim Robinson
Reserve Bank of Australia
GPO Box 65
Sydney NSW 2001 Australia

Andrew K. Rose
Haas School of Business Administration
University of California
Berkeley, CA 94720-1900

Makoto Saito
Graduate School of Economics
Hitotsubashi University
Naka 2-1, Kunitachi
Tokyo, 186-8601 Japan

Jia-Dong Shea
Economics Department
National Taiwan University
No. 21 Hsu-Chow Rd.
10000 Taipei City, Taiwan

Shigenori Shiratsuka
Institute for Monetary and Economic Studies
Bank of Japan
C.P.O. Box 203
Tokyo, 100-91 Japan

Andrew Stone
Reserve Bank of Australia—Economic Research
GPO Box 65
Sydney 2001 NSW Australia

Kazuo Ueda
Bank of Japan
2-1-1 Nihonbashi-Hongokucho
Chuo-ku, Tokyo Japan

Tsutomu Watanabe
Institute of Economic Research
Hitotsubashi University
Naka 2-1, Kunitachi
Tokyo, 186-8603 Japan

Ya-Hwei Yang
Chung-Hua Institute for Economic Research
75 Chang Hsing Street
Taipei, Taiwan

Author Index

Subject Index

Page numbers in italics refer to tables and figures.